The Complete Black Book of Russian Jewry

The Complete Black Book of Russian Jewry

Ilya Ehrenburg
Vasily Grossman

Translated and edited by David Patterson

With a foreword by Irving Louis Horowitz
and an introduction by Helen Segall

Transaction Publishers
New Brunswick (U.S.A.) and London (U.K.)

Library of Congress Catalog Number: 2001052299
ISBN: 0-7658-0069-1
Printed in the United States of America

Library of Congress Cataloging-in-Publication Data

The Complete black book of Russian Jewry : Ilya Ehrenburg and Vassily Grossman ; translated and
    edited by David Patterson ; with foreword by Irving Louis Horowitz and an introduction by Helen
    Segall.
        p. cm.
    Includes bibliographical references (p.).
    ISBN 0-7658-0069-1 (alk. paper)
    1. Jews—Persecutions—Soviet Union.   2. Holocaust, Jewish (1939-1945)—Soviet Union—
Personal narratives. 3. Soviet Union—Ethnic relations. I. Erenburg, Il'ia, 1891-1967. II. Grossman,
Vasilii Semenovich. III. Patterson, David. IV. Chernaia kniga.
English.

DS135.R92 C647 2001
940.53'18'0947—dc21   2001052299

Contents

Part 2: Belorussia

Part 6: The Soviet People are United

Part 7: The Annihilation Camps

Translator's Preface

With the help of my friend Dr. Helen Segall—who is the author of the introduction to this volume, a close friend of Irina Ehrenburg, and herself a survivor of the Holocaust—in early 1997 I made arrangements to fly to Moscow for a June meeting with Ms. Ehrenburg. The purpose of my appointment was to discuss my work on an English translation of her complete edition of *The Black Book* that her father Ilya Ehrenburg had prepared in collaboration with Vasily Grossman. But after making all the necessary preparations for the trip—which included obtaining an invitation from the president of a college in Russia—the Russian officials inexplicably refused me permission to enter the country. Later that summer I was at Yad Vashem in Jerusalem studying the Ehrenburg archives and other material related to *The Black Book*. As I pored over a set of manuscript pages, a librarian came up to me and handed me a clipping from a recent Russian newspaper. It was the obituary for Irina Ehrenburg: she had passed away on the very day that I was supposed to have met with her.

This turn of events increased my determination to undertake the daunting task of translating a volume of more than 360,000 words into English. These words, moreover, are not just any words. They speak from a time when the very meaning of words was under assault, when words like *left*, *right*, *oven*, *cold*, *hunger*, *resettlement*, *special treatment*, and others took on meanings they never had before. Although the materials prepared by the volume's Soviet contributors reflect a clear Soviet bias, it is still perhaps the best single source of information on Nazi activities in Eastern Europe. I cannot say that I wanted to do the translation (indeed, who would *want* to live with these accounts day after day?); but I knew that someone *had* to do it, despite all the difficulties involved. I knew that if these witnesses had the courage to speak, then we must find the courage to listen, and to listen carefully.

In addition to living with texts that were emotionally harrowing and intellectually intimidating—in addition to tracking down data on dozens of people, places, and events—the translation involved certain linguistic challenges. *The Black Book* contains letters, diaries, affidavits, reports, testimonies, and articles written by numerous authors, each with his or her own characteristic style; conveying their styles and linguistic levels was often difficult. Of course, like any translator who takes up portions of a text that others have translated, I am indebted to the efforts of previous translators. In this case I owe much to the work of John Glad and James S. Levine, the translators of the English edition of *The Black Book* published by the Holocaust Library in 1981. They prepared a fine edition with few errors and omissions. As Helen Segall points out in the introduction, however, the Holocaust Library edition was not a complete edition. Thanks to Irina Ehrenburg's hard work and sheer devotion, a complete Russian edition of *The Black Book* was published in Vilnius in 1993. This volume is a translation of that edition.

Sections of *The Black Book* that appear here for the first time in English include the following:

1.   The Germans in Radzivillov (Krasnoarmeisk) (pp. 93-98)

2.   German-Romanian Brutality in Kishinev (Moldavia) (pp. 99-105)

3.   Leaders of the Underground Fighters in the Minsk Ghetto (pp. 140-56)

4.   The Young Women from Minsk (pp. 156-57)

5.   In the Village of Gory (pp. 160-61)

6.   From Materials Compiled by the Special State Commission on the Verification and Investigation of Atrocities Committed by the German-Fascist Invaders (pp. 195-99)

7.   The entire section on Lithuania (pp. 241-377)

8.   The Report of the Special State Commission for the Verification and Investigation of Atrocities Committed by the German Fascist Invaders and Their Accomplices in the Monstrous Crimes of the German Government in Auschwitz (pp. 502-16)

9.   The Warsaw Ghetto Uprising (pp. 544-60)

Portions of the text set of in curved brackets ({ }) are also newly translated into English, and extensive notes have been added for the first time at the end of each section. Most of these notes are the fruit of the labor undertaken by Irina Ehrenburg when she was preparing the Russian edition for publication in Vilnius; dates, figures, names, places, and other data in these notes are for the most part based on her research.

One striking discovery to be made by students, teachers, scholars, and other readers who engage the testimonies in this book is this: the crimes perpetrated by the Nazis and their accomplices were not unimaginable—on the contrary, the imagination was the only limit to what they perpetrated. For they had no other limiting principle to curb their actions against humanity. When the Crusaders, for example, slaughtered Jews on their way to the Holy Land, they had somewhere in their tradition the teaching that Jews also have a soul and that murder is wrong. The Nazis had no such limiting principle that someone could invoke to say, "We are going too far!" On the contrary, the principle that guided the Nazis in their actions was "Thou shalt murder Jews." To do otherwise would amount to remiss in one's duty. For the Nazis, the was no "too far." Reading these texts and testimonies, one realizes that murder was not a byproduct of National Socialism—it was its very essence.

The material contained in this volume, therefore, not only attests to the Nazis' massive, murderous project to exterminate every Jew in Europe and ultimately on the face of the earth. Beyond that, these texts bear witness to a singular, definitive feature of the Holocaust: the Nazis set out not only to annihilate human beings but to eradicate the very notion of a human being. Indeed, in 1935 the Union of National Socialist Attorneys proposed that the term *Mensch*, which means "human being," be eliminated from the legal code, since it obscured the Party's view on what constitutes a person—a view diametrically opposed to the teaching of nearly four thousand years of Jewish tradition. Under the Third Reich there was not enough room in the universe for both views. Therefore the Jews posed not only a racial problem, nor even merely a moral problem—they posed a cosmic problem.

According to the Nazi view, the value of a human being derives from an accident of nature, from race. Hence an Aryan has more value than a non-Aryan—to be sure, an Aryan *has no essential connection* to a non-Aryan; and within the Aryan race (which is not a race at all but a political and ontological category) the value of a "person" rests upon a will to power. According to the view set forth in Jewish tradition, on the other hand, a human being has infinite value because a human being is created in the image of an infinite and holy being. Further, every human being has an origin in a single human being, in Adam; therefore each of us is connected to the other as a family is tied to one another. The other human being is *essentially* my brother, sister, mother, father, son, daughter—in a word, a member of my family. Thus each of us is placed in the care of the other, and the value we take on is a matter not of power but of truth—the truth of our responsibility to and for one another. Thus, briefly stated, the horror of the catastrophe known as "the Holocaust" is that it entails an assault on the very values that would make other human catastrophes horrible, and not just historical tragedies, cultural anomalies, or other objects of academic curiosity. For without the absolute value of the other person and the subsequent responsibility to and for the other, we need not be horrified by catastrophes that do not immediately concern us.

Beyond its historical data and Soviet slant, the testimony contained in *The Black Book* makes it an essential part of any effort to achieve some level of understanding of an event that will shape humanity's thinking about itself for generations to come. Having translated this collection, I have come to realize hat one cannot claim to know something about the Holocaust and know nothing about *The Black Book*. That is why making this volume available in English—the language of most of the thought and study on the Holocaust—is so needful. And now that needful task has been accomplished.

David Patterson
The University of Memphis

Foreword

The Totalitarian Collusion:
The Complete Black Book of Russian Jewry

The fate of East European Jewry between 1939 and 1945 can readily be described as an unenviable "choice" between liquidation at the hands of the Nazis and denigration at the hands of the Communists. In such mortifying conditions, most Jews who had the chance to migrate from German-occupied to Russian-occupied territories did so—in sorrow—but also in realization that their options were severely limited under the Nazi-Soviet Non-Aggression Pact engineered by German Foreign Minister Joachim von Ribbentrop and his Soviet counterpart, Vyacheslav Molotov. But on the fateful day of June 22nd, 1941, when the Nazi Wehrmacht invaded Soviet-occupied Poland, thus signaling the next and decisive stage of World War II, even that narrow window of opportunity for Jews to survive rapidly closed.

It is estimated that at least one million Russian Jews perished during the Second World War. This was second only to the three million Polish Jews who died in the same period. Thus these two countries of Eastern Europe, with four million Jewish dead, account for two-thirds of the estimated six million Jewish souls killed in the Holocaust. These estimates are soft, not because the numbers are spurious; they are quite exact. Rather, it is that geographical borders between Poland and Russia were porous. This was especially the case in the relationship between Eastern Poland and the Ukraine. What aided and abetted the destruction of this critical majority of Europe's Jews were longstanding traditions of anti-Semitism and xenophobic nationalism that were widespread in both Poland and southeastern Russia. Local populations delivered up their Jews as sacrificial offerings—not exactly a twentieth-century invention.

For reasons of their own, both the Nazi regime and the Communist system viewed the existence of Jewish life—its economic strength and its cultural formation—as an alien force.

Indeed, they were certainly factors that impeded the onslaught of totalitarianism in both countries. Under such conditions, the analysis of the Holocaust is also a study of dictatorships—rivals in terms of one another, united by a common disdain for what the Nazis called the "international Jewish cabal" and what the Soviets termed "bourgeois cosmopolitanism." It is in this set of complex circumstances, and in full knowledge of the deadly animosities that managed to forge alliances at the expense of Jewish communities and cultures, that the extraordinary efforts of Vasily Grossman and Ilya Ehrenburg to document the Holocaust in Russia was undertaken.

The Columbia Encyclopedia identifies a plague as "any contagious, malignant, epidemic disease, in particular the bubonic plague and the black plague (or Black Death), both forms of the same infection.… In the black form of plague, hemorrhages turn black, giving the term 'Black Death' to the disease." *The Black Book of Russian Jewry* describes the epidemiology of the disease of anti-Semitism, a plague imparted by humans against fellow humans. The Jews of Russia long suffered from this disease, but it burst forth as a plague with the arrival of the Nazi German invasion of Soviet Russia. The soil for this contagious, malignant epidemic was well prepared by several hundred years of pogroms and random (and some planned) assaults against Jewish life and property by Russian rulers and bandits. But it took the Nazi system to initiate a plague, or what we refer to as the Holocaust. *The Black Book of Russian Jewry* is a massive work on the conversion of the disease of anti-Semitism into systematic executions. The slaughter of people affected much greater numbers than was usual for the regions of Russia where Jew hatred was only randomly found in the tsarist past. While the hemorrhaging did not stop with the defeat of the Nazi *Wehrmacht*, the end of the war did slow the slaughter of innocents sufficiently to bring the Holocaust to a close.

The study of the Nazi Holocaust of the Jewish People during World War II is both a special feature of that humanly inspired plague and part of the general character of warfare in the technological epoch. Similarly, *The Black Book of Russian Jewry* embodies the two star-crossed horrors of world war and systematic annihilation. Like others of this genre, this book examines numbers, peoples, terrain, and plunder. The study of genocide is not a "science"—whatever that poor misbegotten word has come to mean in our vocabulary. Rather the routinization of genocide bears witness, in a variety of forms from the historical to the ethical, to the deepest, darkest recesses of dehumanization. This work by Ilya Ehrenburg and Vassily Grossman covers that portion of the Holocaust that took place during the Second World War that was visited upon the Jews of Russia—or as it was known during that period, the Union of Soviet Socialist Republics. It shows us that even within the unitary character of totalitarian systems, there are marked differences in the conduct of conflict and in the treatment of peoples.

The actual mass murder of Jews, what has come to be known as the Holocaust, began after the German invasion of Russia. That singular event triggered the deliberate and systematic effort to destroy all Jewish people, not only in Russia but also throughout Europe. The *Einsatzgruppen,* or "Special Action Groups," had as their express singular task the destruction of Jewish life in every town, village, and hamlet occupied by German forces. News of the mass murders began filtering into the West as early as November 1941. But for Jews the world over, this start of the Holocaust was intuited and felt, if not quite understood, on that grim day of the invasion of Russia.

The Nazi onslaught into Poland and then Russia—from June 1941 to May 1942—corresponded with a shift in German priorities if not policies. The gas chambers set up by the Nazis actually went into full-scale operation when the war aims of the Nazis shifted from victory over the Allied Powers to victory against the Jews, meaning the physical and cultural liquidation, of the hapless Jews of Europe. Lucy Dawidowicz, in *The War Against the Jews: 1933-1945*, demonstrates that at this point the top priority of the Nazis became the Final Solution, even though it crippled their conventional war effort. Raul Hilberg documented this shift in Nazi policy aims in *The Destruction of European Jewry*. Thus while the war and the genocide were coincidental in space, they moved in opposite directions with respect to significance over the course of time. The pathology of hatred overwhelmed the politics of combat. In the process, a new stage of human conflict became standardized: the slaughter of innocents rather than the competition of armed combatants became the touchstone of the century itself.

The Wannsee Conference held on January 20th, 1942 ratified the shift in Nazi war policies from victory over the Allies to the destruction of Jewish communities. But even the document planning the systematic murder of the Jews, contained ambiguities. There are reasons for statistical discrepancies in the number of Russian Jewish dead. These vary from the already mentioned porosity of geographical borders between the Baltic states, Poland, and Russia, to the summary execution of males simply for having been circumcised—whatever their religious background. The Nazi *Wehrmacht* also counted the Romany (so-called Gypsy) people as Jews. Many Jews were not counted at all, but were simply presumed to be part of the human price of warfare. Then there was the thorny issue of whether the Nazi plan to make Europe *Judenfrei* (Jew free) included the liquidation of Jews who had intermarried and others who were only partially of Jewish ancestry. But these are after all quantitative details—the mortification of the flesh, the destruction of Jewish life, was the overriding qualitative fact of Jewish life throughout Europe within a half year of the start of the war inside Russia. Ilya Ehrenburg and Vasily Grossman were among the earliest chroniclers "on the ground" of the character of the Holocaust as it was taking place.

Ehrenburg, with his journalistic appreciation of Russian communities, and Grossman with his novelistic concern for individuals with names and personalities, uniquely constructed and reconstructed the murders as they were taking place, leaving for later generations the larger, metaphysical questions of meaning. Their tactics enabled the two authors to avoid an open break with fundamental axioms of Marxism-Leninism-Stalinism—for the Soviets, too, had a reverential regard for the "science of society"—at least its science of its society. Indeed, we now know that with the aid of key personnel of the Jewish Anti-Fascist Committee, formed as a wartime arm of the Soviet regime to enlist the aid of world Jewry against Nazism, information on atrocities inside Russia were provided to the authors of *The Black Book*. We must appreciate too, as R.J. Rummel reminds us in *Death by Government*, that civilization had few categories for identifying the Holocaust as it was taking place. Indeed, Ehrenburg and Grossman repeatedly noted the hideous mindlessness, the randomness of the Nazi killing machine. In such a climate, these two highly secularized Jews do little more than serve as witnesses to the mass murder of their people—a level of killing that far exceeded the already widespread pogroms against the Jewish people in the tsarist era.

When the German invasion of Russia began I was three months away from my twelfth birthday. The United States was still at peace, and would be for another six months until the Japanese attack against Pearl Harbor. Isolationist temperament was arguably the most powerful force in the country. Indeed that temperament was in no small part aided and abetted not only by the America First Committee on the Right, but also by the American Communist Party and its various satellites on the Left. Thus, the Nazi decision to cross the border of the USSR came as a thunderclap on the American political scene as well. With one act, Jews of all persuasions—from zealots to secularized Zionists, from the working-class Jews in the needle trades to the middle-class shopkeepers—were melded into one. It is as if all Jews understood intuitively that the invasion of Russia was at its heart and soul a war against the Jewish people. Again, in personal terms my childhood friend, Arthur Grumberger who attended religious day school, and I, who attended the secular Workman's Circle Jewish school (as an appendage to public schooling) bonded as never before. With noteworthy exceptions, such as Winston Churchill, this understanding among the Jewish people only rarely permeated rulers and citizens of the Allied powers as a whole.

Arthur and I charted the German invasion of Russia on a daily basis. I voraciously followed Max Werner's brilliant military analyses in the newspaper *PM*—and clipped out the near daily maps with arrows big and little pointing at the heart of Russia. First at White Russia, then at the Ukraine, and finally directly pointing eastward to the prize of Moscow itself—they captured my imagination. Perhaps the low point came with the evacuation of the political machinery from Moscow to Kuibischev, the temporary capital several hundred miles to the east, and deep in the heart of Russia. Even lacking exact data, I well understood that the fate of Russia and the survival of its Jews were intertwined in a special tenuous way. Everything depended on the outcome—not of the war as such, but of a particular battle in a particular railroad town in a particular hamlet I knew from my parents and relatives to be largely inhabited by Jews. These memories came flooding back in reading the microscopic analysis in the Ehrenburg-Grossman volume. Place names and human names that filled my childhood once again came alive. The struggle to publish this mighty effort is finally put to rest with my pre-teen tremors. *The Black Book of Russian Jewry* is a testament to an age.

As assuredly as Aleksandr Solzhenitsyn's *The Gulag Archipelago* documents the Soviet assault on the Russian peoples, so too does the work of Ehrenburg and Grossman presage that effort. In the great tradition of the Russian novel—from Tolstoy to Dostoyevsky, from Pushkin to Chekhov this work carries the conscience of nineteenth-century realism through more than one hundred years. That tradition helped define a world soaked in competing ideologies and aggressive fanaticism. It is little wonder that the Russian people revere their novelists in a way that the rest of humanity can only envy. It was their ticket to sanity and to wisdom. That is the tradition within which this monumental work is written. Now, more than a half century after its preparation, the Ehrenburg-Grossman volume can be seen as part of the triumph of life over death that so marks the history of the Russian literary tradition. The Holocaust in Russia tested that tradition. It was not found wanting.

But there were other traditions in Russia above and beyond the literary one. And these were more insidious. There was the tradition of Great Russian national chauvinism that prevented the correct measurement of the Nazi devastation of Russia's people and armed forces. There was the tradition of Marxism, with its mean-spirited anti-Semitism well rooted in Marx himself, which drowned the history of the Jews in vicious stereotypes. There was the long history of oppression of the Jews under tsarism, including ghettoization, economic quotas, and random slaughter of Jewish communities. There was Stalinism, which emerged in the post-World War II climate as a cult of personality far beyond anything experienced during the

Leninist revolutionary phase. Stalinism also came with an anti-Semitic backlash, marching along a trajectory of extermination plans of its own.

All of these virulent streams of Russian and Soviet prejudices came together in the post World War Two crackdown on figures such as Grossman who were falsely charged with treason and espionage because of his involvement in the Jewish Anti-Fascist Committee, and because of their heartfelt response as Jews to Nazi atrocities on occupied Soviet territory. Stalin had created the committee to rally support for Russia during the World, but he then disbanded it after the war, as his paranoia mounted about Soviet Jews. All of this is documented in the Annals of Communism Series, especially the volume edited by Joshua Rubenstein and Vladimir P. Naumov on *Stalin's Secret Pogrom.* As author of *Tangled Loyalties: The Life and Times of Ilya Ehrenburg,* Rubenstein is a highly qualified commentator on this unique aspect of Soviet Communism. Indeed, were it not for the timely demise of the Soviet dictator in 1953, historians uniformly agree that the purges resulting from the so-called "Doctor's Plot" (the presumed effort to kill Stalin by medical means) and the various show trials in Eastern Europe (in which a preponderance of those executed were Jewish), would have likely spread to the Jewish masses. In such a climate and without the countervailing need any longer to show the wartime Western allies a liberal face, the interest of the Soviet dictatorship for books like *The Black Book of Russian Jewry* ended. Such a book was also embarrassing to the post-Nazi German regimes of Konrad Adenauer in the West and Erich Honecker in the East—both of whom were in search of a muted, if not sanitized, German past.

Given the Stalinist cast of mind that prevailed at the close of the war, Ehrenburg in particular, and to his lasting credit, Grossman far less so, became architects of a myth that Soviet life was the model antithesis to the Nazi tyranny. Despite all that subsequently took place, that myth still fuels those who prefer to see the twin pillars of twentieth century totalitarianism as somehow polar opposites. The Stalinist regime portrayed the Second World War as essentially a simplistic conflict between capitalism run amok and communism fighting the popular class battle. If the imagery of the bourgeoisie in collusion with the Junkers doing battle against the proletariat and Bolsheviks was to be maintained, what was one to do with evidence of a specific assault by the Nazi armed forces against a specific people—the Jewish people? The Stalinist answer was immediate and clear: suppress such views as heretical and erroneous. This was exactly the fate of *The Black Book of Russian Jewry*. The press plates were removed from the printing plant in 1946—one year following the conclusion of hostilities. This book was viewed as a danger to the Communist regime and its narrow mechanical commitment to social class as the only explanatory variable.

The Black Book of Russian Jewry became a weapon in the hands of Soviet anti-Semitism instead of as originally intended a tool for understanding the history and fate of Jewish community life in the USSR. This neat bit of ideological trickery was performed by the Soviet insistence that the Jewish Anti-Fascist Committee was a "center for nationalistic and espionage activity". Under the supervision of Stalin and his legal henchman, Andrei Vyshinsky, the leaders of this tool of Soviet wartime policy became the victims of post-war xenophobic nationalism. In this monstrous episode of legal murder identification with *The Black Book of Russian Jewry* became a touchstone of Jewish "nationalism". This is all fully and tragically documented in the remarkable trial records of The Jewish Anti-Fascist Committee provided by Joshua Rubenstein and Vladimir Naumov in *Stalin's Secret Pogrom.*

An intellectual trap was set by a Leninist-Stalinist formulation of the "national question". It waited only to be sprung on those peoples who took seriously the idea of a national culture for Jews within a larger federation of Soviet peoples. Birobidzhan was to be set aside by the Association for Jewish Colonization in the Soviet Union as a "promised land". It was, in the words of the martyr, Peretz Markish to be a "cherished fatherland within the borders of the great Soviet Union". The myth of a Jewish Autonomous Province on the vast expanses of the Far Eastern Territory" had much in common with the Nazi propaganda machine claim that the resolution of the Jewish Question would be through their removal as a people to Madagascar, where presumably they could also enjoy the fruits of their autonomy. But in a rare post-war moment, Markish said what all Jews who are free know all too well. " There are no two Jewish peoples. The Jewish nation is one. Just as a heart cannot be cut up and divided, so one cannot split up the Jewish people into Polish Jews and Russian Jews. Everywhere we are, and shall remain, one entity." Thus in one fell swoop, the myth of national liberation within the Soviet family of nations became the crime of cosmopolitanism, of a worldview that transcended and ultimately discarded the charade of a Jewish nation deprived of its Hebrew origins and ancient roots.

In *The Passing of an Illusion: The Idea of Communism in the Twentieth Century,* François Furet brilliantly describes the quandary and ultimate the fate of writers like Ehrenburg and Grossman. Stalinism continued and even accentuated rather than resolved the problem of Jews in Soviet Russia. Even those dedicated to the Communist regime, the Red Army, and the tradition of Chekhov and Tolstoy could not reverse that trend. They became reluctant partners to the illusion rather than the solution. Furet's description, coming at the conclusion of an extended examination of Grossman and his work, sums up the situation bluntly: "Stalin's regime emerged unaltered from its victory. Indeed, it added another group to its panoply of hatred and persecution: the Jews, or at least the Jews who managed to survive the Nazi genocide. Soviet anti-Semitism was stronger, and was more encouraged by those in power, after the war than in any other period of the USSR's history. It would culminate in the massive anti-Zionist campaign between 1949 and 1953. How could Grossman, a Russian Jew who was the most assiduous witness of the Jewish tragedy, be allowed to appropriate Stalingrad, that monument to the glory of the Stalinist regime? The war exacerbated the fate of the nation. Won thanks to the extraordinary virtues of a naive people that had put its faith in Stalin, it led to a reinforcement of totalitarian power comparable to that of Nazi Germany" Thus a combination of large scale factors came together to make *The Black Book of Russian Jewry* a non-book in a Russian context. The suppression of this book, and the recording of horrors it details, served multiple ends: it relieved former Nazis from standing trial for war crimes, and enhanced Communists actively involved in expanding the Soviet empire into the heart of Central Europe. Those who knew of the Ehrenburg-Grossman work did not care; and those who cared did not know. That was the fate of a landmark book—and of a people who had come to see Communist Europe as another charnel house rather than a resting-place for the weary.

The Complete Black Book of Russian Jewry is an anomaly, a holy book, a last will and testament of more than a million victims of Nazi tyranny prepared by two "secular" Jews, dedicated to the myth of a national minority without a moral identity. But God's choice of reporters has seen greater ironies and more far-fetched choices. The weight of the catastrophe is such that Ehrenberg and Grossman were wise enough and sufficiently talented as writers to avoid even a hint of exaggeration or tendentiousness. The awfulness and randomness of the individual deaths revealed the grand plan of the Hitlerites. The determinism of the collective design in its very imperfection, in allowing people to slip through the Gordian knot, provided human witnesses, or if you will, the empirical evidence, to the atrocities being committed on a routinized, daily basis.

So here, at the end of the day, sixty years after the Nazi onslaught in Russia commenced, with its single-minded effort to remove the Jewish people from history, body and soul, we finally have the full documentation of what took place. This story is not revealed on military maps and nor in political communiqués about the glorious struggles of the Soviet homeland, but on the bloodied ground of towns and hamlets hardly known. Those of us who watched the maps as children intuitively sensed the magnitude and consequences of the invasion of Soviet Russia by the Nazi Germany. Now we have the completion of that record. While the bizarre Soviet notion of posthumous rehabilitation of people it liquidated can hardly mitigate this horrid Hitler-inspired nightmare, perhaps the more than one million murdered Russian Jewish souls can rest a little more easily with the complete publication of the Ehrenburg-Grossman material. I doubt seriously that those of us who live will be able to say the same after reading this testament offered to the present about evils performed in the all too recent past.

Acknowledgements

I would like to record my gratitude to three people who made this project possible. First and foremost to David Patterson in Memphis, Tennessee. He worked on the translation, editing, and reconstruction of this massive, disorganized text in single-handed isolation. Professor Patterson makes us realize again that acts of scholarship are not confined to the well-funded research centers of the world, but start and finish with the private person. Second, is the editorial work of Laurence Mintz of Transaction. He was uniquely able to undertake the editorial work involved as a result of his deep commitment to the project, knowledge of the Russian language, and an elegant sense of rendering prose in appropriate English. Finally, to Joshua Feigenbaum, my former student, continuing good friend and supporter of this project and of Transaction and its mission from the outset. Without his assistance I seriously doubt that the work would have been completed and presented to the public in so appropriate a fashion.

Irving Louis Horowitz
Princeton, New Jersey
June 15th, 2001

References

Davidowicz, Lucy. *The War Against the Jews: 1933-1945.* New York: Holt, Rinehart & Winston, 1975.

Ehrenburg, Ilya and Vasily Grossman. *The Complete Black Book of Russian Jewry.* New Brunswick and London: Transaction Publishers, 2001.

Furet, Francois. *The Passing of an Illusion: The Idea of Communism in the Twentieth Century.* Chicago: University of Chicago Press, 1999.

Hilberg, Raul. *The Destruction of European Jewry.* Chicago: Quadrangle Books, Publishers. 1961.

Horowitz, Irving Louis. *Taking Lives: Genocide and State Power* (5th edition). New Brunswick and London: Transaction Publishers, 2001.

Laqueur, Walter (editor). *The Holocaust Encyclopedia.* New Haven and London: Yale University Press, 2001.

Rubenstein, Joshua and Vladimir P. Naumov (editors). *Stalin's Secret Pogrom: The Post-War Inquisition of the Jewish Anti-Fascist Committee.* New Haven and London: Yale University Press, 2001.

Rummel, R.J. *Death By Government: Genocide and Mass Murder since 1900.* New Brunswick and London: Transaction Publishers, 1994.

Solzhenitsyn, Aleksandr. *The Gulag Archipelago, 1918-1956: An Experiment in Literary Imagination* (in three volumes). New York and London: Harper & Row, 1973-1978.

Introduction

This edition of *The Black Book* is a tribute both to the memory of victims of the Nazi Holocaust in the territories of the former Soviet Union and to the collecting and recording of that event by Ilya Ehrenburg and his co-reporters. It is also a tribute to the tenacity and dedication of his daughter Irina, whose tireless efforts rescued the manuscript from an obscure fate. It is this triumph of truth and the resurrection of millions of voices from silence that is presented here.

A compilation of letters, diaries, memoirs statements, testimonies of victims and witnesses, notes, fragments, pleas for help as well as calls for remembrance and revenge, *The Black Book* came into being during the war years, 1941-45. It also includes testimonies about rescuers, articles about some of the death camps, and selections from a "Report of the Extraordinary Government Commission [. . .]," as well as articles and documentary materials focusing on testimonies of the criminals. The book reflects the horrors of Nazi atrocities against the Jews, their mass murder and torture, and reveals all the horror of their designs not only upon the Jews but upon humanity. The voices that rise up from these pages, mostly those of victims, are voices from the grave crying out to be heard. The compilation of these materials forms the basis of what has became known as *The Black Book*.

Ilya Ehrenburg felt it his obligation and a debt to his fellow Jews to make the world aware of the tragedy that befell them during the Holocaust. One of the most influential writers living in the Soviet Union at the time, Ehrenburg began collecting these materials during the war (1942-1943). It is at about then (1943) that the title of the work is first mentioned. Later, under Ehrenburg's leadership, a Literary Commission of the Jewish Antifascist Committee was formed. This Commission, together with a number of other writers, undertook the task of collecting and editing *The Black Book*. In 1945 Vasily Grossman, a well known Russian writer, took over the editorial work. By 1946 the book was completed and, under Ehrenburg's and Grossman's editorship, presented for publication. The censor's approval was granted, the type plates were set, and the galley proofs printed and corrected. It was scheduled for publication in early 1947, but as fate would have it, Stalin's policy towards the Jews suddenly changed. Jews were labeled enemies of the people, international spies, and other Soviet pejoratives. Thus speaking sympathetically about the Jews and their fate became an anti-

Soviet act. Publication of *The Black Book* was forbidden. In 1948 the type plates were destroyed, along with all existing copies of gallery-proofs. Until his death in 1967, however, Ilya Ehrenburg persisted in his hope to see the complete manuscript of *The Black Book* published in Russia—something that has yet to come to pass.

I first heard about *The Black Book* from Ilya Ehrenburg's daughter Irina, whom I met in the summer of 1981. Starting with that meeting, during my annual summer visit to Moscow, and every year thereafter, *The Black Book* was always a subject of our conversations.

After her father's death, Irina, took up the task and continued in the hope that the forbidden manuscript would be found and published. In 1970, while going through her father's archives, Irina found folders containing parts of *The Black Book*.[1] She was afraid that they would be confiscated, so, with the help of a foreign diplomat, she smuggled them out to the Yad Vashem Archives in Jerusalem, where they became part of the Ehrenburg Collection. This manuscript—together with another brought there in 1965,[2] supplemented with materials from articles published by Ehrenburg in *Znamia* and in Yiddish in *Emes*, as well as material from the 1946 Romanian version—was published in 1980 in Jerusalem by the Tarbut Press as *Chernaya kniga, The Black Book*. In 1981 an English translation was produced in New York by the Holocaust Library. It was this book which has become *The Black Book* for the English speaking reader and student of the Holocaust.

In 1990, thanks to *perestroika, glasnost*, and later the collapse of the Soviet Union, a complete copy of the original gallery-proofs was brought to Irina by a friend who claimed to have "found" it among his father's papers. The rest is history. Between 1990 and 1993 Irina spent days and nights with a magnifying lass, straining her weak eyes in an effort to proof read the manuscript, correct spelling mistakes, restore correct names of towns and villages in rural areas of Ukraine, Belarus, Lithuania, Eastern Poland, and other parts of the Former Soviet Union. She even enlisted the help of friends traveling to those areas in order to correct errors that had crept into the original manuscript because of illegible, or indistinct handwriting. In the meantime, the Jewish Lithuanian[3] publishing house Yad decided to publish this work. It came out in Russian in 1993. Almost immediately thereafter, it was translated into French, German, and other languages, and now, finally, into English. The fulfillment of Irina Ehrenburg's dream materialized during the last days of her life when, in June 1997, she learned that David Patterson, had found an American publisher who agreed to publish the book in English translation. This was a moment of great joy for Irina. Her wish to have the complete *Black Book* published was about to be realized. She died that same month knowing that success had been achieved.

Scholars writing about *The Black Book* often comment on its unique fate and its connection to history and Stalin's policy against the Jews. With this publication, the version of *The Black Book* originally slated to come out in 1947 has finally appeared. Currently, at least four earlier versions carrying the same title exist. Including this publication, there are now five versions of *The Black Book*, all produced between 1946 and 1993.

The recurring use of the same title has created confusion for readers. Two versions of *The Black Book* were published in 1946, one in Romanian as *Cartea Neagra* in Bucharest, another "in English in New York."[4] Both of these versions are incomplete, and contain primarily materials published in the Soviet Union by Ehrenburg in *Znamia* and *Emes*. The third version of *Chernaya kniga—The Black Book*—was published in Jerusalem in 1980 and in English in New York in 1981. This third revision was based on the materials brought to Yad Vashem in

1965, and on the folio containing *The Black Book* materials sent to Yad Vashem by Irina Ehrenburg in 1970. It is incomplete since it lacks over a third of the materials contained in the original *Black Book* initially slated for publication in 1947.

To confuse matters still further, there is a fourth version of the book, the so-called *Neizvestnaya chernaya kniga*, or *The Unknown Black Book*, published in 1993. This was compiled by Ilya Altman and edited by a most distinguished group of Holocaust scholars. It was published jointly by Yad Vashem and GARF (State Archive of the Russian Federation). This book includes materials from the GARF archives which had been collected by Ehrenburg and the Antifascist Jewish Committee for *The Black Book* but not included in the version prepared for publication in 1947. It also contains materials from the Ehrenburg collection at Yad Vashem. This work is distinguished by its inclusion of valuable materials which could not have been published during the Soviet period because of their implication of Soviet citizens, Ukrainians, Belorussians, Lithuanians, Latvians, Estonians and others in the crimes committed against Jews in their regions. The similarity of the title and its organization and type of material included, all suggest this to be an extension of *The Black Book*.

In 1993, the original *Black Book*, the version which had been initially approved for publication in 1946 and then forbidden in 1947, was finally published by the Jewish publishing house Yad in Vilnius. It is this edition which you have before you. It contains all of the entries carefully selected by Ehrenburg and Grossman in 1945 and 1946. This is the book which Ilya Ehrenburg, and after his death Irina Ehrenburg, dreamed and worked to have published. This is the original *Black Book*. Its appearance some forty six years after its scheduled publication is a reversal of the order in which events normally happen. The book which should have been published first has been published last. This task is completed. Now, thanks to the translation presented here, the English reader is able to enter the horrible world of the Holocaust and hear the voices of its victims and witnesses as Ilya Ehrenburg, Vasily Grossman, and members of the Antifascist Jewish Committee originally intended.

Helen Segall
Dickinson College

Notes

1.   Personal communication with Irina Ehrenburg, & *Chernaya kniga*, 1993, p. 111.
2.   *The Black Book*, 1981, p. xxiv.
3.   Ehrenburg had a special relationship with Lithuanian Jews, especially with Lithuanian Partisans and the Jewish Museum in Vilnius which temporarily housed parts of the manuscript of *The Black Book*.
4.   *The Black Book*, 1981, p. xxiv.

Introduction to the 1993 Russian edition of *The Black Book*

The history of *The Black Book* resembles the history of our own country. It too contains many facts that are yet to be revealed, or, as we are now accustomed to saying, many dark spots. I have questioned the people who contributed to it, read various items as they have been published, and examined numerous archival materials. I have subsequently managed to restore the intricate epic known as *The Black Book* to its general wholeness.

Those who were on the front during the war sent Ilya Ehrenburg[1] a vast quantity of documents found in the territories freed from the occupation forces. In their letters they related what they had seen and heard. From the materials sent to him, Ehrenburg gathered together diaries, letters from the dead, and testimonial evidence relating to the annihilation of the Jews by Hitler's minions. And he decided to publish those materials in *The Black Book*. Working with author Vasily Grossman,[2] Ehrenburg took up the task of selecting the most striking material, abridging it, and clarifying those passages that were difficult to understand. Grossman and Ehrenburg enlisted a group of writers and journalists in this work, and the Literary Commission of the Jewish Anti-Fascist Committee was formed.

In 1943 Ehrenburg wrote to one of his readers: "I am working on *The Black Book*."

Early in 1944, under the headline "Murderers of Peoples," the magazine *Znamya* published several excerpts from the forthcoming book. The collection of materials was completed and the struggle for its publication began. In that same year Ehrenburg appeared at a meeting of the Literary Commission. Judging from the shorthand minutes of the meeting, he had this to say: "I was told, 'Do the book, and if it is good, it will be published.' But I don't understand what 'if it is good' means. This is not a novel, whose contents are unknown."

In 1945 the existence of the Literary Commission was cut short, and the publication of *The Black Book* was entrusted directly to the Jewish Committee, which at that time was headed by S. Lozovsky.

To all the members of the former Literary Commission Ehrenburg sent letters expressing his gratitude for their help. Then he added, "I am deeply convinced that the work you have undertaken will not disappear from history."

On 5 April 1945 Lozovsky wrote to Ehrenburg suggesting that two books be published: one containing only documents, the other materials prepared by Grossman and Ehrenburg.

On 26 February 1946 a resolution was issued by the new commission organized under the Jewish Committee: "Neither of the variants of *The Black Book* circulated for examination fully represents the edited materials. The commission believes that in the selections presented it is unnecessary to relate the tales about the vile activities of those who were traitors to our homeland."

Nevertheless in that same year the first part of *The Black Book* came out in Romania, while in Moscow Strongin, editor of the Jewish literary publishing house Der Emes, informed Grossman that he was indeed sending him the original *Black Book* for typesetting. The financial accounts of I. Pfeffer, a member of the Presidium of the Jewish Antifascist Committee of the USSR, confirmed that *The Black Book* was coming out in Russian in Moscow through Der Emes publishing house and that it was "in production."

In 1947 Ehrenburg handed over to the Vilna Jewish Museum for temporary storage and for their own utilization two albums consisting of 413 pages and containing materials from *The Black Book*.

In his book *People, Years, Life*, Ehrenburg wrote, "On 20 November 1948, when the Jewish Antifascist Committee was closed down, the typesetting for *The Black Book* was scattered, and the galley proofs and manuscript were taken away." At that same time portfolios of the materials from Vilna were returned to Ehrenburg.

In 1960 the Historical Museum of Vilna requested that Ehrenburg lend them the documents he had compiled on the fascists' annihilation of the Jewish communities. After a year Ehrenburg demanded the return of the material. "I need it for my work," he wrote to the museum. They returned the portfolios.

In his letters from 1965 Ehrenburg reports, "Negotiations are being conducted with the APN[3] regarding the publication of *The Black Book*. But nothing has come of it."

The manuscript ended up in Jerusalem, and only in 1980 did the Israeli publishing house Tarbut release *The Black Book* in Russian. As indicated in the preface to that edition, however, some of the material never turned up in Israel.

As I was going through my father's archives in 1970, I discovered some portfolios labeled *The Black Book*. Knowing that the KGB would be interested in them, I entrusted them to the care of various people. In the early 1980s I forwarded the materials to Jerusalem, to Yad Vashem, the Institute dedicated to the memory of the victims of Nazism and the heroes of the resistance, for I knew that there they would be kept safe.

In January of that year one of my friends sent me a copy of *The Black Book* that was circulated in 1947; Grossman had given it to him some time ago. In it was written in somebody's hand, "As per corrections for printing. 14.VI.47." There was an illegible signature. Based on that copy recovered by some miracle, this book was compiled.

In his memoirs Ehrenburg wrote, "I devoted much strength, time, and heart to the work on *The Black Book*. . . . I used to dream that *The Black Book* would be published."

After more than forty-five years his dream has come true.

Irina Ehrenburg

Notes

1. Ilya Grigorevich Ehrenburg (1891-1967) was a prominent and controversial novelist, journalist, and poet. At times a defender of Stalin, he was also the first to publicize the destruction of a generation of writers during the Stalinist period. His novel *The Storm* (1947) contains some of the first descriptions of Nazi atrocities; it was followed by his best known novel *The Thaw* (1954) and by his memoirs *People, Years, Life* (1961-1965).
2. Vasily Semyonovich Grossman (1905-1964) was a novelist and short story writer who dealt with themes of the Soviet struggle. During World War II he was a correspondent for the journal *Krasnaya Zvezda*. Although he was a loyal communist for many years, his last novel *Everything Is in Flux* (published posthumously) is a severe indictment of Soviet society.
3. Soviet censorship office.

From the Editors of *The Black Book*

The Black Book tells the tale of the pervasive mass murder of Soviet Jewish citizens organized and executed by the German fascist forces in the temporarily occupied territories of Russia, the Ukraine, Latvia, Lithuania, and Estonia.

In some cases the accounts deal with the fate of Soviet Jewish citizens deported to annihilation camps in Poland (Auschwitz, Treblinka, Sobibor). Although these camps were located in Poland and not in Soviet territories, the editors considered it necessary to include a description of them in the book.

In a number of places those doomed to death mounted a fierce armed resistance.

In the light of that resistance, there emerged a struggle to halt the flow of trains to Treblinka and other annihilation camps; that struggle, in turn, often gave rise to preparations for general uprisings. For just such reasons the Warsaw Ghetto Uprising took place: here too the deportation of Warsaw Jews to Treblinka gave rise to preparations for the uprising. Because it clearly characterizes analogous events that occurred in the Soviet territories occupied by the Germans, the editors have included in the book a piece on the Warsaw Ghetto uprising, even though it may violate the strict organizational principle of breaking down the description of events according to occupied Soviet territories. The great victory in Stalingrad generally inspired revolt. Like a flash of hope, the knowledge of it brought light to the darkness of the camps and ghettos.

The sum of materials included in *The Black Book* may be divided into three categories.

The first category consists of letters, diaries, transcripts of statements and depositions of witnesses, including eye-witnesses and victims who escaped from the fascist violence. Many of the letters come from the pens of people executed by the Germans. These letters were turned over to the editors of *The Black Book* by friends and relatives of those who perished.

The second category consists of selections written by Soviet writers. These selections were based on depositions, letters, diaries, and transcribed accounts. These materials were presented to the writers by the editors of *The Black Book*. Everything set forth in these selections is in keeping with those materials. In some cases the writers spoke personally with the witnesses. They examined sites of mass executions, ghetto areas, and annihilation camps; they were present at the unearthing of mass graves, for the compiling of official reports, and so on.

In the third category are materials that the editors of *The Black Book* presented to the Special State Commission on the Verification and Investigation of Atrocities Committed by the German Fascist Invaders. These materials include depositions given during the official inquiry by those who directly organized and perpetrated the murders, as well as depositions of witnesses.

In preparing *The Black Book* for publication, the editors have set for themselves the following goals.

The Black Book is presented as a memorial to be placed upon the countless mass graves of Soviet people who were tortured and murdered by the German fascists.

A document incriminating the fascist villains, *The Black Book* provides an account of the bloodiest crimes of the German fascist government. The book should stir an abhorrence and a loathing toward the savage ideology of fascism and should serve the great life-affirming idea of the equality of people and peace among them.

[*The Black Book* is presented as material for the prosecution of the criminal fascist organizers and participants in the murders of millions of women, old men, and children.][1]

Note

1.   Portions of the text that appear in squared brackets are from the 1946 variant of the text, which was smuggled out of the Soviet Union and sent to Yad Vashem in Jerusalem.

Preface

I

During the years of its domination German fascism transformed entire lands and regions into wastelands, destroyed hundreds of cities, demolished the capitals of many European countries, and burned tens of thousands of towns and villages. During the years of its domination German fascism destroyed millions of human lives. If we take a mental glance at those European countries where the Hitlerites ruled and consider the utterly brutal atrocities, if we measure the sheer enormity of the destruction of cultural values shared by all humanity, it may seem that everything that happened was the outcome of madness, the result of insanity. It may seem that during those years elemental forces, the forces of chaos, ruled over Europe like an uncontrollable hurricane. The crimes are so inhuman, the destruction so senseless and massive, that such a thought automatically enters one's mind. It seems that human reason has no part in this, that by its very nature it cannot be part of this. Such, however, is not the case. The whirlwind that passed through Europe did not arise spontaneously. The whirlwind had its organizers. Atrocities never before seen by humanity were founded upon the elaborate reasoning of the advocates of racist theory and the theory of living space for the German people. These theories were preached and cultivated by the leaders of German Fascism, by Hitler, Göring,[1] Rosenberg,[2] Streicher,[3] Goebbels,[4] and many others. Hundreds of books were written, research institutes were created, and academic departments were organized for the validation of racist theory. Ancient and modern history, jurisprudence, the laws of economic development, the history of philosophy and the history of culture, religious beliefs, and the ethical and moral precepts of humanity were all revised by the advocates of racism. The people of the world now know what racist theory and the theory of "living space" for the German people are, what fascist justice, ethics, and all such elements of fascist ideology are. The ruins of Europe and countless mass graves attest to all of this.

The principles worked out by the Nazi theoreticians found their realization in German legislation; in the activities of Reichsführer SS Himmler[5]; in the actions of his deputy Kaltenbrunner[6]; by the regents of the occupied states such as Rosenberg, Koch,[7] Frank,[8]

Seyss-Inquart[9]; in the hundreds, thousands, and tens of thousands of members of the Gestapo[10]; in the officers of SS[11] troops; in the leaders of the SA[12] and SD[13]; in the gendarmes; in the police battalions and regiments; in the offices of the commandants; and in the countless Brigadenführers, Obersturmbannführers, Rottenführers, Ober- and Unterscharführers, Sonderführers, and so on.

The mass murder and forced enslavement of millions of people had a timetable and standards regulated according to the fulfillment of monthly and quarterly deadlines. The transport of millions of people condemned either to death or to slavery required the coordinated planning of train schedules. Chemists, experts in thermodynamics, engineers, and building specialists participated in the construction of gas chambers and crematoria for burning bodies. These structures were carefully designed, and the designs were submitted for examination and approved. A technology of mass murder was worked out according to specific functions, as is usual in the process of mass production. Money and valuables belonging to those who were murdered were deposited in government accounts; furniture, personal items, clothing, and shoes were sorted, gathered into warehouses, and then distributed. After placing their orders, agricultural installations, military enterprises, and soap factories received and distributed women's hair, ashes, and the crushed bones of those who were murdered. No, it was not a whirlwind that swept through Europe. It was the theory and practice of racism. It was a plan and the realization of that plan. It was an idea and the fulfillment of that idea. It was a design and an edifice constructed according to that design.

At the cost of tremendous sacrifice, only the stubborn, bloody struggle of the freedom-loving people of the world, above all of the Soviet people, demolished the edifice constructed by the German fascists and destroyed the executioner's block that Hitler erected in the heart of Europe.

Hitler, his general staff, his field marshals, and his advisors considered the Red Army and the Soviet state their primary, mortal enemies. Preparing a treacherous, lightning assault on the Soviet Union, Hitler mobilized the military power of Germany and its satellites to suppress the resistance of the Red Army with a surprise attack and superior power.

In the deadly throes of a terrible struggle the Red Army displayed a selflessness and courage never before seen in the world. The Red Army pitted military technology developed by the young Soviet industry against German military technology. The Soviet people and the Red Army pitted the Soviet humanism in which their soldiers, officers, and generals were educated against the dark ideas of racism. The Red Army pitted a remarkable Stalinist strategy that reflected a full, far-seeing, profound understanding of the dynamic forces of conflict against the dull strategy of the German fascist command.

On the battlefields the great ideas of progress, democracy, national equality, and the friendship of people triumphed over the forces of darkness and reactionism, and the Soviet people have been and will be the bearers of those ideas. The Soviet people will struggle without compromise against all the attempts of reactionaries and imperialists to revive the ideology and the practice of fascism. All the honest democratic powers of the world support the Soviet people in their struggle.

II

From the first days when they seized power, even during their struggle for power, the Nazis declared the Jews to be the principal cause of all the evils that have befallen humankind.

The advocates of racist theory mobilized all their resources: lies, wild and senseless slander, medieval prejudices long since overcome, the provocative conclusions of a fanatic pseudo-science—in a word the entire arsenal employed from ancient times by reactionaries, obscurantists, and political outlaws who wish to hide from the people the true aims and the real reasons for organizing their criminal game. Why has reactionism always appeared under the aegis of anti-Semitism? Because reactionism has never stood in defense of the genuine interests of the broad masses of the people; because reactionism always fights for the interests of separate, privileged groups, strikes out against the interests of the people, against the objective laws of social development, against truth. In such a struggle, of course, it is impossible to appeal to the rational judgment of society, to a sense of justice, or to the laws of humanity and democracy. In such a struggle it is necessary to appeal to prejudice, to lie, to indulge base instincts, to deceive, and to engage in unbridled demagoguery. Therefore, with its intention of casting the people of Europe into the carnage of brother against brother, German fascism resorted to inflaming the passion of racial hatred, to reviving anti-Semitic ravings and prejudices, and to deceiving the masses. This was done in order to obscure the consciousness of the masses of the German people; to strengthen them in the delusion of their imagined superiority over the rest of the people of the world; and to instill in them feelings of cruelty, pride, and contempt for humanity. This was done in order to demolish and tear asunder the idea of the brotherhood of the workers of the world.

The demagogic principle of racial dissidence, racial hatred, racial superiority, and racial privilege was adopted by Hitler as the basis for the Nazi party and its government policies. The German race—the "master race"—was declared to stand at the pinnacle of the racial pyramid. Then came the Anglo-Saxon races, which were regarded as inferior, and then the Latin races, which were of even less value. At the base of the pyramid were the Slavs, a race of slaves. The fascists positioned the Jews opposite all people inhabiting the world. Fascism took the Jews to be guilty of utterly fantastic crimes: of aspiring toward world domination and the enslavement of all the people of the world. The fascists declared themselves to be the defenders of humanity against the Jews. Racial distinctions, the distinctions of blood, were declared to be the decisive elements in the whole historical process. From the standpoint of Hitlerism, history is the history of the struggle among the races; the laws of history lead to the triumph of a superior race over the inferior races, to the annihilation and disappearance of the inferior races.

Here we should recall the words of Stalin, written in response to a request from the Jewish Telegraphic Agency in America:

> In answer to your question, nationalistic and racist chauvinism is a vestige of customs characteristic of a period of cannibalism. As the extreme form of racist chauvinism, anti-Semitism is the most dangerous vestige of cannibalism. Like a lightning rod protecting capitalism from the blow of the workers, anti-Semitism benefits their exploiters. Anti-Semitism is dangerous for workers, a false path leading them from the true way and luring them into a jungle. Therefore, in keeping with their international outlook, communists cannot help but be the implacable and sworn enemies of anti-Semitism. In the USSR anti-Semitism is prosecuted in the most severe manner as a phenomenon deeply hostile toward the Soviet order. In accordance with the laws of the USSR, active anti-Semites receive the death penalty.
>
> J. Stalin

These words were written by Comrade Stalin on 12 January 1931, when the German fascists were fanning the fires of racial hatred with all their might, as they prepared to seize power. History has demonstrated whose side truth was on. The fascists have always striven to relegate the relationship with the Jews to a special section of their racist program. Always and everywhere—in their attack against the workers, in their violence against the intelligentsia, against the progressive course of science, literature, and art, in the programs they inflict upon universities and institutions of learning, and in their revision of school programs—the fascists have made noise about the Jews. Always and everywhere the Jews have been declared to be the universal source of evil: in the trade unions, in government institutions, in factory shops, in the editorial offices of magazines and newspapers, in commerce, in philosophy, in music, in legal societies, in medical science, in the railroads, and so on.

Under the pretense of doing battle with the Jews fascism has raided, destroyed, and burned out the spirit of resistance, the spirit of protest. In the territories occupied by German fascist troops, the distinction between the Jews and other nationalities was constantly made. Why was this done? These acts of violence were committed in order to create the impression that the German fascists set the destruction of the Jews as the primary aim of their activities in the territories, as if to divert the blow from the rest of the people.

Undertaking the greatest provocation in history, fascism wanted to hide its true face from the people of the world. Fascism wanted to strike from human consciousness the great concept of "man."

In 1935 the Union of National Socialist Jurists proposed to eliminate from the German civil code the concept of "man," having replaced it with other concepts, for the concept of "man," in the opinion of the German fascist jurists, "clouds and distorts the distinction between a member of a tribe, and imperial citizen, a foreigner, a Jew, and so on."

But fascism did not succeed in eliminating the concept of "man."

III

The consistency in the activities of the German fascist government leaves not a shadow of a doubt that in a gradual, step-by-step manner Hitler and his cohorts planned the murder of millions of people. On 15 September 1935 in Nuremberg the Reich Citizenship Law was passed with the signatures of Reich Chancellor Hitler and Reich Minister of Internal Affairs Wilhelm Frick.[14] The second paragraph of this law reads: "A Reich citizen is someone only of German or kindred blood who through his behavior demonstrates that he is willing and able to faithfully serve the German people and the Reich." Through this law German Jews, foreigners, and all Germans who were hostile toward the Hitler regime were at once deprived of German citizenship.

The fourth paragraph in Hitler's Citizenship Law reads: "Only those who have German blood flowing in their veins can be a German citizen. Therefore Jews cannot belong to the German people."

At the same time that the Law of German Citizenship was passed, on 15 September 1935 the Law for the Preservation of German Blood and German Honor went into effect. This law was issued with the signatures of Chancellor Hitler, Internal Affairs Minister Frick, Justice Minister Gürtner,[15] and the Führer's Deputy Hess,[16] an official with no credentials. The first paragraph of the law forbade marriages between Jews and German subjects with German and kindred blood. The fifth paragraph stated: "Those who violate the prohibition set forth in Paragraph I will be sentenced to hard labor." Another paragraph declared: "Jews are forbidden to fly the national flag of the Reich or to make use of the colors of the Reich."

From then on laws, decrees, and explanations rained down as though from a cornucopia. Newspapers and legal publications began to glow with such terms as "full Jew," "mongrel Jew," "three-quarters Jew," "half Jew," "one-quarter Jew," "pure-blooded German," "German-related blood." A decree enacted on 14 November 1935 declared that Jews were deprived of the right to vote and that they were forbidden to hold civil service positions. It was announced that as of 31 December 1935 all Jews working in government offices would be retired. For those born of mixed marriages, calculations were made to determine the percentage of Jewish blood in their ancestral line. Ancestors' marriages going back to 1800 were subject to investigation. The grandfathers, great-grandfathers, and great-great-grandfathers of anyone wishing to enter into marriage were examined in detail. Next came new prohibitions against working. Jewish doctors were forbidden to treat "Aryans." Prohibitions against working in the universities, publishing books, and giving lectures came crashing down on Jews in the sciences, literature, and the arts.

This was the initial period of legislative and administrative restrictions, the period of isolating the Jews, of expelling them from all areas of science, industry, and social life.

While all of this was taking place, the Hitlerite government and Nazi Party were organizing and provoking open acts of violence: pogroms, massacres, the pillaging of stores and apartments, and murder. Wave after wave of pogroms swept through Germany. Their organizers and perpetrators were members of the Gestapo, Storm Troops, and activists of the Nazi Party.

At the same time—hidden under the black fog of racial hatred and demagogic harping on the defense of blood, state, and German honor—the resistance of the German people and all democratic organizations was crushed and destroyed. Tens of thousands of the leading proponents and progressive activists were imprisoned in concentration camps and executed for high treason. The process of the fascist takeover of trade unions, of state and private institutions, of the arts and sciences, of secondary and post-secondary schools, and of all areas of social life proceeded without exception in a manner parallel to the pogroms and anti-Semitic activity of the German government.

Perhaps never before in history has the connection between reactionism and anti-Semitism been so graphic and concrete; perhaps never before has it been so obvious that the anti-Semitic campaign was undertaken to conceal a general assault on the rights and freedom of the working classes.

The second period of Nazi policies regarding the Jews corresponded with the beginning of World War II, with the German invasion of Poland, France, Norway, Belgium, and a number of other European countries. German imperialism moved on to the open implementation of their plans for aggression. During this period the concepts of "living space," "the superiority of the German race," and "the master race" were unfolded in concrete form. There was talk of the world hegemony of Germany, of the power of German imperialism over all the people of the world.

The attack on the freedom of the people of the world was underway. The people of the world were convinced that German fascism was resolved to take any terrorist measures and would not hesitate to use any form of violence in order to realize its aims.

They demonstrated their resolve.

The German ax was hanging over the people of Europe. True to their tactics, the fascists loudly proclaimed the cruelest forms of terror against the Jews while quietly preparing the massacre of enslaved people. New provocations began on an unprecedented scale. Although multiplied many times over, the initial period of the persecution of the Jews was reminiscent of the anti-Semitic activity of the Black Hundreds[17] in tsarist Russia during the difficult days of reactionism; but the stage they now reached surpassed the darkest times of the Middle Ages. Ghettos were organized in the region of eastern territories. Millions of Polish Jews were driven into the ghettos. The Germans then began transporting Jews from Germany, Austria, and Czechoslovakia to these Polish ghettos. The Jewish inhabitants of small towns and villages were concentrated into large ghettos. More than half a million people lived in the Warsaw Ghetto alone. In the Lodz Ghetto there were approximately two hundred fifty thousand. The populations of the ghettos in Radom, Lublin, and Czestochowa numbered in the tens of thousands. Stone walls were erected around the ghettos, and bits of glass from broken bottles were affixed to the walls; the walls were enmeshed with barbed wire, through which in some places ran high voltage electricity. At the gates stood SS guards with automatic weapons. All the Jews living in the ghetto were required to wear distinguishing signs: a six-pointed star sewn to the clothing on the chest and on the back.

Life for millions of people passed by under conditions of unprecedented deprivation. The suffering from cold and hunger was terrible. But no less terrible were the moral torments of a people utterly deprived of all rights, excluded from social and industrial life, stamped with the mark of prisoners, left to stand outside of all laws. The very first winter in the ghettos brought epidemics and hundreds of cases of death by starvation. In those days people who thought the ghettos would exist for a long time were regarded as pessimists. Most people assumed that the ghetto was a temporary, "special measure" connected to the war.

But even the darkest pessimists did not guess the true intentions of the Hitlerites.

The concentration of the people into the ghettos was merely a preparation for the complete extermination of the Jewish population. It was a link in a chain of premeditated measures, just one more step that drew millions of people closer to the place of execution. The fascist occupiers of the captured territories once again made use of methods already employed in Germany. Beneath the thunder of Judeo-phobic drums, beneath the din of malevolent slander, and in the poisonous haze of anti-Semitic lies, they quickly and methodically dealt with hundreds of thousands of Polish intellectuals and activists for democracy. They screamed about reprisals against the Jews; at the same time they placed the people of Poland and Czechoslovakia in shackles. In books and newspapers they printed descriptions and photographs of the Warsaw Ghetto, and inconspicuously, on the sly, they murdered Poles and Czechs.

At that time, in the quiet of Berlin offices, detailed plans for the final, decisive stage of the massacre were being carefully worked out; sites for the construction of annihilation camps and death factories were being considered; methods of mass murder were being approved; Himmler and Eichmann[18] were organizing Einsatzgruppen[19] and SD commandos; and designs for gas chambers and crematoria were being examined.

On 22 June 1941 German fascist troops invaded the land of the Soviets.

This was the greatest effort fascist Germany made in its struggle for world domination. Hitler proclaimed this to be a Blitzkrieg, declaring that by the end of 1941 the USSR would cease to exist. After the defeat of the Soviet Union, resistance on the part of England and America would become useless. The fascists assumed that the Blitzkrieg had entered into its decisive phase. Never had the fascists' racist propaganda reached such a scale as at this time. Instructed beforehand down to the finest details and armed to the teeth, SS bands,

Einsatzkommandos, Einsatzgruppen, and SD units awaited the order to murder. In June of 1941 Hitler gave that order. On a scale never before seen by humanity, there began a massacre of millions of Soviet citizens, chief among whom were communists, military commissars, and Jews.

This slaughter was a link in the sweeping chain of terrorist measures by which the German fascists wanted to paralyze the will to resist among freedom-loving Soviet people. Using unheard-of cruelty, the fascists wanted to stun the Soviet people. Streams of blood were flowing. The fascists slaughtered Russians, Belorussians, and Ukrainians by the hundreds and thousands.

A secret order given by Hitler prior to the invasion of the Soviet Union allowed all reprisals to be made against the inhabitants of Soviet cities and towns. In accordance with this order, military courts received instructions to ignore the complaints of the Ukrainian, Russian, and Belorussian population against the lawless acts committed by the soldiers and officers of the German army. The plundering, arson, murder, humiliation, and violence perpetrated by the Germans on Soviet soil were not regarded as crimes—they took place with the permission and with the blessing of Hitler, his field marshals, and his generals. Hundreds and thousands of villages and settlements were set aflame. Entire regions were turned into "desert zones." In the area between the Desna and Dnieper Rivers the Germans leveled almost all the trees to the ground. Vast regions of the Smolensk and Orlov districts were transformed into uninhabited wastelands. The German forces consciously condemned residents in these areas to the greatest of suffering, to extinction by starvation, and to the bitter cold of winter. Millions of people who had lost their homes lived in the forests in earthen shelters and abandoned dugouts. Economic policies adopted by the Germans in villages and towns were incomparable in their cruelty: work was the forced labor of a prison camp, a curse hanging over the peasantry. Using whips and clubs, German police supervisors in charge of agricultural units would drive the peasants out to work, bringing down on their heads dozens of the cruelest blows for the smallest infractions of the forced labor regimen.

Blossoming industrial regions were laid waste, and beautiful cities were destroyed; doomed to death by starvation, townspeople poured into the villages in search of food. But even the villages were almost completely plundered. Day and night transports loaded with stolen grain, factory equipment, household fixtures and utensils, historic treasures, and works of art set out for Germany. Conditions of infinite cruelty were created for prisoners of war captured from the Red Army. In the camps thousands of people perished from hunger and disease. Mass executions of unarmed prisoners were periodically organized; hundreds of thousands of people near Vyazma, in Minsk, and in the Kholm region perished from such forms of punishment.

The Hitlerites regarded all of this murderous work as a preliminary preparation for the take over of the "eastern area." In many places the murder of the local residents—of Russians, Belorussians, and Ukrainians—was merely the first step toward the realization of Hitler's intended program of the eventual extermination of the Slavic people. With regard to the Jews, fascism implemented its bloody plans immediately and universally. Throughout the areas occupied by the Germans, the entire Jewish population was marked for extermination. Everyone, without exception, was taken away to be executed. Children who did not yet know how to walk, paralytics and the sick, and decrepit old men who were unable to move on their own were carried to the places of execution on sheets and were transported on trucks and carts.

Executions were carried out in precisely the same manner in places that were separated by hundreds and sometimes even thousands of kilometers. Such complete uniformity attests to the fact that instructions were secretly worked out beforehand. The executioners followed these instructions. The shape and the depth of the pits, the procedure for conveying people to the execution sites, the explanations that the Germans gave to the people taken to be executed—who were often unaware of their fate until the last minute—all of it was carried out in the same manner in thousands of cases.

In the occupied areas of the Soviet Union, the confinement in the ghettos immediately set up by the Germans was brief. It was followed right away by murder. The ghetto was simply a place for gathering together those who were condemned to death. It was convenient to take people from the ghettos to be executed; in the ghettos it was easier to control all segments of the population; in the ghettos those who were capable of resisting could be separated from helpless children and old men. Only in the western regions of the occupied areas of the Soviet Union—in cities such as Minsk, Kovno, Vilna, Shiauliai—did they set up ghettos that lasted one or two and in some cases three years. As a rule, in the eastern regions of the occupied areas of the Soviet Union, murder followed in the occupied city soon after the arrival of German civil authorities, Gestapo, SD Einsatzkommandos, gendarmes, and police units and battalions. Normally only two or two and a half months would go by from the time of the occupation of a city to the mass executions. This time period consisted of several stages. First, eight to ten days after the soldiers had come, the Gestapo would arrive. Himmler's hyenas preferred not to expose themselves to danger in those areas where a military victory had not been firmly established. A little time was then needed to coordinate the work of the Gestapo, the police, and the commandant's office. Immediately after the organization of a punitive and investigative network, the resettlement of the Jews into the ghetto would be announced. This resettlement took two or three days, sometimes a week. While the resettlement was underway, the Germans were secretly and eagerly making preparations for murder, selecting and preparing an execution site. Sometimes anti-tank trenches served as mass graves, sometimes a natural pit or ravine. In most cases, however, the graves were dug. From their shape and size, these graves looked like deep trenches. The work of digging the graves was done by peasants driven from their homes in neighboring villages, by Red Army prisoners of was, or by Jews brought from the ghetto. None of those who worked on them ever suspected the true purpose of these trenches; they assumed that it was something connected to the usual sorts of work done in times of war. After the completion of these preparations, only one thing could cause a delay in carrying out the executions: the inability of the SS, police units, and SD Einsatzkommandos to keep up with the huge number of mass murders, for millions of men, women, children, and old people were doomed to death at the same time.

In some cases the mass murder was carried out in an even shorter period of time. One need only recall Kiev, where, with immeasurable cruelty, the murder of many tens of thousands of people was carried out nine days after German troops had taken the city.

It can be said with complete certainty that never in the history of humanity was there a crime such as this. Never before has the world seen such a conjunction of the sadistic debauchery of murderous criminals and the premeditated measures taken by a ruling government. The population of the occupied areas was stunned by the monstrosity of these crimes. Often the victims themselves could not believe until the last minute that they were being taken out to be executed, so monstrous and incomprehensible was the murder of millions of innocent people.

The Black Book contains the story of a German officer who attests to the fact that Himmler himself would check to see whether the rate of murder was going according to schedule and that Himmler severely criticized an SS figure who had fallen behind schedule in the mass murder of the Jews.

The Germans tried to keep the doomed people ignorant of the fate that awaited them until the last minute. There existed a single, meticulously conceived system of deception. Rumors circulated among the people doomed to death, saying they were concentrated in one area to be exchanged for German prisoners of war or to be taken away to work on farms, or to be sent off to transit camps in the western regions of the occupied territories. A day or two prior to the mass executions the Germans would start building bathhouse or other places for public use to avert any suspicion. People taken out to be executed were told to pack warm clothing and to bring a two-day supply of food, even though they had only a few hours left to live. Those condemned to death were formed into columns and presented with a false itinerary, namely that they were to proceed on foot to the nearest train station and there climb aboard a train. When the column of people with warm clothes and foodstuffs went out to the highway, there was an unexpected change in direction: they wound up in the forest, standing in front of freshly dug graves.

If the doomed were taken by train to the execution site, they did not know until the last minute where they were going; they were assured that the train was taking them to a new place of work, to a farm or a factory.

At the annihilation camp Treblinka a phony train station—complete with ticket windows, train schedules, and so on—was built, so that those getting off the transport were unable to orient themselves right away and realize that they had been brought to a dead end. In some cases people were forced to write letters to relatives prior to their deaths, so as to allay suspicions and anxieties.

The logic of such a system of deception is quite clear. The Hitlerites were afraid of resistance and uprisings.

In the eastern regions of the occupied Soviet territories, where murders were carried out immediately after the arrival of the invaders, the Hitlerites often succeeded in using such a system of deception. So far from their minds was the thought that they were all doomed to execution—and the monstrous massacre was upon them so suddenly—that they were unable to organize any resistance against their executioners. Such was the case in Kiev, Dnepropetrovsk, Mariupol, and many towns and villages along the left bank of the Ukraine. Also on the side of the Hitlerites was the fact that Jews capable of fighting at the time of the invaders' arrival were in the ranks of the Red Army, and those capable of work had been evacuated along with industrial plants, factories, and Soviet offices. And so those who fell under the blow of the executioners were the weakest, the most helpless, and the most disorganized: the elderly, ailing invalids, minors, and women burdened with large families consisting of the sick and people incapable of work. Motorized SS units, police brigades, Gestapo commandos, storm troops, and guard detachments—all of them armed with automatic weapons—inflicted their terrible, murderous designs upon these people, upon the helpless and the unarmed. Most horrifying was the discrepancy between the might of the executioners armed with every type of military technology and the weakness of their victims, between the fascist horde with every detail of its murderous scheme worked out and the lack of preparation among those who suddenly stood before a mass grave with their children and their elders.

Nevertheless, even under such hopeless conditions, condemned people tried to fight, resist, and carry out acts of vengeance. Women defending their children attacked armed SS men, fought with them, and perished from the stabs of bayonets or fell under a hail of bullets. In the western regions, where ghettos existed not for days or weeks but for many months and sometimes even years, the Jewish struggle against the invaders was highly organized. Underground fighting organizations were created in many cities, such as Minsk, Vilna, Bialystok, Kovno, and numerous others. Underground fighters in the ghettos established connections with resistance organizations beyond the boundaries of the ghettos and created fighting and sabotage groups. Facing the greatest of difficulties, underground fighters obtained rifles, pistols, grenades, and machine guns. In some cases the production of weapons and explosives took place inside the ghettos. Underground ghetto fighters engaged in the sabotage of factories and railroads, organized bombings and fires, and immobilized various operations serving the German army. Many times the underground ghetto fighters established contact with partisan units and sent them men, weapons, and medical supplies.

Inside the ghetto the underground fighters set up secret radio stations, received bulletins from the Soviet Information Bureau, and published illegal pamphlets, newspapers, and calls to arms, all of which prepared the people who were capable of fighting for uprisings. Jews who managed to escape from the ghetto joined partisan units; there is a great deal of testimony on their joint actions with partisans in Belorussia, Lithuania, many areas of the Ukraine, and the forests of Bryansk and Smolensk.

Under such inhuman conditions, organizing the underground, obtaining weapons, and establishing military connections demanded tremendous effort and great deal of time, experience, and skill.

Within the walls of the ghettos, the struggle against the invaders took on quite a varied character.

[The battle of ideas came to be regarded as a fundamental form of protest. The German fascist authority deprived the Jews confined to the ghetto of all human rights, equated them with animals, and condemned them to conditions under which neither livestock nor wild animals could survive.

Cultural life emerged in the ghettos as an ideological protest against the degradation of people to the level of bestial existence. In the ghettos, underground lectures and theatrical performances were arranged, and schools were organized so that children dying of hunger could learn. All of this affirmed a sublime human dignity and the spiritual right of the insulted and the injured to remain human beings unto their last breath. Many pages in *The Black Book* are devoted to describing the underground cultural life in the Vilna Ghetto. One might think that organizing schools and lectures for people doomed to death was meaningless. But such thinking is wrong.

The spiritual and intellectual life sustained by cultured people under these inhuman conditions was the foundation and pre-condition for the organization of partisan military resistance.]

Other fundamental forms of resistance included various ways of sabotaging German orders, hiding and destroying valuables subject to confiscation, concealing work skills that might be useful to the invaders, and damaging or destroying tools, raw materials, and production levels in various business enterprises.

There are many examples of such forms of resistance. Literally thousands of cases can be cited in the Minsk Ghetto alone, where people working under the muzzles of fascist machine guns and rifles, in the grip of unheard-of terror, fearlessly and stubbornly, every day and every hour, damaged and destroyed equipment and production levels in business enterprises. This form of resistance sometimes bore an elemental character, arising as it did from the close confinement of large numbers of ghetto prisoners aching to do battle against the German invaders.

Naturally, wherever the underground resistance organization engaged in sabotage and diversionary tactics, the effect and scale of the diversions increased significantly. Better organized, these prisoners of the ghetto burned warehouses, disabled electric power installations, and, during railroad loading operations, rendered useless tank engines, firing mechanisms, and the like.

The next and highest level of resistance was the preparation for an armed struggle and finally armed resistance itself—an uprising. Preparations proceeded in various ways: distribution of underground pamphlets and calls to arms; recruitment of people for fighting units; military training; preparation of explosives and devices for hand grenades, bombs, mines; procurement of pistols, automatic weapons, machine guns, and mortars from outside the ghetto walls. Armed struggle took two forms. The first form consisted of armed individuals and organized groups going out to join the partisans. This form of struggle was practiced in Minsk, Kovno, and many other ghettos. Hundreds of people joined the partisans. The scope of the partisan struggle was great indeed. At the same time, members of the underground figured out ways of continually helping the partisans not only with people to join their fighting ranks but with medical supplies, clothing, and weapons. The second form of struggle consisted of uprisings within the ghetto itself. These uprisings usually coincided with periods when the fascists were preparing and implementing mass executions and "Aktions."[20]

The Black Book contains tales of uprisings in various ghettos and camps: Bialystok, Warsaw, Treblinka, Sobibor, and others. These accounts, of course, cannot convey the full picture of the armed struggle. Cases of uprisings number in the dozens. The course and duration of the uprisings varied, ranging from fierce one-day battles using hand grenades and revolvers, as was the case in Lutsk, to combat of the type in the Kremenets region, where Jews who had escaped into the mountains held out for many days. One of the greatest and most striking of all the uprisings was the Warsaw Ghetto Uprising.[21] This uprising developed into forty days of extensive combat between the Jews and German tanks, artillery, infantry, and aviation units. In most cases the results of the ghetto uprisings were the same. The uprisings ended in the deaths of their heroes. Known beforehand by the ghetto fighters, the tragic outcome of the uprisings only underscores the greatness of their struggle.

By the end of 1943 the German fascist authorities had almost completed the total and universal murder of the Jewish population of the eastern region of the occupied territories; by the beginning of 1944 the extermination of the Jews in the western region had already been achieved.

While they were murdering the Jews—and remaining true to their usual methods—the German fascist authorities inflicted the greatest atrocities and acts of violence upon the Russian, Ukrainian, and Belorussian population of the occupied Soviet lands. Hundreds of thousands of prisoners of war were tortured and murdered. Hundreds of thousands of peasants, workers, and intellectuals suspected of involvement in the partisan movement or of being sympathetic toward the partisans were subjected to the severest of tortures, torments, and finally execution. The term *partisan village* arose. There were hundreds of such villages; the Germans burned them to the ground. Four million people driven off into slavery endured the greatest humiliation, suffering, and hunger, and many of them were subjected to beatings and torture. Thus in the final stage of its existence German fascism tried again and again to use pogrom-like actions in order to conceal the terrorist measures taken against the people living in the occupied regions.

One of the sections of *The Black Book* introduces a number of testimonies as to how Russians, Belorussians, Ukrainians, and Lithuanians aided the Jews during the worst time of the debauchery of racist terror. In their wisdom the people understood why the fascists were undertaking this monstrous, bloody provocation. The pure heart of the people shuddered at the sight of rivers of innocent blood. Elderly peasant women and young women on the farms, workers, teachers, doctors, professors, and priests often risked their own lives and the lives of their families (the occupiers equated hiding Jews with hiding partisans) to do everything in their power to save these doomed people. Hundreds of Jewish children were saved by Russians, Belorussians, and Ukrainians who claimed these children as their own, hiding them for months on end and at times even for years. In the midst of the black cloud of racist insanity, in the midst of the poisonous fog of hatred for humanity, shined the eternal, inextinguishable stars of reason, goodness, and humanitarianism. They proclaimed the death of the old kingdom of darkness and the light of a new dawn. The fascists were powerless to extinguish or drown in a sea of blood the forces of good and reason living in the soul of the people. Only the moral rabble, the moral lowlife of society, the dregs of humanity, outlaws and sadists, heeded the criminal call of Hitler's propagandists.

The forces of darkness have now been shattered. The armies of freedom-loving people have crushed Hitler's black hordes. Moving from the Volga to the Elbe and engaging in heavy, bloody fighting, the Red Army dealt the mortal blow to the German fascist troops. This unparalleled feat of the army that stormed Berlin, the capital of world obscurantism and world reactionism, will be recorded on golden tablets of humanity for centuries to come. As long as people exist on earth, this feat will not be forgotten.

The victory over German fascism is not only a military victory. It is a victory of the power of progress over the power of reactionism. It is a victory for democracy and humanity, a victory for the idea of the equality of all people. The defeat of fascist Germany in war is not only a military defeat of fascism. It is the defeat of the ideology of racist terrorism. It is a defeat of the ideology of the domination of the "master race" over the people of the world.

The day of judgment has come, the day of retribution.

Those who planned, organized, and implemented crimes against humanity have been brought before the court of the people in Nuremberg.

The court held up an endless list of monstrous crimes for all the world to see. The court demonstrated that the storm that raged over Europe had its organizers; that the murder of millions was conceived in cold blood, planned in cold blood, and carried out in cold blood. The court sentenced the chief perpetrators of these monstrous crime to death. This sentence pronounced by the court has been ratified by the will of humanity.

Millions of murdered innocent people, whose ashes have been buried in the earth and scattered over fields and roads, believed that the hour of reckoning would come. As they stood along the edge of a mass grave, crossed the threshold into a gas chamber, or approached a bonfire in their final moments, those who were doomed hurled curses upon their executioners and warned them of the inevitable retribution.

And retribution came. The triumph of justice after the terrible years of Hitler's dominion gives us reason to look toward the future with hope and faith.

May contempt for the terrible ideas of racism live eternally in the heart of humanity.

May the memory of the suffering and the agonizing deaths of millions of murdered women, children, and old people be preserved forever. May the holy memory of those who were tortured become the formidable guardian of good; may the ashes of those consumed in the flames find their way into the hearts of the living and call forth the brotherhood of people and nations.

Vasily Grossman

Notes

1.   Hermann Göring (1983-1946), a World War I fighter pilot and a major architect of the Final Solution, was Hitler's chief deputy.
2.   Alfred Rosenberg (1893-1946), chief Nazi ideologist, elaborated the notion of *Lebensraum* or "living space."
3.   Julius Streicher (1885-1946), Nazi ideologist and propagandist, was the publisher of the viciously anti-Semitic paper *Der Stürmer*.
4.   Joseph Goebbels (1897-1945) was the Minister of Propaganda under the Third Reich.
5.   Heinrich Himmler (1900-1945) was head of the SS (*Schutzstaffel* or Defense Corps), the arm of the Nazi government that was given the task of implementing the Final Solution.
6.   Ernst Kaltenbrunner (1903-1946) succeeded Reinhard Heydrich as the Chief of Security Police on 30 January 1943, after Heydrich's assassination in 1942; in charge of the extermination of the Jews, Kaltenbrunner reported to Himmler.
7.   Erich Koch governed conquered territories in the East, from Brest Litovsk in the north to the Black Sea in the south, and was responsible for overseeing the implementation of policies regarding the Jews in that region. He was arrested by the British, extradited to Poland, and given a life sentence to serve in Mokotow prison; he died sometime after 1967 in prison.
8.   Hans Frank (1900-1946) was head of the *Generalgouvernement* or the conquered territories of Poland. At the Wannsee Conference, a meeting held on 20 January 1942 to discuss the logistics of implementing the Final Solution, Frank requested that the Jews of the *Generalgouvernement* be the first to be marked for extermination.
9.   Arthur Seyss-Inquart (1892-1946) was commissioner for the Netherlands, where he ruthlessly recruited and exploited slave labor; he was condemned to death at the Nuremberg trials.
10.   The Gestapo—*Geheime Staatspolizeiamt* or Secret State Police—was established by Himmler as a secret police unit on 26 April 1933; in 1934 Himmler appointed Heydrich as chief of the Gestapo.
11.   The SS—*Schutzstaffel* or Defense Corps—was initially organized in 1927 within the SA (see note 16) as a unit of armed guards for the Führer. Under the leadership of Himmler, who became head of the SS in 1929, it grew into a massive organization whose primary purpose was to kill all the Jews of Europe.
12.   The SA—*Sturmabteilung* or Storm Troops—was the early military, terrorist arm of the Nazi Party.
13.   The SD—*Sichersheitsdienst* or Security Service—was the branch of the SS that was entrusted with nearly all intelligence work and was given the task of implementing the Final Solution; it was established in 1934, with Reinhard Heydrich as its head.
14.   Wilhelm Frick (1877-1946) was with Hitler from the time of the Munich putsch of 1923; in 1943 he was given governing authority over Bohemia and Moravia after Himmler ousted him from his position as Minister of Internal Affairs.
15.   Franz Gürtner served as Minister of Justice from 1933 to 1941 and was instrumental in drafting and passing all major anti-Semitic legislation, so that everything done to the Jews of Germany was legal.
16.   Rudolf Hess (1894-1987) was a close friend to Hitler from the early 1920s; he served as Hitler's secretary while Hitler was writing *Mein Kampf* in prison; he died in Spandau prison.
17.   The Black Hundreds were groups of militant, fanatic anti-Semites in early twentieth-century Russia and were responsible for numerous pogroms against the Jews, including the Kishinev pogroms of 1903. Among them were high-ranking military and police officials.

18.   Adolf Eichmann (1906-1962) was an SS specialist in Jewish affairs and was responsible for the deportation of hundreds of thousands of Jews from Hungary and other areas. He was captured, tried, and hanged by the Israeli government.

19.   The Einsatzgruppen were formed by Heydrich (see note 10) as special SS units, whose task was to follow the German army as it marched eastward and to slaughter the Jewish population. Six Einsatzgruppen followed the army into Poland in 1939 and four into the USSR in 1941.

20.   *Aktion* or action is a term used to refer to the purging or liquidation of a ghetto.

21.   The Warsaw Ghetto uprising was the first armed civilian uprising against the Nazis; it began on 19 April, Passover Eve, and ended on 16 May 1943 with the razing of the entire ghetto.

Part 1

The Ukraine

Kiev: Babi Yar

German troops entered Kiev on 19 September 1941.

{On that very day and in that very hour the Germans broke into stores on Bessarabka Street and looted them. House porters would not let residents out of their courtyards. Here on Bessarabka Street several Jews were detained. Nesya Elgort returned home from Bessarabka Street (to No. 40 Saksaganskaya Street) and found everyone in her huge family gathered together. Looking upon all her children, as though longing to hide them away from the enemy, the old grandmother Dina Shmulevna cried out, "My God, where shall we flee?"

On 21 September family head Berl Gertsvich and his daughter Nesya-Roza went to Stalinka to check on their apartment. Toward evening Roza returned and told the family that the Germans had taken their father away to some place unknown. The next morning Roza decided to make inquiries about her father. But she did not know where to go. She and her brother Ilyusha went to the commandant. He asked her about only one thing: her nationality. Once he discovered that she was a Jew, he drove her away from the premises.

On Lenin Street she saw Germans beating some Jewish men on the legs and forcing them to dance. Then they forced the men they had beaten to load heavy crates onto a truck. The men collapsed under the unbearable load. The Germans beat them with rubber truncheons.}[1]

On 22 September the people of Kiev were awakened by a powerful explosion. Smoke and the smell of something burning came from the direction of Kreshchatik Street.

{On the streets adjoining Kreshchatik the Germans drove people into the flames. A German ran past the building where Nesya Elgort was standing on Saksaganskaya Street. He glanced at her, raised his hand to his cheek, and in the direction of the explosions shouted, *"Partisan, Jude, kaputt!"*}

On that very day the Germans posted an announcement written in Ukrainian on the walls of the buildings. It stated that Jews, communists, commissars, and partisans would be wiped out. {A reward of two hundred rubles was offered for each partisan or communist turned in. Such announcements were also posted on Red Army Street and other streets of the city.

Life in Kiev became intolerable. The Germans broke into homes, seized people, and took them away to some unknown place; these people never returned. The Elgort family moved out of their apartment and into a cellar. It became Nesya's job to obtain food, since she did not look Jewish. The Elgort family spent several days in the cellar under such conditions. Whenever Nesya happened to go out, the house porter Pavlo Davidchenko, who knew about the family's predicament, would say, "What are you hiding here for? You'll still be transported out of Kiev."

Meanwhile, collaborating with the Germans, he continued to clean the apartments of the building assigned to him.

One day while out looking for her mother-in-law Gitl Elgort (who had left to inquire about her apartment on Zhilyanskaya Street) Nesya unexpectedly ran into her father. His appearance horrified her. He had been captured by the Germans and thrown into a damp cellar along with a group of Jews, among whom was a rabbi; there they were mocked and humiliated. Several of the men were tortured, but Nesya's father and the rabbi were saved by some miracle. Tears ran down the old man's sunken cheeks as he told his story.

On 22 September}a mass beating of the Jews took place in the streets of the city near the water towers and in the parks.

On the second or third day of the German occupation, many residents of Kiev, especially in the areas of Podol and Slobodka, saw the bloated bodies of old men and children who had been tortured to death floating down the Dnieper. {On Friday and Saturday, 26 and 27 September, Jews who went to synagogue did not return home. Evgeniya Litoshchenko, a citizen of Kiev, testified that her neighbors, an old man named Shneider and Mr. and Mrs. Rosenblat, did not come home from synagogue. She saw their bodies in the Dnieper. This was confirmed by T. Mikhaseva. Synagogues were surrounded by Germans and Ukrainian policemen with automatic weapons. In several places in Kiev bags containing religious articles washed up on the banks of the Dnieper.

Whenever the police or Gestapo agents spotted someone with dark hair, they demanded to see a passport. Jews were beaten and taken to the police station or to Gestapo headquarters. At night they were shot.

On the fifth day after the arrival of the Germans in Kiev, V. Liberman took advantage of the fact that his house register had been burned and a new house manager had been named: he decided to pretend to be a Karaite[2] and changed his name from Liberman to Libermanov.

On 24 September he left his home, walked down Korolenko Street, and turned onto Tolstoy Square. A tall man wearing a cap and a black coat walked up to him. The man ordered him to stop and demanded to see his passport. Liberman refused to show his passport to someone unknown to him. Indeed, he did not have his passport with him; he kept it hidden at home. "I am an agent of the Ukrainian Political Police," the man declared in an irritated voice. "Show me your passport. I suspect that you are a Jew." Liberman answered, "I am a Karaite by nationality; my passport has been stolen." The police agent ordered Liberman to follow him.

As he was walking down Kreshchatik, Liberman saw a car with a huge megaphone making frequent stops; a loud voice was coming over the megaphone, shouting, "Report the whereabouts of communists, partisans, and Jews to the Gestapo and to the police! Report them!"

The police agent took Liberman into a movie theater on Kreshchatik not from Proresnaya Street. A Gestapo soldier—a tall, muscular man—gave him a sharp blow in the back and shoved him into the foyer. Liberman went through the foyer and into the auditorium. More than three hundred Jews were sitting there. Most of them were old men with gray beards. All of them were sitting in deep silence. Liberman sat down next to a young Jew, who whispered to him, "They're going to take us to Syrets to work, and tonight we'll be shot."

Liberman walked up to a broken window in the foyer of the theater and, secretly hoping to see his wife, looked at the people walking up and down Kreshchatik Street. He happened to notice a resident from the building where he lived going past the theater and called him to the window. Without explaining the reason for his arrest, Liberman asked the man to tell his wife that he was being held in the theater.

Soon, sneaking along the street, Liberman's wife Valentina Berezleva came up to the window. Taking advantage of the fact that no one was in the foyer, Liberman said to her, "Valya, I've been passing myself off as a Karaite. Go get signatures from Mikhailov, Goncharenko, and Pasichny certifying that I am a Karaite. The Gestapo agents are preparing a bloody fate for the Jews."

Berezleva went over to the Gestapo agents and offered them an impassioned plea to set her husband free, declaring that she, Valentina Berezleva, was a Russian and that her husband was a Karaite. Before she could finish, one of the Gestapo men shoved her as hard as he could. She fell down the steps of the theater and struck her head on the sidewalk. Then she went home.

Liberman sensed that every passing hour drew him and the Jews in the theater closer to death. But chance saved him and all the others. At two o'clock in the afternoon on 24 September a very loud explosion went off near the theater. Liberman jumped out the broken window. Terrified people were madly rushing up and down Kreshchatik. A woman covered with blood and a man with no hands ran by. Thick, yellow clouds of smoke billowed through the street. A second explosion came immediately after the first. Twenty or thirty minutes went by. With a cry of "*Feuer!*" [Fire!] the Gestapo agents abandoned their posts at the theater entrance and fled. Once they saw that the Gestapo agents had run away, the Jews hurried off to their homes.

Upon arriving home, Liberman discovered that his wife had burned his passport, all his documents, his articles, and photographs of his parents. Liberman's friends—A. K. Mikhailov, D. L. Pasichny, and F. I. Goncharenko—had provided him with their signatures certifying that he was a Karaite.

Liberman decided not to show his face in the courtyard or on the street. His wife camouflaged the entrance to their small kitchen, and for days on end he sat there like a prisoner, looking out the narrow window at a small patch of blue sky.}

In the evenings the sky was tinged with the crimson reflection of a gigantic fire. Put to the torch, Kreshchatik was ablaze for six days.

On 27-28 September 1941, a week after the Germans' arrival in Kiev, announcements printed in bold letters on coarse blue paper, in Russian and Ukrainian, appeared on the walls of the buildings:

Kikes of Kiev and the surrounding area! On Monday, 29 September, at 7:00 A.M. you are to appear with your belongings, money, documents, valuables, and warm clothing on Dorogozhitskaya Street next to the Jewish cemetery. Failure to appear is punishable by death. Hiding kikes is punishable by death.

There was no signature on this terrible decree that condemned seventy thousand people to death.

The Gestapo continued to perpetrate such outrages on the streets and in the buildings of Kiev until 29 September.

{On 28 September at the Galitsky Market, the Germans detained seventy-five-year-old Gersh Abovich Grinberg (22 Volodarskaya Street), the head of a large family, among whom are many engineers, doctors, pharmacists, educators, and writers. They robbed him, stripped him, and tortured him to death like animals. Grinberg's wife, an elderly lady named Telya Osinova, never heard from him again. She spent the day baking, cooking, and packing things to get ready for the trip. Within twenty-four hours, on 29 September, she perished at Babi Yar.}[3]

On Zhilyanskaya Street the Germans seized engineer I. L. Edelman, brother of the well known pianist and Kiev conservatory professor A. L. Edelman. They threw him head first into a barrel standing under a drainpipe and drowned him.

B. A. Libman tells a story about one Jewish family that was hiding in a basement for several days. The mother decided to take her two children and go to the country. Some drunken Germans stopped them at the Galitsky Market and subjected them to a cruel punishment. They cut off the head of one child and killed the other right before the mother's eyes. The woman went out of her mind and held the bodies of her dead children to her bosom. Once the Hitlerites had had their fill of the spectacle, they murdered her too. {After hurrying to the site where his family had perished, the father was also murdered.

Two days prior to the events at Babi Yar the elderly musician Efim Borisovich Pikus went to the German commandant to obtain permission to stay with his sick wife L. G. Pikus; she was not strong enough to go outside. The old man did not return home. His wife and son were dead within two days.

Many Kievans knew the attorney Tsiperovich, a highly educated man who lived at 41 Pushkin Street. He and his wife were shot.

The Germans pursued the pianist Bella Zinovevna Grinberg and her cousin Rozalie Naumovna Kapustina into the Lukyanovka cemetery. They never returned.

The young writer Mark Chudnovsky was not able to be evacuated from Kiev at his assigned time because he was ill. His wife, a Russian woman, would not let her husband go to Lukyanovka alone; she knew what awaited him there. "We spent days of joy together," she said to him, "and I won't abandon you now." The two of them went to Lukyanovka and there died together.}

The fascists shot Professor S. U. Satanovsky of the Kiev conservatory and his family.

{Anatoli Sandomirsky, a mathematician and chess player, lived at 36 Saksaganskaya Street. Having been sick with encephalitis for several years, he was bed-ridden. The Germans carried him outside; he perished on the street.}

The SS dragged a paralyzed old woman named Sofya Goldovskaya out of her home at 27 Saksaganskaya and murdered her. She was the mother of ten children.

Another old woman, Sarra Maksimovna Evenson, had been an organizer of political circles, a propagandist, and the editor of the newspaper *Volyn* in Zhitomir during the pre-revolutionary period. She wrote many articles (under the pseudonym of S. Maksimov). {She was the first to translate Feuchtwanger[4] and a number of other writers of the new age into Russian. She had thoroughly mastered the West European languages and corresponded with dozens of artistic and cultural figures.

Because of her advanced years and ill health, S. M. Evenson was not allowed to be evacuated from Kiev. She had not left her home for the last two years.} The Hitlerites threw this woman who had great-grandchildren from a third-story window. {An elderly lady named Khana Itskovna Kaganova, the mother of an army doctor, and Mednikova, the mother of several soldiers, were denounced by the house manager Gontkovsky (12 Tarasovskaya Street) and savagely tortured by the Germans. The Germans also murdered Regina Lazarevna Magat (10 Gorky Street), the mother of a professor of medicine and biology who was killed on the front.} The well-known attorney Ilya Lvovich Babat and his two granddaughters, Polina and

Malvina, died from German bullets. {Germans and house porters working for the police took old people who could not move from their apartments and left them on the streets and sidewalks. The old ones died from cold, hunger, and the indifference of those around them.

The composer and conductor Chaim Yampolsky worked for many years on the Radio Committee and in the orchestra of the Kiev Circus. Yampolsky is the author of major compositions, primarily on Jewish and Ukrainian themes, and his renditions of Jewish folk songs are quite popular. The brother-in-law of the world-renowned violinist Miron Polyakin, Yampolsky was Polyakin's first teacher and the first to open the way for Polyakin into music. Chaim Yampolsky's children are musicians: Vera, Vladimir, and Elena are pianists, and Gerts is a violinist. The Germans showed up for the old man at the Radio Committee. They took him away immediately after rehearsal, and Yampolsky never returned.

Bella Aleksandrovna Libman (who now works in Kiev as a secretary-machinist) writes about her father, son-in-law, and other relatives who perished:

The residents of the apartment building where we had spent so many years say that Papa understood perfectly why the Jews, these eternal martyrs, had been gathered together. It is said that he wept so uncontrollably that even the most hardened of people could not look upon him without losing their composure. He went off to the cemetery with several elderly residents of the building, under the eyes of whom I grew up. I know of a building at No. 6 Volodarsky Avenue in which fourteen Jewish families perished; my aunt Sofya Shumaya and her husband were among them. One of the survivors was a Russian woman, an old nanny who had brought up my aunt's children, who are now soldiers in the Red Army. The nanny accompanied my aunt and uncle to the cemetery.}

Moisey Grigorevich Benyash, a professor of bacteriology renowned throughout Europe, also perished at that time, along with his sister and niece.

But all this was just the prelude to mass murder. At dawn on 29 September, the Jews of Kiev were moving slowly along the streets from various parts of the city toward the Jewish cemetery on Lukyanovka. Many of them thought they were being sent to provincial towns. {Some of them understood that Babi Yar meant death. Therefore on that day there were many suicides.}

Families had baked bread, sewn knapsacks, and rented wagons and carts for the journey. Old men and women walked along supporting each other. Mothers carried their infants in their arms or pushed them in baby carriages. People were carrying sacks, bundles, suitcases, and boxes. Children plodded along with their parents. Young people brought nothing with them, but the elderly tried to take everything they could from home. Leading them by the hand, grandchildren walked with old women who were pale and had difficulty breathing. Those who were sick or paralyzed were borne on stretchers, blankets, and sheets.

A crowd of people flowed along Lvov Street in an uninterrupted stream, as German patrols stood on the sidewalks. {The number of people moving along the pavement from early in the morning until late at night was so great that it was difficult to cross from one side of the street to the other.} This death procession continued for three days and three nights. The city had fallen silent. Like streams flowing into a river, crowds flowed onto Lvov Street from Pavlovskaya and Dmitrievskaya, from Volodarskaya and Nekrasovskaya. After Lvov they came to Melnik Street and then went up a barren road through stark hills to the steep ravines known as Babi Yar. As they approached Babi Yar, a murmur mixed with moans and sobbing grew louder and louder.

An office with many desks was set up in the open air. From the gates that the Germans had placed at the end of the street, the crowd could not see these desks. People were separated from the crowd in groups of thirty to forty and escorted under guard to be "registered." Their documents and valuables were taken away from them. Indeed, at this point, the documents were thrown to the ground. Witnesses say that the area was covered with a thick layer of discarded papers, torn passports, and union cards. Then the Germans ordered everyone, without exception—girls, women, children, and old men—to strip naked; their clothes were gathered up and placed in neat piles. Rings were torn from the fingers of the naked people, both men and women. Then the executioners placed the doomed people in rows along the edge of the deep ravine and shot them at pointblank range. The bodies fell over the cliff. Small children were pushed into the ravine alive. Many went insane as they approached the execution site. {Many of those whom they had not yet rounded up soon found out what was happening at Babi Yar, and they prepared themselves for it. Old men dressed themselves in black, gathered in buildings to say their prayers, and then went out to Lvov Street.}

Nevertheless, many Kievans did not know until the last minute what the Germans were doing at Babi Yar.

Some said it was a mobilization of labor, while others said it was a resettlement. A third group maintained that the German command had made an agreement with a Soviet commission to do an exchange: a Jewish family for each German prisoner of war.

A young Russian woman named Tamara Mikhaseva, the wife of a Jewish commander later killed in the Red Army, went to Babi Yar with the intention of passing herself off as a Jew: she thought she would be exchanged along with the others and would find her husband on Soviet soil.

When she reached the other side of the fence, Tamara came to her senses. She stood first in one line to hand over her belongings and then in another to be registered.

Next to her was a tall old woman in a hat, a young woman with a small boy, and a tall, broad-shouldered man.

The man took the little boy into his arms.

Mikhaseva went over to them and {asked, "Will we be exchanged this month?"

The man looked at her. "Are you Jewish?"

"My husband is Jewish."}

The man looked at her very intensely and said, "You must leave here. Wait a moment, and we'll leave together."

He picked up the little boy, kissed his face, and said farewell to his wife and mother-in-law. He said something in German, harsh and authoritative, and the guard opened the gate.

This man was a Russianized German; he had accompanied his wife, son, and mother-in-law to Babi Yar.

Mikhaseva followed him out. From the direction of Babi Yar they could hear the barking of many police dogs, the noise of automatic weapons, and the cries of those being murdered.

The crowd moved toward them. The entire street was covered with people. Dance melodies blared over louder speakers to drown out the screams of the victims as they perished. {On Ovruchskaya Street a man who was bringing his wife, son, and mother-in-law to Babi Yar stopped and pointed at the crowd moving along slowly, solemnly, and silently, resigned to their fate. He said to his family, "You are to live. I, a German, am to live. But they are being taken out to be shot."}

There are stories of some who were saved by a miracle. Nesya Elgort of 40 Saksaganskaya Street was walking toward the ravine, clutching her trembling son Ilyusha to her naked body. All of her relatives and loved ones had been lost in the crowd. With her son in her arms, she came up to the very edge of the ravine. Half out of her mind, she heard the shots and the cries of the dying, and she fell. The bullets missed her. Warm bodies covered with blood were lying on top of her. All around her were piles of hundreds and thousands of murdered people. The bodies of old men were heaped on the bodies of children and the bodies of infants on their dead mothers.

"It is now difficult for me to comprehend how I got out of that pit of death," Nesya Elgort recalls, "but I obviously crawled out, driven by an instinct for self-preservation. That evening I found myself in the Podol district with my son Ilyusha beside me. I truly cannot understand by what miracle my son was saved. It was as though he had become part of me, and he did not leave me for a single second. A Russian woman who lived in Podol, Mariya Grigorevna—I don't remember her last name—took me in for a night, and the next morning she helped me to get to Saksaganskaya Street."

Here is another story of a woman who was saved from Babi Yar.

It was already completely dark when Elena Efimovna Borodyanskaya-Knysh arrived at Babi Yar with her little girl.

"Along the way they added about 150 people to our group, maybe even more. I shall never forget one girl; her name was Sarra, and she was about fifteen years old. It is hard to describe the beauty of this girl. Her mother was pulling at her own hair and crying out in a heart-rending voice, 'Kill us together!' They killed the mother with a rifle butt. Taking their time with the girl, five or six Germans stripped her naked, but I saw nothing more than that.

"They took our outer clothing from us, confiscated our belongings, and, after escorting us another fifty meters, they took away our documents, money, rings, and earrings. They started pulling out one old man's gold teeth. He resisted. Then a German grabbed him by the beard and threw him to the ground; the German stood there with tufts of the old man's beard in his hands. The old man was bleeding profusely. When my little girl saw all this, she started to cry.

"'Don't take me there, Mama, they're going to kill us! Look, they're killing the old man!'

"'Don't cry out, my dear little one,' I begged her. 'If you cry out, we won't be able to run away, and they will surely kill us.'

"She was a patient little girl and walked along quietly, trembling all the while. She was four at the time. Everyone had been stripped naked. But since I was wearing old underwear, they let me keep it.

"Around midnight, in German, came the command for us to line up along the edge of the ravine. I didn't wait for the next command but immediately tossed my little girl into the pit and then fell in after her. A second later, bodies started falling on top of me. Then it grew quiet. About fifteen minutes went by, and then they brought in another party. Again shots rang out; again the bloody bodies of dead and dying people began falling into the pit.

"I could feel that my daughter wasn't moving. I leaned up against her, covered her with my body, and, squeezing my hands into fists, placed them under her chin, so my little girl wouldn't suffocate. My daughter started to move. I tried to raise myself up, so as not to crush her. There was so much blood all around us. The shooting had been going on since nine o'clock that morning. Bodies were lying on top of me and beneath me.

"I heard someone walking over the bodies and swearing in German. A German soldier was using a bayonet to make sure there was no one was left alive. It turned out that he was standing on top of me, so the bayonet missed me.

"When he left, I raised my head. There was a noise in the distance. The Germans were arguing over how they were going to divide up the things they had stolen from us.

"I freed myself, got up, and took my daughter in my arms; she was unconscious. I walked along the steep bank. I had gone about a kilometer, when I noticed that my daughter was hardly breathing. There was no water anywhere. I wet her mouth with my saliva. I went another kilometer and began to gather dew from the grass to moisten my little girl's lips. Little by little she started to regain consciousness.

"I rested and then walked farther. Crawling through the ravines, I reached the village of Babi Yar. I went into the yard of the brick factory and hid in a basement. I stayed there for four days without food or clothing.

"My little girl and I started to swell up. I had no idea of what was happening around me. Machine guns were firing somewhere. On the night of the fifth day I crawled into the attic of a building and found a worn-out knit skirt and two old blouses. I put one blouse on my little girl in place of a dress. I went to see my friend Litoshchenko. She was horrified at the sight of me. She gave me a skirt and a dress and hid my little girl and me. We stayed with her under lock and key for more than a week. She gave me some money, and I went to another friend, Fenya Plyuiko, who was also a great help to me. Her husband was killed at the front. I stayed in her apartment for a month. Her neighbor did not know me. Whenever she was asked who I was, Fenya would say, 'My sister-in-law from the country.' After that I moved to Shkuropadskaya's place. I was with her for two weeks. But everyone knew me in Podol, and I could not leave the house in the daytime."

Hiding behind a gravestone in the Jewish cemetery, Dmitri Pasichny saw the Germans shoot the Jews. {He could not watch for long. On his way home Pasichny saw a crowd near the university. A lanky German was inviting people to go into the library. Pasichny went into the building. On the floor lay a Jewish man and a Jewish woman covered with blood. You could see from the size of the Jewish woman's stomach that she was pregnant. On a wide table in the middle of the room lay a pile of gold coins and paper money. Red banners stood in the corners of the room. A tall German went over to the Jewish woman lying on the floor and kicked her hard in the stomach with his boot. In broken Russian he shouted, "There they are, kikes and communists robbing the people! Just look at how much money they have!" This rude provocation from the SS stirred feelings of contempt in Pasichny, and he quickly left the library building.

Pasichny's wife Polina and her mother Evgeniya Abramovna Sheveleva are Jews. In an effort to save them, he hid them in a closet and spread the rumor that they had gone to the cemetery throughout the apartment building. Pasichny kept his wife and mother hidden there for a month. Later he managed to move them to the home of some friends on Lvov Street; after spending several months there, they moved to the priest's house at the Prokovskaya Church in Podol. Father Glagolev, the priest at the church, is the son of a priest who appeared as an expert witness at the Beylis[5] trial; he made it possible for Pasichny's wife Polina and her mother Evgeniya Abramovna to stay in the rectory until August 1942, that is, up until the time when Pasichny decided to take them to Kamenets-Podolsk. Father Glagolev saved many other Jews who turned to him for help.

The Germans annihilated the Jews of Kiev. But they carefully packed and shipped out extremely valuable Jewish books from the major libraries of Kiev, so that by working through agents from neutral countries they could sell them to America and thus obtain hard currency. That is how the Germans resolved the "Jewish Question" in Kiev.}

After the murders at Babi Yar the Germans and the Ukrainian police went searching for new victims. Hundreds of Jews who had managed to escape the executions at Babi Yar perished in their apartments, in the Dnieper, and in the ravines of Pechersk and Demievka; they were also shot in the streets of the city. The Germans were suspicious of everyone, and the documents of anyone who looked Jewish were subject to a thorough examination. Those who were under suspicion were shot upon the first denunciation. The Germans not only searched apartments but went into underground vaults and caves; they blew up floors and suspicious walls, attics, and chimneys. {They wanted to erase every trace of the Jews of Kiev and thus wash away all evidence of their crime.}

Fate has spared some of those Jews who escaped from Babi Yar so that humanity may hear the testimony from the lips of the victims and the truth from the eyewitnesses.

Two years later, as the Red Army was approaching the Dnieper, the order to destroy the bodies buried at Babi Yar came from Berlin.

Vladimir Davydov, who had been a prisoner in the Syrets camp, relates how in the fall of 1943, when they realized they would have to give up Kiev, the Germans rushed to hide every sign of the mass executions at Babi Yar. On 18 August 1943 the Germans took three hundred prisoners from the Syrets camp and shackled them in leg irons. This group of prisoners was escorted only by the officers and non-commissioned officers of the SS. The prisoners were led out of the camp and transferred to dark earthen bunkers surrounded by barbed wire. Germans with machine guns were on duty day and night in the tall watchtowers surrounding the bunkers. On 19 August the prisoners were taken out of the bunkers and escorted under heavy guard to Babi Yar. There they were given shovels. Then the men realized the terrible task that was upon them: they were to dig up the bodies of the people shot by the Germans at the end of September 1941.

When the prisoners had uncovered the first layer of earth, they could see tens of thousands of bodies. The prisoner Gaevsky went mad upon seeing the piles of bodies. The bodies were tightly stuck together from having lain under the earth for so long, and they had to be separated with gaffs. From 4:00 A.M. until late that night Vladimir Davydov and his comrades labored in Babi Yar. The Germans forced the prisoners to burn the remains. Two thousand bodies at a time were piled on top of stacks of firewood, and then gasoline was poured over them. Gigantic bonfires burned day and night. More than seventy thousand bodies were consigned to the flames.

The Hitlerites ordered the bones that were left after the bodies were burned to be ground up with large rollers, mixed with sand, and scattered over the surrounding area. Himmler, the Chief of the Gestapo himself, came from Berlin to inspect the quality of this terrible work. On 28 September 1943, as the task was approaching completion, the Germans ordered the prisoners to once again fire up the ovens. The prisoners realized that now they were the ones to be executed. The Germans wanted to murder the last living witnesses and then burn them in the ovens. Davydov had found a pair of scissors in a dead woman's pocket. With those rusty scissors he unlocked his leg irons. Then the other prisoners did the same. At dawn on 29 September 1943, exactly two years after the mass murder of the Jews of Kiev, Davydov and his comrades ran from the bunkers and raced toward the walls of their cemetery. Stunned by the sudden escape, the SS were unable to open fire with their machine guns right away. They killed 280 men. But Vladimir Davydov and eleven other men managed to climb the walls and run away. Residents in the area near Kiev sheltered them. Later Davydov was able to escape from Kiev and lived in the settlement of Varovichi.

[Not all the bodies were burned; not all the bones were ground to dust—there were too many of them. Even now anyone who comes to Babi Yar will see bits of skulls and bones mixed with charcoal. He will find a boot with a decayed human foot in it, as well as slippers, galoshes, scarves, and children's toys. He will see the cast-iron gratings torn from the cemetery wall. Those cast-iron gratings served as the oven racks on which the exhumed bodies of those murdered during the terrible September days of 1941 were burned.]

An article based on documentary materials and depositions from the
people of Kiev. Prepared for publication by Lev Ozerov.[6]

The Murder of the Jews of Berdichev

Thirty thousand Jews—half the population of the city—lived in Berdichev before the war. In most of the villages and towns of the southwestern region, in what used to be the Pale of Settlement,[7] Jews comprised no less than sixty percent of the total population, a higher percentage than in Berdichev. But for some reason Berdichev was considered the most Jewish city in the Ukraine. Before the revolution anti-Semites and the Black Hundreds called it the "Jewish capital." After studying the distribution of the Jewish population prior to their mass murder of the Jews, the German fascists took special note of Berdichev.

The Jews of Berdichev were on friendly terms with the Russians and Ukrainians in the city and in neighboring settlements. Throughout the entire history of its existence, there had never been any nationalistic excesses in the city of Berdichev.

The Jews worked in the factories: in the Ilich Leather Works, one of the Soviet Union's largest leather factories; in the Progress Machine Factory; in the Berdichev Sugar Factory; and in dozens and hundreds of factories and workshops producing leather, tailored goods, boots, hats, metal products, and cardboard. Even before the revolution, Chuvyaks, the famous soft slippers made by the craftsmen of Berdichev, were sent to Tashkent, Samarkand, and other cities in Central Asia. The craftsmen who made fashionable shoes and the specialists in colored paper decorations were also widely known. Thousands of Jews of Berdichev worked as masons, stove setters, carpenters, jewelers, watch makers, opticians, bakers, barbers, porters, glaziers, electricians, locksmiths, plumbers, and loaders.

The city had a large Jewish intelligentsia. There were dozens of experienced senior physicians, including therapists, surgeons, pediatricians, obstetricians, and dentists. There were bacteriologists, chemists, druggists, engineers, technicians, bookkeepers, and instructors in numerous technical schools and high schools. There were foreign language teachers, music teachers, and tutors who worked in nurseries, kindergartens, and playgrounds.

The Germans showed up in Berdichev unexpectedly, when German tank troops penetrated into the city. Only a third of the Jewish population was able to get out. The Germans entered the city on Monday, 7 June 1941, at seven o'clock in the evening. Waving their arms and laughing, the soldiers shouted from their vehicles, "*Jude kaputt*!" They knew that most of the Jewish population was still in the city.

It is difficult to convey the psychological condition of twenty thousand people who have suddenly been declared to be outside the law and entitled to absolutely no human rights. To the Jews, even the most terrible laws that the Germans imposed on the residents of the occupied territories seemed to be an unattainable blessing.

First of all, the Jews were forced to pay an indemnity. The military commandant demanded that they deliver fifteen pairs of patent leather shoes, six Persian rugs, and 100,000 rubles within three days (judging from the insignificance of this indemnity, this was simply an act of extortion on the part of the military commandant). Whenever passing by a German, a Jew had to remove his hat. Those who did not comply with this demand were subjected to beatings and forced to crawl on their stomachs along the sidewalk and pick up trash and manure from the pavement with their bare hands; old men had their beards cut off. After escaping from Berdichev on the sixth day of its occupation and making his way through the front line, the cabinetmaker Gersh Giterman told about the crimes that the Germans first perpetrated upon the Jews. German soldiers drove Jews out of their apartments on Glinok, Bolshaya Zhitomir, Malaya Zhitomir, and Shteinovskaya streets; all of these streets lead to the Zhitomir highway, where the leather factory is located. The people were taken to the factory's tanning shop and forced to jump into large pits filled with caustic tanning acid; those who refused were shot, and their bodies were thrown into the pits. The Germans involved in this atrocity took it as a "joke": they were tanning Jewish hides, so to speak. Similar "jokes" were committed in the Old City, that part of Berdichev located between the Zhitomir highway and the Gnilopyat River. The Germans ordered old men to put on their tallis and tefillin[8] and conduct a religious service in the Old Synagogue: "Pray to God for forgiveness for the sins you have committed against the Germans!" The doors to the synagogue were locked, and the building was set on fire. The Germans played a third "joke" near the mill. There they seized several dozen women, ordered them to undress, and announced to these miserable souls that those who could swim to the opposite bank of the river would be allowed to live. The river along the mill is very wide, due to the stone dike that dams it. Unable to reach the other bank, most of the women drowned. Those who did mange to swim across to the west bank were immediately forced to swim back. The women would sink to the bottom and drown as their strength gave out; all the while the Germans looked on in amusement. And so they had their fun, until every last woman had drowned.

Another example of such a German "joke" is the death of an old man named Aron Mizor, a butcher who lived on Belopolskaya Street.

A German officer had come to rob Mizor's apartment and had ordered his men to carry away the goods, while he himself stayed behind with two other soldiers to have some fun. Since he had found the knife that the butcher used on domestic birds, he discovered Mizor's profession.

"I want to see your work," he said, and he ordered the soldiers to bring in three small children who belonged to a neighbor. "Butcher them!" he commanded.

Mizor thought the officer was joking. But then the German hit the old man in the face with his fist and repeated, "Butcher them!"

Mizor's wife and daughter-in-law began to weep and beg the officer. The German said, "You must butcher not only the children, but these two women as well!"

Mizor fainted and fell to the floor.

The officer took the knife and hit the old man in the face with it. Mizor's daughter-in-law, Liya Basikhes, ran outside and begged passersby to save the old couple. When the people entered Mizor's apartment, they saw the dead bodies of the butcher and his elderly wife lying in a pool of blood: the officer himself had demonstrated how to use the knife.

The residents of the town thought the mockery and murder that took place during these first days had not been ordered. They tried to complain to the German authorities; they tried to seek help against these arbitrary acts of violence.

The minds of thousands of people were unable to accept the terrible fact that Hitler's government itself encouraged and approved of all of these monstrous atrocities. They could not grasp the inhuman truth that Jews stood outside the law—that torture, violence, murder, and arson were perfectly natural with respect to the Jews. They went to the military commandant in charge of the city's government. Representatives of the German authorities drove away the petitioners, cursing and mocking them.

Horror was hanging over the city. Horror entered every home. It hovered over the beds of those who slept; it rose with the sun and walked the streets at night. The hearts of thousands of old women and children would tremble whenever they heard the stomping of soldiers' boots in the night or the barking of German speech. Both dark, overcast nights and nights of the full moon were horrors; the early mornings, the light of midday, and the quiet evenings in the native city also turned into horrors. Thus fifty days went by.

On 26 August the German authorities began preparations for a general "Aktion." All over the city they had posted announcements ordering the Jews to move into the ghetto that had been set up in the Yatki area, where the city bazaar is located. They were forbidden to take any furniture with them. Yatki is the oldest part of the city, with unpaved streets and mud puddles that never dry up. It consists of ancient shacks, little one-storied houses, and old buildings made of crumbling brick; the courtyards are filled with junk, trash, manure, and piles of garbage.

The resettlement lasted for three days. People loaded down with bundles and suitcases slowly moved along Belopolskaya, Makhnovskaya, Uchilishchnaya, Grecheskaya, and Pushkin streets; along the Bolshaya and Malaya Yuridika; along Semenovskaya and Danilovskaya streets. Adolescents and children supported decrepit old and sick people. Paralytics and those who had no legs were carried on blankets and stretchers. Another stream of people flowed in from the Zagrebelny area of the city across the Gnilopyat River.

Many dozens of people were crowded into tiny shacks, including nursing mothers, bedridden sick people, and blind old men. Cage-like rooms were crammed with household goods, feather beds, pillows, and dishes.

Ghetto laws were announced. People were forbidden, under the threat of severe punishment, to go beyond the borders of the ghetto. Food could be purchased at the bazaar only after six o'clock, that is, only when the bazaar was empty and there was no more food.

No one who had moved into the ghetto, however, realized that, according to a plan already worked out down to the last detail, the resettlement was merely the first step toward the murder of the twenty thousand Jews left in Berdichev.

One resident of Berdichev, a bookkeeper named Nikolai Vasilevich Nemolovsky, went to the ghetto to visit the family of his friend, an engineer named Nuzhny who had worked at the Progress Factory before the war. Nemolovsky relates that Nuzhny's wife cried a great deal and was very upset because her ten-year-old son Gerik had been unable to continue his studies in school since the fall.

The whole time Father Nikolai, bishop of the Berdichev Cathedral, and an old priest named Gurin maintained contact with the physicians Vurvarg and Baraban, a woman doctor named Blank, and other representatives of the Jewish intelligentsia. {They tried to baptize them or provide them with Christian baptismal certificates.} The German authorities explained to the Archbishop in Zhitomir that the slightest attempt to save the Jews would be subject to the most severe punishment, including death.

According to the priests, the elderly physicians of Berdichev lived in the constant hope that the Red Army would return. On one occasion they were comforted by news someone supposedly heard over the radio that a message demanding a halt to the mistreatment of the Jews had been delivered to the German government.

By that time, however, the Germans had brought in prisoners of war from Lysaya Gora to dig five deep trenches in the field near the airport, where Brodskaya Street ends and the paved road to the village of Romanovka begins.

On 4 September, one week after the ghetto had been set up, the Germans and the traitors on their police force ordered fifteen hundred young people to be sent to agricultural jobs. The young men and women gathered up bundles of food and bread, said their farewells to their relatives, and set out. On that very day they were all shot between Lysaya Gora and the village of Khazhino. The henchmen had prepared the execution so cleverly and so precisely that the doomed ones had no idea of the murder that awaited them until the very last minute. The Germans explained to them in detail where they would be working, how they would be broken up into groups, and when and where they would be issued shovels and other work tools. It was even hinted that once the work had been completed, each of them would be allowed to take some potatoes back to the old ones who had stayed in the ghetto.

And, in the short life that was left to them, those who remained in the ghetto never found out about the fate that had befallen their youth.

"Where is your son?" one old man would ask another.

"He went to dig potatoes" was the usual reply.

The execution of the young people was the first in a chain of premeditated measures that had been planned for murdering the Jews of Berdichev. Nearly all of the young men and woman capable of resistance had been eliminated from the ghetto.

For the most part, those who remained in Yatki were old people, women, and school children. Thus the Germans were able to guarantee themselves complete impunity when carrying out the mass executions.

Preparations for the "Aktion" were finished. The pits had been dug at the end of Brodskaya Street. The German commandant briefed city government representative Reder (a Russianized German who had been taken prisoner during the First World War) and police chief Korolyuk (a traitor) on the plan of operation. These people, Reder and Korolyuk, took an active part in the organization and implementation of the executions. On 14 September SS units arrived in Berdichev, and all the city police were mobilized. On the night of 14-15 September troops surrounded the ghetto area. At four o'clock in the morning the signal was given for the SS and the police to start breaking into the apartments, get the people up, and drive them into the bazaar square. The executioners murdered many of those who could not walk, frail old people and cripples, right in their homes. The terrible wailing of the women and the crying of the children woke up the whole city. Residents living on the most distant streets awoke and listened in fear to the groans of thousands of people merging into a single soul-shaking cry.

Soon the bazaar square had filled up. Reder and Korolyuk stood on a small hill surrounded by guards. People were brought to them in groups, and from each group they selected two or three who were known to have special skills. Those selected were taken aside, to the section of the square next to Bolshaya Zhitomir Street.

The doomed ones were lined up in columns and marched under a heavy SS guard through the Old City and down Brodskaya Street in the direction of the airport. Before lining them up in columns, the SS ordered the doomed people to set their valuables and their documents on the ground.

The ground where Reder and Korolyuk stood became white with certificates, passports, identification papers, and union cards.

Four hundred people were separated from the group, including the elderly physicians Vurvarg, Baraban, Liberman, and the woman doctor Blank. In addition, there were artisans and craftsmen well known in the city: the electrician and radio repairman Epelfeld, the photographer Nuzhny, the shoemaker Milmeister, the old mason Pekelis and his two sons Mikhel and Vulf, and other masters famous for their work as tailors, shoemakers, and locksmiths, as well as a few barbers. These specialists who had been separated out were allowed to take along their families. Many of them were unable to find their wives and children, who had gotten lost in the huge crowd. According to the testimony of witnesses, heart-rending scenes soon followed. Trying to make themselves heard over the crowd gone mad, people were shouting out the names of their wives and children, and hundreds of doomed mothers held out their sons and daughters to them, begging them to taken the children as their own and thus save them from death.

"You cannot find your own children in such a crowd anyway!" screamed the women.

Meanwhile trucks were moving down Brodskaya Street along with the columns marching on foot; in them were helpless old people, small children, and all those who could not walk the four kilometers from Yatki to the execution site. The image of these thousands of women, children, and old people plodding along is so horrible that even today witnesses who recall it turn pale and weep. The wife of the priest Gurin lived on the street along which they were driven to their death. Having seen these thousands of women and children crying out for help and knowing that among them were dozens of her own friends, she went mad and over the next several months was in a state of mental shock.

{At the same time, there were shady criminal types who derived material benefit from this great misfortune; greedy for gain, they got rich at the expense of the Germans' victims. Policemen, their family members, the German soldiers' mistresses, and other shady types rushed in to rob the vacated apartments. Before the eyes of the living dead they carried off dresses, pillows, and feather mattresses; some of them walked right past the guards and took scarves and knitted woolen jackets off the women and girls awaiting execution. By this time the head of the column had reached the airport.}

Half-drunk SS men led the first group of forty people to the edge of the pit. The first volley of automatic fire resounded. The execution site was set up fifty to sixty meters from the road traveled by the doomed. Thousands of eyes saw murdered children and old people fall. Then new groups were taken into the airport hangers to await their turn.

Groups of forty people were led out of the hangars. They had to walk some three hundred meters over a bumpy, uneven field. While the SS men were murdering one group, a second group, their outer clothing already removed, was waiting in line several dozen meters from the pit, and a third group was being taken out of the hangars.

Although the overwhelming majority of the people murdered that day were helpless old people, children, and women with little ones in their arms, the SS still feared resistance from them. The murder was organized in such a way that at the execution site there were more executioners with automatic weapons than there were unarmed victims.

The monstrous slaughter of the innocent and the helpless went on all day; all day the blood flowed. The pits were full of blood, for the clay soil could absorb no more; blood flowed over the edges of the pits and formed large puddles on the ground, as it ran in little streams and collected in low-lying areas. Those who fell wounded into the pits did not die from the SS bullets but drowned in the blood that filled the pits. The executioners' boots were soaked through with blood, and the victims walked to their graves through blood. All day the mad screams of the murdered hung in the air. Peasants on the surrounding farms fled from their homes so as not to hear those wails that no human heart could bear to hear. All day people walking in an endless column past the execution site saw their mothers, sisters, and children already standing at the edge of the pit to which fate would bring them in an hour or two. And all day the air was filled with words of farewell.

"Good-bye! Good-bye! We'll soon meet again!" they cried from the highway.

"Good-bye!" answered those who stood over the pit.

Terrible shrieks reverberated in the air; they cried out the names of family members and shouted their final farewells.

Old men prayed loudly, never losing their faith even in those hours marked by the rule of the devil.

On that day, 15 September 1941, twelve thousand people were murdered in a field near the Berdichev airport. The vast majority of those who were murdered were women, children, and old people.

All five pits were filled with blood; mounds of earth had to be piled on top of them in order to cover the bodies. The earth moved, as though breathing convulsively. That night many of those who had not died crawled out from under those burial mounds. Fresh air had penetrated through the newly turned earth and reached the upper layers of those who lay beneath it; the air strengthened the ones who were only wounded, whose hearts continued to beat as they lay unconscious. They crawled out of the grave and over the field, instinctively trying to get as far from the pits as possible. Their strength failing them due to the loss of blood, most of them died there in the field, a few dozen meters from the execution site.

At dawn peasants driving into the city from Romanovka saw the entire field littered with bodies. Later that morning the Germans and the police took the bodies away, killed those who were still breathing, and buried them again.

Heaving from the pressure inside, the earth covering the graves cracked open three times within a short period; a bloody fluid oozed over the edges of the pits and ran over the field. Three times the Germans rounded up the peasants and forced them to pile new mounds of earth on top of the huge graves.

We have information on two children who stood at the edge of these graves and were saved by a miracle.

One of them was named Garik, the ten-year-old son of the engineer Nuzhny. His father, mother, and little six-year-old sister were executed. When Garik approached the edge of the pit with his mother and sister, his mother tried to save him by shouting, "This little boy is Russian! He is my neighbor's son!"

The voices of others of those who were doomed to death chimed in with her, saying she was telling the truth.

An SS man shoved the little boy aside. The boy went off and lay in the bushes near the road until dark. Then he went to the city, to the building on Belopolskaya Street, where he had spent his short life.

He went to the apartment of Nikolai Vasilevich Nemolovsky, a friend of his father; no sooner did he catch sight of familiar faces than he fell into a faint, choking on his tears.

He told the story of how his father, mother, and sister had been murdered, of how his mother and people he did not even know—people who were now dead—had saved his life. He sobbed all night; jumping up from his bed, he would try to return to the execution site.

The Nemolovskys hid him for ten days. On the tenth day Nemolovsky found out that the brother of the engineer Nuzhny was among the four hundred craftsmen and skill laborers who had been allowed to live. He went to the photography studio where Nuzhny worked and told him that his nephew was alive.

That night Nuzhny came to see the boy. As Nemolovsky was describing to the writer of these lines the meeting between Nuzhny, who had lost his whole family, and his nephew, he burst into sobs and said, "It's impossible to tell it."

A few days later Nuzhny came for his nephew and took him to his place. Both of them met with a tragic fate: the uncle and his nephew were both shot at the next execution.

The second child to escape from the execution site was the ten-year-old Chaim Roitman. His father, mother, and little brother Borya were murdered before his eyes. When a German raised his automatic weapon, from the edge of the pit Chaim said to him, "Look, a watch," and he pointed at a shiny piece of glass nearby. The German bent over to pick up the watch, and the boy took off running. Bullets from the German's gun tore through his cap, but the boy was not wounded; he ran until he fell unconscious. He was saved, hidden, and adopted by Gerasim Prokofevich Ostapchuk. Thus he was perhaps the only one of those taken out to be shot on 15 September 1941 who was still alive when the Red Army arrived.

After this mass execution, Jews who had fled from the city, as well as residents of villages where the total slaughter of the Jewish population was taking place, went to the empty ghetto to try to save themselves. Someone had convinced them that there, on the streets set aside for the Jews, they could escape death. But soon the Germans and the police came once again and once again their bloody atrocities began.

Little children had their heads crushed on the stones of the pavement, and women had their breasts cut off. Fifteen-year-old Leva Milmeister was a witness to this slaughter; he was wounded in the leg by a German bullet while running away from the execution site.

Round-ups of the Jews who had been secretly staying in areas of the city forbidden to them began at the end of October 1941. Not only the Germans and the police but members of the Black Hundreds conducted these round-ups. By 3 November two thousand people had been herded into the old convent of the order of the Discalced Carmelites, which stands on the steep bank of the river and is surrounded by a tall, thick fortress wall. The four hundred skilled workers whom Reder and Korolyuk had selected at the time of the execution on 15

September were brought here with their families. On 3 November the people who had been driven into the convent were ordered to place all the money and valuables they had in a special circle drawn on the floor. A German officer announced that anyone hiding his valuables would not be shot but would be buried alive.

After that they began taking people out to be shot in groups of 150. The victims were formed into columns of two and loaded into trucks. First the men were taken, approximately eight hundred of them, and then the women and children. After four months of German butchery; after terrible beatings, torture, hunger, and thirst; and after having lost their loved ones, some of those imprisoned in the convent were so crushed mentally that they viewed their death as a deliverance. People got into the death line without attempting to delay the moment of death for even an hour or two.

One man who had forced his way to the exit cried out, "Jews, let me go first! In five minutes it will be all over. What is there to fear?"

On that day two thousand people were shot; among them were Dr. Vurvarg, Dr. Baraban, the dentist Dr. Blank, Dr. Liberman, and the family of the dentist Dr. Rubinstein. This execution took place outside of town, near the Sakulino farm.

With this new execution, as before, there was a selection held at the very edge of the pits; this time the Germans separated out 150 craftsmen and skilled specialists.

They were taken to the camp at Lysaya Gora. The finest specialists from other regions were gradually gathered into this camp. There was a total of about five hundred people in the camp.

On 27 April 1942 all registered Jewish women who were married to Russian men, as well as all children born of mixed marriages, were shot. There were about seventy of them.

The camp at Lysaya Gora was in operation until June of 1942. On 15 June the Germans took machine guns and executed the last of the craftsmen and their families, and the camp was closed. Once again the Germans and the police held a selection at the execution site, where sixty of the best of the best craftsmen and artisans were separated from the rest—tailors, shoemakers, electricians, and masons. They were locked up in a prison and forced to attend to the personal needs of the SD and the Ukrainian police.

The fate of these sixty Jews who were left alive was decided later. The Germans shot them during the first advance of the Red Army on Zhitomir. {The old electrician Epelfeld, known throughout the city, died at this execution.} Thus, operating according to their preconceived plan, the Germans slaughtered the twenty thousand Jews of Berdichev, from decrepit old people to newborn babies.

Out of the twenty thousand only ten or fifteen people survived the occupation. Among those who were saved were Leva Milmeister, the fifteen-year-old boy mentioned above, the ten-year-old Chaim Roitman, and the brothers Vulf and Mikhel Pekelis, who were the sons of Berdichev's stone mason and oven maker.

In conclusion, we present a few lines printed on 13 January 1944 in the Red Army newspaper *Za Chest Rodiny* (*For the Honor of the Homeland*):

Among the first to break through to Berdichev was Lieutenant Bashkatov's company. Isaak Shpeer, a native of Berdichev, served as a private in that company. By the time he reached Belopolskaya Street, he had killed three German machine gunners. The Red Army soldier's heart sank as he looked around. The street he had known since childhood lay in ruins. He went over to Shevchenko Street. That is where his parents' home had been. The roof, walls, and shutters were still intact. There Shpeer found out from the neighbors that the Germans had murdered his mother, father, sister, and little Borya and Dora.

The Germans still held Lysaya Gora. The next morning the soldiers crossed over the ice of the Gnilopyat River and stormed Lysaya Gora. Isaak Shpeer was in the front ranks. He crawled up to a German machine gun position and used hand grenades to kill two gunners. His leg was torn open by a piece of shrapnel from a mine, but he kept on fighting. Shpeer shot one more German and then died when he was hit by an exploding bullet, there at Lysaya Gora, where his mother was murdered. Private Isaak Shpeer was buried in his native city on Belopolskaya Street.

Vasily Grossman

Talnoe

Anyone walking along the high embankment of the railway line that runs near Talnoe can see the slaughterhouse building standing by itself on the slope of a hill outside the city. Here the great tragedy of the city of Talnoe took place: the murder of many thousands of innocent people at the hands of the Germans. Talnoe is located in the Kiev district, and more than half its population was Jewish. Of the entire Jewish population only one man was left alive: Yulin, the butcher from the slaughterhouse.

On 19 September 1941 the German commandant of Talnoe issued an order requiring all Jews residing in the city to register with the authorities. When the Jews gathered on the square in from of the commandant's headquarters, it was announced that they would be sent in several groups to Uman. Old men unable to work were separated out and taken to the movie theater and to the club; the next day they were all shot.

On the other side of the Kulbid Forest, several kilometers outside of town, is the village of Belashki. Here, near the village of Belashki, the Jews that were led out of Talnoe were brought to a halt, and all of them—more than a thousand men—were shot down with machine guns.

Mariya Fedorovna Rosenfeld, who is now the chief accountant and Deputy Secretary of the Regional Committee of the Young Communist League in Talnoe, was married to a Jew. She herself is Ukrainian; her maiden name is Moskalenko. The Germans forced Russian and Ukrainian women who were married to Jews and had children into three apartments in a single building; in addition to the woman and children, some old men were there also. Approximately one hundred people crammed into a few small rooms awaited the hour of their death.

On 17 April 1942, [Hitler's birthday],[9] at five o'clock in the morning everyone in the building was taken out to the courtyard. They started taking the children away from the mothers whose husbands were Jews. The little Moskalenko-Rosenfeld boy was five years old; their little girl was three. The Germans had conceived a punishment for the mothers that was more refined than plain murder. The children were thrown into a truck in piles, like logs of wood. Then they were taken away. Near the city slaughterhouse, in that terrible and cursed place that can be seen from the high embankment of the railway line, all the children were shot. The mothers were left alive. Their souls had already been murdered, and the Germans were certain they would never recover.

The photographer Pogoretsky, a Russian, was married to a Jewish woman; his son was shot along with the boy's mother, and the father was left alive. Partisans killed the village elder and German collaborator in Glibochek. The next day the Germans completely wiped out two Jewish families: the Sigalovskys and the Khersonskys. A Jewish woman named Ratushnaya was hanged, and for a long time her body was left to swing outside the commandant's headquarters. She had an empty bottle tied around her neck; the German to whom Ratushnaya was supposed to deliver a bottle of milk thought the milk was not thick enough. This is how the SS would murder Jewish children: with one hand an SS man would pick up a child by the hair, and with the other he would take a pistol and shoot the child in the ear. When he saw a boy who had ringworm on his head, an SS man tried to pick him up by the ear. That did not work, and the child fell; then the German stripped the boy's pants off and crushed his genitals with the heel of his boot. "Try reproducing now!" he said to the laughter of the other German soldiers.

Vladimir Lidin[10]

Resistance in Yarmolitsy (Kamenets, Podolsk District)

In Yarmolitsy the Jews resisted for two days. Arrangements to have weapons were made beforehand; the Jews had brought them along with their household goods. It all took place in the cantonment. The Jews killed the first policeman who came in to select a group for extermination and threw his body out the window. An exchange of gunfire broke out, during which several more policemen were killed. The next day truckloads of policemen from surrounding areas were brought in. Only toward evening, when the Jews ran out of ammunition, were the police able to break the siege and penetrate into the cantonment. The slaughter of the Jews lasted for three days. During the resistance sixteen policemen were killed, including the chief of police and five Germans.

Suicides were observed in other buildings in the cantonment. A father threw his two children out a window, and then he and his wife jumped together. As she stood in a window, one girl cried, "Long live the Red Army! Long live Stalin!"

Prepared for publication by Ilya Ehrenburg

How the Woman Dr. Langman Perished (Sorochitsy)

A gynecologist named Lyubov Mikhailovna Langman lived in Sorochitsy. The people loved her, and for a long time peasant women hid her from the Germans. Her eleven-year-old daughter was hidden along with her.

When Langman was in the village of Mikhailovka, a midwife came and told her that the village elder's wife was having a very difficult delivery. Langman explained to the midwife what had to be done, but the mother's condition was getting worse by the hour. Faithful to her duty, Langman went to the elder's cottage and saved both the mother and the child. Afterward the elder told the Germans that a Jewish woman was in his hut. The Germans took Langman and her daughter out to be shot. At first Langman pleaded, "Don't kill my little girl!" But then she held her daughter close to her and said, "Shoot! I don't want her to live among the likes of you!" The mother and her daughter were murdered.

Prepared for publication by Ilya Ehrenburg

In the Town of Chmelnik (Vinnitsa District)

Before the war ten thousand Jews lived in the little town of Chmelnik in the Vinnitsa district; they made up the majority of the population. Jews had lived there for many years, from generation to generation; they were bound to the Ukrainians and Russians through friendship and love.

During the years of Soviet rule the little town grew and developed both economically and culturally.

In Chmelnik there were factories that produced textiles, furs, and furniture; there was a manufacturer of machine parts, a brickyard, and two sugar refineries, as well as many craft guilds. In all of these enterprises Jews worked alongside Ukrainians and Russians as laborers, technicians, and engineers.

The entire town knew and respected the Jews known to be Stakhanovites,[11] inventors, and conscientious workers.

The town had a cinema, a theater, three middle schools, two seven-year elementary schools, and a large, beautifully organized hospital. [The sum of this orderly and rational way of life tumbled into the abyss on 22 June 1941. Almost none of the Jews managed to get out; when the Germans entered their native town, their mental anguish and affliction were overwhelming.]

July days are blessed days in the Ukraine; that is when nature generously shares its wealth and its beauty with humanity. But even nature understood what terrible days had fallen upon the earth. On 18 July 1941 a hurricane unlike any that had ever been seen struck this land; torrents of strong, cold autumn rains poured down.

The Germans burst into the town.

By 21 July 1941 all Jewish men, women, and children over five years of age were required to wear a white armband fifteen centimeters wide with a blue embroidered six-pointed star on their left arm.

The first decree announced that Jews did not have the right to buy anything in the market except potatoes and peas. But soon a second decree declared that any Jew caught in the market would receive twenty-five to fifty lashes. Thus the Jewish population was condemned to starvation.

A special decree absolutely forbade the peasants to enter into any kind of business or personal relations with the Jews. Any peasant who stepped into the house of a Jew received twenty-five to fifty lashes; sentences were carried out immediately.

The general plundering of the Jewish population began: all Jews were required to hand over their bicycles, sewing machine, and phonographs within twenty-four hours.

Even more devastating was the categorical order that the Jews turn in absolutely all their plates, spoons, forks, and soap. The plundering of the Jews was not always carried out in an orderly fashion; police burst into homes, breaking down windows and doors, and took everything they wanted. What they could not take they destroyed.

The Germans and the police went into every home and forced the Jews out to work. [They were sent to repair blown up bridges, wash floors, and dig gardens.] Some jobs were for purposes of humiliation: Jews were forced to fill containers full of holes with water. The "work" was absurd and pointless, and yet the Jews received kicks and blows when they could not keep up with it.

On 12 August 1941 the Gestapo arrived in the town.

One evening three Jewish boys were sitting on a bench outside a building. One of them was Musya Gorbonos. He was a quiet, good boy and an excellent eighth-grade student. A policeman went up to the boys. He turned to Musya and asked for a smoke. The boy told him he did not smoke.

The German fixed his gaze upon the boy and shot him. Musya Gorbonos was the first victim. The population was seized with fear and horror.

The Jews were ordered to register with the authorities. On the first day 365 men and two women were selected from the crowd.

A monument to Lenin stood on a boulevard in the central part of Chmelnik. It was a favorite place for young people to take a stroll.

The Germans chose this very spot for the public humiliation of the Soviet people.

The 367 Jews who had been selected were driven out to the boulevard. Beaten with rifle butts, they were forced to join hands, dance, and sing the International. Old men had their beards torn out, and young men were forced to eat the hair from the beards.

Afterward they were all taken to the regional Cooperative Society building. Here the Jews were herded into the glass warehouse, where they were forced to dance barefoot on broken glass and on specially prepared boards with nails sticking out of them. Thus the Germans debased these people in such a vile and terrifying fashion before executing them. At six o'clock in the evening the tormented people were taken outside of town. There, along Ulanovsky Road, pits had been prepared. The executioners forced the Jews to strip naked and dance once again.

Before they died, some of those who were doomed cried out, "Long live Stalin! He will win the war anyway! May Hitler rot!"

On that day the Gestapo and their minions murdered 367 Jews and forty Ukrainians who were members of the Party.

With the formation of the Litin Gebietskommissariat the persecution of the Jews assumed a more calculated character.

First of all, an order was issued, according to which all Jews living in the center of town has to move to the outskirts within three days.

On 25 December came the deposition requiring all Jews to hand over warm clothing for the German army.

The Germans seized ten women and one man, took them to the police station, stripped them naked, and threw them into a cell. From nine o'clock in the morning until six o'clock that evening policemen would go into that cell and beat those poor people. Then the tortured victims were thrown out into the freezing cold.

"Collections" for the German army continued.

But all of this was still only a prelude to the total extermination that awaited the Jewish population. It was reported that a sick man named Abramovich might have a weapon. The invalid was dragged out of his house; a gallows had been set up in the middle of the street. Before his died, he was ordered to say a last word.

Terribly sick and barely alive after having been beaten, the old man found within himself the strength to declare in a clear, pure voice, "May the fascists and their 'ober-bandit' Hitler be swept off the face of the earth!"

On Friday, 2 January 1942, the Litin Gebietskommissar Witzermann arrived in his yellow car.

He summoned the Jewish elder and imposed upon him a new contribution.

In addition, he ordered that the Jews be moved immediately from the new part of the city into the old area, where a ghetto had been set up.

The decree ordered categorically that all Russians and Ukrainians paint a cross on their doors and that anyone who allowed a Jew into his home would be severely punished.

Several days went by. The came the "Aktion."

Deep snowdrifts, wind, a snowstorm, piercing cold. People were afraid to leave their homes, as if they had a presentiment of the horror and the misery that awaited them on the following day.

At five o'clock in the morning the streets were surrounded by the Gestapo, their minions, and the Litin police, all led by the Gebietskommissar Witzermann.

Soon the bloody action was underway. Sleeping people were dragged from their beds without even being allowed to get dressed. The old and the sick were shot on the spot.

The temperature had fallen to thirty degrees below freezing, and yet everyone had been mercilessly driven outside. People were barefoot. Some had on only one shoe, and others wore galoshes on their bare feet; some were wrapped only in a blanket, and others were in their nightshirts. Many tried to run, but they were shot down.

A survivor named A. Beider relates, "At six o'clock in the morning I heard shooting. When I opened the door, a policeman holding a rifle was shouting, 'Everybody out!' They took me to the building next door. No matter how much I begged for permission to go with my family, so it would be easier for my wife to lead our children to their deaths, I got nothing from them except blows from their rifle butts. In the most terrible hour of my life I was violently torn away from my wife and our three beloved children. I managed to escape from the column. The air trembled with screams, cries, and groans. A German woman, the wife of the chairman of the city council, was herding the children. As she moved them along, she was saying, 'Quiet, children, quiet.'

"Once the crowd had been herded into the square, the Gebietskommissar ordered the list of specialists who would be allowed to live to be read. The rest were led into the pine forest about three kilometers from town. Pits had already been prepared there. Along the way the Gestapo mercilessly beat and humiliated the people.

"A Gestapo man was herding the two Lerner sisters along by poking them in the back with a dagger.

"A four-year-old boy named Shaim, who had no father and whose mother had been murdered by the Germans, marched in the column with everyone else, like an adult, toward the pits. . .

"As they lined up in a row next to the pits, people were forced with threats and blows to undress themselves and their children. It was horribly cold. Children cried out, 'Mama, why are you undressing me? It's cold outside!'

"Every fifteen to twenty minutes carts loaded with clothing that had belonged to the murdered people left for the warehouse."

On that day, 9 January 1942, 6,800 people were murdered.

On 16 January another 1,240 were murdered. There was no limit to the cruelty of the Gestapo and the police. Doctor Abramson's mother, a woman of sixty, failed to immediately obey an order to come out of a cellar where she had sought refuge; she was deaf and could not hear the order. A Gestapo man seized her by her gray hair and cut off her head with a saber.

He stood there, right in front of the people, holding up her gray head.

Several victims managed to hide in cellars and attics that belonged to peasants; many wandered in the fields, without any shelter. More than a few froze to death; they were not found until the following spring, when the snow melted.

Among those who managed to hide and save themselves were the Goldman children. They lay hidden under a bed for several hours. Finally the older boy, a twelve-year-old, said that they should go see where their father was. At that moment a policeman came into the room. He stabbed the boy with a dagger; the child simply cried, "Oh!" and died.

When it got dark the little girl took here five-year-old brother and fled to the home of some people they knew in Slobodka. Few Jews living on Evreiskaya Street escaped the initial "Aktions." The German chief of gendarmes told the Jewish elder Elzon to have the Jews report to the police station for documents. Then the Jews, he assured them, would be left alone. But if an unregistered Jew should be caught, the elder and three other Jews from Evreiskaya Street would be shot. The people were issued blue documents that had to be stamped at the police station every day at eight o'clock in the morning. [The promises, of course, had no real meaning; the savage and arbitrary humiliation of the Jews did not stop. On 25 January 1942 a Gestapo agent noticed the rabbi of Chmelnik, Rabbi Shapiro. He dragged the rabbi out of his shelter, began beating him, and demanded gold. Finally, he took the rabbi out into the street and drove a knife into his throat. Shapiro's body lay there for several days; the Germans would not allow him to be buried. On 5 February the Jewish elder was ordered to bring twenty-four women to clear the stadium of snow. The girls who showed up for the job began clearing away the snow with shovels. A policeman did not like that and said he would have the women work in manner more preferable to him.

He ordered the women to dance in the deep snow; then he told them to lie on their stomachs and crawl around in the snow. As the poor women were lying in the snow, the policemen started kicking them with their metal-tipped boots.

Over the next few months the Jews felt the sword of Damocles[12] constantly hanging over them.]

On Friday, 12 June, at five o'clock in the morning Hungarian soldiers who had arrived in the city the previous day surrounded Evreiskaya Street and began herding the people toward the police station, supposedly to be registered once again. Outside the police station the men were separated from the women and children. The men were taken away, and the women, children, and old people were loaded onto trucks and driven into the forest.

It was a clear, sunny day. The little ones, who understood nothing of what was taking place, ran around the pits, played, and gathered flowers.

On that bloody Friday 360 people were murdered. [The German-Hungarian bandits tore the children to bits and threw pieces of their bodies into the pit.]

Early in 1943 the Germans decided to liquidate the ghetto once and for all.

On 3 March at seven o'clock on the morning police officer Schur ordered the guards not to allow the Jews to cross the bridge. People were forced into the street; policemen holding guns and axes surrounded their homes.

Trucks pulled up. Those who hesitated for even a moment were beaten with rifle butts and axes.

On that day another 1,300 people perished. It was terrible to look upon Evreiskaya Street. The pavement ran red with blood; littered with broken dishes and smashed furniture, it bore the remnants of the senseless and vile destruction of human life and the labor of human hands. . . . After the slaughter 127 men and eight women were left; they had been designated for work in the shops and factories.

These specialists were taken to a school that had been converted into a camp. The camp was carefully guarded day and night; the windows were covered with barbed wire. In spite of such tight security, however, sixty-seven people escaped within two weeks. [Several of them fled to Romanian territory, that is, to the territory that the Germans had temporarily handed over to the Romanians.]

Some of them ran off to join partisan units. The Jews of Chmelnik selflessly fought in the ranks of the people's avengers. Once an active worker in Chmelnik's social welfare organizations, Weissman hid in the village of Kurilovka until October 1943. He obtained some weapons and gathered together eleven strong, reliable comrades who were prepared to follow him through fire and water. On 25 October Weissman and his group went into the woods. A Jewish girl from Litin named Kalikhman went with them.

Assigned to the Khrushchev Detachment, Weissman received his first combat orders from the partisans: he was to derail military trains running along the Zhmerinka section of the railway.

Weissman derailed three of the enemy's military trains. Soon Weissman and his group received a new operational assignment: to provide the partisan unit with food. A great deal of courage and resourcefulness was necessary for such a task.

Weissman operated literally under the noses of the Germans without getting caught.

Two other residents of Chmelnik, Izya Reznik and Leva Kneloiz, fought in the Lenin Partisan Detachment.

[The German bandits tormented and physically destroyed the Jewish population. But they had no power over the honor and the soul of the people.]

Two Jewish women, Sima Mazovskaya and Rakhil Portnova, fought in the Menshikov Detachment. They took revenge on the enemy for all the country's suffering and misery, for their people and their native city.

In Chmelnik the violence continued, aimed at the remaining small group of Jews, whose difficult lives dragged on in the camp. The Gestapo showed up on Saturday, 26 June, as it was just getting light. The Jews were all forced into the street. Fourteen people were selected, and the rest of them were loaded onto a truck. The people knew that they were being taken to their death; silently they made their farewells to one another.

In the woods the pits had already been dug.

Thirteen people tried escaped from the execution site; four managed to get away and hide, while the others were shot during the escape. [On that day fifty people were murdered.]

That night the four who escaped the execution went into a village. The peasants fed them, gave them clothes, and hid them. The peasants had been threatened with death simply for talking to Jews, to say nothing of actively helping them. They were all people who had no regard for danger. [They despised the Germans' cannibalistic decrees and helped the Jews as brothers.] Having escaped an "Aktion" on 3 March for a second time, A. Beider relates, "From the 3rd of March until the 23rd of June 1943 my brother and I hid in the village of Kurilovka, where we were born. Without any regard for danger, the Ukrainians Ivan Tsisar, Emelyan Shavchuk, Trofim Orel, Nina Kirnitskaya, Sergei Bratsyuk, Viktor Bezvolyuk, and Marko Sichenko saved our lives and were prepared to share our fate. The peasants often went into town and brought back various bits of news. On 15 April Yarina Tsisar came and told us that our uncle was in the camp. We were overjoyed and decided to save him. On 20 June, Marko Sichenko went to Chmelnik, abducted our uncle as he and others were being led out to work, and brought him to us. [We decided to join the partisans."

The fugitives, however, were unable to find the partisans and join them.]

After going through many ordeals, the fugitives wound up in Zhmerinka in the Romanian occupation zone. There they lived in the ghetto and engaged in the hardest of labors. They had to work at night all the time.

On 16 March 1944 the Romanians left Zhmerinka, and the Germans arrived. On the following day they announced that all Jews between the ages of sixteen and sixty had to report to be registered once again. Everyone who showed up was murdered. [The bloody German "new order" had begun.] The ghetto was seized with anxiety and horror; everyone knew that the end was near.

This time, however, a true salvation came. The Red Army was approaching Zhmerinka. On 20 March, the German authorities fled from the city in fear.

A. Beider relates, "On 21 March, we heard the voices of our brothers. When the Red Army soldiers saw the barbed wire surrounding the ghetto, they asked, 'What is this?' We answered, 'A ghetto.' 'What is a ghetto?' they asked. Then we explained to them that Jews live here. The barbed wire was torn down at once."

[Fighting was still going on in the city. Once freed from their dungeons, the Jews immediately joined in the battle.

Fighting alongside Red Army troops, they liberated the railroad station, where the Germans had dug in. Fritz took to his heels. Jews helped to carry wounded Red Army soldiers out of the line of fire. Doctor Malkin and Jewish nurses took up their posts and did not leave the field hospital.

The shooting stopped. Zhmerinka had been won back from the invaders. The city took on a holiday atmosphere. Everyone was competing with each other to invite the Red Army soldiers into their homes. Exhausted and worn out from suffering, the people gazed at their liberators with love.]

According to Beider's account, the company commander "gave a speech and uttered words that the Jews had not heard for two years and nine months." They were words about inviolable friendship, about the equality and brotherhood of peoples—about the great law of Soviet life.

Reported by A. I. Bekker,
prepared for publication by R. Kovnator

In the Village of Yaryshev

Yaryshev is a small village. A Jewish collective farm was there. It had craft guilds. It had a school with ten grades. People lived in peace and happiness.

On 15 June 1941 the Germans and Romanians broke through to Yaryshev. On the first day they were there they shot twenty-five people. But the most terrible events came later. As the Jews were led out to work, they would be ordered to lie down, stand up, and lie down again. Whoever did not lie down instantly was shot on the spot. Six moths later the Jews were forced into a ghetto. Hunger, cold, tears. On 21 August 1942 a punitive detachment arrived. They rounded up the Jews and told them, "Collect all your valuables. You are being assigned to a work detail." They were led down Zhukov Road, as if they were on their way to the train station. They came to a fork in the road; the way to the cemetery was to the left. They were commanded, "To the left!" At that point a mathematics teacher named Gitya Yakovlevna Taleisnin turned to the doomed people and offered them these words: "Our brothers are on the front. They will return. The Soviet authority still exists. It is immortal. Stalin still exists. He will not forget this."

She was murdered along with her six-year-old son Leva. Then the others, more than five hundred people, were murdered. Eight people were miraculously saved. They will never forget Gitya Yakovlevna's words.

Reported by O. Yakhot and M. Brekhman,
prepared for publication by Ilya Ehrenburg

In the Settlement of Tsybulevo

Approximately three hundred Jewish families lived in Tsybulevo in the Vinnitsa district. The winter of 1941-1942 was a severe one. The Germans forced unclothed women and barefoot old men to work. Once they selected approximately one hundred children and took them out to a field. A short while later the policemen returned and told the mothers, "Go on, go and fetch your puppies. . ." The mothers raced to the field screaming. They saw the bodies of their dead children in a pit.

All the Jews were murdered in the spring of 1942. They were taken outside the settlement, stripped, and executed. The children were placed in cages and hauled away on carts. These little ones were buried alive.

Tamara Arkadevna Rozanova hid a Jew in her cellar. The Germans had burned down her house. Rozanova was saved only by chance.

Hadya Rozanova relates, "They took Dusya Kapitovskaya and her baby boy out to be shot. Dusya's husband was an officer at the front. The little boy was only eight months old. Dusya tossed him over the heads of some Germans who were passing by and cried, 'Dear people, please save my son! At least let him live!'

"The baby fell to the road. A German walked up. He grabbed the little boy by the leg and smashed his head against the side of a car. . ."

There was a nineteen-year-old student named Lyusya Sapozhnikova. As Lyusya was being led to the execution site, she shouted, "Shoot, murderers! But know that Stalin will come!" With those words she died.

Prepared for publication by Ilya Ehrenburg

In the Village of Yaltushkov

I questioned the neighbors, who were spared by some miracle, and I discovered the whole truth.

My kinsmen were tortured for a long time. The ghetto was set up near the bazaar, sectioned off by a high barbed-wire fence. People there were starving.

On 20 August 1942 everyone was taken to the train station. They had to walk four kilometers, and rifle butts were used to drive children and decrepit old people; everyone was ordered to undress. . .

I saw scraps of clothing and underwear.

In order to economize on their bullets, the Germans stood people four deep and then shot them; those still breathing were buried alive. Small children were torn to pieces before being thrown into the pit. That is how they murdered my little Nyusenka. Other children, including my little girl Adusya, were shoved into the pit and covered over with earth.

Two months later my wife Manya was among those who were taken away from the village of Yakushintsy. There was a concentration camp at Yakushintsy. The people there were humiliated, and then they were all murdered.

There are two graves next to each other. In them lie 1,500 people. Adults, old people, and children.

Only one thing remains for me: vengeance.

From a letter written by Soviet War Hero Second-Lieutenant Kravtsov,
prepared for publication by Ilya Ehrenburg

In My Hometown (Brailov)

One warm spring day about seven years ago I went to visit my parents. I had been in the city of Kirovograd on a business trip. I had finished my work and was getting ready to go back to Moscow, when the thought occurred to me that I might stop by home for a few hours. I could see my relatives and have a look at my favorite childhood places.

By the next day I was having dinner at home. The old folks were very happy about my unexpected visit. All my relatives, neighbors, and friends came to see me. My mother bustled about the house and spent a great deal of time in the kitchen preparing a sweet-and-sour meat dish for me. She said that when I was a little boy I loved it. To tell the truth, I had managed to forget that.

They quizzed me about how I lived, what was going on in the wide world in general and in Moscow in particular, and whether I had seen anyone from our village. While we were chatting, the postman came by and delivered two letters. One of them was from me: I had written that I would be in the Ukraine on business and that I did not know whether I would be able to drop by. The other letter was from America. The name of the sender was printed on the large envelope: Brailov Landsmanschaft Committee in the United States of America.

{Signed by the president and general secretary of the Committee, the letter informed us that letters and reports from the homeland had been read at a general meeting and that it was decided to send us fellow countrymen greetings for the coming Passover, along with $1,000. Two hundred dollars were to be given to Rabbi David Liberman, and another hundred were to be used to buy a wedding gift for a certain girl. My father was authorized to divide up the rest of the money among orphans and the people most in need by Passover, so that they all could celebrate the holiday.}

I must admit that I found this letter to be rather amusing. I thought to myself: the authors left Brailov forty years ago and live far away in America, where they are now quite busy with their affairs. And yet they took the time to come together from various cities for their annual conference in noisy New York, where they show such a naive interest in the details of the life and living conditions in such a small village. But I caught myself thinking that I too had taken three trains and raced several hundred kilometers just to spend a few hours in the place where I grew up. . .

More than once during the war I remembered that letter from America. For nearly three years I had received no letters from Brailov; the Germans were in my hometown. But, oh, so often I would think about that little village in the Vinnitsa district, where I spent my childhood years! I thought about my father, mother, and sister, all of whom stayed there. No matter where I was during the war—in the forests of the northwest, in the streets of Stalingrad, or on the Donets steppe—in my thoughts I was home. I would think of the day when I would go back home, open wide those familiar doors, and say, "Is there anyone home? Come on out a greet me!"...

On 23 March 1944 at twilight, I saw Brailov in the distance. I had recently been wounded, and it was hard for me to walk; my right foot was swollen, and I could hardly pull it from the sticky black earth. Finally I came to a road sign; on it was written just one word: Brailov—that combination of letters so dear, with so many memories tied to it.

I had to cover three hundred kilometers to get there from a different section of the front. My car had gotten stuck in the mud, and I trudged the last ten kilometers on foot. I knew that the Bug River formed the border between the German *Generalgouvernement* and the Romanian-governed territory of Transnistria; I also knew that there were still several ghettos left in Transnistria. But in Vinnitsa the border ran somewhere west of the Bug. In which part, then, lay Brailov: in the German *Generalgouvernement* or in Transnistria? No one could answer that question for me. I had only a few hundred meters left to go before I would reach the village and have the answers to everything.

A few minutes later, however, I came to another road sign. It was written in German and in Ukrainian: "A Town Free of Kikes."

Immediately everything became clear.

{I called out to a bright-looking youngster who was peeking out from a hut and told him to bring an axe and chop down the sign.

"Is it really permitted to do that, sir?"

"It is not only permitted," I said, "it is absolutely necessary. Besides, what the sign says is not true. You see, I have come back to Brailov, which means that there is at least one Jew here."}

More than once I had entered liberated cities. I knew very well the feeling of excitement that comes when you enter a city that has been wrested from the enemy's hands and returned to the homeland. But I do not think my nerves had ever done such a turnabout on me as they did on this occasion. Here I knew the history of practically ever home. There was Yakov Vladimir's house. I had visited that home many times; I prepared for my exams and had many good times there. Now the house was dark and deserted. Over there, in the next house lived Aizik Kulik, a friend from my school days who later became a railroad engineer. I looked through the window: half-rotten pieces of broken furniture lay on the floor; apparently no one had been here for a long time. The next house had belonged to the watchmaker Shakhno

Shapiro—not a soul was to be found there now. The tailor Shneiko Priputsky used to live across the street—the same scene there. . . .

I traveled the road from the Volga to the Carpathians with the Red Army. I have seen before my eyes the destruction of Stalingrad, the ruins of Rzhev and Velikie Luki, and the ashes of Poltava and Kremenchug. By now the sight of ruins was nothing new to me. But what I encountered in my hometown shook me to the core. From Mirgorod to the Dnieper, along a strip one hundred kilometers wide, the Germans had burned the all forests to the ground. In the summer of 1943 not a single hut was left standing; the Hitlerites had created a "wilderness zone." But from under the rubble of these burned-out Ukrainian huts, from somewhere beneath the earth, a peaceful wisp of smoke worked its way upward. People had built up hearth and home in the depths of an abandoned bunker; little children were running about, and dinner was cooking in clay ovens. You could believe that life would return here. Let all the huts and barns be burned to the ground and the farms' beehives and storehouses be broken to bits. People will endure nevertheless. I give you my personal guarantee: life will return.

But here I was walking about in a village that was completely intact; there was even glass in the windows of many houses. But I did not meet a single living soul. My footsteps sent a lonely echo throughout this wilderness. To realize what this meant, one had to know the customs of the cities and towns in the south. The main street had always been a place to meet with others and to go for walks. Now I was the only one walking the streets. From time to time a solitary cat would scamper across the street.

As I walked on, I was afraid to turn my head to the right, where the house in which I was born was supposed to be standing, where the people closest to me had lived. Indeed, the house was there, nearly undamaged on the outside. I walked up to the windows and looked in; the walls were stained with traces of blood, and down feathers were scattered all over the floors. There was nothing left for me to ask about. Indeed, whom was I to ask? Iosef Sukonnik or the hatter Grutskin? They had been neighbors. And then there were the apartments belonging to the Lener, Goldman, Lumer, and Kharnak families. But nowhere was any trace of life to be found.

For half an hour I wandered about the once noisy village, utterly alone. It started to get dark, and I went to a village nearby to spend the night. A peasant woman took me in and gave me a brief history of the destruction of the Jews of Brailov. I asked about the fate of families I had known, about first and last names.

"And how do you know all of them?" she asked. "Have you been to Brailov before?"

"Yes, I have been here before. More than once I have come here. You used to have a paramedic here named Gekhman. Did you know him?"

"How was it possible not to know him? Everyone knew him."

"Where is he now?"

"Murdered."

"Have you heard anything about his wife?"

"They cut her throat."

"What about the paramedic's daughter, the student?"

"She is there, where everyone else is. . . "

After that I could ask no more. The peasant woman looked at me long and hard and then quietly said , "Forgive me, but are you not the son of our paramedic?"

"Yes, my name is Gekhman."

"You look so much like your father!"

I do not know how, but soon everyone in the village knew I had returned. Many people came to the hut where I had stopped over. There were many I knew, many who remembered me. All night long we talked about the war, about people in the war, and about the victory that would come.

The next morning I went back to the village. Suddenly someone called out to me in Yiddish. "Comrade Gekhman!"

Five people ran up to me: three men, a woman, and a teenage girl. They rushed up to hug and kiss me, and then suddenly they all broke into sobs and pressed themselves close to me. For them I was not only an acquaintance from the local area, I was a close and dear kinsman. Our parents, brothers, and sisters were all buried in the same terrible pit.

I recognized the tailor Abram Tsigelman right away. His older daughter and I were in the same class in elementary school; after that I was often a guest in their home. I had no recollection at all of the second man. Realizing this, he shook his head bitterly and asked, "Don't you recognize me, Gekhman? Yes, it is hard to recognize me now. My name is Bas, Moses Bas. The barber. How many times have I cut your hair?"

I would never have thought that a man could change so much in three years. He stood there with his back bent and his eyes downcast. Before me was a man who had lost the foundations of his life, who no longer had any confidence in his strength or in his right to exist on earth.

"You are looking at my rags? Yes, I was once considered a gay blade, but I have not changed my underwear in the last year and a half."

These were practically the only residents of Brailov left alive.

We counted up all the people of the village on our fingers and figured out that only twenty-one had survived....

Over the course of several years my father had described [to the Brailov Committee in the USA] all the affairs and events that took place in Brailov. The Germans executed my father. Now he will no longer write anything ever again, and I, his son, have resolved to take it upon myself to describe how the village of Brailov perished. Here I neither invent nor add anything; I simply relate what witnesses have told me.

The Germans entered Brailov on 17 July 1941. It turned out that a major portion of the population had not been evacuated and was still there. I have often asked myself why so many did not get out of there and move as far as possible away from the brown plague. Why didn't my relatives get to the East? Evidently there were many reasons: for one thing, my mother was seriously ill, and my father and sister did not want to leave her alone, sick and defenseless. So they decided to share her fate with her.

Approximately fifteen people were killed on the day the Germans entered Brailov—Iosif Sukonnik, Ilya Paltin, Isaak Kopzon, and others. German soldiers walking down the street would check to see if their rifles were in working condition by shooting people on the street. Thus fifteen people were exterminated. [The village woke up, and everyone immediately realized that a storm cloud was hanging over them.]

Soon the German commandant arrived, along with the police, and the "new order" was established in Brailov. In a Jewish village the "new order" looked something like this: all Jews had to wear on their backs and chests a larger six-pointed star (a "Magen David"). No one had the right to go beyond the limits of the village or to associated with the Ukrainian population of neighboring settlements. Although a bazaar has existed in the center of Brailov from time immemorial, no Jew could show his face in the bazaar without fear of getting hit by a German bullet. For only ten minutes per day, at the sound of a police whistle, were the Jews allowed to run to the bazaar. The German commandant Kraft derived a great deal of pleasure from this spectacle. By the third or fourth minute the policeman would blow the whistle to signal that their time was up; throwing down their purchases, everyone would quickly run away from the bazaar. Then it would be announced that the second signal was a mistake, and everything started all over again. Thus Commandant Kraft amused himself.

Every day, by order of the commandant, more than a thousand residents of Brailov went out to hard labor. But not on a single day did all of them return home. Either German soldiers riding by would "hunt" them, or the police would finish off the exhausted and tortured people. Once a month the residents of Brailov received an "order" from the local commandant's office warning them that if the items listed in the "order" were not delivered to the commandant's office by the designated date, then everyone would be shot.

I saw one of these "orders," the one for November. Items on the long list included ten gold women's watches, twenty gold bracelets, a grand piano for the officers' club, two automobiles, and three tons of gasoline.

The November "order" was filled, as was the December "order" after it. To this day I cannot understand how the community, forbidden to go beyond the confines of the village, could obtain automobiles and gasoline during the war. The community's elder Iosif Kulik and his assistants are no longer alive, and there is no one left to ask how they did it. Khana Kulik, a student and the only survivor from that family, says that her father never indicated how he managed to obtain the things listed on the Germans' "orders."

"Don't ask about it, Khana," he once told her. "It's enough that I be the one to go insane. Don't trouble your head with it."

One freezing February night police and Gestapo men surrounded Brailov; by dawn the slaughter had begun. In the words of a policeman whom I interrogated, this was the "first Aktion." Each policeman received an order to go around to two or three Jewish apartments and herd everyone out to a gathering place on the square. Anyone who was unwilling or unable to go was to be finished off on the spot, but it had to be done silently, with a bayonet, rifle butt, or dagger.

At six o'clock in the morning, my father was awakened by the sound of rifle butts pounding on the door. Two policemen burst into the room.

"Out on the square, quickly! Everyone!"

"My wife is sick. She cannot get up."

"We know what to do with the healthy and what to do with the sick."

Using their rifle butts, they drove my father into the street. My sister Roza started to quickly get dressed. Just then she saw one of the policemen raising a dagger over our mother. She rushed over to save our mother, but they hit her in the head with a rifle butt and drove her barefoot into the freezing cold; she was wearing nothing but a light dress. Roza fell. Father picked her up and helped her get to the gathering place on Torgovaya Square opposite the Catholic church.

The residents of Brailov were driven there. But not everyone. Many, like my mother, were murdered in their homes. A policeman lined up the Bakaleinik family outside their building and bet another policeman that he could kill them all with one shot from his machine gun.

After checking their list for an hour and a half, the police announced that three hundred people would be selected to work for the German army—mostly tailors, shoemakers, and furriers, as well as their families. The rest would be executed. The procession set out under heavy guard. It happened that my father and sister were walking at the head of the column; behind them was Oskar Shmaryan, a sixteen-year-old relative of ours from Kiev who had come to Brailov for the holidays. The column stopped at the pharmacy; the police chief remembered that he had forgotten Iosef Shvarts, who lived outside the village near the Orthodox cemetery. He sent a policeman to get Shvarts. Within a few minutes Shvarts arrived with his wife, and they were placed at the head of the sad procession.

Everyone walked silently, concentrating on their last steps and casting a final farewell glance toward their hometown, toward life. Suddenly a song rang out above the column. A girl's voice was singing about the homeland, about its wide-open spaces; about its forests, seas, and rivers; about how a person can breathe freely in this land. It was my sister Roza singing.

I have questioned several witnesses and have verified this fact several times very carefully and scrupulously. Everything was exactly as I have recorded it here. My sister was never considered a singer. On that terrible morning she had spent about two hours in the freezing cold barefoot and hardly dressed. By that time her feet would already have been frostbitten. Why did she start singing? Where did she find the strength for this one last feat?

The police ordered her to be quiet, but she went on singing the song. Two shots rang out. My father picked up the dead body of his only daughter. For the last kilometer and a half of their journey he carried in his arms a burden most precious and most sacred to him, all the way to the execution site. . . .

When the column reached the excavated pit, the first group was ordered to strip naked, place their clothing in a single pile, and lie down at the bottom of the pit. My father carefully lay my sister's body into the pit and started to undress. About a dozen peasant sleighs came up from the direction of the village to transport the clothing of the murdered to police warehouses. At that moment a slight interruption occurred at the edge of the pit: a young girl named Liza Perkel refused to undress and demanded that she be shot in her clothing. She was beaten with rifle butts and poked with bayonets, but they could not make her undress. She grabbed one Gestapo man by the throat, and when he tried to get her off of him, she sank her teeth into his hand. The Gestapo man cried out, and some other executioners came to his aid. There were many of them, all armed to the teeth, but the girl would not back off; she would not give in to the enemy.

The killers threw Liza Perkel to the ground and tried to tear her dress off. She managed to free one of her legs for a moment, and with all her might she kicked one Gestapo man in the face. Commandant Kraft decided to restore "order" himself; he walked up, issuing orders with every step. The girl rose to her feet; blood was flowing from her mouth, and her dress was torn to shreds. She calmly met the gaze of the approaching commandant and spat in his face.

A volley of gunfire rang out. Liza Perkel died on her feet, meeting death in battle. What could this young, unarmed girl have done against a mob of executioners? But the Germans did not succeed in breaking her will! [Her last wish came true, that the Germans would not be able to force her to degrade herself. They could kill her, yes; they had the weapons. But they did not have the power to shatter her will, her dignity, and her honor.]

My father decided to take advantage of the fact that the attention of the commandant, the Gestapo, and the police had been distracted. Having caught sight of a peasant woman whom he had once treated, he whispered to her, "Gorpina, hide the boy," and he pushed Oskar Shmaryan into the pile of clothing. The peasant woman quickly threw someone's overcoat over him and laid him in the sleigh along with the pile of clothing. She hid him for several days and gave him clothes to wear; soon the boy left to join a partisan unit. He is still alive. I found out from him how my family died. Oskar Shmaryan saw my father in the last minute of his life. . . . My father did all that he could, down tot he last moment. He saved one more avenger, young and implacable, for our people in their fight against fascism.

After approximately two hundred people had been executed, the next in line was the community's elder Iosif Kulik. The police and the Gestapo stopped to consult each other about something, and then the police chief said, "Kulik, you and your family can go back to the village; you'll continue to represent the community, as before."

Kulik's wife took her shawl from the pile of clothing and with trembling hands hurriedly started to wrap it around herself. It seemed to her that by some miracle they had been unexpectedly saved at the very edge of the grave.

"Basya, throw down the shawl," he husband said to her in a quiet but stern voice. Then, turning to the policemen, he replied, "When you execute two thousand of my people, there is nothing left for me to do in this world as elder of the community."

"Don't you want to save your own life?"

"The people chose me to represent the community, and I shall stand where the majority of them stand."

"I'm asking you for the last time, Kulik: will you go back to the village?"

"Only if you allow the Jews to live."

Iosif Kulik—the last elder of the Jewish community in Brailov and father of four sons, all of whom became engineers and are now soldiers in the Red Army—was executed along with his wife.

Yakov Vladimir and his family approached the execution site. The policemen thumbed through the list and spoke among themselves for a long time.

"Vladimir, you were told to stay in the village. We don't have any other tailors who make women's clothes."

"I'll stay if you let my family stay with me."

"They can stay with you."

"My daughter Sonya? And my grandchildren?"

"No, she is no longer in your family. She has a husband in Leningrad."

"She is my daughter, flesh of my flesh. I won't stay without her."

The altercation between Yakov Vladimir and the police went on for five minutes. They needed this highly skilled tailor: a lot of clothing had been stolen, and the police wanted to have it re-sewn for their wives and mistresses. [But their thirst for blood was even greater than their lust for profit.] Yakov Vladimir was shot with his wife, children, and grandchildren.

The "Aktion" was coming to an end, when an eighty-year-old man named Chaim Arn ran up to the execution site with a Torah scroll in his arms. The police had not found him at home that morning, and he had been sitting in his cellar until noon. When he went out to the street, it was deserted.

"Where are all the people?" he asked Doctor Yanitsky's son, who happened to be passing by.

"What do you mean 'where are they'? They are being shot behind the mill."

"Then I'm the only one left! No, I won't be the only one left!"

And he picked up a Torah scroll and ran off. [The only thing he asked of the police was that he be allowed to lie in the pit with the Torah.] And so they shot the old village *balagole*[13] Chaim Arn, as he stood and embraced the Torah.

More than two thousand people were executed on that day. It all took place on 12 February 1942, [which was the 26th and Shevat 5702 on the Jewish calendar].

The pit was not filled in. They were waiting for a convoy to return from the village of Mezhirov with the Jews from there. Two policemen were left to stand guard at the pit. The next morning a woman covered with blood crawled out of the pit. She had lain under the bodies for twenty hours, and even though she had been wounded, she still found the strength to climb out and crawl off to the side. She was Cheselnitsky's daughter-in-law, a woman doctor who had come from Kiev for a visit the day before the war broke out. She begged the policemen to give her a chance to try to reach the village, but they threw her into the grave and shot her.

The local residents have confirmed that for three days the earth covering the pits moved and that the sounds of groaning and wheezing could be heard coming from them. . . .

In addition to the three hundred people that the Gestapo had left in Brailov, more than two hundred came out of their cellars and hidings places toward evening. A ghetto was set aside for them. Only the mind of a monster could have conceived the "laws" that were implemented for this ghetto. It was forbidden to take the dead out of the ghetto; [they had to be buried deep in the earth and the site had to be filled in.] Wherever a child happened to be born, the whole family was shot. If even a few grams of meat or butter, if a single chicken egg, were found in a house, the whole family was taken out and shot.

A month and a half later there was a second "Aktion." This time, of the fifteen tailors, five were selected; of the eighteen shoemakers, six; and so on. Those who could fled from Brailov. The Rov River, which flows through the village, forms the border with Transnistria, and about three hundred people crossed it. Most of them found refuge in the Zhmerinka Ghetto. The last of the Jews of Brailov were executed in April. A month later the Romanian gendarmes from Zhmerinka turned over 270 Brailov residents to the German police; they were taken to Brailov and executed along the same steep granite slope.

In June of 1942 the Germans placed a sign at the entrance to Brailov: "A Town Free of Kikes." It was time for me to leave.

"I have a big favor to ask of you," the tailor Abram Tsigelman turned to me. "You were friends with my children and knew my family well; I can open up my heart to you. You know that I cannot bear to live in this world. I'm sixty years old now. I am left alone in my old age, without family, friends, or relatives. I have no one to live for. But a fury seethes in my soul. Can it be that Brailov—a town that has produced twenty-five doctors, twenty engineers, God knows how many lawyers, artists, journalists, and military commanders—can it be that Brailov will turn into a desert? You are leaving. But I don't want Brailov to be without Jews, so I shall stay. Even if I'm the only one at first. All I ask of you is this: help me to get back my sewing machine. I saw it in the house of a former policeman. No need to worry: the tailor Tsigelman knows how to make a living for himself. In my free hours I shall sit over there, at the mill, beside the pit. Everything I had—your whole family too—is buried there."

Within a few hours the sewing machine had been returned to Tsigelman's home. As I was leaving, I could hear its pumping sounds. The only tailor left in Brailov was at work.

Efim Gekhman

What I Survived in Kharkov

The Germans entered Kharkov on 24 October 1941. It is difficult to convey the horror that took hold of me. You see, [as a Jewish woman], I was in a situation with no exit and was forced to stay in the city.

The fascists showed their true colors from the very first day. Bodies were swinging from gallows in the city squares. The next day the Germans began their plundering. It was impossible to stay in your apartment without hearing a knock at the door and the cry of "Open up!" They took everything, including food and clothing. Then they started taking hostages. The Hotel International was filled to overflowing with the unfortunate victims. The windows were broken, and in the rooms there was no place to sit or lie down. Those who were arrested were beaten during interrogations. They were held for ten days, and then, already half dead, they were shot.

One day some people were gathered on the square in front of the Regional Council Head-quarters, where there was a radio. I happened to be walking by on my way to fetch some water. Suddenly we saw a young man climbing down a rope from the uppermost balcony. At first we did not understand what was happening. [We thought it was some sort of stunt.] Then we heard a heart-rending cry: "Save me!" The unfortunate man was hanged from the balcony. Then people hurried home terror-stricken....

It was the morning after I had a bad dream, as though in the dream I had had a presentiment of the future: they demanded that ten Jews from our building report for work. I was not among them. After work those people were sent to the Hotel International as hostages. I began to await my turn.

On 15 December they demanded that all the Jews in our building turn themselves in as hostages. I decided to commit suicide rather than place my life in the hands of those criminals. I had no poison, but I found a razor. I cut my wrists about ten times but, due to my inexperience, I could not cut through a vein. I bled so much that I lost consciousness. A knock at the door woke me. I was told that on this day, 15 December 1941, all Jews must leave the city and go to the barracks behind the Tractor factory, which was twelve kilometers outside of Kharkov. Blood was flowing from my wounds, and I had trouble collecting myself. I set off for Golgotha.

It is difficult to describe the scene: fifteen thousand people, maybe more, walking down Old Moscow Street toward the Tractor factory. Many were dragging various things along with them. Among them were the sick and even paralytics, who were carried in the arms of others. The road from Old Moscow Street to the Tractor factory was strewn with the bodies of children, the old, and the sick.

By nightfall we reached our new residence. I walked into the barracks. Instead of windows there were large openings without panes, and the doors did not close. There was no place to sit. An icy wind was blowing. I was weak from the loss of blood and fell to the ground unconscious. I was awakened by screams, the screams of a woman and her baby. More and more people were arriving; it was very crowded, and in the darkness someone had fallen on the woman and her baby. The little one cried out, and then, seeing that the infant was not moving, the mother screamed, "Save my baby! She's all I have left! They hanged my husband and son!" But what could be done? Lights were forbidden. The baby girl died.

I was stuck in a bad barracks. There were fifty of us. The lucky ones had brought beds that could sleep five or six people. It became freezing cold. I slept on the floor, and my hands and feet grew numb.

A new ordeal awaited me. I have a sister. She had been baptized thirty years earlier, and her papers indicated that she was Russian. I was lying on the floor thinking back on the past. Suddenly someone pushed me; I looked up and saw my dear and only sister. She spent four days in the barracks with me. There were some good people there, and they helped her to escape. Since she had a Russian passport, it was easier for her than for me get help. In order to avoid calling attention to ourselves, we did not say goodbye to each other. I simply looked at her, longing to say everything with my eyes.

The wounds on my wrists would not close. I was suffering from cold and hunger. The Germans would allow us to go to the market or to fetch water if we bribed them. Sometimes the Germans murdered people. I once saw a little boy walking by. A German shouted at him, "Hey, kike, come here!" When the boy went up to him, the German threw him into a pit, held him down with his foot, and shot him. Prior to the order for the general execution of everyone, they killed about fifty people per day. Once they announced, "If the crying of a single child should be heard at night, everyone will be shot." But how could we expect babies not to cry? It was impossible to change their diapers, and they lay wet in the freezing cold; after all we had endured, their mothers no longer had any milk, and there was nothing to feed them.

I managed to move to a different barracks, to No. 9. It was the last one marked for execution.

The Germans planned to take us to our deaths by means of a deception. During the third week they announced, "Those who wish to be transported to Poltava, Lubny, or Romny for work, step forward." It was as though a needle had pricked my heart. Eight hundred people signed up. I saw how they were loaded into trucks without being allowed to take their things with them.

We soon heard shots. The next day they no longer asked who wanted to leave; they seized women, tore their children from them, and threw them into vans. The men were herded away on foot.

Gathering my strength, I went to the barracks next door. It was hell: one large mass of dead people, dishes, pillow down, food scraps, clothes, and excrement. In one corner a dead woman was lying on a bed, her hands hanging down, with a baby sucking on one of her dead fingers. In another corner an old man lay dead.

I do not remember running back to my own barracks. At that point I wanted very much to live. I envied the dogs and cats—they had a right to life, and no one hunted them down, while I had to die simply because I was a Jew.

Every day, from early in the morning, we sat and waited for death. Once we were given a reprieve. The rumble of artillery could be heard coming from Saltov. The doomed people thought our troops were approaching. They were saying, "We are saved!" They wept and embraced each other. I must have had strong nerves to hold up under all that.

Finally it was the day before the last day. That evening a young pregnant woman was brought in and placed in our barracks. The next morning she went into labor. I could not fall asleep because of her screams. That night I decided to run away.

I got ready early in the morning; I put a sheet in my coat pocket for bandaging my wounds and headed for the road. Gestapo men with guns stood at every turn. What was I to do? Where could I go? I did not have long to think; every second was precious. At that moment an officer called the soldiers away to sort through some Jewish belongings that had been piled onto a truck. I crouched down on the ground and crawled to the ravine. The Germans returned. I burrowed into the snow and covered my self with the sheet. I lay like that in the freezing cold until dawn. As soon as it started to get light, I crawled to the other side of the ravine. With difficulty I climbed out. It was unbearably cold, and there were no guards along the ravine. With a sinking heart I walked through the settlement. [I was afraid of every glance.]

Where could I go? Everyone would be afraid to give me shelter; the penalty for that was death. My closest friends were the people in Kirill Arsentevich Redko's family. They hid Jews at the risk of their own lives. They had been denounced and barely escaped death themselves. I knew about this and did not want to get them into trouble. [I went to some friends who lived with me before the Germans came. They used to say they would hide me if anything should happen, but now they turned me away without mercy, even though I told them it was late and that I could be arrested.]

Where could I go? It would soon be night. I did not have time to get out of the city. I found an outhouse that consisted of three compartments. I spent three days and nights there. It is difficult to describe my agonies. It was bitterly cold, and the wind cut right through me. I grew numb. I had neither a crumb of bread nor a drop of water. They could find me at any moment. On the fourth day I began to freeze to death.

Suddenly I felt warm. I heard myself saying, "Water! Just a drop of water!" . . . I do not know how I lasted till morning. I forced myself to get up from the filthy floor and go out. I went to Kirill Arsentevich's house. With every step I fell down. It is a good thing that they lived near the place where I had hidden. They gave me a warm reception. I spent three days with them, my soul taking a bit of a rest; in that home I felt like a human being again. They gave me some food, and, their hearts filled with pain, said goodbye.

My legs could hardly hold me up; they were like logs. I headed in the direction of Lyubotino. It was terrifying to walk without knowing where to go. Who would give me shelter? What use was I to anyone? And what about a passport? . . .

Somehow I made it to Korotich. I decided to find a place where no one would notice me and there freeze to death. But first I wanted to take a chance at the most distant hut. And that is just where I got lucky. They let me spend the night. A heavy snowstorm came up toward morning; the woman took pity on me and let me stay in the house. I spent three weeks with them. The Germans often came to the hut looking for partisans. It was a miracle that they did not find me.

I had to leave the house, but I could not walk: my feet had turned into a charred mass of flesh with pus oozing out. As I was leaving, the old woman said to me, "Wait." She took me to a hut that a doctor had made into a laboratory. After examining me, the doctor said, "Your feet are done for." That was like a death sentence; what was someone in my situation to do without her feet? I would like to tell more about the doctor; unfortunately, I do not know his surname, but his first name was Petro. He sent me to the Lyubotino hospital and came to treat me. He was a Soviet. He guessed who I was. When a nurse who had taken down my name whispered something to him, he told her, "That does not concern us; our duty is to help this woman."

That is how I ended up in the Lyubotino hospital. I lay on a soft bed, and no one drove me away. They fed me twice a day; although it was swill, it was warm. And so I lay there from 7 February to 2 July 1942.

It is terrible to recall how they amputated the toes from both of my feet, and then how they filed the bones. For a month I had a temperature of 40 degrees centigrade. All I could do was lie on my back, unable to sleep from the pain. I wanted only one thing: to die in the hospital. After all, if they were to release me, where could I go? I envied every dying woman on my ward. It was then that I realized what a blessing it is to die a natural death. When they brought in patients from Kharkov I hid my head under the blanket and peeked out with one eye; what if I should see a familiar face? The hospital personnel treated me wonderfully and did all they could to help me. The surgeon also cared a great deal.

Once they brought in a woman from Kharkov who was near death and who soon passed away. She was thirty-eight years old. All the while I was pursued by the thought that her passport could save me. I got that passport.

After leaving the hospital, I spent two weeks in a nurse's home. Then I set out on the road. I had decided to try to find my sister. I guessed where she had gone. [And now I could go anywhere I wanted: I had a Russian passport.] But traveling was not easy. The wounds on my feet had not yet healed, and I had to go on foot; I was hungry too. By the time I reached Merchik, I felt that I was too weak to go any farther. I wanted to board a train, but a German asked me if I had a pass. He threw me off the train car. The police advised me to ask the commandant for a pass, but the commandant turned out to be an animal. Without even hearing me out, he yelled, "Get the hell out of here!"

I sat in the station until evening and then went to the building were the railroad workers lived. There I met a good woman: she gave me food and let me stay until morning. She helped me to get a pass too.

I could not imagine such happiness! Could it really be that I would soon see my dear and only sister? But what if these animals had killed her? The train pulled out of Kharkov. I hid in a corner, for fear that someone might recognize me. At two in the afternoon I arrived in the village of Smorodino. I wandered about the streets, until I suddenly realized that I would not find my sister. After all, I could not ask about her, since that would arouse suspicion.

A woman noticed the harrowed look on my face and asked, "What's the matter?" I told her I was tired and hungry. She took me to her home. Food and bread were set before me. I was ashamed of how I devoured it all. I said, "Please forgive me; after eating like this just this once, I'll never do it again." I spent a month and a half there, cooking and cleaning. That woman played a big role in deciding my fate: it turned out that she knew my sister.

How can I describe our reunion? I wanted to throw myself on her, to hug and kiss her; after all, each of us had thought the other was dead. But our conversation was cold; we acted as though we scarcely knew each other. It took a great deal of will power.

I lived in Smorodino a year and three months. I was a cook, a nanny, and a beggar seeking shelter at every turn.

I saw how the German barbarians forced young people into slavery. Immediately after being examined, the boys and girls were locked up in a special building and were not even allowed to say goodbye to their families. Whenever relatives ran after the youngsters, the criminals would shoot at them. There were many cases in which teenagers maimed themselves or ended their lives in suicide rather than be sent to Germany. When the trains pulled out, there were terrible scenes. A groan would rise up from the station. The unfortunate children would cry out, "Where are you taking us, you murderers?" Relatives were not allowed to go near the train cars.

The front grew closer. We spent two weeks in a cellar. Two artillery shells hit our house. At last our troops entered Smorodino. My soul was filled with such happiness! Our troops!

Once again I am in my native Kharkov. I can freely walk about the streets and look everyone in the eye.

Kharkov, November 1943
Reported by Maria Markovna Sokol, prepared for publication by Ilya Ehrenburg

Pyotr Chepurenko, Witness to the Piryatin Massacre[14]

On 6 April 1942, the second day of Passover, in the city of Piryatin of the Poltava district, the Germans murdered 1,600 Jews—old men, women, and children who were unable to flee to the east.

The Jews were taken down Grebenovskaya Road to Pirogovskaya Leveda three kilometers outside of town. Large pits had been dug there. The Jews undressed. The Germans and the policemen divided up the victims' belongings on the spot. The doomed people were herded into the pit in groups of five and shot with machine guns.

The Germans brought three hundred residents from Piryatin to Pirogovskaya Leveda to fill in the pits. Among them was Pyotr Lavrentevich Chepurenko. He tells the following story:

"I saw how they did the killing. At five o'clock in the afternoon they gave the order: 'Fill in the pits.' Screams and groans could be heard coming from the pits. Suddenly I saw something: my neighbor Ruderman was rising up from under the earth. He was a driver at the factory. His eyes were filled with blood. He cried out, 'Kill me!' Someone behind him was also crying out. It was Sima the cabinetmaker. He had been wounded but not killed. The Germans and the policemen began killing them. A murdered woman was lying at my feet. A little boy around five years old crawled out form under her body and cried out in despair, 'Mommy!' I didn't see anything else: I fell unconscious."

Prepared for publication by Ilya Ehrenburg

The Death of the Jewish Collective Farm Workers in Zelenopol

Zelenopol is an old Jewish colony. A rich collective farm known as "Emes"[15] rose up here and flourished. Before the war Jews, Russians, and Ukrainians lived together at Emes. They prospered and were happy. It was a joy to behold this family of friendly, contented people.

And then the Germans invaded Zelenopol. Many of the Jews were evacuated. All that remained were a few families and old people who did not want to be separated from the earth on which they were born. Among the most decrepit of the old ones were Idl Kalmanovich, Grishe-Leib Kozlovsky and his wife, Shleima Kamsoryuk and his wife, and others.

As soon as the Germans entered the colony, they decided to "cleanse the air and the earth" of Jews. But murder was not enough for them. According to their scheme, those condemned to death would be forced to pass through a round of torture. Idl Kalmanovich was an old religious Jew respected by all. The Germans spread his tallis out on the ground and ordered the old man to roll around on it and then to get down on his knees before those criminals. He refused to do it. Then they shaved off his gray beard. Even that was not enough for them. They took a razor and skinned his face, sliced his cheeks, and cut off his ears. Not once did Kalmanovich ask the Germans for mercy, despite the horrible torture.

Shleima Kamsoryuk was a disabled worker and an honorable man. The butchers tormented him relentlessly. They literally cut him into pieces.

Those who were left among the living wandered around for a long time in freezing cold and terrible weather. The same fate, however, befell them.

Khana Paturskaya's family was savagely slaughtered. Her older daughter Rakhil, a girl of sixteen, was violated and then shot. Her two boys and her mother were also shot. Her younger daughter Tanya was hanged right before her mother's eyes.

A total of seventy-four Jews and fourteen prisoners of war were tortured to death. Many others in the area perished, since it is a national Jewish region.

Prepared for publication by Ilya Ehrenburg

Letters from Dnepropetrovsk
Letters from the Indikt couple

1

I was born in 1895. During the war I lived in Dnepropetrovsk and worked in the food cooperative shop. [I was entrusted with the task of having the shop's equipment hauled off, and I loaded it onto a train car. But the car was not hooked to the train, so I was left there with the equipment.]

On 24 August 1941 the Germans entered the city. I did not go outside because they were arresting Jews. [My wife is Russian, so she could walk about the city; she told me about everything.]

On 26 August I decided to go to the cooperative, where I worked. She told me that a seventeen-year-old Jewish girl had been raped and murdered in the courtyard that morning. [She said: "You can see for yourself, if you like."] I went home and did not set foot out of my house after that.

On 25 September the city commandant issued an order: the Jews had to pay a tribute of thirty million rubles. The Jewish community was to collect the money. My wife wanted to go to the community, but I told her, "It isn't necessary. Whether we bring the money or not, they will kill us either way."

My wife found work for me at the other end of the city. My surname is Indikt, but now I became Indiktenko.

On 12 October my boss told me, "Leave." I left with my wife. It was night, and we heard terrible cries. On the morning of 13 October it was still dark when they knocked on the door and shouted, "Come out!" The police were surprised to find that my wife's name was not on their list. I told them that she is Russian. I knew they were taking me to be shot. They led me to the department store, where there were already a lot of Jews.

There were fifteen hundred to two thousand Jews in the first group. I was in the second group. We had not yet reached the Jewish cemetery, when we heard shots and cries of grief. We decided to run for it. Many of us were shot. I managed to escape.

For two days I wandered the steppe, until I fell into despair and returned home. It was night when I got there; I tapped on the window. I stayed in the attic for a month. Then we decided that I must leave the house since the landlord was getting suspicious.

My wife obtained a worker's identification booklet, which enabled me to change my name and nationality. Then she found a passport for me with the name of Stupki, born in 1905. Sometimes my age aroused suspicion.

I worked for three months in one place; then my supervisor told me to leave. By that time my wife had found an isolated little house on the edge of town. It had no floor, but she made a floor out of boards. Three boards under the bed could be raised up, so I could hide under the floor. In order to keep anyone from occupying the second room, we made it into a shed and kept the chickens, a dog, and a cat there.

I must say a few words about the dog, since she played a part in saving my life. Her name was Alma, and she was quite vicious. No one would come into the house until the dog was tied up. That gave me enough time to crawl under the floor.

A policeman lived next door to us. Knowing that his neighbor was a woman living by herself, he would come to my wife, try to force himself on her, and then curse her when she refused. I sat in a hole and had to just listen when he would say to my wife, "You whore, what do you mean by pretending to be an honorable woman? How long are you going to keep leading me around by the nose?"

Once my wife took all she could stand and said, "Get the hell out of here!" He called her a "big-nosed Jew" and left. I crawled out of my hole and laughed. {First of all,} I had never heard my wife insult anyone like that. {Secondly, I thought this might be our last night, since I was sure the policeman would come back with his friends; but that didn't happen. My wife did not think it would happen, because she had prayed so fervently to God.}

I spent two years in that hole. During the last months my nerves were giving out. Many times my wife suggested that we poison ourselves, but I talked her out of it. Finally our troops arrived.

31 June 1944
[Mikhail Petrovich] Indikt

2

My name is Nadezhda Ivanovna Indikt. I was thirty-four years old when the Germans arrived, but, due to the conditions that arose, I looked terrible; I did not wash, and I walked around in torn clothes; from minute to minute I waited for death.

When I was living with my husband in the little hut, my neighbor, who was a policeman, came and said, "Listen, I've been told that your husband is a kike and your son is a kike and that he is hiding in Odessa." I grabbed him by the sleeve and cried out hysterically, "Let's go to the Gestapo!" Then I started to drag him out the door. But he said, "Let go of me, you louse," and left.

Whenever our airplanes flew over Dnepropetrovsk, I prayed to God to let the bombs fall right on our heads.

I often walked a long way for food, while my husband stayed in the hole.

Once in the wintertime, during a hard freeze, I set off for the village. No one was allowed to stay out overnight without special permission. Someone finally took me in; I was frozen to the bone. I climbed up on the stove to sleep and got carbon monoxide poisoning. I managed to get out of the hut and was feeling bad; I could not walk, but I had to walk. I did not have the right to die, and I started to pray, "God, save me for Misha's sake! What is happening to him? Oh, how he must be waiting for me!" At that moment a cart pulled up and gave me a ride.

What else could I do? I just cried and cried. In Kamenskoe I saw an announcement that any Russians hiding Jews would have their entire families shot, down to newborn babies. As I walked along, only one thought entered my head: is Misha still alive? I thought of how happy he would be to see me, but when I got there, he merely touched my face with his hands and stared at me like a madman, the tears streaming down his cheeks. For my face was frostbitten.

I never went out unless my purse was filled with food and money: I would search for Jews. To get money, I sold our things at the bazaar and hired myself out for work.

Once I was walking down the street with my neighbor Varya. I trusted her. I saw a young man walking along and looking all around. I said to Varya, "Wait, I think he's a Jew," and went up to him. He asked where the commandant's office was. I realized from his accent that he was a Jew. He said he had come here from the Crimea, but when he arrived at the train station they told him he had to have a pass from the commandant. I begged him not to go there because they were shooting Jews; I gave him a hundred rubles and urged him to make his way only along side streets. He did as I told him. I went home and burst into tears: "God, why are people suffering?"

It was hard on my husband. I was gone all day, the house was locked up, and he would listen for every little noise. I would not even open the smallest windows, so he had no fresh air. But it was even harder on me: I walked all over the city and saw everything. I went to see my aunt at No. 84 Prospekt; a German unit was positioned there. They were taking Jews away to work. My aunt and I quietly gave the Jews food to eat; we slipped them bread, lard, and tomatoes. The German officer was very cruel, like no one else in the world. There was nothing the Germans would not do to Jews! They would harness them to a large van and made them pull it. They would pour soup into a trough, so that the Jews would have to lap up their food on all fours.

I went to all the camps. Once a German shot at me; three bullets flew right over my head. There was a camp near the prison; there I saw many carts arriving, and I asked where they were coming from. They said from far away. There were only men in the carts; their families had been shot. I gave them food. The Germans noticed. I told them I was selling tobacco because I had small children. A German hit me, and I ran away. When I got home, I told my husband about the suffering of this humanity.

Among the Jewish prisoners was a boy of about fifteen. His mother had long since died, and his father was at the front. He had been living with his little sister and his grandmother; his grandmother was Russian. When the Germans arrived, someone turned him in, and the boy was taken away. As the prisoners were going to work one day, the boy saw an old woman on the street, rushed over to her, and cried, "Grandma!" They started beating him, and the little grandmother fainted.

An old woman lived on Khersonskaya Street with her daughter and two grandchildren. I used to help them. Once the old woman was trying to thank me and started crying. I kissed her. People saw me [and started shouting.] I had to run away. I hid in the cemetery and decided not to go home until late that night. I used to be afraid of the dead, but now, as I sat in the cemetery, I said, "I have done nothing wrong, but you, dear departed ones, can do nothing for me." [When I got home, my husband said, "You'll get yourself killed, and your kisses will not help them." But I told him that my kisses were more precious than money because every-one had turned away from these people as if they were lepers.]

I took food to a certain family—an old man, his daughter, and two grandchildren.

I obtained a passport for my husband, but it had to have a photograph. I found a man on the outskirts of town who said he could do anything. I told him that the collective farm workers came to me and that they needed photographs for officially stamped German documents. We agreed that I would bring the people to him, and for three photographs he would be paid five hundred grams of lard, two hundred of which would be for me. After looking to be sure the coast was clear, I led my husband to the photographer. He took his picture; I gave him the lard and got two hundred grams back.

My husband started learning how to do engraving. He made a stamp for registration per-mits, and we used it for anyone who needed it. I would still go out looking for Jews.

Many times the Gestapo conducted searches on our street. I would lean through the win-dow to fasten the lock on the door and pray to God. Whenever the Gestapo went up to our neighbors, they would tell them, "A single woman lives there, and she works," and then they would leave.

I would say to my husband, "Let's die peacefully. I cannot live and look upon all this any longer." My husband said we would all survive and live with our people. He read German newspapers, and I had to buy him a paper without fail. If I did not get it, he would look at me with reproach: "You didn't bring it?"

I told him there was nothing of interest in it, only lies. But he learned to read it so well that for him every word took on special significance. He would say to me, "You will see, in the next issue it will say that the front is closing in and that such and such a town has been abandoned." And that is just what would happen. Then he would tell me, "It doesn't matter, our troops will be here."

I found out that a certain German needed a cleaning woman, and I was hired. This German owned a chemical factory. As it turned out, he had blank official forms and a metal stamp. I got a hold of all of it. The typewriter was in German, and it was hard for me to write with it; I ruined many forms before I was finally able to write with it and use the metal stamp. After that I quit the cleaning job.

I had to go to the police station to fill out an application and get my residence permit stamped. The first question they asked me was the nationality of my husband. I replied, "Bul-garian, of Romanian descent." The policeman told me, "That's impossible, I am Bulgarian myself." Then I said, "You must not know the history of your own people very well. Bulgaria shares a border with Turkey, and when the Turks were slaughtering the Bulgarians, as the Jews are being murdered now, the Bulgarians fled to Romania and became Romanian citi-zens." The policeman told me, "Thanks for the lecture," and stamped my residence permit.

Our offensive had begun. We prepared to leave by going under the ground. We dug a tunnel from the cellar to the water well.

My husband had to stay there, and I brought him food. During the last days my husband began babbling; he would say just one phrase over and over, until he lost consciousness:

"We're going to survive, we're going to survive."

It is impossible to describe everything. We lived through that terrible misery and waited until at long last our troops arrived.

2 August 1944.
N. Indikt
Prepared for publication by G. Munblit[16]

The Day of 13 October 1941

The Story of A. M. Burtseva

I was not able to be evacuated from Dnepropetrovsk before the Germans got there, because at the time my daughter was dangerously ill. My mother and father, as well as my thirteen-year-old brother, stayed with me. They did not want to leave without me.

When the Germans entered the city they immediately ordered all the Jews to wear white armbands with six-pointed stars on their sleeves. Some resisted, as they did not want to wear the armbands; I myself saw one of the German bandits murder a young girl in the street because she refused to wear it.

Then the Jews were forced to pay a tribute of thirty million rubles. Next the humiliation and plundering began. On one occasion some SS men burst into our apartment and took my mother and father to the police station. They were beaten and, after having all their valuables stolen, were released. After that my mother and father were afraid to show themselves on the street.

Thus we lived, fearing for our lives and for the lives of our children, until 13 October 1941.

By that time my husband (who is Russian) had found a room where no one knew us and where he planned to move us. But we did not have time to carry out the plan. At six o'clock in the morning there was a knock at our door; they told us to collect our things and go to the department store on Marx Street, where all the Jews were supposedly being gathered and forced to pay the tribute.

When we arrived at the store, the huge four-story building was already overflowing with people. There was an especially large number of elderly people and women with children. Everyone's possessions were taken away from them at the entrance. Since I had no posses-sions, they did not let me into the store, so I stayed outside in the crowd of several thousand people. After a short time those who were in the store were also brought out into the street. I located my mother and brother; we could not find our father. After that I never saw him again. We were formed into a column of six people across and led somewhere under an armed escort. My mother tried to convince me that I should give my daughter to someone I knew on the street, so that somehow she could be sent to my husband. I tried to get a look at the faces of the people headed toward us; soon I caught sight of a neighbor who was searching the column for his wife (a Jew) and child. I handed Lenochka over to him; then I saw my husband walking alongside the column, and he took Lenochka by the hand. After a few minutes a friend of my husband's showed up next to me (I was walking on the outside of the column, so he could come up to me); he tried to persuade me to quietly remove the armband from my sleeve and flee. He said they were taking us to be slaughtered. But I did not want to leave my family and continued walking in the column. Then my mother, who was listening to our conversation, started pleading with me to run away. "You cannot help us anyway," she said. "You must do it for Lenochka's sake."

At that moment a truck full of old people and children drove past us. Suddenly one of the old people in the truck jumped to his feet, took out a razor, and slit his own throat. A German shoved him into the cab to keep anyone from seeing him, and the truck drove on.

When we got to Yurevskaya Street I took off my armband and quietly slipped out of the column; then I went to the address that my husband's friend had given me.

I stayed there for two weeks. Only rarely did my husband come to see me, since we were afraid that he might be followed. Then he brought me back home, where I stayed for two months without leaving the room, hiding in cupboard every time I heard footsteps on the stairs. But Lenochka got sick, and I had to go out to get food for her. I was saved by the fact that I do not look Jewish, as well as by the fact that our neighbors were good people who did everything they could to help us.

Thus, in continual fear and awaiting death every day, I spent two years. This life also affected my child. If I should be delayed somewhere for a short time, Lenochka would become hysterical and start screaming, "They've murdered my mother!" At times it seemed like we could not bear it any longer.

Everyone I walked with in the column suffered a horrible fate. They were all shot in an antitank ditch outside of town. My family came to the same end.

The Story of I. A. Revenskaya

To my great sorrow, I did not manage to get out of Dnepropetrovsk with my family in 1941. On the day the Germans entered the city I was in my nephew's apartment. That evening several Germans and Hungarians showed up and announced that they had been given the right to take possession of everything in the Jewish apartments. {The traitor Abalakov, who lived in the very same building, had brought them. He died in 1942.}

Several days later a census of the Jews living in Dnepropetrovsk was taken, and the Germans began forcing us to do work that could only be described as prison labor. Those who did not have the strength to work the Germans beat to death.

Then came the fatal day when the Jews were ordered to gather at the "Lux" store with their belongings and enough food for three days.

That day was very much an autumn day. There was rain mixed with snow, and a wind was blowing from the south.

As we approached the store building, I saw that it was surrounded by police. I decided it would be better to poison myself than to place my life into the hands of the Germans.

I returned home, and there my neighbor P. I. Kravchenko advised me to leave the city; he gave me a letter for a woman he knew who lived in the village of Krasnopol eight kilometers outside of Dnepropetrovsk. I spent two days in Krasnopol; then I had to flee from there, since the Germans were missing eight hundred Jews and had started looking for them in the surrounding villages.

When I returned to the city I found out that all the Jews who had gone to the department store that day had been shot. I had no place to go: it was impossible to return home, and for a long time I wandered around the back streets trying to come up with something. But what could I come up with here?

I decided to die. I managed to get a bottle of ammonia; I went to the city park, sat down on a bench, and drank in down in one gulp.

Apparently I was groaning, because some Germans came up to me. The first thing they asked was whether or not I was a Jew. I could no longer speak and just shook my head no. Then they sent me to the hospital. I spent one day in the hospital. In the morning a nurse came and told me that the German doctors were about to make their rounds and that I should leave as soon as possible.

Once again I found myself on the street; once again I had no place to go. I had not eaten anything for twenty-four hours because my throat was burned and in the hospital they would not give me anything to eat.

As I was wandering the streets, I ran into a group of men who turned out to be Red Army soldiers who had escaped from a prisoner of war camp. They were planning to go home to their villages, and they let me join them.

I set off, at first with them and then by myself; after I had gone six hundred kilometers I arrived at Nikolaev, where I had once lived for nineteen years.

Here some friends hid me and then obtained a false passport for me; in a word, they did everything to save my life.

During all this time I endured and witnessed so much grief that it would take a very long time to write it all down. And is it really possible to convey on paper what I experienced when I saw, for example, two Gestapo men chase a young girl through the snow wearing only a nightshirt and carrying a small baby in her arms, or when in Nikolaev I saw them throw the four best doctors in the city into a truck and take them away to be shot?

I am now fifty-two years old, and I have lived a hard life. I have been a witness to two wars, but what I was forced to see and experience in the fascist hell still makes my blood run cold.

The Story of B. I. Tartakovskaya

The Germans entered Dnepropetrovsk on 24 August 1941. From the very first day of their arrival, there was torture, plundering, and murder. Wearing the white armband with the six-pointed star on their sleeve (we were ordered to wear it under penalty of being shot), the Jews did not dare to go fetch water from the municipal faucet and were afraid to go out on the street even to get bread.

Soon all the Jews were ordered to assemble at the "Lux" store. I was told that it was for the purpose of setting up a ghetto. After gathering together a few things, my two children and I went to the store. There they put us into a column and led us off somewhere. The Germans answered all our questions about where we were going simply by saying, "To a camp." When we passed the Jewish cemetery and came out onto an empty area next to the railroad tracks, we heard shots. Then we realized why they had brought us here. Since it was getting dark in the yard, however, our turn had not come yet. The crowd of several thousand people was driven up against some kind of fence and surrounded on all sides. It was cold, and people stood shoulder to shoulder in the icy mud; those who were sick and dying lay down in it. My younger little boy was sitting on my back, and the older one (he was three at the time) stood with his face pressed against my knees. That is how we spent the long autumn night.

When dawn broke German soldiers carrying cases of ammunition showed up on the lot. They held the cases up to us and laughed. Then they started herding us toward the pits at the end of the lot. The crowd dashed to one side; the weak ones fell under the feet of people gone mad with horror; screams, shots, and the cries of children could be heard. The Germans dragged the old people and children who had been crushed by the crowd into the pits and buried them along with the ones who had been shot. I fell to my knees and hugged my children; I thought I was going out of my mind from horror.

At that moment someone came up to me and said he would take my children and me away from the crowd. To this day I do not understand how he did it, but after a short time we found ourselves standing with him at the cemetery next to the road. Then we saw a cart driven by a young peasant. We asked nothing of him, but he himself offered to take my children and me to the city. I said farewell to our savior, and we set off.

When we got home I found my husband in tears. They told him that we had been taken not to a camp to be shot. My husband is a Ukrainian, and we had hoped that he would have been able to help my children and me to escape from the camp.

The next morning we all left the city and went to Sumy, where my husband has relatives. We traveled without money or papers, and we were on the road for a month and a half. In Sumy no one bothered me for a while. Then we found out that I had been denounced. Once again we fled, and for a long time we wandered about the villages and towns.

How can I describe the joy we felt when in one village we met a Red Army detachment?

My husband is now in the army, and I am working in the infirmary. I am only twenty-seven, but already I am an old woman. I live only for my children and for the day when the Hitlerite beasts will be punished. But no, they are not beasts. For beasts do not gnaw on those who are down, and anyone who throws living children into a grave is not worthy of being called a beast.

Prepared for publication by G. Munblit

A Letter from Military Officer Granovsky (Ekaterinopol)

Preserve this letter. All that remains of our beloved Ekaterinopol is my letter, some ruins, the graves of our countrymen, and the little girl Sonya. There is only grass in the places where we grew up, went to school, and loved each other, and our dear ones lie beneath the earth.

Ekaterinopol is no more; the Germans destroyed it. Only the little girl Sonya is left.

When I arrived in our village—it was 9 May 1944—I could not find our house. A barren place. . . I walked among the ruins searching for people but found no one; they had all been shot. No one came out to meet me, no one extended a hand to me, no one congratulated me on our victory.

Then I met Sonya Diamat. She is fifteen now. She was saved by a miracle; three times the Germans led her to her death. She told me about the tragedy of Ekaterinopol.

The SS came and began their searches, plundering, and pogroms. All the Jews were herded into special camps. In Zvenigorodok there was a camp for people unable to work. There they had locked up old people, sick people, women nursing babies, and children up to fourteen years of age.

Those who could work ended up in the camp near the train station.

On 6 September 1941 the first group was shot in Ekaterinopol: communists, activists from the collective farms, and many Jews.

Everyone who was in the Zvenigorodok camp was murdered in April 1942. They murdered the eighty-year-old Khana Lerner for being too old and the month-old Manya Fininberg for being too young.

In the camp at the train station they were tormented for a long time, forced to work eighteen to twenty hours per day, and constantly taunted. Girls were raped. Old men were flogged with birch rods. Finally, in the autumn of 1942, everyone from Ekaterinopol, Shpola, and Zvenigorodok was shot—two thousand people.

Do you remember the old barber Azriil Pritsman? He was seventy years old. Before he died he cried out, "Go ahead and shoot me! My sons will avenge me!" His five sons were at the front. And the cooper Golikov! He was eighty years old. The Germans wounded him, but he got up, covered with blood, and cried, "Keep shooting, you scum! You won't take me with just one bullet!" Golikov has twenty-eight relatives at the front: sons, grandson, sons-in-law, and nephews.

Our first collective farm worker, old Mendel Inger, met the enemy with pride. It was on the day the Germans arrived. Mendel was seventy years old. He refused to speak with them. They shot him immediately.

As I stood next to the graves, it was as though I could see my relatives and countrymen. They were speaking to me from beneath the earth: "Vengeance!" I promised them that I would avenge them. Twice in my life I have sworn an oath of loyalty to my people: once when I was entrusted with a formidable military vehicle and a second time at the graves of Ekaterinopol.

[Abram Granovsky],
prepared for publication by Ilya Ehrenburg

The Diary of Sarra Gleikh (Mariupol)

8 October. The Germans are in the city. Everyone is home except Fanya, who is at the factory. She went to work this morning. I wonder if she is alive. And if she is alive, how can she get here, since the streetcars aren't running? Basya is at Ganya's, who is sick with typhus. At six o'clock this evening Fanya came home; she walked all the way from the factory. The Germans had been in the factory since two this afternoon; the workers and other employees were in the bomb shelter. The factory director tried to organize a fighting unit and handed out weapons, but it seems that nothing came of it. The Germans killed Garber, secretary of the Molotov Regional Soviet, in the Soviet chairman's office. Ushkats, the chairman of the city council, managed to escape.

9 October. There is absolutely nothing to eat in the house. The bakeries in the city have been destroyed; we have no electricity and no water. The bakery in the port is operating, but the bread is only for the German army. Yesterday the Germans posted announcements declaring that all Jews must wear a distinguishing sign, a white six-pointed star, on the left side of their chest; to leaves one's house without it is strictly forbidden. The Jews are not allowed to move from one apartment into another; all the same, Fanya and her maid Tanya are moving from their factory apartment to Mama's.

12 October. The Jewish community has been ordered to elect a governing council of thirty men. The order states that the members of the Council will answer with their lives for "the good conduct of the Jewish population." Doctor Erber is the head of the Council. Except for Fain, I don't know anyone on the Council.

The Jewish population must register at points designated by the Council. Several streets are consolidated around each point. Our registration site is No. 64 Pushkin Street. The book-keeper Bots, the lawyer Zegelman, and Tomshinsky are in charge of it. Fanya has to go to a special registration point at the factory. The chairman of the factory registration point set up by the Council is Doctor Belopolsky. Spivakov is a member of the Council. So far there has been no mass repression. Our neighbor Traevsky says that the Gestapo unit has not arrived yet; after that, things will be different.

13 October. Germans came to our house in the night. Anti-aircraft guns began shooting at nine o'clock in the evening. We were all dressed. Vladya was sleeping; Papa went out into the yard to see if anyone was in the bomb shelter and ran into three Germans. They were in the yard looking for Jews. Papa's appearance solved their problem; he led them to the apartment. Pointing a revolver in our faces, they asked where we kept the butter and sugar; then they started smashing the doors of the armoire, even though it was unlocked. They took everything that Basya had; she was at Ganya's. Basya was there day and night. Then they started on our things. We were left literally with nothing but what we had on; two of them relentlessly looted our home of everything down to the meat grinder.

After tying everything up in a tablecloth, they left. Everything in the house was scattered, strewn, and smashed. We decided not to clean it up; if more Germans should come, then they would see right away that there is nothing left for them to take from us. The next morning we found out that there was indiscriminate plundering throughout the city. The plundering continued into the afternoon. They took everything: pillows, blankets, food, clothing. They went around in groups of three or four. They could be heard coming from far away: their boots thundered.

After the Germans left, Mama cried and said, "They do not even considered us people; we are doomed."

14 October. The marauders came again in the night. Fanya's maid Tanya saved some things that were still there by claiming they were hers. The Germans left empty handed. They stopped in at the Shvarts home and took pillows and blankets.

The Gestapo is in the city now.

The Council was issued an order to collect from the Jewish population two kilograms of hot peppers, 2,500 cases of black ointment, and seventy kilograms of sugar within two hours. They went from house to house and collected the items; everyone who had something gave it. After all, the Council members answer with their lives for "the good conduct of the Jewish population."

The Council registered nine thousand Jews at the registration points. The rest of the Jewish population either left the city or went into hiding.

17 October. Today it was announced that tomorrow morning all those who are registered must bring their valuables to the registration points.

18 October. This morning Mama, Papa, Basya, and I went to the registration site. We turned over three silver tablespoons and a ring. But even after we handed over our silver, they would not let us leave the yard. Once the entire population had turned in their valuables, they told us, we would have to the leave the city within two hours. We were to walk to a nearby collective farm, where we would all be resettled. We were ordered to take along warm clothing and enough food for four days. We were to assemble with our things in two hours. There would be trucks for old people and women with children.

Any Jewish woman whose husband is Russian or Ukrainian is allowed to stay in the city, as long as her husband is with her. If her husband is in the army or is away for some other reason, then the woman and her children must leave the city. If a Russian woman is married to a Jew, then she may choose either to stay or to go with her husband. The children would have to stay with her.

The Royanovs came and asked Fanya to give them her grandson. Papa insisted that Fanya go with Vladya to the Royanovs. Fanya categorically refused; she cried and begged Papa not to force her to go to the Royanovs. She said, "Without you I would lay hands on myself anyway; I wouldn't be able to live. I shall go with you." She didn't give Vladya to the Royanovs but decided to keep him with her.

Fanya's maid Tanya followed behind us, begging us to give Vladya to the Royanovs and promising to take care of him. Fanya wouldn't hear of it.

We stood in the street until evening. Everyone was herded into a building for the night; we found a spot in the cellar. It was dark, cold, and dirty.

19 October. It was announced that we would continue on tomorrow morning; since today is Sunday, the Gestapo are resting. Tanya, Fedya Belousov, and Ulyana came; they brought a food package. In all the bustle yesterday, Fanya had left her watch on the table. They gave Tanya a spare key to the apartment, since all the other keys had been turned in yesterday at the registration point.

The Gestapo had posted specially printed signs on the apartments of all the Jews: "All Unauthorized Persons Are Forbidden to Enter." Therefore it was necessary to go in secretly.

Friends and acquaintances brought everyone parcels; many got permission to take more things from their homes. The number of people kept increasing.

The police allowed the Council to organize the preparation of hot food.

They also let them get horses and carts. According to their instructions, all sacks and bundles going on the carts had to have names clearly written on them in Russian and in German; one family member would ride with the belongings, and the other would go on foot.

Vladya can't stand it here any longer and is begging to go home. Papa, Shvarts, and Nyusya Karpilova's stepfather went in together to buy a horse and wagon. They won't allow us to go out the gates; Fedya Belousov made the purchase. Nyusya managed to slip out the gate, but she returned distraught: she said we should never have come here and that many people she knew were still in the city; she said she even met them on the street.

Tomorrow morning at seven we must leave our last haven in the city.

20 October. It rained all night. The morning was gloomy and gray but not cold.

The entire Council left at 7 A.M.; then the trucks with old people, the trucks with women and children, pulled out. We had to walk nine or ten kilometers, and the road was terrible.

Judging from the way the Germans were treating those who brought us packages and had come to say good-bye, the future does not bode well. The Germans took clubs and beat everyone who had come to see us and drove them out of the building. The question arose as to whether Mama and Papa should get on a truck with Fanya and Vladya.

Mama and Papa left at nine in the morning; Fanya and Vladya were held up and will go on the next truck. V. Osovets and Reisins are in charge of the truck. There are fewer and fewer people left in the yard; the only ones left are those who, according to the Germans' explanation, are to stay with the belongings. Shmukler, Vainer, and R. and L. Koldobsky came over to us; I expressed my apprehension for the lives of the old ones, as there was a bad rumor going around. They say the trucks are going down a slope. Someone suggested that they are going to take us outside the city and destroy us.

Vainer looks terrible; it turns out that the Gestapo released him just yesterday. Several Germans came into the yard and started chasing everyone outside with clubs; the cries of those who were beaten could be heard coming from the building. Vasya and I went out. Fanya and Vladya were next to the truck. V. Osovets helped them get in, and they left. We went on foot, and the road was terrible; after it had been drenched in the rain, it was impossible to walk, hard to even raise a leg from the mud. But if you stop, you get a blow from a club. People were beaten regardless of their age.

I. Raikhelson was walking next to me and then disappeared somewhere. Next to us were Shmerok, F. Gurevich and his father, and L. Polunova. It was about two o'clock when we came to the Petrovsky Agricultural Station. There were a lot of people there. I rushed off to look for Fanya and the old people. Fanya called out to me. She had been looking for the old ones prior to my arrival but could not find them. They were probably already in the barn, where they were being taken in groups of forty to fifty.

Vladya was hungry; it was a good thing I had some apples and toasted bread in my coat pocket. That would be enough for Vladika for a day; it was all we had anyway. We were forbidden to take packages of food; the Germans took everything away from us when we left, even the food.

Our turn came. When we headed behind the barn, our eyes met with an entire scene of insane horror, of wildly insane [and acquiescent] death. Mama and Papa's bodies are lying here somewhere already. Having sent them ahead on the truck, I had shortened their lives by a few hours. The Germans herded us toward the trenches that had been dug for the defense of the city. Now the trenches were used to accommodate the death of nine thousand Jews; they would not be needed for anything else. They ordered us to undress down to our underwear; then they went through our clothes looking for money and documents and forced us to the edge of the trench. But there was no longer any real edge: for half a kilometer the trench was full of people dying from their wounds and begging for another bullet to finish them off, since one was not enough. We walked over the bodies. In every gray-haired woman I thought I saw Mama. I flung myself on the corpses, with Basya right behind me, but the blows of a club returned us to our places. At one point I thought that an old man with his brains oozing out his head was Papa, but I couldn't get close enough to tell. We began to say our farewells and managed to kiss each other. We remembered Dora. Fanya did not believe that this was the end: "Can it be true that never again will I see the sun and the light?" Her face was a dark bluish-gray, and Vladya kept asking, "Are we going swimming? Why did we undress? Let's go home, Mama, it's not good here." Fanya took him by the hand; it was hard for him to walk on the slippery clay. Vasya would not stop wringing her hands and whispering, "Vladya, Vladya, why is this happening to you? No one even knows what they are doing with us." Fanya turned around and replied, "With him I can die in peace, knowing that I am not leaving him an orphan." Those were Fanya's last words. I couldn't stand it any more; I clutched my head and started screaming wildly. I think Fanya had time to turn around and say, "Quiet, Sarra, quiet." And with that everything came to an abrupt halt.

When I regained consciousness it was already twilight. The corpses lying on top of me were quivering; it was the Germans walking over them and shooting them at every turn. I gathered from the Germans' conversation that they wanted to make sure the wounded would not be able to leave during the night. They were worried that not everyone had been killed, and they were not mistaken: many were only wounded. They had been buried alive, for there was no one to help them or answer them as they moaned and begged for help. Somewhere above the corpses children were crying. Most of them, especially the babies whose mothers held them in their arms to protect them (they shot us in the back), had fallen, now buried under the bodies of their mothers; buried alive under the corpses, they were smothering.

I started to crawl out from underneath the corpses; I had torn the nails from the toes of one foot (but I did not realize it until I reached the Royanovs on 24 October). Once I had crawled out, I looked around: the wounded were writhing, groaning, trying to get up and falling down again. I started calling out to Fanya in the hope that she might hear me, when a man next to me ordered me to be quiet. It was Grodzinsky; they murdered his mother, and he was afraid that I would attract the attention of the Germans with my shouting. A small group of people who had thought it jumped into the trench at the first volley and came out unharmed. They were Vera Kulman, Shmaevsky, and Tsilya (I don't remember Tsilya's last name). The whole time they were asking me to keep quiet, and I begged everyone who came out of it to help me look for Fanya. Grodzinsky, who was wounded in the leg and could not move, advised me to leave. I tried to help him, but I couldn't do anything by myself. After two steps he fell; he refused to go any farther and urged me to go on and catch up with those who had already left. I sat there and listened. I could hear the voice of some old man: "*Laitelakh, laitelakh!*"[17] In that word, repeated over and over, there was so much horror! From somewhere in those depths someone was crying out, "Don't kill me. . ." I happened to catch up with V. Kulman. In the darkness she had gotten separated from the group of people she left with. Wearing only our slips and covered with blood from head to toe, the two of us began searching for shelter for the night and set off toward the sound of a barking dog. We knocked at one hut, but no one answered; then at a second hut [but they ran us off; and finally at a third], where we were given some rags to cover ourselves and told to head for the steppe. That is just what we did. We made our way through the darkness to a haystack and stayed there until dawn. In the morning we returned to the farm, which turned out to be the Shevchenko farm. It was located not far from the other side of the trench; all day long we could hear the screams of women and children.

23 October. We have been on the steppe now for two days, and we don't know the road. Today, as we were moving from haystack to haystack, V. Kulman came upon a group of men, one of whom turned out to be Shmaevsky. Naked and covered with blood, they had been here the whole time. We decided to set out for the Ilich Factory during the day because we could not find the road at night. On the way to the factory we ran into a group of teenage boys. One of them advised us to stay on the steppe until evening, and then he went away; another told us that we should leave as quickly as possible, since that his friend had deceived us and had gone to get the Germans. We hurried off. On the morning of 24 October I reached the Royanovs. They took me in. When they found out about how everyone died, they were horrified. They fed me and put me to bed.

Prepared for publication by Ilya Ehrenburg

Odessa

I

Near Odessa a broad plain extends into the distance. Only now and then does a small hill, colored green with a patch of woods, rise up; after that the Black Sea steppe stretches out from the sea, to the estuaries, to the Bug River.

Everything here is in open view. For a person pursued by death in the form of a German or Romanian executioner, it is hard to hide in these places.

Flying over in an airplane, you can see scattered farms, co-ops, settlements, and villages, such as Dalniki, Sortirovochnnaya, and Sukhie Balki. Farther on, closer to the Bug are Berezovka, Akmechetka, Domanevka, and Bogdanovka.[18]

There was a time when these names had a peaceful sound and aroused fear in no one; but now they cannot be uttered calmly; each of them is associated with murder, agony, and torture.

Here there were death camps. Here people were tortured and torn limb from limb; children's heads were smashed, and people were burned alive, gone mad from suffering, horror, and unbearable torture.

Out of hundreds of thousands only a few dozen survived. From them we have learned the details of the bestial violence.

In all the testimonies and written accounts of the witnesses who remained, in their letters and memoirs, we encounter over and over the same assertion that they do not have the strength to convey what they have lived through.

"I would have to have the expertise of an artist's brush to portray the scenes of horror that took place in Domanevka," says Elizaveta Pikarmer, a woman from Odessa. "The finest workers and the best scientists perished here. Their insane delirium, the expression on their faces, their eyes shook even those who had a strong spirit. One day, twenty-year-old Manya Tkach had a baby while lying on a dung heap next to a pile of corpses. By evening the woman was dead."

V. Ya. Rabinovixh, a technical editor at an Odessa publishing house, writes, "A great deal could be written, but I am not a writer, and I do not have the physical strength. For as I write, I see it all again right before my eyes. There is not enough ink and paper to write down everything in detail. There is not nor will there ever be a man who can paint a picture of the inhuman suffering that we, the Soviet people, have endured."

And yet they cannot remain silent: they write. And there is nothing to be added to what they have told.

The old physician from Odessa, Izrail Borisovich Adesman, dictated his memoirs to his wife Rakhil Iosifovna Goldental, who is also a physician.

Lev Rozhetsky, a seventh-grade student at Odessa School No. 47, wrote essays describing his life in death camps from Odessa to Bogdanovka.

Odessa's tragic dates are: 16 October 1941, the day Romanian troops occupied Odessa; 17 October 1941, the day Romanian authorities announced the registration of the Jewish population; and 24 October, the day the Jews were sent to the Slobodka ghetto, the doorway to the annihilation camps spread out over the plain of death outside the city. The expulsion of the Jews to the camps began a short time later.

The night of 17 October was a terrible one for the Jews who had been unable to evacuate. It was terrible indeed for the old men and women who were in no position to leave, for the mothers whose children could not walk yet, for pregnant women, for the sick confined to their beds.

It was a terrifying night for Fudim, a mathematics professor stricken with paralysis. They dragged him out of his bed and into the street; there they hanged him. Professor Ya. S. Rabinovich, a neuropathologist, threw himself out a window, but, unfortunately, he was still alive. "Although he was badly crippled, he was still conscious and breathing. An armed guard stood beside his broken body. They spit in his face and threw stones at him."

Once they had occupied Odessa, the fascists began by killing the physicians first. These professional murderers hated those whose calling was to prolong people's lives and alleviate their suffering.

Sixty-one doctors and their families were murdered during the first few days.

On the list of the dead were the names of doctors known from childhood to every Odessan: Rabinovich, Rubinshtein, Varshavsky, Chatsky, Polyakov, Brodsky. . . . Doctor Adesman was saved only by being assigned to the hospital in Slobodka as a consultant. Prior to that, however, he had to endure all the derision and torture that came with registration; later he experienced all the horrors of Domanevka, one of the most terrible death camps on the Black Sea plain.

On 17 October 1941, the day after the Romanians occupied Odessa, the registration of the Jews began.

There were several registration points. From these points some people were taken to the gallows or to mass graves; others were sent to the prison. A few were allowed to return to their ransacked apartments, which amounted to nothing more than a postponement of their deaths.

"The registration point where they dragged my wife and me," Doctor Adesman relates, "was in a cold, dark school building. More than five hundred of us were gathered there. We had no place to sit. We spent the night standing, squeezed tightly up against each other. We were worn out with fatigue, hunger, thirst, and ignorance of our situation. All night long you could hear the crying of children and the groaning of adults.

"The next morning several groups like ours were combined to form a column of three or four thousand people. We were all herded into the prison. Among us were very old people, cripples on crutches, and women nursing babies. In the prison many died from exhaustion and beatings.

"Many took their own lives."

On 23 October 1941 partisans blew up the Romanian headquarters, killing dozens of Romanian soldiers and officers. The invaders flooded the city with Jewish blood in reprisal.

Posted on the walls were announcements declaring that, for every Romanian officer killed, three hundred Russians or five hundred Jews would be hanged. In reality this "estimate" was increased by ten- to a hundredfold.

On 23 October 1941 ten thousand Jews were led out of the prison. They were all cut down by machine guns outside the city. Again, on 25 October, several thousand Jews were taken outside the city and locked inside a barn; then the barn was blown up with dynamite.[19]

The technical editor V. Ya. Rabinovich, who in the summer had gone with his children to Arcadia (how monstrous this idyllic name sounds in the face of the German-Romanian oppression!), describes the city during the first days of the occupation:

"On 23 and 24 October you could see gallows everywhere you turned your eyes. There were thousands of them. At the feet of those who were hanged lay the bodies of those who were tortured, mutilated, and shot. Our city presents a terrible spectacle: it is the city of the hanged. For a long time they put us on display by parading us around the streets. The Germans and the Romanians explained, 'All these Jews—these old men and women, these women and children—are the ones who started this war. They are the ones who attacked Germany. For this all of them must now be destroyed. . . .' They shot us even as they were leading us around. The murdered fell; the wounded crawled off. Thus the group proceeded down New Arcadia Road toward the sea (toward the resorts). They came to a deep pit. The order: 'Strip naked! Quickly, quickly!' Screams. Farewells. Many purposely tore the clothes they wore; for this they were stabbed with bayonets. The murderers needed their things.

"The Romanians and Germans tested the strength of their bayonets on tiny children. A mother was feeding her baby, when a Romanian soldier tore it from her breast with his bayonet and flung the infant into the pit of the dead."

Two other witnesses, Bolshova and Slipchenko, relate [how the number of Jews in the city became smaller and smaller. Every day groups of ragged people were led down the street. The hellish machinery of annihilation was operating smoothly.]:

"There is a short man walking in the crowd, his head drawn back deep into his shoulders. He has a high, protruding forehead and pensive eyes. Who is he? A barbarian, a murderer, a criminal? No, it is the great scientist and neuropathologist, Doctor Blank, [who was so devoted to science, his patients, and his clinic that he had disregarded the approaching danger.] He fulfilled his duties as a physician to the very end and never abandoned his patients. Another doctor was walking next to Doctor Blank; on his sleeve he wore an armband with the sign of the Red Cross. He was an older, heavy-set man with a bad heart; he was having trouble breathing. Gradually he fell behind, and a Romanian gendarme beat him over the head with a cane. Using the last of his strength, the doctor quickened his step but soon fell. . . . They beat him with a cane about the eyes. 'Kill me!' he howled. And two bullets pierced his head.

"There was another one: a tall, thin old man with clear, intelligent eyes. The Russian women wiped away their tears as their eyes followed him. Doesn't every mother know him? It is Doctor Petrushkin, the old pediatrician."

There was no slander, no absurdity, that the invaders would not heap on the Jews.

Anna Margulis, an elderly woman who used to be a stenographer at the Marti Ship Factory, relates the following:

"On 29 October 1941 my dying father tried to light a lamp. The burning match fell from his weak hand and set the blanket on fire. I put it out in a second. That night my neighbor, a Romanian, went to the police and told them I had tried to burn down the building. The next morning I was arrested and thrown into prison, where there were thirty women. During the interrogation they started beating me with clubs, rifle butts, and rubber hoses. I lost consciousness.

"That night, when it was pitch-black all around, a bunch of Romanian soldiers burst into our cell. After throwing their coats on the damp floor, they started raping the girls. We older women (I was fifty-four) sat and cried. Many of the girls went insane."

But all of this was just a prelude to the horror of the ghetto, and the ghetto itself was the threshold to the plain of death.

"The Jews who died during the first days of the occupation were much more fortunate than their comrades." This phrase from one of the Jews of Odessa needs no explanation.

"Everyone was forced into the Slobodka Ghetto: women about to give birth, paralytics and cripples, people with infectious diseases, mental patients. Some walked under their own power, and some were led by loved ones; others were carried in people's arms. Only a few had the good fortune of dying in their beds. On the day of their arrival in Slobodka the people realized that in the ghetto there would be no 'life.' There were not enough quarters. People were crowded together in the streets. The sick moaned and collapsed in the snow. Those who had fallen were trampled by fascists on horseback. You could hear the crying of freezing children. Screams of horror, please for mercy.

"By the evening of the first day the streets of Slobodka were littered with the corpses of people who had frozen to death. You could hear the wailing of people as they were being driven out of Odessa and into the death camps. Slobodka had been transformed into a gigantic trap: there was no place to hide. Romanian gendarmes and policemen were everywhere."

Doctor Adesman was a consultant in the ghetto hospital. The hospital was a gathering place for the dying. When the Jews were expelled from Odessa, those who did not manage to die were sent to the water-transport workers' hospital; there they were killed. Doctor Adesman himself was sent there with the last group on 11 February 1942. He remembers: "At the Sortirovochnaya Station we were transferred into boxcars and transported to Berezovka. From there they herded us on foot. With knapsacks on our shoulders we dragged ourselves twenty-five kilometers into the dark, cold night along a road covered now with deep snow, now with ice. Brief stops cost us dearly: we purchased them from the gendarmes with the last of our belongings. We arrived in Domanevka as beggars."

Here they were placed in half-dilapidated houses without windows or doors, as well as in sheds, cow barns, and pigsties.

Disease began to cut people down: dysentery, typhus, gangrene, scabies, furunculosis. Victims of typhus were scattered around the sheds in their agony and delirium with no one to look after them. And no one paid any attention to the corpses any longer.

In other memoirs we read:

"Boarding began at the Sortirovochnaya Station. So many people were crammed into the car that we stood motionless, pressed tightly up against each other. The car was sealed shut from the outside with a heavy bolt, and the people were left in complete darkness. But gradually in the half-darkness you could make out the frightened eyes, open wide with terror, and the faces of women and children covered with tears. The train set out. Faces lit up with hope. Old women exclaimed, 'God will help us!' People began to hope that they were actually being taken to a place where they would be able to work and live. The train moved slowly. Where was it going? Every jolt, every stop, aroused terror. What if we should suddenly be derailed? Or what if the train caught fire? Our only hope was that they would have pity on the train. But where was it going anyway? People were growing more and more numb from the cold, more and more stiff from not moving. Children were crying, asking for something to eat, something to drink. First the youngsters and then the adults started relieving themselves right there, as nature required.

"Suddenly you could hear groans and pleas for help. It was a woman writhing in serious labor pains, but there was no one to help her. Finally came the creaking of the bolt, and those who were left alive were driven out of the train car. Now they were going on foot, driven along by the clubs of the gendarmes, who were raining blows down on the enfeebled and freezing people. As for the people, they dreamt of only one thing: to reach the ghetto. To stop, to move no more. Meanwhile they kept falling, falling. . . .

The roads were thickly strewn with bodies and looked rather like a battlefield; the only difference was that on this field lay not the bodies of soldiers but the pitiful little bodies of babies and the doubled-up figures of old people."

The entire plan for the expulsion of the Jews from Odessa was designed and calculated precisely so that as many people as possible would die a so-called "natural death." The group assigned to the Berezovka region was led across the steppe for three days, in a blizzard and through the snow, despite the fact that the settlement designated for the ghetto was only eighteen kilometers from the station.

A report submitted by jurist I. M. Leenzon, who visited Odessa in May 1944, states that "the number of Jews exterminated in the city of Odessa is approximately 100,000."

II

Lev Rozhetsky, a student in the seventh grade at Odessa School No. 47, composed sketches, songs, and poems, mostly in his head; some of them, however, he wrote down on scraps of paper, boards, and plywood. "Of course, I did it under the threat of death, but I wrote two anti-fascist songs: 'The Sky Reached High' and 'Nina' (in memory of a woman who went insane). Sometimes, on sad occasions, I found ways to read my poems to my comrades. It was such a joy to me when people would sing my songs and read my poems in the midst of their tears and moans."

Rozhetsky tells how he was beaten half to death when some of Pushkin's poems were found on him. "They wanted to kill me, but they didn't."

A youth hardly more than a boy, he was in many death camps and described them in detail. From his sketches we can clearly imagine the entire chain of hell that ran from the Black Sea to the Bug: Sortirovochnaya, Berezovka, Sirotskoe, Domanevka, and Bogdanovka. "I want every letter of these names," he writes, "to be inscribed and sealed with utmost clarity. These names must not be forgotten. Here were the death camps. Here innocent people were exterminated by the fascists for no other reason than that they were Jews."

The number of Jews murdered in Domanevka reached fifteen thousand; in Bogdanovka 54,000 Jews were murdered. On 27 March 1944 representatives of the Red Army and the local authorities drafted an official report on the killing.

"On 11 January 1942," writes Lev Rozhetsky, "my mother, my little brother Anatoly, who was just getting over typhus, and I were herded off to Slobodka. They came for us at three A.M.

"It was horribly cold; the snow was up to our knees. Many old people and children died right there, under the howling of a blizzard on the edge of the city, in Peresyp. The Germans laughed and took pictures of us. Those who were able managed to make it to the

Sortirovochnaya station. A dam had been blown up along the route we took. [An entire river had formed.] The people were drenched and freezing.

"The train was waiting for us at the Sortirovochnaya station. I shall never forget the scene: pillows, blankets, coats, felt boots, pots, and other things were scattered all over the platform.

The freezing old people could not get up and were groaning softly and pitifully. Mothers were looking for their children and children were looking for their mothers in the midst of shouting, crying, and shooting. One mother was wringing her hands and tearing her hair: 'My little girl, where are you?' A child was rushing about the platform screaming, 'Mama!'

"When we got to Berezovka the doors of the train car opened with a creak; we were blinded by the bright glow of flaming bonfires. I saw people running around engulfed in flames. There was a sharp smell of gasoline. They were burning people alive.

"This slaughter took place at the Berezovka station.

"Suddenly there was a powerful jolt, and the train moved farther and farther away from the bonfires. They were taking us somewhere else to die."

Commenting on Domanevka, Rozhetsky says it occupies a "place of honor" among the death camps. He describes it in detail:

"Domanevka is a black and bloody word. Domanevka was a center of death and murder. Thousands of groups were driven here to their deaths. One transport followed another ceaselessly. Three thousand of us set out from Odessa, of which only a handful reached Domanevka. A small village, Domanevka was a regional center. It is surrounded by hilly fields. There are woods, small but beautiful. Rags and bits of clothing still hang in the bushes and branches. Here lies a grave under every tree. . . . People's skeletons can be seen."

On the outskirts of Domanevka there were two half-destroyed stables known as the "Hills." Even in the Domanevka Ghetto these were terrible places.

In Rozhetsky's memoirs we read:

"We were not allowed to leave the barracks; we were up to our knees in mud, and excrement was piled everywhere. Bodies were lying around, as in a morgue. Typhus. Dysentery. Gangrene. Death.

"Gradually the corpses formed such mountains that they were terrifying to behold. Old people and women were lying there in a variety of poses. A dead mother held a dead child in a tight embrace. An old man's gray beard stirred in the wind.

"Now I wonder: how did I keep from going mad? Dogs ran in and out of the area day and night. The dogs of Domanevka grew fat as sheep. Day and night they fed on human flesh and gnawed on human bones. The stench became unbearable. [One of the policemen petted a dog and said, 'Well, Polkan, did you get enough kikes to eat?'"]

Twenty-five kilometers from Domanevka, on the banks of the Bug, lies Bogdanovka. Here beautiful park lanes lead to the edge of a ditch where tens of thousands of people found their grave.

Those marked for death were stripped naked and led to the pit, where they were forced to their knees, their eyes facing the Bug. They were shot in the back of the skull with hollow-pointed bullets. The bodies were dumped down below. [They would murder a wife before her husband's eyes. Then they would murder the husband.]

The Stavki pig farm stood, as Rozhetsky put it, "like an island in the desert of the steppe." Those who survived the Hills perished at Stavki.

The people were herded into the pigsties. They were held in those filthy cages until merciful death relieved them of their suffering.

"The camp was surrounded by a ditch. Anyone who dared to cross it was shot on the spot. They allowed people to go for water ten at a time. Once, having noticed that one too many went out and thus violated the 'order,' a policeman shot the eleventh person. It was a teenage girl. 'Oy, Mama, they've killed me!' she screamed. The policeman went up and finished her off with his bayonet.

"Those who managed to survive were sent to do the most difficult and most torturous work.

"I remember how we used to pull up to the barracks. I would lead the horse by the reins, and Mama would push the cart from behind. We picked up the bodies by their arms and legs and threw them onto the cart; once the cart was filled to the top, we would take our load to the pit and dump it."

Elizaveta Pikarmer relates:

"A neighbor from my building and her baby and I were the first to come to the edge of the pit, even though we stood in a crowd of hundreds. But at the last minute a Romanian horseman holding a piece of paper in his hand rode up to the guards. And the prisoners were led away to new torments. The next day they threw all of us into the river. After giving our torturers the last of our possessions, we bought ourselves the right to get out of the water. Later many died of pneumonia."

In Domanevka the fascists tore babies in half and smashed their heads against stones. Women had their breasts cut off. Entire families were either buried alive or burned to death in the bonfires.

The elderly Mr. Furman and his eighteen-year-old daughter Sonya Katz were promised that if they danced, then they could prolong their lives. But their lives were not prolonged by much: two hours later they were hanged.

Doomed to death, people moved like automatons; they took leaves of their senses, raved deliriously, and had hallucinations.

The commandants of the village of Gulyaevka, Lupescu and Plutoner Sandu,[20] would send their minions into the death camp every night to bring them pretty girls. The next morning they took a special delight in watching the girls in the throes of death.

The typhus victims were lying everywhere with no one to look after them. "Death cut people down by the hundreds; indeed, it was difficult to distinguish the living from the dead or the healthy from the sick."

Tanya Rekochinskaya wrote to her brother in one of the army's field units:

"My two children and I were forced from our apartment into the horribly freezing winter cold and transported on foot 180 kilometers from Odessa to the Bug. My little girl, who was just a baby, died on the road. My little boy was shot along with the other children in the transport. It was my lot to live through all this.'

And yet these horrors were not enough. An anxious cry penetrated the unreal existence of the death camp, penetrated the silence broken only by the groans and the wheezing of the dying: "The village is surrounded. Romanian and German colonists from Kartakaevo have arrived with machine guns."

Policemen on horseback drove all the Jews into a barn and from there to the death trenches. Some decided to die proudly: they did not lower themselves to pleading for mercy and showed their executioners no fear of death. Others wanted to drown themselves. The men calmed the women, and the women calmed the children. Some of the smallest children were laughing. With a bloody slaughter awaiting them, the laughter of these children seemed dreadful indeed.

"Mommy, where are they taking us?" the voice of a six-year-old little girl could be heard.

"They're taking us to a new apartment, sweetie," the mother would calm her. . . . Their new apartment would be deep and damp indeed. And from the window of their new apartment her little girl would never see the sun, never see the blue sky.

And now the trenches. The entire procedure for this murder of humanity was carried out with German accuracy and precision. Like surgeons performing an operation, the Germans and Romanians donned their hospital gowns and rolled up their sleeves. Those doomed to death were stripped naked and lined up along the trenches. Thus they stood before their tormentors, naked, trembling, and awaiting their deaths.

They did not waste their lead on the children. They crushed their skulls against posts and trees and threw them alive into the bonfires. The mothers were not killed right away, so that first their poor hearts could bleed at the sight of the deaths of their little ones.

One German woman from Kartakaevo, a colonist who had been declared a kulak and had lost her farm, was especially cruel. "It was as if she were drunk with her own cruelty: screaming wildly, she would crush the skulls of little children with such blows of her rifle butt that their brains were scattered over a wide area."

[In the summer of 1942 the inmates at Domanevka looked so terrible that on the day they were expecting the Governor of Transnistria they ordered the Jews to leave the village and stay five to six kilometers away until evening.]

The people in the death camps were plundered of their belongings before they were annihilated. The soldiers and the police took money for everything—for a sip of soup, for an hour of life, for every sigh and every step. In March 1942 Elizaveta Pikarmer fell ill with typhus and sent along with other patients to a place where the victims of typhus were dumped. Six of them, who did not have the strength to walk, were shot. "I too fell into the mud," says Pikarmer. "But for twenty marks a policeman helped me up and dragged me to the top of a small hill."

On 7 May 1943 an order was issued declaring that all those who were still alive were to be sent to work on a farm. "Here our situation improved a little, since we had a chance to bathe in the Bug River every day after work, and once a week we could boil our rags. From hemp we made skirts, blouses, and shoes. . . ."

But this proximity to the Bug that had brought the people such joy in the summer of 1943 would also bring them new horrors.

"On 23 March 1944 a punitive detachment of the SS crossed the Bug: we Jews were condemned to death. There was no hope for salvation from anywhere. All along the road we met groups of prisoners who were being herded in the direction of Tiraspol. Their hands and faces were swollen from cold and hunger. We did not have the strength to continue and begged to be shot on the spot. The women and children were loaded onto trucks and taken to some unknown destination. There were only twenty of us left with a German non-commissioned officer, and we continued on our way. We had not eaten for two days, and we were shivering from the cold. We were losing our minds."

But freedom was approaching. On 1 April the Red Army arrived.

III

On the plain of steppe in the Odessa district, not far from the Kolosovka railroad station, is the village of Gradovka.

In the summer of 1944 Lieutenant Colonel Shabanov was passing through. Just outside the village he saw three ovens designed for baking limestone; they were overgrown with weeds and thistles. In the shafts of the ovens Shabanov could see pieces of charred bones: forearms, shoulder blades, and vertebrae. Small fragments of skulls crunched under his feet. The ground was so thick with them that they were like seashells on a seashore.

That was all that was left of the people who had been burned there.

Here the murderers did not need any complicated, specially equipped crematory ovens with "Cyclone" vortex ventilation; they made do with these simple ovens for their bloody task.

The chief executioners in this region were German colonists. There were many of them here. Interspersed with the Russian names of settlements and villages were German names: München, Radstadt, and so on. Along with their names the Germans brought to the Russian soil the bloody cruelty [that characterizes these "Aryans"].

The land that gave them shelter these people stained red with innocent blood. They went off to the ovens in the steppe as if they were on a holiday. They plundered with relish. They murdered with delight. In Gradovka those who were condemned to death were not held for long. Here a "conveyor" method was in operation. People were burned as quickly as a set of ovens could handle them. Each "batch" took about three days. While one oven was heating up, an execution was taking place in another.

People were stripped naked in front of the ovens, lined up along the edge of a shaft, and shot with machine guns at point blank range; most of them were shot in the head. Fragments of skull bones flew in every direction, and no one bothered to pick them up. The bodies fell into the oven shafts.

Once a shaft was filled to the top, the bodies were doused with kerosene. Bundles of straw had already been placed in the corners of the shaft. Fat melting from the bodies stoked the flames. The entire area was laden with smoke and poisoned by the stench of burning human flesh.

Everything that had belonged to those who were murdered was taken to the train station, sorted into piles, and loaded onto trains. The whole operation went off methodically and with expertise. [The people in Germany and Romania were probably quite pleased with the goods that were sent to them. The only drawback was that their new things smelled like something burning.]

Approximately seven thousand people were consumed in the three ovens. In Radstadt and Sukhie Balki the number of those who perished reached twenty thousand.

Colonel Shabanov concludes his report by saying:

"I saw many things during the war, but I cannot convey what I experienced when I visited the ovens. But if I, a mere witness who arrived late on the scene, experienced all this, what must the condemned have felt and endured just before their heads were shattered and they tumbled into the flames? It is said that one woman grabbed one of the executioners and pulled him into the oven's gullet with her."

[Barges loaded with Jewish women and children set out for the open sea. Half an hour later they returned empty and picked up another group. Again they would set out; again they would return. Interned Jews were forced to clear mine fields; not one of them was spared. What eyewitness testimonies, indictments of brutality, or official reports will describe all this? Who will paint a picture of the transports stuffed to overflowing? Their doors sealed shut, the train cars would sit on the tracks without moving for several days. Bodies were thrown from the trains and burned in bonfires on the steppe. From the Black Sea to the Bug, the entire plain was lit up by the flames from these fires.]

Death by fire, cold, hunger, thirst, maiming, torture, shooting, hanging. . . . every kind of death, the entire bloody arsenal of torture, every manner of torment—all of it was leveled at helpless, unarmed old people, women, and children.

IV

Terrorized and awash in blood, Odessa was transformed into a torture chamber. Taken over by the invaders, the Odessa newspapers were filled with savage rantings about the "Jewish menace." As the Führer stated it, in the new Europe even the skeleton of a Jew would be a rarity found only in a museum of archeological antiquities.

Under such conditions the Russians and Ukrainians were threatened with death for any sympathetic word or compassionate glance offered to the Jews, for every drop of water and crust of bread given to a Jewish child. Nevertheless, risking their very lives, the Russians and Ukrainians helped the Jews: entire families were hidden in cellars, where they were fed, clothed, and given medical attention.

"To you I just want to say thank you, Shura, and to you, comrade Chmir, for hiding us. Every day you, our protectors, read the decrees issued by the German and Romanian beasts, and you knew the danger you were in. But, risking your own lives, you helped us anyway. Thank you." Thus wrote Rabinovich. He has written unforgettable pages of testimony condemning the savagery perpetrated by the German and Romanian invaders in his native city.

Elizaveta Pikarmer was saved from death by a Russian woman who was an acquaintance of hers. [Elizaveta Pikarmer was saved from death thanks only to the fact that she happened to be seen in the death camp by a Russian woman who had been a patient at the sanatorium where Pikarmer used to be a head nurse.]

The Ukrainian Leonid Suvorovsky, an engineer at one of the factories in Odessa, was very well known among the Jewish population of Odessa. Suvorovsky not only warned his Jewish acquaintances not to go the registration sites, the Romanians had ordered them; he took many into his apartment, which at night he made into a headquarters for manufacturing false papers and documents for dozens of Jewish families. With the help of his Russian and Ukrainian friends, Leonid Suvorovsky harbored and fed twenty-two Jewish families by selling cigarettes and even his own clothing during the day. Suvorosky was finally arrested by the German-Romanian authorities and sentenced by a military court to seven years of hard labor. But even on the eve of his arrest, Suvorovsky managed to find shelter for Jewish families.

With the help of a group of trusted friends, Yakov Ivanovich Polishchuk dug a large cellar in an unfinished building in the very heart of the city; there he hid sixteen Jewish families for two years. Although his life was in danger day and night, Polishchuk brought them food. All sixteen families were saved.

An old couple named Varvara Andreevna Lapina and Andrey Ivanovich Lapin hid Jewish children in their rooms. Once the danger had become too great, Lapina sent the children to a safe place in the country. She was arrested but never divulged a word about their whereabouts. Varvara Andreevna Lapina was shot.

A longshoreman named Konstantin Spandenko and his friends carried out several daring attacks on the Odessa prison, where thousands of Jews had been interned. Some of them managed to join up with partisans.

The plain of the steppe did not provide the partisans with a defensive position, but its earth hid them in its bowels. Abandoned stone quarries and Odessa's famous catacombs were transformed into partisan enclaves interconnected by underground tunnels.

The Romanians and Germans grew afraid as they sensed that the ground under their feet was filled with danger. The partisans would emerge from the catacombs to blow up buildings and attack prisons.

The Kantorovich sisters, two Jewish girls named Elena and Olga, joined with their brother, his friend Skuli, a Greek postal clerk, and several others to form a resistance unit to fight the invaders. Twice arrested under the "accusation of being Jews," the Kantorovich sisters escaped both times and established contact with partisan units in the catacombs near and far. Elena and Olga had a radio receiver and a typewriter hidden in the cellar of their apartment in the city. From there summaries of the Soviet Information Bureau broadcasts were circulated throughout the city in ways that baffled the invaders.

These bulletins found their way into the streetcars, the bakeries, the movie houses, and even the prison, where they would be smuggled inside loaves of bread and items of clothing. Taking up the struggle shoulder to shoulder, their Russian and Ukrainian comrades worked alongside young Jewish men and women in this fatally dangerous work.

Lev Rozhetsky, a schoolboy who passed through every circle of the fascist hell, envisions a monument erected "over the infamous Bogdanovka pit, one of the many pits in the death camps. . . ." For this monument to the victims of fascism he has dedicated the following lines:

> Whoever you may be, stop
> And draw nigh, noble traveler,
> To this grave cold and gloomy.
> From the depths of your sorrow, look around.
> Though seized with rage and passion,
> Let not a tear cloud your eye.
> In mute homage honor
> The ashen dust of these people.

The Romanian and German fascists spared no effort to transform Soviet Odessa into the city of Antonescu, capital of the notorious Transnistria. But the city did not surrender; it lived and fought and won, together with the entire country.

Vera Inber[21]

[Chernovitsy under the German-Romanian Occupation

On 4 July the first German-Romanian military units entered North Bukovina from various directions; by 6 July they were in Chernovitsy. One of the first steps taken by Hitler's chief commanders was to announce that the Jewish people no longer had any legal status. A wave of pogroms, unheard of till now, swept through the local towns and villages. In the town of Gzudak there were approximately 470 Jewish families; all except three people, who managed to escape, were murdered. In many villages not a single Jew was left alive. In Chernovitsy more than 6,000 people were murdered.

The Romanian peasant Korda Nikola, who worked at the "Kadrom" rubber factory during the Romanian occupation, has said that in his native village of Voloka not one of the Jews was left alive. In some settlements individual Jews were saved thanks to their neighbors, who hid them in cellars and haystacks.

When representatives of the civil authorities finally arrived in Bukovina, the Jews who were still alive were taken away, some to the village of Storozhinets, some to Bayukany. They were soon placed in camps adjacent to the villages. They stayed in the camps for several days (11 days in Storozhinets) and were subjected to inhumane degradation. Then the camps were liquidated, and the Jews were herded into the ghetto.

In Chernovitsy, where there were approximately 60,000 Jews, men and women were arrested in the streets, forced out of their homes, and taken to the police station; from there they were herded in groups of 50 to 300 to various work sites under armed guard. Romanian women, who had gradually inundated the city and now occupied Jewish apartments, came to the police station, where they were assigned 20 to 30 Jewish men and women to clean their apartments of the filth "left behind by the Bolsheviks." A very large number of Jews were turned over to the German commandant, who forced them to build a railroad bridge across the Prut River. Many perished in the river's turbulent waters, but many more died from inhumane treatment and exhaustion. There were no stores open in the city; only some bread shops. But they would not sell bread to Jews.

One of the first steps taken by the Romanian National Bank was to order that Soviet currency be exchange at a designated rate. When the Jews, however, came to change their currency, their money was simply taken away from them.

Every morning as the Jews were going to work they would run into police patrols. Ignoring the identification cards issued at the work sites, the police would savagely beat them and drag them off to the police station. Only from there, under guard, could the Jews then go to work.

A few weeks later an order issued requiring all Jews to wear a patch with the Star of David on the left side of their chest. This star, in fact, placed the Jews outside the protection of the law; attacks on them increased significantly, since the criminals were certain they could act with impunity. Jews caught without a star or who were not wearing it in the proper place were hauled off to concentration camps. . . . General Galatescu, who was the governor of Bukovina at the time, even issued a special order that was widely distributed and published in the local press. The General demanded that the star be securely sewn at all six points and worn in the proper position, for it had been observed that some Jews did not display it prominently enough and would even remove it from time to time.

Poverty steadily grew among the Jewish population, and most of them were literally starving; they lived solely on pitiful handouts from compassionate neighbors. . . . Jews had to work without pay. Some doctors were allowed to practice, but the word *Jew* had to be clearly marked on their signs. Jewish doctors were strictly forbidden to treat non-Jewish patients. It was forbidden to worship in the synagogues, and as soon as the German-Romanian troops arrived in the city, they burned down the municipal synagogue.

Placards warning against "Bolshevist acts of sabotage" were posted everywhere. They threatened to shoot twenty Jewish and five non-Jewish hostages for every such act. The prisons were filled to overflowing. . . . A very large number of people were taken as hostages, and most of them were murdered.

Among them were Mark, the Chief Rabbi of Chernovitsy, and Gurman, the Chief Cantor. After a short while the authorities set up the so-called "Jewish Council," which was chaired by Doctor Neiburg. The Council consisted mostly of former Zionist leaders. It was supposed to serve as a mouthpiece for the invaders in their relations with the Jewish population. The one thing that the Council did accomplished was the preservation of five Jewish institutions (the Jewish hospital, the maternity home, the home for the aged, the insane asylum, and the orphanage), which they managed to do under very difficult conditions.

One decree resulted in the confiscation of all Jewish real estate. Jewish homeowners had to pay rent to live in their own apartments. Any Romanian could take any Jewish apartment that happened to catch his eye and seize everything that was in it.

So things went until 10 October 1941, when the Jewish Council was instructed to verbally inform all the Jews that they must move into the ghetto, in the area where the poorest segment of the Jewish population lived. In the early morning hours of October 11 crowds of people set out. In their arms and on their backs they carried bedding and bundles of clothing. Some took their things along in wheelbarrows, hand carts, and baby carriages. The military authorities released several tanks to rumble up and down the streets to frighten the people.

No orders were published with regard to the establishment of the ghetto. Only three days later in the Bucharest newspaper *Curentul* did there appear a brief notice stating that "necessary measures" had been taken "in the most humane manner."

Pointing out the absence of an official order, some Jews tried to stay in their apartments. After 6:00 P.M. on 11 October, however, by which time a tall wooden fence had been erected around the ghetto, the gendarmes removed those Jews from their apartments and escorted them into the ghetto. As a punishment they were not allowed to take anything with them.

The living conditions in the ghetto were unbearable; five to eight families were forced into small rooms. The entrances to the ghetto were closely guarded, and not one of the Jews dared to leave.

Two days later, a member of the Jewish Council came to announce that, according to a decision from the authorities, all the Jews of Bukovina, including those in South Bukovina, would be moved to so-called Transnistria, that is, to the region between the Dniester and the Bug occupied by the Romanians. The resettlement would be carried out primarily by rail, but since railways were not available in many areas and there was no other means of transportation, part of the trip would have to be made on foot. It was recommended, therefore, that those making the trip take along only the hand luggage that they could carry themselves. So-called group leaders were designated to organize the move and to oversee the preparations for departure.

The next morning the Jews were forced, under pain of death, to hand overall their valuables: gold, jewels, foreign currency. That same day a transport of Jews from other cities passed through Chernovitsy. The deportation of the Jews of Chernovitsy began a day later. Long columns of people beaten down physically and spiritually, surrounded by an air of death, stretched through the streets to the freight station. Reporters from German and Romanian newspapers took photos of the "event" and glorified it in their newspapers as "a wise solution to the Jewish problem" in Bukovina.

The first transport left on 14 October 1941, the next on 15 October. On the evening of 15 October Doctor Traian Popovici, then mayor of Chernovitsy, appeared in the office of the Jewish council and informed them that he had received permission from Bucharest to allow several thousand Jews to remain in Chernovitsy. In accordance with the mayor's instructions, a list of the Jews was compiled according to age and profession; as a result, 17,000 Jews remained in the city. Among them were representatives of various professions, as well as people over sixty years of age, women more than six months pregnant, nursing mothers, people on government pensions, and former reserve officers.

The fact is that in the majority of cases permission to extend one's stay in Chernovitsy was sold for fantastic sums. People who did not have the means to pay could not get permission, even if their profession or living conditions were in keeping with the mayor's instructions.

In the Jewish hospital, for example, women from Bessarabia had served as nurses for a very long time, for ten to twenty years. At the time when the ghetto was set up the hospital was so overcrowded that patients were spread throughout the halls and were even in the garden.

At the time some of the natives of Chernovitsy and even several "ladies of society" devoted themselves to working as nurses in order to personally care for sick relatives.

When the issue of obtaining permission to stay arose, almost all the natives of Chernovitsy received the appropriate documents; the Bessarabians, however, were communists and did not merit that kindness.

What was the fate of the Jews who stayed in Chernovitsy? It must be kept in mind that the Romanian authorities were faced with the task of restoring trade and industry to the city. In order to draw Romanians into trade, it was decreed that all Romanians directing commercial enterprises in Chernovitsy would be exempt from military service. The enticement worked. Within a very short time many stores opened in Chernovitsy. For the most part they were stores that had previously belonged to Jews, who no longer had the right to own businesses. It was the same with industry: all industrial operations that had previously belonged to Jews were seized by the state and then leased or sold to Romanians at ridiculously low prices. The new Romanian industrialists, however, were unable to handle their new assignments without the help of specialists and skilled workers, who could be found only among the Jews. Each Romanian businessman was given the opportunity to keep "his" Jews on the job.

Jews who received permission to live in Chernovitsy were allowed to keep their families with them, that is, underage children, wives, and, in some cases, parents. All other Jews were gradually sent away. The deportations dragged on until mid-November, when, due to difficulties with the transports, they came to a halt. Thus there were still about 5,000 Jews left in Chernovitsy who did not have permission to stay. Some of them were people in hiding to avoid deportation; others were invalids who could not move.

Those who had permission to stay in Chernovitsy could leave the ghetto and return to their apartments, which had been totally looted. A commission was immediately established to see to it that permits were properly issued. The commission convened in a large chamber in the town hall under the directorship of the governor and with the participation of representatives from the municipal and military authorities, as well as the Sigurantà (the secret police). The commission annulled and revoked a number of permits that were determined to be improper. Those who had held them were immediately sent to Transnistria. The same lot fell to all who were on the Siguranta's "black list."

This revision had not yet been completed, when it was announced that all Jews remaining in Chernovitsy without official permission had to be registered. They were subsequently issued permits of a different type; the permits were signed, however, not by the governor but by the mayor Traian Popovici (hence these were known as Popovici permits). This second census determined that there were approximately 21,000 Jews in Chernovitsy, of whom around 16,000 had Galatescu permits and 5,000 had Popovici permits. The liquidation of the Chernovitsy Ghetto was by no means an act of goodwill but was simply the result of an order from the Sanitation Department intended to prevent epidemics.

Over the next two and a half years one revision followed another, each of which brought with it new oppressions and persecutions. Every Jew was required to have numerous documents and identification cards. A special department of Jewish affairs was set up in Bucharest, the head of which had served as a government minister. It must not be forgotten that all of these documents were sold for huge sums of money; endless petitions had to be submitted with the proper stamps, all for the sole purpose of extorting more and more money. On top of that, "surtaxes" were levied on every document.

With the exception of the physicians, no one had the right to be self-employed. Many hundreds of Jews were forced to work for no wages in various military and municipal establishments; often they even had to pay to secure for themselves a semblance of half-humane treatment from their bosses.

For people working in trade and industry the following rules were established: it was forbidden to employ a Jew without special permission from the labor exchange. In order to obtain such permission, it was necessary to wade through massive formalities and to prove that the Jew in question was "irreplaceable" and that the employer was unable to hire a Romanian for the job; after all that was done, it was still necessary to obtain permission from the Sigurantà. Every Jew, whether a laborer or a clerk, had to have his double, a Romanian whom the Jew would train in the shortest time possible and thus prepare his own replacement. All Jews of draft age (19 to 55) had to pay a military tax of 2,000 to 12,000 lei. Men who were not working in any businesses were sent inland to work and had to provide their own food and clothing at their own expense.

Such was the condition of the Jews up until June 1942. By that time Governor-General Marinescu had succeeded in removing Mayor Popovici. Immediately he issued an order to send to Transnistria everyone who had a permit signed by Popovici. At the same time, those whose work permits had been revoked, as well as invalids who did not wind up in work battalions, were also deported. Altogether approximately 6,000 Jews were deported in June 1942.

That same year a small group of Jews fleeing from Poland—60 to 80 people—arrived in Chernovitsy. Although Polish citizens were under the protection first of Chile, and then of Switzerland, Marinescu handed the Polish Jews over to the Germans, who immediately sent them back to Poland. Even the police chief, who escorted those poor people to the Polish border, said that never in his life had he seen anyone treated with such cruelty. He declared that if he should ever be given such an assignment again, he would rather commit suicide.

And so by August 1942 only about 16,000 Jews were left in Chernovitsy. In addition, the number of restrictions placed on Jews steadily increased. Thus Jews were forbidden to be outside at unlawful hours, that is, from one o'clock in the afternoon until ten the next morning. Workers were issued special passes, which, however, would allow them only to go to work and back. Jews did not have the right to go outside the city limits. In April 1942 a Jewish religious committee was formed; their job was to carry out the orders of the authorities.

Among the functions of the committee was the mobilization of Jews for work battalions. The committee also had to collect the numerous financial contributions that the Jews were forced to pay. In the spring of 1943 a new General-Governor, Dragalina, was appointed in Chernovitsy. Dragalina is on the list of the top ten war criminals published by the Soviet government. He assumed his duties as Governor of Chernovitsy at a time when it was clear that Germany would lose the war and that, for the war criminals, the hour of reckoning was approaching. For that reason Dragalina refrained from making the regimen established for the Jews any worse. During an inspection tour of the concentration camps he even released some of the Jews who had been sent there for refusing to wear the yellow star. In January 1944 he finally gave the order to remove the yellow patches.

As the front drew closer to Bukovina in March 1944, the Jews grew afraid that the Germans would destroy the city and all its residents, just as they had done with all the other Ukrainian cities. Dragalina promised to evacuate the Jews, but in fact he issued very few passes; the ones he did issue were distributed mainly among members of the committee. When, however, the Red Army crossed the Dniester on 24 March, several hundred Jewish families managed to escape from the city during the general panic. On 26 March advance units of the Red Army penetrated the outskirts of Chernovitsy; after a three-day battle waged outside the city, the Germans retreated and did not have time to harm the population. . . . The destruction in the city was not very extensive. The Germans had burned down two factories, the telegraph station, police headquarters, and two apartment buildings downtown. The day before their retreat they also burned down the Archbishop's residence; it was an act of provocation calculated to stir up excessive measures against the Jews. But the watchman was able to contain the fire and exposed the criminals.

An illegal communist organization existed in Chernovitsy during the German-Romanian occupation; eighty people belonged to it, including Jews, Poles, and Ukrainians.

Reported by E. Grosberg,
prepared for publication by L. Goldberg[22]]

The Story of Rakhil Fradis-Milner (Chernovitsy)

We lived in Chernovitsy. The enemies arrived on 6 July. We could not be evacuated: my husband worked in a military garage, and my little boy was sick.

The Jews were driven into the ghetto and from there were sent off to Transnistria. We were in the first group.[23]

The Romanian gendarmes came during the night. We knew that death awaited us, as our three-year-old child quietly slept. I woke him, gave him a toy—a teddy bear—and told him we were going to visit his cousin.

We were taken to a stone quarry in the Tulchin district. We spent ten days there with almost nothing to eat; we made borsch from grass. Lunatics from the asylum were sent with us; [they were not fed], and they were strangling each other. Then we were transferred to Chetvertinovka, since a new groups of Jews from Chernovitsy had arrived at the stone quarry.

We were all housed in the villages of the Tulchin district, in stables and pigsties. We were beaten and tormented. In mid-August 1941 two cars carrying German officers arrived; they called us out and asked whether we wanted to work. They told us they would take us to work and would feed us well.

On 18 August they sent trucks; German commanders from Vinnitsa also pulled up in two cars. Old people, the sick, nursing mothers, and mothers with many children were separated out; those who could work and mothers with one or two children were herded off on foot.

When we crossed the Bug river, people were separated forever: many husbands were left without their wives and children without their parents. We were lucky: my husband, my little boy Shura, and I stayed together. We arrived in Nemirov. There was a camp there for the local Jews, two or three hundred of them, all young and healthy (the rest had already been murdered). We were taken into the yard; there we spent the night. At dawn we saw the Jews of Nemirov dressed in rags, with wounds on their bare feet. When they saw our children, they began to weep and cry out. Mothers remembered their own little ones, who had been tortured to death. It was hard for us to believe their stories. One said that his wife and three children had been murdered; another told how his parents, brothers, and sisters had been murdered; a third said that his pregnant wife had been tortured.

By morning Ukrainians had gathered outside the camp. With his golden hair and blue eyes, my little boy stood out. They all liked him, and one of the Ukrainian women told me, "Have pity on the boy and give him to me. You'll be killed anyway." But I could not give up Shura.

At three in the afternoon they took us to the old synagogue; it was full of feathers from torn pillows. Blouses, children's shoes, and old dishes were scattered everywhere, but most of all there were feathers. It turned out that the Jews of Nemirov had been forced into the synagogue, and from there they were sent to be executed. The nice things were taken away and the old things left. They searched the pillows for gold, and that is why they were all ripped apart. They surrounded us with barbed wire and locked us in. Police Chief Henig and his assistant "Kroshka"[24] arrived.

In the evening they brought in old people, the sick, and children [whom the Romanians refused to leave on their side of the river]. It was a terrible sight. . . .

On the morning of 20 August they took a head count: about two hundred people were suited for work, which left a hundred among the old and the sick, as well as sixty children. Police Chief Henig smiled and said, "Just one more indelicate question: which of the women are expecting?" Blau, a woman in her eighth month and the mother of a five-year-old, gave him her name. He wrote it down and then ordered everyone to get ready to go to work without their children. Only the nursing mothers stayed behind. I decided, "Let them shoot me, I'm not leaving Shura behind." A young woman came up to me with tears in her eyes and said, "I have a baby ten months old. I am afraid if I stay behind, they'll shoot me." I suggested that she leave her baby with me.

[I stayed in the camp. The others went to work on the road crew and did not return until it was nearly dark.]

Any contact with the local population was forbidden. Once a day they distributed pea soup without salt or fat and a hundred grams of bread. Children were dying from hunger. Fortunately, a few Ukrainian women tossed some fruit and bread to the children. As the only one who knew anything about medicine [(I am a pharmacist by training)], I was appointed camp physician; on occasion I had the opportunity to go to the pharmacy, so I could sneak in some food for the children. But it was just a drop in the sea. People worked like slaves and could not even wash themselves. One step out of line, and they got the stick. At night the guards would get drunk and beat everyone. The German authorities took away everything that was of any use. [On 6 September an adjutant of the Chief of Police came to check the list of people in the camp. He called on me to help him make out the names. Shura started crying; I waved him away to show him that he should not stand next to me. The German noticed and said, "Let the boy come to his mommy."]

The SS men carefully examined the rows of people going to work; they took away all the children and nearly all the old people. Six mothers went to their deaths with their children; they wanted to make their little ones' last moments a bit easier. Sarra Kats of Chernovitsy (her husband was at the front) went to her death with six little boys. Vainer went with her sick little girl. Lerner, a young woman from Lipkany, begged the executioners to let her die with her twelve-year-old daughter, the beautiful Tamar.

Once, as the workers were setting out for work, they saw some trucks carrying old people and children from the camps in Chukov and Voronovitsy. Standing at a distance, the workers saw how the trucks stopped, how the Germans started shooting. Later they told how the executioners made the condemned ones strip naked and how they threw babies alive into open graves. Mothers were forced to watch as their children were murdered.

A friend of ours from Edintsy—a lawyer named David Lerner—was in the Chukov camp with his mother, wife, and six-year-old daughter; [his wife's parents, the Akselrods, were there too]. When the children were being murdered in September, they managed to hide their little girl in a sack. The little girl was very smart; she kept still and quiet and was saved. For three weeks her father carried her to work with him; all the while the child lived in the sack. After three weeks our beast Kroshka came to take away everything of value. He went up to the sack and kicked it; the little girl cried out and was discovered. The executioner was enraged; he beat the father, beat the child, and took away all their things, leaving the family practically naked. Nevertheless, he did not kill the little girl; she stayed in the camp and spent the entire winter in terrible fear, awaiting her death every day. On 5 February, during the second "Aktion," the little girl and her grandmother were taken away. The child was seized by a crazed fear of death. She screamed so much on the way to the sleigh that her little child's heart could not endure the terror, and it burst. She was already dead when her grandmother bore her in her arms to the fatal pit. When her mother found out, she went insane; they shot her, and soon afterward murdered the father. That is how this family perished.

On 13 September, at two o'clock in the afternoon, a car pulled up; it was Police Chief Henig, Kroshka, and his assistant Willy. They announced that on 14 September all the children and all those who were unable to work would be sent to another camp, so that they "would not interfere with our work." They compiled a list of the sick, the elderly, and the children. Those who were left were examined, like horses. Anyone who did not step lively or for any reason did not please them was put on the black list. We understood everything. My husband grabbed Shura, put his hand over his mouth, and crawled over the wire.

It was the night of 13 September in the large, two-story synagogue. There was no light. A few people who had bits and pieces of candles lit them. Every mother held her child in her arms and said farewell to him. Everyone knew that this meant death, but no one wanted to believe it. The old rabbi from Poland was reading the prayer ["On Children"], and old men and women joined in with him. There was wailing and heart-rending cries; some of the older children tried to console their parents. The scene was so terrible that even our hardened guards fell silent.

On 14 September people were awakened before dawn and herded off to work, so that they would not interfere. . . . I also went. I did not know what had become of my husband and child, whether they were alive or had fallen into the clutches of the murderers. Some of the mothers went to work with their children; some of the old women put on their finest clothes and also set off for work in an attempt to escape death.

[When we returned to the camp that evening, it was quiet and empty, like a cemetery. Soon the Police Chief arrived and summoned me. He asked where I had been and where my little boy was now. I told him I had been at work and that he knew better than I where my little boy was. He said nothing and left.]

That night my husband returned. He had left our little boy with a Ukrainian woman named Anna Rudaya, who promised to find a refuge for him. We managed to throw all of our things to her over the fence, so our child was taken care of for the time being. The next day Kroshka showed up and searched the cellar, the attic, and everywhere else for my little boy. "Your little blondie wasn't on the truck," he told me. "I know your little boy very well." He had noticed him during a roll call. They did not find Shura.

Anna Rudaya took my little boy to Polya Medvetskaya, to whom I am forever indebted. She took care of him for six months like he was the apple of her eye. . . . He called her Mama and loved her very much.

On 21 September they transferred us to the village of Bugakov. A different German commandant was there, but he reported to the Nemirov authorities: Henig, Kroshka, and Willy. I was appointed medical aide to the facilities in three Jewish camps: Bugakov, Zarudenets, and Berezovka. It is hard to describe what people endured in those camps. The Germans told me, "Cure them with the whip." A few of the old people who had escaped being shot could not stand up under the hard work and collapsed. They were driven to work with clubs. On Saturday the elderly Mr. Akselrod was driven to work with clubs. He died on Sunday. The old Brunvasser woman had thrombosis of the veins in both her legs. They dragged her by the hair and threw her down the stairs; she died two days later. Soon all the old people died. The young fell ill. There was no warm clothing, and it was freezing cold. They beat us. The senior overseer Maindl tormented us more than anyone else; he tortured my husband in particular and called him the "damned engineer."

I never saw my little boy and was going out of my mind at the thought that the Germans might have found him. In early January I managed to secretly visit him. As I approached the gate, my heart was beating so much that it felt like it would leap out of my throat. I looked around to check whether anyone could see me. Medvetskaya opened the door and shouted, "Shura, look who has come to see you." But Shura did not recognize me; he was quiet and sad and hid behind Polya. Only when I took him by the hand and removed my shawl did he begin to remember everything. Medvetskaya told me that he did not leave the room, that he did not even see the yard. They taught him that he was a nephew from Kiev and that his name was Aleksandr Bakalenko. Whenever strangers would come, he would hide. As I was leaving, Shura gave me an apple: "For Papa." He asked me whether it was true that all the children were killed, and he mentioned his friends by name. I warmly thanked Medvetskaya and left.

I went from camp to camp trying to alleviate the suffering of the sick as best I could. But there were more and more of them, [the sick and the barefoot—their last pair of boots or shoes had been taken away. . . . In the morning the sick could not get up.] The commandant asked me for a list of the sick; knowing that a list meant certain death, I did not give it to him.

[Many realized that we would not escape death. Our only hope was that the Red Army might come, even though we were certain that the Germans would kill us at the last minute.]

Late in the evening on 2 February a policeman took me aside and said, "Doctor, see to it that tomorrow everyone who can stand on their feet goes out to work." I realized that this was a serious matter and tried to warn the sick, but they did not believe me. My husband was sick, and he stayed behind; nearly all the sick stayed behind. At twelve o'clock the next day a convoy of sleighs carrying many policemen pulled up, with the German Maindl at their head. Willy also came from Nemirov. I heard Maindl say, "The sick and the barefoot. . . ." I hid, so that they would not force me to point out the sick. It was horrible. Half-naked people were dragged out into the snow. They took everyone who was more than forty to forty-five years old, as well as everyone who had no shoes or clothing. In the yard they were divided into two groups: those who could still work and those who would die. Next to me stood my friend [Mrs. Grinberg from Bucharest], a beautiful woman of thirty, well dressed, but with torn shoes. They noticed her and dragged her over to the group marked for death; then they dragged me behind her, because I too was wearing just an old pair of flannel slippers. She kept saying, "I'm healthy," and they kept answering, "You have no shoes."

I thought of little Shura, and that gave me strength. My husband stood in the group of those who could work. At the last minute, as they were taking us to the sleighs, I managed to run over to the other group and hide. My friend tried to do the same, but they saw her and severely beat her. A young girl of eighteen begged for permission to go to her death with her mother. Permission was granted. Then, when she was sitting in the sleigh, she grew afraid and wanted to go back, but they would not let her. One woman took poison and tried to give some to her daughter, but she refused to take it. A man tried to escape and was shot. After an hour the group marked for death was taken away, and those who remained were herded back into the camp. [When the healthy ones returned from work at ten o'clock that evening, they saw that their mothers, sisters, and fathers were no more.]

We were transferred to Zarudenets; two-thirds of the people in the camp there had been shot in order to make room for us.

I had gone there on 1 February to look after the sick, and a terrible scene rose up before my eyes. The people were barefoot and covered with rags; their bodies were mutilated with mange and covered with various kinds of sores that you would never encounter under normal conditions. They sat on the floor on some kind of rags and were very seriously concentrating on killing lice. They were so occupied with their work that they did not even notice my arrival. Suddenly there was movement and shouting; the people jumped up, their eyes aglow; some were crying. What could it be? The bread had arrived, and—oh, what joy!—there was a whole loaf for each person! This was unprecedented, something new; salvation was likely near—or so these poor people thought. It turned out that it was due to the usual German efficiency. The Germans knew there would be an "Aktion" on the fifth and that for several days they would not know the exact amount of bread that would be needed, since they could not tell beforehand how many people would be left. So they decided to distribute an "advance" of a whole loaf of bread. . . .

We learned of this calculation only after we found ourselves in the Zarudenets death camp.

Along the way, they once again took everyone who could not walk and put them on the sleighs. People marked for death were gathered together in Chukov; they were from Nemirov,

Berezovka, Zarudenets, Bugakov. They were held there for two days, naked, without food or water, and then murdered.

When we were at work Meister Dehr told us that he had been present at the execution (he call it "die Aktion"); he said it was not as terrible as we think. We later found out that, although they were classified as employees of the Schter firm, Meister Dehr and Maindl were actually SS men....

In the twilight of the winter dawn, when it was still dark, we were driven to work with whips. Miserable people hurriedly tied bags of straw around their torn shoes so their feet would not freeze. They wrapped pieces of old blankets around their head and tied a rope around their waist.... We were counted several times and then herded out to the road. It was hard for these tormented people to raise themselves up; their feet—covered with wounds and wrapped in wet rags and straw—could hardly move through the deep snow. And still it snowed; it snowed without end. They drove us on for five kilometers. Once we reached the work site, we breathed a sigh of relief, took out our shovels, and started clearing away the snow. Suddenly there was a commotion: "The Black One is coming" [(Maindl)]. All eyes were filled with fear; the shovels were moving furiously, and everyone was trying to grow smaller, less noticeable, so as not to draw attention to himself. "Stop working," he shouted. "You have to go eight kilometers from here and clear the road."

The steppe was endless and white, the snow was deep, and the snowflakes churned in the storm, so that you could hardly see a thing. In the sleigh sat the tall black German [with a long whip in his hand, furiously driving two hundred shadows of wretched human beings]. My feet were getting heavier, and my heart was about to burst through my chest; it seemed like we would never make it to the end of this wild march. [But the instinct to live is powerful; we struggled on and finally came to the designated site. The sleigh stopped], and a vicious, mocking gaze fell upon the tormented people....

[I went to work with the others clearing snow.]

On 8 February a woman I did not know came up to me and said, "I am Polya Medvetskaya's sister. Take Shura. My sister was denounced, and she hid him with a distant relative." She said that several Jewish children had been hidden in Nemirov, but they were found, and on 5 February all of them were killed at Chukov. Only Shura was left.

What could I do? When I was working as a doctor in the camps, sometimes I would go out to the peasants and treat them. It was very dangerous for me to do this, since Maindl told me, "If I should find out that you have been in a Ukrainian's home, I'll shoot you on the spot." But there was no physician in these villages, and I could not refuse them whenever they asked me to come and help a sick person. Kirill Baranchuk's family lived near our camp. I often went there because Kirill had a sick father. Baranchuk once told me that he would like to take people like us, hold us close to his chest, and carry us across the Bug. I remembered his words. I asked Polya Medvetskaya's sister to go to Baranchuk and tell him that I am begging him on my knees to go to Nemirov and take the boy in for a few days. We would think of something later.

Kirill saved Shura. He brought him back from Nemirov wrapped in his big fur coat. His wife and two children, Nastya and Nina, surrounded my little boy with warmth and love. They came out to the road and said that Shura was alive and asking for us.

We decided to escape: we had to save Shura.

At 2:00 a.m. on 26 February my husband said, "Get up." We waited until the policeman went inside to warm himself and then climbed over the wire. We went to Kirill Baranchuk. He was very good to us, even though it could have meant death for him. We stayed with him for four days and gathered our strength; on 2 March Kirill Baranchuk and his uncle, Onisy Zamerzly, took us to Perepelitsy, toward the Bug. The village was full of German border guards, and none of the peasants would let us in. We knew we had nothing to lose, so at three in the morning we just started across the Bug. With our child in his arms, my husband led the way. It was a dark night. The ice was beginning to thaw, and I fell through into the water up to my knee, but I did not cry out. Shura noticed, but he too remained silent. Finally we made it to the other shore.

Some peasants took us into their hut, where we warmed ourselves and rested. Then they gave us some peasant clothes. We set out on foot for Mogilev-Podolsky, posing as refugees from Kiev. On 10 March we arrived in Mogilev [and ended up in the ghetto]. There we suffered more derision and torture, but we endured until the Red Army came. Then we could live free. . . . But the terrible wounds will remain for the rest of my life: my parents, my two younger brothers, my older brother and his wife, their two children—the younger of whom was a talented musician—all died at the hands of the German. My husband's mother and sister perished as well.

My heart is like a stone. I believe that if it were cut, it would not bleed.

Prepared for publication by R. Kovnator [and I. Ehrenburg]

The Extermination of the Jews of Lvov

The Germans entered Lvov on the morning of 1 July 1941.

[The Germans marched, sang, and spread terror everywhere. No one would come out of his house.]

There was a German patrol on every corner. A Hitlerite demonstrated to a bunch of city hoodlums gathered around him how they were going to hang the Jews. He kept shouting, "Juden kaput!" {Everyone was having a good time; all of them were laughing.}

The round-up of the Jews began. Working with the Gestapo, the local fascists started dragging Jews from their apartments and taking them off to the Lvov prison and to various barracks.

At the entrance to the site where they had been gathered the Jews had their clothing torn off and the money and valuables taken away from them. The fascists beat people bloody and tormented them in every way imaginable. [They forced them to lick the floor with their tongues and to clean the windows with chicken feathers.

The Jews were lined up in a row and forced to beat each other. Whenever the SS men thought the blows were too weak, they would drag the victim in question from the line and demonstrate on him how to beat someone to death. The rest of them would then be forced to hit each other in the face while the executioners laughed. After that they were shot.]

In the first Aktion, known as "Bloody Tuesday," five thousand Jews were murdered.

The unfortunate people who were left did not even have time to recover from the shock, when, on Thursday, 5 July, men and women were taken away, supposedly to work. They gathered on the square next to Polchinskaya Street; after two weeks of torture, they were led away and shot. Several men managed to escape. The SS took anything they liked from the Jews' apartments and loaded it onto trucks.

Regular army troops carried out the initial pogroms and plundering.

Behind them came the Gestapo and the German administrative staff.

On 15 June 1941 Lieutenant General Friedrich Katzmann,[25] the primary executioner of the Jews of the Western Ukraine, issued an order stipulating the following:

1.   All Jews over twelve years of age had to wear a white armband with a six-pointed star embroidered on it. Appearing on the streets without the armband was punishable by death.

2.   Under the pain of death, Jews were not allowed to change their place of residence without the permission of the German Office for Jewish Affairs.

Friedrich Katzmann was the head of the Office of Jewish Affairs for all of the Western Ukraine. He appointed his own deputies: Lex in Tarnopol and Krüger in Stanislav. In every city and town he had his own subordinates who organized the concentration camps and the systematic extermination of the Jews.

In Lvov the head of the Gestapo was Major Engels; his office was located on Polchinskaya Street.

The executioners tried to fragment the Jewish masses by dividing them into groups in order to kill even the thought of any possibility of organized resistance. They created the appearance of safety for those whom they wanted to use and thus distracted their attention from the true state of affairs.

[Among the Jews there were many metal workers, mechanics, and master craftsmen who were needed in German industry. The Germans used their labor in factories and military installations. Among the Jews there were, of course, many healthy and robust people, whom the Germans took away to do the unskilled labor required in the concentration camps.]

The first to be murdered by the Germans were old people, children, women, and people who were sick and unable to work. They were killed during the pogroms, taken off to prison, and led into the "forest of death."

[The Jewish worker was very profitable for them: in most cases he not only did not receive any wages, but he had to paid for his "Arbeitskarte" himself, just to postpone death for a short while or to avoid the camp, where death also awaited them.]

If a Jew could not produce his work certificate during a round-up, he was shot.

From December 1941 every working Jew had to wear an armband with the letter *A* ("Arbeitsjude") and his work certificate number embroidered on it. Anyone who did not have the armband designated by the Arbeitsamt was killed during the liquidation operations.

The unemployed forged work certificates and embroidered armbands similar to those issued by the Arbeitsamt.

It was discovered, however, that spies were denouncing them to the officials at the Arbeitsamt. Then the previous certificates were annulled and "Meldekarten" were handed out to replace them. In this way the Germans maintained strict control over all the "Arbeitsjuden" and all the "Nichtsarbeitsjuden."

A Jewish worker was not paid for his labor. Nor did he always receive the 100 grams of bread that was allotted to him each day.

In addition to wearing the armbands, as of November 1941 Jews working for German companies had to wear a white patch embroidered either with the letter *W* (Wehrmacht) or with the letter *R* (Rüstung), [which indicated that the Jew was working directly for the arms industry.]

The Germans partitioned off the ghetto area with a high fence.

On 12 November a large number of armed Gestapo men appeared at the gate. They detained everyone who was going out to work. If a person did not have a patch with a *W* or an *R* on it, he was taken away to be executed. Twelve thousand people perished as a result of this two-day check at the gate.

In December the ghetto was closed. Two sentry booths for Gestapo guards were set up at the gate. It was permitted to leave the ghetto only in groups in the morning. By the end of December the Germans had begun transferring workers into barracks. Every business enterprise was assigned a barracks. Thus the workers were separated from the non-workers. The former were housed on Zamarstynovskaya, Loket, Kushevich, and Kresovaya Streets; the latter in Kleparov.

The Germans used their agents to spread provocative rumors about setting up a ghetto for "Nichtsarbeitsjuden" (for those who were not working); this calmed the poor, tormented people down a bit and ignited a faint hope in their hearts.

But every hope disappeared after the tragic events that took place in Kleparov.

On the night of 4 January 1942 shooting broke out in the streets of the ghetto. It was the signal for a new "Aktion."

On the morning of 5 January the "January Massacre" began. The workers were herded off to work, and the Germans started hunting down the rest.

During the "liquidation campaign" of November Jews were taken to Belzec[26] and murdered. But many Jews broke through the boards in the train cars and escaped; the Germans never caught them. In order to prevent it from happening again, the Germans conducted the January "campaign" in a slightly different manner. They killed the Jews locally, hauling them off, for example, to Pyaskova Gura. The Germans burned down the houses in which no Jews were found. Those who had been hiding in secret passageways, in cellars, attics, or ovens perished in the flames.

The unrestrained representatives of the "master race" did not spare a single woman during this "campaign." They raped and murdered the women or threw them into burning houses.

All of Kleparov was ravaged; the only things left were the streets with the barracks.

About twenty thousand Jews were now left to live on a few small streets; they endured the most varied forms of torture before going to their deaths.

German policemen stood around the guard booths with leaders of the ghetto. They were checking to see whether the "R" and "W" patches had been forged. It was very easy to tell.

Many embroidered these letters themselves in order to make it possible for them to leave the ghetto each day and go to the "Aryan sector" with the group of workers. Those who remained in the ghetto risked their lives, since the Germans would search the barracks every day and send everyone they found to the prison. The letters issued by the German establishments had been embroidered by machine with a special stitch, and no one could duplicate them with perfect accuracy. Scharführer Siller was a specialist at catching people with a phony "R" or "W"; because he was so highly skilled at catching Jews, he was transferred to the Janowska camp.[27]

.... Prison. Dark, miserable rooms with neither bunks nor benches. Damp, with a putrid smell; small barred windows, through which no light penetrated. The prison was located on Lontskaya Street. It was surrounded on all sides by SS men and a gang of German soldiers, who pulled the shoes and clothing off every new arrival.

In the cell prisoners were not allowed to speak with one another. Those who were arrested were given no food. Why feed them? The Germans were calculating and stingy. Those who fell sick in prison were murdered and then hauled off to the cemetery at night.

Mr. Engels himself often visited the prison. Jews were brought out to the yard for this criminal's amusement. He would torment them and beat them bloody. He liked to play with his victim, promising him life and freedom as he looked for a spark of hope in the prisoner's face. Then he would laugh and kill the man with a bullet from his revolver.

Whenever the prison would become full to overflowing, the Hitlerites would conduct "purges" or "transports." The prisoners were loaded into trucks and taken in groups to Pyaskova Gura, where they were shot.

And yet the prison was always full. If anyone should go out on the street without an armband, it was off to prison! Anyone whose armband was too narrow or who did not bow low enough to a German, he too was off to prison! An SS man would burst into an apartment and arrest a family member. "Why?" the victim would ask. "Don't you know? Because you're a Jew. Sooner or later—it is all the same—you must die."

Chief Engels did not resort to mass pogroms. He arranged "purgings" in the prison. In that way he murdered thousands of old men, children, men, and women.

In the fall of 1941 General-Governor Frank issued an order concerning the forced labor of Jews in the concentration camps in the territory of the Western Ukraine. By the beginning of 1942, the Lvov, Tarnopol, and Stanislov areas were interconnected by a network of concentration camps.

The most terrible of them was the camp in Lvov on Janowska Street; it was called "Janowska" for short. Several thousand Jews from the Western Ukraine were taken there; they were supposed to level a hilly area in order to prepare the site for a new camp. Starving people, worn out from beatings, labored there until they were utterly exhausted. They slept on the ground under the open sky until they finished building their barracks.

The work went on the whole fall and though the winter. People died from hunger and cold. New throngs of Jewish workers were brought in to take the place of those who died.

Every morning before work there was roll call, or the so-called "Appel." All the work units were gathered together with their "group leaders" or "Oberjuden." The "Oberjude" reported who was present in his group to the SS man on duty. After the report, the SS men conducted "morning exercises." After jumping exercise of various sorts and the endless repetition of the order, "Auf, Nieder,"[28] those who were sick and weak were fished out. They were taken to the wire fence, where they were lined up and shot with a machine gun. The dead were then laid out in rows; the living marched off to work. Along the way those who were limping were culled out. They too were murdered. Only the strong and the healthy made it to work.

After the campsite had been prepared, it was paved with tombstones taken from the Jewish cemetery.

Even the dead [Jews] the fascists did not leave in peace. In many cities and villages of the Western Ukraine tombstones were used to pave roads. Once the work of leveling the area was done, the camp was surrounded by barbed wire. The fascist police stood guard.

From the main entrance to the camp one path led to barracks and the kitchen and another to "Death Square," from which people were taken to the hills and shot. Around the camp stood one- and two-story watchtowers for the guards; from the watchtowers the guards could see the entire camp, so that escape was practically impossible.

[The camp had a very gloomy look: the watchtowers, the dismal barracks, people in a silent delirium, and the unbearably saccharine smell of dead bodies.]

Around the vast open yard that served as the site for the morning headcount stood approximately twenty barracks for the inmates. In each of the barracks there were plank beds with several tiers, on which was scattered a small quantity of filthy straw. Behind the barracks was a kitchen, where a watery swill was cooked twice a day; in the morning they handed out two pieces of stale ersatz-bread.

"Newcomers" slept on the bare ground.

The SS criminals who worked in the camp were the most highly honored students of the masters at Dachau[29] and Mauthausen.[30]

After quickly graduating from Janowska "university," the former pupils of Gebauer, the head of the camp, went off to various parts of the Western Ukraine to set up their independent "operations."

Inexperienced SS men were brought to Lvov; there they would master the art of murdering and torturing their victims. Once their superiors reached the conclusion that the young SS men were sufficiently trained, they would send them to do their bloody work in a the provincial camps. On the other hand, whenever someone in the provinces had achieved some renown as a refined executioner and a master of his "trade," he would be sent to the Janowska concentration camp. There his less "talented" colleagues would greet him with respect. There executioners generally competed with each other in the perfection of their means and methods of torture.

Under the direct supervision of Katzmann, Himmler's pupils devised special forms of torture, such as "races" and "boards," that exceeded the usual program. These were most often conducted on Sundays.

"Races" consisted of having to run for three or four hundred meters past the SS, who would stick out their feet to trip the runners. If a runner stumbled, he was taken behind the wire fence and murdered. [There were many such victims, for their mutilated feet were so swollen from hunger that the inmates could hardly drag them along.]

The torture known as "boards" consisted of the following: on Sundays, exhausted from their weekday labors, the Jews had to carry logs prepared for the construction of barracks from one place to another. Moving at a run, each man had to bear 150 kilograms on his shoulders. Whoever could not stand up under the weight would get an SS bullet. The Germans' drunken orgies were terrible. On the days of their orgies the SS did not shoot anyone. They pierced the inmates' skulls with lances or smashed them with hammers; they would strangle them or crucify them, driving nails into their living bodies.

Each SS man had his own passion. Gebauer would strangle his victim in a barrel between two boards; others would hang him by their feet; still others would shoot the poor man in the back of the head. The twenty-three-year-old SS man Schönbach devised completely new methods. One Sunday he tied a man to a post and beat him with a rubber truncheon. When the man lost consciousness from the blows and his head slumped over, Schönbach revived him and gave him food and water, so that after a minute or so he could torture his victim again. All the prisoners were gathered into a circle to witness their comrade's terrible suffering. The poor man was guilty of urinating behind the barracks. He had disrupted order in the camp. [A guard noticed it. They tried him on Sunday. They tied him to the post, where he was tortured all day. Blood gushed from his mouth and nose.] Toward evening Schönbach grew tired. He ordered everyone to disperse and placed a guard next to the dying man. The next morning their eyes met with a terrible scene: the bloody post with pieces of a human body hanging from it.

When command of the camp was turned over to Scharführer Willhaus,[31] murders were committed on a massive scale.

From time to time the prisoners were examined. The sick and emaciated were shot with machine guns.

[Jews from the ghetto looked for various ways of saving themselves. They hid with Polish and Ukrainian friends, fled under false names, and made their way into partisan units.]

The prisoners in the camps did not wear armbands. They were issued a number, and a yellow patch was sewn on their back and on their chest. Their bodies were draped in rags.

A prisoner in the camp lived behind a barbed wire fence. He could not break out and was so oppressed mentally that it was difficult for him to even think about resistance.

Thanks to the self-sacrificing, heroic efforts of the Jewish poets, S. Fridman and A. Laun, partisan groups were formed within the camp. They even managed to obtain weapons. Unfortunately, the Germans picked up the organization's trail and shot all the prisoners in their barracks. After that the Germans showed up in the camp more often, and they were always armed. When the attorney Mandl was led to his death, at the last moment he cried out, "Long live the Soviet Union, long live freedom!" His cry resounded throughout the camp [and had a great impact. It was as though people had awakened from a deep sleep, and even those whom the murderers considered their submissive victims realized that passivity only played into the hands of the Germans.]

The resistance organization began recruiting young men from among the inmates to fight against the Germans. One young man, a butcher from Lvov, attacked a Gestapo man and strangled him. In the Chvartakov camp a young Pole shot the camp commandant. Such incidents were occurring more and more frequently.

Jews marked for "liquidation" were brought to the assembly point in the Janowska camp. At the entrance a German with a pencil on his hand pedantically counted them and made a note of the doomed people. The young men were left in the camp; all the rest were taken to the train station, where they were loaded into the local trains cars. [Everyone knew what this meant.] In the camp tragic scenes broke out. People were crying. Some went insane and were dancing around and laughing out loud. Hungry children were wailing incessantly.

A chief executioner in the Janowska camp, the "musician" Rokita,[32] once stepped onto his apartment's balcony overlooking the camp. He was having trouble sleeping after lunch. Very calmly and for a long time he fired a machine gun into the crowd.

Many Jews were deported from Lvov under the pretense of "resettlement" and annihilated.

The August sun burned unmercifully. People were fainting from thirst and begging for water, but the executioners who were standing guard remained cruel and merciless. The trains departed at night. People had all their clothing taken away from them. Along the way many broke planks off the cars and jumped from the train. They ran through the fields naked. The

German guards, who were usually in the last car, shot bursts of machine gun fire at them.

The railroad tracks from Lvov to Rava Russkaya were littered with Jewish bodies.

All the new trains carrying Jews from Brussels, Paris, and Amsterdam ran through Rava Russkaya. Transports from Tarnopol, Kolomya, Sambor, Brzeżany, and other cities in the Western Ukraine.

[Fifteen kilometers from Rava Russkaya and Belzec Jews who had been transported under the pretense of "resettlement" were taken out of the train cars;] Belzec was a terrible extermination site for the Jews, and the Germans kept it top secret.

But the railroad workers who drove the trains filled with the condemned victims told their relatives the truth about the extermination of the Jews at Belzec.

The Jews were taken into an enormous hall that could hold up to a thousand people. The Germans had led electric wires along the walls of the hall. The wires had no insulation. The same wires also ran across the floor. As soon as the hall was filled with naked people, the Germans ran a powerful electrical current through the wires.

It was one huge electric chair, the likes of which no criminal fantasy has ever dreamt up.

In another section of the Belzec camp was an enormous soap factory. The Germans picked out the fattest people, murdered them, and boiled them down for soap.

Artur [Izrailevich] Rozenshtraukh—a bank clerk from Lvov, in whose words we relate this testimony—held this "Jewish soap" in his own hands.

The Gestapo thugs never denied the existence of a "production process" of this kind. Whenever they wanted to intimidate a Jew, they would say to him, "We'll make soap out of you."

In early February 1943 the management of the ghetto was turned over to SS officer Grzymek, a Volksdeutsche from Poznan. Tall, heavy-set, and always with a machine gun in his hands, he was terrifying.

Grzymek loved cleanliness. By his order signs were posted on the fence surrounding the ghetto: "Work! Cleanliness! Discipline! There must be order!"

He would ride around the ghetto on horseback, surrounded by his entourage. During roll call he would break the windows in the houses and shoot at people.

Under Grzymek going out to work became pure hellish torture.

Sometimes he would force the Jews to pass through the gate with their "W" and "R" patches in their hands so he could check their authenticity; other times they would have to hold their work permits high above their heads.

Grzymek issued a decree: everyone had to have his head shaved. A barber stood at the gate and cut a strip down the middle of the head of everyone who passed through.

An orchestra played military marches as people passed through the ghetto gate to go to work. One had to march to this music in an orderly manner. Whoever failed to do so became the victim of Grzymek's rubber truncheon.

Every wing of the ghetto had a watchman and a cleaning lady. The streets were swept clean, and the houses were whitewashed; Grzymek supervised all this himself. But scattered in the terrible darkness of these whitewashed houses were half-dead people swollen from hunger and doomed to death.

Typhus broke out in the ghetto. Nearly the entire population came down with the disease. [There was a hospital in the ghetto. But everyone knew that it was a place of death. Many died, and those who were left became cripples.] The sick were not treated; instead, from time to time they were hauled of to Pyaskova Gura and shot.

Friends and relatives would hide a sick person in a shelter, where he would suffer the cold and often go without food.

His employer would cross the sick person's name off the list of workers and turn it in to the Gestapo. A special commission of SS men would search the apartments for the sick person. An SS officer named Heinisch, as big as a bear, was renowned for his searches for the sick. Those who had lost consciousness he would shoot on the spot; those who were recuperating he would send to the prison.

Honest Poles and Ukrainians were deeply disturbed by these unprecedented crimes, by the mass extermination of completely innocent people. It became necessary to somehow exercise some influence over the local population. That was the task of the press: the German paper called the *Lemberger Deutsche Zeitung*, the *Gazeta Lwowska*, and the *Lvivskiye Visti*.

Every day in the disgusting pages of these papers there appeared Judeophobic notices and articles describing how "German genius is demonstrating its implacability toward the inferior race" (the Jews) and how "historical justice is punishing the damned kikes with a German hand."

These articles had only one purpose: to arouse the hatred of the Poles and the Ukrainians toward the Jews.

Katzmann published a notice stating that hiding Jews was punishable by death.

The German newspapers conducted an "elucidation campaign." They wrote that the German was carrying out the liquidation of the Jews for the sake of the Aryan peoples. "Jews have long been preparing to rule over the world." [In order to demonstrate this stupid notion, they inserted some quotes from the Bible and the Talmud.]

The Germans wrote that they were "liquidating" the Jews in response to the pogroms that they had inflicted upon the German population in Bydgoszcz, Poznan, and other cities. [But no one reacted to this stupid provocation.]

Under conditions of the most terrible savagery and monstrous violence the Jewish population tried in every possible way to save itself from extinction. Many left Lvov and went to stay in Warsaw, Krakow, Czëstochowa, and other cities in Western Poland under assumed names. Others, also using assumed names, moved to the "Aryan section" of Lvov, [where they lived and worked posing as Poles and Ukrainians.] The Gestapo soon found out about all this; [the Germans decided to put an end to "false Aryans."] The Germans flooded Lvov with secret agents, who eagerly carried out the mission entrusted to them. They hung around the streets, the post office, and the train stations in huge numbers. They rapaciously eyed every person suspected of being of Jewish origin. They took their victims to the "Kripo" (Kriminalpolizei), where officials would quickly determine whether the person in question was a Jew; as for women, they were tortured until they themselves did not know whether they were Jewish or not. The Germans generously rewarded agents [who caught "false Aryans."] But it happened that Jews too rewarded the agents—with bullets. On Streletsky Square a secret agent went up to a young Jew who had forged ["Aryan"] documents and demanded to see his papers. The agent had obviously recognized him as a Jew. Instead of his papers, however, the Jew immediately pulled out a revolver, killed the agent, and ran away. The story of Lina Haus, a teacher in the Jewish high school, created a sensation in Lvov. Lina was posing as a Polak and living on Yakhovich Street. She had changed her name and was working for a German firm. A secret agent became suspicious of her. He went to her house to check her papers.

He was found dead, with a towel wrapped around his neck. The Germans put up wanted posters with her picture on it and promised a large sum of money to anyone who brought her in. But it was all in vain: Lina Haus had disappeared.

It happened that Jews who knew French very well would change into French military uniforms and go to live with them in a concentration camp.

Many Jews hid among the Poles and Ukrainians. No matter how much the Germans tried to corrupt the souls of the people with the threat of death, execution, treachery, and greed, the people remained brave, honorable, and capable of heroic deeds. The Polish intelligentsia saved many Jewish children from death. [For the most part, however, and for obvious reasons, they could take in only girls.]

Several Polish priests took Jewish girls and hid them in churches; they saved those children from death. More than one of those noble people paid with their own lives for saving Jewish children. . . .

After the Germans were defeated at Stalingrad, a committee for armed resistance against the Germans was organized in the Lvov Ghetto. Among others, the Jewish poets Ya. Shudrikh and S. Fridman served on this committee.

The organization was in contact with the Polish committee and began publishing an underground newspaper that was circulated from hand to hand. Revolvers were purchased with funds raised by the committee; several people who worked for German military organizations managed to steal some weapons. Soon secret military training was underway. Delegates from the committee made their way into Brody to make contact with the Volhynia partisans. Among them was the physician Lina Goldberg, who enthusiastically set about organizing a partisan movement in Lvov. The flow of weapons into the ghetto went without interruption. People returning from work would sneak in a gun instead of food. During a search at the gate the SS once found a weapon on a teenager. They shot him on the spot. From that day on there were frequent searches in the barracks. A cache of weapons was found on Lokietek Street. The Germans searched for the organizers but could not find them.

People started fleeing the ghetto both in groups and individually. . . .

The committee searched for every means of transferring people to Brody, which was the center for armed resistance. Three trucks were rented for a great deal of money and with the greatest precaution. The first three transports of ghetto fighters went very well. They quickly and boldly joined the partisans. In this group were many young people who knew the roads and the trails in the area very well.

The partisans successfully attacked German farmsteads and obtained provisions. They set up ambushes and took weapons from the German soldiers.

They were not alone in their struggle. Representatives from the Volhynia partisans were sent to supply them with explosives—with tolite and dynamite—for sabotage.

The Brody partisans once attacked a German outpost near Brody, right on the border between the *Generalgouvernement* and the "Ostgebiet." The guard was killed, and machine guns and grenades were confiscated. The partisans became a threat to the Germans throughout the region.

The German gendarmes did everything they could to discover the partisan unit's whereabouts. But it was impossible to find the their headquarters. They managed to move from place to place.

When the committee received word that the final liquidation of the ghetto was near, they decided to go into the forest and continue the struggle. The poet Ya. Shudrikh was supposed to have been in a group of seventeen people who were planning to leave.

Their departure was scheduled for 8 May 1943 at six o'clock in the morning. But on that morning the truck carrying the partisans was surrounded by the SS on Zyblikevich Street. The partisans saw that they had fallen into a trap and decided that their lives would come at a high cost to the Germans. Shooting broke out, and several SS men were fatally wounded. A new SS unit arrived to help the Germans, and they disarmed the partisans. They killed every last one of them. At dawn on 9 May the Brody forest was surrounded by a battalion of German infantry.

The fighting against the far superior German forces lasted for three days. Only a few partisans managed to break through the lines, make their way to the Lublin forest, and there continue their struggle. The rest died a heroic death with their weapons in their hands. Not a single one surrendered alive to the Germans.

Sensing that their end was near, the Germans began hastening the murder of the Jews.

One ghetto after another disappeared: Przemysl, Sambor, Rudki, Brzeżany, Tarnopol, Jaworów, Żólkiew, Przemyślany, Jaryczów.

Just before the liquidation of the ghetto in Lvov, it suddenly grew very calm. Grzymek rarely came outside. [There were no guards at the gates. The Germans organized soccer games and concerts in the ghetto.] The SS no longer burst into Jewish apartments. Everyone knew, however, that this was the calm before the storm. On 25 April the Germans took the last four thousand people imprisoned in the Janowska camp to Pyaskova Gura to be executed.

On 1 June 1943 at 3:00 A.M. the SS entered the ghetto to finish the bloody task they had started in 1941. It was the final liquidation. [They took everyone, even those who were working in German businesses.] Certificates with the SS stamp and patches with a "W" and an "R" were annulled.

The liquidation "campaign" was led by Katzmann, Engels, Lenard, Willhaus, Inguart, and Schönbach. All day SS units and fascist police searched homes and threw grenades into cellars where people were hiding. On the third day fire trucks entered the ghetto. Jews were being burned alive. Lokietek, Kresowa, and Sharanovich streets were burned to the ground. The people hiding there were choking from the smoke and at the last minute came running out of the fire. The Gestapo did not shoot; they tried to take their victims alive and then throw them back into the flames.

During the first days some tried to resist. Those who had weapons began shooting in a confused manner. Two policemen were killed, and several SS men were wounded. This only made the executioners even more furious. They killed women and children by throwing them off balconies; they took axes and chopped off men's heads. The streets of the ghetto were littered with bodies.

The sky above the ghetto grew black with the smoke from the fires. For a long time the cries of children being murdered rose up to the heavens. They received no answer.

We have told the truth. This fascist crime cannot be hidden from humanity, even though the murderers tried with all their might to leave not a single living witness.

Witnesses survived. They include Naftali Nakht, a teenager from Lvov, who escaped and joined the partisans; Leopold Shor, also a refugee from Lvov; Likhter Uri, who was saved from the executioners when he joined up with the partisans in the Zolochevsky forest; Artur Rozenshtraukh, a bank clerk from Lvov; Lily Herts, who spent thirteen days in a sealed hiding place in the ghetto.

This crime can be neither forgotten nor forgiven by humanity.

Reported by I. Herts and Naftali Nakht
prepared for publication by R. Fraerman[33] and R. Kovnator

Thirteen Days in Hiding: The Story of Lily Herts (Lvov)

We are sitting in our hiding place. Murders are taking places in the streets of the ghetto. You can hear the Germans shooting and the cries of the people they are killing.

Our hiding place is in the attic. It has two sections separated by a brick wall. The entrance is well masked.

There are about forty of us, and it is very stuffy. We have very little water.

The Germans rest at night, so it is quiet until morning.

At about five o'clock the sounds of something like someone ringing a bell start to reach us. At first the sounds are faint and isolated; then they turn into a terrible cry rising up from somewhere, drowning out even the shooting. It is the cry of someone being murdered.

In the hiding place no one moves. The Rozenbergs' tiny baby quietly moans. Finally he breaks out crying, and we are all in the power of the squealer: he can give us away. We give the mother some sugar; someone else offers her a bottle of milk—anything to quiet the child.

Very late at night, when everything is quiet, we come out of the hiding place. The doors to the apartments are opened. We squeeze together on the messed up bed to get some sleep after a torturous day.

But soon the shots can be heard again. We quickly go back into the hiding place; it is so crowded there.

The footsteps of the police grow louder and louder. They have been looking for us, but they cannot find us. Furious over their failure but certain that someone is in the building, they bellow, "Come on out! You stupid people! We'll shoot!"

The baby starts crying. We go numb with fear. This is the end. They are going to find us. What shall we do?

We will not come out. Let them shoot us.

"Open up! Hurry! [You damned kikes!"

Someone pushes the door open.]

The Germans do not come in. They are afraid.

The baby is crying at the top of its lungs. I say farewell to my husband.

The Germans have come up on the roof and are taking it apart, so they can shoot from there. The rafters over our heads have already started to creak. Everyone rushes to the door in a panic.

I try to hide. There is no one in the attic. I crawl under the mattress in the corner. Maybe they will not find me. But someone is pulling on my coat.

We find ourselves in the small hallway. My husband is standing across from me, leaning against the wall. He is pale and says nothing. I go up to him, and once again we say farewell.

They count us: one, two, three. . . eight. . . [thirty-five.]

Suddenly there is a commotion. Someone is running up the stairs. Iska shields me with his body and pushes me through the open door of another apartment.

"Save yourself, if you can!" he says and then disappears. I run through the kitchen and into a room. Everything is scattered everywhere. I crawl under a pile of pillows and feather quilts and lie there without moving a muscle. I hear nothing and feel nothing. My body has turned to wood; only my heart is beating. I am suffocating. My mouth is parched. I wait. I know they will notice that someone is missing and will come.

God, what is that? Shooting, and it sounds so close. It must be in the kitchen.

"You can't even get drunk around here," someone says in German.

He is looking through the cupboard. He is looking for vodka. Then he comes into the room. He looks all around. I hold my breath. If only it would be quick! Let him shoot, but just let it be quick! I gulp. He stooped down, and he has something, some paper in his hands; it is money. My leg is sticking out from under the quilt, and I cannot pull it back in. If he trips over it, I am dead.

But no! He is going away. He is really going away. Just one more minute of intense hiding. I listen with all my strength at how quickly the footsteps fade down the stairs. At last it is completely quiet. I crawl out, but there is no time to rest. I must find a good hiding place. I get up. There is still someone in the room. It is Bronya, Iska's sister.

"By what miracle did you wind up here?"

"Iska pushed me in here at the last second."

We do not have time to talk. We run back to the attic. Behind the brick partition there are still some people whom they did not find. They are the owners of the building. . . . We knock.

"Let us in! Quickly! The Germans could come back!"

There were still sixteen people in the hiding place. Men, women, children, and a three-year-old boy, Dzyunya. We do not talk. The June sun burns mercilessly through the roof.

The night we longed for has come. We creep out from the hiding place and collect some water in a bottle, so that we shall have a supply for the next day.

In the attic we sleep the sleep of the dead. Even after the sun shines through the cracks, we are still asleep.

Lyusya anxiously awakens us.

"Get up! To the hiding place, quickly! Some sort of fire trucks are here."

Once again we crawl into our lair. We hear explosions. It is the Germans chasing people out of their hiding places with grenades. After the explosions we hear screams and groans. We hear the Germans shouting.

"Leonard, look, I dropped her with one shot, and she was really far away!"

"Aha!" yells another German. "Flutter out, little birds! That's it! And now we'll roast you over the fire, [you damned kikes!"]

"Just don't throw me into the fire! Shoot me! O, God!" a woman's cries come from above.

A thin wisp of smoke comes through the cracks in the roof. It stings my throat, which is already dry from thirst and fear.

Little Dzyunya has his hands clasped over his mouth. He knows he must not say a word. Large beads of sweat fall from his face.

"Maybe it would be better to go out. Isn't it better to die from a bullet than to be burned alive?" I say.

"We won't go out," says Bronya. "The Germans won't burn our building: it's right next to a German hospital."

"They'll burn us alive. Open up!" Lida pleads.

"Let's burn it down!" we hear the voice of a German on the roof.

"More gasoline!" a fireman shouts.

There is an evil sound; a liquid sprays out of hose and hits the roof. It comes through the crack and drips on our steaming heads. Strangely, it refreshes us.

"This isn't gasoline, it's water!" we tell each other with gestures. They wanted to scare us. They thought we would hear the order to burn the place down and would come out.

If only the ones standing on the roof do not find us! But they continue to pour on the water, and the sound of the water drowns out our breathing.

"Stop the water!" a fireman shouts.

Apparently they are protecting our building from the fire so that it will not spread to the hospital.

The voices fade away.

All we can hear is the rumbling of red-hot tin, the roar of the flames, and the screams of dying people.

Late at night we come out of the hiding place to look through the openings in the roof; we can see Loket Street in flames.

From somewhere at the end of the street we hear the voice of a dying boy: "I beg you, just one more bullet! I beg y-y-y-oo-o-ou-u-u, just one more bu-u-u-l-l-let!"

Toward morning the screams of burning people subside. Our hiding place has been transformed into a real hell. We are tormented with hunger and thirst, and the lice feed on us relentlessly. We are sweating and suffocating from the heat.

Dzyunya keeps asking for sugar and water. He is pounding on his mother and pulling my hair. We speak in whispers. Someone is wailing half aloud. Those who are mourning their dead children lament and moan in a whisper.

"If only I could strangle one of these murderers with my own hands, how sweet would death be to me then! But I just sit here and wait helplessly," says Lida.

Evening comes. For the first time I go downstairs. My head is spinning. We have not eaten now for several days. I must find some underwear so we can change clothes, because the lice will give us no peace. I sneak into my apartment without making a sound, so that the German patrols will not hear me.

In the darkness I find a jar of sugar and take it for Dzyunya. Something white is hanging from a clothesline. Underwear! I greedily grab hold of it and go back to the attic.

The underwear is torn from my hands. We change into it immediately.

"God, is it possible for a human being to feel so good!" one woman exclaims. "Go back down. Don't be afraid. Maybe you'll find something to eat. That would be a real joy!"

Once again I go down the stairs, this time into another apartment; I trip over the body of a murdered woman. There is something soft and cold under my hand. I hurry back upstairs without any bread. I no longer want anything to eat.

I am standing in the little hallway that leads out to the balcony. I can hear shots. It is the Hitlerite guards shooting at someone trying to escape. . . .

Someone must have spotted us during the night, because just before morning on the seventh day we could hear Germans talking right next to us.

"There are probably Jews here. We have to check it out very carefully."

"Who wants to fool around with them? Use the grenades!" a German gives the order.

We hear one explosion, then another. One grenade blasts through the roof. Dust comes down from the vibrations and settles on our faces.

We keep quiet. You will not frighten us. We have nothing more to fear. Little Dzyunya, our little hero, helps us. He calms down the others.

"Mama, if I sit quietly, will you give me some sugar?"

"I'll give you all you want."

"Mama, will we kill all the Gestapo will we get out of here?"

"Yes, just sit quietly. . ."

{"We'll burn them too. That'll be good."

"Don't talk that way. Sit still."

"Why do they burn people, then? We should do it to them too!"

"What are we to do with him?" the mother asks in despair. "He keeps running off at the mouth."}

At the time the ghetto was still on fire. We heard the voice of a man outside whom the Germans were murdering. Before he died he asked the murderers for water. What a strange man!

Something unimaginable is happening with our little Dzyunya. He is chattering and crying. They are searching our building again, pounding on the ceiling, walls, and floor.

"Tell me a story! Do you hear? Or I'll scream!" says little Dzyunya.

"Look, sweetie, as soon as it gets quiet, I'll tell you a wonderful fairy tale."

"I want it now. Do you hear. Or I'll start screaming!"

Suddenly there is a knock above us. Everyone falls silent in horror.

In a whisper I start to tell a fairy tale, drawing out every word. I am trying to hold the little boy's attention for as long as possible.

"You know, Dzyunya," I say to him, "when we come out of the hiding place, Papa will come, and he will buy you a pony."

Also drawing out his words, Dzyunya answers, "You're lying. Papa won't come: the Gestapo killed him."

"Dzyunya, pull my hair," I tell him.

He pulls my hair. But this does not distract him for long.

His face is burning. He is drinking water constantly. We are even wiping the water off of him. But it is all in vain. He turns around and cries out at every sound coming from outside.

We are utterly exhausted from fear, hunger, and thirst.

{"We must poison him," says someone. "He can't take this torment. He'll be the death of himself and us too."

His mother jumped over to her little boy. No! She would not allow it! If you have enough poison for her too, then go ahead. But there is enough poison for only one, and it belongs to Lida.}

Toward evening the Germans enter our building. They are talking loudly, as usual.

Suddenly Dzyunya gets up and looks around with insane eyes.

"Now," he says, "I'm going to scream real loud, so they'll come!"

We cover his mouth. His mother pleads with him, kisses him, and cries. Nothing helps. He bites her hands and kicks her stomach.

How great our suffering must have been, for even a little boy to go insane!

He died. Late at night his mother takes little Dzyunya's body down to the cellar and buries it.

On the thirteenth day, a Sunday, the ghetto falls silent. A German patrol is running up and down the streets, but seldom are shots heard. We decide to escape that night.

The night is favorable toward us. There are no stars, no moon, no fires. We listen carefully to be sure there are no guards nearby. But all around there is only silence, interrupted now and then by a single shot.

"We are most likely going to our death," says Lida.

"Better to die from a bullet than to die here from filth, hunger, and fear," says Bronya, who all the while has kept up our courage.

We divide up into two groups. They go to the right, and we go to the left. I feel as though I have been buried all these days, and that now I have emerged from a grave. Across from us is Loket Street. It would take only a few steps to get there. But we are in no condition to move. Bronya pushes us from behind. We walk in single file, clinging to the walls of the buildings. Fires are still burning in several places; they light up the ghetto to scare escapees.

Lvov is asleep. Blinds are drawn over the windows of the apartments. Some drunken men come out of a building. They are singing loudly. We squeeze through a gate, so they will not notice us. They go by. I know of a little house nearby; it belongs to a Polish woman. She will probably help us. I knock on the window.

"Who is it?" she asks.

"It's me, Lily. Open up, I beg you!" I say quietly.

The lady takes us in. She brews coffee, fries some eggs, and puts everything out for us on the table.

"I'll hide you in the hay shed, since there is an order forbidding us, under pain of death, to take Jews into our apartments," she says.

The hay shed will be fine for us, if only they do not find us.

We sit there, hiding in the hay, and speak in whispers.

At about ten o'clock in the evening I go to the lady of the house. I want to know if she has any information about Iska. I creep up to the back window and quietly tap on the glass. I cannot be seen from there, and in that little corner I can talk with her.

Suddenly Germans on motorcycles ride into the yard.

"Someone must have informed on us," the thought flashes through my mind.

I am not wrong. One of them goes straight to the hay shed and pulls Bronya out.

"I beg you, please spare me. I'm only twelve years old. What could my life matter to you?"

"Shut up! Damned bitch!"

From my corner I can see all of this. Bronya is standing there pale and erect.

"Where's the other one?" a German asks.

"She left this morning. I don't know where she is."

"We'll find her!"

They shove Bronya with a rifle butt, and she goes, stumbling. Once again I am saved.

Prepared for publication by R. Fraedman and [R. Kovnator]

My Comrade the Partisan Yakov Barer (A Letter from Boris Khandros)

I was born in 1924. When I was fourteen I became a member of the Komsomol.[34] I wrote poetry. In 1941 I graduated from high school. I volunteered to go to the front. I was wounded in the leg during the siege of Kiev. An old lady hid me and nursed me back to health. The front was far away. I returned to Pridnestrove. A village schoolteacher named Tamara Buryk and I organized a resistance group. We survived the hard summer of 1942. Once again I was fighting the Germans.

I met Yakov Barer early in 1944. He was a strong, well-built youth. He spoke German beautifully. He joined our unit and fought courageously. On 17 March 1944, I was seriously wounded in the chest; a bullet had pierced my lung. Yakov carried me away under fire.

Yakov lived in Lvov. He was a furrier. After 1939 he was able to go to school and was preparing to enter the university. But then the Germans came. Like all the Jews of Lvov, Yakov was doomed.

The Germans took him to work one day. When he returned home that evening, neither his grandmother nor his thirteen-year-old brother was there; they had been taken to Belzec, to the "death factory." Jews from Lvov, as well as from Poland and France, were murdered there. Soon Yakov too was on his way there. But he jumped from the train.

In the autumn of 1942 Yakov wound up in a concentration camp near Lvov. The commandant of the camp never sent Jews off to be shot. He would walk up to the doomed man and talk about plans for improvements and the humanity of the Führer; as soon as the man started to believe in his salvation, the commandant would strangle him. He was nicknamed "the strangler." He had a glass booth built on a high platform. A Jew would be placed in the glass booth: there he would die before everyone's eyes. The strangler forced the Jews to dig deep pits and then fill them in again with earth. Once the Jews were digging up the ground along the edge of the camp. Yakov hid; the column went back to the barracks. He heard the guard call out. Then he jumped up and killed the German with his shovel. He took the guard's uniform and checked the name on the pass: Max Waller. Then Yakov headed for the barracks where his younger brother and eight of his friends from Lvov were kept. He started speaking to them in such a foreign voice that even his brother did not recognize him. "Get your stuff together!" he ordered them. Silently they all set out on their last journey. The sentry at the gate was not surprised; Jews were taken out to be shot every night. "What are you doing, brother," the sentry joked, "purifying the air?"

That was Yakov Barer's first feat.

Yakov decided to head east. They came to a railway freight station. Yakov noticed a crate of books in one of the cars bound for Dnepropetrovsk. Nine Jews hid behind the crate, while Yakov, wearing the SS uniform, stood guard.

They split up in Dnepropetrovsk. Yakov stayed with his brother. They wandered around for a long time. Yakov had to get rid of the SS uniform: the gendarmes were arresting deserters. In September 1943 they reached Pervomaisk. There Yakov befriended his former teacher Mikolaichik. Yakov obtained a radio receiver; they listened to the Soviet bulletins and passed the news on to others. The SD took an interest in Yakov. He left, but the Germans killed his younger brother.

I have seen the photographs and documents on the Germans that Yakov killed. Yakov does not like to tell about what he did during the war; it is very hard for him to recall the deaths of his friends and relatives.

He and I parted in the hospital. He went west with the Red Army. One thing kept him alive: the longing to see a Soviet Lvov. . . .

22 July 1944
Prepared for publication by Ilya Ehrenburg

In the Penyatsky Forests: A Letter from an Intelligence Officer (Lvov District)

Two villages were located in the Penyatsky forests. Each was four kilometers from the other. In the village of Guta Penyatsky there were 120 farms; not a single one is left. In that village lived 880 people, both Poles and Jews; they are no longer alive. The Germans surrounded the village, poured gasoline over the houses and sheds, and burned them down with the people inside. Of the 120 farms that were in the village of Guta Verkhobuzhsky only two are left. Not a single one of the residents of Guta Verkhobuzhsky was saved. Not far from these villages, I, Matvey Grigorievich Perlin, an intelligence officer in the Red Army, happened upon two earthen shelters in the forest, where eighty Jews were living. Among them were seventy-five-year-old women, teenage boys and girls, and small children; the youngest was three.

I was the first member of the Red Army they had seen in more than three years of suffering the daily threat of death; they were all trying to squeeze in closer to me, to shake my hand and offer me a few warm words. These people had survived in these holes in the forest for sixteen months, as they hid from persecution. There had been more of them, but only eighty were left. According to their own words, of the forty thousand Jews of the Brodsky and Zolochevsky regions, no more than two hundred people survived. How did they survive? The residents of the villages in the surrounding area gave them provisions, but they did not know exactly where they were hiding. Whenever they came out of "their" woods or went "home," they would cover their tracks with snow that was sprinkled through a specially made sieve. They were armed with a few rifles and pistols. And they did not pass up an opportunity to diminish the number of the fascist beasts.

During the entire three years they spoke only in whispers. They were not allowed to speak in a loud voice even inside their earthen huts. Only when I came did they begin to sing, laugh, and speak in a full voice.

I was especially moved by the impassioned impatience and the firm faith with which these people awaited us, the Red Army. Their songs and their poetry, their conversations and even their dreams, were filled with this longing. The three-year-old Zoya did not know what a house was; she had never seen a horse until I rode up. But when she is asked who will surely come, she answers, "Father Stalin will surely come, and then we shall go home."

Prepared for publication by Ilya Ehrenburg

The Germans in Radzivillov (Krasnoarmeisk)

It is a beautiful autumn morning. All the Jews of Radzivillov (Krasnoarmeisk) are hiding in their homes. From the corner where my family is huddled, troubled whispers can be heard.

"They're coming, they're coming! What'll we do?"

Cars full of Germans have pulled into the courtyard; one of them jumps out and knocks on the door. Panic fills the apartment. My old grandmother goes to open the door.

"Why did you make us wait?" shouts the German, and a whip lashes across her shoulders. She falls unconscious. Mama and my aunt run to her with some water, while the German proceeds with his search: he is looking for men. Seeing that it is no use, my father comes out himself. The German beats him with the whip and yells, "You stinking muzhik, march to the courtyard!" And he shoves my father toward the door with his foot.

A nail was sticking out from the door; it left a bloody scratch on my father's face. Mama wanted to run up to him, but the German shoved her away; then he went out with my father, and they left.

It is impossible to describe the day that we endured. In the apartment there was a deathly silence. It was already getting dark, when we heard the sound of a knock; I could not stand it and started sobbing heavily. Mama opened the door and cried out in shock. In the doorway stood Papa, but what a sight he was: barefoot, without his coat, covered with blood.

Without saying a word he came in and sat down in a chair. My cousin cried out:

"Uncle, where are your boots?"

"There will be others, little kitten," Papa replied.

The German bandits had stolen his coat and boots; his pants were torn from whip lashes, and the blood had not been washed off his face. The whole day he had been carrying stones for the construction of a barracks, and he had been ordered to report for work again the next morning.

Such was our first meeting with the Germans.

But we did not know that this was just the beginning of our sufferings.

Papa worked without receiving any pay for his labor. Mama went around to peasant friends and sold things; we had to live somehow.

The German authorities entered the city, along with the militia, gendarmes, and the police. They tormented the population more and more with each passing day, plundering their homes and taking whatever struck their fancy.

The SS men, with the death's head on their uniforms, arrived in July. They came in the night for some Jews: six women and eighteen men. During the day Jews were placed under arrest; in the evening they were taken away somewhere in a truck. The next day a woman who lived next door to four policemen overheard them talking:

"We need to wash this Jewish blood off our hands."

For a long time we could not believe that the men and women had been murdered, but we soon found out that they really had been taken into the Brodsky forest and forced to dig pits; then they were shot and buried in those pits.

Not long after that Gebietskommissar Dubensky arrived in our city; he took thirty people prisoner and ordered the Jews to bring him thirty thousand marks within two hours, or else the prisoners would be killed.

People ran around like madmen, pawning their most precious objects for a pittance in order to raise that sum. Once he received the money, the Gebietskommissar left satisfied, but four days later he returned with new orders: all gold, silver, and nickel, as well as all furs, were to be handed over. The Jews, moreover, were forbidden to show themselves on the street without wearing the six-pointed star. We were forced to wear two pieces of these rags, one on our chest and one on our back.

All of the orders were carried out, but two of the prisoners arrested that time were still not released. Still it was not enough even for the Germans.

{We were forced to wear yellow badges sewn to our clothing, one on the chest and one on the shoulders. You would walk down the street with these badges, and every little nobody would yell out, "Jew, Jew!" They had the right to hit you and thrown stones at you, because you were not considered a human being. Meanwhile the Germans, with their fat bellies, would stand there and laugh.}

In March 1942 a new order was issued: the police were to go through the village with carts and haul off all the beds, dishes, and food from Jewish houses.

We took our things to some peasant friends for safekeeping: Anna Moroz from the village of Bogaevka and Lena Mostenchuk and Gubskaya from Barany.

This plundering was horrible for us; at the time, however, we did not know that now they would take our possessions but later they would take our lives.

At the end of April the Radzivillov officials received a new order from the Gebietskommissar: to free up two streets from the "Aryan" sector and there house all the Jews. One street was for workers ("Fachers") who would be issued the so-called *Arbeitskarte*; the second street was for the "unemployed." A wire fence three meters high was to surround the streets, and this area would be designated as the "ghetto."

With a great deal of difficulty, five thousand people were resettled into these two small streets.

There were three or four families in every lodging.

The "unemployed" already felt a great threat approaching and were running around trying to obtain an Arbeitskarte, so they could cross over to the other side.

The ghetto was supposed to be sealed on 24 May. With some trouble, my father managed to obtain an Arbeitskarte for two of us. He received some help from a Ukrainian bailiff who once worked with him in the accounting office of a lumber manufacturer. But we never ceased to worry and to wait.

In the early morning hours of 2 June all the local authorities, along with Gestapo agents who had arrived, were drinking in the German dining hall; at 4:00 A.M. the ghetto was surrounded. {There were only six Ukrainian militiamen on the workers' side; on the other side there were 130 bandits of various kinds: Germans, policemen, and newcomers.}

At 6:00 A.M. the authorities arrived with the police and the gendarmes. Still drunk, they poured into the ghetto and began driving people into the square with whips. The wailing and weeping of children, the wild screams of the bandits—all of it was horrible. I managed to hide in a neighbor's home; I saw everything through the window. On the square were children, young girls, and old women. I saw my friend; she was clinging to her mother and weeping bitterly. The Germans lifted children up in the air with their bayonets, {and the drunken militiamen were standing around with their boss, roaring with laughter.} The older children were beaten into unconsciousness. Many of the women lost their minds: they were screaming, singing, laughing insanely. Some started strangling their own children. It was impossible to bear. My friend ran to the fence, thinking she could climb over it; but a shot rang out, and she fell dead.

That was the first shot. The Germans had gathered all the people together and started to herd them out of the ghetto. Those who tried to escape were killed. The people were driven down the street and out of town; the entire city could hear their screams and groans. They were taken to three pits that prisoners had dug beforehand, without knowing for what purpose they had been forced to dig them. Everyone was shoved up to the pits and ordered to undress. They were forced by twos to lie down in one of the pits; then they would get two bullets. Those who were next were ordered to lie down on top of the bodies, until all three pits were full. Trucks pulled up; they gathered all the clothing and hauled it back to the empty ghetto.

We know these details from a girl who managed to escape; she was one in three thousand. Indeed, we could hear the screams and the shooting ourselves until two in the afternoon.

The orphans of people who had been murdered wandered the streets; those whose closest relatives had perished were sobbing. Waiting for such a fate to befall us as well, we did not sleep at night.

On one occasion my mother woke me in the night. Panic. Everyone get dressed. The ghetto is surrounded. Germans are breaking in and yelling, "Crawl out, you damned Jews!"

You can imagine what we felt. But it turned out that the Germans had come for some workers to load six train cars with potatoes. Like cattle our men were driven through the street with whips. We wept the entire night, thinking that they would never return. But they came back the next morning, exhausted, beaten, and covered with blood. It was a false alarm, but we lived in the constant expectation of death.

In August there was a rumor that once again the prisoners were being forced to dig pits. This time people were not going to wait to be driven to the pits, where they would be murdered; instead they ran off to the villages in the area. Many ran to Sestratin, where Jews were working at the peat-processing center. After all, there was a forest nearby, and one could escape, unlike here in this damned ghetto. Mama and I escaped to Sestratin, although working the peat was very difficult. Father stayed home. Then we found out that a new series of murders had actually been planned for August, but the monsters decided against it because there were still eight warehouses of potatoes to be loaded and sent to Germany.

Seeing that everything was more or less peaceful, people started to return. But at the end of September my former teacher Shlezinger arrived from Dubno and confirmed that prisoners were digging pits.

A representative of the local government came once again and informed us that sixty people who had tried to escape had been shot and that the same thing would happen to anyone else who tried to run away.

In the early morning hours of 3 November the ghetto was surrounded by trucks and motorcycles; the second in a terrible series of murders was to begin at 8:00 A.M. What would become of our home? Women wept and prayed to God. My father took me by the hand, caressed me, kissed me, and prayed fervently. At 1:00 A.M. someone quietly rapped on the window. We shuddered. Papa opened the door; two Ukrainians, Volodya Semenchuk and Kolya Vovk—old friends of ours—came in. Taking no thought for their own lives, they had come to save us at the last minute.

We packed only a few small bags and left. Despite our tears and pleas, Grandmother would not come with us. We all crept along behind our saviors, not even daring to raise our heads.

There was a place in the wire fence that had already been cut; we crawled out one at a time. We kept on crawling, a whole kilometer and a half, until we were out of the city. Then we stood up.

"Let's go to Brody," said Kolya. Brody is a city eight kilometers from Krasnoarmeisk; there Jews were still living in the ghetto.

Suddenly a man appeared as though he had sprung up from the earth. He came up to my uncle and said: "Yada, don't you recognize me?"

It turned out that it was Misha Domansky from the village of Nemirovka, my uncle's closest friend. He invited him to spend the night. It was another three kilometers to Nemirovka. We separated into two groups. Kolya, my relatives, and I went on ahead. We had not gone a kilometer, when someone rode up on a bicycle and shouted, "Stop!" Kolya turned off to the side, and we kept on walking. The man shot at us; the bullet went right over my head, and I screamed. It was a policeman {whom we knew}; my father gave him a hundred marks, his pocket watch, and his wedding ring. Without saying a word he got on his bicycle quite satisfied and left. Kolya ran up to us, and we happily reached the village.

Misha led us to his house and set us up in a cow shed on a bed of straw. Then our saviors said good-bye and left. But we did not sleep all night; we knew that during those minutes thousands of innocent people were being led to their deaths.

Misha had a large family: a father, mother, and wife; a little boy, sister, and younger brother. The next morning Misha and his father brought us breakfast and said, "People, you have no place to go. Stay with us. As God wills, so shall it be; whatever we have to eat we will share with you."

We started crying; my uncle thanked them, and we stayed. The Domanskys built us a shelter in the straw. Misha went into town; he came back and told us there were no more Jews there—just the trucks returning with their clothing.

Thus began our new life in the shelter. Our wonderful Misha tried in every way to make our lives better; he even got newspapers for us. True, the news did not make us happy; at that time the Germans were at the gates of Stalingrad. But Misha assured us that that soon we would be free of the German monsters.

Winter came, and we had nothing to keep us warm. Misha brought us his feather quilt, pillow, and blanket; he gave the men his long underwear. He cared for us like we were his own family.

{Thus we spent eight months. As we expressed it later, our lives were happy as long as Misha was with us. At that time bandits had already started showing up, and our Kolya was among the bandits. I do not know why he now wanted to kill us, since he had saved us earlier. Misha found out about it when Kolya went to him and told him to hand us over. That was not the kind of man Misha was, however; he moved us to another spot in the barn, showed Kolya the empty hiding place, and said, "I ran them off long ago." Only then did Kolya leave him alone and stop looking for us, since he was certain that we were not there. We had been saved for the second time. But then a new misfortune came to pass. On the night of 27 September 1943 the bandits came with Kolya to see Misha and said, "You are a communist, which means you must pay for your sins; you'll come with us and we'll put a bullet in your head. Get ready for it tomorrow." And they left. Misha ran to us; he wept like a child. He said good-bye to us, kissed everyone, and said, "People, I am certain that I am going to my death. The whole time we have been together, you have awaited our liberators; now I am going away, to what I do not know." He kissed my uncle once more and left. For a long time we could not come to our senses. A bad premonition was whispering in our ears. My cousin was weeping bitterly; she understood everything perfectly, even though she was only five years old. Indeed, only after he had gone did we realize what our hiding place had meant. True, the old head of the house, Misha's father, started caring for us as Misha had. But there was already a nest of bandits right there. They were sleeping in the loft just above our heads. We did not sleep nights; we held on to the beams so we would not disturb the straw and wake them up. Meanwhile the house that belonged to Misha's mother-in-law was burned down, and she and her son moved in with us, that is, with our host. She wandered around the yard more and more often, looking everywhere, until we were afraid that she would find us, since her son was also a real bandit. Because of her, our hostess, Misha's mother, could not bring us anything to eat or drink, and we grew hungry. As for Misha, there was no news about him.

In November shooting suddenly broke out in our village between the Germans and insurgents. Twelve Germans were killed; the rebels did not lose anyone. The Germans gathered up their dead and left.}

That night the townspeople left for other villages in order to save themselves from the vengeance of the Germans.

At three o'clock in the morning two German trucks arrived, and the Germans started setting fire to the houses on the outskirts of the village. Ours was the ninth one in line. We awaited our turn, but we were not yet fated to perish: the Germans stopped at the eighth house and left. We were saved for the third time.

The village remained empty for two days; then the residents started coming back. Seeing that her home was still intact and we were still alive, our hostess joyfully offered her daughter Nadya's hand in marriage to our friend Volodya Semenchuk, who had been asking for her hand for a long time.

Nadya was a beautiful eighteen-year-old girl. Volodya was only twenty-three. They told us that Novograd-Volynsky had been liberated by the Red Army. This was a great joy.

We stayed in our shelter from 3 November 1942 to 8 February 1944. Dubno had already been liberated when one night the {local authorities} came to our place with Germans. They moved the cattle from the barn into a cow shed and brought twelve horses into the barn; then they started rearranging the straw and nearly found us.

We had to leave; otherwise, had they found us, they would kill the people hiding us, noble, honest people. On 8 February I left first. Our hostess took me into her home. I speak Russian very well, without any Jewish accent. I lived with her openly, posing as her niece from Zhitomir; I took an assumed name and obtained false papers.

My mother and aunt also went off, out in the open, to the village of Levyatin; my father and uncle went to Bogaevka; my sister went to the house where our hostess's daughter lived. I helped with the housework, but I could not bear the light and walked around like a blind person. This is no joke: I had spent a year and a half in the thick darkness of our lair.

I found out that just eight days before the Red Army arrived in Bogaevka, the Germans hauled off all the men, and my father and uncle were murdered. They had endured so much torment only to die a terrible death on the eve of their liberation.

Four days before the Red Army arrived in Krasnoarmeisk I received a letter from Mama in Sestratin. She told me she was alive and asked me to take care of myself. My joy was indescribable, but it did not last long. Two days later I found out that my mother and aunt had been murdered. We, my little sister and I—their unhappy children—were the only ones left.

We longed for that miracle, for the happy moment, when our dear Red Army would come to liberate us. {Now I have the task of raising my little sister myself. I have some things that I left with peasants, with Lena Mostenchuk, Anna Moroz, and Bubskaya. I went to them to get my things back, but in vain. Despite my tears and my pleading that they put themselves in our position and return the things for which our parents had worked so hard, they will not give them back to me. The Red Army authorities are also cold-blooded in this regard. The school year has begun, but neither my sister nor I are going to school; it is simply impossible. I have to think about how to earn a crust of bread, not about school. We have no clothing, and winter is approaching; other people are using our things, people hardly touched by the war, people who still have their families with them—not like us.

There is no news about Misha, and our first savior, Volodya, is now in the Red Army.}

Reported by Lyusya Gekhman,
prepared for publication by Mariya Shkapskaya

A Letter from Syunya Deresh (Izyaslav)

Hello, Uncle Misha!

I am writing from my home town of Izyaslav, which you would not longer recognize. {Only the miserable half of our village remains. But why was it left there at all? It would have been better for it never to have existed, better for me had I not been born into the world! I am no longer the Syunka you once knew.} I no longer know who I am myself. It all seems like a dream, a nightmarish dream. Out of eight thousand people in Izyaslav, only our neighbor Kiva Feldman and I are left. My dear Mama and Papa, my sweet brother Zyama, Iza, Sarra, Borukh—all of them are gone. . . . You sweet, dear people, how very hard it was for you! . . . I cannot come to my senses, I cannot write. If I were to begin to tell you what I have lived through, I do not know how you could comprehend it. Three times I broke out of a concentration camp; more than once I have looked death in the eye while fighting in the ranks of the partisans. But a bullet from Fritz took me out of the action. But I am healthy now; my leg has healed, and I shall seek out the enemy to take my revenge for everything. I would love to see you if only for five minutes. I don't know if I'll be able to. . . . {For now I am staying at home, although all that is left of our so-called "home" is a ruin. I received a letter from Tanya. She was very happy that she still has some family left.}

I am waiting for an answer to my letter. My dear, sweet ones, is there any way we can see each other sooner? . . . Uncle Misha, remember that our most evil enemy is the fascist cannibal. What a horrible death all our loved ones died!!! Kill the fascist, cut him to pieces! Never fall into his hands. This letter is incoherent, as my life is incoherent and [worthless]. Nevertheless I am still alive. . . . For the sake of vengeance. Goodbye, Uncle Misha. I so much hope to see you soon. Greetings to everyone, everyone, everyone! I feel as though I have returned from the next world.

I am now beginning a new life—the life of an orphan. How? I myself do not know. Write as often as possible; I await your reply. Why don't Uncle Shloime, Iosif, Gitya, and the others write?

With warm greetings,

Your nephew Syunya Deresh

P.S. My address is the same. But whichever address you write to, I'll get it anyway, since there is no one here but me.

14 March 1944
Prepared for publication by Ilya Ehrenburg

Letters from Orphans

In 1941, when the Germans occupied the Ukrainian village of Kalinovka in the Vinnitsa district, they forced all the Jews to go to work. They tortured us and beat us with whips. They gave us leaves and grass to eat. Jews were harnessed to a cart and had to pull Germans along. They did not have the strength for it and were murdered. In 1942 they herded us into the ghetto. We could not leave there. Many died of hunger. Then they drove us into the stadium. The young men and women were murdered, and the children and old men were take away to the forest. There they completely surrounded us, shouted "Jude" at us, and started killing us. Children were thrown into a pit. I ran away. A German chased me. I climbed up a tree, and he did not see me. I saw how they murdered all the Jews; for three days blood flowed into the earth. I was ten years old at the time; I am twelve now.

Nyunya Dovtorovich

When the war began in 1941, they came to Mogilev-Podolsk and drove all the Jews into the Pechera camp in the Tulchin region. They tormented us; they shot my parents. They forced us to work. Little girls had to dig peat with their bare hands. We worked from four in the morning until late at night. At one point we overheard them saying that the summer season was coming to an end and that all the "Juden" would be killed. We ran off in all directions. They chased us, and many of us were killed. A certain Ukrainian saved me; he took me into his house and hid me. His neighbor told the Germans that a "kike" was in his house. A German came to shoot me, but the Ukrainian started fighting with him, and I ran away; I ended up in Romanian territory.

Roza Lindvor, 15 years old

I was born in the little village of Vagila on the Seret River. I am now fifteen years old. I have yet to see anything good. They took all of us and sent us to the Edintsy camp. I suffered and saw death right before my eyes. Then they took us to the bright Ukraine, but for us it was dark. In a single day both my beloved parents died there. Five of us were orphaned. I was not far from death. What was lost will never return.

Enya Valtser
Prepared for publication by Ilya Ehrenburg

German-Romanian Brutality in Kishinev (Moldavia)

On 18 June 1941 Kishinev was occupied by German-Romanian troops. The first thing the military authorities tried to determine was how many Jews and communists were left in the city.

Within a few days a ghetto was established, in accordance with the order of the commandant of the city, Colonel Tudose. The ghetto included the Old Bazaar, Old Armyanskaya Street, part of Armyanskaya Street (lower Kharlamovskaya), all of Irinpolskaya, Kodinarskaya Street, and a row of streets adjacent to the area. The ghetto was enclosed by a barbed wire fence. There were two or three exits, around which guards were posted.

On 21 July soldiers armed with rifles surrounded the Ilinsky Bazaar, the square next to it, Prunkulovskaya and Pavlovskaya streets, and a row of other streets where Jews lived. The soldiers went into every courtyard and drove out all the Jews, without exception—the sick, the old, the lame, the blind, and the paralyzed, as well as women and children. The whole crowd was herded down Ilinskaya Street to Drovyanaya Square; there they were photographed in the presence of several prominent German officers.

A few days after the establishment of the ghetto Colonel Tudose ordered forty-four young men and women to be gathered together. They were the flower of the intelligentsia of Kishinev. All of them were taken outside of town in trucks. An officer ordered ten of them to be separated from the group. They were taken over to the side. Then the officer turned to everyone and gave them a short speech he had prepared.

"You are all communists, for you are all Bessarabians and Jews. With impatience you have awaited the arrival of the Soviet forces, and now you expect them to save you. But in vain. You mocked Romanian officers and the Romanian army when we left Bessarabia. Now the moment has come when you will answer for everything. Nothing and no one can save you."

The officer ordered the doomed people to be shot by the ten who had been taken aside. Colonel Tudose was present at the execution.[35]

A short time later the commandant of the ghetto ordered a large group of people to be taken out of the ghetto for road work. Among them were M. N. Yaroslavsky, the attorneys E. P. Grobdruk and V. N. Tselnik, and others. They were taken to Gidyach, where there is a stone quarry. Along the way they were tormented in every possible manner; they had cigarettes thrown at them, and the guards spit in their faces. When the poor people tried to protest, the guards beat them severely. Many of them ended up with broken ribs and arms; blood flowed from them in streams.

The tortured, hungry, wounded people were brought back to the ghetto. The next day they were all taken out of town again to be shot, down to the last one. There were more than three hundred people in the group.

In the ghetto the Jews had to wear special badges. The badges were of various colors that changed almost daily. Each day the badges changed from this to that color. It was very difficult, since people would be severely punished for the slightest mistake or smallest omission; simply stated, they would be beaten half to death.

There were no baths in the ghetto, and people went for weeks without washing. As the result of systematic deprivation, people in the ghetto fell ill from the unhygienic conditions. Epidemics spread: typhoid fever, abdominal typhus, and dysentery. There was a high mortality rate in the ghetto; no fewer than thirty people died every day.

The head of the Jewish Council was the popular social activist G. S. Landau; the Council decided to open a hospital. But no sooner was the hospital set up than the commandant of the ghetto confiscated literally all of the beds, linens, and medications. They were taken away under the pretense of "military exigency." The sick were treated entirely without ceremony: they were thrown from their beds, and their gowns were torn off of them.

The Council opened a second hospital. Doctor Gorenbukh was appointed director. Doctor G. Shafir was in charge of therapeutics, and acting as surgeon was Doctor S. I. Michnik-Landau, wife of the Chairman of the Jewish Council; Doctor Berman, a woman, was the intern.

The population of the ghetto was in fact doomed to hunger.

By order of the ghetto commandant, it was forbidden to sell food to Jews before eleven o'clock in the morning; by one in the afternoon there was no more food to be had. There were, however, some peasants who had no regard for the danger and brought provisions to the condemned people. At great risk to her life, Vera Platonovna Klimova got food into the ghetto. This simple, noble woman helped the residents of the ghetto a great deal.

Early each morning Germans and Romanians showed up in the ghetto to take men, women, and children to do their housework. The workers received neither money nor sustenance for their labor. The commandant made a note of those who were impudent or disobedient and settled things with them at the first opportunity; the "guilty parties" disappeared forever.

At eight in the evening life in the ghetto came to a complete halt. None of the captives had the right to leave his dwelling, under penalty of being shot on the spot.

Drunk out of their minds, the officers and soldiers would break into the apartments at night, wreak havoc and shout insults, rape girls before their parents' eyes, throw things around, and then disappear.

In September 1941 an unexpected order came from General Antonescu, stating that the Jews in the ghetto were to be gradually moved to the other side of the Bug. Near the Visternigen station on Ryshkanovka Street they set up a "customs house," through which everyone designated for transfer across the Bug would pass. All who went through the "customs house" were stripped naked; their clothes and all their belongings were confiscated. The wretched people were then sent on their way, but they never reached the Bug. Many of them went to their eternal rest in the Orgeevsky forest, where they were slaughtered and shot; the rest were drowned in the Reut River.

Such bloody events transpired rather often whenever Jews were transferred to a camp.

The German-Romanian authorities also amused themselves by harnessing weak and exhausted people to a cart and forcing them to pull along important functionaries and members of their household. The wretched people were unable to endure this torture.

Some of the prisoners of the ghetto managed to escaped into the city and hide with non-Jewish friends. The authorities hastened to inform Antonescu of such cases. Antonescu then issued an order that if any Christian should be found hiding Jews, then he and the Jews would be shot on the spot. After the order was issued, there were more and more searches in the city; the situation became more and more strained.

One of the prisoners in the ghetto—I. F. Ludmer, an intelligent woman who had served under the Soviets in a finance office—managed to escape from the ghetto on 23 October 1941, at great risk to her own life. She headed for Timiryazev Street, where her friend Sofiya Konstantinovna Kristi lived.

Antonescu's order was widely known throughout the city; nevertheless S. K. Kristi decided to save Ludmer no matter what. For the next seven months Ludmer hid with Kristi without going out of the house for days on end. Kristi gave Ludmer her papers, and so Ludmer was officially transformed into Kristi. Kristi's integrity and selflessness saved the life of a Jewish woman.

G. S. Landau, head of the Jewish Council, was responsible for providing the Jews in the ghetto with the necessities for life and for equally distributing food and script among these captives. The food and money came from Bucharest, where, under the leadership of Doctor V. Filderman, the local Jewish Council had taken upon itself the task of providing goods for the residents of the Kishinev Ghetto. The attorney A. Shapirin was sent to Bucharest to obtain their help. All this, of course, was done secretly. Shapirin would disguise himself in a soldier's uniform and then carefully slip out of the ghetto; then, traveling in a military convoy, he would set out for Bucharest. The officer who allowed Shapirin to join the soldiers on the convey was paid a great deal of money. He had five men marching behind Shapirin, and they did not take their eyes off him, so he would not escape. Using every means they could, the members of the Bucharest Jewish Council provided an envoy who would come back to Kishinev. But for the Bucharest Council the possibilities were limited. By the order of Antonescu, the Jewish population of Romania was taxed beyond its means. All the Jews had to labor in various public works, but, of course, they were paid nothing. Any funds to be used had to be raised.

At the end of 1941, in accordance with arrangements made by Antonescu, the Kishinev Ghetto was liquidated. All the Jews in the ghetto were to be sent to camps in the Ukraine.

It was late autumn. Bitter cold had set in. But the new commandant of the ghetto, Captain Paraskivescu, carried out the order with inexorable cruelty. He openly bragged that he had personally exterminated four thousand Jews. The soldiers were literally mad with rage. Showing no mercy, they tossed sick people from their beds and pushed women who had just given birth into the street; they threw people with a temperature of 40° C onto trucks and tore children from the arms of their parents.

The chairman and members of the Council went to the military authorities and pleaded with them to change the means of evacuation, but in vain. Twelve hundred people disappeared along the way. They were murdered.

Gane Kipervasser, who had been sent to Balta, managed to find her way back to Kishinev. She told the ghetto residents who had not yet been sent to Balta that all the roads beyond the Dniester were littered with the bodies of Jews.

A. S. Goldenberg, director of the girls' high school; the talented poet Ya. V. Oksner (whose literary pseudonym was Jacques Nuar); the journalist E. G. Babad; the lady physician L. S. Babich; Doctor M. A. Talmazsky and his parents A. I. and R. P. Talmazsky; the x-ray physician Doctor S. E. Vasserman, his wife, daughter, and all his brothers who were left in Kishinev; Doctor G. Shafir, his wife, and his little boy; Doctor G. S. Yurkovsky; the families of attorneys G. F. and L. F. Ziskisov and their children; Doctor Gelman and his wife; the artist N. M. Khess; the attorneys E. L. Grobdruk and V. N. Tselnik; A. Shapirin and his wife and daughter; the publisher of abstracts for Russian literature L. I. Grinfeld, his wife, and his brother; the family of G. M. Kresser, whose office was widely known in Kishinev for its translations of texts from foreign languages into Russian (the mathematician E. G. Kresser was the sole survivor); A. I. Koropatonitsky; the old physician I. A. Gisnfiner, his brother V. A. Gisnfiner, and his brother's family; the journalist S. E. Puterman and his two sisters; the dentists N. O. Shteinberg-Rabinovich and his son; L. and S. Vainshtein (husband and wife); I. Ya. Tetelman and his family, Galperin and his family; the old dentist G. A. Levin and his wife; S. G. Malamud; the cantors A. I. Chervinsky and Kh. Tsipris; V. N. Vaisman, his wife, and his sons; Yu. N. Vaisman, his wife, and his sons; the widow R. A. Levina and her children; the teacher S.

Gamza, his wife, and children; L. Gorenshtein and his wife; the pharmacist M. Rozenblat; the sculptor and philanthropist famous in Kishinev, M. G. Grinshpun; the cooperative head V. G. Solomonov and his daughter; the engineer A. M. Shvartsman; the banker trusted throughout the all of Kishinev society, G. K, Lindenbaum and his wife; and many, many others—all perished in the ghetto.

According to the testimony of Doctor S. I. Michnik-Landau, two or three days after the Gestapo installed themselves in Kishinev, they settled matters with a large group of intellectuals. They arrested the attorney Aron Roitman, Kleiman, Doctor Kraminsky, the attorney Pinchevsky, Doctor Korimsky, Doctor Milgrom, Michekhin, Kaufman, Markov, Land, Blank, Efrusi, the attorney Yu. M. Slutsky, and Rirkelman. All of them were take to the headquarters of the Sigurantsa,[36] where they were held for several hours; then they were taken out and ordered to run. But no sooner did they start to run than shots rang out. They were all murdered.

Many of the intellectuals could not stand the physical and moral shock. Seeing no possibility of resisting all the horrors and the arbitrary violence to which they were doomed in the ghetto, they committed suicide. Among them were Jewish Council Chairman G. S. Landau; the lady physician Gifeisman; Doctor V. B. Patin and his wife; Doctor Zinger and his wife, who was also a doctor; the lady doctor S. Ya. Fleksor-Khazan-Erlikh and her husband, an agronomist; the physicians B. R. Abramova-Voinova and Sofiya Isaakovna Grinfeld; and many others.

According to the data compiled by the city commission that conducted an investigation into the atrocities committed in Kishinev by the German-Romanian fascist criminals, 9,299 Soviet citizens were forced into slavery; 879 people were shot in the Jewish cemetery, 350 on Strashensky Road, 2,015 on Prunkulovskaya Street, and 519 on Sadovaya Street. Fifteen thousand Soviet citizens were murdered in the ghetto.

Drawing on information from their investigation into the fascist crimes committed in Kishinev, the city commission compiled a list of the German-Romanian barbarians and the accomplices to their atrocities and brutalities:

1.   Marshall Ion Antonescu, Commander-in-Chief of the Romanian fascist troops, organizer of mass shootings and of the annihilation of Soviet citizens and military personnel.

2.   Professor Aleksiyan, governor and organizer of mass shootings.

3.   General Petr Dumitrescu, commander of the fascist army.

4.   Corps General N. Chuperka, VO commandant.

5.   Lieutenant Colonel Raika-Gorya, military magistrate and procurator.

6.   Captain Emil Kurulesky, jurist and military procurator.

7.   Brigadier General I. Arbore, chief of staff.

8.   Tudose, prison warden who carried out the torture and shooting of Soviet citizens and who buried people alive.

9.   Lieutenant Colonel Fedor Pogotsa, chairman of the military tribunal.

10. Major Ion Kozma, jurist and military procurator.

11. Captain Radoga, procurator.

12. Major Ladesko, vice chairman of the military tribunal (who handed out death sentences and had Soviet citizens tortured and shot).

13. Captain Luka Popescu, commissar, chief of police in the Fourth Precinct of the city of Kishinev, who supervised the arrest of Soviet citizens and engaged in torture.

14. Luchescu, prison warden, who supervised the arrest and torture of Soviet citizens.

15. Barbalits, senior superintendent of the prison, who tortured and tormented prisoners.

16. Major Muntyan, who supervised the shooting of Soviet citizens and tortured prisoners.

17. Lieutenant Colonel Dumitrescu, commandant of the ghetto, who supervised brutalities and tortures inflicted upon prisoners, as well as the shooting of Soviet citizens.

18. General Procurator K. N. Dardan, who supervised the mass shooting of Soviet citizens, particularly from the Jewish population; Dardan was originally from Bessarabia and served for a long time as the procurator of the Kishinev tribunal.

19. General Procurator Yunka, guilty of the same crimes as Dardan.

20. Undercomissar Katulchan, organizer of tortures and humiliations.

21. Ponko, procurator who supervised the shooting of Soviet citizens.

22. Paraskivescu, captain of the gendarmes, who tortured people who were arrested.

23. Marinescu, military procurator.

24. Vasilescu, procurator.

25. Minevich, prison supervisor.

26. Ivan Goltsev, commissar of the Sigurantsa.

27. Morarnu, commissar of the Sigurantsa.

28. Dumitrescu, commissar of police.

29. Ionescu, commissar of police.

30. Stoiko, commissar of police.

31. Borodin, procurator for the Sigurantsa.

32. Lieutenant Colonel Fedor Iogan, chairman of the court.

33. Captain Pogoltsan, procurator.

34.   Beiu, procurator.

35.   Konstantinescu, secretary of the military tribunal.

36.   Ivan Mazilo, chief of the military prison.

All of those listed above are guilty of supervising the torture, humiliation, and shooting of innocent Soviet citizens and Soviet military personnel.

L. Bazarov

Notes

1.   Portions of the text that appear in curved brackets are from the 1945 variant of the text, which is based on material from the State Archives of the Russian Federation. These sections often contain accounts of complicity with the Nazis on the part of Russians, Ukrainians, Belorussians, Lithuanians, etc.; they appear here for the first time in English.
2.   A Karaite is a member of a sect of Jews that arose in the eighth century of the common era in reaction against rabbinical Judaism. The Karaites recognize the authority only of the Torah, and not of the Talmud and other rabbinical texts and teachings. In the ninth century the great Jewish thinker Saadia Gaon refuted the Karaite position, and since that time the Karaites have not been part of the Jewish fold. The Nazis did not regard the Karaites as Jews.
3.   On 29 and 30 September 1941 nearly 34,000 Jews were murdered at Babi Yar; by the end of the slaughter more than 100,000 had perished on that site.
4.   Lion Feuchtwanger (1884-1958) was a German author perhaps best known for his historical novel *Jud Süss* (1925); he fell out of favor with the Nazis when he wrote a satire of Hitler's Munich putsch called *Erfolg* (*Success*, 1930).
5.   In 1913 Mendel Beylis, a Jew from Kiev, stood trial on a blood libel charge, that is, the ritual murder of a Russian boy; he was acquitted.
6.   Lev Adolfovich Ozerov (b. 1914) was a poet who wrote an important and powerful poem on the massacre at Babi Yar.
7.   After the third partition of Poland, on 23 December 1791, the Russian government decreed that Jewish settlement would be limited to Belorussia, the Ukraine, and the newly acquired Baltic territories; thus began the Pale of Settlement. The Pale was abolished in 1915.
8.   A *tallis* is a prayer shawl and *tefillin* are phylacteries that Jews wear in prayer.
9.   Adolf Hitler was actually born on 20 April 1889.
10.   Vladimir Germanovich Lidin (1894 – 1979) was a prose writer and a correspondent for *Izvestia* during the war.
11.   Named for Aleksei Stakhanov (1905-1977), a Stakhanovite was a Soviet worker who was recognized by the government for his diligence and enthusiasm.
12.   Damocles was a courtier of the elder Dionysus of Syracuse (405-367 b.c.e.). After he had extolled the good fortune of royalty, the king invited him to a sumptuous meal; as he ate, Damocles happened to look up to see a sword hanging by a hair suspended over his head.
13.   *Balagole* is from the Yiddish word for "coachman."
14.   A variation of this piece was originally published under the title "The Land of Piryatin" in Ilya Ehrenburg's book *The War* (Moscow, 1944), pp. 117-18.
15.   *Emes* is the Yiddish word for "truth."
16.   Georgy Nikolaevich Munblit (b. 1904) was a prose writer and critic; during the war he worked as a journalist.
17.   *Laitelakh* is Yiddish for "dear people."
18.   The names are infamous. Akmechetka, for example, was one of the Romanian death camps in Transnistria, south of the Bug River; about four thousand people died there from hunger and disease. Domanevka was also a Romanian camp south of the Bug. In January and February 1942 eighteen thousand Jews were murdered there; most of them were from Odessa and surrounding areas. Bogdanovka was another Romanian camp in Transnistria. From 21 December to 31 December 1941 approximately 54,000 Jews were murdered there.
19.   Irina Ehrenburg notes that German occupying forces entered Odessa on 16 October 1941. The next day, on 17 October, three to four thousand Jewish men were shot. On 22 October the Romanian military headquar-

ters was blown up; sixty-six German and Romanian officers and soldiers died in the explosion. Over the next three days Romanian military units shot approximately 35,000 Odessa Jews.

20. It is possible that here Plutoner is not the man's first name but rather designates his rank, since a plutoner was also a rank assigned to a non-commissioned officer in the Romanian army.

21. Vera Mikhailovna Inber (1890 – 1972) became famous during the war years as an essayist and journalist.

22. Leib Goldberg (1892 – 1955) was a prose writer, translator, and journalist. He wrote in Yiddish and translated Sholom Aleichem into Russian; he was very active with the Jewish Anti-Fascist Committee.

23. After Rakhil Fradis-Milner moved to Israel in 1960, she corrected this line to point out that her deportation took place on 7 June 1942, by which time 50,000 people had already been deported from the region.

24. Literally "crumb."

25. In 1941 SS Brigadeführer Friedrich (Fritz) Katzmann was named head of the SS and the police in the "Galicia District" (the Western Ukraine). By 1943 he had orchestrated the murder of more than 434,000 Jews; he was also responsible for the deportation of more than 20,00 Jews to concentration camps.

26. Belzec was one of the six extermination camps located in Poland. Killing operations began at Belzec on 17 March 1942; by July 1943 approximately 600,000 Jews had been slaughtered there.

27. Two hundred thousand Jews were murdered in the Janowska camp; of all the camps in Europe, it is the only one still functioning as a prison. For an excellent account of the tribulations in the Janowska camp, see the memoir *The Death Brigade (The Janowska Road)* by Leon Wells (New York: Holocaust Library, 1978).

28. "Up, down."

29. Built in March 1933, Dachau was the first concentration camp to go into operation, and many camp officials received their training there.

30. Mauthausen was built soon after the German annexation of Austria in March 1938; it was designed for "extermination through labor."

31. SS Obersturmführer Gustav Willhaus succeeded F. Gebauer as commandant of the Janowska camp.

32. An assistant to the camp commandant, SS Obersturmführer Richard Rokita was a musician in a nightclub before the war.

33. Ruvim Isayevich Fraerman (1892 – 1972) was a prose writer and journalist; in 1941 he joined the National Guard.

34. The Komsomol was the Communist Youth Movement.

35. This execution took place on 1 August 1941.

36. The Sigurantsa was the Romanian political secret police, which was advised by the German Gestapo.

Part 2

Belorussia

The Minsk Ghetto

On 28 June 1941 German tanks rumbled through the streets of Minsk. Unable to leave, approximately 75,000 Jews and their children were left in the city.

The first order issued was that, under the threat of being shot, all men between the ages of fifteen and forty report to a registration point. On 7 July 1941 the Germans burst into Jewish apartments, seized the first men they saw, loaded them into trucks, and took them away. The next day a second declaration was issued, announcing that, due to their Bolshevik connections in Minsk and surrounding areas, one hundred Jews had been shot.

The oppression started from the moment the Germans entered the city; people were robbed, beaten, and shot for no reason. Special torments were inflicted upon the Jews.

The apartment building at 21 Myasnikov Street was quite crowded; more than three hundred people lived there. On 2 July 1941 the building was surrounded. The residents (adults, old people, and even children) were taken out into the courtyard with no explanation and ordered to stand with their faces to the wall. A military unit of forty men held them for six hours. During that time (under the pretext of searching for weapons), clothing, linens, blankets, footwear, dishes, and all foodstuffs were confiscated. The stolen goods were loaded into two large trucks and hauled away. Only when it was all over were the people released. They looked upon their ravaged apartments in sheer astonishment.

That night groups of four or five men returned; they went to the Graiver, Rapoport, and Kleonsky apartments and demanded that they turn over the rest of their belongings. "Silver spoons were left here. . . . Where's the suit? What have you done with the silk?" the bandits shouted.

A large school building is also located on Myasnikov; its windows look out on the courtyard of an apartment house. From the windows one can see the interior of the apartments where people live. The Germans positioned themselves in the school and, simply for their own amusement and delight, picked out certain residents in the apartments. For a whole day they shot from the windows, aiming at mirrors, furniture, and people.

In keeping with the order, hundreds and thousands of men crowded into the gathering point. All of them were sent to the camp at Drozdy. There Soviet people—Belorussians, Russians, and Jews—were subjected to humiliation and violence.

After a while the Russian men were released, but the Jews remained in the camp. Those who were left were divided into two groups: white-collar workers and blue-collar workers. The first group was loaded into trucks, taken out of the camp, and shot with machine guns.

More than three thousand men were gunned down. Among them were talented people—engineering professors from the Polytechnic Institute; candidates for degrees in technological sciences, such as Aizenberg and Pritykin; Priklad, who held a doctorate in mathematical sciences; and many others.

The second group, which consisted mainly of skilled laborers, was taken out of the camp under armed guard and locked up in the city prison. As they were led through the streets, women and children came running out of the houses to see if they could recognize friends and relatives. The guards shot those who were coming out to meet them. They led the men down Kommunalnaya Street. Zyskind's fourteen-year-old daughter ran outside and stood at the gate in the hope that she might see her father. A shot rang out, and the girl fell dead.

Partisan Comrade Grechanik related the following account of the days that the men of Minsk spent in the Drozdy camp:

"After we had marched a kilometer outside of the city, the guards stopped us and said: 'Whoever has knives, watches, or razors must put them in his cap and hand them over.' The people did as they were told. Of course, those who still had their wits about them hid their watches and razors. Many people had buried their belongings in the ground rather than hand them over to the Germans. The Germans turned our pockets inside out, collected all the items in the caps, and checked wallets. We were standing in a field surrounded by guards. Group after group of people continued to arrive. It was cold that night in the open field, and people were lying next to each other to keep warm. Thus we spent the first night out in a field. Day broke. There were a large number of us, but we received nothing to eat. People asked for water, but they gave us no water. As soon as anyone would walk up to ask, the Germans would shoot. Thus ended the second day. The second night fell. People were lying there cold and hungry. Some were dressed warmly, while others had on just a summer shirt. Day broke. People kept arriving. A German showed up with a bucket and started distributing water. People crowded around him so much that they nearly knocked him over. Again those reptiles shot at them.

"The third day. People were hungry. It was already twelve noon. The weather was warm and pleasant. Suddenly an officer appeared with an interpreter and announced that from ten in the morning till four in the afternoon relatives would be allowed to bring food packages into the camp. In the distance we could see women with baskets and children with bottles of water, but they were not allowed to approach us right away. They were stopped and checked for what they were carrying. It got noisy. Everyone was trying to get to the women and children. We cheered up a little. Those who received something to eat ate with relish and shared with those who did not get anything. It grew noisier in the field; the children were asked to bring the water. They brought it, and we drank with pleasure. But people could hear women crying. They asked, 'Why are you crying?' And immediately they were answered: 'Our husbands and children are no more; they have been murdered.'

"The day ended. The women and children were driven away. The fourth night fell. The people lay on the field. We heard footsteps, Germans shouting, and rifle shots. Suddenly we saw what it was: they were bringing in Red Army soldiers who had been taken prisoner. But they were not allowed to mix with the civilians. The morning of the fourth day came. Some Red Army soldiers wanted to see the civilians, but they were shot at as soon as they made a move. Thus more than ten men were murdered that day. The women came again with food and drink. And so the fourth day ended. The fifth night began. As soon as it grew dark, the Red

Army soldiers began running toward the civilians from all directions. The German fired, but the soldiers paid no attention. They ran over and immediately lay down. The civilians gave them bread, water, and salt. Thus the civilians spent the whole night with the soldiers, almost till morning, when the Red Army prisoners ran back; again the Germans shot at them. The fifth day began. The weather was not very clear. The Germans continued to bring people in, both military and civilian. Suddenly a large column was led in. It was a group of people dressed differently from the rest of us. With sacks and bags. We talked with them. They said they had come from the west, trying to flee from the advancing Germans. They said many had died along the way.

"Again the women came with food. Some of them brought raincoats. And suddenly it rained. It was cold and damp. People were lying in it. And so the day passed. The sixth night began. It was dark. The Red Army soldiers ran over to the civilians. The Germans shot at us. Again shouts were heard. It turned out that somebody's sack had been cut open; the sack contained biscuits, and the hungry people rushed for them. There was a loud commotion, and shots were fired; about fifty people crawled away from the crowd and then started running. But the Germans saw them and started firing their rifles. It was very dark. The Germans killed only three, and the rest got away. Thus the sixth night passed.

"The seventh day dawned. It rained that morning. [We saw the women and children in the distance. They were coming closer. People were waiting impatiently. It was already ten o'clock, but they had allowed no one into the camp; all of them had been detained. In the distance a column of people was approaching. They were dressed in ragged civilian clothes; some of them were barefoot. As they passed the women who were trying to get in to bring food to their relatives, shouts could be heard. They fell upon the women and children to take their baskets from them. The Germans forced the women back and let the people into the civilian area of the camp. Only then did we realize who they were. They were people whom the Soviet authorities had sent into forced labor. Then] in the distance we saw a Gestapo unit on motorcycles, bicycles, in cars, and on foot. They approached us. Shouts could be heard: 'Fall into ranks four deep!' They were swinging rubber truncheons. First the soldiers and then the rest of us were lined up and led far into the field. We went two kilometers. The wounded were lying along the path; they were screaming and moaning, but the Germans would not allow anyone to break the column to help them. They set up camp next to the Svisloch River. The soldiers were on one side and the civilians on another. And so the day ended.

"The eighth night fell. People were lying down. They had been warned not to stand up, or they would be shot. The Germans often used their machine guns. We could hear people crying out, 'They've killed him!' As it happened, people would get up to relieve themselves, and they would be shot. One man was lying there. A bullet had hit him in the small of his back and come out his stomach, tearing out his intestines. He was still alive and asked people to note down his address and write to his wife and children, telling them how he died. A German came up, laughed, and asked, 'Who took a knife and cut his stomach open?' Thus ended the eighth night.

"The ninth day. People did not ask for water; they could get it from the stream. A German stood by the stream and allowed people to get a drink one at a time. We heard a truck pull up, and the interpreter shouted several names through a megaphone: doctors, cooks, bakers, electricians, plumbers. They were ordered to go over to the truck and were told that they could go home under the condition that they report for work.

"Another truck pulled up. It carried Germans with a movie camera. They started throwing biscuits to the prisoners of war, and the prisoners grabbed at the biscuits. The Germans filmed them. But suddenly there was gunfire. An officer was in the truck; when they threw the biscuits and the Red Army soldiers started grabbing at them, he shot them in the hands. Then he got down from the truck and examined their hands; those who had only flesh wounds were led to one side, and those who had been hit in the bone were sent to another. The ones with flesh wounds he ordered to be bandaged; those who had been hit in the bone he shot, right in front of everyone. He had shovels handed out to the Red Army soldiers and ordered them to bury the dead.

"The tenth night fell. It was very dark. Once again the military prisoners ran over to the civilians. In the noise and the shooting that followed, many of the military prisoners—about three hundred men—crossed over to the other side of the stream. There was a small wooded area right along the bank. Suddenly a shot was heard coming from the woods. The prisoners and the stream were lit up by searchlights from three different directions, and machine guns began firing. Bullets were flying over the heads of the crowd. People were clinging tightly to the earth. Those who were lying on higher ground crawled to lower ground. But nearly all the prisoners who tried had already managed to get across the stream and into the wood. Only two were killed in the stream; they did not get away. The shooting stopped, and the searchlights were turned off. The prisoners of war ran back to their places. The night ended.

"The eleventh day began. The weather was bad. Some officers had come. They were going to speak. A German guard was sitting on the other side of the stream, washing his feet in the water. Suddenly we heard the drone of an airplane and several explosions. The guard grabbed his boots and ran into the woods. The officers got into their car and drove away without saying a word. When people saw the guard grab his boots and run, they burst out laughing. The women came again. They brought food and underwear; some of them brought warmer clothing. The day ended.

"The twelfth night. The prisoners of war ran over to the civilians. The civilians gave them food. A large number of the military prisoners changed into civilian clothes and stayed with the civilians. And so the night ended.

"The thirteenth day. It was already ten o'clock, and they had not let the women in. A car drove up, and it was announced that the Poles were to gather on the left and the Russians on the right. A spot next to the stream had already been prepared for the Jews; it was roped off. And so we started splitting up.

"Germans with rubber truncheons were everywhere; they drove the Jews into the roped off area, beating them with the truncheons. Anyone who resisted was beaten to death or shot. Suddenly from the car came an announcement that we would be allowed to go home. The Poles and the Russians were to be in the first group; nothing was said about the Jews. They began releasing the Poles. With that the day ended.

"The fourteenth night. It was dark and cold. The prisoners of war ran over to the civilians. The Germans shot at them. Suddenly we heard a steady round of gunfire coming from the other side of the stream. We asked the military prisoners what it could be. They said, 'The Germans are shooting the political instructors and the officers.' The shooting lasted almost the entire night.

"The fifteenth day. It rained that morning. The women had come once again. The sentry was checking what they had brought. They brought food. Some of their provisions were confiscated, and then they were allowed into the camp and were shown where to take their goods. Some of the women were looking for their loved ones and could not find them. They had been murdered. The women went away crying. It grew warm. A German was posted next to the stream but would not let anyone near the water. He pushed every man who approached him into the stream fully clothed and told him he would have to dive under three times before he could have some water. The crowd went up to him. He jeered at them and ordered them to jump in. The number of Poles in the camp was growing smaller and smaller. And so the day ended.

"The sixteenth night fell. It was dark and rainy. Again the Red Army soldiers ran over to the civilians, and the civilians gave them food; many of them changed into civilian clothes.

"The rain poured down all night. And the night ended.

"The seventeenth day. Toward ten in the morning a car pulled up with an interpreter, who announced that all the Jews—engineers, physicians, technicians, bookkeepers, teachers, all the intelligentsia—had to be registered. They would be released from the camp and sent to work. And so they started registering. There were three thousand of them. Later we found out that the intelligentsia were all shot. The women brought food. A heavy rain started to fall. We were all soaked. Some of us shaved. A group of women gathered around three of the men who had shaved; they changed into women's clothing, with large scarves over their heads, and some old women led they off by the hand. They carried baskets with pots in them and headed for the exit. The guard paid no attention. We watched them intensely. They got through, and everyone breathed a sigh of relief. About twenty men got out of the camp that day. All of the intelligentsia had already registered; they were gathered together and separated from the workers. The workers were also registered. It started getting dark. There was no one left in the field, except the Jews and the prisoners of war. Suddenly a shot rang out: a guard had recognized a man dressed in women's clothing and killed him. Then it began. Clubs in hand, the Germans ran for the Jews. They searched us for razors and confiscated cups, raincoats, and good boots. The people were shoved around and in the confusion threw their razors and valuables into the stream. With that the day ended.

"The eighteenth night. It was dark. It was rainy. The Red Army soldiers ran over to the civilians; this time, however, they did not change into civilian clothes, for only they and the Jews remained in the field, and a bitter fate awaited them both. The Jews gave them food. They lay down and warmed themselves with us; it was dark, but we could hear the rumbling of trucks. The Red Army soldiers ran back to their area. The trucks pulled up to the intelligentsia, piled them in, and hauled them away—to work, they said. But now we know what this 'work' is. About twenty minutes after the trucks left we could hear machine gun fire; fifteen minutes after that the same trucks returned and hauled away more people. Thus all of the intelligentsia were taken away. Dawn broke. An officer showed up and selected two hundred workers. He sent them off to 'work' on foot and announced, 'All the Jews will be taken to a new site tomorrow. It will be warm there, and you will be out of the rain. You will be taken through the city. Be sure that today you tell your wives, relatives, and friends that tomorrow you will be led through the city. If anyone should come up to you as you pass through town, both of you will be shot.' They were already beginning to take away the prisoners of war. The women arrived. They brought food. Many were crying, for their relatives, husbands, and children were no more. They were told that tomorrow we would be led through the city and that they were not to approach us; if they did, they would be shot. They left crying. The last day in Drozdy came to an end.

"The nineteenth night. The prisoners were taken out of the camp. The trucks' headlights were turned on. They spent the whole night loading the Red Army soldiers. No more were left in the field. Just the Jews. The next morning a Gestapo unit showed up; they were all wearing red silk neckties. They lined up the simple Jewish people in rows and led they away. Guards lined the entire road to the prison. The people were taken up to the prison gates. The Gestapo opened the gates, and they all passed into the prison yard. The gates were closed."

The workers spent several days in the prison. Then some of them were released and sent to work; others were loaded into trucks, taken outside the city, and shot.

According to the orders of the German authorities, the entire Jewish population had to register with a specially created Jewish Council (*Judenrat*). The order warned that any Jews who did not register would be denied apartments at the time of resettlement. Upon registration the Jews were to provide their first name, last name, age, and address.

The Jewish Council was created in the following manner: the Gestapo seized ten men from off the streets and took them to government headquarters; they informed them that they were to be the Jewish Council and that it was their responsibility to carry out all instructions from the German authorities. Anyone guilty of the slightest infraction would be shot.

Ilya Mushkin, the former Assistant Director of the Ministry for Commercial Trade, was appointed chairman of the Council.

By 15 July 1941 the registration of the Jews was complete. From that day forward, under pain of being shot, Jews had to wear a yellow patch of strictly defined dimensions (ten centimeters in diameter) sewn on their chest and back. Instructions were issued forbidding Jews to walk on the central streets of the city. On the other streets they could walk only along the pavement. They were forbidden to say hello to non-Jewish friends. Then the German authorities issued the order to set up the ghetto.

In addition, the Jews were forced to pay a tribute in gold, silver, Soviet currency, and certain types of bonds.

Crowds of Jews poured out of their old places of residence, leaving behind their apartments, furniture, and possessions; they took with them only the most necessary items. They had no form of transportation and had to carry their things on their shoulders. Each person, not counting the children, was allotted one and a half square meters in the ghetto apartments.

The resettlement did not take place without harassment. A strictly defined area had been designated for the ghetto, but people would no sooner settle into an apartment than a new order would be issued, now excluding some streets from the ghetto while including others.

For two weeks, from the 15th to the 31st of July 1941, the Jews endured the torment of moving from place to place. By 1 August 1941 the resettlement of the Jews was completed. In cases of mixed marriage the children stayed with the father; if the father was a Jew, the children went with him into the ghetto, and the mother stayed in the city. If the father was not a Jew, then the children stayed with him in the city, and the mother had to move into the ghetto. In one known instance Professor [Afonsky], a Russian married to a Jew, went to the German commandant's office and purchased the release of this wife from the ghetto. She was permitted to live with her husband and daughter in the city (outside the ghetto) on the condition that she be sterilized. The operation was performed by Professor Klumov under German supervision. This case was unusual. Professor Afonsky had a large sum in gold coins, which he put together with money he received from the sale of his property; he gave it all to the Germans as a ransom.

The ghetto contained the following streets: Khlebnaya, Nemigsky Lane, part of Respublikanskaya, part of Ostrovsky, Yubileinaya Square, part of Obuvnaya, Shornaya, Kollektornaya, the Second Opansky Lane, Fruktovaya, Tekhnicheskaya, Tankovaya, Krymskaya, and several others. These streets were isolated from the city center, from the trade and industrial enterprises. The cemetery, however, was included in the ghetto territory.

The ghetto was surrounded by a fence made of five strands of barbed wire; the punishment for going beyond the fence was death by firing squad. Any association with the Russian population was equally punishable. The Jews were forbidden to engage in trade or purchase food outside the ghetto under penalty of death by shooting. [The firing squad became a constant companion of Jewish life.]

Cherno, a laborer, had six people in his family: two adults and four children. His wife Anna could not stand to see her hungry children suffer and went outside the ghetto to seek help from her Russian friends. On her way back the police stopped her and confiscated everything she had; then they took her to the prison and shot her. The same fate befell Rozaliya Taubkina, who crossed the fence to meet with Russian relatives.

As soon as the ghetto was fenced in, the plundering and violence began. At all hours, day and night, Germans would drive up in cars or come on foot and go into Jewish apartments, where they took themselves to be the absolute masters. They plundered and confiscated anything in the apartment that pleased them. With the robbery came beatings, humiliations, and often murder.

At night the Germans would attack Jewish homes and murder the residents. The murders were carried out in especially cruel fashion: they gouged out eyes, cut off tongues and ears, and cracked open skulls. The Jews' suffering was particularly severe on Shevchenko, Zelenaya, Zaslavskaya, Sanitarnaya, Shornaya, and Kollektornaya streets. The Jews defended their apartments by making double doors with iron bars, and when the bandits knocked they refused to open. They arranged for lookouts and formed self-defense groups, but the force of arms was too great; doors and windows were broken down, and the bandits burst into their homes.

The Germans broke into the apartment were the lady physician Esfir Margolina lived, beat everyone, and killed two people. Margolina was seriously wounded; they put four bullets in her. They tortured the Kaplan family on Zaslavskaya Street for a long time; they gouged out the father's eyes, cut off the daughter's ears, and crushed the skulls of the rest of the family; after that they shot everyone.

A camp was set up on Shirokaya Street; there Russian prisoners of war and Jews were forced to do hard, exhausting labor. Jews were forced to carry sand and gravel from one place to another and then back again; they also had to dig holes without shovels. Once a day the workers were given two hundred grams of bread and some murky water that passed for soup.

Gorodetsky—a former member of the White Army and a thief, rapist, and murderer—was appointed commandant of the camp and chief of the ghetto.

Professor Siterman, a doctor of medicine and one of the most renowned specialists in Belorussia, did not succeed in evacuating from Minsk. As soon as Gorodetsky and the Gestapo discovered his whereabouts, they began to torment the professor. Gorodetsky burst into his apartment, took whatever he wanted, and severely beat the old man. Gestapo agents went to Professor Siterman's home, took him away, and forced him to do filthy, backbreaking work, cleaning excrement from cesspools and toilets with his bare hands. In August 1941 Siterman was placed in a toilet and photographed with a shovel in his hands. He was once forced to crawl around on all fours in the middle of the ghetto square; they put a soccer ball on his back and took his picture. A few days later a car came for him, and they took him away; his relatives were told it was "for a consultation." The professor was never seen again.

All the men in the ghetto were registered with the Jewish Council's labor department. This office was subsequently designated the "labor exchange." From there people were sent to do hard labor both in the military sector and in the camp on Shirokaya Street.

On 14 August a rumor spread throughout the ghetto: the men were going to be rounded up. And, in fact, part of the ghetto had been surrounded, and many men had been loaded into trucks and taken away. The Gestapo explained that they had been taken for work on military projects. What the Gestapo called "work" meant death in every other language.

On 26 August 1941 at 5:00 A.M. cars started speeding up to the ghetto. Within five minutes the ghetto was surrounded by cars, and Gestapo agents were getting out of them. They broke into Jewish apartments and shouted, "*Männer*!" ("Men!"). They took all the men to Yubileinaya Square, beat them, and then took them away.

On 31 August 1941 the round up was repeated. Once again the ghetto was surrounded by cars. This time they took not only men but also several women. While they were at it, they plundered Jewish apartments.

The people seized during these three round-ups were taken to the prison and shot (a total of about five thousand people).

The Germans were trying to create a mood of panic among the Jews, to fetter their thoughts and actions, and to plant in them the idea that for them all was lost, that there was no way out. Beginning in August 1941, however, the gathering of forces for organized resistance against the enemy was underway. The communists who had stayed in Minsk agreed to call a party meeting at the end of August. They met in the building at 54 Ostrovsky Street. Among them was Vaingauz, one of the Soviet People's Commissars in Belorussia; employees of the Bialystok Textile Factory—Shnitman, Khaimovich, Feldman; and Smolyar, an employee of the Soviet Writers' Union.

At the meeting it was decided to create an underground party organization. [They set for themselves, first of all, the following tasks:

1. To dispel the mood of panic among the Jews.

2. To set up the systematic distribution of leaflets.

3. To establish contact with the communists in the Russian sector.

4. To establish connections with partisan units.

5. To set up a radio receiver.

The party organization's first steps were crowned with success. The Germans issued an order that all valuables—gold, silver, and jewels—be surrendered, but the underground party organization resolved that the valuables would be sent to partisan units. And some of those valuable were in fact delivered to the partisans.]

The underground party organization then began the systematic distribution of leaflets.

The leaflets were read with great interest and circulated from hand to hand. Whenever people met, instead of offering the usual greeting they would ask, "What is the news today?"

The word *naes* [news] was heard everywhere. In the leaflets the Jewish underground published the latest news from Moscow radio broadcasts that they picked up over their secret radio receiver. The leaflets were copied and passed on from house to house. Vaingauz was named editor of the leaflet.

Kirkaeshto, one of the leaders in the ghetto's underground party group, was killed in September 1941. Misha Gebelev, an instructor from the Kaganovich Regional Party Committee in Minsk, took his place in the party leadership.

He was assigned the task of establishing contact with communists outside the ghetto. The question of convening a joint party conference was raised.

In order to save the Russian communists from the German prison, Gebelev risked his life by going throughout the city, locating apartments, and hiding his comrades in them. Some of them he hid in *malinas*[1] in the ghetto. Just outside the ghetto they set up reserve apartments, where communists from the "Russian sector" and communists from the ghetto conducted their work.

In September contact was established with a partisan unit that was operating in the east. Guides from the unit came, and the first group of people from the ghetto was sent to join the partisans; there were about twenty of them, mostly communists and people with military training: Shnitman, Khaimovich, Gordon, Lenya Okun, and others.

The underground party group resolved to organize systematic help for partisan units in the form of warm clothing and items such as soap and salt.

The underground group viewed the Jewish Council (*Judenrat*) as an organ of the occupying authorities; nevertheless they found elements that they needed within the Judenrat, people who were ready to aid the partisan movement and to direct Jewish families to partisan units. The initial contact was made with Mushkin, the chairman of the Jewish Council; later Ruditser and Serebryansky, who were in charge of the production section of the Jewish Council, were recruited to help the partisan movement. They turned over to the leaders of the party group items for the partisan units: shoes, leather, underwear, warm clothing, typewriters, office supplies, soap, medications, money, and sometimes even food and salt.

The fascist executioners roamed the ghetto and would not leave the Jewish apartments alone; and yet Jewish women, even the elderly ones, helped the partisans by sewing underwear and camouflaged outfits and knitting socks. Late at night they would sneak into the cellars and work by the light of the moon. The workshops in the ghetto, which were managed by Goldin, operated primarily for the sake of the partisan cause.

At that time the communists of the ghetto and the communists of the Russian sector decided to call a joint meeting for the creation of a single party organization in Minsk.

The twenty-fourth anniversary of the October Revolution was approaching.

On 6 November the rumor spread that on the anniversary of the October Revolution there would be a pogrom in the Minsk Ghetto.[2] Gorodetsky came to the ghetto; he selected the skilled workers he needed and made arrangements for them and their families to be taken to the camp on Shirokaya Street during the pogrom. Several employees of the Judenrat were also sent there.

Here is a brief description of the camp from Comrade Grechanik:

"The camp was on Shirokaya Street. From there no one was allowed to go home. There were prisoners of war in the camp; for the most part, the Germans sent to the camp Russians, Belorussians, and Poles who had resisted the German authorities. Everyone there had red patches sewn onto their clothes. The Germans put some 'Westerner' in charge of the camp.

He made no distinctions: he beat everyone, both Jews and Russians. In the camp they would shoot people for the slightest step out of line. . . .

"Many were sick, and new people were often brought into the camp. In the camp on Shirokaya Street people were quickly used up."

The Jews did not sleep that troubled night; they waited for morning. It had just begun to get light, when big black covered trucks entered the ghetto. The Gestapo agents were armed with whips, revolvers, and light machine guns. On 7 November 1941 the Germans committed their crimes not only against the Jews. Gallows were set up all over Minsk, on the streets, in the parks, in the bazaars, and on the outskirts of the city. Approximately one hundred people were hanged throughout the city that day; from their necks dangled plywood signs with the words "Partisan," "For Associating with Partisans," "Communist," and so on. But the most terrible blow, of course, fell on the ghetto. People were ordered to put on their finest clothing and to dress their children in holiday clothes; they were told to bring even their little infants along. Everyone was lined up in columns four abreast and taken under armed guard to Novo-Krasnaya Street. The Germans photographed one of the columns from a truck that stood next to the park. Machine guns opened up, and the entire column was murdered. Trucks pulled up to Novo-Myasnitskaya Street, and people were loaded onto them. The workers who had already been taken out of the ghetto to go to work that morning found out that a pogrom was underway. At twelve noon, they begged to be given passes for their families and ran back to the ghetto. Many of them found no one in their family at home. It was apparent that they had been taken right from their beds. The workers rushed to the trucks. Some of those who could not find their loved ones asked if they could go with the trucks; perhaps they would find them.

The officer replied that those who had already be taken away were no longer alive. "If you want to go," he said, "you can, but I do not know whether you will return." Many workers saved women, girls, children, friends, and strangers by passing them off as members of their own family.

The trucks went back and forth all day. On that day somewhere between twelve and thirteen thousand Jews were taken to Tuchinka.[3] They were held there for two days. The moans and cries of children, their throats parched from lack of water, echoed throughout the area. On the third day the machine guns went to work. Of the thousands who were taken to be shot, two or three returned.

A boy of about ten made it back to the ghetto. He told his story:

"Many women and children were brought to the barracks in trucks; at seven o'clock in the evening they were taken away. They were held for nearly three days. They were given nothing to eat or drink. Some died during those three days: small children, old men, old women. I was with my mother's sister when they took us away. There were no other trucks behind ours. My aunt picked up the truck's tarpaulin and said, 'Jump, little one; maybe you'll survive.'

"I jumped while the truck was moving and lay there for a while; then I came here."

Here is another story, the story of a woman who was taken into a field to be shot. Her body swollen, she made it back to the ghetto naked and bloody; she had been wounded in the arm. She had seen long, wide trenches; next to them stood Germans and policemen ordering people to undress. As soon as the little children got off the trucks, the policemen took them from their parents and broke their backbones over their knees. Infants were thrown into the air and either shot or caught on bayonets and then tossed into the trenches. Those who had undressed were lined up along the trenches and machine-gunned down. Those who refused to undress were murdered with their clothes on; if they had nice clothing, their bodies were stripped. One woman who had undressed was stood next to a pit and was wounded in the arm; she fell into the pit, and bodies fell on top of her. That night it grew quiet; the shooting had stopped. She crawled out of the pit and made it back top the ghetto.

The following streets fell prey to the pogrom: Ostrovsky, Respublikanskaya, Shevchenko, Nemigsky, Khlebnaya, and others.

Toward evening, on 7 November, the pogrom began to die down.

After the pogrom the Germans set about creating a "specialists area." They referred to all skilled workers as "specialists."

The labor exchange requested lists of Jewish workers from the German managers. The managers gave them the lists, and the labor exchange started issuing special cards for the skilled workers.

Unskilled workers were not given cards. All the non-specialists were order to be transferred immediately to another region. A new resettlement was underway. Everyone understood what this resettlement meant. Women began looking for specialists, and young girls married old men. The Germans condemned many of those without a "specialist" card to death; many of the condemned went insane.

Once the resettlement of the non-specialists was completed, the Germans started issuing address plates to be attached to doors. The plate was attached the door and indicated who lived in the apartment, which ones worked, and who were the dependents. Once all of this had been done, the Germans ordered each resident who was a skilled worker to go to the *Judenrat* and have the number of his building sewn on his chest and back beneath the yellow patch. The number was stamped onto a piece of white canvas.

The Germans warned that if any resident of any building should fail to wear the number, then all the residents in the building with that number would be shot. [The "specialists" and *Judenrat* employees returned from the camp on Shirokaya Street on 8 November 1941.]

Portions of Nemigsky, Ostrovsky, and other streets led into the Russian sector. The ghetto territory was growing smaller. In the ghetto a hard and hungry life went on, but even this life was snatched away from many.

Thousands of German Jews began arriving in Minsk. Their clothing was strange: they wore hooded capes, some in pink, others in dark blue, still others in light blue. The capes were made of artificial leather and had a six-pointed star sewn on the right side of the chest. The people spoke only German. The Gestapo came and drove the Minsk Jews out of their homes on Respublikanskaya, Obuvnaya, Sukhaya, and Opanskaya streets; the new arrivals were housed there. The entire area was surrounded by a barbed wire fence.

People would go up to the fence where the German Jews were quartered. The newcomers eagerly engaged in conversation. It turned out that they were from Hamburg, Berlin, and Frankfurt. Approximately 19,000 of them were housed there during the period of the Minsk Ghetto's existence.[4] They brought with them all their possessions and were told that they would be sent to America, but they wound up in the Minsk Ghetto surrounded by barbed wire. They asked for bread; they thought that the Russian Jews were allowed to freely come and go and could freely purchase food. The Gestapo found "work" for the German Jews. Every night they would come into the ghetto and murder seventy to eighty of the German Jews. The Germans forced them to haul the bodies to the cemetery in baby carriages. Pits had already been dug there, each of which could hold about three hundred bodies. Once a pit was filled with bodies, it was covered over.

20 November 1941. Morning had not yet broken, when the Germans and the police were already wandering certain streets of the ghetto: Zamkovaya, Podzamkovaya, Zelenaya, Sanitarnaya, and others. Once again people were driven from their apartments, lined up in columns, and led away to the graves at Tuchinka. The graves had already been prepared with lime, and people were thrown into the pits alive. They were then shot and burned.

Among the people who were seized on 20 November were good skilled workers whom the Germans needed.

An officer went out to the assembly place, but the people had already been taken out of the ghetto. The officer found out where they had been taken and went outside of the city to the field where they were being slaughtered. It turned out that almost all of his workers had been murdered; but he recognized a few of the men, and it was agreed that they would not be killed. One of them was a highly skilled furrier named Alperovich; another was the barber Levin, who shaved all the officers. The barber's wife and daughter were found also. At first the "chief" of the annihilation operation released only the barber and Alperovich; then, to torment them further, he allowed the barber to take either his wife or his daughter with him. Levin took his daughter. The officer told them to speak to no one about what they had seen. When they arrived at the factory, they were white as a sheet and could not speak. Alperovich fell ill for a long time afterward.

Five thousand Jews perished there on 20 November.[5] People began hiding in specially prepared cellars, pits, and secret rooms known as "malinas"; but the malinas did not save them. The Hitlerites' raids were too sudden. The Germans explained the pogrom of 20 November by saying that "the plan had not been completed" on 7 November; that is, the number of Jews annihilated had been less than what the German authorities demanded.

The pogroms and deaths of several leaders of the underground did not stop the resistance movement. Vaingauz died during the pogrom of 20 November1941; Propaganda Secretary Pruslin[6] (Bruskind), of the Stalin Regional Party Committee in Minsk, was brought into the underground center to take his place. At the end of November the communists convened a general party conference. The conference was chaired by "Slavek." Gebelev was chosen to represent the ghetto party group. From that moment began the systematic smuggling of people into the partisan units. [The general party conference resolved to organize the party into groups of ten. Each group of ten would be headed by a secretary. The groups were to be organized solely on the basis of personal acquaintances and recommendations. All secretaries would report to the commissioner of their zone. There were four zones, including the ghetto. The party conference set up an underground party committee; "Slavek" was chosen as secretary of the committee.

The commissioner of the party's Central Committee in the ghetto was Smolyar, who also served as secretary of the ghetto party group; he was living in the ghetto under the name of Stolyarevich, and his code name was "Skromny." The boiler room in Jewish hospital where Smolyar worked served as their headquarters. There the communists would gather to discuss and decide the most important questions.

Among the leaders of the groups of ten were Naum Feldman, Zyama Okun, Nadya Shusser, Maizels, Rubenik, and others. Emma Rodova was appointed to maintain contact with the communists in the Russian sector. The groups of ten were assigned following tasks:

1. The selection of candidates from among the communists and people with military training to be assigned to partisan units.

2. Gathering weapons.

3. Providing partisan units with material aid in the form of warm clothing.

4. Collecting medications and distributing them among partisan units.

5. The creation of a fund to assist needy communists.

The winter was hard for the residents of the ghetto; they were all suffering from cold and hunger. The Jews who worked in the Russian sector had the opportunity to interact with the Russian population, so they did not feel the hardship quite as sharply; but the Jews who worked behind the barbed wire were starving and in dire need.

Thanks to connections with members of the Judenrat, many people managed to be placed in the city, so they could direct their work in the German establishments toward the struggle against the invaders.

Groups of young people worked in factories producing arms and ammunition and had the opportunity to smuggle out those materials. Women worked in places where they could obtain underwear and warm clothing to be sent to partisan units. Shipments of ammunition and clothing to partisan units were made regularly. The shipments usually went out from the Openheim apartment at 16 Respublikanskaya Street; collection sites were located in the bazaars. As the result of their moving from place to place, contact with several of the partisan units was lost in February 1942. Word was received that the Nichiporovich unit was operating near Dukor. A group of people set out to look for the unit; among them were Doctor Margolin and Skoblo, one of the first Stakhanovites in Belorussia. The group was armed with four rifles and four grenades.

The expedition was not successful. The people were surrounded by the Gestapo, and some of them, including Skoblo, were killed; the rest returned to the ghetto with frostbitten hands and feet and spent a long time in the hospital.]

Meanwhile the underground continued to search for and purchase weapons. Naum Feldman conducted the operation. In keeping with the assignment from the party committee, ways were set up for getting people who could not be sent to partisan units out of the ghetto. At first it was mistakenly assumed that simply getting people outside the barbed wire fence would be enough to ensure their safety.

The underground party committee searched for places to send women, old people, and children. Nina Liss was assigned to this task; she went to West Belorussia to look for villages and farms located far from the railroads and highways.

In February 1942 the Germans arrested Mushkin, the Chairman of the Judenrat. He had been in a very difficult position: on the one hand, he led the struggle against the invaders by providing material aid to the partisan units; on the other hand he had to maintain the appearance of normal relations with the German authorities and pretend to carry out all their orders and directives. He had to hide his work even from some members of the Judenrat, such as Rozenblat and Epshtein.

It was a provocateur that betrayed Mushkin.

Mushkin was tortured for a long time in the prison, but he did not betray his comrades. He endured his suffering in silence. Not until a month after his arrest and torture was Mushkin taken out of the prison; he was shot while trying to escape from the car.

The winter of 1942 set in. . . . It brought hunger, cold, and illness with it. It is difficult to refer to the people's pitiful existence as "life." Homes were filled with the crying of children and the moaning of the sick. People ate the garbage thrown from German kitchens. A common dish among the Jews was potato peels that were somehow made into pancakes or pudding.

Diseases broke out: furunculosis, dystrophy, scurvy, typhoid fever, and typhus. Illnesses had to be hidden from the authorities, since every day the Germans would demand to see lists of patients admitted to the hospital. The Germans were afraid of infectious diseases; the Jews knew that as soon as the Germans found out about an outbreak of typhus, a pogrom would be inevitable. Therefore the Germans did not find out about such diseases in the ghetto. Nevertheless a pogrom of new and horrifying violence befell the Jews.

On the morning of 2 March 1942 cars filled with Gestapo agents pulled up to the ghetto; among them was Obersturmführer Schmidt, who was completely drunk. It was a bad omen. The Jews were terribly distressed. The columns of workers, however, set out for work as usual. The Gestapo agents went to the apartment where the labor exchange was located and started carousing. There was no shortage of vodka and expensive wines. It had all been brought into the ghetto in a truck. Not all of them could fit into the apartment, so some of them remained on the street and in the square. They summoned Richter, Chief of Police for the Fifth Precinct and the man in charge of the ghetto. The Gestapo agents guzzled liquor and stuffed themselves with food; then they went to work. They broke into homes with their whips and revolvers and drove people into the wallpaper factory yard on Shpalernaya Street. Crowds of people—women, children, and the elderly—stood and waited to die. The executioners did not find the residents of two homes on Tekhnicheskaya Street; they were hiding in malinas. The Germans set those buildings on fire and burned the people alive. When the columns of workers returned to the smoldering ruins the next morning, Gestapo men met them at the ghetto gates. Along with the people awaiting their deaths in the wallpaper factory yard, these workers were taken to the railroad tracks, loaded into train cars, and sent to Dzerzhinsk. There they were all shot. Many tried to escape, but the murderers' bullets caught up with them. Thus five thousand people were murdered.

Gestapo agents surrounded a column of workers from the prison; the squad leader for the column was Levin.

Levin used to be an artist and writer who wrote children's books under the pseudonym of Ber Sarin.

Levin demanded that the entire column be released, arguing that his column consisted entirely of specialists. They released Levin, but he insisted that everyone be released. They beat him with their rifle butts and shoved him back. In his hands Levin had a lid from a tin can, and he used it to attack the Germans. Levin was shot right there on the street.

When the bloody job was drawing to an end that evening, the drunken Obersturmführer Schmidt, whip in hand and surrounded by Germans and policemen, shouted in a pure Russian: "More than ever, today was a success, splendid, a success, a success." A policeman was awarded a medal and given a promotion for organizing the pogrom so well and for assisting the Gestapo.

As in the earlier pogroms, the orphanage and the nursing home were destroyed, [and some of the employees of the Judenrat were killed.]

Led by the director of the orphanage, the column of children of all ages, from the very youngest to children of thirteen or fourteen, posed a terrible sight. The children were crying out: "Why? Our people will come and avenge our blood and the blood of our fathers and mothers!" Whips lashed at their heads. Bruised and in rags, their faces swollen from the blows, the children walked on. Whenever one fell behind, he was shot. The whole street was littered with the bodies of children.

A woman who worked in the Amsterdam Orphanage committed suicide by slitting her wrists.

The population of the ghetto was growing smaller. Once again the Germans carried out a resettlement, shifting Jews from one apartment to another, from one area to another. The territory of the ghetto was shrinking; the ring around it tightened.

The pogroms perpetrated by the Gestapo did not stop the work of the communists. The flow of Jews leaving the ghetto for partisan units went one uninterrupted; indeed, more and more were leaving to join the partisans every day. The Gestapo found out about it and answered with bloody terror every time Jews left to join the partisans.

Whenever the Gestapo was on the trail of someone associated with the underground party organization, they held not only him responsible but everyone in the building where he lived or in his work column as well. At night they would surround the building, take all the people out, and shoot them.

At the end of March 1942 a wave of night pogroms broke out. Ghetto residents listened in horror to bursts of machine gun fire in the night and to the screams and groans of people who were shot. Every night you could hear the footsteps of people running to escape the bullets.

Night pogroms took place on 31 March, 3 April, 15 April, and 23 April. Nina Liss died during the pogrom of 31 March 1942; she had returned to Minsk just the day before, after completing her assignment in West Belorussia.

A traitor turned over to the Gestapo lists of people working in the underground party committee, with their addresses. Nina lived at 18 Kollektornaya Street. When the bandits surrounded her building that night, they knocked and shouted, "Ninka, open up!"

The Gestapo demanded that Gebelev, Smolyar, Feldman, and Okun be handed over; otherwise they would shoot all the employees of the Judenrat. [Ioffe, who had been appointed Chairman of the Judenrat, knew that the Germans would carry out their threat. Nevertheless he refused to comply with the Gestapo's demands.]

In the course of engaging in conspiracies, Gebelev had acquired three surnames, so the Gestapo lost his trail. There were many Feldmans in the ghetto. The Gestapo sent three Feldmans to prison; they never returned. Okun was arrested after a brief period of time.

Smolyar (Stolyarevich), the leader of the underground party organization, was very hard to catch. The Gestapo persisted in their demands that he be handed over. Judenrat Chairman Ioffe came up with a plan: he filled out a blank passport for Efim Stolyarevich and smeared it with blood; then he went to the Gestapo and told them that the passport was found in one of the buildings where a night pogrom had taken place and that it was removed from one of the bodies. The Gestapo was satisfied and wrote Stolyarevich off as dead.

Stolyarevich, Gebelev, and Feldman survived and continued the struggle against the enemy.

Feldman was assigned the task of supplying weapons. Groups of people on their way to partisan units were armed with rifles, pistols, and grenades. In addition to acquiring weapons, members of the underground directed their efforts toward obtaining a printing press for the partisans. They managed to get two presses to partisan units; a third press was delivered to the party committee in the city.

One person who played a major role in getting the presses to the partisans was a messenger boy named Vilik Rubezhin. A member of the Young Pioneers,[7] the boy had lost his parents; when the war broke out, he was in a Young Pioneer camp near Minsk. Three times, and at great risk, he pulled sleds through the city carrying typesetting materials hidden under a pile of rags.

In fact, he led a group of thirty Jews to join the partisans. Subsequently Vilik himself went into the forest to join the partisans; he was involved in many acts of sabotage and ambushes. He was awarded the medal of the order of the Red Star.

[The Gestapo justified the night pogroms by saying that they were part of the fight against the partisan units. Indeed, such Aktions took place in the Russian sector as well.] An enemy infiltrated into the party organization in the city and betrayed several members of the underground party committee.

Gebelev brought ten communists from the Russian sector, provided them with Jewish passports, and hid them in malinas in the ghetto.

Especially cruel was the quick and sudden pogrom of 23 April 1942. The murderers surrounded the buildings on Obuvnaya, Sukhaya, Shornaya, and Kollektornaya streets. The pogrom began at five in the afternoon and ended at eleven that night. Five hundred people died.

Another night pogrom, very striking in its cruelty, was conducted by soldiers and police in May 1942. They surrounded two very crowded four-story buildings on Zavalnaya Street and set them on fire from all sides at once; the people inside were burned alive. Several hundred people perished in the flames.

The German thugs rotated; some would leave, others would arrive. And, under the pretense of maintaining order in the ghetto, every one of them was fully engaged in the extermination of the Jews.

Shortly before he left the ghetto, Richter decided to see whether the Jews were complying with the order that required them to go to work. He stopped the first three people he met and took them to the labor exchange office, where he ordered the police to strip them and beat them half to death; then he took one of them out to the square, tied him to a post, and shot him. On the chest of the murder victim there hung a sign that said, "This is what will happen to anyone who dares to refuse to go to work."

Richter's successor was Hattenbach. He issued the order to transform the ghetto into a camp. All of the buildings in the ghetto were renumbered, and in addition to their yellow badges, residents were required to wear the number of their building. Hattenbach personally shot hundreds of Jews for violating this order. Shootings in the ghetto, however, took place for any reason and every excuse. In May three workers were brought in from the Trostyanets camp. They were not feeling well and asked to see a doctor. Hattenbach took them to the cemetery and shot them. There were many such incidents.

Work at the October Factory was considered most desirable. There, in addition to two hundred grams of bread, workers received a mug of hot water and some thin soup for lunch.

In May 1942 thirteen women were fired from the factory. They decided to go with the workers' column the next day and find out why they had been released. They were not allowed to speak to the supervisor and were sent to the prison. For two weeks they were tortured and tormented in the prison; then they were taken under armed guard to the square in the ghetto opposite the Judenrat. The residents were forced out of their homes and onto the square, whereupon the thirteen poor women were shot with hollow-point bullets. The murder victims lay on the square for two days; the Germans would not allow them to be buried.

In April 1942 the Gestapo ordered all the Jews to show up for *Appell*[8] on the square in front of the Judenrat at precisely ten o'clock every Sunday.

These gatherings on the square never took place without people being lashed with whips and beaten with rifle butts. Not knowing what awaited them there, everyone was very worried. Every Sunday at the assemblies Richter, Hattenbach, Fichtel, Menschel, and others would give speeches to persuade the Jews not to flee from the ghetto to partisan units; they said there would be no more pogroms. Every Sunday they repeated exactly the same speech, after which the Jews were forced to perform concert numbers. They would sing and play instruments; some of them were photographed.

One Sunday the police went to check the buildings to see whether all the Jews were at Appell. They found fourteen men in the apartments. They were taken out to the square and paraded in front of everyone; it was announced that they would be taken to the prison, from which they would never return. And so it happened: they were shot. The Appells continued until 28 June 1942. One Sunday in June, after Appell, a group of Jews was lined up at the water fountain on Tankovaya Street. A policeman was walking down Second Opansky Lane with a woman. As they approached the barbed wire, they saw the people standing in line for water; the policeman turned to his lady friend and said, "Watch what a good shot I am." Then he took his rifle and fired into the crowd. A sixteen-year-old girl named Esther fell to the ground. She died an hour later. It was not an isolated incident.

[As a result of the arrest of the Minsk party committee, guides from the partisan units stopped coming, and the connection with the units was temporarily lost. After discussing the situation, the ghetto party committee decided to establish its own base for sending people to the partisan units. Twenty people led by Comrade Lapidus were picked for the assignment. People were to be sent out in a truck. But since there was not room in the truck for everyone being sent, they arranged for an initial group of twenty to be taken forty-five kilometers; then the truck would go back to the fifteenth kilometer and pick up a second group. Feldman, Tumin, Lifshits, and others were in the second group. They did not find the truck at the site agreed upon. The first group got through all right, but the second group came under fire from the Gestapo and traitors. Some of them, including Feldman and Tumin, made it back to the ghetto; the others were killed.]

At the end of April 1942 [the communists who were left in the ghetto decided to reestablish the party organization in the city.] A party meeting was convened in one of the buildings on Torgovaya Street. By the end of the meeting, the party organization was reestablished; it was no longer divided in groups of ten, however, but according to territory and work sites. The party organization in the ghetto was set up as a separate district committee. [At that time a directive had been issued from the Central Committee of the Bolshevik Party calling for the mass smuggling of people into the partisan units.]

With the help of the ghetto's underground party committee, a partisan unit was formed (in the Slutsk area). Jews from the ghetto were sent to this unit. Prisoners of war working in the camp on Shirokaya Street, as well as workers in the felt factory and other establishments, were systematically sent to partisan units.

As the prisoners of war were being sent to their units, Misha Gebelev was arrested; he had devoted his entire life to serving the people and had carried on the struggle tirelessly and courageously.

While the prisoners of war were being smuggled to partisan units, acts of sabotage were taking place at various businesses: at the meat-packing plant, the felt factory, and the distillery. A Jewish blacksmith who worked at the distillery systematically poisoned the liquor that was to be sent to the German soldiers on the front.

The ghetto party committee instructed Naum Feldman, one of the original members of the underground party organization, to set up a partisan base west of the city. Feldman had a difficult time. For two days he waited at the ninth kilometer for the partisan guides who were supposed to take him and his group to the designated site.

Feldman finally found Skachkov's unit; it had just been formed. But Feldman decided to organize a unit himself. He sent messengers to the underground party committee in the ghetto, and they in turn sent him new comrades. The group was already armed with light machine guns, rifles, pistols, and revolvers. At the end of May another unit took those from Feldman's group who had their own weapons. The ones who were left set about searching for arms. Once again the ghetto party committee came to their aid. The connection between the partisan unit and the party committee was never broken. In June 1942 Semen Grigorevich Ganzenko—a prisoner of war in the Shirokaya Street camp for whom an escape had been arranged—was sent to command the unit. The unit was named in honor of Comrade Budenny. Feldman worked in the unit as a party organizer. The unit merged with the Stalin Brigade and became one of its military subdivisions. Ganzenko was subsequently named brigade commander, and Feldman was appointed commissar of one of the brigade units.

All of the escapes from the ghetto entailed colossal difficulties. The ghetto was guarded day and night. Ambushes were set up everywhere.

On 27 July 1942 the Gestapo issued an order: as of 28 July 1942, in addition to the yellow badges and building numbers, all Jews had to wear the following signs: they were to wear red badges, and their dependents and the unemployed had to wear green ones. The workers were to receive their badges at their place of employment; dependents and the unemployed would receive theirs on the square in front of the Judenrat. No one suspected that this seemingly innocent order was a preparation for a terrible slaughter.

28 July 1942 was the blackest day in the ghetto.

The Gestapo and police came into the ghetto that morning after the workers' columns had left. The entire ghetto was enclosed in a tight ring of patrols. The residents were forced out of their apartments and into the square. Large black enclosed trucks—mobile gas units—pulled up. During this pogrom the Gestapo even destroyed the hospital, which had been spared in previous pogroms. The sick were shot in their beds; among them was the award-winning composer Kroshner. Physicians and medical personnel were lined up in a separate column in their white gowns and led out to the square. They were loaded into the mobile gas units and murdered.

Forty-eight doctors were killed; among them were the finest specialists in Belorussia: Professor Dvorzhets, a doctor of medical sciences, and Associate Professor Maizels, a doctoral candidate in medical sciences. Highly experienced, senior physicians also perished, including Khurgel, Kantorovich, Gurvich, Sirotkina, and many others.

The Germans dragged two Jews from malinas. One of them was thrown to the ground and covered with pieces of broken glass; they tried to force the other to stomp on the glass. When they saw that the Jew refused to be his comrade's executioner, the Germans themselves crushed the glass and then murdered both of them.

The terrible, unprecedented pogrom lasted from 28 July until 1:00 P.M. on 31 July. During their brief pauses the executioners drank and caroused.

At 1:00 p.m. on 31 July 1942 the order to halt the pogrom was given, but the fascists' debauchery did not abate. They continued to run from one apartment to the next searching for malinas, dragging people out, and shooting them. Approximately 25,000 people died during this monstrous slaughter.

Lilya Samoilovna Gleizer lived through the pogrom from the first hour to the last. This is how she describes it:

"It rained all night, but on the morning of 28 July it came down even harder. Nature had already begun to weep over innocent blood. That morning everyone who was able left for work with the workers' columns. Once they were out of the ghetto, some of them went to hide with Russian friends. They hid in malinas.

"Based on guarantees they had received, those who were in the workers' columns thought that the children left in the ghetto would not be touched. That morning I went down into a so-called malina that was set apart from the other malinas in our building. It was right under the stove. The entrance to it was so carefully camouflaged that the most experienced detective could not discover it.

"Through the basement walls I could hear the cries of children and the even the muffled conversations of adults. I can say with certainty that, judging from my experience with previous pogroms, these malinas would be discovered if the fascists should look for them.

"People are usually discovered during pogroms because of the children.

"Children cannot sit in complete silence and endure the hunger that lasts for days on end, the unbearable stuffy air, the darkness. They start to get fidgety and cry, which leads to the discovery of the malina.

"Through the wall I could hear people frantically rushing to get ready for something extraordinary. Everywhere the sound of bustling, doors creaking, people crying, excited talking could be heard. You could hear policemen forcing people out of the building and into the street. You could hear screams, people begging them to leave the very old ones and the little children; but all the crying and pleading for mercy was drowned out by the unconstrained swearing of the policemen. After an hour everything became quiet. Out of curiosity I crawled out of the malina and into the room. A hush had descended on this building where nine hundred people lived; it was as if all of them had died. The street, too, was quiet and empty. I stood there a minute: I thought I heard something. It was the hysterical cries of a woman begging for mercy; then came a long, drawn out noise followed by several rifle shots. I quickly crawled back into the hole that was my savior. From the malina I could hear the sound of gunshots gradually becoming louder. I realized that the police had returned to make a second, more careful search and that they were shooting anyone they found.

"After a few minutes I could hear the sound of footsteps on the stairs in our building. Dishes crashed, and rifle shots rang out; I heard the quick, sharp crack of doors broken in and the guffawing of the policemen. It went on for several minutes, and then the noise started to die down; the 'bobiki,' as the policemen were usually called, had left. A few more rifle shots could be heard in the building, and then everything grew as still as death.

"A quiet set in; now and then you could hear the faint crying of people in the neighboring malinas. My curiosity changed into fear. Again I crawled out of my malina. Suddenly I heard a noise from the apartment next door. After standing there for a moment and listening, I realized that it was the insane woman; she was my neighbor, and she had lost her mind when her husband had been shot right before her eyes during the first days of the ghetto. Listening for the slightest sound, I tiptoed like a cat up to her door. I cracked it open and saw her; she was walking around the room with a sleeping baby in her arms. By sheer chance the police had not noticed her. 'She must have been fated to live,' I thought. She did not see me; talking to no one, she was begging for food. I burst into tears at the sight of this mad woman with the little one in her arms; I was overcome by an infinite compassion for her. I remembered that in my cupboard I had a crust of the sawdust bread that the Germans fed to Jews and prisoners of war. In an instant I sprang to my cupboard and brought her the bread; I showed it to her, using it as a lure to get the insane woman into my malina and save her. We had no sooner crawled in than we heard knocking on the outside door and the Hitlerites barking, 'Aufmachen!' [Open up!] After a few moments you could hear the pounding of rifle butts. I crawled even farther into the hole and pressed against the earthen wall, trembling with fear. We heard the Germans break into the room and start firing into the walls, ceilings, and floors. These Germans were specially trained to find malinas, and they were known for their brutality. The Hitlerites shouted and swore furiously; from their garbled speech and swearing I could tell that they were drunk.

"Now in my malina, the mad woman's baby was frightened by the gunshots and started crying loudly.

"His mother put her hands over his mouth, but the Hitlerites had already heard him. They stood still for a moment and then started ripping up the floor over my malina, swearing violently.

"'We're dead,' the thought ran through my head. After tearing the boards out of the floor around the stove, the Hitlerites tossed in several hand grenades. The explosions uncovered malinas next to mine, but not mine, since the shock from the explosion had caused the layer of ground that served as my roof to collapse. Then began the terrible firing into the malinas. The Hitlerites were not moved by the pleas of women and children begging for mercy. They threw several more grenades into the underground opening, through which the moaning of the wounded and pleas for mercy could be heard. Again the explosions shook everything, and my malina was uncovered. The moaning and pleas stopped for a moment. Again the silence set in after the explosions had deafened me, but then, all of a sudden, I could hear the snarling and swearing of the fascists: 'Herausgehen!' [Come out!] But all that was heard in reply was the heart-rending screams of the wounded. After repeating the order and getting no results, the Germans came down into our cellar; they shined their flashlights into the darkness where the pleas and groans of the dying were coming from. I clung tightly to the cellar's earthen wall and held my breath when I saw the beams from the flashlights. The Germans did not find me, since I was behind a corner in the cellar. After yelling 'Herausgehen!' several more times, they finished off the dying with daggers and went back upstairs.

"Possessed by the madness of destruction, the Hitlerites began to smash dishes, tear up furniture, and break windows. Then they broke into other apartments in our building, and the same horror was repeated. After several hours everything grew quiet. From time to time the silence was broken by faint moans from the neighboring malinas. Alone with the dead in the darkness, I became terrified and hurriedly crawled toward the door that had been blown open by the grenade blasts. A faint light was coming from there; it lit up the cellar. I stumbled over a woman stretched across the very entrance to the malina. It was the mad woman I had tried to save. Her body was riddled with shrapnel from the grenades; apparently she had died instantly. Next to her lay the dead body of her baby.

"I crawled into my room. It was littered with pieces of broken dishes and furniture; the floor and everything else were covered with a thick layer of lime, as well as with feathers and down from blankets and pillows. The windows and window frames had been smashed out, and there were gaping holes in the walls and ceiling from grenade blasts. My head started to spin. I buried my face in my hands and nearly fell onto pieces of the broken door; but the thirst for life drew me out of my swoon. After regaining my senses, I rushed up to the attic. From the attic I saw the pogrom continuing in other buildings on our street. I could hear the scattered, uninterrupted sound of grenade explosions and machine gun fire. The street was covered with the bloody bodies of women and children. The Hitlerites were dragging all sorts of items and bundles from the buildings; they loaded their loot into carts and hauled it away. Even this, however, was not the pogrom itself but only the beginning of the pogrom."

At noon everyone in the ghetto was herded onto Yubileinaya Square. Huge tables, decorated as if for a holiday, had been set up there; they were laid with all sorts of fine foods and wines. At the tables sat the leading perpetrators of a slaughter never before seen in the world.

In the center sat Richter, the head of the ghetto to whom Hitler had awarded the Iron Cross. Next to him were members of the SS and one of the chiefs of the ghetto, an officer named Rade; the fat pig Bentske, chief of police in Minsk, was there too. [Not far from this demonic throne stood a specially constructed platform. The fascists forced the composer Ioffe, a member of the ghetto's Jewish Council, to speak from the platform. Having been deceived by Richter, Ioffe began by calming the anxious crowd, explaining that today the Germans simply wanted to conduct a registration and exchange of identity badges. Ioffe had not yet finished trying to calm them down, when] covered trucks—mobile gas units—entered the square from every direction. [Immediately Ioffe realized what this meant. He cried out to the agitated crowd, through which the phrase "mobile gas units" spread like lightning.

"Comrades! They've deceived me. They are going to kill you. It's a pogrom!"]

The insane crowd scattered in all directions, seeking salvation from a horrible death. Everyone was confused, and people were rushing all around; an infinite number of six-pointed yellow stars were flashing by. Having already surrounded the square, the fascists opened up a steady stream of fire on the defenseless people. Nevertheless the people pushed forward. Hand-to-hand combat broke out between the unarmed people and the fascists, who were armed to the teeth. Many of the fascists had to pay dearly before the crowd could be brought under control. The entire square was littered with bodies and flowing with blood. The Germans lined up endless rows of women and old people in front of dozens of mobile gas units.[9] The children were separated from the adults and forced to stand on their knees with their hands up. Weak and exhausted, the little ones started to cry; immediately their little arms grew tired and fell. For this they had their throats cut or their backs broken; or a fascist would raise a small child up over his head and thrown him down on the cobblestone pavement as hard as he could. With such a blow the child's skull would break into pieces, and his brains would fly everywhere. The mothers standing in line for the mobile gas units who saw it either went insane or attacked the Germans like tigers. They were murdered with machine guns. Those who refused to crawl into the gas trucks suffered a horrible death. They were dragged over to the tables, behind which drunken toasts were being made to the sound of accordion music. The drunken Hattenbach, Richter, Rade, and others would pronounce the sentence: "Cut off the nose and ears," "Beat them to death with fists and whips," and so on. The sentences were carried out immediately either by the judges themselves or by the Gestapo, police, and garrison soldiers.

[Upon witnessing this bloody spectacle, Zorov—once named the People's Artist of the Republic—rushed at the fascists with a curse on his lips. He bit them with his teeth, beat them with his hands, and kicked them with his feet; he was knocked unconscious and thrown into a gas truck.]

So it went until late in the evening. The square was emptied, and the organizers of the massacre fell asleep at their festive tables. The pogrom quieted down. Constant perpetrators of violence in the ghetto, the soldiers from the Minsk garrison were still poking about looking for valuables. Every last child who was forced to hold his hands up over his head had been murdered in the square. The mobile gas units were no longer returning. They had taken away everyone who was not murdered in the square, at Trostyanets, or at Tuchinka.

That night members of the Jewish police who were still alive were ordered to clean the blood and the bodies off the square. The order was carried out by the next morning. The morning of 29 July came. The day was a gloomy one, as though it were a premonition of the continuation of the massacre. The darkened sun peeked out from time to time and then hid again behind the black storm clouds. The ghetto was deserted.

At ten o'clock in the morning the German trucks began rumbling onto Yubileinaya Square. Commanded by the chief of police and Bentske—a German officer, executioner, and mayor—groups of soldiers from the Minsk garrison once again set about their looting and searching for malinas. Since it was about to rain, the tables were moved from the square into the committee building. Old people, women, and children found in the malinas were taken there to be slaughtered. Many hiding places were uncovered that day.

The Germans and the police burst into the ghetto hospital, which had not been touched on the first day of the pogrom, and killed all the patients and hospital staff with their daggers.

On 1 August, after four days of slaughter, the Germans once again set up tables laid with food and wine on Yubileinaya Square. All the same leaders were seated there.

The Gestapo and the police were ordered to round up the last inhabitants of the ghetto hiding in malinas.

On this last day of the pogrom the fascists surpassed all limits of the human imagination in the crimes they committed. Before the eyes of mothers, who either fainted or went insane, the drunken Germans and policemen raped young girls without a trace of shame either in front of each other or in front of onlookers. They took their knives and cut out sex organs, forced bodies, both dead and alive, into the most disgusting poses, and cut off noses, breasts, and ears.

Mothers threw themselves on the fascists in fits of rage and then fell dead with their skulls crushed.

Decrepit old men and women were beaten to death with rubber truncheons and leather whips. The hysterical screams, cries, and curses went on all day; the playing of dozens of accordions could not drown them out. It was all over by three in the afternoon. An hour later, Richter's assistants had left the ghetto.

After the slaughter the Gestapo ordered all the establishments where Jewish workers had been during the four-day pogrom to return them to the ghetto.

The workers' columns headed toward the ghetto that evening. They all walked slowly, in complete silence, their eyes looking down toward the ground. Thus they approached the checkpoint at the entrance to the ghetto. Who would meet them at the gate?

Ordinarily all the unemployed people in the ghetto would crowd around the control point to meet the columns of workers returning from hard labor. Mothers, wives, the elderly, fathers, children, sisters, and brothers were glad to see each other alive again after a fourteen-hour separation. But this time there was no one standing at the gate.

Only at the checkpoint did a German guard run out, give his metal-tipped boots a loud, firm click, and salute the officer at the head of the armed escort. The officer returned the salute and ordered the guard to open the gates. The columns entered the silent ghetto. The streets were littered with pieces of smashed furniture, scraps of paper, books, and broken dishes. Feathers from quilts and pillows, along with bits of broken household utensils, covered the pavement and sidewalks.

Cupboards, buffets, and tables were sticking half way out of broken windows and by some miracle were just hanging there. And everywhere, everywhere, lay the bodies of the ones whom the returning workers longed to see. They were lying in huge pools of blood. The German officer who led the columns had apparently never seen such a sight, for he suddenly screamed and fell to the blood-soaked pavement in a fit of hysterics. A shudder went through the column, and it came to a halt. The women became hysterical and fell into heavy sobbing; the men groaned as they wrung their hands and tore their hair. From the time of its creation, had the world ever seen such a portrait of horror?

Insane, people rushed to their apartments hoping to find their relatives safe in the malinas. But, hidden away in stoves, under the floor, and between the walls, the malinas had been blown up with grenades. There the workers found the remains of loved ones whose bodies had been torn apart by the explosions. Most of them, however, did not find a trace of their loved ones. Their loved ones had been taken to Trostyanets and Tuchinka in gas vans; after suffocating in the "death trucks," they had been robbed, stripped, and dumped into pits.

Even the pogrom of 2 March paled next to the bloody slaughter of July.[10]

By the first of August only 8,794 Jews remained out of 75,000.

German Jews also perished in the pogrom: three thousand of them were poisoned in the mobile gas units. They had been told to gather together their things, supposedly for a work assignment. Hattenbach and the Obersturmführer said a few words to them on the square; then they were loaded into the gas trucks and poisoned.

There were changes in the German butchers. Richter left, and Hattenbach took his place; then came Fichtel, then Menschel. Each such departure and arrival cost more human victims.

In January 1943 the police found the bodies of two Germans on the street. The Gestapo responded to this act with terrible reprisals. On 1 February 1942 at 3:00 P.M. the mobile gas units entered the ghetto. Gestapo men got out; at their head was the bloody Obersturmführer Miller.

People were driven from their homes and into the street, where they were seized and thrown into the gas vans. The following day there were four hundred fewer people in the ghetto.

Shortly afterward fifty-three Jews from Slutsk arrived in the ghetto. They had been designated as "specialists." They told about the horrors of the gradual liquidation of the Slutsk Ghetto. In their stories they often mentioned the name Ribbe, a Gestapo agent distinguished by his unimaginable cruelty.

In the first half of February 1943 two previously unknown Germans appeared on the streets of the ghetto. On their clothing they wore the insignia of the Gestapo. They stopped a woman, searched her, found eight marks, took the money, and went on. Another woman ran into them; she had a four-year-old son. The Germans asked her why she was not working. (One of them spoke Russian; it turned out that he was the translator Michelson.) The woman showed them a certificate of illness, but they both attacked her, beat her up, and dragged her and her son to the cemetery, where they shot the mother and child. On their way back from the cemetery they met a boy of about fifteen, who was carrying two logs. "Where did you get the wood?" "My boss gave it to me at work." They took the boy to the cemetery and shot him. That night when the workers returned from work the Jews among them who were from Slutsk recognized their executioner. "It's Ribbe, with his translator Michelson," they said. "If he is here, then the complete liquidation of the ghetto is about to begin."

It was indeed Hauptsturmführer Ribbe, winner of many decorations for his pogroms, and his assistant and translator Michelson.

With the arrival of Ribbe, the Jews did not know a single minute of respite. Those who assisted him in the massacre of the Jews were Michelson, the re-appointed police chief Bunge, and his deputy Corporal Scherner.

Shots could be heard in the ghetto from early in the morning until late at night; people fell dead at every turn. If Ribbe did not like someone's face, he shot him; if a man's clothing was not as Ribbe thought it should be, he shot him; if his badge was not sewn just the way Ribbe wanted it, he shot him.

The streets were empty; people were afraid to come out of their apartments, but that did not save them. Ribbe and his gang would burst into the house. If they found a German-baked roll, they shot someone; a pat of butter for a sick child, they shot someone; a map or a reader, they shot someone.

Wracked with hunger, Jewish children went outside the ghetto to beg and plead for a crust of bread. They would usually gather at the railroad bridge in the evening and wait for the workers' columns to return with them to the ghetto. In February Ribbe organized a round-up of the children; those caught in the Russian sector were loaded into a truck, taken to the Jewish cemetery, and shot. Whenever the children were thrown into the truck, they screamed, "Kind sirs, don't beat us, we'll get into the truck ourselves!"

On 19 February Ribbe was going around to the establishments where German Jews were working; several young and beautiful girls and women caught his eye.

He selected the most beautiful women in the ghetto: twelve German Jews and one Russian Jew named Lina Noy. Ribbe ordered them to report to the labor exchange at 6:00 P.M.

Ribbe showed up at the exchange with Michelson. Not yet realizing their fate, his victims awaited him. It was noisy outside; the workers' columns were returning home, and many of them stopped and waited; they were all interested in why Ribbe had summoned the most beautiful girls and women. Ribbe gave the order to take the women by the hand and slowly lead them down Sukhaya Street. A groan went through the ghetto: Sukhaya led to the cemetery.

It was a terrible procession: thirteen young beautiful women slowly walking toward the gates of the cemetery. One of the German Jews asked for permission to say goodbye to her husband. Ribbe said okay. Her husband was brought to the cemetery and shot before her eyes. The animals stripped the women naked and started taunting them; then Ribbe and Michelson personally shot them. Ribbe took Lina Noy's bra and slipped it into his pocket. "To remember a beautiful Jewish woman," he said.

That same evening, on 19 February 1943 at 11:00 P.M., a truck carrying Gestapo agents pulled into the ghetto. After picking up Epshtein, a traitor who regularly helped them, they headed for the building at 48 Obuvnaya Street. The building was surrounded; the people were taken outside and lined up in a column four abreast. All the residents of the building, 140 people, were murdered. Only two women, a man, and a little boy survived that night. The Germans sealed the building. On 20 February 1943 Ribbe posted an announcement stating that weapons had been hidden in No. 48 and that for this all the residents were shot. The order demanded that all guns be turned over; anyone who was afraid to hand in his weapon himself could have it delivered anonymously. The order warned that any instance of failing to hand over guns would result in immediate mass executions. The Jews read the order with loathing and horror, but not a single person turned over a weapon, even though weapons came into the ghetto every day and were sent on to partisan units.

Ribbe liquidated the ghetto in a leisurely, methodical manner. He took over the workers' columns; every evening he and Michelson met the workers and searched them. If Ribbe found some potatoes, a bottle of milk, or some fat on one of the workers, the "criminal" was taken to the cemetery and shot; the food was hauled off to Ribbe's or Michelson's apartment.

Ribbe maintained that he was persecuting only those who were involved in political activity or who were part of the partisan movement. Whenever Ribbe determined that someone was missing from a column, he would shoot the whole column. Columns from the distillery, the prison, and many others were destroyed that way. Jews working in the prison were warned that they did not have the right to divulge what they had seen in the prison. In order to isolate them and prevent them from having any contact with the Jews in the ghetto, they were forced to live in prison barracks.

In accordance with an order issued by prison warden Ginter in May 1943, all the Jewish workers were lined up, stripped naked, and loaded into a truck; then they were taken outside of town and shot.

"They knew too much," said Ginter.

After that he went to Epshtein at the Judenrat to get more workers. A new group of people was sent to the prison. Three weeks later they were shot.

Soon Ribbe ordered all children without parents to be brought to the labor exchange. The ragged, hungry children were brought there; some children whose parents were still alive were among them. The children were taken to the prison in a truck, and from there they were taken out to be shot.

After this murder mothers were afraid to leave their children at home and took them to work, often carrying them in sacks. The German Scherner once went up to a truck and dragged a six-year-old boy from a truck, threw him to the stone pavement, and stepped on his neck; he trampled the boy with his boots and tossed the child's dead, mangled body to the side.

The next day Bunge met the workers' columns, seized an eleven-year-old boy, took him to the cemetery, and shot him. After returning to the columns, Bunge grabbed a second boy by the hand and headed for the cemetery, but they never got there: Bunge shot him on Sukhaya Street. According to Ribbe, the elderly and the unemployed were a burden on the ghetto. He considered even those who did not work for good reason or who had an official exemption from work for two or three days to be unemployed.

One hundred fifty of the "unemployed" and the elderly were taken to the prison and shot. The ghetto was dwindling; each day the number of those left alive grew smaller. The prediction made by the Jews of Slutsk turned out to be true: Ribbe was sent to Minsk to liquidate the ghetto.

Carrying out his political agenda, Ribbe tried to keep any word of his evil actions from getting out of the ghetto. But he could not hide it.

Inspector Schultz was a German officer in the Luftwaffe. He made an agreement with the Jews working for him to get them out of the ghetto. He loaded thirty-seven Jews into a truck and armed them with machine guns, revolvers, and rifles; he seized a radio receiver for himself and went off with the Jews to join a partisan unit. Incidents such as this were altogether exceptional, but we thought it was necessary to mention it.

After the elderly and the children of the unemployed, it was the physicians' turn to die.

At the end of April 1943 Ribbe ordered a list of the physicians to be brought to him. A few days later, new instructions were given: all the doctors were to report to the Judenrat. From there they were taken to the Gestapo.

Ribbe called Epshtein's attention to the fact that among the physicians were elderly people such as Doctor Gekhman and the invalid Doctor Kontsevaya (she walked with a limp); he asked Epshtein to take care of them and lead them through the city so that they would not grow tired and fall behind.

Everyone was amazed at the monster's show of concern—amazed and frightened. Ribbe ordered the doctors to be at the Jewish labor exchange that day at 4:00 P.M. When they arrived, Ribbe and Michelson were already waiting for them. The doctors were quickly divided into groups. The elderly ones (Gekhman, Shmotkina, Kontsevaya), the pediatricians Savchik and Lev, many specialists in internal medicine, ear specialists, and dentists were all sent to one side.

The ones selected were taken to a bunker (a place next to the labor exchange where prisoners were held). As soon as it got dark, their families were sent for. Among those brought in were Lev-Mlynsky (the historian and scholar) and his two children, Doctor Shmotkina's son, and Doctor Savchik's three children—approximately one hundred people in all. At around five in the morning, before the workers' columns had left, Bunge and Scherner arrived with a police unit and took the doctors and their families to the prison. There they were stripped, beaten, and killed.

When the doomed physicians and their families were being led to the prison, Doctor Savchik's twelve-year-old daughter cried out, "It's all right, Mommy, be brave. Our blood will be avenged."

Next in line were the orphanage and the home for the disabled. At eleven o'clock on a clear, moonlit night at the end of April 1943 a car and a truck pulled up to the large two-story building where children, invalids, and service personnel lived. Ribbe and Michelson got out of the car; they walked over to the building, pointed it out to the men in the truck, and left. The building was on Zaslavskaya Street right next to the Russian sector. The police cut through the barbed wire fence and surrounded the building. The children and service personnel were seized naked and thrown into the back of the truck. The invalids, the sick, and very small children were shot on the spot. It was all over within an hour. The truck left for the prison. No one ever saw those children again.

The next morning Bunge and Scherner came to check out their night's work. Among the bodies, which were literally swimming in pools of blood, they found a few seriously wounded women and immediately finished them off.

Next to the large stone building stood a small hovel; it served as the isolation ward for the orphanage. In it were thirty sick children. They started shooting them, and when they ran out of bullets, Bunge and Scherner stabbed them with their daggers.

[Only the hospitals remained.]

In May Ribbe came to the hospital; he was interested in the condition of the sick and asked to see their wards. Two days later at exactly twelve noon on a clear, warm day the residents of the ghetto heard shots coming from the direction of the hospital for German Jews. Everyone rushed over there. A large black gas truck was parked in the hospital yard. The German Jews said that Miller, Ribbe, Michelson, and four others who were dressed in civilian clothes, with machine guns hidden under their coats, entered the hospital and the orphanage and shot the sick and the children point blank. Having committed their murders in this hospital, the bandits went straight across the street to the hospital for Russian Jews. The sick jumped from the second-story windows, and some of them survived. All the rest were shot.

The hospital personnel were told to remove the bodies, wash off the blood, and put everything back in order, so that things could be restored and made ready to receive new patients by 4:00 P.M. Said Ribbe, "The German authorities do not carry out pogroms, but we need healthy, not sick, people."

After these liquidations, Ribbe became occupied with the German Jews. He used to say to them, "What are you doing? Where do you work? If it is too difficult, we'll give you easier work: we'll send you to the camp to peel potatoes."

After a lunch with vodka and wine, he went out into the yard at 2:00 P.M. and ordered his assistants to get ready for the operation. Meanwhile he decided to have some fun. Ribbe thought he would like to hear a concert. Just at that moment the violinist Varshavsky walked by; after him came Barats, a violinist from the Minsk Philharmonic. As he walked by the German Jewish ghetto, he saw the people being gathered together and realized they were preparing the next pogrom.

They stopped him unexpectedly. In vain Barats tried to tell them that he had not played in two years and was in no condition to play. They forced him. Pale, with tears in his eyes, Barats played before his executioners. When the concert was over Ribbe released Barats and went with his unit to the German Jewish ghetto. Ten minutes later, a crowd of people with children, packages, and bundles were locked into the bunker. After a few more minutes, large enclosed truck pulled up; they started loading people into it and taking them to the prison. A deathlike silence set in. Richter and Menschel checked the German Jews into the prison; they stripped the doomed people, hosed them down with water, taunted them, and then shot them. One hundred seventy-five people died in the massacre.

Despite the terror and daily murders, people tried to fight and escape from the ghetto.

When the Pakhomenko Unit and the National Unit, commanded by Zorin, were organized in Pushcha in April and May of 1943, special efforts were made to get Jews out of the ghetto. Zorin knew about the sufferings of the Jews in the ghetto; he had endured them himself. Zorin systematically sent guides to bring everyone they could out of the ghetto: old people, women, and children. His unit numbered as many as five hundred. Many Jewish partisans became excellent fighters: they destroyed railroad tracks, as well as trains carrying military supplies, troops, and equipment for the German army.

Many died in their attempts to escape from the ghetto. Fourteen Jews worked at the *Verpflegungsamt*:[11] shoemakers, tailors, blacksmiths and house painters. Among them were the communist Uri Retsky and his fried Ilya Dukorsky. Retsky would often tell his comrades at work that he would give up his life at a very high price and that the Hitlerite who raised his hand to him would die. . . .

He made a Finnish knife that he always carried with him.

These men worked on Dolgobrodsky Street, but for lunch (which consisted of watery soup) they had to walk several blocks to the bakery. {During a lunch break Retsky once ran into his old friend Savich, who used to manage the Belgosstroy Cafeteria. Savich claimed to be a patriot to the Soviet Homeland and said he had connections with partisan units and guides. He offered to obtain a large quantity of weapons for some money. Retsky arranged to meet Savich two days later, so that Savich could give him a final answer to his request for weapons and a guide. After thinking about Savich's proposal, Retsky decided to check up on him; he had a bad feeling about Savich. But the traitor Savich was way ahead of Retsky: two days later he went to the Verpflegungsamt with his boss Kovalev (a local German) and a whole band of Gestapo agents. Kovalev quickly entered the workshop. Savich stood there and watched him. The rest of the bandits surrounded the building. Kovalev began looking around. Retsky understood everything. He exchanged glances with Dukorsky.}

Dukorsky slammed the door shut, and Retsky grabbed his knife; he started stabbing Kovalev with it, who just stood there bleeding. The others came running. They shot Retsky and Dukorsky on the spot and tried to seize everyone else.

The workers Bykhovsky and Zilbershtein cried out to their comrades: "Don't let them take you alive, run, don't cry, don't beg for mercy!" Everyone ran. The police did not capture anyone alive; [people were jumping over fences and barriers. At the third fence a bullet caught up with Misha Belostoksky. Among the workers was a twelve-year-old boy named Blyakher; he ran, but a bullet cut him down too.] {Kovalev was awarded the Iron Cross for his battle against the partisans.}

Solomon Blyumin, who managed the housing section of the Judenrat, did everything he could to help the partisan movement. When the party organization was destroyed and the partisan guides sent to the ghetto were killed, contacting the partisans became extremely difficult. Blyumin decided to ship some weapons out of the ghetto and to send the communists left in the ghetto with them. {With the help of a friend, a certain Sonka, Blyumin got in touch with two truck drivers, Ivanov and Kuzminov. They both worked at the housing bureau in Minsk. Blyumin met with them many times to work out a plan for forging papers and escaping from the ghetto. Blyumin wanted to ship weapons out of the ghetto and to send the communists left in the ghetto with them. Not wanting any more people than necessary to meet with the truck drivers, Blyumin meet with them himself.}

It was difficult for Blyumin to leave the ghetto: everyone there knew him and loved him.

Tall and handsome, his appearance stuck in everyone's memory. The departure date was set for 8 May. [The trucks pulled into the ghetto, but not the ones that Blyumin and his people were supposed to leave on. They were mobile gas units with Gestapo agents and the traitor Ivanov.] At six in the morning the Gestapo surrounded the block where Blyumin lived.

As soon as Blyumin stepped out his door, blows from rifle butts descended upon him; he fell, stunned and bleeding. They tied him up and threw him into a truck along with his family and all the residents in his building.

Blyumin spent three weeks at Gestapo headquarters. For three weeks, day and night, they tortured him, demanding information about his accomplices, his connections, and the weapons. Blyumin suffered in silence; in silence he endured the torture; neither a word nor a sound fell from his lips. When the butchers were convinced that they would get nothing out of him, they took him out to the cemetery in broad daylight and shot him. His body was thrown into a pit. It was difficult for people to identify their Blyumin. He had been tall and broad-shouldered, but he had been brought to the cemetery emaciated and toothless. The people stole Blyumin's body from the mass grave and buried him with honor.

In June 1943 guides from the partisan units asked for medications and a doctor. Anna Isaakovna Turetskaya was chosen. She used to be the manager of an orphanage. With pride the children and her co-workers referred to her as "our Nyuta" and "our Mommy." A beautiful, intelligent woman, she found something in common with everyone; she knew how to comfort people in hard times and cheer them up, how to kindle hope where it seemed that there could be no hope.

She was happy to serve her people during those difficult days. Four times Turetskaya tried to take her group out of the ghetto, but every time she met with failure.

Finally, at eleven o'clock on the night of 16 Jun 1943, a group broke out. Two kilometers from the ghetto they ran into Scherner and a police unit, who were out checking guard posts. The guide was killed. Turetskaya was wounded in the leg, and everyone else scattered. The wounded Turetskaya crawled away and hid in a pit. The bandits searched for her for three hours. They found her and took her to the Fifth Precinct police station, where they beat her severely and threw her to the stone floor. Teretskaya lay there, mutilated and bleeding. Scherner tortured her for days, asking in Russian and in German where she was going, whom she was with, whose orders she was following. His every word was accompanied by blows; they rained down on her head. Scherner kicked her wounded leg with his boots. Struggling to gather her blurred senses, Anna Isaakovna told him that in her condition it was impossible to answer his questions. Scherner realized that he would get nothing out of her. The next morning her dragged Turetskaya into a car and took her to the Jewish cemetery. She was carried to the massive pit on a stretcher. There Nyuta began to speak. To the question of who she was with she answered, "All of my people were with me. I do not know their names; you will murder me, but after my death they will hate you even more. Look at your hands: they are covered with blood. How many children have you strangled? I am not afraid of you; the Soviet people will surely avenge us. Kill me!" Gathering together her last ounce of strength, Nyuta Turetskaya raised herself up and calmly waited for the bullet.

Scherner fired and killed her. The Jews stole her body from the mass grave and buried it separately, in a grave adorned with grass and flowers.

The Jews who survived the Minsk ghetto will never forget their Nyuta.

The liquidation of the workers' columns began in June 1943. On 2 June the Germans assembled seventy women under the pretext of sending them to work at a radio factory; twenty were sent to the factory and fifty were sent to the Gestapo. Surrounded by Gestapo officers, Ribbe notified the women that they would be loaded into a truck and taken to work outside of town, where they would be well fed. The trucks pulled up, and the women saw the mobile gas units that were so familiar to them. The women realized that they were not being taken to work but to their deaths.

Many were shot on the spot; they rest were forced into the truck and murdered. Only one of the fifty women—Lile Kopelevich—managed to get away. She hid between some trucks that were parked in the yard.

From that moment the systematic slaughter of the workers' columns began. Ribbe went around to the firms where the Jews worked and took down their names. One after another, after Ribbe's visit, the columns disappeared.

Ribbe showed up in the German Jewish ghetto in September 1943 and selected three hundred of the youngest and healthiest men. They were loaded into trucks and taken away. A few days later the same thing happened in the ghetto for Russian Jews. Two trucks pulled up, the men were loaded into them, and they were taken to the camp on Shirokaya Street; a few days later they were taken away from there.

On 12 September the German Jews were informed that they must get ready for their departure to Germany. They got ready and quickly collected their belongings; on 14 September they were loaded into mobile gas units and taken to their deaths.

By 1 October only two thousand Jews remain in the ghetto.

Once again, and for the last time, the ghetto was surrounded by the Gestapo on 21 October 1943. All the people, every last one, were loaded into trucks and taken to their deaths. Whenever no one was found in an apartment, the building was blown up with grenades, so that anyone hiding in malinas would die in the rubble.

21 October 1943 was the last day of the great tragedy. The Minsk Ghetto was no more. The last of its inhabitants perished. Not a single living soul was left in the Minsk Ghetto; only the ruins were left as reminders of the suffering and the terrible torment inflicted upon tens of thousands of Jews in Minsk for two and a half years.

Materials provided by A. Machiz, Grechanik, L. Gleizer, and P. Shapiro,
prepared for publication by Vasily Grossman

Leaders of the Underground Fighters in the Minsk Ghetto

Note: The Editors believed it was expedient to include with the selection "The Minsk Ghetto" excerpts from G. Smolyar's book Avengers of the Ghetto. *The author of the book was an active member of the Minsk underground. This article sheds detailed light on the work of the Bolshevik underground fighters in the ghetto, who were dedicated to delivering more and more fighters, weapons, medications, and clothing to the partisan units.*

In August 1941 the Soviet people—that is, the communists—in the Minsk Ghetto convened their first meeting for the purpose of initiating underground activity.

Few people attended the meeting. All of us there trusted each other, since we had become very close through years of working with each other. We knew Yasha Kirkaeshto from Bialystok and Meier Feldman from years of underground activity in West Belorussia. We often met with Boris Khaimovich in the ghetto and knew that, like Evsei Shnitman, he was a determined man and ready to start work immediately. Notke Vaingauz did not attend the meeting. His situation was especially difficult. As the editor of the children's newspaper *Pioner*, he was know by all, young and old.

The Gestapo undertook a relentless search for communists, and Notke was in extreme danger. He and I would meet in a malina in Novo-Myasnitskaya Street; it was in an attic by the chimney. His comrades furnished him with papers indicating that he was a stonemason. His views on our most urgent tasks were known and were expressed at the meeting. There were two other communists who did not attend the meeting: Khaim Aleksandrovich, an old and experienced party worker, and the writer Girsh Dobin. At the time both of them were prisoners condemned to forced labor.

The speeches at the meeting were brief. For us the main thing was clear: despite the terrible conditions in the ghetto, Stalin's rallying call of 3 July 1941 obligated us to work and to fight. We were of one mind in our striving to find a means of making it possible for the greatest possible number of Jews to break out of the ghetto and join the people's struggle against the Germans.

We considered it absolutely necessary to gather together and train a broad selection of dedicated activists who were prepared to fight against the German invaders.

At the meeting it was decided to set up and organizational center composed of three people: Ya. Kirkaeshto, N. Vaingauz, and E. Stolyarevich (who served as secretary).[12] Each of them was given a specific assignment: Notke Vaingauz was to compile summaries of reports from regular radio broadcasts for the widest possible distribution among the population; Yasha Kirkaeshto was to obtain illegal equipment, apartments [malinas], and a typewriter; Efim Stolyarevich was to organize party groups and establish connections with the Russian sector.

We were determined to fight to our last breath, and, if captured, we would not be taken alive.

As we left the meeting, we were all overwhelmed by the thought of the great responsibility that we had taken upon ourselves.

Nearby, at 46 Respublikanskaya Street, another group of communists was meeting at practically the same time. Attending the meeting were old, experienced comrades who knew each other from their work in a free Soviet Minsk. At the center of this circle of communists was Naum Feldman. The group included the old printer Getsl Openheim, the shoemaker Eselevich, Lena Maizelis, Zyama Okun, Misha Chipchin, Volf Losik, and others. They had strong connections with a group of Jewish printers.

At their first meeting it was decided to set up a printing press in the ghetto for distributing leaflets, printed reports of news from the front, and calls to resistance against the Hitlerite monsters.

Each day Komsomol member Misha Arotsker, the printer Kaplan, and Lena Maizelis rought pocketfuls of type and other printing materials into the ghetto. They established connections with a Russian comrade, who within the circle of conspiracy was known as the "Colored Cap." (His real name was Andrei Ivanovich Podpryga, and he later joined the partisans.) From him they obtained everything they needed to set up a well-equipped printing press.

The truth began to find its way into the ghetto from two different sources; spirits were raised, and faith and hope shined brighter. Our radio technician Abram Tunik built a radio receiver inside a stovepipe in one of the homes on Tatarskaya Street (later, when he had joined the partisans, Tunik was seriously wounded in a battle with the Hitlerite bandits). The antenna was twisted around a wire used to hang out cleaned underclothes.

Notke Vaingauz gathered the latest news from the front, reviews of military actions, and lead articles from *Pravda*. These materials were quickly distributed not only in the ghetto but also among the Belorussian population. In the ghetto people became accustomed to new and regular reports; they would grow worried and depressed if for some reason there was no news.

Information was passed along by word of mouth; sometimes it reflected not only the objective situation but also the hopes and fears of the commentators.

We also set up a youth organization. It was led by Emma Rodova (a former member of the District Committee of the Voroshilov Komsomol); David Gertsik (whose nickname was Zhenka), a seventeen-year-old member of the Komsomol who was a "guest" in the ghetto, since he was living in the Belorussian sector on a false passport; and Dora Berson (a former secretary for the Komsomol organization at the Oktyabr Clothing Factory). This trio diligently set about their work. Nonka Markevich, a fifteen-year-old Komsomol member, set up a radio receiver on Flask Street (in the ghetto); his group was busy with the distribution of summaries of broadcasts from the Soviet Information Bureau. For the most part, printed material was distributed by the young, who were constantly maintaining ties with their Belorussian and Russian comrades at school and in the Komsomol.

Our secret and impassioned aim was to establish connections with the Belorussians and the Russians as fighting allies and to gain access to the partisans.

An old friend who was a student at the Belorussian Drama Studio came to the ghetto to see one of our Komsomol members. He was from one of the partisan units; they wanted us to prepare a false passport for their commander. That was the first thread in our bond. Moishe Levin, the author of children's books (his pen name was Ber Sarin), performed this task perfectly, and we were able to provide a false passport not only for the comrade who had come to see us but also for our own people who often had to go outside the ghetto.

In early September 1941 a new messenger from the partisans arrived in the ghetto. He was Jewish youth who went by the name of Fedya. (It was not until we met him at a partisan parade after the liberation of Minsk that we managed to learn the details of his biography. His surname was Shedletsky. He was orphaned as a child and was brought up in the Minsk orphanage. In June 1941 he left to join the partisans.)

For those of us who were languishing in the ghetto it was a great joy to see a determined, good-natured Jewish youth without a yellow badge. We sent a letter to the commander of the unit informing him that we would place all our resources at his disposal. We asked that he take from the ghetto battle-ready people who were eager to join the ranks of the partisans.

We issued an order for our people in the ghetto to collect weapons, medications, boots, and warm clothing. We wanted to be ready to supply the commander's unit with the help they needed as soon as he asked for it.

The Hiterlite overlords of the ghetto were becoming more and more brutal. More frequently and more persistently each of us witnessed death unfolding before our eyes, yet we were filled with courage. We believed that we would succeed in joining the ranks of the people's avengers.

Every day people in the ghetto were hunted down. The degenerate Gorodetsky and his gang would come in from the concentration camp on Shirokaya Street. Right away they would start hunting people down to rob and kill them. Yasha Kirkaeshto died in one such round-up. He tried to run away, but a hollow-point bullet caught up with him. He fell dead not far from the apartment where we held our first meeting. It seemed that there was no one in the ghetto who did not know Yasha, and many people gathered together for his burial. We buried him quietly, without words. On his freshly dug grave we placed the inscription "Fallen in Battle."

Mikhel Gebelev took Yasha's place in the leadership of our organization.

After Yasha's death we selected the hospital for infectious diseases as our meeting place in the ghetto. From the time of the First World War we had known of the Germans' terrible fear of contagious diseases. Doctor Kulik, the head of the hospital, did not have to give the matter a moment's thought: he placed himself and all his resources at our disposal. We expected nothing less of Kulik.

We made the hospital's boiler room into our headquarters. Modest and selflessly devoted, Liza Ris always stood watch at the door; her nine-year-old daughter Rita, who also "knew how to keep quiet," helped her. . . .

We had strong connections in many places, both inside and outside the ghetto.

We had three trusted comrades in the German police station: Grisha Dobin, Avraam Gelman, and Zaskin. Thanks to their help, we knew ahead of time about the evil actions that the Germans were plotting against the people in the ghetto, as well as against the partisans....

At seven o'clock on the morning of 7 November, the anniversary of the Great October Revolution, the ghetto was encircled by Gestapo and police; they started hauling people away in large black trucks.

On that day twelve thousand Jews were taken from the ghetto to be executed.

The evening twilight came more slowly than usual. It was quiet in the ghetto, as if not twelve thousand but all eighty thousand Jews had been butchered that day. There was no sign of life anywhere, not a fire, not a rustle.

But Soviet people lived in the ghetto, and they had much hope and faith in victory.

David Gertsik informed us that a Russian comrade was waiting for us in an apartment outside the ghetto (on Abutkovaya Street); he wanted to talk about matters that would be of interest to all of us.

After taking off our yellow badges and changing our clothes, we went over the ghetto fence with David (Zhenka).

Within a minute we could tell that this was a meeting with a comrade, as in the good old days. A young man of about thirty was looking at us in a very friendly and affectionate way; he called himself Slavek. He was in civilian clothes, but it was apparent that he had only recently removed his military uniform.

A young woman wearing a red beret was sitting in the room and carefully listening to our conversation. She noticed that we were exhausted. A few days later she sent us some food in the ghetto.

One other young man took part in the conversation; he was primarily interested in the work that our young men and women were doing.

Their warm-heartedness and brotherly concern for our lives were deeply touching.

I told Slavek that we wanted to get our brothers and sisters out of the ghetto, that we wanted to be part of the people's struggle against our hated enemy. We have wonderful people, and we can procure weapons. Slavek listened to us in silence.

"We'll meet again," he said as he left. "Zhenka will be in touch with you."

We exchanged a warm handshake and parted.

Another five thousand Jews were murdered on 20 November 1941. Among them was our beloved Notke Vaingauz. Our radio receivers were destroyed in the ransacked apartments of the demolished area. . . .

Could it be that we were condemned to die before we could realize the dream of our lives?

We brought in Motya Pruslin, the former head of the propaganda department of the Stalin Regional Party Committee, to take Notke's place; he arrived from the village of Uzda. He told us, by the way, about a young man, a Jew, who attacked the villains at the edge of a mass grave at an execution site. Many of those who were doomed took advantage of the commotion and escaped.

The call went out to the ghetto:

"Arm yourselves!"

After the slaughter of 20 November there was an incredible demand for revolvers, grenades, cartridges, and even rifles. Weapons were purchased with money, watches, suits. . . . The stonemason Mikhl Rudinsky spent his entire savings of twelve thousand rubles on a rifle.

A short while later David Gertsik brought us a note: "Send your delegate to a meeting at the address that will be passed on to you orally, and use the password that you will be given. Slavek."

We authorized Gebelev, an old party worker from Minsk, to attend this meeting.

He returned from the meeting beaming. His dark expression had disappeared; he had grown lively and cheerful. At the meeting he met ssome of his old comrades. They decided to organize a broad, illegal network of people in groups of ten through the city, including the ghetto, and to appoint a centralized leadership. If it should turn out that in the city such a centralized leadership already exists, then a new "reserve committee" would be set up. At the meeting it was also decided to establish connections with partisan units and to put together an underground paper and printing press.

The first three groups of ten in the ghetto were headed by members of our organizational group.

One morning in November we set up a reinforced guard in the vicinity of the Jewish cemetery. Through a place in the wire fence that had been cut beforehand Gertsik (Zhenka) entered the ghetto; right behind him, wearing a yellow badge on his chest and shoulders, came Slavek. In Doctor Kulik's room we held the first meeting between the ghetto's organized leadership and a representative from the General Committee. We told them about the situation in the ghetto. There was very little time; we had to save everyone we could.

We outlined our most urgent tasks: (1) to select as many battle-ready and morally upright people as possible and prepare them to join the ranks of the partisans (this would be the responsibility of the secretaries of the groups of ten); (2) to make every effort to collect enough clothing and weapons so that no less than half those sent to partisan units will be at least be armed with revolvers; (3) to create a reserve supply of medications and prepare medical workers (with military doctors having top priority) to be sent to partisan units; (4) to set up a welfare fund for the terrible poverty that plagued the ghetto.

We discussed the question of our relationship to the Judenrat. We agreed with Slavek's view that it was necessary to identify trustworthy Soviet members of the Judenrat, to establish connections with them, and to use them for our work. Such connections would enable us to warn the Jewish population of danger before it hit and to weaken the Germans' terrorist activities. With all the German decrees issued in the ghetto (such decrees were issued every day: at the tannery, the textile mill, the furrier, and so on), most of the funds raised in the ghetto had to be transferred to the city committee to aid the partisan movement. We also took upon ourselves the task of outfitting a printing press for the entire city.

We drew strength and courage from knowing that we were no long alone, that our Belorussian comrades had come to our aid. Now we were certain that we could stand our ground in this unequal fight!

In spite of the savage terror, the living thread of friendship between the Jews and the Belorussians was unbroken.

People would come out from the Belorussian courtyards situated next to the ghetto and, taking advantage of a moment when the police could not see them, would exchange a few kind words with their Jewish friends or throw some food over the barbed wire fence.

Once, as a peasant was walking down Zelenaya Street along the border of the ghetto, he saw a Jew he asked, "Could you please go and see if Yankel Sloushch's family is still alive?" He was told that the whole family had been killed. But the peasant did not leave. He called out to a woman passing by with her children and said, "Wait a minute, I'm coming over to you right now." He took a sack of potatoes, then a sack of cabbages and beets, and threw them over the fence. Then he said, "Eat and be healthy! Hold out! Maybe we'll survive all this. . . ."

Nikolai Romanovich Shchasny would ride up to the ghetto from the side that borders on Shornaya and Abutkovaya Streets. He brought food for a doctor from Ratamka, Dory Alperovich, as well as for others who were from his town: Pliskin, Kats, and Bogdanov. Once he even slipped past the border to place an especially valuable gift into the doctor's hands: he had brought Dory Alperovich a revolver. Nikolai Romanovich Shchasny also saved sixty Jewish children.

The Hitlerites sent a teacher from a Belorussian school on the Red Beacon collective farm in the Minsk region to the concentration camp on Shirokaya Street.

The teacher became a chauffeur in the camp.

The teacher started taking Jews out of the camp in the car that he drove.

He saved Lev Beilin, a future partisan fighter in the Budennovsky Unit, and many others.

The Jews referred to Mariya Adamovna Yasinskaya's apartment on Berson Street (naar the Gestapo) as the "subsidiary ghetto." When, after being sentenced to death, Isroel Goland managed to escape from the concentration camp on Shirokaya Street, he hid with Mariya Adamovna. When our contact Klara Zheleznyak had to be registered under a false passport, it was taken care of in Yasinskaya's apartment. When it was necessary for Mikhel Gebelev to stay in the city, he would spend the night with Mariya Adamovna. This fearless, noble woman later left with a group of Jews to join a partisan unit.

Many Belorussian women lived in the ghetto, wore the yellow badge, and endured all the misfortunes because they did not want to be separated from their Jewish relatives.

Without the brotherly help of the Belorussians, not a single Jew would be left alive. And thousands are still alive!

Our organization in the ghetto, including Komsomol groups and comrades outside the party, initially numbered about three hundred people. These were dedicated, battle-ready, fearless people with strong ties to the ghetto population.

The leader of the organization divided the tasks among themselves. Gebelev worked on maintaining the strongest possible connections within the ghetto. Motya Pruslin organized propaganda activities. Efim Stolyarevich was in charge of the groups of ten and directed people to partisan units. Naum Feldman took on the duty of providing material aid to those who joined the partisans; he was especially concerned with obtaining items in short supply in the ghetto. Zyama Okun was busy organizing an underground press.

Given the exceptionally difficult conditions in the ghetto, the success of our operations depended on maintaining good connections. To this end we organized a special women's group. The task of tying together all the loose ends was placed in the hands of Emma Rodova. Although prior to the war she had no notion of what underground activity entailed, this twenty-year-old girl had the talent and ability of a born conspirator. She understood the language of instructions and knew how to make concise reports on following them. Emma found it insulting to be asked whether she understood an order. On such occasions she would sometimes frown and leave the room, often without even saying good-bye. Exceptionally modest and undemanding when it came to satisfying her own needs, she invariably refused any offer of material aid; we knew, however, that Emma was going hungry, that she was subsisting on just a handful of potato skins per day.

With Nina Liss it was a completely different story. She did not know what a conspiracy was. Inexhaustible energy raged in this young woman, whose eyes were as blue as the heavens. No sooner would she take on an assignment than she would become unbelievably excited, and soon everyone knew what she was working on. She also had to take care of her five-year-old little girl and her elderly mother, who was seriously wounded by a bandit's bullet during one of our terrible nights. We assigned Nina to work outside the ghetto and, at times, outside the city. As with all our contacts, we provided her with a false passport; she had a face like a peasant and could move around freely outside the ghetto.

Our "diplomatic courier" was the peaceful, business-like Khasya Bindler. Her tasks included maintaining connections with the employees of the Judenrat, the Jewish police, the ghetto workshops, and so on.

Fat Klara (the author does not know her last name) dealt primarily with economic issues. She often had to carry "forbidden" things (white camouflage coats, ammunition, and so on); then she looked even fatter than usual.

A special women's group under the supervision of Mikhel Gebelev was set up for establishing contacts with the Russian sector. This group included an amazingly courageous girl named Anya, as well as Klara Zheleznyak-Gorelik, Berta Libo, and Slava Gebeleva. These women had to have a special talent for disguising themselves, since they often had to go outside the ghetto several times a day right under the noses of the police.

Well-established connections helped us to carry out our work under conditions of unceasing terror.

All of our groups of ten were energetically engaged in selecting people to be sent to partisan units. There were daily examinations of weapons and medications obtained by the groups of ten.

Mirkin arranged for several people from his group of ten to work in a German establishment; every day they left the establishment with their pockets full of bullets. Comrade Kagan's group was soon fully armed with loaded weapons. Those in Naum Brustin's group had fifteen grenades. Many initiatives were undertaken by the young journalist Iosif Mindel, who created a special "arsenal" in the vicinity of the Jewish cemetery.

The stockpile of military supplies also grew in Naum Feldman's group of ten. People in his group smuggled weapons out of the German camp at Krasny Urochishch; they had purchased them from the Hitlerites and secretly transferred them to a well-hidden warehouse on Respublikanskaya Street. In the ghetto, right on Zelenaya Street, comrades from the Rolbin group dug up six rifles and several hundred cartridges that had been buried under the ground.

They had established direct contact with a group of Belorussian comrades on Peresl. They sent their liaison Lilya Kopelevich there every day.

Our young people took up many initiatives. Valik Zhitlzeif's Komsomol group managed to obtain thirty rifles and a large supply of ammunition. Nonke Markevich's group (which included Sanya Kaplinsky, Sholom Gringauz, Yasha Lapidus, and others) left the ghetto; with the help of their Belorussian school friends Vitya Rudovich and Kolya Prishchepchik, they buried 540 cartridges, an ammunition belt, twelve rifle bolts, two grenades, and other items near Mogilevsky Road.

The tailor Avraam Gelman took a sub-machine from the arms warehouse of the German police; at the time getting a sub-machine gun was the dream of every partisan. Two young workers—Shie, who later died a heroic death as a partisan in the fight against the Hitlerites, and Leibl Shafran, who worked in the peat factory outside of Minsk—found a heavy machine gun. They took it into the ghetto a piece at a time.

Another one of our missions was not left unfulfilled: finding medications. The first ones to answer the call were medical workers: the physicians Kulik, Minkin, Zibtsiker, Alperovich, Kerzon, and Lifshits, as well as the nurses, and the pharmacists Khinyuk, Tsilya Klebanova, Khayutin, and others. They gathered iodine, bandages, and various salves for frostbite, mange, insect bites, and the like. Every group of ten set up its own medications fund; some of it they stole from the Hitlerites, the rest they collected from the populace.

At the same time we undertook the huge task of stockpiling clothing for our comrades sent to the partisan units, as well as for the units themselves.

In keeping with the Hitlerites' orders, there were workshops making shoes, clothing, underwear, and warm hats under the supervision of the Judenrat. In the ghetto there was also a soap factory and a bakery.

Once we had established close connections with comrades on the Judenrat, we in fact became the heads of the workshops. There were often times when partisans wearing German uniforms would pull up to a workshop in the ghetto and haul off whole truckloads of clothing, shoes, soap, and salt. In addition, our groups of ten organized the voluntary donation of clothing among the populace.

In the attic of the hospital we collected fur coats, quilted jackets, warm trousers, hats, and so on under the pretense of having to disinfect them.

The partisan units were constantly asking us to help them obtain radio receivers. Comrade Segalchik, who worked as a radio technician in the German Commissariat, worked on this project. He started bringing radio parts into the ghetto. In spite of strict supervision, our comrades who worked at the radio factory also smuggled radio tubes, condensers, and batteries into the ghetto.

We expanded our propaganda efforts, too. Once again, with the help of Comrade Tunik, we set up an underground radio receiver on Shevchenko Street.

A law student named Khonon Gusinov was appointed radio operator. We provided him with a typewriter, and twice a day he received bulletins from the Soviet Information Bureau. From time to time Khonon would also get a lead story from Pravda, and we would pass it on, along with other important materials, to the city committee.

An exceptional event not only for life in the ghetto but for all the Soviet people of Minsk occurred when we received Comrade Stalin's report on the 24th Anniversary of the Great October Socialist Revolution. It happened like this: A group of Jews was being led to work. A peasant carefully approached the column. He slipped a folded piece of paper to one of our comrades and whispered, "Take it. . . . Maybe you can make something of it. . . . I found it in the field. . . ."

It was a Polish translation of Comrade Stalin's report. We translated the report and distributed it everywhere. Many knew the report by heart.

During hours of hard labor endured by the people locked in their ghetto cages, Comrade Stalin's words would be passed from mouth to mouth like glad tidings, words declaring that Hitler's Germany was sure to collapse under the weight of the crimes they were committing.

The groups of ten headed by Zyama Okun and Naum Feldman worked in the printing office in the city. They quickly organized the distribution of printed materials that might bring hope to the ghetto. After a while so much printed material piled up in Zyama Okun's malina that he had enough for his own printing office. Comrade Slavek told us about all of this, and it was Zhenka (Gertsik) who got everything moved from the ghetto to the city. The committee demanded that we provide a qualified worker for the printing office. We picked Misha Chipchin for the job; he was the former director of the Comrade Stalin Printing Office, the largest in Minsk. Misha Chipchin parted from his family, whom he was no longer able to see, and went underground. The printing office was set up near the ghetto in the malina on Ostrovskaya Street. They immediately issued a call to arms and sent out bulletins with information on the situation at the front.

Once these materials arrived in the ghetto in printed form, everyone was certain that Soviet airplanes from the "Great Land" had dropped them from the sky.[13]

One of the most powerful turning points for the Minsk underground was the release of the first issue of the illegal newspaper *Zvyazda*, which prior to the war had been published in a brief two-page issue by the Belorussian Central Committee of the Communist Party. We received a great tribute. The pride of our comrades who took part in setting up this newspaper beamed throughout the ghetto.

We devoted much attention to caring for our comrades in need. The problem of hunger grew in the ghetto with each passing day. People received only a hundred grams of bread and a few spoonfuls of ersatz soup per day. Thousands of Jews who had been saved from pogroms in various places were in a horrible position. More and more often we saw people in the ghetto who were bloated from starvation. Along Glukhy Drive, on the way to the cemetery, we constantly saw people who transporting the dead on sleds or handcarts. There were fifteen to twenty such funerals in the ghetto every day.

The dead were buried in one large mass grave.

The ghetto hospital was overflowing. It became necessary to set up a surgical area for the sick. Since the Germans had issued a warning that in case of an epidemic the entire ghetto would be quarantined, the outbreak of such an epidemic was of particular concern to everyone in the ghetto. . . . We announced to the Judenrat that anyone who dared to inform the Germans of the epidemic would be mercilessly destroyed as an enemy of the people. At the same time we gathered together a group of the most supportive physicians and told them that in the reports they had to submit to the city authorities every day there should be no mention of the typhus epidemic. The physician's diagnosis should indicate influenza, inflammation of the lungs, dystrophy and other such "legal" diseases. All the doctors who were working with us agreed; knowing that we were capable of acting in a decisive manner, the rest remained silent. . . .

A talented and well-known Belorussian actor named Zorov was a member of the Judenrat. He maintained contact with us and wanted to join a partisan unit. We proposed that he set up a cafeteria where the most needy could get a morsel of warm food and piece of bread. We appointed Zyama Okun and Khasya Binder to set up the cafeteria and Rozenberg (who later perished as a partisan) to manage it. They were loyal men.

The medical students G. Solomonik and S. Yakubovich (both of whom later left to join the partisans) enthusiastically set about organizing a disinfection center. Without a thought for themselves doctors and nurses labored to stem the tide of the epidemic.

A large group of our underground workers suffered from terrible poverty.

We required all the "specialist" workers to place themselves at the service of their needy comrades. As a result we set up a fund that enabled us to assist many of our comrades and their families. Among those involved in offering this help were comrades Ruvim Geiblom, Grish Dobin, Avram Gelman, Zaskin, Nokhim Goldzak, Avrom Shlyakhtovich, Riva Norman, and others.

A man going by the name of Gusakov was once lying seriously ill in the hospital. When one of the nurses looked at him, she thought he looked very much like one of her close friends. She quietly called out to him: "David." The patient shuddered and in a voice barely audible said, "Quiet." It turned out to be David Ratner, a well-known Komsomol worker and former member of the Central Committee of the Belorussian Komsomol. He related a story that was very common in those days. He had been surrounded and taken prisoner. As he was being led on foot over the railroad bridge into Minsk, he gathered his last ounce of strength, jumped off the bridge, and escaped. He had not eaten for twelve days. Now he was dying. We provided help for Ratner-Gusakov. But it was too late. He expired right before our eyes.

We also arranged for aid to the famous Belorussian composer Kroshner. But he was not destined to rise from his deathbed. The Hiterlites shot him in the hospital.

A group of our Russian and Belorussian comrades turned up in the ghetto one winter morning. A blind man could tell that these were "forest brothers." They had people who were in urgent need of medical attention. Doctor Kulik's personal quarters in the hospital were immediately transformed into an emergency room. The ones who could stand on their own two feet or who did not require complicated surgery were initially denied medical assistance. The problem was worse for those who were seriously wounded or very sick; they had to be put into the hospital. Nevertheless, we dealt with the problem of getting them admitted. With the help of our people in the Judenrat, Emma Rodova obtained signed blank documents for the ones who had to get into the ghetto to receive medical attention. We provided these comrades with the best and broadest range of medical and material aid. The fund we had set up, therefore, proved to be indispensable.

Although our underground activity in the ghetto developed along many different lines, we did not forget our basic task: to get people capable of fighting to the partisan units in the forest. With the help of the city committee, we merged groups from the ghetto with Belorussian groups that were systematically leaving the city to join partisan units. Every week people were sent from the ghetto to a secret meeting point (in the Storozhovsky Market) to meet with guides from partisan bases.

The city committee also connected us with an underground group of railroad workers headed by Comrade Kuznetsov (he was later the commissar of the Voronyansky Partisan Brigade). The railroad workers loaded our people on the tenders of the steam engines and took them to railroad stations in the vicinity of partisan bases. More than five hundred people were transported from the Minsk Ghetto to partisan units in such a manner. Everyone who left was bound by a solemn oath: to set an example of daring, courage, and combat ability in their units; to forever remember those who were left in the ghetto; and to use all their power to get the largest number of people into the forest to join the partisans' fight as quickly as possible.

The storm clouds were gathering over our heads. Mushkin, the chairman of the Judenrat, was arrested; this was a huge loss for the population in the ghetto.

At just about the same time we received word that Zhenka (David Gertsik) had been arrested. In a letter from prison he wrote that the Gestapo had cruelly tortured him but he had betrayed no one. "Continue our work, dear comrades, and do not worry," wrote this modest seventeen-year-old youth. "Our enemies will get nothing out of me." The Gestapo tortured him to death.

The Gestapo issued an order for five thousand Jews to assemble, supposedly to reported to work, by ten o'clock on the morning of 2 March. They stipulated that those who were already working at German establishments were not to be included in this number. Judenrat member Dolsky asked the patently naive question of whether old people and children could be included in the five thousand, to which the Gestapo answered, "It doesn't matter."

It was clear to us that the Germans were planning to exterminate the entire population of the ghetto a segment at a time.

Working through members of our organization, we immediately warned the people in the ghetto about the terrible danger. We ordered Zyama Serebryansky, the head of the ghetto guards, to select the most reliable of his guards and, when the time came, have them give the signal that the perpetrators of the pogrom were on their way. We recommended that on the afternoon of 2 March as many people as possible be taken out of the ghetto to work at places owned by our Belorussian friends. . . .

A malina for a hundred people, with an exit into the city, was set up in a Judenrat workshop. Hiding places were also prepared among the ruins on Myasnitskaya Street.

After the workers' columns left on the bloody day of 2 March 1942, the Gestapo arrived and demanded "their" five thousand Jews, since "the train was ready to pull out. . . ." The Gestapo bandits spread out through the ghetto, firing their pistols and sub-machine guns indiscriminately. Like vultures they swept down on the little ones in the kindergarten and savagely beat them to death. Then they formed a special children's column with the manager of the orphanage Fleishner and the physician Chernis at its head; the two of them held the smallest of the children in their arms. Thus they were all led to their execution.

Not far from the Judenrat, at 35 Ratomskaya Street, the Germans threw children alive into a pit and started covering them with sand. Soon the chief executioner of Belorussia, Kube, arrived. This sadist tossed candy to the children as they were buried alive in their grave. . . .

Darkness fell. In keeping with Kube's instructions, the returning workers were not allowed into the ghetto. At the gates on Shornaya Street they were ordered to lie down in the snow. The terrible execution began. On that spot we later found the murdered Komsomol leaders David Plotkin and Khaya Botvinnik.

Moishe "Ber Sarin" Levin worked as a painter in the Minsk prison. He was the leader of a column.

We decided to send him to a big partisan group, since, in addition to being a writer and an artist, he had good military training and was an excellent topographer. On 2 March the prison warden took him out of the general column to save him, since he needed Levin as a skilled worker. But Levin took his place in the column and died with everyone else.

After the horrible slaughter of 2 March it was clear that the last days were at hand.

After the second of March the dispatches of people to the partisan units proceeded even more intensively than before. Comrade Kagan's group of armed men was sent to the Uncle Vasya Brigade. We sent out a second group with the special assignment of creating a new partisan unit; it was led by some of our activist workers, such as Motya Pruslin, Khaim Aleksandrovich, Meier Feldman, Lena Maizelis, Girsh Dobin, and others. We sent a third group—led by Naum Feldman, Getsel Openheim, and V. Kravchinsky—into a different region; after receiving no word from them, we sent another group after them. They could not make it without sacrifices. Comrades Sukenik, Arotsker, Pesin, and Girsh Skoblo (one of the first Stakhanovites in Belorussia) all perished from enemy bullets. Comrade Skoblo's feet had become frostbitten, and he could no longer walk; that was when the Gestapo fell upon him.

We sent Sonya Levina, a Komsomol member, with Vitya Feldman to the Staroselsky Forest to establish connections with the partisans. Following a recommendation from the city committee, we decided to organize our own bases for Jewish partisans, so that we could get more people out of the ghetto.

We sent forty people armed with grenades, rifles, and revolvers into the forest outside of Minsk. They did not, however, manage to establish contact with any partisans, so we ordered our comrades to return to the ghetto. Some of them refused to come back. Misha Yufa, a former employee of the Minsk Polytechnic Institute, selected a group of armed men and set out with them in search of a partisan unit.

As the group was returning, they were followed by Hitlerite cyclists. In the clash that followed one of our activists, the journalist Iosif Mindel, was killed; he had smuggled many weapons out of the ghetto.

Neither this nor other setbacks, however, weakened our resolve. Every group sent into the forest confirmed our leadership abilities. The Judenrat dining room became the gathering point for those who were to be sent to the partisan units. Every evening, as the workers' columns were returning, candidates for dispatch to the partisans gathered in the dining room. We spoke with every comrade individually, checked his weapons, and gave him a warning: "Death lurks at every turn; but it is better to die in battle than to be strangled like a rat in the stinking ghetto."

Wearing a white band on their sleeves instead of a yellow patch, a group of "mongrels"[14] (E. Narusevich, D. Baran, and others) followed our instructions for taking groups of people from the ghetto to the forest. Thanks to printers such as Kaplan, Pressman, Rapoport, and others, the shop where we forged documents was able to obtain blank forms from various German military establishments. Thus we were able to supply every woman leaving the ghetto with papers affirming that she was being sent outside the city to get firewood or peat.

Our people in the Judenrat proved to be a great help in getting people to the partisan units. The baker provided people leaving with a two-day supply of bread. This was no small accomplishment in the ghetto! Workshops provided heavy clothing, warm hats, and felt boots. Komsomol member Sima Shvarts organized a large group of women who sewed underwear, mended clothing, and knitted woolen gloves, socks and other items. Another group, organized by Rokhl Kubina and Tsilya Botvinnik, collected warm underwear, mended clothes, and so on. A small storeroom belonging to Ida Aler was transformed into a secret sewing shop, where they sewed camouflaged outfits. Young girls collected sheets from people's homes. No one asked why or for whom all this was necessary; everyone gave freely, with words of blessing on their lips.

Trading at the walls of the ghetto (which was brought to a halt every day by gunfire) took on larger and larger proportions. People were buying guns—the new "Soviet passport," as they were called. People traded the last of their possessions for a revolver, a grenade, or some cartridges.

At one of the meetings at the ghetto's underground center we called upon Isroel Lapidus and commissioned him to select people to be taken from the ghetto into the forest to set up a new base for the mass movement of people out of the ghetto.

Mikhel Gebelev established contact with a reliable man who worked in the rehabilitation department of the German municipal office. He promised to get Jewish children into Belorussian children's homes.

To this end two women's groups were set up: one in the ghetto, for the transfer of children, and the other outside the ghetto, made up of Belorussian women who received the children and took them to a designated site.

Every morning, even before the workers' columns set out, Riva Norman, Genya Pasternak, Gisha Sukenik, and others stood ready at the boundary of the ghetto. Patiently they awaited the signal. There, beyond the ghetto, lived the Belorussian Voronov family. They had all taken it upon themselves to fight against the Germans. The father worked for an illegal printing press; the son was busy sending people and arms to partisan units. The son's wife took messages to comrades who had been arrested and hid people who were in danger. Every morning she stood at her post and gave her Jewish comrades the signal indicating whether or not the coast was clear for moving out the children. Belorussian comrades met in her home; among them were Mariya Ivanovskaya, Tatyana Gerasimenko, Lelya Revinskaya (the woman in the red beret whom we saw on the day of our first meeting with Slavek), and others.

Asya Pruslina, Lena Ginzburg, and Genya Sultan were also busy making arrangements for the children. Within the first few weeks they alone managed to get seventy Jewish children out of the Minsk Ghetto.

Soon after the bloody Aktion of 2 March mass arrests began in the city. Some of our comrades from the Belorussian underground came to us and asked that we hide them for a while in the ghetto. We set up several malinas for them that had been hit during the various raids of 2 March. From one of our comrades, whom we hid in a cellar under the apartment of the well-known sculptor Brazer, we found out that nearly all the members of the underground military council had been arrested. We received an urgent message from Slavek: the enemy had gotten into our organization and had infiltrated almost the entire military council of about thirty men. People who had received their assignments from the partisans had penetrated into the city. Slavek decided to abandon the city, join a partisan unit, and from there establish contact with us. "Continue your work, dear comrades of the ghetto," Slavek ended his letter to us. "And if we should die, the Red Army will avenge us!"

Some time later we learned that Slavek and Revinsky were on their way to an apartment, where they were to await a contact from a partisan unit, when they were arrested by Gestapo agents.

Soon after that we received more news: the Gestapo had surrounded Volf Losik's apartment. This was a terrible, unexpected blow for us. Losik had spent all his time smuggling weapons into the ghetto. He led a group of comrades who worked at a German military depot in Krasny Urochishch. A shipment of grenades had been delivered just hours before the Gestapo arrived at Losik's apartment. We immediately warned all our comrades who worked on obtaining weapons and who had any contact with Losik. We even managed to retrieve Losik's wife and children from the enemy's clutches. The Gestapo agents searched everywhere and turned everything upside down but found nothing. It turned out that the grenades had already been hidden in a safe malina, and the Hitlerites were unable to find them.

The Gestapo surrounded Nonka Markevich's apartment (on Zelenaya Street); they found several hundred cartridges and a radio receiver. The Gestapo agents led away Markevich, his mother, and his ten-year-old brother Khaim with their hands bound behind their back. Terrible blows rained down on the head of the fifteen-year-old Komsomol member.

When Markevich arrived at the Judenrat, he shouted out, "You may kill me, but my comrades will be left to avenge me!"

On 31 March 1942 at 11:00 P.M. the ghetto was awakened by gunfire.

The next morning we beheld a horrible scene: the ghetto guards, the German Jews, and passersby were carrying the bodies of those who had been murdered to the Jewish cemetery.

It seems that the Gestapo had surrounded the courtyard of the building at 18 Kollektornaya Street, where Nina Liss lived. Gestapo agents cried out, "Ninka, open up," and then started breaking down the tightly sealed door. The residents of the building were taken out into the courtyard in their underwear.

After savagely beating the doomed people, the Gestapo shot them all down. Only our Fat Klara was saved; she hid among the bodies of the murdered (later she was killed on her way to join a partisan unit).

On that same night, as we learned from G. Ruditser, the Gestapo went to the homes of Tulsky and Z. Serebryansky and arrested them; taking their prisoners with them, they then went around the ghetto looking for Mikhel Gebelev, Zyama Okun, Efim Stolyarevich, and Naum Feldman.

We met briefly with Gebelev and Zyama Okun and decided that all of us had to hide immediately.

Mikhel Gebelev and Naum Feldman hid in a tried and true malina on Zamkovaya Street. Zyama Okun tried to get there too, but he fell into the hands of the Gestapo along the way. With the help of Doctor Kulik, Efim Stolyarevich was taken to the hospital on a stretcher and placed in the ward for patients with infectious diseases. On the night of 2 April a terrible execution took place at 20 Kollektornaya Street, where Naum Brustin, a secretary for one of the groups of ten, lived. He and all the residents of the building were killed; many of them were to have gone to join partisan units within a few days. Then came the horrible nights on Krymskaya, Tankovaya, Abutkovaya, Ratomskaya, and other streets.

On 7 May 1942 gallows were erected on the squares and plazas of Minsk. From them hung the bodies of the leaders of the Minsk Underground Military Soviet. Among those executed was a fervent patriot of the Soviet Motherland and friend to the people of the Minsk Ghetto: Slavek. Many of our comrades were executed as well: Ekelchik (a member of the city committee), Zyama Okun, Zyama Serebryansky, and Girsh Ruditser.

A short time later the comrades met at an apartment on Torgovaya Street to discuss the problem of resuming military activity. Among those who attended the meeting were workers from the previous city committee who had escaped the shootings. At the meeting it was explained that contacts with the partisan units had been lost. It was necessary to start all over again but without repeating the mistakes that had led to failure and arrests. We proposed that three basic measures be taken: (1) all military activity with new and existing partisan units should be placed in the hands of the committee; (2) the organizational structure should be altered, so that instead of groups of ten, groups should be organized in business firms and factories; and (3) in the light of the special circumstances facing the Jewish population, the ghetto should be designated as an independent organizational unit. We resolved to continue establishing bases for getting battle-ready people out of the ghetto.

Our work progressed at a heightened tempo. Although Mikhel Gebelev was regarded as a ghetto worker, he in fact became one of the leaders in the citywide organization. He would not allow himself a minute's rest and scorned the danger that followed his every footstep. He organized the dispatch of battle-ready Soviets to the partisan units. The women in the ghetto collected clothing, which was sorely needed by the partisan fighters. Our "passport bureau" provided them with "irreproachable" papers. The work increased rapidly every day, and with it came an increase in. . . carelessness. And that led once again to a severe blow.

The Komsomol headquarters was located in a well-camouflaged cellar on Zamkovaya Street. Their leader was the tireless but inexperienced Valik Zhitlzeif. These youths prepared weapons, provisions, and everything else needed by those who were sent into the forests to join the partisans. But the Gestapo was on their trail, and the Komsomol malina was surrounded. The Gestapo ordered our young comrades (there were twelve of them) to surrender. A battle broke out. All twelve of the Komsomol youths were armed with grenades; they had four rifles in addition to those that were stored in the cellar, as well as two cases of cartridges, two radio receivers, and some provisions. The one-sided fight lasted a long time. None of the Komsomol members surrendered, and all expect one died. Zyama was still alive but was seriously wounded; at the time he had just made contact with the Lapidus Partisan Unit, so that the whole group could go into the forest to join them. We had him taken to the hospital.

He recovered there. He was then sent to join Feldman's unit but was killed along the way.

At just about that time the Gestapo discovered our radio receiver. Instead of going into the cellar, they threw grenades into the whole building. The disciplined, daring, and dedicated Khonon Gusinov died at his battle station. Once again we had lost the ability to systematically spread throughout the ghetto information on what was happening at the front and about life in the "real world."

In addition to the task of sending people to the partisan units on a regular basis, we were faced with the problem of bringing the fight to where we were through acts of sabotage in the factories and business establishments.

We had our people at the so-called "Jewish Labor Exchange": Mirra Strogina and Roza Altman. With their help we managed to have our comrades sent to work at the firms where we were planning acts of sabotage.

Lena Maizelis, Nadya Shusser, Fanya Gurvich, Sonya Teishova, Fanya Chipchin, Esther Krivosheina, Dora Berson, Lena Pevzner, Genya Yudovina, and Sarra Yudovina worked at the old Bolshevik Factory. Our comrades systematically undermined the materials—primarily leather goods—that were made there. Every day they took from the factory warm underwear, gloves, socks—anything the partisans could use.

At the same factory a group of men led by David Lerner was working independently of the women's group. The men's group was involved with "cruder" work. They removed several fully equipped field telephones from the factory and took them to the partisans; they poured sand and molten glass into machinery; they sabotaged entire batches of manufactured goods that were supposed to be sent to the front. Our laboratory in the ghetto supplied Lerner's group with a special liquid that would eat holes into leather and synthetic materials.

We organized several sabotage groups at the old October Factory. These groups included the shoemakers Zilbershtein, Shapiro, Noterman, and N. Luft; the tailors Misha Grichanik and R. Sukenik; the house painter Iosif Tishlman and his sixteen-year-old son; S. Peisakhovich; and others. We gave these groups an assignment: to drag out as long as possible the number of days required to fill their orders and to sabotage manufactured goods and materials. In addition, all of them took boots, shoe soles, and coats for our comrades who were going off into the forest.

Thanks to sabotage carried out by our people, the factory's electrical equipment was systematically destroyed. A group of Belorussian comrades played an active part in this work; they were led by Comrade "Nikolai" (Gerasimenko), Secretary of the underground Stalin District Committee. At the same factory a group led by Khaim Gravets was smuggling out weapons.

A special group worked in the German system of field communications. This group was led by Ruvim Geiblyum (he later died in battle as a partisan). With his help we obtained detailed plans for a communications network running from Baranovich to Minsk to Smolensk and from Vilna to Minsk to Smolensk. This group also passed on to us important information on the German mine fields in the Minsk area. We in turn sent this information to the city committee, which found it to be extremely valuable.

At the same time wet stepped up our efforts to free the Soviet prisoners of war. In addition to clothing and papers, we supplied them with the names and secret addresses of contacts.

Mikhel Gebelev fell into the enemy's clutches while preparing a large group of prisoners of war to be sent to the Budenny Partisan Unit. This was a terrible blow not only to those of us working in the ghetto but to the city's entire underground organization.

Gebelev had been one of the primary organizers of underground activity since the disasters of March. Mikhel Gebelev was a tireless worker. In broad daylight, when hordes of Hitlerite dogs swarmed in the streets, as well as after midnight, when the echo of every rustle had died out in the half-dead city, Gebelev was making his way from the ghetto to the city and back again.

The police seized Mikhel at the ghetto border.

One of the most heroic sons of the Minsk Ghetto perished. He devoted his entire life, without respite, to the struggle to free his native land from the Hitlerite yoke, to free his brothers and sisters.

But the struggle continued more stubbornly and more persistently than ever. Thousands of people tore themselves from the deadly grip of the Minsk Ghetto to join the battle waged by the disciplined ranks of the partisans and the great army of the people's avengers. We sent our contacts out of the ghetto on a mission to find more ways of getting Jews to the partisan units. By an order from the headquarters of the Frunze Partisan Unit (which operated in the Koidanovsky Forest in the Minsk district), groups of Jews from the Minsk Ghetto were organized into two new units: the Dzerzhinky Unit and the Sergei Lazo Unit. A stream of people flowed from the ghetto into these units.

The people of the Minsk Ghetto not only felt it—they knew it for a fact: the hour of the Hitlerites' final massacre of the Jewish population was growing near. With each passing day the exodus from the ghetto into the forest became more and more massive. Women, children, and the elderly would set out often without a guide, not knowing their way through the partisan forests.

About five hundred Jews gathered near the village of Vertinka (near the place where the Budenny Unit was situated). With the help of the commander of the Budenny Unit, some of the people obtained arms. They became the new Parkhomenko Jewish Partisan Unit. The rest of them, under the command of the Minsk worker Sholom Zorin, were sent to the Nalibokskaya Woods to form Jewish Unit No. 106.

Under the command of Comrade Golitsev, the Kutuzov Unit also came to the aid of those who were left in the ghetto. Contacts from that unit repeatedly came into the ghetto to take people out.

During the last days of October 1943, when partisan contacts were approaching the ghetto, they discovered that this time they would have to return to their unit without carrying out their assignment: there was no more Minsk Ghetto. The last of the Jews had been slaughtered by the fascists.

The partisans, including those who had escaped from the ghetto, responded to this news by taking a solemn oath to fight even harder against the Hitlerite cannibals for the total liberation of the Soviet earth from the fascist scum.

G. Smolyar

The Young Women from Minsk

On Sunday 16 July 1944[15] there was a rally in Minsk to celebrate the liberation of the city. The rally included a grand parade of partisans, among whom was the Jewish partisan unit commanded by Sholom Zorin, a carpenter from Minsk.

In this unit were more than 650 people who had escaped on various occasions from ghettos in Minsk, Borisov, Lyuban, and Cherven. One hundred fifty of them, both men and young women, took part in military operations. The rest—women, children, and the elderly—lived in partisan camps and worked at making boots, sewing clothes, and other tasks needed by partisans throughout the region.

In the front row of the unit on parade were three young women wearing men's boots and trousers and German jackets; they were carrying German submachine guns.

This is what they related about themselves.

Sonya Kats, age twenty, was resettled in the ghetto along with her parents. Her father was shot during their first days there. On 11 August 1941 a boy from her village of Koidanov came to the ghetto and told the story of how all the Jews in the village had been shot and thrown into a pit; many of them, he said, were buried alive. For three hours the earth covering the mass grave would move: people still alive were trying to crawl out of their grave. Among them were Sonya's sister Genya and her girls: Galya, Sima, and Berta. When she found out about the deaths of her daughter and granddaughters, Sonya's mother also died. Sonya was left alone. During the mass slaughter of the Jews of Minsk in November 1941 Sonya and twenty other young women managed to hide in the cellar of a destroyed building on Zelenaya Street; then they escaped from the city.

They were ambushed by Germans along the way, and only seven of them reached the partisans. Sonya was one of them.

She has three blown up bridges, two attack waves held at bay, and dozens of dead Germans to her credit.

"I cannot live any other way," says Sonya. "Now I shall enlist in the Red Army. I cannot live without taking revenge on the murderers."

The Germans shot Emma Shepsenvol's father early on as well; she was left with her mother and her little brother and sister. One day, when Emma was on her way to the market to trade their possessions for bread, she was picked up and taken to the police station. In front of the police station stood sixty drunken policemen lined up in two rows facing each other. Emma was led down the middle of the two rows, as they beat her with whips. She collapsed at the end of the line. They left her for dead; when night fell, she regained consciousness and made her way home. During the second pogrom of 1942 Emma was at a neighbor's house outside the ghetto and thus was saved; but her mother, brother, and sister were murdered. Emma decided to escape. She managed to get as far at the village of Staroe Selo dozens of kilometers from Minsk; there she found the partisans. They sent her to a Jewish unit.

During the first pogrom of 1942 Anna Kaplan hid in the attic of a half-destroyed building. She could hear the drunken SS down below ranting and raving and smashing furniture. They shot her father. Without waiting for the next pogrom, she and her mother and her two sisters fled from the ghetto and joined the partisans. She served as a secret agent the whole time she was in the unit.

Reported by Semyon Bank,
prepared for publication by Vasily Grossman

The Story of an Old Man

I am already close to seventy.

The Germans reached our little village of Pleshchenitsy (Minsk district) on 27 June 1941. As soon as the shooting broke out, we, the old ones, left for a wooded grove five kilometers outside the village; when the battle was over we returned.

They burned down half the village, but my little house was left in tact. My wife and I quietly slipped inside, locked the door, and drew the curtains over the windows; we could still hear shots in the distance. We were seized with horror when they faded into silence: we were now on the far side of the front lines.

The temporary German commandant arrived in Pleshchenitsy and issued an order stating that the Jews must follow a special set of rules. They were to live in a ghetto apart from everyone else and wear yellow identification badges on their chest and back; children also had to wear the badges. Jews were forbidden to walk on the sidewalk. The rest of the population was not only forbidden to do business with Jews but could not even speak to them or respond to their greetings. All hard labor was to be assigned to Jews, who would work without pay.

In the first few days several [Jews and Christians] who had held positions of responsibility under the Soviet authorities were murdered.

A few days later we found out that about two kilometers from us, in the village of Zembin, Jews had been forced to dig a large pit. When they were done, all the Jews of Zembin were herded into the bazaar, supposedly to be registered; then they were taken to the pit and shot. Several of those who had fallen into the pit were still breathing. Children generally were not shot but were thrown into the pit alive. Once the pit was covered over, the earth continued to move and heave for a long time, due to the stirring of people who were still alive. So the story was told by those who had been forced to fill in the pit.

Only ten Jews managed to escape. One of them reached us two weeks later.

Such a heinous crime was unthinkable to us. We wanted to believe it was some kind of accident. Perhaps some Germans had been found murdered in Zembin, and that was why they had dealt with the Jews so terribly. It was known that entire villages and towns had been wiped out for the killing of a single German.

In vain we tried to calm ourselves. The savagery was repeated in the village of Logoisk twenty-five kilometers from us, as well as in several other places. An especially large number of Jews were killed in the city of Borisov, as well as in Smolevichi, Gorodok, and other small towns.

And so we realized that what happened in Zembin was not a chance occurrence, that it was carried out on Hitler's criminal orders. By that time we had moved into the ghetto. Fifty homes had been set aside for the ghetto, with approximately one thousand people living in them.

We knew that the matter would not end with moving into the ghetto and that we would have to drink the cup to its bitter dregs.

Once we saw dozens of policemen from the village approaching with a large number of empty carts. Several families had managed to escape about forty kilometers away to the village of Dolginovo in the Vilnius district, where the mass slaughter of the Jews had not yet taken place. But by evening the ghetto was surrounded, and it was impossible to escape.

Early in the next morning the policemen went around to the Jewish houses and herded everyone into a field. Those who walked slowly were driven with whips. In the field several of the craftsmen—cobblers, tailors, blacksmiths, as well as the elderly—were separated from the others and returned to the village. My wife and I ended up in that group, but our entire family of eight—our daughters and granddaughters—were loaded into carts and taken away. We could not even say goodbye to them or offer them a last embrace. Later the cart drivers told us that they had taken the poor people about fifty kilometers away to a forest near Borisov, where the German murderers were waiting for them. The drivers were sent back with their horses. After that we heard nothing more about our loved ones.

How can I describe my state of mind as we returned home? A death-like silence reigned over the village. My wife rushed about the empty rooms as though looking for her children. The books, the maps, the musical instruments—everything was in its place; but there were no children. She started to tear at her hair and then fainted.

Three weeks went by. The holy days of Sukkot (the Feast of Tabernacles) passed. I was returning home from work with four Jews. Not far from town we were warned: "Run to the forest immediately. The Gestapo is rounding up all the Jews who are left."

I wanted to run home to save my wife or to die with her. My comrades would not let me go and dragged me into the forest with them. The Germans shot at us, but they missed.

Unable to keep up with the young men, I sat in the cold rain until dark. That night I went home. I was hoping that my wife had hidden somewhere near the house and that she would be waiting for me. But I found no one, and the locks on our house had been changed. There was nothing left to hope for. I crawled under a haystack to get warm and to figure out what to do next; I did not want to wait around until morning and fall into the clutches of the Germans. I wanted to live, so that I could see the blood of the innocent avenged with my own eyes. I decided to head for Dolginovo. It was still raining, and I had nothing warm to wear. All I could find was a large sack; I put it over my head, took a staff in my hand, and left my home and birthplace, the only one left from my village. Thus I set off into the darkness of the night.

It took me four days to get to Dolginovo. I walked through woods and fields and spent the nights in the haystacks of peasants, who fed me as they wept over my fate and their own.

I met a relative in Dolginovo. We burst into tears. He had his own bitterness. An SS unit had passed through his town five days before I got there. After they had left, some of the bandits returned and declared that one of their whips was missing; if it did not turn up within ten minutes, they said, several Jews would be slaughtered. They did not find the whip, and the murderers immediately killed five young workers who were on their way home.

One of them was my relative's son-in-law. His young daughter was left alone with her two-month-old baby to grieve for her husband.

I spent the winter in Dolginovo. The Jews did not suffer a total annihilation there; they simply suffered from violence, taxes, and forced tributes.

After the Purim[16] holiday the rumor spread that mass murders were about to take place. We set about preparing hiding places for ourselves, so that we would not fall into the clutches of the murderers. Shortly before Passover trucks carrying Gestapo agents arrived. They began shooting Jews right in the streets, young and old alike. We hid in the attic and looked down on the slaughter through the cracks in the roof.

But it was not enough for the Gestapo. The next morning they mobilized the police from the surrounding villages and spent the entire day searching houses, barns, and attics; they used hand grenades to flush out those who were in hiding. Everyone who fell into their hands was stripped naked, beaten, and driven out of town to be slaughtered. Those who could not move quickly enough were shot on the spot. The walls of the buildings were splattered with the blood of the martyrs.

Outside of town large groups of people were shot and left unburied. Several hundred were driven into a barn; it was then doused in kerosene and set on fire. There were once three thousand Jews in Dolginovo.

In those two black days 1,800 people were murdered, and 1,200 survived. We were among the survivors.

The murderers left on the third day. They declared that, while most of the Jews had been killed, the rest would not be harmed if they would come to register with the police. Anyone failing to do so would be shot.

Almost everyone showed up; a few days later they were resettled in the ghetto, which consisted of forty small buildings. The ghetto was surrounded by barbed wire and a wooden fence. The Jews themselves had done all the labor. Right away, however, we started setting up hiding places. Everyone knew that the cannibals could not be trusted. On one occasion they demanded that we join a military convoy as drivers. No one had any desire to slide down the gullet of the beast. People hid themselves. As my relative was crawling into the attic, they noticed him and shot him in the leg. The following day the murders commenced once again. Another eight hundred people were killed over the next two days, but the Germans simply could not find about four hundred of us.

In the building where I was staying many were so tired that they did not even try to hide. People would say, "You can't save yourself anyway; you're just torturing yourself."

But ten people, including myself, hid in the attic. The bandits broke through the roof and came into the attic several times, but they did not find us. Thus I managed to stay alive once again.

After they left the fascists set up another registration, complete with promises of life. But no one was in a hurry; was there any way we could believe the word of a dog? We began planning an escape, and about two hundred of us broke through the fence and headed for the Belorussian forests. There we met our friends and brothers: the partisans. They gave us a warm welcome; the younger ones among us enlisted in the partisan units, while the children, the sick, and the elderly were given food and shelter. Comrade Kiselev, a good and educated man, was appointed as our political instructor.

We spent the summer and fall in the forests with the partisans. When it turned cold the commander ordered the weakest among us to be taken across the front line and delivered to our dear homeland. A special unit led by Kiselev himself was assigned to this task.

The journey took about two months. We would walk at the night and rest during the day. Each day we entered a new forest. We would cover about twenty kilometers every night; in regions where it was especially dangerous, we covered thirty kilometers. Whenever we came to an area occupied by the partisans, we could pass through during the day and rest with the peasants at night, sleeping three to four people to a hut. They fed us, too. Altogether we covered about three thousand kilometers on foot.

Thus we were saved. Of all I have lived through I, the seventy-year-old Shmuel-Dovid Kugel, bear true witness to the world.

Prepared for publication by Vasily Grossman

In the Village of Gory

Many Jews lived in the town of Gory: workers, lumberjacks, artisans, craftsmen, and farmers from the Cherny Styag farm. Their blacksmiths, boot makers, and village tailors were known far and wide. Who did not know the blacksmith Abram Altshuler? In Gory there was a high school, a library, a large club, a hospital, and a cultured park where people could relax.

In the summer the linden trees were in bloom. In the autumn the dahlias turned red in the front gardens.

On 19 October 1941, early in the morning, the Germans surrounded the village. A German broke into the home of the eighty-year-old Efros. The old man begged. The German grabbed him by the arm and shouted, "Come on!" Efros replied, "Don't touch me! I have enough strength to go to my grave." The Germans drove the invalid Gurevich from the house next door; his wife Mirra was crying. Gurevich said, "Mirra, you mustn't cry." The Jews were taken to the factory. There a huge grave had been dug. An old woman named Rakhlev yelled, "Not a drop of blood will be forgotten! You will pay for all of this. . . ." She was the first one they killed. The Jews undressed. "I'm cold," little children cried out. Khana Gurevich screamed,

"I won't let these reptiles mock my little boy." The aged Efros was the last to be murdered.

On 21 March 1944 the Red Army liberated the village of Gory. They dug up the grave near the factory and discovered a horrible sight. Here a woman with a child in her arms; there a little boy hugging an old woman around the neck, apparently his grandmother. Hundreds of bodies.

A military unit gathered at the edge of the uncovered grave. Officer Konishchev spoke: "Comrades, do not forget this grave! Vow to take revenge on the Germans for the innocent blood of the Soviet people." Ryadovoy Troitsky said: "As I go into battle, I shall always remember this grave." The funeral march ended with the words of this vow.

Prepared for publication by Ilya Ehrenburg

The Murder of the Jews of Glubokoe and Other Villages

On 2 June 1941 the Germans entered the village of Glubokoe. The population was seized with fear and horror. [Belorussians, Jews, and Poles had lived here for dozens and dozens of years.]

The German authorities began by demanding that all grain surpluses be handed over. Each family, regardless of how many were in the family, was allowed to keep only twenty kilograms of flour or grain.

The rest had to be delivered to the magistrate within a few hours. The line of people bringing their "excess" of three or four kilograms was a pitiful sight. The German authorities cruelly enforced their order. Osher Gofman was discovered with a quantity larger than the Germans had stipulated. For this crime they arrested him, as well as his wife, children, and elderly parents. They were led out of town, ordered to dig their own grave, and shot.

Several other families were threatened with the same punishment: the Olmers, the Drutses, the Kantoroviches, the Pliskins, the Ponyatovskys, and others. The police found some bran, for example at the Druts home; the family had not turned it in because they did not realize that it was included in the grain quota.

All of these people were seized like criminals; only after a large bribe had been paid did they manage to escape death.

From the day of their arrival the Germans started rounding up the entire Jewish population [(including the children)] for forced labor.

[Jews were forced to perform tasks that were beyond their strength; while they labored, they were taunted and tormented. In some cases people were beaten unconscious and had to be carried off from "work." Natanzon, Pintov, Ozhinsky, and the attorney Slonimsky were among those unfortunate victims. The German overseers behaved like slave drivers with their slaves, and the Jews had to fulfill their most vile whims: they were forced to sing songs, crawl around on all fours, imitate animals, dance, kiss the Germans' shoes, and so on.]

The invaders had refined every form of degradation. For example, some people at the train station in Krulevshchina were placed under a water tower and drenched in cold water.

Very often the tormented people were forced to go "bathe" in the lake after work completely clothed.

All these things, however, were as yet innocent diversions that the Hitlerites indulged in.

On 22 October 1941 the Gebietskommissar announced that the Jews had exactly half an hour to move into the ghetto. [They were forbidden to take anything but a few sticks of furniture, and that required the permission of a specially appointed commission from the magistrate's office.]

M. Rayak describes this resettlement:

"The city looked like a bazaar. The streets were jammed with furniture! The Jews were carrying their pitiful possessions to the place assigned to them: the ghetto. In the streets there was screaming and shouting, pushing and shoving, like no one had ever seen before. The police, for their part, 'maintained order' by beating people with rifle butts, clubs, and anything else they could find."

The ghetto was horribly crowded; several families were crammed into a single room. The room's furnishings usually consisted of a small table and some benches. Whole families slept on the floor.

At first Jews were permitted to spend a couple of hours at a time shopping in the bazaar; then they were absolutely forbidden to go near the bazaar. Jews were not allowed to buy butter, meat, eggs, or milk.

Contact with the peasant population was forbidden under pain of death. [But, in spite of the cruel measures that doomed the Jews to starvation,] these cannibalistic decrees were circumvented in every way possible.

Although they were threatened with great danger, many of the peasants had food smuggled into the ghetto; some would bring it in themselves. There were times when peasants would put the Jewish badge on their sleeves and bring food to people they knew in the ghetto.

The Rayak brothers related how a peasant named Shchebeko secretly provided their sick mother with milk every day.

The peasant Grishkevich smuggled cabbage, potatoes, and other vegetables to several families; he brought food for the physician Rayak, for the tailor Shames, and for Gitelson.

Whenever such "crimes" were discovered, the guilty party paid with his life. People were beaten to death for being found with a scrap of meat or a pinch of salt. [The Germans maintained this policy throughout their rule.] The wife of Zalman-Vulf Ruderman was horribly beaten for attempting to bring two eggs into the ghetto as she was returning from work. The butcher Sholom Tsentsiper was arrested and shot early in 1943. A guard caught this "criminal" trying to bring a rooster into the ghetto hidden in a sack.

The Jews were absolutely forbidden to eat berries.

It is difficult to believe that people were persecuted for eating a few berries, as if they had committed some terrible crime against the state.

The Glozman family had been tailors in Glubokoe for generations. Honest, hard-working, and masters of their trade, they enjoyed the love and respect of all.

Zelik Glozman had a ten-year-old son named Aron. Looking upon his son's fine work, the father had great hopes for his firstborn. The boy brought home all A's and B's from school; he was always at the head of his class in games and artistic talent.

Then the Germans arrived. Within a few days they were searching all over town for Archik Glozman. The Gestapo agent Hainleit enlisted everyone in the effort to apprehend the little boy for the "crime" of carrying around a few berries in his handkerchief. The boy managed to escape from the guards, and, thanks to some kindhearted friends and with great difficulty, his parents found a hiding place for him.

Both the boy and his parents were subsequently murdered.

[The teacher David Pliskin worked as an interpreter for Commandant Rosentreter. One day in late June 1943 Pliskin walked up to a raspberry bush and picked a few berries. A German engineer from the SD saw him from the window of a house nearby. Foaming at the mouth, he ran out to Pliskin and, cursing him in the foulest language, screamed that Jews were forbidden to eat berries. Pliskin promised that in the future he would strictly adhere to this prohibition from the German authorities.

The German threatened to shoot him, and only due to his "sincere repentance" and the fact that his supervisor put in a word for him was he fined instead of shot. . . . They demanded that he pay two thousand rubles, but after a lengthy argument the fine was lowered to five hundred, which he paid immediately. When Pliskin went to the Gestapo office to pay the fine, he was warned that if such a crime should be repeated he would not escape execution; according to a new decree, any Jews eating berries, fruits, or animal fat would be executed.]

N. Kraut was wounded and then killed for trying to bring a little salt into the ghetto.

In March 1943 the gendarmes and police were searching for Zalman Fleisher, who was accused of buying a slice of butter from a peasant.

Having been warned that they were looking for him, Fleisher managed to escape.

But the crime had to be punished, and Kern, chief of the gendarmes, ordered his men to arrest the first Jews they saw on the street. Levi Drisvyatsky, his eighteen-year-old son Khavna, and Lipa Landau had to answer for Fleisher's "sin."

Drisvyatsky was an educated man—a talmudist, mathematician, and linguist; he was loved and respected by everyone in Glubokoe. He lost his oldest son Ovsei during an Aktion. The death of his son, a talented and highly educated young man, deeply disturbed Drisvyatsky. Life and lost its dearness, and he never recovered from it.

Lipa Landau was a man with a higher education. The German henchmen murdered his wife and children. He himself was saved by a miracle: he crawled out of a mass grave from beneath a pile of bodies. For a long time he wandered about the woods and fields until he finally staggered into Glubokoe. Here he and Drisvyatsky became friends.

And so the Germans arrested them, took them to Gestapo headquarters, and tortured them throughout the night; the next morning they were taken to bloody Borki—the execution site. That was how the Hitlerite "law" avenged the slice of butter that Zalman Fleisher "illegally" smuggled into the ghetto.

The systematic annihilation of the Jewish population began in December 1941 through what was designated by the short and terrible word *Aktions*.

Early one December morning the Gestapo broke into ghetto homes and, without offering any explanation, dragged several dozen people from their beds. These people, who had been declared an "unnecessary element," were forced to walk naked in the freezing cold.

"One woman," writes M. Rayak, "lay down in the middle of the street with her children and cried and screamed that she would not budge. She was beaten unconscious. Everyone was herded off to Borki, where they were shot. The poor children were thrown into the pit alive, and there they were buried alive."

Borki was in a rural area a kilometer and a half from Glubokoe. In more peaceful times it was a place where people would go for a stroll and relax. Now the Germans had transformed Borki into a place of mass murder.

"In Borki," write the Rayak brothers, "the Germans forced the young to dance and the elderly to sing Jewish songs along the edge of a mass grave. . . . After this sadistic torment, they forced those who were young and the healthy to take feeble old people and cripples in their arms and carry them into the pit. Only then could they themselves lie down in the pit. And then the Germans shot them all."

That was how the seventy-year-old mother of the Rayak brothers died; that was how the entire population of Glubokoe was gradually wiped out.

The murders were preceded by unimaginable tortures: people were cut up with knives, placed naked in the freezing cold and drenched with water, and beaten unconscious with clubs and rifle butts.

The fascists took special delight in torturing women and children.

In Glubokoe, as in many other places, the Germans resorted to their usual method of provocation: they divided the people into two ghettos.

The second ghetto, said the Germans, was for Jews who were of "little use" and "little value." In fact, many skilled workers ended up in the second ghetto: cobblers, joiners, and tailors. The Germans decided to undertake and economic Aktion in the second ghetto: people could buy their way out of it.

Thus Jews who could pay the ransom remained in the first ghetto. Those who could not raise the necessary sum either in cash or valuables were sent to the second ghetto, [even though there were highly qualified skilled workers among them.]

The resettlement into the second ghetto took about two weeks, from 20 May to the first week of June 1942. Every day during those two weeks carts carrying old men and women flowed into the ghetto.

Rayak writes, "This terrible spectacle is beyond description. The poor old people just sobbed and begged, 'Where are you taking us, and why? . . . For what sins are you separating us from our children?' Krasnoarmeiskaya Street was filled with the moans of weeping old people and cripples. . ."

After the establishment of the second ghetto, the fascists announced that everyone in the first ghetto would receive a worker's identification card and that the card would guarantee their immunity.

Kopenwald, the executioner of the Jews of Glubokoe, gave the members of the Jewish Council his official "word of honor" that there would be no more massacres of the Jews.

In July 1942 the Gebietskommissar ordered all Jews who were still alive to be gathered into the Glubokoe Ghetto. When he gave this order, the Gebietskommissar assured the Jews that no more of them would be killed. He even issued passes for members of the Judenrat to travel to the forests and villages, so they could seek out Jews who were in hiding and bring them to the camp.

By this time the camp—the ghetto in Glubokoe—had become a well-known Jewish "center"; the surviving Jews from forty-two different towns and villages were gathered here. Here were husbands without wives and wives without husbands. There were husbands and wives who had gotten separated during the slaughter and did not know what had become of one another; now, upon meeting each other once again in the ghetto, they would ask each other about what had happened to their children. There were little boys and girls who had lost their parents; there were infants who had been found under some bushes in the forest and brought to the camp. There were Jews from Miory, Druya, Prozorki,

Golubichi, Zyabki, Disna, Sharkovshchina, Plissa. . . Exhausted, tormented, and beaten down, people had gathered here from all these places. There were also survivors of massacres that had taken place in Dolginovo, Druisk, Braslav, Germanovichi, Luzhki, Gaiduchishki, Voropaevo, Parafyanovo, Zagate, Bildyugi, Shipy, Shkuntiki, Porplishche, Sventsyany, Podbrodzi. . . .

The scheme worked: all the Jews were gathered in one spot.

[It is interesting to note that in Glubokoe the economic effectiveness and benefits derived by the Germans as a result of the Aktions against the Jews were striking.]

For days on end the Germans hauled off truckloads of stolen clothing, shoes, linens, and dishes, as well as sewing machines, machines for making stockings and hats, milling machines, and all sorts of household goods. All of these things sorted through and stored in barns with characteristic German accuracy and precision. A short time later the goods turned up in stores (along Karl Marx Street) where ready-made dresses, shoes, and haberdashery were sold, as well as in furniture stores and stores full of china and glassware.

The laundry where the belongings of the murdered were washed ran day and night.

Jews worked in the laundry (as they did in other "restoration workshops").

Terrible scenes unfolded during the sorting and folding of the clothing. People recognized underclothing and other items that had belonged to their murdered relatives. Rafael Gitlits recognized his murdered mother's undergarment and dress. Manya Freidkina had to wash her husband Shimon's bloodstained shirt. With her own hands the wife of Milikhman, the school teacher, had to get her murdered husband's suit into "decent shape."

[Commercial activity was far from dissipating in the German department stores, the *Warenhäuser.*]

A special "Bureau of the Glubokoe Gebietskommissar" was located at 19 Karl Marx Street. The bureau's assignment was to keep order in the workshops, do the bookkeeping, and supervise the workers.

The bureau also had the task of preparing packages that met German specifications, as well as those of private parties, and ship them to Germany.

The bureau's steady customers were Gebietskommissar Gachman; the consultants Heberling and Hebell; gendarme chief Kern; the officers Hainleit, Wildt, Speer, Zanner, Bekkar, Kopenwald, Seif, and Schultz; and many others.

In order to maintain the enormous flow of packages, a special operation was set up to manufacture cartons. Jewish children from eight to twelve years of age worked there. And woe to them if the slightest defect should be discovered in their work! They were punished just as cruelly and mercilessly as the adults were.

Dozens of train cars loaded with cloth, leather, wool, shoes, knitted items, and massive food supplies set out from Glubokoe, Krulevshchina, and Voropaevo. [The Jewish population was ravaged, and the Germans drained every ounce of life from the village. The economy was exhausted, yet German pockets bulged. In addition to the widespread appropriation of foodstuffs and consumer goods, there was a massive plundering of metals.] The Germans set up a special warehouse where they stored metal items: samovars, pots, candle sticks, mortars, copperware, door handles, and the like. In Glubokoe the police went from house to house to check to see whether the population had any metal goods left. All of the stolen metal was loaded into train cars and shipped to Germany.

The German authorities utilized everything. In the summer and fall of 1942 dozens of tons of "light" cargo were sent to Germany: the down and feathers from quilts and pillows that had been ripped open. . . .

The grief and suffering that fell upon the people of Glubokoe was immeasurable.

In addition to physical torments, the Hitlerites subjected the Jewish population to moral torture.

With horrible cruelty they violated not only the living but also the dead.

The Germans forced the Jews themselves to tear down the stone fence surrounding the cemetery, chop down all the trees, and destroy the memorial stones.

On the night of 18 June 1942 there was a bloody Aktion.[17] The earth shuddered from the screams of women and the cries and groans of children. [All of a sudden, in the terrible darkness of the night, the mournful sound of old men chanting *El Mole Rachamim*,[18] the prayer said following a death, could be heard.] Just as dawn was breaking, people were herded off to the execution site at Borki. A young girl named Zelda Gordon bolted for the lake, and others followed after her.

Those who fled were cut down by bullets, and within half an hour the entire field from Borki to the lake was strewn with bodies. Bloody torture awaited anyone who refused to go silently to his death. Samuel Gordon tried to hide in the first ghetto (the Aktion targeted mainly the second ghetto), but he was caught. They beat him severely; then they hooked him around the neck with a poker and dragged him through the streets until he was finished.

Those who were still alive after this Aktion knew their days were numbered.

Despite the terrible conditions in the ghetto and deprived of all rights, Jews came to the aid of Soviet prisoners of war. There was a prisoner of war camp one and a half kilometers from Glubokoe, in the village of Berezvech. The Kozliner family took bread to them.

The Germans took note of this. The family had seven members. They were all shot.

It was difficult to get out of the ghetto. There were sentries at every turn. The German policy of holding each person responsible for the actions of the other held everyone in the grip of fear and submissiveness. Thoughts of struggle and vengeance, however, were alive in the hearts of the people.

In the spring of 1942 the Jewish youth demonstrated a great deal of resourcefulness and ingenuity in obtaining weapons. One cannot help but recall those heroes who were among the first to offer themselves in sacrifice. Ruvim Iokhelman of Gaiduchishki got a job in the gendarme warehouse; taking no thought for the risks involved, he smuggled out weapons and medications. This went on for a rather long time, until the Germans caught up with him. Iokhelman suffered a terrible death.

Yakov Fridman "specialized" in obtaining weapons in the villages. In the fall of 1942 he joined the Mstitel[19] Partisan Unit and, with no regard for his own safety, fought in its ranks until the arrival of the Red Army.

Moisey Berkon's son-in-law purchased rifles, grenades, and revolvers and delivered a significant number of them to the partisan units.

He was denounced. When the Germans came for him, he put up a desperate struggle. Kleiner of Luchai (near Dunilovich) [also sent weapons to the partisans, but in the fall of 1942 he left the ghetto-camp. He] hit a German who was standing guard, took his submachine gun, and headed for the forest.

In the summer of 1942, with weapons in hand, a group of young people went into the forest to join the partisans. One of the most famous of the partisans to first get out of Glubokoe was Avner Feigelman. Certain spiritual qualities distinguished this young man; he was intelligent, composed, and decisive. He fought in the Voroshilov Brigade. Others who fought with great courage, without fear for themselves, were Isaak Blat (Chapaevsky Unit of the Voroshilov Brigade), Borya Shapiro, and Khasya, a girl from Disna.

Boma Genikhovich of Plissa became one of the people's avengers. A German named Koppenberg murdered his father. The young man tracked Koppenberg down and killed him.

The German fury Ida Oditskaya was famous for her cruelty. She took part in a mass murder and played an active role in the murder and persecution of partisans. Genikhovich and his comrades managed to lure her into the forest. There they conducted a swift but just trial and hanged her.

In September of 1942 another group of eighteen armed people left to join the partisans. Among them were the Katsovich brothers, Zalman Milkhman, Iokhelman, Mikhail Feigal, Yakov Ruderman, Rakhmiel Milkin, and David Gleizer. This group had been in contact with the Mstitel Partisan Unit and sent them weapons.

A few months later another group of eighteen left the ghetto to join the partisans. Among them were Izrael Shlarber, Moisey and Sonya Feigel, Girsh Gordon, Simon Soloveichik, and Girsh Izraelev.

Two days after this group left, the Gestapo surrounded the building where the partisan families of Feigal and Milkin lived; fourteen people were murdered after being subjected to horrible torture.

Iosel Feigelson's sons Zalman and Don went to join the partisans. Tales of their courage spread throughout the area. In July of 1943 the Gestapo savagely murdered their father, their aunt Sarra Romm, and her daughter Nekhama Romm.

On 17 August 1943 in Krulevshchina, nineteen kilometers outside Glubokoe, a heavy battle was fought between the partisans and German units reinforced by the local gendarmes. Kern, the chief of the gendarmes in Glubokoe, was killed in the battle, along with several dozen others. The bodies were brought to Glubokoe.

Jews were forced to dig the graves, and it must be said that this was the only task they ever performed with pleasure.

A fateful day was approaching. The fascists were preparing the final liquidation of the ghetto. Anyone who was even slightly suspicious wash flushed out. They found a radio receiver in Zayats' attic; they beat him and tortured him for several days but got nothing out of him.

At the request of an old peasant friend, the blacksmith Shlema Kuznets started to shoe a horse. A guard spotted him and shot him.

Everyone in town knew and respected the sixty-year-old Mordukh Gurevich. He was a quiet, peaceful, kindhearted man. He lived his entire life in Glubokoe, and the peasants in the area loved and respected him. Once, while he was sweeping the street, he greeted an old friend who happened to be a peasant. They spotted him and arrested him; then they took him to Borki and shot him.

The cheerful, sweet Salya Braun was shot for her friendship with a peasant lad named Vitya Shchareiko.

On 13 August 1943 the ghetto in Glubokoe was liquidated. [The German newspapers reported that in Glubokoe a major enclave of three thousand partisans led by a seventy-year-old rabbi had been destroyed. . . .]

The German fascist troops brought death, destruction, and annihilation everywhere they set foot. The Germans arrived in the village of Krivichi on 2 July 1941.

A few days prior to their arrival, the seventy-year-old Zilbergleit gathered all his strength and made his way to Budslavo, where Red Army troops were positioned; he informed them that German agents had shown up in Krivichi. The information turned out to be extremely valuable: the first Germans in Krivichi were destroyed. The old Zilbergleit paid with his life for his patriotic actions: he was denounced and murdered on the very day that the Hitlerites entered Krivichi.

Wherever they went, the Germans tried to isolate the Jews from the rest of the population.

Every day the residents of Krivichi were forced to hang flags from their houses, first white ones, then black and white—the colors were constantly changing. The Jews had to hang flags that had colors different from those of the rest of the population, so that their homes could be distinguished [from the peasants' homes. Jewish girls were gathered and sent to wash and clean the peasants' homes. "This was hard on many peasants," write the Rayak brothers. "They wanted to refuse the service. They could not reconcile themselves to the fact that their neighbors, with whom they had lived so long in friendship, were enslaved and forced to work for them."

There were five prisoners of war from the Red Army in Krivichi, and the Jews did everything they could to help them.]

Every day the local police brought Jews to the police station; there, for no reason at all, they took birch rods and beat people who were known and respected in the town.

No sooner did dawn break than the Jews would be hauled off to work. Even more tormenting that the forced labor, however, was the humiliation they had to endure. They were forced to dance, run, and sing the Katyusha and the International; while they were working, they were beaten mercilessly with whips and clubs for the slightest error. Nearly every day people were brought home from work maimed and often unconscious.

The Jewish women were sent to work in the fields. Once, in mid-August 1941, the Germans assembled the Jewish girls who were working a garden that belonged to a Roman Catholic priest named Kropovitsky. After work they were locked into a barn, and the Germans tried to rape them; the girls smashed a window and escaped. Bullets were fired at them, and only a few managed to get away.

Jewish property was plundered, and the synagogue of Krivichi was ransacked; highly valuable texts that were kept there were barbarically torn to pieces and burned in bonfires.

[Next in line to fall prey to the police were Rabbi M. Perets and Movsha Dreizin.

Gestapo agents came to Dreizin's apartment; the police were with them. All the people there were forced to stand with their faces toward the wall, and a cabinet full of books was overturned on them. The Gestapo cleaned out the apartment and then left.

In March of 1942 government officials brought twenty carts of plundered goods and valuables from Smorgon to Krivichi. Jews were summoned to unload them.

It was a cold March day, and the Jews were kept outside for several hours in a piercing wind. While they were working, they were forced to run barefoot through puddles; then they had to lie down and get up again repeatedly.]

The first Aktions began in April 1942: the Hitlerites took care of the Gypsies, murdered the prisoners of war, and started on the Jewish population.

The people of the village of Dolginovo died horrible deaths: most of them were burned alive.

Dolginovo is located about fifteen kilometers from Krivichi. The residents of the two towns were very close to each other.

[The few Jews of Dolginovo who survived were a fearsome sight. Less than one hundred were driven into Krivichi. Robbed of their shoes and practically naked, they were forced to crawl around on all fours, sing Soviet songs, and dance.

It is difficult to imagine the general torment to which these Jews were subjected. They had to clean out latrines with their bare hands and haul away the excrement in sacks placed on their shoulders. The onlookers delighted in the suffering of their victims.

On 25 April 1942, about one and a half kilometers down the railroad tracks from Krivichi, the partisans derailed a transport carrying gasoline, and the train burst into flames. The Germans used this as an excuse to undertake a general Aktion against the Jews.]

On the morning of 28 April 1942 the first twelve Jews who happened by were arrested and sent to Smilovichi, where they were tortured and finally shot.

The SS and gendarmes came into Krivichi that day, completely surrounded the town, and forced the Jews into the open square.

The doomed people were forced to strip naked on the square and were then led out to a field.

In the field stood a large barn. The Germans set it on fire and forced the Jews into the flames.

The sight of children being burned alive was horrible!

The twelve-year-old Sarra Katsovich fought for her life with all her might. She ran out of the burning barn, but the police shoved her back in and shouted at the dying child: "Did you think your saviors had arrived?"

Blyuma Kaplan also perished in the fire. But it is impossible to list all the victims.

Girsh Tsepelevich was an active worker when the Soviets were in power. He was a cripple and could not get very far when the Red Army was retreating. He was forced to return to Krivichi. For months on end he hid in a dark, damp, narrow cellar.

He had forgotten what daylight, a bed, and clean linen were like. At night his sister M. Botvinnik would secretly bring him a meager portion of food. When the Aktion of 28 April 1942 broke out, Girsh Tsepelevich realized that it was senseless to go on struggling for his life.

The Germans and the police were searching for Jews everywhere and dragging them out of their malinas. Girsh Tsepelevich knew that the hours of his life were numbered, and he did not want to be taken alive. So he took the poison that he always carried with him.

Moshe-Leib Shud hid in an attic for a long time. His hiding place was discovered during a massive search. Shud knocked down the policeman who found him and ran away. He was captured. He suffered a cruel death: they threw him into a fire alive.

On 28 April 160 Jews were killed; the same fate awaited the rest. Of the 420 Jews in Krivichi, 336 perished.

Only those who managed to escape to the partisans survived. In April 1942 ninety young men and women left to join the People's Avenger partisan brigade. They fought selflessly and courageously, avenging the blood of their loved ones and the humiliation of their people.

Eleven Jewish women worked in Slobodka, eleven kilometers from Krivichi. They managed to fool the German guards and escape to the forest to join the partisans.

Five children worked in the little town of Pokut (about four kilometers from Krichivi). When the Germans liquidated the ghetto, they took care of even the children. Only one little boy, Gevish Gitlits, escaped and reached the partisans.

The fascists literally wiped entire Jewish towns from the face of the earth. In a single day the two thousand Jews of Miory and the five hundred in Braslav were annihilated. In Dur there were 2,200 murdered. The ghetto-camps in Plissa, Luzhki, and Novy Pogost were completely liquidated.

The slaughter of the Jews in the villages was horrible: people were thrown alive into fires. In the village of Sharkovshchina people had their tongue cut off, their eyes gouged out, and their hair cut off before they were killed.

The cruelty of the invaders could be seen in the way they would force Jews to do work that was not only beyond their strength but was completely useless and pointless. People were awakened at night and forced to carry around water in leaky buckets.

Weak women were forced to carry heavy stones and boxes full of sand from one place to another only to find that neither the stones nor the sand was needed for anything. The work had only one purpose: to torture people.

The fate that the fascists had prepared for the Jews was terrible, and anyone who attempted to help them was subject to execution. The honest, selfless people who saved Jews and thereby exemplified the strength and purity of the human soul must be remembered with the deepest gratitude.

In Borsuchina, Adolf and Mariya Stankevich hid many Jews from the surrounding villages.

People flocked to Statsevich in the town of Sharkovshchina from all directions, and he helped whomever he could. Statsevich died a martyr's death: the Germans hanged him in Glubokoe.

The Jews established contacts with the partisans and joined partisan units.

From the little town of Orany forty people left to join the partisans. The partisan Aizik Lev derailed fourteen enemy transports. He died bravely. His memory endures in the hearts of the people. Other partisans from Orany also fought with courage and daring.

Especially enthusiastic were the Jewish partisans of Dolginovo; Ivan Matveevich Timchuk, commander of the People's Avenger unit, was of great help to them.

The Jewish partisans from Dolginovo took part in many important operations; in May of 1942 they destroyed a sawmill, killed fifteen Germans, and captured a stockpile of ammunition. In November of 1942 they played an active role in the destruction of a German garrison in Myadel; they freed Jews from the ghetto and helped them to get across the front lines.

[In spited of its heavy fortifications, the partisans smuggled type for a printing press out of the German garrison in Glubokoe.]

Under the leadership of Yakov Sigalchik, the Dolginovo partisans killed more than thirty Germans in the village of Litvichi.

From materials provided by the brothers M. and G. Rayak,
prepared for publication by R. Kovnator

The Story of Engineer Pikman from Mozyr

I was born in Mozyr in 1916. I worked as a draftsman. Before the war I worked in Minsk as an engineer-dispatcher. On 25 July 1941 I left the burning city of Minsk and started down the Moscow Highway. It was crammed with refugees. I walked about thirty kilometers and then stopped for the night; the next morning I was on the move again. Fascist airplanes bombed and strafed us. There were many casualties: old people, women, and children. I hid in the bushes. When night fell the bombing stopped.

For four days I wandered about the forest without bread or water. On the fifth day I came upon the village of Skuraty. There were many refugees there. The Germans came and took everyone back to Minsk. They set up a checkpoint along the way and detained all the men.

Minsk was unrecognizable: everywhere you looked there were ruins and charred bodies. Decrees were posted on the walls: all men between the ages of sixteen and sixty-five were to report to the office of the commandant immediately. Anyone who failed to report would be shot.

The men were herded off to a camp. [It was initially set up at the Starorzhevskoe Cemetery. They were held there for twelve days without food or water. When a barrel of water was finally brought in, they all rushed toward it, and the Germans shot at them. Then the camp was moved to the Svisloch River, but they were forbidden to take water from the river.] The Jews were separated from everyone else and severely beaten. Some were used for target practice. I saw my colleague, a technician and stock clerk named Bernshtein, tied to a post and shot at.

A few days later came the order requiring all Jews to register and to make a "contribution." On 15 July all the Jews were forced to move into the ghetto. It was announced that the Jews must build a stone wall sealing them off from the rest of the world. They started building the wall, but then came the order to surround the ghetto with a barbed wire fence. It was announced that any Jew found outside the boundary of the ghetto—man or woman, adult or child—would be shot. [In addition, Jews had to wear yellow circles on their chest and back.]

Seventy-five thousand Jews registered in Minsk. They were housed on several streets. Five families were crammed into every room. People slept standing up. During the day they were herded off to work without any food; at night they were beaten.

I spent three weeks in the ghetto. On 6 August I crawled through the barbed wire fence and began making my way to Mozyr by way of country roads. I walked for a long time and grew very weak, until finally, on 30 August, I made it to my hometown.

My father, grandfather, and great-grandfather were born in Mozyr. I also had an uncle named Rukhomovsky; he was an artist and engraver. He lived in Paris. There, in his old age, he wrote a book telling the story of his life; he spoke lovingly about Mozyr. We were very close to our town.

Mozyr seemed to be completely deserted. There were no Germans in the town: they had moved on toward the east. I ran into some old women and told them who I was. They told me that my relatives had been evacuated. I went to our house. It had already been looted, and looters were still rummaging through other homes. The only ones left from the Jewish population were the sick, the old, and women with children.

Auntie Gasha, a Belorussian neighbor of ours, took me in.

On 6 September, as I was wandering around the empty streets, I suddenly caught sight of some German soldiers wearing camouflaged uniforms. They were walking along and shooting into the windows of houses. They were from a killing unit. Many people were murdered that day: the old shoemaker Malyavsky, a Polish actress who had come from Pinsk, a Belorussian family on Pushkin Street, another Belorussian family on Pyatnitskaya Street, an old man named Lakhman and his wife, and many others. The dogs dragged Lakhman's body down Novostroeniya Street.

Auntie Gasha said to me, "Leave. There is a viper living in this building. She told me, 'When the Germans come, I'll tell them you're keeping a Jew girl here.'" I went to my Grandma Golda Bobrovskaya's house. She was seventy-three year old. She lived on the very edge of town.

On 9 September I went to a street where many Jews once lived. Every apartment was littered with bodies: old women, children, and women with their bellies sliced open. I saw an old man named Malkin. He had been unable to leave Mozyr because his legs were paralyzed. He lay on the floor with his head smashed.

A young German was walking down the street. He was carrying a child no more than a year old stuck to the end of his bayonet. The little one was still faintly crying out. The German was singing and was so carried away that he did not notice me.

I went into several homes; bodies and blood were everywhere. I found some women and children who were still alive, hiding in a cellar. They told me that the old men had gone to the ravines near Pushkin Street.

On 10 September I could hear gunfire all day long: people were being shot. On Lenin Street I saw a sick old man, the hatter Simonovich. The Germans were hitting him with their rifle butts and shoving him forward, but he could not walk.

I went back to my Grandma Golda's. I sat down on the porch and tried to think of a way to get to the front. It was six or seven in the evening. Suddenly I saw Jews being led down Novostroeniya Street. Some of them had shovels, and at first I thought they were being taken out to work. There were about two hundred of them. Bent and bearded old men led the procession; behind them came twelve- to fifteen-year-old boys; then came some men dragging along the sick and the crippled. One tall, thin man was leading two feeble old men by the hand. His walked with his head bare but held high. The Germans beat him with their rifle butts, but never once did he cry out. I shall never forget his face.

They were taken out to the steep slope of a mountain and were forced to scramble up its side. The old men slipped and fell down. They were prodded back up with bayonets, and then I heard machine gun fire.

Within half an hour the Germans were already on their way back from the mountain. They were singing.

As for the people on the mountain, it was said that the Germans threw the old men into the pit alive. When some tried to crawl out, their hands were chopped off at the wrist.

As the fascists were leaving the execution site, I saw two soldiers dragging two Jews up the slope. The Germans were in a hurry, so they shoved the two Jews forward with their rifle butts. As soon as they reached the top, two shots rang out. The soldiers then ran to catch up with their comrades. They too were singing.

Twenty old Jewish carpenters who did not want to fall into the hands of the executioners gathered together in the home of a carpenter named Eli Gofshtein on Pushkin Street. Then they soaked the house in kerosene and burned themselves alive. Their charred bodies were scattered about the ruins, and no one buried them.

I spent the night in a house about a hundred meters from the pit. I heard moaning all night long. More than two years have gone by since that time, and every night I can still hear people moaning.

The next morning Auntie Gasha greeted me with the words, "We're all doomed!" She said the Germans were herding all the women and children to the Pripyat River and throwing them in; children, she said, were raised up on bayonets. Auntie Gasha cried out, "Why the children? . . . Those beasts! They are murdering everyone! . . ."

I returned to Golda Bobrovskaya's. She was praying. Toward evening the Germans and the police arrived. They asked me, "Where are the Jews here?" I told them I did not know because I was not from around here. At that moment they caught sight of old Golda. They pounced on her and started beating her with their rifle butts. I ran away and hid in the corn shed. A neighbor came out and said, "Stay here. They are looking for you."

It was a very bright sunset. I waited for them to come. . .

But they went away. I changed my clothes and got out of town. I decided to make my way to the front. In the village of Kozenki I met a plumber who had come from Mozyr. I had seen him in Bobrovskaya's apartment. He said that old Golda had been stabbed to death with bayonets and her body dumped near the cemetery. The bodies of many old men, old women, and children were there. No one buried them. Pieces of torsos, heads, hands, and legs were just lying around. The Jews of the town had already been slaughtered. Now the killing units were combing the villages. The plumber said, "You are still young. I don't know who you are, but I feel sorry for you. Leave this place."

A Jewish schoolteacher lived in that village. Her husband was a Belorussian, and I went to see her. She was a very beautiful young woman. She had three children, the oldest of whom was six; the youngest was not yet walking. I suggested to her that she leave with me. She replied, "Where can I go with three little ones?" While spending the night in the next village I found out that the killing units had arrived in Kozenki and that the teacher and her children had been murdered.

I saw many things. I saw the ghetto in Orsha. It was even more horrible than the Minsk Ghetto. Freezing old women poked around dead bodies. Girls, bruised and swollen from hunger, would ask, "When are they coming for us?"— to them death seemed like a relief. I saw a prisoner-of-war camp in Orsha. The fascists kicked the prisoners with their boots and beat them with whips and rifle butts. I saw the camp in Smolensk. Mere shadows of human beings had to bury the dead at a rate of three to four hundred per day. {I saw Germans lying back and counting, "One Jew, two Jews. . ."} I was arrested in Pochinok. They tortured me and wanted to know whether I was a Jew. I remained silent. They whipped me and knocked my teeth out. In Pochinok I saw the Germans hang Russians. I saw Germans plunder, murder, and laugh at people's misery. Hungry and barefoot, I headed east. I picked ears of corn in the fields and lived like a beggar. A German car ran me down and broke one of my legs; soon after that I came down with typhus and begged the doctor to let me die.

I reached Orel. I saw the partisans and Soviet people fighting against the invaders. And on 5 August 1943 I saw a miracle: the red star on the cap of a Red Army soldier.

I cannot forget Mozyr: the face of old Golda, the mutilated bodies of the heroic carpenters.

Basya Pikman,
prepared for publication by Ilya Ehrenburg

The Story of Dr. Olga Goldfain

The war caught me in the border town of Pruzhany, where I was working as a doctor in a hospital. On the night of 22 June 1941 I was on duty. At 3:30 in the morning the Germans began to bomb the town.

They entered the town on 23 June; immediately they jumped out of their cars and started plundering the town and beating the Jews. {A group of White Guards was with them; they were speaking French and German as they went up and down the streets inciting people to a pogrom.} We all locked ourselves into our houses.

On the third day the Germans demanded that we hand over all our dishes, knives, spoons, and pots. Two days later they demanded our beds, linens, and such.

The Jews hid in cellars and attics, but the Germans found them, beat them half to death, and dragged them off to work.

After the German army passed through town on 10 July, the Gestapo arrived; what happened next is indescribable. First they seized eighteen Jews, took them two kilometers outside of town, and shot them. We discovered the fate of those poor people ten days later, when we saw a dog dragging around a human arm with a red cross on the sleeve, a doctor's arm.

On 15 July the Germans posted an announcement stating that within three days the Jews were to set up a Jewish Council—a Judenrat—consisting of twenty-four men. If they should fail to form a Judenrat, one hundred people would be shot. None of the Jews wanted to be on the Judenrat. After consulting with some Poles, one Jew decided they should submit a list of Jews without the Jews' knowledge, so that when they were summoned, it would be too late to do anything about it. People with a higher education were put on the list—attorneys and physicians—but when the Germans saw the list, they said they needed skilled workers, not scholars. Within a week the Germans had put together a Judenrat of their own choosing.

On 20 July the Gestapo showed up at the Judenrat office and announced that a substantial tribute would have to be paid within the next three days: {five kilograms of gold, fifty kilograms of silver, and half a million Soviet rubles.} Three days later the Germans collected the tribute but failed to give the Judenrat a receipt. Jews from the surrounding villages asked us to help them pay the ransom. They had neither valuables nor money. We collected all the valuables we had left—brooches, rings, light fixtures and menorahs from the synagogue—and paid the tribute for the villages of Shirokov, Malech, and Linovo.

The Germans would take the Jewish men off to work at five o'clock in the morning; in the evening many would return crippled and beaten.

On 10 August the German High Command posted announcements on the walls of the buildings stating that all Jews in the occupied territories would be moved into a ghetto.

For two months we slept in our clothes, with a small bundle under our heads, ready to leave at any moment.

On 10 October it was announced that a "Judenstadt"[20] was to be organized in Pruzhany; we were to stay where we were, and the residents of Bialystok were to move into our Judenstadt. On 25 October we moved into the ghetto. Part of the ghetto was fenced off with barbed wire, part with a solid wall.

Over the next six weeks the Jews of Bialystok flowed into our ghetto: three thousand widows and two thousand orphans. The Germans set up a checkpoint outside of town, where once again they would mercilessly beat and rob the new arrivals.

At the same time Jews from other towns and villages were moving into the ghetto with the rest of us: Jews from Belovezh, Gainovka, Novy Dvor, Zabludov, Kamenets, Bluden, Malech, Shereshevo, Bereza, Slonim, and other places.

On 3 January 1942 the Germans demanded that we pay a second tribute. They collected our fur coats, all our woolen clothing, and other fur items. A Jewish woman did not have the right to wear so much as a fur button. All cameras, rugs, gramophones, and records, [except those by Mendelssohn], were confiscated. They presented us with a bill for equipping the ghetto, which we ourselves build under the lash; first they collected 750,000 marks and then another 500,000 marks.

On 9 January a German woman named Horn, who was mayor at the time, announced that two thousand Jews would have to leave the ghetto immediately. Thanks to a large bribe that we paid to Horn and the gendarmes, however, those Jews were allowed to remain in the ghetto until spring.

In February a new mayor arrived, a man named Koschman; he immediately demanded a third payment of money and clothing. In addition, a new tax was levied: ten marks per person. For those who had no money, the Judenrat had to pay.

In March Jews from Ivatsevichi, Stolbtsy, and other villages began to arrive in the ghetto. They looked horrible; they were half-naked, and their hands and feet were frostbitten. In April the ghetto was crammed full once again. In May they started rounding up people to be sent to the camps, from which no one ever returned. That winter we cleared snow off the railway lines from the Linovo station to Baranovich; even then young people were being sent to the camps. In the spring and summer we dug peat, took out stumps, cleared a strip in the forest one hundred meters wide along the railroad, filled in pits with sand. . . .

The Germans set up cooperatives for cobblers, tailors, and furniture makers.

The Germans hauled off all the iron to Germany; they dismantled the narrow-gauge railroad line in Pruzhany and shipped it west.

Of the eighteen thousand residents in the ghetto that winter, six thousand died from cold, hunger, and beatings.

At five o'clock in the morning on 2 November the Gestapo surrounded the ghetto and said we were being evacuated. They warned us that we were allowed to take no more than fifty kilograms of baggage. By the time this order was given, all the Jews in the surrounding villages had already been killed, and we knew what lay in store for us. Many decided to die right there and rushed to their medicine cabinets for poison. Forty-seven people took poison and died. I too decided to die. We had a supply of morphine and divided it among ourselves: a gram per person. I swallowed a gram and injected a gram into a vein. Then we locked ourselves in our apartment and tried to poison ourselves with carbon monoxide. The Judenrat found out about it and towards morning opened up the apartment. Everyone was lying unconscious; one lucky soul was dead. Medical personnel treated us for three days, and we returned to life.

On 7 November, I received a note from a friend of mine, a nun named Chubak. She asked me to meet her. I went to the barbed wire fence and saw her. She had brought a liter of vodka for the sentry so that he would let us talk; she gave me three hundred marks for bribe money. I told her how horrible things were and that I did not want to go on fighting for my life; better to leave this life. After we parted, I decided to insult the sentry, so that he would shoot me. At first the guard was amazed that I dared to even speak to him. I started by asking if he really believed what Hitler said about our being biologically non-human. Is it really possible, I asked him, that Germans—who considered themselves a cultured people and the master race—are not ashamed to torture defenseless widows, old people, and children? Could it be, I asked, that he was not aware of the situation the German army was in? After all, they failed to take Stalingrad, they were surrounded in the Caucasus, and they were fleeing from Egypt. It was impossible for them to win the war. I told him that the Führer had infected the whole German people with rabies and that they had truly gone insane, like mad dogs. "Understand me, Sergeant," I said. "I want you to survive, go back home, and remember the words of this little Jewish woman who told you the truth."

But the sergeant did not shoot me.

Then I went to a barber whom I knew, a man named Berestitsky. I knew him to be a man of resolve. I called him out into the alley and said, "I wanted to poison myself, but the poison did not work; I wanted to get shot, but a German bullet could not find me. There is only one other way: to escape from the ghetto. Help me." Berestitsky carefully lifted up the barbed wire, and I crawled under it. I hurried across the street and through gardens and courtyards, until I came to the convent. Soon I was with my friend the nun. She immediately changed me out of my clothes and hid me. They set up three hiding places for me: one in the cow shed, another under the stairway, and a third between two cupboards. I sat locked up and looked out the window the whole time to see who was coming. Whenever I went to the dining room, the doors were locked shut. All this while I had a terrible toothache and could not sleep at night, but there was no way I could see a dentist. A week of constant terror went by. During the day I hid in the room, but at night I went out into the courtyard and listened to what was happening in the ghetto. It was dark and horrifying. All of a sudden there was a fire in the ghetto; machine guns and tanks were positioned all around it, and airplanes were flying overhead.

At the end of the fifth week of my stay in the convent a representative of the Judenrat came to me with a letter from the chairman of the Judenrat [and my husband.] They wrote that the Germans were concerned about my health (the Germans thought I was still sick from talking poison). If I did not return to the ghetto, the entire ghetto would suffer because of me.

I did not have to think about it for long: if the ghetto was threatened because of me, I would go back. But I did not know how to get into the ghetto. The messenger said he would sneak me in disguised as an employee of the commissar who was going into the ghetto to find some good wool to knit him a sweater.

A few hours later I was in the ghetto. [I could not find my way home. It turned out that it was now outside the ghetto wall, so my husband and I were now staying with a friend of mine, a dentist named Nitsberg-Mashenmesser.] {After I returned to the ghetto I found out that Africa was almost liberated and that the Germans were trapped in Tunis. Everyone's spirits were lifted.}

On 27 January 1943, as I was returning from seeing a patient, I heard shooting in the Judenrat office. Twenty minutes later I was summoned there. I found two people wounded and one dead. It turned out that the Gestapo chief, Wilhelm, had shot them: at seven o'clock that evening he had burst into the Judenrat building and accused the Judenrat of giving aid to the partisans. He killed the watchman on the spot and then wounded two members of the Judenrat.

On 28 January at five in the morning troops marched up to the ghetto, and at seven they announced that we were to be evacuated. At eight o'clock a large number of carts pulled into town to haul us away. Gestapo chief Wilhelm ordered them to use only some of the carts; the rest would be brought in on 29, 20, and 31 January.

Five hours later we arrived at the Linovo station, where the Germans ordered us to climb out of the carts. Everyone was beaten unconscious. I received two powerful blows that made my head buzz like a telegraph wire. Seeing that death was near, I left my things on the cart. I did not see my husband.

They kept us at the station for three hours; at six in the evening a train of unheated boxcars arrived. Loading began at seven. On the platform we were stepping over dead bodies. They threw us into the train cars like sacks of potatoes. The Germans tore children from their mothers' arms and killed them on the spot.

At the last minute, just before they sealed the train, I jumped out onto the tracks. My badge was covered with a large kerchief. I quickly made my way down some street and came to a garden; then I walked along a fence and came out into a field. From there I walked only through the fields, since Gestapo agents were on the roads. I later found out that the temperature was minus 22° C. Many times I collapsed from exhaustion.

When I came to a military guard post and tried to go past, I was stopped by the shout of a sentry: "Halt!" Pretending to be a Belorussian, I told him that I came from a neighboring village and that my daughter was having a baby. He decided to let me go ahead.

And so I walked until two in the morning. Finally, I reached the town. For two hours I wandered around the outskirts, afraid of running into someone. Very carefully I went up to the convent. I quietly tapped on the window. The mother superior opened the door for me and immediately started rubbing my hands. I could not eat, but I drank several glasses of cold water. My friend, Sister Chubak, lay me down in her bed, and I fell asleep.

I was awakened the next morning (29 January) by the sound of crying. It was one of the nuns: she was afraid that my return to the convent would mean the death of all of them. Chubak assured her that we would leave the following day. But the nun said, "Doctor Goldfain is doomed to die anyway, and because of her we'll all perish." At that point I interrupted the conversation and told them that if I could jump off a death train, then I could leave this place without causing anyone any unpleasantness.

In town it was announced that all barns, attics, cellars, and outhouses were to be locked up, so that no Jews could hide in them. Dogs were to be unleashed. If any Jews were found in any house, the whole population would be executed.

Ranya Vevyurskaya, a sixteen-year-old servant from the convent, went to a village twelve kilometers away to find a cart for me. She returned late that night and said the cart would be here in the morning. The cart arrived at ten o'clock. I put on a nun's habit and dark glasses. As I sat in the cart, I kept my eyes fixed on the bundle in my hands. Sister Chubak led the way on foot. I left town under the eyes of the Gestapo. Just as I was leaving, a third transport of Jews was pulling out. Once we were outside of town, Sister Chubak climbed into the cart. A Polish woman I knew named Kalinovskaya was headed toward us. She signaled to Chubak that I was well disguised. That frightened me; I was afraid she might turn me in. My companion tried to calm me down. She said that Kalinovskaya deeply sympathized with the Jews in their suffering and that, having heard about the plan to save me, she had made a special trip to be sure that everything was all right.

We traveled until five in the afternoon. The horse was exhausted, and we decided to spend the night in a village nearby. My companion went to the village elder and asked permission for us to spend the night, but he told her every room was full: twenty German gendarmes were staying in the village that night. We decided that it would be better for us to leave, so we got back into the cart and went on. The exhausted horse could hardly drag itself along. We entered the dense Bialowieza Forest. We saw a little house along the road. My companion walked up to the house, and there she met a former student of hers. We were well received and spent the night in a warm place. At dawn we set out once again. We finally came to Bialowieza and headed for the cathedral. Then we left for Gainovka, from there to Belsk, and from Belsk to Bialystok by train. On the train we found out that the Germans had surrounded the Bialystok Ghetto in early February and that a massacre was taking place there.

We went to the convent in the heart of Bialystok. I asked the mother superior to hide me, but she was frightened and ordered us to leave immediately. As we were leaving, I told my companion that we must not reveal our secret to anyone else. We found ourselves in the street that night and did not know where to go. Then my companion recalled that she knew the address of the brother of one of the nuns. He was not home, but his wife graciously took us in. At that very moment the Jews of Bialystok were being slaughtered. The city was filled with Gestapo agents, and the residents were afraid they might be suspected of being Jewish. The train stations had no tickets for sale. We went to the stationmaster and asked him to give us a free ticket, since we were just poor nuns who were forced to beg for charity. At first he refused, but then he gave us the tickets. I was afraid to put the precious tickets in my pocket and held them in my hand the whole time.

And so on 13 February we left Bialystok; the train pulled into the station at Lapa. From there we went by cart to churches in various towns—Dombrovo, Sokoly, Mokini—and then on to Warsaw by train. We were by afraid of being detained by the Government-General, since here they did not ask for passports.[21] From Warsaw we went to Lowicz, where my companion's family lived. We spent six months there; no one knew I was a Jew. I worked as a nurse and had a large practice.

In May of 1944 we decided to move closer to the Bug River, to a town about twenty-two kilometers from Lublin.

The Red Army liberated the town on 26 July 1944. On 29 July I set out—part of the way on foot, part of the way by car—until I finally made it to my hometown of Pruzhany.

Pruzhany had been liberated on 16 July. Of the 2,700 Jews who hid in the forest, only about twenty young men and women returned; the rest perished. The people of the town were very happy that I had come back; my friends, acquaintances, and patients literally made pilgrimages to see me. {But it must also be said that there were some in Pruzhany who were afraid to see me, for I had emerged from *that* world, a witness to the dark deeds of a number of people.}

Prepared for publication by Vasily Grossman

Brest

Depositions and Documentary Testimony of the Residents of Brest

Approximately 26,000 Jews[22] lived in Brest before the war; among them were engineers, doctors, technicians, lawyers, and highly skilled carpenters. No more than fifteen survived, miraculously saved from the violence.

This is what a few of those survivors have to say about the first days of the German occupation of Brest.

Vera Samuilovna Bakalyash:

"On the day the Germans arrived the Jewish population immediately felt the weight of the German paw. The roundups began, and people were hauled off to forced labor. After work they had to dance and crawl around on their bellies. Those who did not obey were savagely beaten."

Tatyana Samuilovna Gutman:

"Life for the Jews was horrible from the very first day. The Germans herded them off to work and tortured them without mercy; they robbed them and demanded gold. Those who did not hand it over were beaten and shot; [cruel as tigers, the thieves ran from one house to the next.]"

Osher Moiseevich Zisman:

"In early July 1941 the Germans rounded up Jews for 'work'; in fact, they herded all the Jews they had captured into the Brest Fortress and kept them there under terrible conditions. For five days, in the July heat, they gave them neither water nor bread; then they shot every last one of them. One Jew did survive; he said that when he crawled out of the mass grave he could see that many of the others were still alive, since only people in the first row were hit. When the Germans started filling in the graves with dirt and hot lime, many people were still alive."

Zisman goes on to write, "In the city of Kobrin in the Brest district, the Germans burned down the Jewish hospital and the rabbi's apartment. Since the local firemen were ordered not to put out the fires, the flames spread through the entire town. The Germans threw Jews into the fire alive."

On 12 July 1941 there was a roundup of the Jewish men in Brest. The sisters Mariya and Sulamif Katsaf write:

"[They were taken from their beds in the night; whoever managed to hide lived for another year.] Five thousand men were taken, including thirteen-year-old boys and seventy-year-old men. Many of the intelligentsia were taken—doctors, engineers, and attorneys, including our good friends: the pediatrician Doctor Gotbetter; Doctors Frukhgarten and Tonenboim, both specialists in internal medicine; the attorneys Berlyand, Adunsky, and Belov; the engineer Mostovlyansky; and others."

Tatyana Samuilovna Gutman writes:

"They organized a roundup and seized five thousand men; they took the men outside of town and shot them. Among them were doctors, engineers, and lawyers."

Osher Moiseevich Zisman writes:

"The German beasts tore out my old father's gray beard before they shot him. The German mad dogs pulled out all my brother's teeth before they shot him; he was a dentist. When he fell unconscious into the grave they pointed at him and laughed, saying he should make himself a set of false teeth."

From the first days of the occupation living conditions for the Jews who were still alive were unbearable. They were all ordered to wear yellow armbands with a six-pointed star; after a short time the armbands were replaced with yellow circular patches ten centimeters in diameter. They had to be worn on the chest and on the back, so that a Jew could be spotted a kilometer away. Jews were forbidden to walk on the sidewalk. "They had the right to walk only in the middle of the street," writes T. S. Gutman. And the Katsaf sisters recall, "This made a huge impression and was considered a terrible humiliation. We did not know what horrors awaited us."

The Jews had not yet been deprived of their lives, but their lives had already been transformed into a hell. This is what the Katsaf sisters relate:

["From the first days of the occupation the Jews were forbidden to go to the market; those who managed to do so were driven away with whips and machine guns."

V. S. Bakalyash adds:

". . . it was forbidden to go to the market, and in the surrounding villages people were not allowed to sell anything to Jews. Those who managed to buy something had it taken away from them."

The Katsaf sisters go on to write,] "The plundering started from the very beginning of the occupation. They took everything: beds, linen, dishes, furniture. No one was given any consideration; they took our pregnant sister-in-law's only bed and blanket. For some, their personal belongings were their sole means of existence, but it was impossible to sell anything since the Jews were forbidden to buy anything.

[And yet there was some semblance of freedom, compared to the life that awaited the Jews.]

At the end of November 1941 the fascist authorities selected several streets in Brest and moved all the Jews to those streets; then they surrounded the area with barbed wire. Thus a ghetto was set up in Brest.

"The police stood at the gates," writes Vera Bakalyash. "They would not allow any Jews to leave the ghetto or any non-Jews to enter the ghetto. Groups under police guard were led off to work; it was forbidden for Jews to walk around town by themselves. If a Jew should manage to buy something on his way back from work, the police would confiscate it; they searched everyone who returned. Ration cards were distributed, allowing each person 150 grams of bread per day."

Sikorsky writes, "Living conditions were a nightmare. People were deprived of every possibility of obtaining any food whatsoever. If anyone had any food in reserve, it was soon confiscated. People were literally starving."

"They herded us out of the ghetto to do forced labor," writes Gutman. "Even teenagers were forced to do the heaviest work. I worked as a loader and received a slap in the face whenever I did not have the strength to carry out an order."

"Jews were forbidden to get married or have children," writes Osher Moiseevich Zisman, "under pain of death by firing squad."

Such was existence in the ghetto. But the unfortunate people endured it, with hundreds of them dying from hunger, unbearable labor, and hellishly vile living conditions. Meanwhile the fascist overlords—calm and cool, attending to every detail, without any fuss or bother—were plotting the last bloody act of the tragedy: the destruction of the Jews.

As for how that act was conceived and carried out, we have an official document prepared after the liberation of Brest by a commission consisting of representatives of the Soviet government, partisans, and citizens of the Brest district:

A Report on the Savagery, Plundering, Torment, and Destruction Perpetrated by the German-Fascist Invaders in the Area of Bronnaya Gora in the Berezovsky Region of the Brest District Chaired by Arkady Ivanovich Taraseivich, the Commission consisted of Vasily Nikolaevich Bury, Chairman of the District Executive Committee; partisan representative Ivan Pavlovich Kashtelyan; and Comrade Novik from the Berezovsky Region.

The following is based on an examination of the sites of mass torture and shooting of Soviet citizens by the German-Fascist invaders and on a series of interviews with local citizens.

In accordance with plans previously drawn up by the German-Fascist invaders, in May-June 1942 the Germans began digging mass graves covering an area of 16,800 square meters; the graves were dug four hundred meters northwest of the Bronnaya Gora train station.

Each day the Germans mobilized six to eight hundred citizens from the villages in the Berezovsky region to dig the graves. In order to finish the job as quickly as possible, the Germans used explosives such as tolite.

Once the digging of the graves was completed in mid-June 1942, the Germans began transporting Soviet citizens to the Bronnaya Gora train station. These citizens were of various nationalities: Russians, Belorussians, Jews, and Poles, from infants to old people.

As the trains pulled into the station, special SD and SS units escorted the cars. The cars came from various parts of Belorussia: from Bereza, Brest, Drogichin, Yanovo, and other places. Soviet citizens were also rounded up and brought to Bronnaya Gora on foot.

The cars in the arriving transport were extremely overcrowded, so that there were dead people among the exhausted citizens. As the transports came in they were directed to side tracks leading to military depots about 250 meters from the main line at the Bronnaya Gora station. The transports pulled up to mass graves; then the Germans unloaded the cars in a special area enclosed by barbed wire.

During the unloading people were forced to strip naked and toss their clothes into a pile. They were taken down a narrow barbed-wire corridor to the pits; after going down the steps into the pits, they were forced to lie faced down close to each other. Once the first row was ready, Germans in SD and SS uniforms shot the people with submachine guns. And so it went with the second and third rows, until the grave was full.

All of this was accompanied by the heartrending screams of men, women, and children.

After a transport had been completely unloaded and all the citizens shot, their clothing and belongings were loaded into train cars and sent to an unknown destination. The scheduling of transports going to and from the execution area was strictly controlled by Heil, the stationmaster at the Bronnaya Gora train station, and by duty officers Pike and Schmidt. [All three were German.]

In order to hide every trace of the crimes committed in the Bronnaya Gora region, the Germans shot the entire civilian population—about one thousand people—living in the vicinity of the former military depots. Altogether there were eight mass graves in the area where the mass shooting took place. The first was 63 x 6.5 meters, the second 36 x 6.5, the third 36 x 6, the fourth 37 x 6, the fifth, 52 x 6, the sixth 24 x 6, the seventh 12 x 6, and the eighth 16 x 4.5. All the graves were 3.5 to 4 meters deep.

From June to November 1942 the Germans shot more than thirty thousand peaceful Soviet citizens in the area of Bronnaya Gora.[23]

When 16 October came, it was time for the people of the Brest Ghetto to say farewell to life. This is how some survivors remember that day:

"On 14 October 1942 anxiety swept through the ghetto. Beyond the barbed wire that surrounded the ghetto something was happening. It was very noisy; police units were everywhere. What could it mean? Toward evening, however, the police dispersed, and the people calmed down a bit. At 6:00 A.M. on the morning of the 16th our neighbor woke us and told that the ghetto was surrounded. It had begun! What happened next is hard to describe. Some hid in places that they had prepared beforehand; those who had no place to hide simply rushed around the streets like madmen." (Katsaf sisters)

". . . on 15 October the ghetto was surrounded by SS and SD troops; at six in the morning the bloody slaughter of innocent people began. Hitler's cutthroats burst into houses and basements and dragged women, old people, and babies into the streets. Then they lined them up and herded them off to be shot," writes Comrade Sikorsky.

Throughout those three terrible years, however, these executioners who were versed in torture and murder—who possessed neither a soul nor a conscience—knew the feeling of fear. An official commission document speaks eloquently of this:

"In order to hide all traces of their savagery, the Germans brought more than one hundred people from various villages in the Brest district to the camp at the Bronnaya Gora train station; these people were given the task of digging up the mass graves and burning the bodies. The bodies were burned in the vicinity of the mass graves, where our citizens had been shot. They burned day and night for fifteen days. In order to fuel the flames that consumed the bodies, the Germans dismantled forty-eight military warehouses and barracks located nearby. They also used a flammable liquid that burned with a dark blue flame. After the work of burning the bodies was finished, the Germans had to shoot and burn all the workers who had dug up and burned the bodies; there were more than a hundred of them.

"The Germans planted saplings in the area where the graves had been and the burning had taken place. All around were found charred bones, barrettes for women's hair, children's shoes, Soviet money, a shoulder blade, and a baby's arm eighteen centimeters in length."

Several people survived: Roman Stanislavovich Novis, Ivan Vasilevich Govin, Borislav Mikhailovich Tsetinsky, Grigory Grigorevich Yatskevich, and others who related everything they saw with their own eyes. They were the ones who led the Soviet investigation commission to another terrible place, to a hill near the village of Smolyarka in the Berezovsky region; it was six kilometers from the Bronnaya Gora station and seventy meters off the Moscow-Warsaw highway. This is what the commission established:

"The Germans transported citizens of Bereza and villages in the Berezovsky region to mass graves in trucks. Using the same methods they employed at Bronnaya Gora, the Germans tormented, tortured, and shot peaceful Soviet citizens not far from Smolyarka.

"A total of five graves containing the bodies of Soviet citizens were found. All the graves had the same dimensions: ten meters long, ten meters wide, and two and a half meters deep.

"The mass shooting of people in the Smolyarka area took place in September 1942; according to the testimony of witnesses, more than a thousand people were killed there. That testimony was confirmed by Ivan Ivanovich Gents, Ivan Stepanovich Gents, Andrei Ivanovich Levkovets, Iosif Yakovlevich Kutnik, and others."

Engineer Kokhanovsky, a resident of Brest, offered the following testimony on the events that took place there:

"[Approximately] twenty thousand Jews were shot during the mass executions; among them were the most highly educated people of the intelligentsia. Having spent a year in the city, I could recognize these faces: Doctor Kalvarisky, a noted specialist in neuropathology; Doctor Ioffe, a therapist; Doctor Manzon; Doctor Kagan; Doctor Keblitsky; Doctor Mechik; the lawyer Mechik; Doctor Rakif; Doctor Kislyara; Doctor Ivanova; Zeleny, a well-known engineer; Berezovsky, an electrical engineer; the economist Zilberfarb; the engineer Filipchuk; the technician Golub; the technician Taran; the engineer Kaminsky; and many others.

"The Germans hated the working intelligentsia. The engineers were forced to clean animal stables, while the townspeople yelled at them, 'Engineer, Engineer!' They were shot both individually and with their families. A Catholic priest was shot. [The Germans destroyed all culture, the educated people, and religion.] Those who were physically healthy were hauled off to Germany for forced labor; those who remain in the city were used to dig trenches."

In Brest the Red Army found people half-dead and swollen from hunger but who, nevertheless were still alive, saved by a miracle from German death. Among them were Tanya Gutman, Vera Bakalyash, the Katsaf sisters, and Osher Zisman. How did these people survive?

"My sister and I and our children hid beneath a building, from which we could see Jews being led away to be shot. At first they forced people to undress and shot them in the ghetto, so the clothing would be left there. In my hiding place I ate raw buckwheat, flour, beets, cucumbers. The children grew dehydrated from hunger. After two weeks of hiding I went out of the ghetto to see what was happening in the world; I got some bread, brought it to the children, and once again left the ghetto. I had to spend the night under the open sky; by then it was freezing outside. For five weeks I managed to sneak in and out and get food for the children, until one day I came back to the ghetto and did not find my children. I wandered about aimlessly, not knowing where I was going. Late that night I decided to go to a Russian family; they took pity on me and hid me in a shed. I spent the whole winter there; then they hid me under the floor in a pit, where I stayed until the Red Army came. When they arrived I came out to freedom; the troops who had stopped in the yard treated me to a dinner, and I became a human being once again."

Thus Tanya described the sheer miracle by which she survived.

"My wife, twelve other women, and I hid in a pit under a small shed. Several of the women went insane; since my wife and I were sick, we had to gather the last ounce of our strength to move to another place, to an attic. Thus we endured seventeen months of misery, in attics, cellars, and outhouses. When the happy day of 28 July 1944 arrived—the day of our city's liberation from the German bandits—I did not have the strength to move. Sick and swollen from hunger, I could not even speak to people. The Red Army soldiers fed me and brought in a Soviet doctor. And so they saved my life," says Osher Zisman.

"I no longer had a husband. My sister and I took our children to the cellar, which had a secret passageway leading to our room. Our aged mother stayed in the house to push a cupboard over the passageway, so that when the Germans came hey would not find us. They took her away. And so we stayed there until 1 November, eating raw beets, cabbage, raw buckwheat, and even flour mixed with salt. I decided to send my nine-year-old son to a village to see some friends. Two days later he returned empty-handed and asked me to go look for bread, saying that he would bring the younger children later. He cried and pleaded so much that I finally agreed to do it. The two of us left; I hid in a village, and he went to get the other children. But when he returned a few days later, instead of my children he brought me a lightning bolt: my children had been detained by the police. For three days I lay unconscious, with a high temperature, but I could not stay there for long; I had to get up and leave. I spent three days in some abandoned water tanks outside of town. In one village I hid until 20 February under the floor of a house that belonged to a good person. One night, however, I had to flee, since for some reason I had been reported, and they were searching for me. I hid underneath a church not far from the village. I spent nearly a month there living on a two-kilogram loaf of bread. Hunger forced me to leave. I collapsed in the woods, utterly exhausted. A woman found me, fed me, and gave me some bread, but she asked me to leave because she was afraid of the Germans. She led me into the woods, where I met some partisans. I lived with their unit until the arrival of the Red Army." That was the "miracle" of Vera Bakalyash's survival.

"On 15 October 1942 at 6:00 A.M. we took our mother and our sister's baby to the hiding place where our sister-in-law lived; since there was no room for us, we left them with some provisions and went outside without knowing what to do with ourselves. At the last moment we got the idea to go up to the attic in our building; sixteen of us spent five weeks there, huddled in a boarded-off corner. It is difficult to imagine the conditions: hunger, cold, filth. But that is unimportant; the main thing is that we witnessed the horrors—that is, we did not see, but we heard every day how seventy to a hundred people would be taken out to the courtyard, ordered to strip, and then were shot and buried on the spot. Workers would come early in the morning to dig the graves. Once we heard a small child crying out, 'Mama, I hope they shoot us soon. I'm cold.' It was November, and they had to strip naked. Mothers undressed their children and then undressed themselves. And so on the other side of the fence across from our building at 126 Kuibyshev Street lie approximately five thousand people. For the first three days Jews were taken from Brest to Bronnaya Gora; trucks were moving constantly, and the entire Aktion was carried out with all the exultation of a great victory, as if they had captured a city or something of the sort. After the Aktion was over you could hear singing and music all night long. Another seventeen thousand Jews from Brest perished in the same way, including twenty-five members of our family. Early in the morning of 20 November 1942 several {Ukrainian} policemen found us, but they did not kill us; they just robbed us. We did not know where to go. Practically naked, we suffered through two years of cellars, attics, and sheds, left outside the most severe cold. It is a miracle that we did not freeze to death. We went six months at a time without changing our clothes. We did not see a morsel of cooked food. If our lives had gone on like that for another two weeks, we would not have made it. But the Red Army liberated us, and our brother, a soldier in the Red Army, is avenging our family and all the Soviet Union," write the Katsaf sisters.

All the while, from every hideout and cellar, from every crack and every pit, people witnessed scenes, each more terrible than the other. Before their eyes unfolded a bloody panorama of executions, a monstrous spectacle of death each day.

"Through the ventilator I saw the German henchmen taunting their victims before they shot them. Under the threat of being buried alive, the people were forced to strip naked. The

Germans did not have enough bullets for everyone, so they covered people with earth and hot lime while they were still alive. I contracted dysentery while staying in the cellar and could not get up, but from the ventilator I saw the Germans herd young girls into a shed next to the mass graves and rape them before shooting them. I heard one girl crying out for help; she punched the German in the snout, and in return they buried her alive," writes Osher Zisman.

"The weeping and shouting of children could be heard everywhere. People were loaded into trucks and hauled off to Kartuz-Bereza. There enormous pits had been dug in the clay. Children were thrown in alive and then killed with grenades; the adults were buried alive," writes Vera Bakalyash.

Of the 26,000 Jews of Best, only twelve to sixteen survived. It is a great miracle that— despite dangers endured every minute of every day, despite the deaths of their loved ones, despite the cruel suffering of their souls and the incredible deprivation of their bodies—these people have a passionate will to live, to carry on the struggle for revenge.

This is the last testimony given to us in the commission's document:

"In the Bronnaya Gora region the Germans destroyed the railways and all the structures at or near the station. Buildings were blown up and burned down during their retreat; they used a special machine to destroy the rails and the ties. The unit designated for the destruction of the railway was called the *Pimaschzug*. The commander of the brigade was Captain Sporberg, a German national. The damage done to the Bronnaya Gora station comes to 1,152,000 rubles. After questioning witnesses and gathering data, the Brest district commission determined that the Germans' mass shooting of Soviet citizens in the Bronnaya Gora region and in the Smolyarka areas of the Berezovsky region was carried out by special units of the SS and the SD under the leadership of the following persons:

1. Mayor Rode, chief of the Brest district police department (until the beginning of 1944),

2. Biner, chief of the Brest district police department (from the beginning of 1944 until the Germans were driven out of Brest),

3. Lieutenant Hofman, chief of the First Precinct of the Brest municipal police force,

4. Meister Golter, Meister Grieber, and Meister Boss, chiefs of the First Precinct of the Brest municipal police force,

5. Lieutenant Preisinger, chief of the Second Precinct of the Brest municipal police force (until the beginning of 1944),

6. SD Oberscharführer Sagatsky (a German), chief of the criminal police,

7. Ivanovsky (a Pole), commandant of the criminal police,

8. SD Obersturmführer Zibel, first deputy chief of the SD,

9. Captain Dauerlein, chief of the gendarmes under the Gebietskommissariat,

10. Gerik, an SD collaborator,

11. Oberleutnant Gardes, chief of the gendarmes in Kartuz-Bereza, and

12. SD officers Grieber and Wanzman (who directly took part in the shootings)."

(Signatures of members of the commission)

These names were preserved in the traumatized memory of the witnesses and now have been made known to us. May they join the ranks of the executioners who will receive a just and deserved punishment.

Prepared for publication by Margarita Aliger[24]

The Tragedy of My Life

A Letter from Red Army Soldier Kiselev

Let me introduce myself: I am Zalman Ioselevich Kiselev, a soldier in the Red Army and a resident of the village of Liozno in the Vitebsk district. I have lived nearly five decades, but my life has been crushed and my days trampled under the bloody German boot. For a long time I studied in the Talmud-Torah, a school for poor children where my poor parents sent me. In 1929-1930 I studied at the regional collective farm school. Under conditions of hard work and severe need, I read books by Victor Hugo, Balzac, Tolstoy, Shakespeare, and Jules Verne. I shall now begin the story of my life's tragedy; I am the main character, and the author of the tale is the war. I was born in 1900 into a wagon driver's family; happiness then was no more than a game, and every year a horse fell dead. As I said, I studied in the Talmud-Torah, and a former student gave me free lessons. In 1920 I went with my mother to visit the small town of Babinovichi. There I grew very fond of a girl, my third cousin; she was tall, full-figured, and had a rather pretty face. She had a nice personality, and I liked the fact that she was not from a wealthy [family], since she would not despise me for my poverty. I think she liked me too. I received a cow as her dowry, and we celebrated our wedding; I had only forty rubles when we got married, but that did not bother us, because our love was more precious than anything. I had come alive; no man was my enemy. I was working day and night, and I was happy. By 1928 I had two daughters, pretty little girls, and my wife was growing prettier every day; I was the luckiest man in the world. I worked at the Belmyastorg,[25] and in the evenings I studied and read books. 1931 was a hard year. I had to give up my studying and go to work stocking groceries; they gave me bread to sustain me, but it was not enough. My wife endured it all with me. Generally I still considered myself a fortunate man and lived in peace; even though I was not rich, I truly had the respect of my neighbors. By 1941 I had a cow, a couple of pigs, beehives, and a garden. My wife worked, and I worked. We had six children: five girls and one boy. As you know, the war broke out, and the enemy attacked our homeland. On 5 June 1941 I went into the army, and my wife stayed in Liozno with our children and my seventy-five-year-old mother. On 12 July the Germans took Liozno. I lost contact with my family. But in May 1942 I received a letter from my wife, who was in the city of Saraktash in the Chkalov district. She sent me greetings from all the children. I was overjoyed, and we wrote to each other for more than a year. I could tell that my wife's letters were full of sorrow; in June 1943 I received a letter saying that my wife Fanyusya Moiseevna had fallen ill and that I should come. We were stationed in the Kursk Bulge, and the situation was tense. I did not go. Two weeks later I received a letter that simply said, "Your family has left Saraktash."

I immediately realized what "left" meant; it was what we call "breaking ranks." I asked the apartment landlord where my wife was living and how many children she had with her. The landlord told me that Fanya was alone, that she had lost the children when they were crossing the front line. This is how it happened: During the first days of March 1942, after the mass murder of my relatives, my family and several other families left with the partisans. They came to the front positions. My wife left the children with my mother and went to a village nearby to get some bread. She spent the night there. But during the night our troops arrived in the village, so that she was not able to get back to the children. Thus my Fanya lived without her beloved children; she did not write to me about it because she did not want to cause me the pain; she took her sorrow to the grave without sharing the pain with me. She was my one true friend in life. I ask you to write the story of her fate in your own words.

20 April 1944
Prepared for publication by Ilya Ehrenburg

A Letter from Red Army Soldier Gofman (Krasnopole, Mogilev District)

I shall write about the tragedy of Krasnopole. 1,800 Jews perished there, including my family: my beautiful daughter, my sick son, and my wife. From all the Jews of Krasnopole, a miracle saved only one: Lida Vysotskaya. She wrote to me and told me everything. I found out that the day before they were executed, when they were no longer permitted to leave the ghetto, my wife, the badge of shame on her chest, managed to make her way into town to get some dried apples for our sick son. She wanted to prolong his life, even if it were just for a day; her love for our son kept her poor heart beating. On 20 October 1941 the Germans rounded up everyone and shot them. For two months the children were tormented before they were murdered. My son was sick for a long time, but doctors saved him. Soviet science saved him. And then those beasts murdered him with a submachine gun.

I am a husband without a wife, a father without children, no longer young, and in my third year of fighting. I have avenged them and will go on avenging them. I am the son of a great homeland, a soldier in the Red Army. I raised my younger brother, and now he is fighting as a lieutenant colonel on the First Ukrainian Front. He is also taking revenge. I have seen fields strewn with the bodies of Germans, but that is not enough. How many of them must die for each murdered child? Whether I am in the forest or in a bunker the tragedy of Krasnopole is before my eyes. Children died there. In other cities and towns children of all nationalities have died. And I swear that I shall take revenge as long as my hand can hold a weapon.

10 March 1944
Prepared for publication by Ilya Ehrenburg

In the Pit

Little Khinka Wrublewicz told her savior, Red Army commander Captain V. Krapivin, her brief but terrible tale. Dressed in rags, she was a strange little creature dressed in rags, with long, tangled hair and bare feet; the skin on her wrists was cracked and bleeding. When she was brought to Captain Krapivin, he did not realize at first that she was a child, a little girl.

Then this wild creature, who had lost every semblance of anything human, began to speak. Step by step, the little girl's tale recreated her journey into suffering and loneliness. Khinka Wrublewicz was born in the small Jewish town of Vysoky Mazovetsk. Her father, a shoemaker, lived there until 1941. Then the Germans came, and their life was transformed. [All the misery of the Wrublewicz family lay in the fact that they were Jews.] The Germans' first concern was to set up a ghetto in the town. The Wrublewicz family included a thirty-seven-year-old father, a mother of forty, three brothers (seventeen, ten, and seven years of age), and Khinka. They lived in the ghetto for about a year, if a half-starved existence shrouded in the constant fear of death can be called living. But this existence came to an end when they began to ship all the Jews in the surrounding area to a place that had become ominous during the occupation: the Red Barracks in Zambrov. Thousands and thousands of people were taken there and then hauled off to somewhere else, never to be seen again. Their fear of Zambrov was so great that along the way Khinka's entire family fled into the forest. After wandering around in the woods for two weeks, they came upon two Polish-German collaborators from Vysoky Mazovetsk: Wysocki and Leonard Szikorski. They grabbed her mother and two younger brothers and took them back to town. As for their unhappy fate, all she knew was that they were sent to Zambrov. Khinka is convinced that the Nazis murdered them.

She, her father, and her surviving older went deeper into the forest, where they dug a pit and spent a year living on berries and handouts they received from going around to nearby villages at night. Their father was soon tracked down and murdered right in front of Khinka and her brother. The children were left alone in the pit. They were surrounded by forest, swamp, and wilderness. . . . After a while, however, another Jew joined them; he too was hiding in the forest from the Germans. But he brought with him more misfortune. Evidently he had been followed: before long two strangers showed up and took from him everything he had. Then they told the Germans where the pit was. That was when the most terrible days in Khinka's life set in. When they heard the Germans approaching, all three of them jumped out of the pit and fled. A dozen machine guns fired after them. Khinka's brother was killed as he ran beside her. She never saw the third occupant of the pit again either. She crawled back to her empty lair on her hands and knees. . . . And so she was alone in the forest. Now she had no mother, no father, no brothers, no relatives. Alone. But if it was frightening in the pit, it was even more terrifying to know that [German] henchmen and murderers were everywhere. Through it all Khinka was sustained by a single hope: that the Germans would be driven away! That is what gave her strength. At night she would go, as before, into a village where a kindhearted woman would slip her a piece of bread.

Imagine! A winter night, the snowstorm is howling, and a hundred-year-old fir is bending under the fierce wind. A small, half-naked, lone figure slides along the snow. Clutching a crust of bread in her frozen little fist, she hurries to her cold, narrow den to get there before dawn breaks; there she sits, cold and trembling, until night falls again.

Our submachine gunners found her in the pit near the village of Golashi, ten kilometers east of Zambrov. . . .

"I don't know if I will ever be able to convey this tragedy the way I myself have grasped it. When she finished telling her story, we front-line soldiers who had seen many things were afraid to look each other in the eye. Standing before this child, we were ashamed that these two-legged insects with their swastikas were still walking the earth, that the author of *Mein Kampf* had not been hanged, that the preacher of racial hatred, Alfred Rosenberg,[26] was still alive."

Thus ends the tale that Red Army commander V. Krapivin recorded from the words of Khinka Wrublewicz after he saved her from a terrible death.

It should be added that the orphaned little Khinka found love and a home with the family of Red Army lieutenant R. Shulman.

Prepared for publication by Valeriya Gerasimova

[The Story of a Little Girl from Bialystok

The memoirs of the ten-year-old Dora Shifrina were recorded in the schoolgirl's careful handwriting in a lined notebook. She writes: "In the building where we lived about twenty men were shot right in front of my eyes. After I saw that, I grabbed my little sister and brother and rushed to our uncle, who lived nearby. It made a horrible impression on me. The screaming and wailing of the mothers and the crying of the little children were horrible. I was overcome by pity when I saw it all. Our whole building with everything we owned was burned down. We stayed with our uncle only for a little while. The Germans carried on terribly. They murdered a lot of Jews; in our yard and the neighboring yard alone they murdered seventy-five people. They seized sixteen thousand people, supposedly for work; they said they would let them go when a ransom was paid. But the never let them go; they murdered them all and burned them. . . .

"When everything was on fire and the synagogue started to burn, the barbaric Germans took men, women, children, and old people and threw them into the synagogue alive."

Dora Shifrina's parents did not survive. They were murdered before her eyes.

The ten-year-old little girl remembers. She will never forget.

Prepared for publication by Valeriya Gerasimova]

Liozno

I was born in 1928 in the little town of Liozno in the Vitebsk district; before the war I live there with my grandmother and grandfather.

The Germans came on 16 July 1941. On the very first day they seized everything we had. They burned down our house.

The first announcement I saw stated that, under pain of death, Jews had to wear an armband with a six-pointed star on their left sleeve. One street was marked off for us to live; six hundred people were housed in thirty to forty small buildings.

In the autumn of 1941 a young German wearing glasses, with a skull and cross-bones on his sleeves and collar, came onto this street. After a lengthy search he seized six old men. Among them were the wood carver Simon, one of the most respected Jews in town; two invalids; and Velvele, who was mentally ill. They locked them into a shed; that evening they took them to the river, where they forced them to crawl on all fours in the icy water. Thus the old men were tortured for three days; on the fourth day they were shot.

The partisans derailed a German train carrying ammunition near the Krynka station. The Germans hanged six of the station's residents and fired explosive bullets into the bodies as they hung there. I shall never forget how a German officer climbed onto the gallows to photograph one of the people they murdered in profile. I saw two pregnant women whose bellies had been cut open. Next to them lay their babies' bodies. I saw the bodies of twenty-five Jews from Babinovichi; the Germans had thrown them from transports along the road from Babinovichi to Liozno. I saw a truck filled with Belorussians on their way to be shot. I have seen many things for my fifteen years.

During the winter the police could break into any home in the ghetto any time day or night. They would break windows, beat Jews with whips and clubs, and force them out into the freezing cold.

In one building, where there had been a shoe shop, not a single window, not a single door, was left intact; yet forty people lived there with the weather at forty degrees below zero.[27] Covered with lice, they slept on rotten, wormy straw.

A typhus epidemic broke out. Several people died every day, and new Jewish families from Vitebsk, Minsk, Bobruisk, and Orsha were herded in to take their place.

On 24 February 1942 at two in the afternoon the Germans and the police began loading Jews into trucks to take them all to one place. I was not home. When I returned, all my relatives had already been loaded into the truck. Russian comrades hid me in a toilet and nailed the door shut. An hour or two later, after the police had given up searching, I crawled out of my shelter. I saw them shoot the Jews; I saw many go insane. My grandmother and grandfather kissed each other before they died. They had loved each other all their lives, even into their old age, and that love endured even unto the last minutes of their lives.

After that I lay unconscious in the snow for a long time. I do not have the strength to describe how I felt. I could not even cry. When it got dark I went to a Russian friend, {Fedosiya Semenovna Dekhtereva}, but I knew that I could not stay with her for long. So I left Liozno and got across the front line.

Now I have no one. But I live in the Soviet Union, and that says everything.

Reported by B. Chernyakova
Prepared for publication by Vsevolod Ivanov[28]

[Letters from Belorussian Children

(From the Starye Zhuravli Settlement, Gomel District)

1

The Germans herded all the Jews into one place and made them work for Germans. Then the Germans came and started to drive out the Jews. One German went up to a shoemaker, and the shoemaker hit him on the head with a hammer, and the German fell down. They shot the shoemaker. The rest of the Jews were loaded into trucks and taken away to be killed. Along the way one woman jumped out of the truck and escaped. They took the Jews to the hospital and killed them there.

V. Vorobeva, 4ᵗʰ Grade

2

The monsters tortured the Jews and beat them with whips. When they were taking them away to be shot, one Jewish woman threw her baby from the truck. People wanted to get the baby, but the Germans wouldn't let them; they took the baby to the pit and killed it. But the mother escaped into the woods. She stayed in the woods until nighttime. Then she came to look for her baby, and the Germans shot her.

Lyuba Maiorova, 3rd Grade
Prepared for publication by Ilya Ehrenburg]

A Letter Written by Zlata Vishnyatskaya Prior to Her Death

I found this letter in the village of Byten in the Baranovich district. It was written by Zlata Vishnyatskaya and her twelve-year-old daughter Junita to their husband and father prior to their execution. The Germans murdered approximately 1,800 Jews from Byten.

Maior Vladimir Demidov

Mister Vishnet. Orange, U.S.A.
(Letter in Hebrew)
31 July 1942

Dear Moshkele and all my loved ones,
    On 25 July a terrible massacre took place here, as well as in other towns. Mass murder. Only 350 people are left. 850 died a terrible death at the hands of the murderers. Like puppies thrown down toilets, children were thrown alive into pits. I will not write much. I think someone may survive to tell you about our ordeals and our bloody end. We have managed to survive for a time. . . but for how long? Every day we wait for death and weep over our dear ones. Your loved ones, Moshkele, are no more. But I envy them. I shall end this; it is impossible to write, and I cannot convey to you our suffering. Be healthy, all of you. The one thing you can do for us is to avenge our murders. We cry out to you: Revenge! I kiss you passionately and bid you farewell before we die.

(Postscript in Polish)
Dear Father,
    I am saying good-bye to you before I die. We long so much to live, but all is lost—they won't let us! I am so afraid of this death because they throw small children into the mass graves alive. Farewell forever. I kiss you, kiss you.

Your J.   A kiss from G.

The Temchin Family from Slutsk

(Passages from Letters Received by the Pilot Efim Temchin)

1

27 September 1944

Hello, Efim. I stopped by the Gorsoviet[29] and found your letter asking about your family. As a warrior with a brave heart, I must inform you that most of your loved ones who stayed behind, like my own, are no longer alive. I hear that you have accomplished great military feats. I always knew you would.

Your childhood comrade,

Anatoly Potekhin

2

2 October 1944

Hello, my dear and only brother, Efim. At last, from the whole family, I have found a human being who is dear and close to me. But the wound in my soul will never heal. You and you alone know how I have loved and respected our family, how Mother often wept over us. Now there is no one left alive. Efim, you cannot imagine how I mourn Mother, Father, Pinkhos, Freida, Nekhama, and Roza. I still have not heard anything about the fate of Manya.

I saw our relatives for the last time on 22 June 1941 at ten o'clock in the morning. Since you went away to school, it has been even longer since you last saw them. I said farewell to them and left for the front. On 24 June we went into battle. On 24 August I was seriously wounded near Chernigov. I spent eight months in hospitals. I went to fight again, and I was wounded again. I am now in Lithuania in a non-combat unit. I am constantly trying to gather details about our family, but with no success. The family was forever on my mind; I remembered them when I rose up, when I sat down to eat, and when I lay down to sleep.[30] But I was prepared for the blow I received when the letter explaining the fate of our family arrived, for I had seen what the Germans do to the Jews. In Kaunas they shot and burned 65,000 Jews. [When the town was liberated, I saw people's charred corpses being dragged away.] Efim, you must get a hold on yourself and be a man. I beg you to get a hold on yourself. You yourself know how I loved the family. Since I was the oldest, I worked harder than anyone else did to help the family when we were home, because I loved our family, especially our mother. A mother is the closest and dearest person in your life. I worked so hard because I felt sorry for Mother. O, Efim, it is such a pity that we do not have even a single photograph of our family, so we might look at it and remember them. Efim, I ask you once again to get a hold on yourself and be a man. Do not take offense at my writing to you this way; you are all I have left. You are a great joy to me.

Your brother,

Leizer

3

29 August 1944
(A letter attached to the preceding one.)

Hello, Leizer. I am answering your letter about what happened in Slutsk. Since your father was a specialist at the pickling plant, he was deemed a skilled worker. Then the Germans arrested him and took him home for a search. He was hardly alive. They seized everything they felt like taking. Four or five days later I heard that he had been murdered. No one told your mother, so she kept going outside and walking around town in the hope that she might somehow come across him. The Jews lost all their cattle. It was very hard on your little children. In early October they set up a ghetto and started moving all the Jews into it. At first there was just the one ghetto, and then there was a second one. One was a field ghetto located outside of town, and the other was in town, where the Jews that worked lived. Life was a little easier in the town ghetto; people went to work and, bit by bit, were able to obtain some food and sell things. It was harder in the field ghetto; they were not allowed to go to town. Your family ended up in the field ghetto, since Pinkhos was the only one who could work, even though he was very young. But there was no work for him at the time. They soon started shooting people in the field ghetto, usually on Mondays and Saturdays; two, three, or four trucks would haul people off to a place in the forest near Bezverkhovichi. Pinkhos managed to get himself a work assignment, and he avoided the first group taken away to be shot. He and the whole family were transferred back to the town ghetto, where they stayed until the last moment—that is, until 8 February 1943, when the town ghetto was completely annihilated. The field ghetto had been destroyed in March 1942. When they were transferred from the field ghetto to the town ghetto, the Germans confiscated many of their belongings. I helped your loved ones; they came to me once or twice a week. But what could I do? I worked as a teacher and received 350 rubles a month, but a kilo of lard cost 500 to 600 rubles and went as high as 1,000 to 1,100 rubles. They sold their sewing machine, the bicycle, and the clock. As for Manya, she is gone. She escaped from a truck that was taking her to be shot and then came to me in tears. I gave her a few things, and she went into the forest.

Your neighbor,
Sulkowski

4

20 October 1944

My dear friend, Efim. I hid in the city, but several pogroms against the Jews took place right before my eyes. The Germans shot your father before the pogroms. We hid with Pinkhos several times during the pogroms. Your mother, Manya, and all the little ones also hid with us. It is very difficult to tell you about this tragedy. It was easier for me, since I was alone. In early 1942 I went to join the partisans. Pinkhos decided to stay for the sake of the family: had he not been working, they would have all been shot. I was the deputy commander of a partisan unit until July 1944.

Yours,
Senya

5

23 October 1944

Hello, Efim. I just came from Slutsk, where I was on leave. Slutsk has been all but burned to the ground; all that remain are a few buildings on Ostrov, Reichany, and Volodarskaya Street. Father was shot in August 1941 in the Monakhov Orchard. They tortured him before they shot him; they broke his arms and legs and then took him home to do a search. Mother, Pinkhos, Freida, Roza, and Nekhama were shot in February 1943 in Makhorty. Roza tried to escape as she was being loaded into the truck, but they wounded her in the leg; she fell, and they threw her into the truck. She was bleeding, and Mother held her in her arms. Witnesses related all of this to me. More than twenty thousand peaceful residents were shot in Slutsk. Efim, it is terrible to see what the Germans did to Slutsk and to hear what they did to the people. It is simply a horror. But Manya is alive! She is in Pinsk. She jumped off a truck and escaped to join the partisans. I wrote to her, and I shall send you her address.

Your brother,

Leizer

6

28 October 1944

Hello, my dearest, beloved brother, Fima. Today I am enjoying a holiday like I have never before enjoyed in my short life. I received a letter from Leizer and discovered that you are alive!

When the damned Germans came, we were all living together; we were even helping Aunt Sonya. Papa was with us, but misery was in store for him. He did not want to work for the Germans, but they forced him because he was the only specialist in pickling vegetables. He worked for just a short time. Then they found out that he had been employed by the Soviets, and they arrested him. On Saturday, 26 July, they brought him home. He had been tortured. His arms and legs were broken. I saw him. Mama begged and pleaded, but nothing helped. They plundered our home, stole everything, and took Father away. Mother said good-bye to him and kissed him. His last words were: "Take care of the children; they are going to kill me."

They shot him in the Monakhov Orchard. It is now a cemetery where thousands of people lie buried. After that we lived worse than beggars. The cursed ones dreamt up a ghetto. It was a place of hunger and cold, with many people staying in a single building, in a barracks. No one was allowed to go out. Then they began to haul people away to be shot. Seven times we were on the edge of death, but somehow we avoided being loaded into the trucks. Simon Strugach became paralyzed in the ghetto, so he had to be carried onto a truck. At that time many of our friends were being killed. Leizer writes than no one except the partisans survived. On Passover 1942 the ghetto was destroyed, and only the workers were left. Thanks to Pinkhos, we were transferred to live with him. But there was no room where he lived. Mama and the children spent the nights in a barn in the freezing cold; sometimes they were even left out on the street. We ate potato peels and bran. It was terrible to see Mama; she was a walking corpse. But the children could not understand any of it and kept asking for food. On Monday, 6 February 1943, they surrounded the whole area and started loading people into trucks. Pinkhos was the first to be taken. Then Mama and the children. That was at nine in the morning. They took me at one in the afternoon. I can still hear the screams of our little sisters as they were being taken out to be shot. Roza was wounded. I was in a truck with children and men who had been wounded while resisting. They took us down the Bobruisk Highway. The truck was covered with a tarpaulin. Two Germans were in the back with us. I decided to jump out. Better to die on the road. The truck was going very fast. I had a razor. I cut the tarpaulin below the window and jumped out. When I regained my senses, the truck was gone. I went to Valya Zhuk and said to her, "Save me!" She and her mother hid me in a shed for six days. Then I stayed with Sulkowski, and after that I went into the forest, where I finally found a partisan unit. I cannot describe everything. I weep like a little child. I was with the partisans until the Red Army came. Now I am working in Pinsk as a bookkeeper for the Red Cross. My dear brother, I beg you, take revenge, revenge, revenge!

Your sister,
Manya

Prepared for publication by O. Savich[31]

From Materials Compiled by the Special State Commission on the Verification and Investigation of Atrocities Committed by the German-Fascist Invaders

Depositions of Soviet Citizens

From the Protocols for Inquest Witness Mira Markovna Zaretskaya

9 August 1944
Zaretskaya: I arrived from Smolensk three days ago. Right now I am living at 5 N. Ostrovsky Street, Apartment 1.

Questions were posed by Brigadier General Burdenko.

Burdenko: Where did you live before now?

Zaretskaya: I lived in Minsk from 1936 on. Most recently I worked in a motor pool for a personnel department and for a department of teaching methodology. My specialty is agricultural engineering and mechanics. I graduated from the Kharkovsky Institute.

Burdenko: What did you see in the concentration camp? How were prisoners of war and civilians confined there?

Zaretskaya: Prisoners of war and other prisoners lived in one barracks. It was very crowded. It was not a barracks really, but more like a shed. Prisoners and soldiers stayed together. The Jews lived over the workshops.

Burdenko: Were the women housed separately?

Zaretskaya: There were no women among the prisoners of war or the other prisoners. The Jewish women lived separately; only families stayed together.

Burdenko: What do you know about the mass shootings and when did they begin?

Zaretskaya: The shootings began in the camps in October 1943. Every day I saw covered trucks taking people from Minsk to be shot and burned in pits. From 23 June on a very large number of trucks came, more than you can count.

Burdenko: Did you see people burned in the crematoria?

Zaretskaya: I myself did not see people burned, but I saw the smoke and the flames, and I heard the shooting.

Burdenko: Did they tell you in the camp how man prisoners had been burned?

Zaretskaya: Very many were burned. I would estimate half a million. From the villages in the area they brought in the families of people who had joined the partisans.

Burdenko: Did the Germans allow you to take messages to the prisoners?

Zaretskaya: Officially it was forbidden, but for a bribe you could get a message past a policeman or a guard.

Question: Did you see poison gas trucks?

Zaretskaya: Yes, I saw the sealed trucks that were used to poison people with gas. I saw them at the workshops. They were large. Each one could easily hold one hundred people. Jews who worked at the SD headquarters had to clean out the trucks after people had been poisoned with the exhaust fumes. They would find hair and a little blood. People can have nosebleeds when being poisoned.

Question: You yourself did not have to clean them out?

Zaretskaya: No, I did not.

Question: What did you do in the camp itself?

Zaretskaya: I was a cleaning woman for the Jews, the prisoners, and others.

Question: During your stay in the camp, 99,000 Jews were brought in?

Zaretskaya: That was not while I was there. That was in 1942, and I was there in 1943.

M. Zaretskaya   *From Special State Commission Document 124, lines 95-98*

From the Protocols for Inquest Witness Lev Shaevich Lansky

9 August 1944

Questions were posed by Brigadier General Burdenko.

Burdenko: When did you first observe the brutality of the Germans?

Lansky: I am from Nesvizha in the Baranovich district. I was in a concentration camp from 17 January 1942, in the Trostyanets camps.

Burdenko: Could you move freely about the camp?

Lansky: I got around.

Burdenko: When did the Germans start burning bodies?

Lansky: I couldn't tell you the exact date. It was about eight months ago. I was there temporarily, from 5 January 1943.

Burdenko: Did they actually burn bodies right before your eyes?

Lansky: I saw it myself. I was working there as an electrician, and whenever I climbed up a pole to work the wires, I could see everything.

Burdenko: Did you see the Germans burning people alive?

Lansky: Yes, they burned people alive.

Burdenko: Where did they burn people alive?

Lansky: In the camp. They would set a storehouse on fire and force people into it. Meanwhile they were gassing people in the mobile vans all the time.

Burdenko: When was the last time they burned people?

Lansky: The 28th of June.

Burdenko: Did you see them burn the last of the women and children alive?

Lansky: Yes. I saw it.

Burdenko: Did you hear the screams, wails, and crying of the children who were led into the flames?

Lansky: Yes. I heard and saw it al myself.

Burdenko: Did you know there was an oven there?

Lansky: There was a pit nine meters by nine meters. We dug it ourselves. That was about eight months ago.

Burdenko: Can you describe how the oven was built?

Lansky: I was not involved in its construction myself, but I could tell from a distance that they used iron rails. They would start it with a small incendiary bomb and then pile on large pieces of wood.

Burdenko: What was the name of the one who conducted the shootings?

Lansky: Reider.

Burdenko: Can you tell me: during the last days before the liberation of Minsk, did they pile up only dead bodies with the logs to be burned or did they burn people alive as well?

Lansky: On the 29th they brought in more people. The infamous Klimov was leading them. They built a barracks a hundred meters long and called it Artsbarak.

Burdenko: And how did they stack people with the logs?

Lansky: I didn't see how they stacked them with the logs; we had already run away. But before I got away, when they were still bringing people into the barracks, I saw blood flowing through the logs.

Burdenko: Did many of you escape from the camp?

Lansky: Four of us escaped. My wife and I and Gumov and his wife (he is now in the army, and his wife is here). Later there were seven German Jews who got out and are now in Moscow.

Burdenko: Tell me, please, how did the Germans treat you? How much bread, soap, water, and so on did they give you?

Lansky: They gave us two hundred grams of bread and some soup each day. We all got soap and clothing from German Jews who had been slaughtered. There were ninety-nine transports of a thousand people each that came from Germany, Austria, and Czechoslovakia.

Burdenko: Where are they?

Lansky: All shot.

Burdenko: How many were burned in Trostyanets, besides the Jews from Germany, Austria, and Czechoslovakia?

Lansky: Around 200,000 people. I don't know exactly how many were shot before I got there; 299,000 people were shot while we were there.

Burdenko: How did the Germans treat the sick? Did they have an infirmary?

Lansky: They had one, but they shot the ones who were seriously ill.

Burdenko: Were the doctors Russian or German?

Lansky: Two of the German Jews were doctors.

Burdenko: Did they speak Russian?

Lansky: One spoke Russian.

Burdenko: Lansky will be called again either tomorrow or the day after tomorrow.

L. Lansky   *From Special State Commission Document 124, lines 149-53*

Protocol of the Interrogation of Ivan Osipovich Kasimov

17 June 1944, Minsk

A native of Kropotkin in the Kybansk district, I. O. Kasimov was born in 1899. He is Russian, a Soviet citizen; not a member of the Party, he has little education and is a musician by profession. He works in a theater for opera and ballet and lives in Minsk at 28 Podzamkovaya Street, Apartment 2.

Regarding False Testimony Presented on Page 136 of the BSSR[32] Affidavits

Question: Did you live in Minsk during the German occupation?

Answer: I lived in the occupied city of Minsk from 1 April 1943 to 3 July 1944.

Question: What do you know about the savagery and brutality of the German-Fascist invaders?

Answer: When I lived in Minsk I witnessed the extreme cruelty with which the German occupying forces treated peaceful Soviet citizens.

In 1942, on the 25th of July, the Germans initiated a pogrom against the Jews that lasted until August—nine days in all. The pogrom was led by the Minsk chief of police and the German mayor Bentske, a native of Königsberg, tall and blond.

German soldiers from the local garrison and workers from the SD killing units carried out the pogrom, while Belorussian police formed a chain around the ghetto.

It is hard to say how many Soviet citizens were murdered. They say it was forty thousand. In any case, after the pogrom the ghetto area was reduced by one third.

The perpetrators of the pogrom did away with their victims selectively. First they registered all the Jews who were sick and unable to move. Those who could not move, who were incapable of working, and who were old were loaded into trucks and hauled off somewhere to be murdered.

Children were murdered on the spot. When the size of the ghetto had been reduced and people started settling into the buildings, in the attics they found the bodies of children no more than a year and a half old. I was walking down Rakovskaya Street during the pogrom on 29 or 30 July 1942, and I saw many bodies being taken to the Jewish cemetery on two-wheeled carts. A twelve-year-old Jew was harnessed to the cart and escorted by the police. This confirms what I said earlier about Germans murdering Jews right in the ghetto.

The reason for the pogrom, the Germans announced, was that they had found a radio transmitter and a store of weapons and that the Jews were in radio contact with Moscow and were planning an armed uprising.

Thus the Germans were provoked into a mass slaughter of Soviet citizens. The newspapers remained silent about the pogrom.

The next pogrom took place in August 1943. The police did not take part in that pogrom.

German soldiers, anti-aircraft gunners, and railroad workers were directly involved in the murders.

I personally saw railroad workers under the command of officers going in and out of the ghetto.

At that time I lived near the ghetto, across from two apartment buildings. Day and night for a week I could hear continuous gunfire, screams, and wails coming from the ghetto. The Germans themselves hauled the bodies of the murdered ones out of town in trucks.

Some Jews hid in pits. The Germans tracked them down with dogs and murdered them. I saw it myself.

Unlike in previous pogroms, in this one some of the Jews resisted. Many SS and Germans were killed. There were several funerals for the dead. Those Jews who were still alive were taken to Trostyanets, where they were murdered.

The Germans treated the Russian-Soviet citizens worse than animals.

In spring 1943 the Germans took fifty families—all the occupants of an apartment building near the Dinamo Stadium—as hostages; all of them were taken out of town and shot. The reason was that they had found the dead body of a German official from the city commissariat in the basement of one of the hotels.

This protocol is written accurately and signed by me, Kasimov.

From Special State Commission Document 124, lines 4, 121-126

In Bialystok

My name is Riva Efimovna Shinder-Voiskovskaya. I was born in Western Belorussian town of Krynki. My parents were not wealthy but tried to provide their children with a good education. Like everyone else in our town, they wanted their children to "be somebody" and avoid the insecure and unhappy life of a "nobody." So I had the opportunity to go to school. I completed high school in Grodno, and in 1923 I graduated from the pedagogical institute in Warsaw. I worked for many years as a history teacher in Jewish schools in Brest-Litovsk and Lodz. I loved my work, and I can say that my students had a very good attitude toward their studies. The classes were quiet, and many of my students became so fascinated with the subject that they read books that were not even assigned. It was very gratifying to see a child's lively and inquisitive mind working and developing. But my teaching was interrupted quite unexpectedly. In 1932 I was arrested for communist activity, and after my release from prison I lost my right to work in the schools. After being unemployed for a long time, I found work operating a grooving machine at a textile factory.

I was living in Lodz when the Second World War broke out. On 1 September 1939 my husband and I left Lodz and headed for Bialystok. We got as far as my hometown of Krynki (it was forty kilometers from Bialystok), where I went to work as the director of a school. Soon after that we moved to Bialystok.

The Germans entered Bialystok on 27 June 1941; almost no one managed to get out. In 1941 there were approximately 100,000 people living in Bialystok, about half of whom were Jews. The Germans immediately began committing one outrage after another; it was clear that the sword of death was hanging over our people. The Hitlerites wanted first of all to wipe out the male Jewish population. They hunted down the men in the streets and in the houses and took them away regardless of their age, health, or social status. Men would go outside and. . . disappear. [At first the men would be picked up under the pretext of sending them to work. But thousands of these men were "transported" to some "unknown destination" and never heard from again.]

The Germans took a special delight and diligence in destroying the Jewish intelligentsia.

The Hitlerites wanted not only to physically annihilate the human being; they wanted first to destroy his dignity, his fighting spirit. Striving to degrade the human being, the fascist monsters dreamt up every moral torture imaginable. The strict order that the yellow star must be worn on the chest and back was issued, no doubt, for purposes of moral degradation. Some were inclined to think that the star had no special significance. They would say, "So let's wear the yellow star. After all, they don't murder or torture us." But that was not true. We experienced a terrible and torturous feeling of shame and disgrace. People would not go outside for weeks on end. This is what happened to me personally: The first time I went out with my "decoration" a group of Germans was crossing the road. They and other passersby rushed at me and began shouting terrible curses at me. I leaned against the wall. Tears of bitterness and indignation filled my eyes; I was unable to utter a word. Suddenly I heard something; someone put his hand on my shoulder. I looked up: it was an elderly Pole. He said, "Don't be upset, my child, and don't be offended. Those who are doing this are the ones who should be ashamed." Then he took me by the hand and led me away.

This encounter made a big impression on me. I realized that not everything was lost yet, that there were still some honest and upright people left. The Hitlerites would not succeed in corrupting and confusing the people with their policies of hatred toward humanity.

From that moment on, thoughts of resistance never left me. I realized that by doing everything possible to resist we could help our own Red Army, that only through such a struggle could we save our dignity and our honor.

On 12 July 1941 my husband was arrested along with several thousand other men.[33] My sorrow was overwhelming. But I saw that it was just a small part of the sorrow that swept over all the people.

My sole desire—a desire that permeated my existence and burned in my blood—was to fight and take revenge against the Germans.

The Germans demanded to be paid an astronomical tribute: one million rubles, as well as several kilograms of gold and silver. All of it had to be handed over within forty-eight hours; if not, then they would burn down the Jewish quarter and destroy the entire Jewish population.

You can imagine how difficult it was to meet such an exorbitant demand. There were times when Poles would come into the Jewish community with gold objects and say, "Take this and save the Jews; they are your brothers and ours." It must be said that during those troubled times the friendship between the Poles and the Jews generally burned bright. The fascists were able to organize only the dregs of society and set them against the defenseless, persecuted Jewish people.

But the best of the Polish intelligentsia, honest representatives of their people, helped us whenever they could.

Once the tribute had been collected, a new order was issued: all the Jews had to move into the ghetto. [Everyone who complied with the order would be allowed three meters of living space, but in fact the "norm" was even less.] Two or more families were crammed into the small rooms. People had to carry their own things into the ghetto; the Germans prohibited the Poles from offering the Jews any help whatsoever. Of course, many of the Poles disregarded the prohibition and gave the Jews carts to use. Some Poles gave me a cart; I also carried a large bundle on my own shoulders.

A Polish woman whom I did not even know came up to me and offered to carry my bundle; in those days German soldiers or local hoodlums would often grab things right out of the Jews' hands.

On 1 August the Jews of Bialystok were sealed into the ghetto.

The ghetto was a prison—no, *prison* is too weak a word for it. The ghetto was hunger, humiliating oppression, shootings, hangings, mass murder.

The people were in the grips of absolute tyranny. The Gestapo would enter homes whenever they wanted and take whatever they pleased. An announcement posted on the ghetto gates declared that it was forbidden to bring food into the ghetto. If anyone were found with even the smallest morsel of food, he would be shot.[34]

They started selecting people for work. People selected were issued passes indicating which streets they were allowed to walk on. Those who were caught walking down a forbidden street were arrested and shot.

Jews were allowed to walk only on the road pavement. I personally know of cases in which people were severely beaten for setting foot on a sidewalk while trying to avoid an oncoming car.

But for all their heinous crimes, the Germans could not destroy the human fighting spirit and love for freedom. Despite all the terror, an anti-fascist organization was formed in December 1941. Polish comrades such as Tadeusz Jakubowski, Niura Czerniakowski, and several others played a big part in the organization. I was the Committee secretary.

In order to maintain contact with Poles and Belorussians, I had to find a way to get in and out of the ghetto. A friend of mine helped me to get a job as a cleaning woman at a factory.

The Committee carried out its work under conditions of inhuman terror and the cruelest of persecutions. The ghetto firmly believed in the victory of the Red Army.

Let us bow before the greatness of these people's spirit!

A good radio link was set up in the ghetto; almost every day we listened to English news bulletins and broadcasts from the Soviet Information Bureau.

The grandson of an old woman named Bramzon worked as a radio repairman in the German *Schloss*.[35]

He received bulletins in German and managed to hear English broadcasts as well. In the evenings, a young Jew would no sooner show his face than not only other young Jews but also elderly Jews would show up at his place. It was amazing how they would take out a map and follow everything with such focused attention—God knows how, in this hell; what joy and delight they took in every little success of the Red Army! Bramzon's grandson was far from being the only or even the main source of information that we got from the radio.

We had our own radioman: Comrade Salman.

His wife and son perished in the ghetto; he devoted his whole life and all his strength to the struggle against the Hitlerite cannibals.

Comrade Salman knew several languages as well as shorthand, which came in very handy.

The radio was located in an underground pit, where there was hardly room for even a single person; he had to write while standing on his knees. It was horribly difficult in the freezing cold of winter, but Comrade Salman was at his post every single day.

We must also remember the Kozhets brothers (who were later partisans in the October 26th Unit); they kept our radio receiver in their apartment for a long time.

Thanks to our dedicated radio personnel, we carried on an intensive propaganda campaign, releasing English news bulletins and bulletins form the Soviet Information Bureau almost every day.

We published Comrade Stalin's speeches and distributed materials on Treblinka and Auschwitz. With the help of reliable people, we received and distributed a large amount of material on Warsaw.

Our "technology" consisted of a typewriter and a duplicating machine; we were not in bad shape in that respect.

In our organization was a chemical engineer named Marusya Davidzon. She worked in the chemical lab in the same factory where I worked as a cleaning woman. I also established contact with a Jewish foreman, and with his help I managed to smuggle a duplicating machine out of the factory. I slipped it into a bag and covered it with a thick layer of wood chips. We were allowed to take such "fuel" into the ghetto.

In addition, our comrades working in German factories used their typewriters to prepare many of our materials.

Frida Fel, Sonya Ruzhevskaya, and Kveta Lyaks formed the core of our technical staff. All of them subsequently died at the hands of the Germans. . . .

My entire family perished in November 1942. First they took away my sisters and their husbands, and then the rest of my relatives. In the beginning they left my brother but took his wife and child; three weeks later they took him too. I was completely alone.

The citizens of Bialystok knew what awaited them. No one harbored any more illusions.

All of us knew that our strength was not comparable to the enemy's, that the enemy was armed to the teeth, and that resistance would mean death. But we were determined not to give up without a fight.

In the apartments of Velvl Messer, Ber Savitsky, and others we held numerous anti-fascist meetings in which we discussed our current situation and the tasks to be done.

With the knowledge and consent of the organization our people carried out many acts of sabotage at textile factories, power stations, railways, and train stations in Lapy, Staroseltsy, and other places.

The ingenuity of our comrades in the struggle against the Germans was inexhaustible.

Ada Lisakovskaya, for example, slipped into the SS kitchen and put poison in a kettle. Fifty Hitlerites were poisoned.

We established contact with the partisans. The connection was set up through Soviet prisoners of war who had escaped into the forest and organized the Misha Sibiryak Partisan Group. Sibiryak was a partisan who had gone into the city to attend a meeting; the Germans found out about it and surrounded the building. Sibiryak jumped out a window, but he was seriously wounded. A Pole took him in, but later Misha fell into the clutches of the Gestapo and died.

The reconnaissance work performed by our anti-fascist organization was very helpful to the partisan movement; later, through the partisan headquarters of the K. Kalinovsky Brigade, we passed on valuable materials to the Red Army headquarters. Aksenovich, Lyarek, Leitish, and others were excellent scouts. Jewish girls displayed wonderous courage and fearlessness; among them were Marilya Ruzhitskaya, Anya Rud, Liza Chapnik, Khaika Grossman, Khasya Belitskaya, and Bronya Vinnitskaya.

With the help of a Polish friend who worked in the German passport office, they obtained Polish passports. So they lived outside the ghetto; naturally, they took advantage of their situation to help our cause.

We helped the partisans a great deal; we supplied them with radio receivers, medications, and clothing.

A remarkable page in the history of our anti-fascist organization and the Bialystok Ghetto is the assistance we gave to the Soviet prisoners of war. A committee of three people was responsible for helping them: a boot maker and Communist Party member from Warsaw named Leibush Mandelblit, an office clerk named Yudita Novogrudskaya, and Belya Kaufman.

The prisoner-of-war camp was located in Bialystok.[36] Officers stayed in the camp, while the other prisoners were taken out to work at various sites. Contact had to be made with the officers. Since the camp was surrounded by barbed wire, that was difficult to do.

[The prisoners of war were starving.]

A sewer worker, whose name I cannot remember, was allowed into the camp and was able to make contact with an officer. He was a member of our anti-fascist organization. We systematically provided him with food and medicine that we had collected.

No matter how hungry they were, there were people in the ghetto who in the name of brotherly love gave up their last bite of food for the Soviet prisoners of war.

At the factory where I worked there was one fellow who was a work foreman for some prisoners of war. We would bring him our rations, and he would pass them along to the prisoners. He once told us that the prisoners had elected a leader who divided the food among them and that they very much wanted to know who was bringing them these things. Later, without the guards noticing us, we sneaked behind some trees near the camp. When the prisoners saw us, it was a very touching scene, they smiled and waved at us.

[Both Polish and Jewish women who worked at the factory were of help.]

The guards murdered one girl who had played an active role in the committee assigned to help the prisoners of war. But this act of violence did not frighten anyone.

We managed to help one group of prisoners escape from the camp. They were privates who lived in the barracks.

In 1942 Soviet airplanes bombed Bialystok; many took advantage of the opportunity and escaped from the camp during the bombing.

In the ghetto the anti-fascist group created the "Self-Defense" fighting unit. We had to arm the fighters in the group. Jews worked in various arsenals, as well as in the barracks. Disregarding all danger, Jews smuggled out weapons from the 10th and 42nd regiments and from the Gestapo's arsenal. The Gestapo often searched people walking down the street, especially Jews. [You can imagine what it meant for a Jew to walk through the city with a weapon; but] the most difficult thing was to get the weapon into the ghetto. After all, a sign was posted at the gates leading into the ghetto: "It is forbidden to bring food into the ghetto. Anyone caught doing so will be shot." You had to risk your life just to bring a few kilos of potatoes. Can you imagine the courage you would have to summon to smuggle weapons into the ghetto? Nevertheless weapons were carried into the ghetto during the day and thrown over the fence at night. Several times Marek Bukh and Shmerl Berkner carried weapons through the city in the daytime.

Berestovitskaya smuggled eight pistols and a lot of ammunition into the ghetto. One night Natek Goldshtein and Ruvim Levin took twenty-four shotguns and twenty rifles from the Gestapo arsenal and brought them into the ghetto; both of them later died heroic deaths as members of a partisan unit. Jerzy Suchaczewski (who later commanded the Jewish partisan group Vpered) smuggled a pistol out of the Museum of Captured Weapons. Motl Cheremoshchny took rifles from the same place. Mulya Nisht, who is known among the partisans as Volodya, smuggled many weapons into the ghetto.

Weapons were also brought in from Polish villages.

Bronya Vinnitskaya transported weapons from Grodno in a suitcase. Under the guidance of the engineer Farber, grenades and explosives were prepared in the ghetto.

It was impossible to supply everyone in the ghetto with firearms. Many homes, however, were furnished with toxic substances. Jews working at the Miller factory brought several hundred liters of sulfuric acid into the ghetto.

Etl Bytenskaya organized self-defense procedures in several buildings along Kupecheskaya Street; she provided residents of those buildings with sulfuric acid and axes.

The most terrible days were approaching. [We knew that the Hitlerite monsters were liquidating the ghettos in various cities. The liquidation of the Bialystok Ghetto began in February 1943; the bloody business was completed in August 1943.

February 1943 was a time of great victories near Stalingrad!]

By six o'clock in the evening of 4 February 1943 the residents of the Bialystok Ghetto knew that the Aktion would begin at four o'clock the next morning. When the Germans showed up, our comrade Malmed was the first to kill a Hitlerite bandit. The Germans shot Malmed's wife and his little girls right before his eyes. They hanged Malmed. His body was left hanging in Belaya Street for seven days (that was how long the Aktion lasted in Bialystok), and the Germans would not allow it to be removed. Hundreds of Poles went up to the ghetto fence to pay homage to the remains of this courageous fighter![37]

Malmed was not the only one. The fascist murderers had to take every building by storm, as if it were a fortress. Many buildings were blown up with grenades or set on fire. Later it became known that the Gestapo did not regard the first Aktion in the Bialystok Ghetto as a success.

The second Aktion began on 15 August 1943. It began suddenly, but that did not help the Hitlerites. The murderers met with gunfire. The Germans brought in tanks and airplanes. The fighting continued for a whole month.[38]

The bright names of the leaders and participants in the Bialystok Ghetto Uprising will endure forever in the grateful memory of the people. Daniel Moszkowicz, the leader of the uprising, and his deputy Mordecai were posthumously awarded the highest honor conferred by the Polish government.[39]

Khelya Shurek and her ten-year-old daughter Bira died heroic deaths along with seventy teenagers; their weapons remained in their hands until their last breath. Velvl Volkovysky saved dozens of people and sent them to the Jewish partisan unit Vpered. He fearlessly sacrificed his own life, as did Kalmen Berestovitsky and Khaim Lapchinsky, who fought with an ax in his hands. Leibush Mandelblit joined the battle, even though he was seriously ill; the artist Maler also refused to leave the battlefield, as did hundreds of others.

{Anyone who knew the terrible living conditions endured by the Jews under the Hitlerite yoke and saw how heroically they fought against the German murderers will know how great was the contribution of the Jews to the defeat of German fascism.}

All the honorable people of Bialystok bowed before the heroism of the Jewish fighters. Many Poles gave us weapons. Wrublewski and Wladek Mstyszewski actively helped the Jews to arm themselves. [Several Polish shoemakers hid in their apartments Jews who were fighters in the anti-fascist movement.] A Pole named Michail Gruszewski and his wife, from the village of Konnoe, hid a group of Jews who had broken out of the ghetto in the forest. They took care of them until they were able to join up with partisans. Doctor Dokha from the village of Zukewicz and the paramedic Ryszard Pilicki helped Jewish partisans who had been wounded.

The Gestapo subjected people in the village of Kremennoe to cruel punishment, but still the people continued to help the Jewish partisans in every way they could.

Those who were able to escape from the Bialystok Ghetto went into the forest. The Germans began to conduct searches. [The Germans captured one girl and shot her.] A forester named Markewicz went out to warn the fugitives not to go past Lesniczewka, since the Germans were lying in wait to ambush them. He hid the Jews and fed them until they could join up with the partisans. The Germans took the forester, his wife, and his little girl from the Three Pillars reserve, stripped them naked in the forest in the dead of winter, and tortured them. But they did not reveal the whereabouts of the Jewish partisans.

I have given only a few of the facts from the story of the anti-fascists' struggle in Bialystok. I have related only a small part of what I have seen with my own eyes, as a participant in the life and the struggle in the ghetto.

Prepared for publication by R. Kovnator

The "Brenners"[40] of Bialystok: The Story of Two Workers in the City of Bialystok, Shimon Amiel and Zalman Edelman

We shall never forget the dark days of the ghetto. We shall never forget the barbed wired that surrounded the streets of Bialystok—Kupecheskaya, Yurovetskaya, Czenstochovskaya, Fabrichnaya, and many others, over which death hung for three years. By the end of 1943 the streets of the ghetto had been emptied; more than fifty thousand of its residents had perished in the ovens and gas chambers of Majdanek and Treblinka and in the "extermination camps" near Bialystok.

On 16 August 1943 the Germans selected forty-three people from the last of the residents of the ghetto. We two workers from Bialystok were among them.

Everyone selected was thrown into prison. The next day we were ordered to forge chains for ourselves; the chains were two meters long and weighed twelve kilograms. They kept us in prison until 15 May 1944.

During the three months prior to that ill-fated day we had been transformed into a special unit. Everyday they took us out somewhere; the whole procedure looked like they were setting us up to be executed. But our fear of death gradually faded. We had lost all hope of being saved. We were constantly being mocked and beaten. Shlema Gelbort and Abram Klyachko came down with a mental disorder. They refused food (a liter and a half of thin soup) and suffered from hallucinations; after about ten days, they died. In spite of the fact that these people had long since lost their minds, the Germans continued to beat and torture them and accuse them of faking it. A state of stupefaction reigned over the rest of the prisoners.

Everyone awaited the same end.

After three months the doomed men lost all resemblance to human beings.

Early one morning Makhol, deputy chief of the Gestapo, showed up in the prison. He ordered us to put on different clothing. Our new outfits had large white patches on the knees and a large white patch on the back. The patches could be seen from a distance of five hundred meters. The clank of the two-meter chains on our wrists and ankles reminded us that any attempt to escape would be futile.

They loaded us into a "death truck" (a type of mobile gas unit) and took us in the direction of Augustow. The truck stopped. When we climbed out we were ordered to fall into formation. We found ourselves surrounded by fifty gendarmes armed with machine guns, pistols, and grenades.

Makhol gave us a speech. He said we would be doing construction work for the next three years. None of us would be shot if the work is done conscientiously. Any attempt to escape was unthinkable, since our chains made it impossible. If by some miracle someone should succeed in escaping, then everyone would be shot. Then the gendarmes took us deeper into the forest under an armed guard; they led us to a hill that we were supposed to dig up.

We were issued picks, spades, and other tools. We started digging into the earth; at a depth of about fifteen centimeters we ran into dead bodies. We were ordered to drag out the bodies with hooks and stack them on piles of wood two meters high. We stacked the bodies so that every other row was wood, every other row was bodies (the wood we cut from the forest). When the pile reached a height of three meters, the wood was doused in kerosene or gasoline, and exploding bullets were planted here and there; then they set the whole thing on fire. An hour later it was impossible to go near the bonfire, since clothing would catch fire within one meter of it. It took twelve to eighteen hours to burn of a batch of bodies. The bones were removed from the ashes and ground into dust in large mortars. Then the ashes were sifted through sieves to look for gold crowns and other items of gold and silver that had belonged to the dead.

We buried the ashes in the same pits from which the bodies had been taken for burning.

The Gestapo ordered the hills over the pits to be leveled. After the pits were filled in, the area was planted with trees and flowers.

The regimen was strict. The Germans were afraid that one of the "brenners" might escape, and they watched them very closely. The Gestapo checked on them several times in the course of a day to be sure the "brenners" were all there. That is what they called those who were burning the bodies.

We were forbidden to speak. They woke us at six in the morning to take us out to the place where we would dig up bodies and burn them

The first three pits in the forest near Augustow contained 2,100 bodies. Most of these people had been murdered with rifles and machine guns. The clothing on their bodies had rotted and decayed. The bodies themselves, especially those buried near the surface, were decomposing.

The bodies were dragged out with the aid of hooks and attached to ropes. A hook or sometimes two hooks would be thrown into the pit to snag a body.

The Germans were careful to see to it that everything in the pits was destroyed.

From the very first days we decided that we must do whatever we could to make known to the world all that was happening here. Once a German walked up to me and said, "You won't be alive anyway. Even if you should survive and tell someone about this, they won't believe you." This statement had a huge impact on me. I decided to do everything possible to preserve some traces of our work. I kept my eye on the gendarmes surrounding us and seized the moment whenever something distracted them. At that instant I would take a hook and toss a corpse's hand, a rib, or a skull into a hole and cover it with sand. My comrades did the same. Within us stirred the faith that one of us would survive and reveal to the court all the horrible things we had been forced to witness.

They took us to villages near Augustow where mostly Belorussians lived. Next to every village was a hill in which murdered Jews had been buried. It is impossible to say how many of these graves there were. From early in the morning until late at night we would burn two to three hundred bodies at a time and then bury the ashes in the pits. Not far from Grodna, near the Staraya Fortress, we burned approximately one thousand bodies. We burned an especially large number of bodies fourteen kilometers from Bialystok in the villages of Novoshilovki and Skidel.

Near Bialystok we dug up a pit that contained seven hundred women. One can imagine what these poor people went through before they were murdered. Their bodies were completely naked. Many of the victims had their breasts cut off and tossed into the pit next to them. [This heinous act of sadism must have taken place near the end of 1943.]

A survivor from the little town of Edvabny, Mikhel Perelshtein, told me he had been in the ghetto on the day that the seven hundred able-bodied young women were selected; they were supposedly being sent to a knitting factory. Along the way they were forced to turn of into the woods, dig a pit, and strip naked. After being subjected to horrible tortures, they were shot.

Near Lomzha, in the village of Gelchino, we dug up four pits; each one was five meters wide and four meters deep. There I managed to hide several legs, a skull, and several ribs. The Germans were nervous; we could tell from their conversations that the Red Army was close by. The haste that we saw in the Germans told us that our days—perhaps even our hours— were numbered. They did not guard us as closely, but it was still hard for us to dream of victory, since we were surrounded by six hundred gendarmes armed to the teeth.

I'll always remember that early morning. At dawn we were digging up a large pit; Makhol showed up before we could finish. He summoned Obersturmführer Schultz Sturmbannführer Lieck, and Head Bandit Tiefenson, as we called him. Makhol began discussing something with them, and we realized right away that something serious had happened. Makhol's nervous tone and several words that we caught from the conversation told us that our end was near. Gudaiski and Paul herded us over to one side with clubs and ordered us to dig a pit four meters wide and two meters deep immediately. It was clear to us that this time we were digging our own grave. Each of us started thinking about how he could tear himself from the clutches of death. We were not able to consult each other or discuss the matter. The slightest word, even a whisper, was punished with a "Gummi," a blow from a rubber truncheon. When the pit was ready we were all made to line up along its edge facing it. Makhol waved his glove, and Zugwachmeister Wacht gave the order: "Into the pit!" I yelled out, "Save yourselves! Run, all in different directions!" Everyone screamed at the top of his lungs, just from the terrible tension, and broke into a run. You could hear machinegun bursts, which brought many of us down, but even the wounded tried to make it into the thick woods about two hundred meters from the pit. Toward evening Edelman and I joined up in the woods. For three days we wandered through the forest, living off roots and leaves. We drank water from puddles and were afraid to come out of the woods. On the fourth day we came to Grabovka, not far from Bialystok. We found out that the Reds had occupied the city that morning. Our hearts beat with tremendous joy, for we realized that we were saved. From our whole group, ten people survived: myself, Edelman, Rabinovich, Gershuni, Felder, Vrubel, Abram, Lef, Shif, and Lipets. Eleven days later we were all back in Bialystok. It is difficult to describe or convey our feelings as we now stood on ground occupied by the Red Army. But even today and probably for the rest of our lives the death order rings in our ears: "*In die Grube marsch*— into the pit march!"

Reported by Medical Service Major Nokhum Polinovsky
Prepared for publication by Vasily Grossman

Notes

1. A *malina* is a hiding place.
2. On 23 October 1917 Lenin attended a Bolshevik Central Committee meeting, at which it was decided to take up arms and stage a revolution. The Bolsheviks began the insurrection on 6 November; on 8 November the government surrendered.
3. Tuchinka is a village not far from Minsk, where approximately 25,000 Jews were shot.
4. From November 1941 to October 1942 more than 35,000 Jews were deported from Germany to Minsk. Some of them were housed in the Minsk Ghetto; others were sent directly to Maly Trostyanets and were murdered there.
5. Records obtained from Russia by Yad Vashem indicate that on 20 November 1941 seven thousand Jews perished at Tuchinka.
6. Matvei Pruslin died in April 1942.
7. Similar to the Boy Scouts, the Young Pioneers was a Soviet organization for children between the ages of ten and fourteen.
8. *Appell* is roll call.
9. According to testimony from SS Unterscharführer Franz Hess, who served in a killing unit, there were three or four mobile gas units and twenty to thirty trucks assigned to take care of the Jews who were shot thirty kilometers outside of Minsk.
10. On 2 March 1942 five thousand Jews were murdered in Minsk; on 28 and 29 June about ten thousand were murdered. Of those ten thousand, about 6,500 were old people, women, and children from the Minsk Ghetto; the others were unemployed Jews from Vienna, Bremen, and Berlin.
11. The *Verpflegungsamt* was a supply office.
12. Efim Stolyarevich is the name used by G. Smolyar, the author of this selection, while he was in the ghetto.
13. In a footnote the author adds, "Later, when we were publishing illegal newspapers and pamphlets in the partisan units, the surrounding population was certain that these materials where coming from 'up above.' The people were surprised that Moscow knew so well exactly what was happening in every little village."
14. In a footnote the author of this selection explains that this was a "group of young men and women who were able to forge documents stating that they were not 'full-blooded' Jews because they had a Belorussian father and a Jewish mother. They were called 'mongrels,' and they did not have to wear the yellow star or live in the ghetto."
15. Minsk was liberated on 3 July 1944.
16. Purim is a holiday celebrated in late February or early March in remembrance of the deliverance of the Jews from a plot to exterminate them in ancient Babylon.
17. On 31 June 1942 Kube, the German General-Commissar of Belorussia, reported to Loz, Ostland Reichscommissar: "In an action that exceeded their authority, the rear zone command has interfered with the liquidation of the Jews of Glubokoe. Without my consent they liquidated 10,000 Jews that we were most assuredly planning to remove in a systematic manner."
18. *El Mole Rachamim* means "God, full of compassion."
19. *Mstitel* means "the Avenger."
20. Literally, a "Jewish city."
21. Since Bialystok was in Soviet territory from 1939 until the German invasion of the Soviet Union in 1941, it was administered by an authority separate from the Government-General, the Nazi authority initially set up to govern the conquered areas of Poland.
22. Other sources put the figure at 21,000 Jews.
23. One cannot help but note the scandal of the Soviet portrayal of the dead as "Soviet citizens," and not as Jews.
24. Margarita Iosifovna Aliger (1915 – 1992) was a Russian poet and translator who, in some of her writings, explored Jewish themes.
25. A meat market.
26. Alfred Rosenberg (1893-1946) was the chief theoretician of the National Socialist movement and minister for the conquered territories in the East. He was tried and convicted of war crimes at Nuremberg.
27. Celsius.
28. Vsevolod Vyacheslavovich Ivanov (1895 – 1963) was a prose writer and playwright.
29. The town council.
30. This is a play on a line from Deuteronomy 6:7, where we are told to remember God's word when we rise up and when we lie down. It is part of the *Shema*, the prayer that begins, "Hear, O Israel, the Lord our God, the Lord is One."

31. Ovady Gertsevich Savich (1896 – 1967) wrote prose and poetry and worked as a journalist during the war.
32. Belorussian Soviet Socialist Republic
33. Between the 5th and the 12th of July 1941 approximately five thousand people were shot in the forest near Bialystok.
34. On 15 August 1941 Jews were forbidden to purchase anything in the Aryan sector; as of 18 August the Jewish community was held collectively responsible for any purchase made by anything outside of the ghetto. At the same time, food rations were severely reduced, first to five hundred grams of bread per day and then to three hundred grams.
35. A castle.
36. The Germans operated a prisoner-of-war camp in Bialystok from August 1941 to March 1943; initially known as Stalag 57, after August 1942 it was renamed Stalag 316. In early 1942 it held more than 11,500 prisoners; by February 1943 only 1,673 of them were left alive.
37. Itskhak Malmed (1903-1943) was a worker and a member of the underground. On 5 February, the first day of the Aktion, he threw sulfuric acid on an SS soldier. The Germans opened fire only to kill their own officer. In reprisal, on 6 February the Gestapo shot one hundred ghetto residents, including Malmed's wife and children. Two days later Malmed was arrested; on 8 February he was hanged on Kupecheskaya Street. The Aktion continued until 12 February.
38. The Bialystok Ghetto Uprising actually lasted for five days, from 16 August to 20 August 1943.
39. Mordecai Tenenbaum-Tamarov (1916-1943) was the leader of the Jewish Fighting Organization in Bialystok. When the war broke out he immediately became an active member of the underground in the Vilna Ghetto. In the spring of 1942 he was in Warsaw, where he organized the Anti-Fascist Block and served as the editor of their paper *Der Ruf*. In December 1942 the Warsaw organization sent him to Bialystok to consolidate the various underground groups there. He was killed in the Bialystok Ghetto Uprising.
40. *Brenners* is a German term meaning "cremators" or "burners."

Part 3

The Russian Soviet Federated Socialist Republic

The Smolensk Area

Shamovo

It happened in the village of Shamovo in the Roslavl region of the Smolensk district. On 2 February 1942 Lieutenant Krause, commandant of Mstislavl, made the following announcement to the police: "All the Jews living in Shamovo must be destroyed." The doomed people were herded into the square in front of the church. There were about five hundred of them: old men, old women, women, and children. Several girls tried to escape, but the police shot them.

They were taken to the cemetery in groups of ten. There they were shot. Among the doomed were the two Simkin sisters. The younger one, Raisa, a student at the Leningrad Pedagogical Institute, was among the first to be murdered. The older one, Fanya, was a teacher. She lived to tell the following tale:

"It was towards evening on 1 February. My sister and I kissed each other and said goodbye: we knew we were going to our deaths. I had a little boy, Valerik; he was nine months old. I wanted to leave him at home in the hope that someone would take him and raise him, but my sister said, 'Don't bother. He will be killed anyway. Let him at least die with you.' I wrapped him in a blanket. He was warm. My sister was the first to be taken away. We heard screams, shots. Then everything was quiet. My baby and I were taken in the second group. They led us into the cemetery. They picked up children by the hair or by the back of their neck, like kittens, and shot them in the head. The whole cemetery was screaming. They tore my little boy from my arms. He fell into the snow. He was cold and hurt, so he cried out. Then I fell from a blow. They started shooting. I could hear groans, curses, gunfire, and I realized that they were checking the bodies to see who was still alive. They hit me twice very hard, but I remained silent. Then they started taking the belongings from the ones they had murdered. I was wearing a shabby skirt; they tore it off. Krause called a policeman over to tell him something. Everyone left. I reached for Valerik. He was completely cold. I kissed him and said farewell. Several people were still groaning and wheezing, but what could I do? I left. I thought they would kill me. Why should I live? I was alone. True, my husband was at the front. But who could know whether he was still alive? . . . I walked all night. My hands were frostbitten. I have no fingers, but I made it to the partisans."

The next morning Lieutenant Krause sent the police to the cemetery again to finish off the wounded.

Two days later four old Jews went to the police station. They had tried to escape death but found no refuge. Shmuilo, age seventy, said, "You can kill us." The old men were taken into a barn and beaten with an iron rod; whenever they lost consciousness they were rubbed with snow to revive them. Then a rope was tied to the right foot of each of them; the other end was thrown over a rafter. Upon command the police hoisted the old men two meters above the ground and then dropped them. Finally, the old men were shot.

Krasny

The Story of Agronomist Sofya Glushkina

Before the war I lived in Minsk. On 24 June 1941 my husband was sent to the front. I left the city with my little boy (he was eight years old) and headed east. I decided to go back to my hometown of Krasny to get my father and brothers. The Germans caught up with me in Krasny; they marched in on 13 July.

On 25 July they announced that the residents of the town were to assemble for a meeting. At the meeting the Germans said that anyone who wished to do so could enter the homes of the Jews. [They also announced that Jews must submit completely to all orders given by German soldiers.]

They began going from one apartment to the next, stripping people, taking their shoes, and beating them with whips.

On 8 August the SS burst into the building where I lived. The were wearing the death's-head insignia. They seized my brother, Boris Semenovich Glushkin. He was thirty-eight. They beat him and then threw him out into the street, where they mocked him and hung a sign on his chest; finally, they threw him into a cellar. The next morning announcements were posted: "All townspeople are invited to the public execution of a kike." They led my brother out; on his chest it was written that he would be executed that day. He was stripped, tied to the tail of a horse, and dragged. He was already half dead when they murdered him.

At 2:00 A.M. the next night there was a knock at the door. The commandant came in. He demanded the wife of the executed Jew. She was crying, shaken by the terrible death of her husband; her three children were crying too. We thought they were going to kill her, but the Germans did something even more vile: they raped her right there in the yard.

On 27 August a special unit arrived. They gathered the Jews together and announced that they must collect all their valuables and hand them over to the Germans; after that they were to move into a ghetto. The Germans sectioned off a small piece of ground, surrounded it with a barbed-wire fence, and put up a sign: "Ghetto. Entrance Forbidden." All the Jews, including the children, had to wear a six-pointed star made of bright yellow material on their chests and backs. Everyone was granted the right to insult and beat any person wearing such a star.

In the ghetto "checks" were conducted at night. People were herded into the cemetery, girls were raped, and people were beaten unconscious. The Germans shouted, "Everyone who thinks the Bolsheviks will be back, raise your hand!" Then they would laugh and go on beating people. And so it went every night.

In February the SS burst in with their flashlights. An eighteen-year-old girl named Eta Kuznetsova caught their eye. She was ordered to remove her blouse. She refused. For a long time they beat her with a whip. Her mother, fearing that they would kill her, whispered,

"Don't resist. . ." She undressed. Then they stood her on a chair, shined their flashlights on her, and started taunting her. It is difficult to tell about this.

The lucky ones escaped into the forest. But what could the old people, women with children, and the sick ones do? I had comrades in Krasny with whom I wanted to leave to join the partisans. We were waiting for warmer weather. But on 8 April 1942 my comrades informed me that a death squad had arrived. We decided to try our luck. I left the town half an hour before it was surrounded. Where was I to go? The police were everywhere. They were hunting us like rabbits. I reached the prisoner-of-war camp; I had connections with them.

They surrounded the town. All the Jews were herded into a courtyard and forced to strip. My father was the first to go. He was seventy-four. He carried his two-year-old grandson in his arms. Evgeniya Glushkina, the wife of my older brother (whom the Germans had murdered in August), took two of her children with her; one was twelve, and the other was seven. A third child, who was just a year old, she left in the crib, thinking that perhaps the beasts would spare the little one. But after they had finished shooting people, the Germans returned to the ghetto to fetch some rags. They saw Alek in the cradle.

A German dragged the baby into the street and smashed his head against the ice. The head of the unit ordered them to chop up the body and feed the pieces to the dogs.

I left to join the partisans. It was hard for me with a child. But under difficult conditions solidarity, comradeship, and human caring come out. There were long marches and many guard posts. I was a messenger. Twice I ran into death squads, but I escaped. My little boy was ready for anything. I told him, "If they take me, if they beat me or poke me with needles, if I cry and scream, you must be quiet." My eight-year-old little boy never complained. He was a true follower of the partisans.

For two years we fought; then came the day when I saw the Red Army.

9 November 1943
Prepared for publication by Ilya Ehrenburg

The Fate of Isaak Rozenberg

Many Jews lived in the village of Monastyrshchina in the Smolensk district. There was a Jewish collective farm there. On 8 November 1941 the Germans slaughtered all the Jews—1,008 people. They shot them with machine guns; children were buried alive. When the policeman Dudin was later caught and asked whether he really threw children alive into the grave, he replied, "I didn't throw them; I laid them down."

Children from mixed marriages were also murdered. Aleksandrovna Dubovitskaya, a pedagogue and a Russian by nationality, was married to a Jew. They arrested her and tortured her. Her children—ages seven, four, and one year old—were all murdered. Dubovitskaya is twenty-seven, but after all she has endured, she looks like an old woman.

Monastyrshchina was burned to the ground; only the stoves of the houses were left. One stove that was left was from the home of Isaak Rozenberg, who worked in the regional civil registry office. He was married to a Russian woman from the Zhiryatino region of the Orlov district. Natalya Emelyanovna Rozenberg had two small children. They survived; their mother managed to convince the executioners that they were from a previous marriage.

Natalya Emelyanovna hid her husband in a pit under the stove. He spent more than two years there. He sat in the hole bent over; there was no room to lie down or to stand up. When he sometimes came out at night, he could not straighten himself out. The children did not know that their father was hiding under the ground. Once their four-year-old little girl peeked into a crack and saw his big black eyes. She cried out in horror, "Mommy, who is there?" Natalya Emelyanovna calmly answered, "It's a very big rat; I noticed it a long time ago."

Isaak Rozenberg used a manganese solution to jot down notes on scraps of the German newspaper from day to day; he recorded stories about his wife and the "new order" in Monastyrshchina. Water often leaked into the pit. Rozenberg had to cough, but he did not dare to cough. He wrote about it. The house was a good one, and the Germans liked it. That was when Natalya Emelyanovna dismantled the roof. Water poured into the house, and the winter was cold, so that Germans left the house.

Natalya Emelyanovna came down with typhus. She was taken to the hospital. A neighbor took in the children. At night Isaak Rozenberg would crawl out and eat glue from the wallpaper. That sustained him for two weeks. But Natalya Emelyanovna was tormented as she lay in the hospital: what if she should give her husband away while in a state of delirium?

In September of 1943 Red Army units came right up to the edge of the village. Monastyrshchina is at a crossroads, and the Germans put up a strong resistance. The battle went on and on. Armed Germans were right outside the Rozenberg house. Natalya Emelyanovna took the children and, like other residents of Monastyrshchina, fled into the forest. She returned when the Red Army had reached the village. She saw the smoking ashes and the stove standing there: they had burned the house down. Isaak Rozenberg died from smoke inhalation. He had spent twenty-six months in the hole under the ground only to die two days before Monastyrshchina was liberated by Soviet troops.

Prepared for publication by Ilya Ehrenberg

Rostov on the Don

On 4 August 1942 an announcement signed by "the Jewish elder Lourié" was posted on buildings throughout Rostov; it called for the registration of the Jews.[1] The announcement stated that Jews could continue to live freely in the city, since "the German command was there in the interest of their safety." Five days later, a new flier went out, also signed by Lourié, declaring, "In order to protect the lives of Jews from the irresponsible actions of enraged elements, the German command must resettle the Jews outside the city and thereby secure their safety." The Jews were instructed to gather at designated points on 11 August 1942; they were to take their valuables, clothing, and keys to their apartments, where their other belongings would remain undisturbed.

Many Jews who were unable to travel stayed in Rostov: old people, the sick, their relatives, women with children. Some immediately understood what the order from the Germans meant. Fedor Cheskis, a researcher at the agricultural institute, cut open his veins and lost a great deal of blood, but he did not die. His wife tried to take him to the hospital in a hand cart, but in vain. A German patrol stopped them. They executed Cheskis and put his wife, a Russian by nationality, in prison. One woman who lived on the Don threw her three children into the river and then jumped in herself. She and one little boy were rescued; the other two drowned.

An elderly couple barricaded themselves in their apartment. The Germans broke down the door, tossed aside the furniture piled in front of it, and took the old couple away. A woman dentist lived on the corner of Budennovsky Avenue and Sennaya Street with her daughter and one-month-old grandson. When she heard about the order, she decided to drown herself, along with her daughter and grandson. The daughter and grandson drowned, but some good people saved the grandmother. Out of her mind, she ran to the hospital where she worked and begged Doctor Orlov to give her an injection of morphine, for the Germans were after her. Those "good people" who had saved her, in fact, called the Germans. The Gestapo took her from the doctor's office to her execution.

Ekaterina Leontevna Itina was eighty-two years old. She lived with two former nuns who loved her and took care of her. She said, "I will not go anywhere. Let them come and kill me." The Germans informed her that if she did not go, then they would take the nuns. Then the old woman went to the assembly point.

Doctor Ingal and Doctor Tiktin, two of the oldest physicians in Rostov, went to their deaths. There was a woman physician named Garkavi, who was considered the best specialist on tuberculosis. Her husband, a Russian by nationality, did not want to part from his wife; they went to be executed together.

A paralyzed old man named Okun lived on Maly Avenue with his wife and granddaughter. The little girl did not want to leave and thus abandon the old couple. When the elderly Mrs. Okun read the order, she started giving away her things to her neighbors. On 11 August she went with her granddaughter to the gathering point. The paralyzed old man was left alone. He asked his neighbors whether his wife would be back soon. The next day a car came for him.

The residents of Rostov who frequently went down Maly Avenue knew an elderly lady named Mariya Abramovna Grinberg. She was always sitting at her window greeting her friends and handing out candy to the children. Everyone loved her. Her children managed to get out, except for her daughter, Doctor Grinberg, who did not want to abandon her aged mother. The daughter went to the gathering point. The old woman could not walk and stayed home. She did not understand why her daughter had left her for the whole day. The old woman asked her neighbors, "Let me stay with you until a car comes for me. . ." When she said that, she did not realize the reason why a car would come for her. [She did not understand why her neighbors turned her away. She said, "I don't recognize you. You are such good people, and you won't take me in just for an evening. . ." That evening they took her away.]

Doctor Ludmila Nazarevskaya relates this story:

"On the morning of 11 September I was walking past the gathering point on Pushkin Street. A truck was parked next to a building. People were crowded into the courtyard. An elderly lady named Rozaliya Oguz, a music teacher, saw me. A half century ago she had given my sister lessons. She was very happy to see me and said, 'Lyuda, you must have come to see us off. Please go by my apartment and tell Goncharova, the woman I live with, that they are taking us to the military offices. Have her bring my sister and me some food.' I promised to do everything she asked and said good-bye.

"I walked a few steps further and saw a mother with her daughter. The mother was blind, and the daughter was deaf. They stopped me and asked where the assembly point was. A tall girl who was walking behind me threw her hands up and cried, 'My God, you poor people, where do you have to go? . . .' She burst into tears and took the poor mother and daughter to the gathering point.

"I set out for the military offices. Traffic was moving continuously down Budennovsky Avenue and on across the Don to Bataisk. A couple of workers walked past me. One was sadly saying, 'It's hard to overpower them. . .' I walked around the military offices—this was fifteen kilometers from town—and saw no one. As I was returning through the workers' neighborhood, I sat down on a bench to rest. Suddenly I saw a group of women, modestly dressed, and several old men; one of them was Doctor Tiktin. I followed them.

"German soldiers were walking in front and behind them. At the head of the whole group was a man in a white shirt. He seemed to be enjoying his role; from time to time he would turn around and wave his hands as if he were directing them.

"Outside of town the road ran parallel to the railway line. Here the bandit in the white shirt stopped me. He called the Germans. They told me I could not go any farther.

"When I was returning to the city I saw several trucks carrying Jews. A teenage boy took his cap off and waved it at the bandit in the white shirt. Perhaps he wanted to say farewell to a living soul? The bandit burst out laughing in reply. I remember the face of a woman in another truck; she was holding a baby in her arms. Her face was tense and had an insane look. The truck sped on, the woman and her baby were jolted as it hit some bumps. In still another truck I saw our old midwife Rozaliya Solomonovna Fishkind wearing a shabby jacket and a white cap. Her face was sad and pensive; she did not see me. . ."

What happened in that place where the Germans would not let Doctor Nazarevskaya go?

It was a sparsely populated region. There were five small houses for railroad personnel; there were several more houses east of the zoological garden and the Olimpiade farm. The people living in all of these places were sent away for two days. Under the threat of being shot they were ordered to lock up their houses and leave. Fearing for their belongings, however, some hid in sheds, gardens, and ravines. They saw everything.

At the same site, next to the Zmiev Ravine, on the eve of 10 August the Germans murdered three hundred Red Army soldiers. The Red Army soldiers were transported there in trucks. Then they were loaded into a special truck designed to gas people. The dead were dragged out of the gas truck. Those who showed some sign of life were shot.

The Jews were ordered to undress. Their belongings were piled to one side. They were shot at the edge of the Zmiev Ravine and immediately covered with clay. Little children were thrown into the pit alive. Some of the Jews were murdered in mobile gas units. One group was led naked from the zoological garden to the ravine. A beautiful woman, also naked, was among them; she was leading two little girls with ribbons in their hair by the hand. Several girls walked arm in arm and were singing something. An old man went up to a German and hit him in the face. The German yelled, knocked the old man down, and kicked him to death.

On the night of 11 August local residents saw a naked woman crawl out of the pit, take a few steps, and fall dead.

The next day the German-operated newspaper the *Voice of Rostov* announced, "The air has been purified. . . ."[2]

Prepared for publication by Ilya Ehrenberg

Doctor Kremenchuzhsky

The physician Ilya Kremenchuzhsky lived in the town of Morozovsk with his wife and two daughters. One daughter's husband was at the front. She was left with an infant. Kremenchuzhsky's wife was Russian. [She survived by a miracle.] This is her story.

"The Germans murdered 248 Jews. But on that night they murdered 73. They came to our house in the evening and shouted, 'Is Doctor Kremenchuzhsky here? Get your family together.' My husband immediately understood everything. In the truck he gave each of my daughters and me a powder containing poison. He said, 'When I give you the signal, take it.' He kept one powder for himself.

"They put us in a cell. It was very crowded. We were all standing up. Under the windows SS men were shouting, 'Now we'll put an end to you. Just wait. . . .' Children were crying. Several women went into hysterics. My younger daughter wanted to take the poison, but my husband tore the powder from her hands and said, 'No, we mustn't. What will become of the others if we poison ourselves? We should support them and share their fate.' My husband did not speak Yiddish; he lived his whole life on the Don. But here he remembered two words: 'Brider, Yidn—brothers, Jews.' Everyone gave him his attention. My husband said, 'We must die with dignity, without tears, without screams. We must not give our executioners that satisfaction. I implore you, brothers and sisters, please be quiet.' A terrible silence came over us. Even the children were quiet.

"An engineer whom we knew was there too. Suddenly he started to pound on the door and cried out, 'There's been a mistake! There are Russian women in here! . . .' A German asked, 'Where?' He pointed to my daughters and me. The German took us down the hall: 'We'll clear this up tomorrow.' Then they started the killing. The Hitlerites were murdering people in the courtyard. No one cried out. I thought, 'Why should I live? But my grandson. . .' I wanted to save my grandson, so we ran away. A teacher hid us. . ."

Prepared for publication by Ilya Ehrenberg

"Where Are They Taking Us?"

In a village near Morozovsk there were children working in the fields. Rumors about the murder of the Jews had reached the village. Six Jewish children, ranging in age from nine to twelve, set out for Morozovsk. When they discovered that the Germans had taken away their parents, the children went to the commandant. From there they were taken to the Gestapo.

Two Russian women were in the cell where the children were taken: a nursery school director named Elena Belenova, age forty-seven, and Matrena Izmailova. The latter relates the following:

"The children were crying. Then Belenova started to calm them down, telling them that Mama and Papa were alive and there was nothing to be afraid of. She sang lullabies to them and caressed them. They fell asleep. But at three in the morning the Gestapo came. The children started to cry out, 'Miss, where are they taking us?' Belenova quietly explained, 'To the village. We're going to work there. . .'

"The bodies of Elena Belenova and the six children were found in a pit near Morozovsk."

Prepared for publication by Ilya Ehrenberg

In Stavropol

On 5 May 1943 I returned to my hometown of Stavropol, which had been liberated by the Red Army. The Germans murdered my entire family: my elderly father, my mother, my brother and his wife and children, and my four sisters and their children, some of whom were nursing infants.

When the Germans occupied Stavropol they set up "The Jewish Committee for the Protection of the Interests of the Jewish Population." They registered all the Jews.

A week later the Germans instructed all the Jews to report to the square at the train station for evacuation; they were allowed to bring up to thirty kilograms of luggage "for resettlement in less densely populated areas." Everyone who showed up was loaded into special vans and gassed. Their belongings were taken to the Gestapo.

Two days later, on 14 August 1942, the Germans instructed all the local Jews to come and receive armbands. They all went, and my family was among them. They were held at Gestapo headquarters; that evening they were told that they would be allowed to go home in the morning. When morning came they were stripped naked, loaded into gas vans, and taken out of town.

Officers and Gestapo men rummaged through Jewish apartments in search of booty.

I want to tell about my mother. She had great-grandchildren; she raised seven children. She was sick the last two years of her life; she almost never left the house and prepared dinner on the stove. Her grandchildren would come to her and bring her flowers. She sat with them, weak but happy. She was seen on her way to the Gestapo. She walked bent over, in a worn housecoat, with a black shawl over her gray hair. How empty and terrible must have been the heart of the person who shoved her into the grave!

My relatives lived a peaceful life; they fixed watches, sewed dresses, and made boot tops. The children went to school and worked in the fields.

Lina, my sister's oldest daughter, was a strong, beautiful girl and an athlete. During the first days of the occupation the German officers were all over her; a proud Soviet girl, she would come home crying over the insult done to her. Then they murdered her.

They also murdered my nephew's little son. He was ten months old. First the Germans announced that all children over the age of eight had to report; then they ordered the women they had rounded up to bring in every child to be registered. And they murdered them.

My mother did not take along one of my nieces. They hid the little girl with a neighbor. The Gestapo found out about it. All evening soldiers with submachine guns searched for the twelve-year-old girl. They did not find her. The next day, in spite of the neighbor's efforts to dissuade her, she went to the Gestapo herself and said, "I want to go to my Mama." They murdered her too.

Reported by A. Nankin,
prepared for publication by Ilya Ehrenburg

The Germans in Kislovodsk

Moisei Samoilovich Evenson, the man who recorded these recollections on the Germans in Kislovodsk, is now seventy-nine years old. He was born in Kovno. He was still practically a boy when he emigrated. He worked for a long time as a reporter in Vienna. Evenson returned to his native land without finishing his degree in philosophy, a subject in which he took a keen interest. He was twenty-one at the time.

He worked for the famous bibliographer and historian of Russian literature S. A. Vengerov[3] and was involved in the creation of the Brockhaus and Efron dictionary. In 1892 he began working as a journalist; he wrote a series of short articles on philosophical questions and on the history of the Jews. Because he was a Jew, the police in Petersburg expelled him to Kiev; in Kiev Evenson worked at the newspaper *Life and Art*.

[In Kiev too, however, he did not have the right to live; this talented writer and father of a family was forced to spend his days and nights at the chess club. The police did not go there to check documents.]

Moisei Samoilovich was forced to move from Kiev to Zhitomir, where he almost single-handedly published the newspaper *Volyn*. The famous Ukrainian writer Kotsyubinsky once worked for this paper. *Volyn* was closed down.

Evenson went back to Kiev and once again wandered the streets.

Evenson's son was killed in 1915 in a battle with the Germans outside of Buchach.

The Revolution of 1917 put an end to the denial of rights to Jews in Russia.

The young republic was engaged in a fierce struggle with its enemies. The German imperialists invaded the Ukraine and tried to rob the Ukrainian people of their freedom. In 1919 Moisei Samoilovich's second son, an attorney and chess expert, died at the hands of our enemies. Evenson left for Baku. He worked at the People's Commissariat for Foreign Trade until 1924; then he retired and lived at the small Minutka train station near the resorts of Kislovodsk. [There he was married for a second time, now to a Russian woman; she saved him during the time of the German occupation. Such was the life of the author of these notes.

Evenson's Story

The Germans broke through to the North Caucasus quite suddenly; until then life in Kislovodsk had been that of a town far from the front. The town was a haven to many evacuees and refugees.

On 5 August 1942 the population found out that the Germans were approaching Mineralnye Vody. The evacuation of people from institutions and sanatoriums began. You had to have a pass to leave, and people were delayed while their documents were being processed.

Many tried to get to Nalchik on foot, but by 9 August German mounted patrols were already watching the roads.

On 14 August German motorcyclists arrived. Behind them came a large number of German vehicles carrying machine gunners and submachine gunners. A transport of infantry arrived, along with light vehicles carrying the German authorities.

Neatly drawn placards were seen on most sanatorium doors; they read, "Occupied by the German Command. Entrance Forbidden."

The German commandant and his numerous departments occupied the city center. Announcements addressed to the population were posted throughout the city. [They said that the German army was waging a war only against the GPU[4] and the Jews. The rest of the population was called upon to preserve peace and order; everyone would have to work. The announcements said that the collective farms were being dissolved and that there would be free competition among the trades and the crafts.] It was announced that any hostile acts toward the occupying authorities would be punished according to military law during times of war. Primary examples of such acts were aid and support given to the partisans and refusal to report them to the authorities; spreading unfavorable rumors about the movements of the German army and the occupying authorities; and any refusal to follow the orders from the office of the commandant or the civil authorities.

Within a few days a newspaper went on sale in Kislovodsk; published in Pyatigorsk, it was called the *Pyatigorsk Echo*. Three-quarters of it were full of anti-Semitic agitation and ridiculously false attacks on the Soviet government.

By the time Kislovodsk was occupied, a rather large number of Jews evacuated from Donbass, Rostov, and the Crimea had already entered town.

One of the first orders issued by the German command was to appoint Kochkarov as mayor. The mayor issued an order for the surrender of weapons, for turning over all property from the sanatoriums, and for the registration of "Jews and persons of Jewish descent."

The Germans appointed the dentist Benenson, who was popular in the town, as the head of the Jewish Council they had established.

Two days later a new order was issued: Jews must have a white six-pointed star six centimeters in diameter sewn on their chests.

And so people appeared on the streets of Kislovodsk already marked by the sign of death.

There was no fuel or kerosene in town. The bathhouses were closed. The price of soap went as high as four hundred rubles for a single bar. The schools were open. The teachers were ordered to introduce corporal punishment into the schools, but they did not submit to this order. There was not enough medicine in the city. There was a horrible unemployment problem.

The Germans announced a forced rate of monetary exchange: ten rubles for one mark.

Deprived of all means of existence, people began selling their belongings. Second-hand stores opened; at first they sold things at 25 percent of their value, then 10 percent and even 5 percent. All prices were falling, and the Germans were buying.

German officers and soldiers from various units turned up in the center of town decorated with all sorts of ribbons and badges. Women came out wearing thin stockings and dress shoes. All able-bodied men and women had to work for the invaders two days a month; soon an announcement was made that it would be necessary to get ahead in their work by several months. Peddlers found their way to the Karachaev mountaineers to sell their wares. Flour became expensive; other goods became cheap.

In the first days of the occupation the Jewish Council was order to hand over fifty men's coats, fifty women's coats, a similar number of shoes, tables linens, and so on to meet the needs of the German command. Next they demanded watches and other valuables. Then people were ordered to go to work cleaning the squares and doing earth-moving projects. They had to do the work with their bare hands.

On 7 September an order came from the commandant's office: "In order to populate certain areas of the Ukraine, all Jews and persons of Jewish descent, with the exception of half-breeds, are ordered to report to the rail-freight station on 9 September. They are to bring their apartment keys attached to tags indicating their name and address. Those who are being resettled may bring with them no more than twenty kilograms per person."

Many knew that this order meant death. Doctor Vilensky and his wife, as well as Doctor Bugaevskaya, took poison. Doctor Fainberg, his wife, and their daughter cut open their veins.[5]

On 9 September as many as two thousand Jews gathered at the rail-freight station. The Jews filed past Gestapo men, who collected their apartment keys. Among those being transported were the elderly Professor Baumgolts, the writer Bregman and his wife, Doctor Chatskin, Doctor Merenes, Doctor Shvartsman, and the dentist Benenson and his family. Doctor Benenson's son was seriously ill and had to be carried on a stretcher. The people approached the train. The Gestapo demanded that they hand over their food and belongings. Timid protests could be heard: "But what about the children's underwear?" The loading continued. A car carrying nine little Jewish girls from the orphanage pulled up. The frightened people grew nervous and started grumbling.

"Why are these little girls being sent away?" shouts rang out.

A Gestapo man answered in Russian:

"If we do not kill them, they will become Bolsheviks."

The train pulled out at one in the afternoon. The guards were in a first-class car. The train passed through the station in Mineralnye Vody and then stopped in a field. The Germans took a look through their binoculars. They found a convenient spot. The train backed up to Mineralnye Vody and took a sidetrack to a glass factory.

"Get out," said the Germans.

[One woman, Debora Reznik, had grown weak from hunger and anxiety; she fell out a rear door into the tall weeds.]

The people got out. The Germans said:

"Hand over your valuables."

The people removed their earrings, rings, and watches and tossed it all into the guards' caps. Another ten minutes went by. A car from German headquarters pulled up. Then came the order: strip down to your underwear. People began to scream and rush around, as the guards herded them into an anti-tank trench about a kilometer from the glass factory.

Children were dragged by the arms; several cars were driving around the field shooting people trying to escape.

The shooting lasted until evening. That night trucks arrived from Essentuki.

They transported 1,800 people from Kislovodsk; from Essentuki they brought 507 adults and 1,500 children and old people. By morning all of them had been murdered.

[Debora Reznik crawled away through the grass. She was practically insane.

She wandered along the roads and stayed alive merely by chance. Perhaps because she did not look Jewish.

An old man named Fingerut also survived.]

In Kislovodsk the Germans kept a few shoemakers and tailors alive. Before they retreated, the Germans summoned them and their families and shot all of them.

Some were saved. Sheveleva, an employee of a Leningrad institute, saved three Jewish children by passing them off as her nephews. Employees at the medical institute helped her to hide the children. The physician Gluzman and his two daughters, one fifteen and the other eight, were saved. A Russian woman named Zhovtaya hid a young Jewish woman and her baby in her home.

[A few Jews survived in the caves.]

The weather was beautiful. The rumor spread that the Germans wanted to set up a resort for Germans only in Kislovodsk. The Russian population would be resettled.

On 6 November a transport of young people was sent to Germany.

Poverty was on the rise in the town; the situation was tense. Shootings were discussed with the greatest of caution, and gunfire could be heard at night.

In December vague rumors about Stalingrad were circulating. Groups of prisoners arrived in Kislovodsk. Soviet aircraft bombed Pyatigorsk. The invaders fell silent and turned pale.

Mayor Kochkarov was removed from office for embezzlement. Topchikov took his place. Many pine trees were cut for Christmas, but the Germans did not engage in any merrymaking that Christmas season. The evacuation began.

On 4-5 January 1943 once again they searched the apartments for Jews and communists. An announcement was posted stating that any rumors concerning the evacuation of Kislovodsk were false; anyone spreading such rumors would be shot.

Explosions were first heard in early January. The railroad bed and the rail-freight station were blown up. Again there were searches. The Germans suddenly fled on 10 January. As a result, many lives were saved. The Germans left many barrels of sauerkraut, cases of wine, and bags of salt at the station. As it turned out, the wine had been poisoned. The salt had also been poisoned, but the cooks noticed that the soup prepared with the German salt was covered with a green film, so that not many were poisoned from it.

By 10 January there were no more Germans in Kislovodsk. Soviet troops arrived. The task of digging up the bodies of those who had been tortured and murdered began.

The bodies of 6,300 Soviet citizens who had been brutally shot were found in the anti-tank trenches. At Mashuk-Gora in Pyatigorsk the bodies of 300 *Russians* were found. At Koltso-Gora in Kislovodsk another 1,000 bodies were uncovered.[6]

What the Germans did in Kislovodsk, Pyatigorsk, and Essentuki they did calmly and methodically.

Prepared for publication by Viktor Shklovsky[7]

Essentuki

The Germans occupied Essentuki on 11 August 1942. A Jewish Council was appointed on 15 August; they conducted the registration of the Jews. They registered 307 people capable of working; added to the children and the elderly, there was a total of about two thousand.

The Jews were told to report to the Council at dawn. They were sent to hard labor. The Germans taunted them and beat them. Lieutenant Pfeifer, the "Overseer of Jewish Affairs," exhibited a particular zeal in this regard.[8] This fat, red-faced German came to the Council with a whip and directed the beatings.

On 7 September, by order of Commandant Von Beck, the Jews were directed to move to "sparsely populated areas." All the Jews were to report to the school just beyond the railroad tracks and bring their things with them (no more than thirty kilograms): a dish, a spoon, and food for three days. They were given two days to get ready.

When he found out about he "resettlement" and realized what it meant, Associate Professor Gertsberg of Leningrad University took his own life. Professor Efrusi and Associate Professor Muchnik of the Leningrad Pedagogical Institute took poison, but they were saved by German doctors, who believed that Jews had to be murdered according to established procedures.

All the patients in the hospital were also supposed to report to the school.

On the morning of 9 September, Jews began gathering at the school. Many were accompanied by Russians, who were crying and saying good-bye. The building was surrounded. The doomed people spent that night in the school. Children were crying. The sentries sang songs. At 6:00, on the morning of 10 September, the Jews were loaded into trucks, without their belongings. The trucks headed for Mineralnye Vody.

A large anti-tank trench was located about a kilometer from the glass factory. The trucks stopped next to the trench. The Jews were stripped and placed in gas vans, where they died of asphyxiation. Those who tried to escape were shot. The children's lips were smeared with a poisonous liquid. The bodies were thrown into the trench in layers. Once the trench was full, it was covered with earth and stamped down with machines.

Among the murdered were scientists and doctors; Associate Professor Tinger; Doctors Livshits, Zhivotinskaya, Goldshmidt, Kozneivich, Lysaya, and Balaban; the jurist Shats; and the pharmacist Solkolsky.

Doctor Aizenberg worked in Essentuki. He was appointed head of a field hospital when the war broke out.

After the Red Army liberated Essentuki, Doctor Aizenberg returned to his hometown. He discovered that the German cannibals murdered his wife and ten-year-old son Sasha. Together with representatives from the Red Army and workers from the glass factory, Doctor Aizenberg set up a memorial plaque at the trench where his family and many others were murdered.

Not only the Jews of Essentuki were buried on that site but also Jews from Pyatigorsk, Kislovodsk, and Zheleznovodsk. Also buried there are the bodies of seventeen railroad workers and many Russian women and children.

Prepared for publication by Ilya Ehrenburg

The Story of Iosif Vaingertner, a Fisherman from Kerch

When the evacuation of the women and children from Kerch began, my wife did not want to go. Our fishermen and canning factory were filling orders from the front, and I could not leave my work. But my wife would not agree to leave me alone in the town.

"If it turns out that you have to leave," she said, "we'll leave together."

When the Germans entered the town, they posted an order everywhere: all Jews, from the elderly to the infants, had to report for registration. Those who could work would be sent to work, and children and old people would be given bread. Anyone who did not have a registration stamp on his papers would be shot.

My family and I went to register.

My heart was heavy. I did not like the fact that very few citizens of Kerch—and almost no

Jews—were to be seen in the streets.

"You know," my wife said to me, "let's go talk to Vasily Karpovich about our little one."

We went to see Vasily Karpovich Klimenko, who lived on our courtyard. He and Elena Ivanovna were an elderly couple who had asked us to drop in to see them several times.

"Bad times are better," they said, "when people stick together."

We did not want to leave home, however, so we took only our younger son Benchik to them. Our older son Yasha was never at home anyway. The schools were closed, and he spent the whole day running around with his friends. Two policemen and a German came to my house one morning. The German read out my name, my wife's name, and the names of our two children from a piece of paper.

"Collect the things you'll need most," he said. "You are being sent to work on a collective farm; your apartment will be occupied by other people. Take your sons with you, Yakov, age fourteen, and Bentsion, age four. Where are they?"

"That's a mistake," I replied. "We have no children."

Just then the thought flashed through my head: what would I do if they should suddenly walk in?

The German jotted something down and ordered us to come with him. The courtyard was completely empty. But I could sense our frightened neighbors secretly watching us from their windows.

They took us to the prison. It was filled to overflowing. We saw all our friends and acquaintances there. Since no one knew why or for how long we had been arrested, the most terrifying thoughts went through our minds. Everyone was agitated because of the crowding and dark foreboding; they were talking loudly, and the children were crying—it was enough to make you go out of your mind.

Toward evening the head of the prison came in.

"There is nothing to get upset about, citizens," he said in a saccharine voice. "Get some sleep, rest up, and tomorrow you'll be taken to your assigned farms to work. You will receive two kilos of bread per day."

The people calmed down. Those who knew each other started making arrangements to get on the same truck together so they could work on the same collective farm.

The next morning five trucks pulled up to the prison. The pushing and shoving were so great that my wife, our friends, and I could not even get close to the trucks. People want to get out of the prison and enjoy the freedom of the collective farm as soon as possible. The strongest ones forced their way to the front, and we remained in the back, even though trucks were coming all day along.

That night someone commented on how strange it was that a truck could make a roundtrip to the farm in just twenty-five minutes. Where could they be taking people in such a short amount of time? The thought was so startling that we were seized with horror. It tormented us the whole night.

The next morning the trucks came again; our friends and my wife and I finally managed to climb into one. I had a bad feeling as soon as we left town. I knew all the roads in the area— we were not going to a collective farm! But before I could give it any more thought, I saw anti-tank trenches and a mountain of clothing next to them.

That is where the truck stopped. We were surrounded by soldiers pointing their rifles at us. Arms and legs, still moving and barely covered with earth, were sticking out of a pit. A girl of fourteen or fifteen from our street turned to me and cried, "I don't want to die!" Her words shook us all so much that it was as if we had awakened from a dream. I shall never forget that girl. Her tearful cry lives in my blood, my brain, my heart.

They began tearing off our outer layers of clothing and herding us toward the pit where people who had been shot were lying. We could hear terrible wails. The soldiers forced us into the pit alive, so they would not have to drag our bodies in later. The ring around us tightened. We were pressed closer and closer against the very edge of the pit, until we fell into it. At that moment shots rang out, and they immediately began covering those who had fallen with earth. I said farewell to my wife. As we stood there embracing a bullet hit my wife in the head, and her blood splattered my face. I held on to her and looked for a spot to lay her down. At that instant, however, I was knocked off my feet, and other bodies fell on top of me. For a long time I lay unconscious. When I came around I had an unusual sensation. I did not know where I was or what had happened. A huge weight was pressing down on me. I wanted to wipe my face, but I did not know where my hand was. Suddenly I opened my eyes and saw stars shining high above me. I remembered everything; I gathered all my strength and pushed away the earth that was covering me. I started digging away at the earth that was around me. I wanted to find my wife. But it was dark all around. Every time my hand felt someone's head, I looked to see if it was my wife. It was so dark! I ran my fingers over the faces; perhaps I could recognize her by touch. I finally found her. She was dead. I crawled out of the pit and started wandering. I saw a light and went toward it; it was a peasant's hut. There were three men and two women there. They asked me about something, but I did not know what to say. Apparently they guessed what had happened. The women took my bloody shirt from me and put iodine on my wounds; they found a fresh shirt and a cap for me fed me. Then I left.

On the road a woman asked me:

"Was Ilya Veniaminovich Valdman taken there with you?"

"Yes," I replied. The woman started wringing her hands and burst into tears.

I walked toward town. I do not know why, but I felt no fear. I wanted to find out about my children. It was night, and I did not want to wake my friends. I saw the ruins of a building that had been bombed, and I went down into the basement.

Early the next morning I tried to get up but could not. My wounds were bleeding, and I had a fever. From the bits of conversation I caught and the screams and terrible wails I heard, I realized that a big pogrom was taking place in the town. As I later discovered, what was happening in town far exceeded anything I could have imagined. The Germans had surrounded the workers' settlement and murdered about two thousand people.[9]

I lay in the basement and could not move. Then something remarkable happened: someone apparently guessed that there was a living creature in the basement. Because from time to time this person would lower a loaf of bread or a boiled potato, an onion or a bottle of water, into the basement. Thus I spent fifteen days. Suddenly it became clear to me that I was rotting away alive. I gathered the last ounce of my strength and crawled out of the basement. I went to a clinic. When I walked into his office, the doctor asked:

"What happened to you? What is that stench?

I showed him my wounds.

"We have no room," he said. "Do you have money and papers?"

"No."

"Then I cannot treat you," the doctor replied. Then he whispered to the nurse to prepare a place for me in the ward right away.

He treated me, even though I had neither money nor papers; I spent two weeks there and came out a healthy man.

I went to see my [Russian] friends; they gave me food, money, and a place to stay.

For thirty-five years I have struggled with the sea, with hurricanes. More than once storms have overturned my boat, but they have not defeated me. So many times was I swallowed up by the waves! And now this contemptible fascist dog wanted to kill me in a single stroke. . . . He would not live to see the day! My brothers and my wife's brothers were fighting at the front, and they already knew what the Germans had done in Kerch.

I started searching for my children. No one knew what had become of Yasha. For several nights in a row I dug through the pits. But how could I recognize anyone in the dark among so many bodies? Besides, dead people often undergo such a change that it is impossible to recognize them. I went to join the partisans. But I did not give up hope on my son; he had grown up on the sea. As for Benchik, everything went as the Klimenkos promised it would.

"No matter what happens to us," they told me when I left my little boy with them, "Benchik will be saved."

Several days after we had been taken away to be shot, the Germans and the police came into the courtyard and demanded that our neighbors hand over Bentsion Vaingertner. A German held up a piece of paper stating that the four-year-old son Bentsion was missing from the family of the fisherman Vaingertner. He demanded to know where the boy was. The neighbors assured him that the boy was taken away with his parents, although they all knew, of course, that the child was with the Klimenkos.

The next day a German came again with a policeman. He showed up unexpectedly, in the middle of the day, when there were many children in the courtyard.

"Anyone who tries to run away will be shot on the spot!" the German warned. Once again he took out his list and began asking every child individually for his name, patronymic, and surname. Benchik was among the children. He looked older than his age.

When his turn came he answered that his name was Nikolai Vasilevich Klimenko. Everyone standing near him, even the children, kept quiet. The German went on to question the others.

The matter did not end there, however. A few days later the Germans went straight to the Klimenkos to take the child that was missing from their list. The Klimenkos insisted that this was their child. They bustled about and produced papers and living witnesses to confirm that the boy was really theirs.

There was a long struggle between the Klimenkos and the Germans over the four-year-old Benchik. Meanwhile the Klimenkos would not be caught napping. They consulted with their neighbors and came to a decision.

After leaving their home in their neighbors' care, they quietly slipped out of town one night with Benchik. Thus they traveled with him until they came to an abandoned collective farm near Dzhanko on the steppes. The Klimenkos had relatives living there, and people knew them.

That is how they saved my Benchik.

Prepared for publication by L. Kvitko[10]

Yalta

On 7 November 1941 the last Soviet steamship left Yalta. Many failed to get out. A black haze hung over the city: the oil reserves were burning. On 8 November the Germans entered the city.

[They starved the Jews and tormented them. No one knew what tomorrow would bring.]

On 5 December the Jews were moved into the ghetto situated on the outskirts of Yalta; they were fenced in with barbed wire.

On 17 December the Germans took the men out of the ghetto and led them down the road to the Nikita Gardens. The truck stopped at the Red Shelter (the guard post for the Massandra vineyards). The Jews were ordered to dig two deep trenches at the bottom of a ravine. When they finished digging, they were shot.

On the morning of 18 December, the remaining Jews of Yalta—women with children and old people—were loaded into trucks. They were forbidden to take any of their belongings with them. [People stuck a piece of bread or an apple into their pocket.] The trucks stopped beside a cliff. The doomed people were stripped and driven toward the edge of the cliff with bayonets. Children were torn from their mothers' arms and thrown over the edge. The rest were shot with machine guns.

It was a clear sunny day. Waves from the sea were splashing twenty meters away. The workers of Massandra and Magarach were working in the vineyards; they saw everything.

By evening it was all over, and the Germans covered the bodies with a thin layer of earth. Fifteen hundred people perished that day.

Then the executioners headed for Magarach. At Elizaveta Poltavchenko's apartment they boasted that they had killed 1,500 people and that soon not a single Jew would be left in the world.

There were many doctors among those who were murdered. The *Tourist Guide to the Crimea* published in 1898 lists "L. M. Druskin—pediatrician" and "A. S. Guryan—female obstetrician and gynecologist" among the practicing physicians in Yalta. Anna Semenovna Guryan managed to get out of Yalta but fell into the hands of the Germans in Kislovodsk, where she was shot. Doctor Druskin was murdered in Yalta on 18 December. He treated children for fifty years. His patients had long since reached a ripe old age. He was shot at the Red Shelter; the bodies of little children were thrown on top of the pediatrician's body.

The winter of 1941-1942 was a harsh and hungry one. Stray dogs dug up graves at the Red Shelter and dragged the bodies out. When spring came, water flowing down from the ravine washed away the earth and uncovered half-decayed bodies. The Germans set off explosions in part of the ravine to fill in what had been washed away.

On one occasion the German police found flowers on a grave. An investigation followed, but the Germans failed to find the "criminals."

Prepared for publication by Ilya Ehrenburg

Fishgoit's Report

Evpatoriya

The Germans entered Evpatoriya on 31 October 1941. Three days later the Gestapo arrived. On the evening of 5 November ten Jews were picked up in the street and made members of the Jewish Council; one of them was my friend Doctor Berlinerblau. The registration of the Jewish population was ordered on the morning of the sixth. The order was posted on the streets. A six-pointed star was drawn at the top of it. All Jews were required to wear the star on their backs; all money and valuables were to be turned over to the Council. They were permitted to keep only two hundred rubles. The order ended by declaring, "Anyone who fails to comply will be shot."

On 19 November an order for the evacuation of the Jews from the Crimea was issued. The Jews were to assemble at Military House; they could bring along an unlimited quantity of their belongings, but they had to turn in their apartment keys to the Council. Everyone was to gather there on 20 November. That morning I was outside, and my eyes met with a horrible sight. Women were carrying children in their arms or leading them by the hand and crying; men were carrying bundles; the sick and the paralyzed were being moved in carts. One young mother with the eyes of a madwoman was leading two children; she was shouting, "Look! My children have two arms and two legs like yours. They want to live. Like yours!" After being taunted and tormented, all of these people were soon annihilated. I survived thanks to the fact that on the day before registration my friends brought me a document from a Karaite woman I know, Doctor Neiman. It was a passport that had belonged to her sister, who was killed by a bomb. With the passport in hand, I walked from Evpatoriya along the road that goes to Simferopol. A woman in the village of Vladimirovka agreed to take me in; it had gotten dark, and I could go no farther. We had no sooner gone to bed than a truck pulled up. The landlady went to answer the door. "You have a *Jude* here?" a German asked. She told him no. Cars and trucks rumbled by all night long. They were looking for Jews. The weather changed radically overnight; a snowstorm had set in. I left early in the morning, and by evening I reached the next village. I managed to spend the night there. The landlady's son returned from Saki that night and said that the Jews there had been shot at five o'clock the previous evening. The next morning I continued on my way. The snowstorm was so strong that three times I was blown off my feet. It was terribly cold, and all I had on was light clothing. And so I walked for three days. Toward evening on the third day I came to Simferopol. The Jews of Simferopol had been shot a month later than the Jews of Evpatoriya. Here Jews had been plundered in an "organized" manner. At the same time, Jews had their apartments broken into and were beaten, robbed, and driven out of food lines by anyone who felt like it. On 10 December people who had broken the curfew (they were allowed to be outside only until 4:00 P.M.) were sent to the movie theater, where they spent the night lying on the floor; the Jews, however, were tied to each other in such a way that they were forced to stand the whole night. The order for the "evacuation" of the Jews came a short while later. For three days I watched people going to their deaths. An old man from a neighboring courtyard came to us for advice on whether he should go to the camp. He had heard that the order did not apply to people more than eighty years of age. We advised him not to go. I felt like hugging this helpless old man. Two days later the Gestapo took him away.[11]

On 7 January I deserted Simferopol and began wandering from village to village. In every one of them I heard about horrors and bloody tortures. I passed by wells and pits filled to overflowing with Jews. At the Politotdel collective farm I learned about the noble actions of several people who took turns hiding Birenbaum, a Jewish shoemaker from Evpatoriya, in their homes: the village elder Kazis (he was later shot by the Germans as a partisan), the farm worker Pavilchenko (a partisan), nurse Ruchenko of Evpatoriya, and the farm worker Nina Lavrentevna Ilchenko.

Ruchenko took Birenbaum to Ilchenko's apartment. There they dug a hole for him to hide in during the searches. In July 1943 Ilchenko had to change her residence for security reasons. She moved to Evpatoriya and rented a small house on the edge of town; she and Birenbaum settled in there. They dug a hole for him in a passageway, with an exit leading outside. She hid the Jewish shoemaker in that hole until the Crimea was liberated. Birenbaum is now a soldier in the Red Army.

I had parted with my son in Evpatoriya; when I found out that he had headed toward Fraidorf, I also set out in that direction. I went passed trenches where Jews and other innocent people were buried. Bloody clothes, shoes, and galoshes were scattered everywhere; the stench was horrible. In the first village I passed through there was a funeral. They were burying eighteen Red Navy sailors who had come to shore to join the fighting; the sailors were hiding in a haystack, when the Germans burned them alive. The Jews had been shot on all the collective farms. Only on the Shaumyan Farm were there any Jews left; they were from the mountains. They were shot later, in 1942. I spent entire days on the steppes, eating frozen corn; at night I would go into the villages to stay. I told everyone that I was looking for my sister, who had fled Evpatoriya after the attack. I tried to stay in several villages, but the elders would not take me in, since my passport was not stamped with the Germans' registration seal. I went on and knew that sometime someone in some village was going to recognize me and I would be hanged or thrown down a well. I searched for my son in village after village but found no trace of him. I reached the point where I would roar like a beast in the steppes and scream out for my son. It brought me a moment of relief. They began hunting down the Jews hiding in the villages. Every time I heard about a Jew being arrested, I rushed to that village to see if it was my son. I lived through my son's execution dozens of times. Each time I found out that the person arrested took his own life (there were many such cases), I was glad in the hope that it was my son. I no longer dreamt of my son's salvation; I merely hoped that he might kill himself rather than suffer torture at the hands of the Germans. In Fraidorf I found out from a cook working for a killing unit that for twelve days the gendarmes brought Jews here to be shot and thrown down wells; they smeared the children's lips with poison. In the village of Imansha, as one witness told me, children were thrown into a well alive, since they had nothing to smear on their lips. Several adults went out of their minds and jumped into the well themselves. Moans and scream could be heard coming from the well for several days. The same farm worker showed me a dog that had belonged to a Jew from Imansha; for five days the dog lay at the well and howled. Jews were brought from the Tartar and Jewish areas of Munus to the Russian section of Munus, where there was a well. They were lined up three abreast; those standing in the rear had to throw the bodies of the ones who had been shot [up front] into the well. A girl who had seen everything from an attic told about it.

One old man fell behind as they were being led to the well; a Gestapo man murdered him with a rifle butt.

Not far from Nikolaev I saw an old Jew frozen to death on top of a burial mound. As I later found out, he was lucky to have escaped the fascist executioners. In Kori I learned about the tragedy of three small brothers, ages eight, ten, and eleven. The three little boys ran away when their parents were taken to the well. That had been in the autumn; when the dead of winter set in, they returned to Kori. They came back because they had no place else to go.

They went to their parents' home. A new owner was living there. For a long time the children stood outside their hut without asking for anything; they did not even cry. Then they were taken to Fraidorf and murdered.

Once, as I was wandering about the steppes, I found a packet of fliers; one of them had Comrade Kalinin's New Year's speech.[12] From it I found out about the victories of our Red Army. I felt like a human being again; his opening of "Dear brothers and sisters" seemed to be addressed to me personally. At that moment I imagined I could see our mighty Red Army with Comrade Stalin at its head moving toward me. I hid two of the fliers and, now in better spirits, I went on. A thick fog moved in, and I lost my way. If I were to stay on the steppe, I would either freeze to death or fall into the hands of police patrols. For a long time I stood in one spot, not knowing which way to go. I prepared a knife to slash my wrists. Suddenly I heard a dog barking somewhere in the distance, and I set out in that direction. By the time I reached the village, the fog had lifted a little. It was the village of Krasny Pakhar. I went to a hut and asked to spend the night. The owners agreed. That evening I spoke with them at length; they said I could stay with them, but I would have to take care of their baby and give them something in return. I offered them my watch; they accepted it and agreed to let me stay and to feed me (if the village elder would allow it). The next day I met the elder, Ivan Nazarovich Novogrebelsky. He agreed to let me stay, in spite of the fact that I was not registered with the Germans. From the first words he spoke, I sensed that Novogrebelsky was one of us. I started visiting him and his wife. His wife, Vera Egorovna, was also a very kind person. I found out from them that the Germans had plundered the population, confiscated the livestock and poultry, and levied exorbitant taxes. The commandant beat people. Corporal punishment was commonplace. I saw a woman who had to lie on her stomach for a whole month after corporal punishment. The Germans began shipping many young people off to Germany.

I once secretly visited my friends in Evpatoriya, the ones who had obtained my passport for me; I got some morphine from them. My situation in the village was becoming more and more dangerous. On my last visit to Evpatoriya I found out from a neighbor that my son had left the Crimea in February with the intention of getting across the front line. It was like a mountain had been lifted from my shoulders. When I returned to the village, I dropped by to see Novogrebelsky, and he offered to let me spend the night. That evening he revealed a secret to me: he had a radio. They had an organization that, in addition to the elder himself, included his son, an old partisan named Suslov (who worked as a bookkeeper), the elder's wife, his mother-in-law, his brother-in-law, the farm worker Oksana Nikitich, and three people from another village. Novogrebelsky began to receive bulletins; he had me translate them [into German]. Suslov typed them, and others distributed them among the villages. I was happy to be doing even this small task; it provided my existence with some justification. I also translated into Russian our fliers that had been dropped from the sky for the Germans. Suslov typed them.

But this way of life did not last long. Toward the end of September, when passports were being registered in the village, the registrars from Evpatoriya recognized me. A few days later I fled. Novogrebelsky gave me a certificate stating that I worked in the labor exchange. I joined up with two women who were leaving for the Ukraine; they had passports, and the Germans had evacuated them to our village. With great difficulty we managed to get across the Perekop. We reached Rubanovka in the Zaporozhskaya district, where I met one of our prisoners of war who was making his way from a camp to the front line. . . .

After our liberation, fate bestowed a great joy upon me. I found out that my son had made it to our people, that he studied in Nalchik and was a lieutenant, and that he had been seen on the Southern Front in 1943. Whether or not he is still alive, I do not know. I have received no information about him. But the thought that he tore himself from our shameful captivity and that he was defending his homeland was an enormous source of happiness for me.

1944

Prepared for publication by A. Derman[13]

Murder in Dzhankoy

Before the war broke out we used to sing a beautiful, cheerful song about the Jewish peasants of Dzhankoy. The song would end with a joyful refrain of "Dzhankoy, Dzhankoy." But then the beast Hitler came and slit the throats of the Jews of Dzhankoy.

Grigory Purevich, a mechanic at the tractor station that served the Jewish collective farms in the region, lived in Dzhankoy during the mass murders.

He took me to the Jewish camp and told me the following tale:

"Here in the attic of the creamery, in the heart of Dzhankoy, the Germans imprisoned many hundreds of Jews who and been driven here from the surrounding villages and towns. It was so crowded and hard to breathe that it was unbearable. The children were exhausted from hunger and thirst. Every morning we discovered several dead people. As for me, it was like this: several days before the Germans arrived the director of the Koleiskaya mill offered me a job. My wife and children stayed in town; she is Russian. How could I, at the age of sixty, be part of an evacuation? Somehow we would get through these hard times. . . . I went to the director of the mill and spent several days there. But when all sorts of talk started going around, I did not want to endanger the people who had sheltered me, so I returned to Dzhankoy.

"When I got home the Germans were there.

"'Who are you?' they asked.

"'The owner!' I said.

"And they kicked me out. I did not see my wife, my two daughters, or my little boy. They were hiding.

"{I went to a neighbor's home. 'What are you doing here?' she asked. There is no room for you here now.'}

"I spent three days in someone else's demolished room near my home—without food, without water, without any news of my family. Then the Germans left, and I went back to my own apartment. The members of my family came out of hiding.

"Two days later the police came.

"'Who are you?'

"I showed them an old paper from my savings account that said I was a Karaite. They looked it over and left.

"All the Jews of Dzhankoy were already locked up in the creamery. They were forced to do hard labor such as dragging stones. The overseer saw to it that only one person carried even the heaviest stones. Anyone who collapsed under the weight was shot on the spot.

"They came to take my Karaite neighbor and me to the Gestapo.

"'I am a Muslim,' my neighbor declared.

"'And you?' they asked.

{"'I am a Muslim too,' I said.

"'Why are you lying?' said my neighbor. 'You're a kike!'}

"They let my neighbor go and took me to the creamery.

"Once I got to the damned attic and saw what was going on and what had become of the healthiest and strongest farm workers within two or three weeks, I nearly went out of my mind. Several people were bustling about in a corner. It turned out that the shoemaker Kon had hanged himself. . . . I knew this young, cheerful man. This shook me, but the others acted as if it were perfectly normal. Here I met Jews who had been evacuated from Dzhankoy. Many of them were from the collective farms in the area; there were non-Jews as well. Non-Jewish peasants were held here for helping Jews and giving them food.

"The Russians and Ukrainians did not stand out from the mass of pale faces. Their eyes, like the eyes of everyone else, were full of anger and sorrow. After all, they say, misfortune is the great equalizer.

"I tried to get work, and I got it: paving the road. It is better to die outside than in an attic.

"The Germans would select groups of people, including children and the elderly, and herd them out to the anti-tank trenches outside of town. It was winter, and there was snow. People were hungry and sick and could hardly drag themselves along. But they were forced to move on. A child of three or four fell behind. A German beat him with a rubber truncheon. The child fell, got up, ran a few steps, and fell again. Again the rubber truncheon came down on his back.

"The Germans lined the people up along the trench and began shooting them. The children went running in all directions. The Germans flew into a rage and ran after them; they shot at them and grabbed them by the legs and beat them against the ground.

"We were working on the road that goes from Kerch to Armyansk. All along the way we saw many Red Army prisoners who had been tortured and murdered.

"Toward evening they took us back to the attic. A bookkeeper from the creamery was there, a Russian name Varda. They had come for his Jewish wife and child. He started to object and grabbed a gendarme by the throat. 'Take me too!' he cried out. So they took him.

"One night a young woman named Katsman went into labor. Whenever her quiet weeping would erupt into screams, everyone could hear it. Her husband Yakov Katsman, a young combine worker from the Jewish farm, was somewhere on the front in the ranks of the Red Army. People thought of him all the time. . . . He never could have imagined that his wife would give birth to their first child in this tomb.

"At dawn the senior gendarme and his assistants arrived to take over the operation of the camp. The gendarme went up to the mother and turned the newborn babe around to have a look at him; then he took a rifle from one of his assistants and drove the bayonet into the baby's eye.

"Redchenko was the 'quartermaster' for the camp. He pretended to be mean, but in fact he helped people as best he could. Every day he would slip them some bread and sugar, so deftly that no one ever guessed when or how he did it.

{"There was a village elder in the attic, supposedly a Jew, whose name I don't even want to pronounce. He went to the Germans and informed on Redchenko. Redchenko was taken to the Gestapo. The bandits beat him half to death.

"Redchenko returned to the attic with his face bloody and so swollen that you could not see his eyes. He lifted up his shirt, and we saw that his body was covered with wounds. 'Look,' said Redchenko, 'how your elder repays me for helping you.'

"The unhappy residents of the attic were infuriated. They searched for the elder, their eyes filled with rage. People rose up from their places; you could hear curses and cries of 'Where is he,' 'Have him summoned,' and 'Find him and bring him here.' Before long the scoundrel showed up. Everyone went over to him and dragged him to the place where Redchenko was lying bloody and beaten.

"After taking a minute to draw a breath, the people suddenly raised their hands and rained blows down on the traitor's shoulders. Everyone wanted to have a part in taking revenge on the villain.}

"Every day several dozen people were selected from among us and taken to the trench made into a grave. Every day we had to endure inhuman torture and degradation. We were forced to do things that are impossible to mention without disgust.

"I obtained a piece of electrical wire, and one day at dawn I tried to hang myself. But people heard my death rattle and took me down. That morning I was beaten for it, and three of my ribs were broken. I did not have the right to take my own life; that right belonged only to the Germans.

"One day trucks pulled up, and they began taking people from the attic and cramming them into the trucks. Everyone knew that they were being taken to their death. Large German units guarded the building and the road leading to the mass grave. At first some of the people tried to flee anywhere they could during the confusion. Some managed to get away; I was one of them. I went home but could not stay there. A friend of mine, a farm worker named Onishchenko, happened to be in Dzhankoy at the time and came by to see me.

"'Come stay with us,' he said. 'I'll hide you.'

"I went with him and spent six months at his place. Then he brought my whole family to the village. Many Jews were hidden and given work on this collective farm. A trustworthy Soviet hand protected them there.

"An old Russian named Sergeenko arrived there with his wife and three children. We found out that two of his children, little boys of six and seven, were not his after all but were Jewish children. As the Jews were being driven to their death in Simferopol, Sergeenko's wife snatched the two little boys from the crowd and took them home with her. Since it was dangerous to stay in Simferopol with two Jewish children, Sergeenko's whole family moved out here to the village. Here they were given work on the farm.

"In this village we could openly rejoice whenever we saw Soviet airplanes flying overhead. In this village we awaited our liberation. The memory of the joyous day when the Red Army arrived in our village will remain in our hearts all our lives."

Prepared for publication by L. Kvitko

How Dr. Fidelev Was Murdered

Fifty years ago a younger doctor named B. N. Fidelev arrived in the Crimean port of Feodosiya. He had chosen pediatrics as his specialty, but fate would have it otherwise. A ship from Jaffa had brought plague to Feodosiya, and it was lurking everywhere in the innermost recesses of the port. The port was closed off, and the sick, as well as those who had been in contact with them, were placed in quarantine. There was an area on the beach surrounded by a high wall; from time immemorial it had been used to isolate people who had come down with cholera and the plague. Doctor Fidelev voluntarily entered this dark realm with its stone barracks, a cemetery covered with quicklime, and a laboratory that served as headquarters for the ones who were fighting the terrible disease. . . . Fidelev spent three months in quarantine, and many people died all around him. Many others, however, owed their lives to the talented, self-sacrificing young doctor. Doctor Fidelev became an epidemiologist; thanks to his efforts the Feodosiya quarantine area was renovated and transformed into one of the best medical observation stations on Black and Mediterranean Seas. . . .

Deeply believing in the value of the Crimean sea air and sunshine, Fidelev managed to get a new municipal hospital built on the coast just outside of town. It had large rooms with windows overlooking the sea. Lawns and flower gardens spread out around the building. Over the years tall acacias, poplars, and cypresses sprang up around the hospital building. . . .

When the war with the fascists broke out Doctor Fidelev was serving as chief physician at the Feodosiya municipal hospital. Soon its wards were full of people wounded during the bombing of settlements in the surrounding area. . . . Feodosiya itself was swallowed up by the howl of sirens, the roar of anti-aircraft fire, and the explosions of bombs.

When the Germans reached the Perekop, Doctor Fidelev was advised to leave.

"I have never been a deserter," he replied, "and I shall not abandon hundreds of patients to their fates. That would be deserting them in the hour of their peril."

On the third day after the Germans took Feodosiya they issued an order requiring all Jews to report to the city prison for "deportation to the north." Their apartments were to be left untouched, and they could take with them only a change of underwear, a coat, and food for several days.

Doctor Fidelev and his wife went to the prison. After their papers were examined, however, the doctor was told to go home. . . .

That evening Chizhikov, an old repairman from the quarantine area, paid a secret visit to Fidelev.

"The Germans want to set up disinfectant chambers in the quarantine area," he said, "but they are having trouble doing it. They don't have the blueprints, and some of the equipment has been damaged. Someone told them about you. But I wanted to warn you that, apparently, the chambers they are preparing are not for disinfection. . . . When they were testing them, I saw them take Isaak Nudelman there. Then I saw them throw his dead body into the sea. . . ."

The Germans did in fact demand that Doctor Fidelev help them set up the disinfectant chambers.

"It is to disinfect your countrymen before they are deported," they explained.

"No," the doctor answered.

They arrested him and his wife and led them down the town's main street. Some Romanian soldier yanked the fur hat off the doctor's head. The autumn wind blew through the old man's thick white hair. There was not a person in Feodosiya who did not know Fidelev, and everyone who saw him silently removed his hat, for everyone knew where the old couple was being taken. They walked past the Fidelev Clinic and the clinic at the tobacco factory, which was also organized thanks to his efforts; they went past the nursery that he directed.

The prisoners were not taken to the prison but were placed in one of the cellars in the former clinic. The Germans [probably] subjected the old doctor to the cruelest tortures, but

Fidelev refused to help them with the quarantine area. Several days later the doctor and his wife were tied up with telephone wire and thrown into the well in the clinic's courtyard; it was used to dump water that had seeped into the cellars. It took only eight hours for a pump to fill this wide pit to the level of a man's height. Through a crack in the fence a cleaning woman from the clinic who lived next door saw the Germans shove the bound old couple into the pit; she heard the electric pump running all night, huffing and puffing as it did its work. . . .

Doctor Fidelev drowned in the liquid filth that filled the pit. He had devoted his entire life to the struggle against the enemies of humanity, against diseases, and he stood fast when he came face to face not with a pulmonary illness or the bubonic plague but with a new variety of disease: the "brown" plague.[14]

The Germans were crushed in the Crimea and thrown into the sea; once again the city hospital, named in honor of Doctor Fidelev, is operating. . . .

Reported by A. Morozov,
prepared for publication by A. Derman

The Painter Zhivotvorsky

I spent my childhood and youth in Dzhankoy. It was a town of hard-working craftsmen, and life there was rich and happy. The one most beloved in the whole town was Naum Zhivotvorsky, the "happy painter."

Zhivotvorsky was an amazing artist, inexhaustible and devoted to his work. He painted bright placards that made every passerby stop and look. He painted alluring posters for the movie theater and fantastic decorations for club parties; by the time he got through with them, the carriages from the collective farm were so beautiful that it looked like they were on their way to a wedding.

I never saw Zhivotvorsky in a bad mood. He may have had his bad days, but he used to say, "Let my sadness stay with me and my joy go out to people." He loved people, and people loved him. In the evening Zhivotvorsky would go for a walk along Krymskaya Street, the main street in town, with his whole family. Beautiful and dark-skinned, his cheerful wife walked next to him. Their children formed a small noisy crowd that surrounded them; they had four tanned boys and three girls, who were as beautiful as their mother.

Zhivotvorsky was proud of his family and his many relatives.

In August 1941 I was passing through Dzhankoy on my way to the Perekop. A German bomb had destroyed the kindergarten building in the center of town. One wall had collapsed, and the roof had been blown off. Scattered everywhere were twisted children's beds and tiny tables, chairs, and toys. On the inner walls was an artist's painting of everything that represents the wealth of the Crimean steppe. Huge striped watermelons lay in a heap of colors beside a shed in a melon field; tomatoes were ripening in gardens; there was yellow squash and pods of field peas bursting open. A side wall was covered with a painting of two seas. One was the Azov Sea and the other the Black Sea. Fishing boats with sails aslant glided over the water's mirror-like surface; navy vessels with cannons stood motionless; and a huge steamship with the name *Ukraine* written on it had billows of smoke rising from its three stacks. The Crimean steppe lay between the seas; it too was reminiscent of a sea. Golden stalks of wheat stretch out their ears of grain toward combines that moved over the steppe like sail-boats.

"The children probably liked this very much," my comrade remarked. "Who did it?"

"Zhivotvorsky," I assured him.

And I was not mistaken. A resident of Dzhankoy who was passing by said, "Yes, he painted it."

For three years I did not hear a word about Zhivotvorsky. And then a letter finally arrived:

"Dear countryman, someone told me that with his own eyes he had seen you killed. But you are alive, and that is wonderful. I cannot tell you how happy I am.

"Perhaps you have already forgotten me, but soon you will remember. After all, you will recall that I was always around people, and people remember me because I was so noisy. But now there is not much left of the old Zhivotvorsky. A great sorrow has overwhelmed me. I am even surprised to still be alive and breathing, eating and joking with my comrades.

"In April of this year I fought at the Perekop and forced a crossing of the Sivash; now I am back in my beloved native town of Dzhankoy.

"The city was destroyed. Everything was burning. I rushed to my home. It was unharmed and still on one piece; the flowers I had painted on the shutters and the mean dog I had drawn on the gate were still there. I opened the gate and went into the garden. A strange little boy was standing there looking at me, smiling; but I could see nothing. Blinded by fear, I was unable to ask him anything.

"My soul grew empty and cold, as if a hard freeze had frozen me solid; even my tears were frozen.

"Then, my dear countryman, I found out that the Germans had murdered my wife and children, my sick mother and old father, my sisters and their little babies—altogether forty-two people whom I knew. I do not know the fate of the others.

"At that point I decided that life was not worth living, and I wanted to do away with myself. But then I thought that it was not proper for a soldier to die in such a manner. When I was in combat again and saw the Germans, I no longer wanted to die. I fought the Germans, and when I attacked them I shouted, 'Judgment is coming!' And so I pressed on to the very tip of the Crimea, to Cape Kherson; here, on the shore next to Sevastopol, I killed a German and said, 'The sentence has been carried out. Let the others tremble! The judgment is coming! I will reach your Berlin yet!'

"I was awarded a medal, and the regiment commander ordered me to take a rest in Yalta. But I went with the commander to a new area of the front. Now we are moving farther and farther toward the West, and every day we conduct a trail in the field.

Reported by L. Feigin,
prepared for publication by A. Derman

Notes

1.   The announcement was made "by the authority of Dr. Lourié, Head of the Judenrat."
2.   Between fifteen and sixteen thousand Jews from Rostov were murdered.
3.   Semem Afanasievich Vengerov (1855-1920) is famous for his work on such figures as Ivan Turgenev and Nikolai Gogol, as well as for his encyclopedic dictionaries and handbooks on Russian literature.

4. The Soviet secret police.
5. Doctor Fainberg and his wife and daughter tried to kill themselves by slashing their wrists and taking morphine. The Germans, however, found them and sent them to the hospital. After the family recovered, the Germans shot them.
6. Note once again the tendency to refer to the murdered as "Soviet citizens," and not as Jews. According to the "Acta on Soviet Citizens Shot by the Hitlerites in Koltso-Gora from 15 January to 7 July 1943," 349 bodies of people had been shot were discovered.
7. Viktor Borisovich Shklovsky (1893 – 1984) was a prominent prose writer and literary theorist.
8. In a trial held in Pyatigorsk in 1968 Pfeifer testified that on 1 September Mineralnye Vody was "cleansed" of its Jews; on 2-5 September Essentuki and Zheleznovodsk; on 6-8 September Pyatigorsk; and on 9 September Kislovodsk. "I cannot say how many were destroyed altogether," he asserted. "Seven or eight thousand, I think. Perhaps twelve thousand."
9. The records of the State Commission for investigating these crimes show that a total of 14,087 people—the vast majority of whom were Jews—were murdered in and around Kerch over a period of two years.
10. Leib Kvitko (1890 – 1952) was a Yiddish poet and activist with the Jewish Anti-Fascist Committee.
11. According to an SD report dated 20 January 1942, "Simferopol, Evpatoriya, Alyshta, Karasubazar, Kerch, Feodosiya, and the other population centers in the Western Crimea have been cleansed of Jews. From 16 November to 15 December 1941, 17,646 Jews, 2,604 Crimeans, 824 gypsies, and 212 communists and partisans were shot. A total of 75,881 people were executed."
12. Mikhail Ivanovich Kalinin (1875-1946) was a champion of the peasant class after the 1917 Revolution. He served as President of the Supreme Soviet from 1938 until his death in 1946.
13. Abram Borisovich Derman (1880 – 1952) was a Chekhov scholar and prose author.

Part 4

Lithuania

The Vilna Ghetto

A. Sutskever, translated from the Yiddish by M. Shambadal and B. Chernyak

The First Days

The persecution of the 80,000 Jews of Vilna began on the very first day of the Germans' arrival.

The fascist police threw the Jews out of all the places of business and confiscated goods from the Jewish merchants. Decrees were posted on the walls of buildings:

Jews are forbidden to talk on the telephone.

Jews do not have the right to ride the train.

Jews are not to be seen in public places.

Jews must turn in their radios.

Jews cannot be admitted to the university.

Throughout the city the inscription appeared: "No Jews allowed."

The newspapers ran vicious, hateful articles on the Jews.

On 4 July 1941 an order was issued: All Jews, regardless of age or sex, must wear a yellow badge on their chests and backs.

The badge had to be ten centimeters by ten centimeters. In the center there had to be a yellow circle with a six-pointed star. The pattern for the badge was available in all the police stations.

The order went into effect on 8 July 1941. Anyone who failed to comply would be severely punished.

A few days later Commandant Niemann issued another resolution. The decree regarding the yellow star on the back and chest would be changed; instead, a white star in a blue circle was to be worn on the sleeve. A day later this order was also changed: once again the requirement was to wear the yellow badge on the chest and back.[1]

It was not by chance that these orders were changed so frequently. The Germans wanted to degrade, humiliate, and confuse the Jewish population in every way possible so as to claim more and more victims, for the people were physically unable to comply with the daily changes in the orders. Subsequently, those who were guilty of wearing the wrong badge were arrested.

No sooner did the series of orders regarding the yellow star end than a new order came out: Jews do not have to right to socialize or speak with non-Jews.

Jews do not have the right to sell anything. All moveable and non-moveable Jewish property would henceforth belong to the German government and would remain with the previous owners only for safekeeping. They must see to it that the property is carefully protected. As indicated in Paragraph One, Jews are prohibited from visiting the market.

Anyone who violates this order will be shot.

On 8 July 1941 Khingst,[2] who was appointed Gebietskommissar (commissar for the region), visited Vilna.

Khingst managed to make his presence known on the very first day. On Gospitalnaya and Novogorodskaya Streets, where many Jews lived, monstrous pogroms were carried out. They were led by Schweinberger[3] and Weiss,[4] both of whom were professional murderers. In addition, the new satrap demanded a huge tribute from the Jewish population.

More orders followed:

Jews were permitted to be out on the city streets only until 6:00 P.M.

The Jews were forbidden to ride on trolley cars, and they could walk only on the street pavement, in single file.

Mitskevich, Zavalnaya, Shirokaya, and Slesapnaya Streets, as well as Kafedralnaya and Vokzalnaya Squares, were completely closed to Jews.

The Vilna Gestapo had a special office where, under the guidance of Sturmbannführer Neugebauer, German "professors" were specifically invited to develop plans for the more effective torture and mass annihilation of the Jews. Professor Hogarth of the University of Berlin, an agent of Himmler himself, created a "codex," where in five hundred paragraphs he outlined a system for the mass destruction of people.

A Vilna Jew named Kamermakher, who had been doing forced labor in the Gestapo's courtyard, told me that while he was in the ghetto he was somehow able to take a look at Hotgarth's codex. Here are several paragraphs that he memorized:

Himmler's order cannot be carried out simply by shooting the Jews. First the Jews must be tortured. The longer the Jews are subjected to torture, the better.

There were no direct orders indicating that the Germans had to personally participate in the executions. On the contrary, it was preferable for the Germans simply to direct it; others should perform the slaughter itself.

Procedures for disposing of the dead should be conducted in secret. No one should know about it, so that those who were still alive would not try to hide.

The same "codex" has a special section.

The gist of it is this: the Vilna Jews are the most dangerous in the world. If only ten Jews should survive in Vilna, then the aim of the Germans' operation would not have been accomplished. Any compassion shown for the enemy is a betrayal of the state.

In addition to physically exterminating the Jewish population, the Gestapo took up the task of destroying its morale and disgracing Jewish history for all eternity. For the Gestapo this was every bit as important as the physical extermination itself.

In order to carry out the laws and decrees issued by their special office, the Gestapo set up a section for Jewish affairs.

Gestapo officer Schweinberger was entrusted with the task of organizing the German Lithuanians. Schweinberger was a tireless worker. He set up his headquarters at No. 12 Vilna

Street, where the Ipatingas Buris—or, as it is more commonly known, the Ipatinga, meaning "special unit"—was located.[5] He divided the Ipatinga into two sub-units; one was assigned to shoot the Jews, the other to perpetrate acts of violence against them.

The "Hunters"

"Hunters" started poking around the streets of the city. Their job was to seize Jewish men and take them off to work. The work itself, however, was of no interest to the new authorities. It was simply a prudent, cold-blooded means of delivering the Jews into the clutches of death.

Workers were initially given certificates that kept them from being arrested.

Soon the Jewish population was divided into two groups: those who worked and those who were hiding in malinas. Whenever the hunters discovered a Jew who was hiding, they would tell him to grab a towel and a piece of soap and then take him to the Lukishki Prison, where Schweinberger in charge.

They conducted their work according to a predetermined system. In the Ipatinga set up a card file in which they entered the name, address, and year of birth of everyone who entered the prison, including the names of the hunters. On the reverse side of the card Secretary Norvaisha wrote the letter L or P in red pencil; the letter L meant that the victim was in the Lukishki Prison, and P meant that the one picked up had already been sent to the annihilation camp at Ponary. The hunter received ten marks for every Jew captured and sent to his death...

"The hunters were masters of their craft. Not only did they seize people and doom them to death, but they tormented them as well."

On the eve of the Day of Atonement (Yom Kippur) they brought mandolins to the condemned people and forced them to play along the road to the prison. In the second ghetto[6] the following occurred: A Jew named Gershon Shmukler hid behind a cabinet during a routine raid. A hunter found him, however, and dragged him into the yard. The Jew had three ten-ruble gold coins and tried to buy his way out. At first the hunter did not want to hear about it, but then he softened. Once the gold was in his pocket, however, the hunter declared, "It's not enough. I won't let you go."

Shmukler had no more money.

Then the hunter knocked out Shmukler's gold teeth, picked them up, and left.

On the night of 24 October 1941, the night of the "Yellow Passes,"[7] the hunters and their dogs were searching the ghetto for hiding places and found a malina. They broke through the boards with axes and went inside. A woman who had just given birth lay moaning on a bed of straw; the infant was still attached to the umbilical cord. The woman pleaded, "Don't hurt me. After all, you are human beings, you have children..."

Her pleas were ignored. They tore umbilical cord off the baby, threw him and his mother onto a truck, and hauled them off to Ponary.

In the Lukishki Prison

Where they took the ones who got caught, no one knew. They were taken away to "sign up for work" in the Lukishki Prison. Many went to register on their own, preferring that to a life of perpetual fear of being caught by the hunters. "The hardest labor," they reasoned, "is better than hiding in a pit and dying a slow death." But the prison, too, meant death.

On 31 August 1941 Schweinberger, his adjutants Weiss and Göring,[8] and a special infantry battalion from the Ipatinga surrounded the old Jewish quarter—Evreiskaya Street, Strashun Street, Myasnitskaya, Stekolnaya, Gaon Street, Dominikansky Lane, and Nemetskaya Street. Approximately ten thousand Jews were taken to the Lukishki Prison.[9] My wife, who had the misfortune of being sent to the prison but the good fortune of being set free, later described what she saw:

"As we approached the prison, two rows of policemen in civilian clothes met us in the Lukishki Market. We were forced to pass between the rows to receive our initial 'greeting.' A policeman hit me in the head so hard that his stick broke. Many old people and children fell in the marketplace and did not make it to the prison. They made us drag them along behind us. Children were lying next to their trampled mothers.

"Finally we came to the prison. As soon as we were inside the gates, they ordered us to put down the parcels we had brought and to remove our outer clothing. Then some other doors opened, and they kicked and shoved us into a large room overflowing with people who had been beaten. I could not move; I could not even take a step.

"The next night, his sleeves rolled up like a butcher's, Schweinberger came in holding a whip in his hand. He went to the middle of the room, where a woman had fainted, and stood on her body. Then he ordered everyone to turn their faces to the wall and bellowed, "I will torture to death anyone who raises his head!'

"Without showing the slightest concern for the ones he was savagely beating, he lashed out with his whip and barked commands: 'Get up! Sit down! Get up! Sit down!'

"After one such beating a young woman hanged herself with her baby's swaddling clothes.

"Schweinberger came back for more. People would pray and cry out, 'Shema Yisroel!'[10] They awaited death as their sole deliverance. They longed for death more that people on death row long for life. But Schweinberger would not grant them an easy death.

"He held us for weeks. Every night he would come, and the torture would begin again. Those who did not stand up or sit down precisely on command got a taste of Schweinberger's gilded dagger. Then they were dragged down the long, bloody corridor and thrown into the latrine.

"A guard collected a fee at the doorway to the restroom. Soon they started accepting the price of ten rubles only in gold. Not even water was free. Watches and rings were paid out for every drop.

"I noticed the two performers Khasha and Kadisha huddled in a corner, now crying, now singing some sad song.

"Several Jews who managed to avoid going to prison were worried about their loved ones who had fallen into Schweinberger's clutches and tried to buy off the Germans.

"Oberleutnant Wagner from the Burbishk forts agreed to release eight Jews for a very high price. With the permission of Schweinberger (with whom he shared the ransom), he walked around the room and called out eight names. When he called out Goldberg—a woman from No. 60 Kalvariskaya Street who had already fallen prey to Schweinberger's dagger—I shouted, "Here." The Oberleutnant cried, "You live! Get out!' Schweinberger personally escorted us the gate and announced that we were free.

"He said, 'Be careful. I know everything. If you say a single word about anything you've seen here, then I would not want to be in your brothers' place!'

"At that he pointed toward the prison, from which came the sounds of a slaughter house.

"As she was passing through the gate, one woman's shawl got caught on a button on Schweinberger's overcoat. The killer grabbed her and screamed, '*Zurück!* Go back!'

"The button cost her her life."

Schweinberger

He was a "beauty," this German officer. Up until 1939 he was a policeman in Berlin. Then he graduated from the Nazi Party school in Nuremberg. He was tall and elegant, with skin as soft as a young girl's. Whenever he spoke, he would not look a person in the eye but would look to the side or up and down. Jews who were building a garage in the courtyard of the Gestapo offices relate some surprising things about Schweinberger. He ordered them to call him "Father," for example, because it made him feel good. Schweinberger was very sensitive. He once heard a Jewish woman singing at work and gave her a gold brooch that he had just taken from a murdered woman.

"Your voice brings tears to my eyes," he told her.

I happened to meet Schweinberger three times. The first time was on the night of the "Great Provocation," 31 August 1941. His whistling whip lifted me up off my bed: to the slaughter, immediately!

The second encounter took place several days after the establishment of the ghetto. Someone had told him that a "foreign" Jew was hiding at No. 4 Rudinskaya Street. And that was something he had forbidden. I was the "foreign" Jew; I was afraid to stay where I had been assigned to stay, so I went to spend the night with my wife's parents.

Schweinberger burst into their apartment with a revolver in hand. I slipped into the kitchen and locked the door behind me. The ceiling was glass; I jumped up on the table, knocked out a pane of glass with my head, and climbed up. Schweinberger broke down the door and fired at me. I looked down at his shiny snout and then escaped along the roof.

The third time I saw Schweinberger was on Rosh Hashanah (the New Year) 1941. Accompanied by his companions Weiss and Göring, he had come to inspect the ghetto. He thought that there were still too many Jews, and he demanded that the sick and the old people be handed over. Without waiting for the order to be carried out, he summoned the Gestapo's "Black Raven," which was what they called the vehicle that took doomed people to Ponary; he himself set about selecting the victims. Taking a great risk, I ran to the other side of the street and hid behind a wall opposite the Jewish hospital; from there I could see Schweinberger.

He stood motionless, like a stone sculpture, with a medal shaped like a sword gleaming on his chest. His adjutants Weiss and Göring stood on either side of him and obeyed his short, sharp orders. Jews were dragged out of attics and chimneys on their hands and knees—the old, the sick, the dying—and thrown into trucks. Schweinberger only glanced at them. His stone eyelids were lowered. Now and then his gaze scanned the victims with cold disdain.

I saw them drag out my friend's parents: the mother of Bentsion Mikhtom, an artist and writer who belonged to the Young Vilna circle.[11] Then there was the writer A. I. Grodzensky, who was also the editor of the newspaper the *Vilna Courier*. Two of the "hunters" carried him out by the arms, and two others had him by his wooden prosthetic legs. Not until they reached the truck did they finally pull the legs off. At that Schweinberger finally raised his head for the first time; he ordered Göring to throw the legs into a basket.

Ponary

Ponary is an area seven kilometers outside of Vilna along the Grodnensky Highway. To the right the Vilnia River winds along its hilly banks. The entire area bespeaks a picturesque beauty. Adam Mickiewicz wrote poetry in praise of it. It is said that Napoleon declared he would like to take Ponary into his hands and carry it back to France.

The Germans fell in love with the site: on the right there was the road along which victims could be conveniently hauled, and on the left was the Vilna-Warsaw railway just a quarter of a kilometer away. From there the Germans laid rails leading to a large pit.

Once the death factory had been prepared and the word *Ponary* resounded with horror throughout the population, the Germans published a map of the city that included no trace of Ponary. In Ponary's place there was simply a green spot with the word *Forest* written on it. It was as though Ponary did not exist.

Three Stories of People Saved from Death

1. The Story of Motel Gdud

It was July 1941. All Jewish men between the ages of sixteen and sixty were required to work for the Germans; otherwise the "hunters" would take them. So as soon as we obtained a pass that would prevent our arrest, my father and I set off to work at the airfield in Porubanek.

Once, as a friend and I were walking down Bokshto Street on our way home from work, a taxi pulled up beside us; three officers stopped us and told us to get into the car. After picking up six more Jews, they took us to the Bernardin Garden. There were around five hundred Jews there. They kept us there all night under a tight police guard. Exhausted from the intense heat of the day and the hard work at Porubanek, I fell asleep. When I opened my eyes the sun was already up. Before me stood the Black Raven, the truck with the little latticed portholes. The door in the rear of the truck was open; a German officer with a skull and crossbones on his cap set an iron footstool at the door and ordered us to climb in one at a time. After thirty-five had been loaded, the officer raised his hand, even as the thirty-sixth man was standing on the stool. The Officer pushed him off and locked the door; then he climbed into the cabin with the driver, and the truck pull off.

The truck was painted black inside and out. It had no benches to sit on—just six seats for the guards. We were forbidden to speak. The guards would poke us with their bayonets for the slightest movement. After about ten minutes the Raven stopped, and the officer unlocked the door. The guards jumped out and stood to one side; they were not allowed into the camp area. I saw a barbed-wire fence and a wooden gate; on the gate was a plywood sign that said, "Warning! Danger! Minefield!"

The guards stayed behind, and we went on; the door to the truck was left unlocked.

The truck stopped a second time. Schweinberger walked up to the door; whomever he pointed to had to go with him.

I was the seventh one called. Through the open door of the truck I could see them shooting my friends. Each one was ordered to undress in a ditch that led to a huge grave. Schweinberger would then lead the naked man to the pit and shoot him in the back of the head.

Then my turn came. Naked, I approached the pit; I could hear the screams of people who were still alive. I heard a shot. I thought I was dead. Apparently I fell a split-second before he fired, and the bullet missed me. I could hear Schweinberger talking with the soldiers standing next to him. A few seconds later a body in its death throes was weighing down on me; someone's blood was on my lips... . At that moment I lost consciousness. When I came to, the sun was high in the sky. I could see it through the blood that was clouding my eyes. The shooting had stopped. A light breeze refreshed me a bit. Then I heard gunfire. It was the guards randomly firing into the mass grave. I was slightly wounded.

Again the shooting stopped. The executioners—some of whom were in military uniforms, other in civilian clothes—sat down at the edge of the grave and started drinking vodka. After getting drunk during their guard duty at the mound, they left.

Finally everything was quiet. Naked, I tore myself out of the grave and crawled through the grass toward the bushes, as far as the wire fence. In the distance I saw the "Raven" approaching with a new cargo of doomed people.

A Pole whom I did not know took me into his home; he bandaged my wound and gave me some clothes. I spent the night there. At dawn the next morning, I drank some milk and set out for the city.

When I told my father about everything that happened at Ponary, he refused to believe me.

2. *The Story of Khiena Katz*

During the Aktion of 24 October 1941 the Germans came to our home and ordered us to come with them. I asked if we should take anything. The robbers said that if we had any gold, it would probably be useful in our new place.

Our whole family—my parents, my sister, and my children—was taken with all the other residents in our building to the Lukishki Prison. They made us undress to our underwear. Our clothes were quickly taken away. They beat us with iron clubs. Weiss showed up at dawn and ordered us to get dressed. We told him the guards had taken our clothing. He started screaming:

"Who dared? You'll have to go to work the way you are! You'll have to be taken in trucks... ."

The children and the men were separated from us. Still undressed, we were loaded into the trucks and taken somewhere. Once in the truck, Weiss announced:

"Know that I am your father! I am taking you to the factory to work. What sort of work it is, you will soon find out."

He pulled a bag from his pocket and gave each of us a piece of candy. Many began to trust Weiss; they stopped weeping and started talking about their new work. Some were even smiling. As for me, I did not believe a single word. I knew I had come to the end of the line. I must admit, however, that I took the candy. I thought: "If it is poisoned, then so much the better—they won't torture me; if it isn't, I can suck on something sweet in my last minutes." When we reached Ponary, they herded us into the ditch with whips.

"This is where you will work!" Weiss laughed at us. He ordered us to removed our under-shirts and wait our turn. Weiss threatened to gouge out the eyes of anyone who refused to obey the order. And immediately he carried out his treat on one woman.

About two hundred women were in the ditch. There were also a few children. They had been separated from the women in the prison, but several women somehow managed to hide their children, and now the little ones were clinging to their mothers.

At first everyone was sobbing and wailing, but they gradually grew quiet. Two hundred paces away an execution was taking place. I saw them murder my father with my own eyes. He was first stunned by a blow from a crowbar and then shot. Covered with blood, he fell on top of a dead body.

My sister was lying down, resting next to me. Her two-year-old little boy Moishele was sobbing at her breast. When the shooting had died down a bit, I suddenly heard my sister singing something. She was rocking her little boy to the tune of a familiar folk song:

Tra-la-la, sweet little girl
Tra-la-la, sweet little bird,
I have lost my true love,
My sorrow is oh so bitter.

One woman took out a piece of bread and started eating it. Others followed her example. Our turn came toward the end of the day. We were led to the huge grave in groups of ten; it was thirty to forty meters long. The ditch became deeper as it led closer to the grave; where the two met it was about seven meters deep.

Our group was last. Weiss came over and ordered us to line up. He was holding some sort of cloth and tore it into ten pieces to blindfold us. I was the first in line. My mother and sister were behind me.

"Hands on your hips!" Weiss ordered as he led us forward. I stepped on bodies that were not yet cold.

Suddenly the order rang out: "Fire!"

Behind me my sister cried out, "God!"

I felt her fall. I fell beside her and lost consciousness.

When I came to, it was dawn. The dead were lying on top of me, covered with lime. I recognized my sister. Moishele looked as if he were dozing at her breast. I crawled out from under the heavy pile of bodies and went to the ditch to look for some clothes. I found a nightgown and put it on; then I found an old shirt, and, wearing nothing else, I ran away, back to the ghetto. There I spent a whole month in the hospital.

3.   The Story of Solomon Garbel

On 5 April 1942 four thousand Jews were executed; they were supposed to be taken to Kovno but were taken to Ponary instead.[12] The next day Weiss rode into the ghetto on a bicycle and ordered ten Jewish men to come and bury the ones who had been murdered. So we set out, with Weiss leading us.

We began seeing bodies half a kilometer from Ponary, near the railroad lines; they were the ones killed while trying to escape. There was a sign hanging on the gates leading to the execution site: "Entrance is forbidden even to German officers!"

Rails were laid passing through the gates, so that the trains carrying the victims could pull right up to the pits. The farther we went, the more terrible the scene that unfolded before us. The grass was red with blood. The entire field was littered with bodies. The trees were splattered with brains. Mutilated children lay beside the tree trunks, many of whom were torn in half, with one leg lying here, another there. There was a whole pile of children's heads. Identification papers, visitor's cards, photographs, and banknotes were scattered everywhere.

In one spot lay the body of a German with his throat torn out: apparently a Jew had killed him.

Weiss gave us vodka and said, "Work diligently! See to it that the bodies are undressed and neatly buried. Place the coats to the side, men's coats in one pile and women's coats in another. If you happen to find any gold, put it in the bucket. Anyone who dares to take anything for himself will be shot."

He led us to the closest mound. Then he pointed out various areas that had been covered over and announced: "That is where the Jews captured by the 'hunters' are (he used the Yiddish word for 'hunters' and smirked). Farther on are the gypsies. Over here are the ones who said, 'We'll never surrender!'—that is, the Poles. Here lie the hunters who turned on us. And here prisoners of war. Over there, however," he pointed in the distance, "no one lies buried. But not for long. There are still many more people left in the world!"

Among the bodies there were some people who were still alive. We did not know what to do with them. Many were wearing a tallis. Others had letters in their pockets that they had written on their way to their execution. I remember one letter that said, "Jews, they are taking us to be shot! Avenge us! Flekser from Sventsyan."

Curled up among the blood-stained packages that we loaded into the train cars was a little boy who was still alive; he had hidden, and they did not noticed him. His name was Berele Goldshtein from Mikhalishek.

When he realized that we were Jews, he started begging us, "Save me!" We hid him from Weiss and got him back into the ghetto.

We buried about five hundred people. They were scattered all over the field; having tried to run away, they were still dressed. The others were lying in a ditch; all that remained to be done was to pour lime over them. We were certain that we would never return from that place, that Weiss would have us shot. But suddenly he came up to us, drunk, and said, "You are the only ones ever to visit Ponary and return home."

At the exit I saw a terrible sight.

The mass grave in which we had buried the Jews started moving and was heaving higher and higher... .

Weiss calmed us down: "It's just the bodies swelling and making the earth rise."

Murer

Murer was twenty-four years old; he worked under Gebietskommissar Khingst as head of Jewish affairs.[13] His father "worked" as an executioner in one of the German provinces. The son carried on the tradition of the father "with honor." He was trained with the Hitler Youth in Nuremberg, where he studied the theoretical aspects of the "Jewish Question." He was an officer assigned to Neugebauer's staff; he took Professor Hogarth's place after the professor had left. It is said that spread out on a large table Himmler has a map with a little flag marking every single spot where there are Jews. Every day he removes a few more flags, indicating that in those places the Jews have been exterminated. In accordance with orders issued, men like Murer were sent to those places to develop the procedure for annihilation that men like Schweinberger and Weiss were to carry out; and they followed their orders down to the last detail.

In accordance with an order from Murer, on 4 July 1941 the first Judenrat was established. A member of the Judenrat named Doctor Yakov Vygodsky—one of the most respected citizens of old Vilna—went to Murer to request that some of the most monstrous orders be revoked.[14] Murer calmly listened to him; then he slapped Doctor Vygodsky across the face and threw him down the stairs.

Murer loved to mock his victims. He would suddenly pull up to the ghetto gates and subject the Jews returning from work to a search; whenever he found a bit of food, he would personally escort the guilty party to the prison.

On one occasion, after conducting a search of twenty workers, Murer caught one of them with a kilogram of flour. The entire group was sent to Ponary, where Murer personally carried out their extermination. When the victims were tallied, however, it turned out that there were not twenty but twenty-one.

"*Donnerwetter*!" Murer cried. "An innocent man has been shot!"

Sometimes he would check for yellow passes. If it happened, for example, that the corner of a pass had been torn, he would not let the victim out of his clutches. If he should find money or flowers on a Jew, he would order the criminal to be whipped. He especially liked to watch girls getting lashed and would yell, "Harder! Harder!"

He was a frequent visitor in the ghetto; he had his own key to the gate. He liked to set up a bench at No. 6 Strashun Street; there, with arms folded across his chest, he would eye the young women walking by. Sometimes he would reach out to touch them and say, "You're too fat. I'll help you lose weight."

When he visited the workshops he would make people crawl under the tables and howl like dogs. At the same time, this sadist was so "generous" that he set up a playground for the children in the ghetto.

After a certain provocation, four thousand people were supposed to go to Kaunas but were sent to Ponary and shot; Murer offered his apologies to Gens,[15] the Chief of the Jewish Police Force, for the "mistake." Then he added that after the war the ghetto would be expanded to include Stefanovskaya Street.

Schweinberger's Successor Martin Weiss

Once Schweinberger had accomplished his mission in Vilna, he was sent to the front. According to stories told by his lover, his own comrades shot him.

He was replaced by Martin Weiss, Chief of the Ipatinga and Master of Ponary.

Although Schweinberger graduated from a special training school, he could have learned a lot from Weiss, who was just a sergeant major.

Weiss loved his work. He built himself a cottage at Ponary, not far from the mass graves. An unusual, black blood flowed in his veins!

He was a native of Karlsruhe. He worked as a tinsmith. He was less than forty years of age and had two children.

Using the pretense that a Jew had killed a German, he ransacked Novogorodskaya Street. Five hundred Jews were shot and several thousand were marched off to Lukishki Prison. He ordered them to remove their belts and to place their hands behind their heads, so that they could not hold their pants up. Rabbi Segal led this procession down Novogorodskaya Street.

On 6 September, the first day of the Jews' transfer into the ghetto, Weiss was walking along leading a little girl by the hand; she did not have a yellow badge. The girl was a twelve-year-old pupil at the Vilna Technical School.[16]   Apparently assuming that Weiss was a "good German," she thought he was saving her from the hunters. She was mistaken. Weiss stood her up against a wall and shot her.

Zelda Eingorn escaped from Ponary; she hid in the bushes as they shot her family. She told me how Weiss murdered Tserna Morgenshtern, a remarkably beautiful eighteen-year-old girl who was the daughter of a Vilna schoolteacher.

... She was walking along with her mother and her little brother. The doomed people had to undress at the very edge of the pit. The Germans gouged out the eyes of people who disobeyed. They were especially insistent that young girls undress. It was evening, and the moon had risen. As Tserna approached the pit half-dressed, Weiss ran up to her, grabbed her by the hand, and pulled her over to the side. He wanted to save her. Tserna tore herself away: she wanted to die with her mother and brother, who had already been shot. Weiss would not let her.

"Such a beautiful girl should not die," he insisted.

Tserna sobbed and tried to get away, but Weiss was holding her too tightly.

"Look at how wonderful life is!" he said, pointing at the trees with the dark blue moonlight shining on them. "And you are a young girl. You look so lovely in the moonlight."

And so, like a love-struck youth, he rambled on about the beauty of life in this world, while at the same time he was quietly pulling a revolver from his back pocket; he shot the girl in the back of the head. Then, roaring with laughter, he shoved the girl, who was lying there in agony, into the pit.

Weiss was advancing his career. He was promoted from a simple sergeant major to a Sturmbannführer. He now wore silver bars on his shoulders and on his chest the Order of the Sword and Swastika.

He regarded all of these things as marks of distinction. He personally took part in all the executions and killed thousands of people with his own hands.

Weiss was not prejudiced with regard to nationalities. When it came to killing, he did not make any distinctions among people. However, he did not have enough Gypsies in his collection. So he arranged to have them rounded up in the forest and brought to him at Ponary along with their horse-drawn carts. He took five hundred Polish priests and monks from the Benedictine monastery, led them to the Lukishki Prison, and ordered them to undress. After taking away their clothes, he made them put on outfits with a yellow badge on the chest; the new clothes had just been taken from murdered Jews. Then Weiss hauled them off to Ponary and shot them as Jews. A Jew named Brenaizen, who at the time was in the prison, told me about this.

To Wiess's "credit," it should also be noted that he was the one who set up the German brothel at No. 9 Suboch Street, where he put a sign on the door that read "Entrance Forbidden to Civilians."

Weiss came by the "goods" for his establishment in a very simple manner: he and his gang surrounded the Zeleny Luch café one night and took away all the girls and women, whether they were accompanied by men or not. Someone named Leskauskas, a man with a wife and five children, was appointed director of the "house."

The "house" was exclusively for the use of the Gestapo and the SS. They paid with coupons that they received with their food ration cards. The girls were not allowed to set foot outside of the "house." They were awarded medals for good behavior. In order to keep them from running away, they had a special sign branded into their legs.

There came a time in Weiss's career when his star began to grow dim. Neugebauer reproached him for failing to liquidate the ghetto and for replacing Kittel.[17] Weiss moved to No. 10 Ross Street and there raised flowers in the Gestapo gardens.

The Fate of the Elderly

On 17 June 1942 Weiss took eighty-six elderly men and women out of the ghetto and hauled them off to Pospeshki, five kilometers from Vilna. He also ordered food and pots and pans to be brought to the old people. Nurses in white uniforms took care of them. Weiss doted on them so much that he brought them thirty-three kilograms of butter.

The old folks' home in Pospeshki became an enigma in the ghetto. No one could understand what it might mean. A day passed, then two, then three. Living in the nice wooded setting, with good food, the elderly men and women began to grow healthier. Among the residents of the "home" was ninety-year-old woman whose parents had baptized her at the age of nine. Weiss found her in a Polish poorhouse and in the twilight of her life reminded her of her Jewish origins.

The mystery was not solved until the seventh day. Weiss showed up with a group of foreign guests and correspondents to photograph the old men and women. After that they were taken to Ponary.

Degner

A German from Hamburg, Sergeant Major Hans Degner, was the foreman in charge of the airfield at Porubanek, where several hundred Jews worked. His sister Helen worked for the Gestapo, she personally shot people with a machine gun. Degner was the terror of the Jewish workers. He tormented and tortured the people for so long that they could not take it any more; they complained about him to Murer, who told him that he must stop because it was interfering with the work at the airfield. After that Degner found even worse ways of torturing his victims.

Several Jews were once late for work; to punish them and to set an example, Degner selected a row of twenty men and gave them a speech. "You Jews must be taught a lesson," he said, "for absence from work is an act of sabotage."

He picked ten men from the row of twenty and shot them. The ones he picked, however, depended on the Jews themselves. He commanded them to run around the airfield for one kilometer. The ten who came in first, he said, would be allowed to live; the rest would be shot.

Sitting on his bicycle, Degner shouted, "Run!" And twenty men forced themselves to break into a run. Degner rode alongside them as if he were judging their athletic abilities.

The miserable men ran with every ounce of their strength. Among them were adolescent youths and old men in their fifties. One of them fell down: he was having a heart attack. A second one collapsed at the finish line. But Degner had tricked them: he shot the ten who finished first and "had mercy" on the rest.

Grounds for the Arrest of Jews

Watching the Jews' every step, an agent who noticed a Jew without a yellow badge or a Jew buying food from a peasant would take his victim to the police station. If the "criminal" should be unable to buy his way out at the police station, he would be handed over to the Gestapo.

At Gestapo headquarters there was a similar procedure, according to which the man's guilt was monstrously exaggerated. One who was charged with buying a loaf of bread, for example, would be charged with purchasing weapons; or, as it happened to my wife, instead of being charged with going outside without having her yellow badge properly sewn on, she was accused of distributing illegal literature. By then it was very difficult to slip out of the scoundrels' clutches. Sturmbannführer Maier[18] would interrogate the victim, and then he would send the protocol of the interrogation to the Gestapo chief, Obersturmführer Neugebauer. Then Neugebauer would make a note in red pencil: B. B., meaning *Besondere Behandlung*, or "special treatment," that is, death.

Weiss's Inoculations against Typhus

It was the Passover season. Weiss arrived at the concentration camp at Kailis[19] and announced that an epidemic had broken out in the city. The following day, he said, mothers should dress their children more warmly than usual and take them to the clinic, where they would receive inoculations.

Suspecting nothing on that bright spring day, the women cleaned up their children, got them dressed, and combed their hair; then they took them to the clinic. They waited outside the fence surrounding the camp.

Meanwhile the director of the clinic, Doctor Schultz, telephoned Weiss to inform him that the children had arrived.

Within five minutes a Black Raven arrived. Weiss went into the clinic, seized the children and began throwing them into the vehicle. The mothers could see what was happening. Screaming and sobbing, they lunged forward to save their children, but Weiss ordered his men to shoot them. Some of them still managed to get to the truck. They struggled to get inside; Weiss "took pity" on them and let them accompany their children to their deaths.

The truck pulled away, and Weiss stayed behind. According to the list that he held in his had, he was still sixty children short. So he went off to the camp to get another group.

The Story of Fruma-Riva Burshtein of Novogrudok

When I heard that all the children were to be sent to the clinic, I knew that something was amiss. After all, Kailis had its own doctor and field hospital; why should the children be taken to the German hospital? I decided to wait and see what was going to happen, even though Richter had announced that anyone who did not comply with the order would be severely punished.

As soon as the screams could be heard coming from the hospital, I realized that the monsters had plotted something horrible. I took my three grandchildren and hid them in a malina. Then I ran out to the courtyard. Richter and his henchman Weiss were poking around the courtyard with their list in hand and shouting that they did not have enough children. If the children were not turned over this very minute, they would send in a unit of storm troopers to shoot down everyone in the camp. No one, however, gave up her children. Then Weiss blew his whistle; a mass of Germans who had been awaiting his signal poured into the camp. They went into all the buildings and drove the adults out into the courtyard while they went on searching.

I stood there and thought that a miracle might suddenly happen, and they would not find my children. But at that very moment I could hear the little ones crying. The monsters brought them out and placed them to one side. They had herded the entire population of the camp into the courtyard to divide us into two groups: on one side stood children and old people, and on the other the young healthy ones. As I am no longer a young woman, they put me with the elderly.

I waited for a minute and then grabbed my youngest grandson (it was impossible to save the others); we headed for the crowd of young people, who had not been marked for murder. But Richter stopped me and asked: "Where do you think you're going?" I told him I had just gone over to give a little boy something to eat and that now I was returning to my group.

The Jews who were allowed to remain among the living shielded me. My two-year-old grandson did not make a sound the whole time. Suddenly a truck pulled up, and the Germans began throwing the children and the old people into it. I saw them throw my two other grandsons into the back of the truck. They cried out, "Grandma, we're afraid!" But there was nothing I could do for them. I was still worried about the one I held in my arms. Richter—or "Golosheika," as we called him—recalled that I had gone over to give some food to a little boy, and he was looking for me.

Four times a day they came to look for our children. I hid my little one in a basket in the lavatory. He spent ten days there. Then we slipped out of the camp and hid in the city with a friend of mine.

Golda Krizhevskaya (As Told by Her Father Avraam Krizhevsky)

When the Gestapo first burst into the Kailis concentration camp and started gathering up the children, they did not shoot my Golda. She was tall enough to pass as an adult, and so she remained in the camp. But Golda did not want to be separated from the children. She would sing to them and secretly put on shows for them in the attics.... She would say:

"I'll never leave the children, even if we have to die together."

When they were dragging the children out of the cellars and the malinas, tearing them from the arms of their sobbing parents, and throwing them into the trucks, Golda did not want to hide. No matter how we tried to hold her back and hide her, she refused. Finally Weiss noticed her and shouted:

"Hey, you, get over here!"

And so they took here to the train station with an entire class of schoolchildren. The Polish engineer who had been with the children to the very end of the line later showed up at Kailis and asked if anyone knew Golda Krizhevskaya. He said:

"The children were screaming and crying on the train. But Golda calmed then down and comforted them. She assured them that the Germans would pay dearly for everything and that the day of liberation was near.

"The sound of folk songs and melodies from the revolution could be beard coming from the transport almost the entire way. Golda was leading the singing."

The Extermination of the Children in the HKP[20] (As Told by Strolik Zelikman)

On 27 March 1944 at about half past six in the morning, Sergeant Major Richter drove into the camp courtyard and examined all the gates. Then he left, but soon he was back; he had soldiers with him, and he positioned them in various spots. I was in the bathroom lighting the heater. When I heard them say that the camp was surrounded, my heart came to a stop. I ran out of the bathroom. Just then a truck carrying thirty to forty policemen in dark blue uniforms drove up.

I went to the building where my mother was staying and found her crying. We were convinced that the camp would be liquidated; in our souls we felt we were staring death in the face. We put on as much clothing as possible and agreed to seize the slightest opportunity to escape. If they should put us on a train, we would jump off. Meanwhile policemen and Germans flooded into the rooms. They ordered the women and children to assemble in the tailors' workshop. Suddenly the rumor spread that this time they were going to take "only" children and old people.

What was I to do? How could I save my mother? I took her into the bathroom, laid her down in a corner, and covered her with a blanket. I was not thinking about what would happen to me this time: first of all, I was a worker, and secondly, I was no longer a child.

I came out of the bathroom and looked into the shelter. I noticed that the ladder leading into the attic had disappeared. I asked, "Who's there?" Pilka Rudenskaya answered:

"It's us. Come hide!"

I do not know why, but for some reason I decided not to go into the attic. I went over to the locksmith shop (according to the work list, I was a locksmith). The window in the shop looked out onto the square.

Old women and children were being led away. They were all carrying bundles. Their heads were bare. The SS and the police were lined up across from them. People had gathered around the window of the locksmith shop; they were holding their heads in their hands and pacing around the shop. I saw them taking Yabrova away. Her son was standing at the window; he started beating his head against the wall. One hour went by, then two. After searching one building, the police proceeded to another. Weiss was walking around in the workshop to see whether there were any children hidden there.

Now he was in the carpenter shop next door to us. We could hear a child's cries coming from there. Weiss had found a little boy and was dragging him out by his arms. He turned the boy over to his assistant as he entered our workshop. I stood there as though paralyzed; I did not know what to do. There he was: Weiss, holding a large ax in his hand. For the first time I beheld his hideous face, with those eyeglasses resting on his nose. He ordered all of us to go into the next room; he seized several at the door and hurled them into the yard. It was my turn. I stretched on my tiptoes with all my strength in order to look taller, but you cannot fool Weiss: he pointed me toward the door, and the SS threw me into the yard. I tried to run, but they blocked my way; I turned to go in another direction, but they caught me. And so I wound up at the fence with a crowd of children. "It's over," I thought to myself, "there is no breaking free from their clutches." And yet I felt lucky: the SS guard turned away for a moment, and I bolted once more for the gates, but again without success: someone grabbed me and knocked me to the ground with his gun. (Later I found out it was Lukoshyus, one of the leaders of the Ipatinga.) I lay there half-dazed. But the villain was not satisfied; he dragged me by the arm over to the barracks, all the while laughing at me.

They had brought a table into the barracks; Weiss was seated at it. The sorting process began: children were sent into the barracks, and the women were released. If a woman should follow her child, the child was taken away from her by force. My turn came, and he pointed me toward the barracks. Again I tried to run away, but an SS man grabbed me. In the barracks I curled up in a corner. I tried to think of a way to escape. Where could I go to hide? Suddenly I noticed a loose board in the ceiling. Without losing a second, I slipped through the opening and into the attic. Others crawled in behind me. Soon the attic was full. I could hear the sound of motors: the Black Ravens had arrived.

It was all over by evening. I crawled out of the attic and went to my mother; I was over-joyed to see her. She had lain there in the bathroom the whole time. Schirmmeister Drisher, who was conducting the search, did not find her.

One that day 150 children were taken from the camp (among them were two who belonged to the actor Bergolsky). Mrs. Bass refused to turn over her little boy. No matter how severely Weiss beat her, she would not give up her child. A Black Raven finally swallowed her up along with her little boy.

Weiss shot another woman on the spot for calling him a child murderer; her name was Zhukovskaya.

Shmulik Kotlyar (As Told by Zelik Levin)

One day Weiss came into the ghetto to select men for resettlement in Estonia. Shmulik Kotlyar was going from house to house looking for his father. But instead of finding his father, he ran into Weiss.

"You're going to Estonia, too!" Weiss shouted.

"But Mr. Weiss," Shmulik pleaded, "I'm only ten years old!"

"Ten years old?" Weiss repeated, looking the boy up and down. Suddenly another Jew caught his attention. Shmulik seized the moment and slipped away.

Six months later, when the slaughter of the children and other "elements incapable of work" began, Weiss once again ran into the little boy. Shmulik and his friend Marek Levin were looking for a place to hide.

Weiss smiled:

"Ah, there you are! Now you will come with me! Your friend too!" And he grabbed Marek.

Shmulik started begging him:

"Mr. Weiss, I'm fifteen years old!"

Weiss burst out laughing:

"So, you've aged five years in a few months? No, it'll do you no good."

And he led the boy away to the black van.

Shmulik knew he had nothing to lose. He jumped off the van, grabbed Weiss around the neck and started kicking him in the stomach. Marek did the same.

For a moment Weiss fell into a state of utter confusion. But, with the help of Gestapo men who arrived on the scene, he regained his senses and beat the boys off of himself. As a punishment for their resistance, he did not throw them into the truck but strangled both of them on the spot with his own hands.

Leibl Finkelshtein (As Told by Basya Finkelshtein)

As soon and the women and children were ordered into the courtyard, Leibl said to me:
"We cannot just hide ourselves—we have to save others too."

He led his little brother and me out to a woodshed, hid us behind a pile of wood, and then disappeared.

I anxiously waited for him to come back, but he did not show up. By now I assumed that they caught my dear Leibl. It turned out, however, that something else had happened.

In the courtyard he picked up the ax that Weiss used to chase after the children. Then he gathered together a couple of dozen children; one of the adults joined him, and Leibl led them all to an attic. He tried to break through the roof with the ax so that he could crawl out, but then he noticed that there were two huge vats in the attic; they were water vats to pump water to the bathroom, and one of them was empty. Leibl immediately decided that he could find no better shelter. But how could he climb into a vat that was three meters deep? Leibl quickly crawled down from the attic to look for a ladder; he found one and returned to the attic. With the help of the adults, he moved all the children to the bottom of the vat; he lowered the ladder in after them, so no one would notice it.

Someone informed Weiss that some children had slipped into the attic. He immediately burst into the attic to look for them, but he found nothing. Just to be thorough, Weiss tapped against the side of the vat with his cane and said:

"Come on out, children! I have some candy for you."

But even the two-year-old babes did not make a sound.

The Fate of the Children Who Were Taken Away

Railroad engineer Yuzef Rintsevich, who drove the trainload of children, later related:

"Two hundred children from Kailis and the HKP were taken to the German hospital in Krakow.

"There the children were divided into two groups. One group was used for drawing blood for wounded German soldiers; the other had the skin removed from their faces by German specialists for cosmetic surgery on soldiers who had been wounded and burned."

Clothing

The clothing from the murder victims was gathered into piles in front of Gestapo head-quarters, where Jews from the ghetto had to sort through it. Maier, a German from Vienna, supervised the work. Shoes, coats, and even change left in their pockets were separated out.

Any identifying marks were removed from the clothing, so that in Germany, where these goods were to be sent, no one would guess where the clothing had come from. Maier enjoined the workers to save for him the many varieties of a certain type of badge: he collected them.

The badges came in various forms. There was the white square with a yellow circle and the letter *J* (*Jude*) in the middle, the dark blue band with the white six-pointed star, the yellow star and the black circle and the word *Jude* worn by Czech Jews, yellow patches shaped like the

Star of David, red square-shaped badges, and so on. Then there were tags with numbers on them that people in Vilna wore around their necks instead of badges. Different kinds and colors of documents and certificates were gathered together and handed over to Maier, who was a devout Catholic, so that future generations would have something by which to remember the old Europe.

The Gestapo agents often fought over the dresses and tore them, even though every one of those thieves had already managed to plunder the Jews of all their goods. Weiss, the chief plunderer, had a special assistant whose assignment was to go through the pockets of the people who had been shot. Only then was the clothing sent on to the Gestapo.

Kittel

Kittel was an actor. He graduated from the theater school in Berlin and from the plundering school in Frankfurt. On Sundays he played songs on his saxophone at the Vilna radio station. Kittel was not only the youngest of his colleagues; he was the most zealous. Neugebauer entrusted the liquidation of the Vilna Ghetto to Kittel, not to Weiss. Weiss was good whenever he met with no opposition. Knowing that there was a partisan organization in the ghetto, Neugebauer turned to Kittel, whose reputation extended from Riga to Lodz to Warsaw.

At first glance, you would never guess that Kittel was an executioner. Constantly smiling with his dazzling white teeth, he was perfumed, elegant, polite, and refined.

Here is an example of his style. He and Weiss once went to the Jewish labor camp at Bezdany. He summoned a Jewish barber and asked him for a shave. When the barber finished the job, Kittel offered him a cigarette and politely asked:

"Need a light?"

"Yes," the barber replied.

"Then have one!" Kittel cried, and with a shot of his revolver the barber fell to the floor.

The shot also served as a signal for Weiss and his troops to begin their massacre.

When the destruction of the Vilna Ghetto was underway, Kittel ordered a piano to be brought out into the yard, and he sat down to play. The hunters had surrounded a malina and were bringing out a Jewish boy. When he saw Kittel sitting at the piano, the boy threw himself to his feet and begged for mercy. Kittel pulled out his revolver, and, as he continued playing with his left had, he shot the boy with his right.

After the liquidation of the ghetto, only three concentration camps containing three thousand Jewish "specialists" remained in the city. As Kittel was walking with a young woman one day, he spotted an elderly man and woman and a little boy on the other side of the street. Suspecting that they were Jews, Kittel stopped them and had them sent to the concentration camp at Suboch, where he determined that their name was Zalkind and that up till now they had been hiding in a malina. He ordered a gallows to be erected in the middle of the yard and summoned sixty SS men from the Gestapo. When everything was ready and the yard was full of SS surrounding the doomed Zalkinds—husband, wife, and child—Kittel said:

"For having violated my order and hiding in the city, you will now be hanged in front of everyone."

Kittel went over to the gallows to be sure that the rope was strong; then he began the execution process. The child was the first to be hanged. Then the mother. When the noose was tightened around the father's neck, the rope broke.

Kittel ordered a new noose to be made. But as soon as Zalkind was hanging from it, the rope broke again.

Kittel was simply amused by it all.

"If the rope should break a hundred times, I'll hang you a hundred times," he said. And he ordered the hangman to prepare another rope.

Once it was all over with Zalkind, Kittel lined up the Jews, counted off fifty, and announced:

"Let this be a lesson and a warning to all who are contemplating escape. If one more Jew should be found in the city, a hundred will pay."

The fifty Jews counted off were then loaded into a Black Raven. According to the Jewish poet Khaim Semyatitsky, the author of *Outstretched Arms* and *Drops of Dew*, there were forty-nine.

The Germans posted an announcement at the gates of the ghetto:

"Beware. Jewish Quarter. Danger of Plague. Entrance Forbidden to Non-Jews."

It is impossible to count all the decrees and orders that were hanging over the heads of the residents of the ghetto. I shall present only a small sample of this legislation and let a normal person try to sort through it.

The Jews were forbidden to look out any window facing the area outside the ghetto. These windows were to be hermetically sealed with putty or glue.

Jews were forbidden to speak German.

Jews were forbidden to discuss politics.

Any Jew engaging in conversation or other dealings with a non-Jew would be shot.

Jews were forbidden to wear a moustache or beard.

It was forbidden to eat fat.

Jewish women were forbidden to color their hair or lips.

It was forbidden to pray.

It was forbidden to study.

Beginning at the age of six, all Jews had to wear a yellow star both in the ghetto and outside of it. The star had to be carefully sewn on the left side of the chest. Jews had to remove their hats for any German they happened to see in the ghetto.

It was forbidden to bring flowers into the ghetto.

Women were forbidden to give birth. Those who had babies would lose their lives along with the infants.

When the Gestapo officially informed hospital director Doctor Sedlis that Berlin had issued an order forbidding Jewish women to give birth, a shock wave went through the ghetto. What would happen to those who were pregnant, and what would be done with the newborns? And yet the people in the ghetto tried to avert this cannibalistic order in every way they could. They hid women and their infants in a secluded place, where the mothers could nurse the little ones. Once the babies had grown a little, they were listed in old ghetto registers.

Jewish women retained their right to motherhood. A child was the very personification of life, of the future, of the immortality of the people.

Mirra Bernshtein, a well-known educator in Vilna, did not miss a single day with her pupils.

The school that she had operated for many years was moved into the ruins of a house of prayer that had been destroyed. In the beginning she had a hundred and thirty students. They were divided into groups according to their age and developmental stage. While one group studied, the other cooked food and mended clothes. The pupils were very attached to their teachers and viewed them as men and women who had taken the place of their murdered parents. Every morning before classes began Mirra would count her students, and every day the number gradually grew smaller. But they continued to study as long as they were alive.

In October 1941 Mirra invited me to the school for a show. I did not recognize what I had seen only as a half-destroyed building. Plants were hanging from the walls. The windows were lined with flowers in flowerpots. Everywhere there were posters with quotations from Jewish classics.

By then there were only forty children left in the school. They were dressed in their holiday outfits. They all had flowers painted on their chests.

In the middle of the show a noise was heard outside. The performance continued; only when a bullet broke a windowpane did Mirra go outside. The street and courtyard were full of Germans. They were seizing people and dragging them into trucks that were parked at the gates.

Mirra returned, went to the stage, and said:

"Children, the monsters who want to slaughter us are now in the ghetto. Do not cry out or start running around. Calmly and quietly crawl underneath the stage. The littlest ones will be taken care of first, and then the older ones."

Mirra spent the entire night watching over the children. She had decided that if the Germans should break into the school, then she would offer herself up as a sacrifice for the sake of the children. Perhaps the Germans would think that there was no one left there and leave.

This time they were all around the building. They managed to round up their quota, however, so they left the ghetto.

I used to think that someone who was sentenced to death would give no thought to artistic creation. Life convinced me otherwise. I saw for myself that humanity would never abandon the spirit of building and creating.

Two days after my mother was murdered a young stage director named Viskind came to call on me and comfort me. He invited me to come and meet some Jewish actors. They were planning to set up a theater.

I looked at him in utter surprise:

"A theater? In the ghetto?"

"Yes," Viskind repeated. "We must do our part to resist the enemy, using this as a weapon. We must not give up for an instant. We shall create our theater; we shall inspire the ghetto to rejoice."

I agreed to serve as artistic director for the proposed theater.

What words must we use to approach our audience so as not to profane or defile the mourning of an entire people? What power could we use to captivate the ghetto resident and awaken in him a consciousness of his people's heroic history so as to help him gather the strength to fight in the name of life, in the name of the future?

When the Gestapo terror began, many of the musicians of Vilna buried their instruments in the ground.

Later, when the Jewish population had been driven into the ghetto, they were able to make their way through the sewers and into the city; they dug up the instruments they had hidden and brought them back into the ghetto.

The sounds of a symphony orchestra conducted by Volf Durmashkin began to be heard in the ghetto.

Some musicians were among those subjected to forced labor in the city. From there they brought into the ghetto a piano that they had found in an empty Jewish apartment. It was dismantled, and each musician smuggled in a piece of it. In the ghetto there were specialists who were able to put the piano together again.

There were seventeen pieces in the orchestra for its first performance (which took place on 15 March 1942); it was truly a festive occasion. They played the *Causien Sketches* by Ippolitov-Ivanov, *Jewish Potpourri* by Max Geiger, and a portion of Franz Schubert's *Unfinished Symphony*.

For the inhabitants of the ghetto, the music of the symphony orchestra was like mountain air for people suffering from lung disease. They longed to take up the struggle for such beauty.

There were two choirs in the ghetto. They also gave a series of concerts, at which Jewish songs stifled by the Germans loudly resounded.

On 17 February 1942 a group of artists and authors was created in the ghetto. It had more than a hundred people it in—writers, musicians, performing artists, painters. It was chaired by Zelig Kalmanovich.[21] The entire aim of the organization was to free the artistic elements in the ghetto from the pervasive atmosphere of oppression. Kalmanovich spoke of the swift and certain victory of the Red Army, which would bring freedom to the Jewish people. It was necessary to go on working in the name of that liberation and to strengthen the people's spirit.

The leaders of the group gathered the works of their murdered comrades. They undertook the creation of a chronicle of the works of all the writers, artists, musicians, and scholars whom the Germans had murdered; they also compiled an album of artistic works from the ghetto.

After hearing the news of Stefan Zweig's[22] suicide on our underground radio receiver, we organized an evening event in his memory. The musicians played a march by Chopin, and the actors performed scenes from Zweig's play *Jeremiah*.

Evenings devoted to individual writers in the ghetto were also organized; the discussions following these productions often continued late into the night. In addition to these events, the group organized several gatherings in the theater; these events were dedicated to the memory of our great writers, including Mendele Mokher Seforim,[23] Peretz,[24] Sholom Aleichem,[25] and Bialik.[26]

The library of the Society for the Advancement of the Enlightenment stood on Strashun Street long before the war. When the Jews were forced into the ghetto, they discovered that the library had been destroyed: hundreds of books lay scattered in the street and courtyard.

Herman Kruk,[27] a librarian who had been evacuated from Warsaw, diligently undertook the task of rebuilding the library. On 10 September 1941 the library was once again lending books.

People who in normal times would rarely pick up a book now became avid patrons of the library. A book came to be one's friend and teacher in that sad and sorrowful life that befell everyone.

In underground shelters, by the glimmer of a wretched candle stub or by a scant beam of light that penetrated through some crack, the people of the ghetto read books.

On 1 October 1941 three thousand people were taken out of the Vilna Ghetto to be slaughtered. On 2 October the library lent out ninety books. On 3 and 4 October a massacre took place in the second ghetto. On 5 October the library lent out 421 books. By November 1941 the population of the ghetto had been reduced by 40 percent, but the library's circulation was up by a third. According to information provided by the library, literary classics and children's books were in the greatest demand.

By November 1942, when the ghetto had been in existence for hardly more than a year, the number of books circulated by the library reached 100,000. The library arranged an evening of celebration in honor of the occasion and awarded books as prizes for the first and last borrowers.[28]

The Germans systematically slaughtered the residents of the ghetto. Among the victims of this barbaric fascist terror was Vilna's entire intelligentsia. Of the three hundred people who were culturally active (educators, writers, musicians, scholars, artists) almost no one survived. Of the several thousand children who attended the ghetto schools, only two or three dozen survived. Of all the members of the literary group, only two survived. Of the musicians and the jurists, no one survived.

In Alfred Rosenberg's Office

The people in Rosenberg's office in Vilna (the Einsatzstab Reichsleiter Rosenberg) made their own contribution to the Gestapo's activities. Their assignment was to seek out and destroy everything of any Jewish cultural value. The Germans were to wipe from the face of the earth five centuries of Jewish culture in Vilna.

In January 1942 Doctor Poll, Director of the Frankfurt Museum for the Study of Peoples of the East, arrived in Vilna. A collaborator on the malicious newspaper *Der Stürmer*, he brought with him an entourage of "scholars" for his special assignment; among them were Doctor Miller and Doctor Wolff (both from Berlin). Sporket and a man named Gimpel joined him later.

In order to do their "scientific" work, the fascists needed twenty people from the ghetto to gather up everything of Jewish cultural value in the city. This group of twenty was to sort through the items, packed them, and send them to Germany.

Doctor Miller demanded that the twenty include five people well versed in Yiddish and Hebrew who were also able to examine ancient texts and manuscripts. I tried to get into that group of five. I had but one aim: to save everything that could possibly be saved. I knew very well what this German "concern" for culture meant from the way they treated people. Not only that, when I was in the ghetto I had heard that in the city they were using library books as fuel for heating their stoves.

I set out for Rosenberg's office on Zigmund Street. The first assignment that the head of the office, Doctor Miller, gave me was to burn the wealth of the medical library at the University Hospital.

Doctor Poll ordered us to group all the Jewish books into a special "ghetto." He ordered the forty thousand volumes from the world-renowned Strashun Jewish Library to be dragged out to Universitetskaya Street, along with all the books from hundreds of synagogues.

Out of more than 100,000 books, Poll sent only about twenty thousand in eighty-four crates to Germany. The rest of them, including priceless and irreplaceable editions, he sold to the New Vilna Paper Mill as waste paper for nineteen marks per ton.

Manuscripts, engravings, and paintings met the same fate.

The Germans transformed the building of the YIVO Institute into a barracks.[29] They tossed all the archives, documents, and collections into the cellar as rubbish. Doctor Gotthart, a consultant to Himmler, quickly subjected the institute to a search for Jewish gold. Seeing that there was a fireproof cabinet in the cellar, he sent for a locksmith to open it. When they broke through the door of the cabinet, the doctor was disappointed to find only some manuscripts by Sholom Aleichem and Peretz looking him in the face, as if they were mocking him... . Enraged, he threw them to the floor and trampled them with his feet.

The YIVO Institute had collected books, manuscripts, painting, and sculptures from all the Jewish museums, libraries, and private homes. When the works of M. Antokolsky[30] were brought there from the Ansky Museum, Doctor Poll smashed a large number of the sculptures on the floor. Lead plates of the complete text of the Talmud—which took the Romm family of printers more than twenty years to create, using old typographic techniques—were sold as scrape metal by the order of Doctor Poll for thirty-nine marks per ton. He sent six crates of ancient manuscripts and rare editions to Berlin. At the train station, however, his associate Sporket, a former leather dealer, dumped this cargo from the crates and replaced it with pigskin, which he sold on the black market in Germany.

A short time later Sporket was appointed manager of Rosenberg's office. He turned over five hundred Torah scrolls to the local tannery to be used for shoe soles. He ordered the ancient bindings of parchment from Venice and Amsterdam editions to be torn to pieces. By his order, marble memorials and gravestones from the Zarechensky Cemetery were sent to Germany to be used for street pavement.

Rosenberg's office hunted down the printed Jewish word with the same zeal and relentlessness that the Gestapo exhibited when tracking down every last hidden Jew. The Rector of the Vilna University told me that after Rosenberg's office had taken from the library all the books either written in Hebrew or written by Jews, the Gestapo's bloodhounds came and searched every corner—even tore up the floor—see whether some Jewish books might still be hidden there.

Just as the Gestapo slaughtered thousands of people of other nationalities in their effort to exterminate all the Jews, Rosenberg's office was not satisfied with the destruction of Jewish libraries and museums. They ravaged and destroyed other national and cultural institutions, such as the Polish Museum of the Association of Science Lovers, the famous Polish publishing house Yuzef Zavadsky, the Tomasz Zan Library in Poland, the Library of the Evangelical Church, and others.

During the year and a half that Rosenberg's office was doing its work, our group managed to save many things of cultural value; we hid them inside of walls and buried them in basements and cellars in the firm conviction that soon the day would come when free men and women would return them to the light for the sake of the people and all humanity.

We hid the most valuable books and manuscripts under our clothing and brought them into the ghetto. Somehow I got Sporket's permission to take a little waste paper with me into the ghetto for lighting stoves. Sporket granted my request and wrote a note so that the gendarmes at the gate would not take the package of paper away from me.

This package of "waste paper" contained letters from Tolstoy to the philosopher Vladimir Solovev (I found them in the snow outside the Strashun Library); manuscripts by Sholom Aleichem; letters written by Gorky, Romain Rolland, and Bialik; editions from the fifteenth and sixteenth centuries; a painting by Repin; the diary of Doctor Herzl; the world's only manuscript written by the Vilna Gaon; drawings by Marc Chagall; and dozens of other priceless works.[31]

With permission from Sporket, we were able to take out "waste paper" every day. Of course, we managed to remove from the building only a small portion of the wealth it contained. We built a cement malina underneath the building and hid there about five thousand of the most valuable books written in various languages.

In May of 1943 a delivery from the Smolensk Museum arrived in Vilna; it consisted of several boxes of manuscripts and paintings. My comrades and I managed to take three of the boxes directly from the train station to the city archives and hide them under a bundle of documents. These boxes, which I later recovered, contained a diary kept by one of the servants to Peter I,[32] chronicles of the Church dating from the fifteenth and sixteenth centuries, paintings by Repin and Levitan,[33] and many other valuables from the museum. I later removed some of these treasures from the archives and buried them in the ghetto.

In one of the museums of Vilna, whose holdings we transferred to Rosenberg's office, we came upon documents signed by the famous Polish freedom fighter Tadeusz Kosciuszko.[34] That was in the spring of 1943, at the height of the debauchery of fascist terror. I gave the document to a Polish woman who was hiding twenty Jews. She fell to her knees and kissed the precious relic so dear to her Polish heart. The next day the woman sought me out and told me that when she showed Kosciuszko's signature to the members of the underground organization she belonged to, it was as if lightning had struck a keg of gunpowder. Her comrades asked her to tell me that not only they but their children and grandchildren would remember this precious gift and would be forever grateful in their hearts.

Among those who helped to save our cultural wealth from the Hitlerites were Z. Kalmanovich, R. Krinski, the docent of the University of Vilna Mariya Abramovich, and the famous Lithuanian poet Kazys Boruta.[35]

I turned over the most valuable manuscripts written by the great Yiddish author Peretz to the Lithuanian journalist Shimaite[36] in May 1942. She often came to the German establishment where I worked and would leave with packages that I had prepared for her.

Among the ghetto archives that were preserved I found a letter she had sent to a teacher named Nina Gershtein the day after a performance that Shimaite had attended. Here is a fragment from the letter that clearly characterizes this wonderful human being:

"Dear Nina! Do not be offended that I address you by your first name, even though I am not a personal friend of yours. I was enchanted and inspired by the wonderful performance, especially the dramatic staging of the Jewish folk songs. One would have to belong to a people of great talent to create such works of art amidst the nightmare of the ghetto.

"Like the remarkable Jewish youth, I believe that in the end the wall will come down, and brotherhood will rule among all the peoples of the world."

Martyrs of the Ghetto

Tiktin

I taught literature to a group of teenagers, most of whom were from the junior high school. We put together an evening of literary readings in the ghetto.

Zalman Tiktin, a sixteen-year-old boy who had lost his parents in the first ghetto massacre, was caught up in the preparations for the evening. From the forced labor site at Burbishki, where he worked loading and unloading military supplies, he managed to bring a bouquet of flowers into the ghetto. He hid the flowers under his jacket, so that the gendarmes at the gate would not find them. The penalty for attempting to bring flowers into the ghetto was twenty lashes.

These were not ordinary flowers; they were taken from the graves of the two Gordon brothers, who had been fatally wounded by a bomb at the munitions depot where they had worked. The explosion destroyed the whole depot. Oberleutnant Wagner, the head of the depot, concluded that it was just an unfortunate accident. But Tiktin knew very well that it was no accident. One of the brothers who died had secretly told him that he was going to blow up the German depot, even if it should cost him his own life.

Tiktin belonged to the partisan organization. The youngest member of the group, he was a real devil when it came to obtaining weapons. But little did anyone know that this sixteen-year-old lad intended to blow up the Gestapo building. Zalman once told me about it.

He explained his plan to me in detail. A group of Jews was assigned to forced labor in the courtyard of the Gestapo building. It would not be difficult to get in with them. He had made all the arrangements with one of his friends who worked in the yard, and the two of them were going to blow up the building.

I advised Tiktin not to undertake anything on his own. He belonged to an organization and should submit to their group discipline; he should inform them of his plan. Tiktin told me that he had already asked their permission to blow up the building, but they turned him down and warned him that he should not take upon himself anything that would be a risk to his life. But he was aflame with youthful enthusiasm. I felt that the matter could not end well. I convinced him not to be too hasty. You have to be careful about obtaining grenades: you are putting the lives of twenty thousand people on the line.

The day after we spoke Tiktin set out for work as usual—to load and unload military supplies. They were waiting for a colonel who was supposed to come to inspect the warehouses. Wagner wanted to demonstrate to him his cleverness; he had spread the warehouses out on various sites. Several days after the colonel left, the Oberleutnant ordered the Jews to move all the military supplies back to the old warehouse at Burbishki. Wagner knew how to pull the wool over the administration's eyes; his one goal was to avoid getting sent to the front.

Toward evening, before he went home, Tiktin noticed that a train car had just pulled up along the tracks leading into the warehouse. If a train car had been hauled in here, it must mean that it was carrying combat goods. Tiktin slipped away from his group, and, without being noticed, he sneaked over to the train car. The car was closed with a lead seal. Tiktin bit through the seal with his teeth and broke into the car. He looked around: no grenades today. Just some blasting caps and bullet belts. Well, these would have to do. In any case, he did not want to leave the train car empty-handed. They could find a use for the blasting caps in the ghetto; they did not have enough for their own grenades. Loaded to the teeth, he got out of the train car; then he managed to jar the warehouse door loose, get across the ditch, and head for the edge of the woods. But at that point a sentry noticed him. The sentry opened fire and wounded Tiktin; a dozen armed guards pounced on the boy.

They threw Zalman into the prison. Meanwhile Wagner had informed the Gestapo that all the Jewish workers were being detained. Suddenly those who were under arrest looked over at the prison where Zalman was being held: there was an explosion, and Zalman himself jumped out and threw himself at the Germans. Having stunned them with his daring, he dove into the nearest bushes and from there rushed toward the railroad tracks that ran along the ravine. In the green light his white shirt was the perfect target for his pursuers. But Zalman ran in a zigzag motion and managed to get across the railway and go down into the ravine. There he was hit by several bullets and fell into the grass.

Kittel showed up. When he found out that Tiktin was still alive, Kittel had him taken to the prison hospital. Every day Kittel visited him; he brought him food and sweets and asked whom he was stealing grenades for. But the boy was not seduced by the gifts and did not answer any of Kittel's questions. He simply lay there, turned toward the wall, acting as though he heard nothing. But once, when Kittel was especially persistent, he answered:

"I stole them in order to get even with you. You murdered my parents."

Levitskaya

Who in Vilna has not heard of the singer Lyuba Levitskaya? Her radio concerts and performances were loved by listeners. She taught classes in voice at the Vilna Conservatory. She was invited to give concerts in Moscow.

I had not seen her in the ghetto for a while. She was hiding with some friends of hers—some non-Jewish musicians—on the outskirts of town. When the mass beatings began, she moved back into the ghetto.

In January 1942 we were preparing a concert. I invited Lyuba to perform with the Jewish folk singers.

There is no forgetting that concert.

Every word, every sound, invoked the images of those who had perished. No one took any thought of the fact that at any moment we could be surrounded and dragged off to the pit at Ponary. The concert was, of course, illegal, and was held without Murer's knowledge. Levitskaya gave a marvelous performance of folk songs overflowing with a hope and a faith that brought healing to all.

A year went by. Lyuba was supposed to sing the lead role in an opera performance that had been secretly organized. Lyuba was worried: how would her voice sound? It used to be that when she was nursing her throat, it was dangerous for her to go outside in damp weather. Now, living in a barracks, she was suffocating from the dust. During a massacre in the ghetto she lay hidden in a garbage pit. When the second pogrom hit the ghetto, she went into a cellar, where Schweinberger stomped on her with his boots and stabbed her with a dagger. That time she was saved by sheer accident. She spent a long time in the ghetto hospital after that, all the while spitting up blood...

When a music school opened in the ghetto, Lyuba began conducting classes in voice.

It was the eve of the show; Lyuba could not wait for the work day in the barracks to end... The show was a source of great joy for her, but today Lyuba had another reason to rejoice: a friend of hers from the city had brought her a bag of peas for her old mother.

With her yellow six-pointed star on her chest, Lyuba hurried down the street.

When she reached Rudnitskaya Street she caught Murer's attention as he was passing by in his car. He stopped the singer, examined the number on the piece of tin hanging around her neck, and checked to see whether the star was sewn on precisely according to the regulations. Then he searched her coat. He confiscated the bag of peas, ordered Lyuba to get into the car, and took her to the Lukishki Prison.

She spent a month in prison. Every day people were taken from her cell to their death. Lyuba knew that never again would she sing in the ghetto of her own free will. Her days, perhaps even her hours, were numbered. So now she sang in her cell, she sang for her sisters, who were doomed to death, so as to bring some relief to their tormented souls...

Weiss, who at the time was chief of the Sonderkommando, personally escorted her to Ponary. Weiss drove the truck. Next to him sat his lover, a thirty-year-old Gestapo woman from Hamburg named Helen Degner.

Once inside the barbed wire fence that surrounded the pits, Helen ordered Lyuba to strip naked. Lyuba did not obey her right away. Then Degner took out her dagger and threatened to gouge out her prisoner's eyes if she did not undress immediately... Lyuba took her clothes off and, naked, moved forward toward her grave. There, covered with lime, lay the bodies of those who had been shot. Weiss and Murer stood to the side peering through their monocles. Helen Degner, a former student at the University of Hamburg, smiled and cut down Lyuba with a long blast from her submachine gun.

A Mathematician

Young Zalkindson was a surgeon. He was reputed to be the best in his field, but more than anything else he loved mathematics.

He performed numerous complicated operations in the ghetto hospital. He operated on and cured the sick while the healthy were being slaughtered in the streets.

In the ghetto Zalkindson began a huge research project on astronomy. He refused to report for forced labor: better to die than to aid the murderers with his own hands. He also refused the few grams of bread and the horsemeat, and he never registered with the ghetto authorities. He slept during the day, and stayed up at night. During those hours when the ghetto was cooling off from the oppressive heat of the day's despair, Zalkindson would write.

At dawn he liked to play the violin: Zalkindson was a pretty good musician.

When the ghetto began to go into the throes of death, I started looking for a way to save the mathematician. A friend of mine who lived in the city, Yuliyan Yankovsky, took it upon himself to hide six Jews in a specially equipped shelter. The plan consisted of the following: Yankovsky had a friend who worked on the police force and who helped the partisans. He lived by himself. There was a bathroom in his apartment. They decided to take out the door to the bathroom, fill it in with a wall, plaster it over, and hide six Jews inside.

That night I went to see Zalkindson and introduced myself to him. After explaining to him the plan, I told him that he would be one of the six people that we wanted to hide in the shelter.

"Never in my life have I gone into hiding," he replied. "As long as I am engaged in my writing, death has no power over me. And when it is done, I shall have no more reason to live."

Zalkindson took a wadded up piece of paper from his vest pocket and said:

"Potassium cyanide."

After a moment of silence he added:

"If you are so concerned about me, then I ask you: deliver this work to my mathematics teacher, and let him keep the manuscript."

I took Zalkindson's thick notebooks filled with his writing, hid them away, and took them to Professor Rudnitsky.

A week later the professor turned up in the courtyard of the Jewish Scientific Institute, where I was working as a forced laborer. He called me over to him and said:

"The day you brought me Zalkindson's work was the happiest day of my life. I have examined his work, and its author will be valued for his merit."

The earth in the ghetto trembled. Death was a daily visitor. The youth fled into the forest. The old ones dug shelters for themselves in their cellars. But the walls of the buildings that concealed the living were broken down. On one occasion Kittel surrounded the ghetto with machine guns.

Young Zalkindson fell as one of his victims.

The United Partisan Organization of the Vilna Ghetto (UPO)[37]

The First Proclamation

"We shall not allow ourselves to be led as sheep to the slaughter!

"Jewish youth! Do not believe the liars! Of the eighty thousand Jews of Vilna only twenty thousand are still alive. Before our very eyes they have taken away our parents, our brothers, and our sisters. Where are the hundreds of people seized by the city police for work? Where are the women and children taken away on that terrible night of the first massacre? Where are the Jews who were led out of the synagogue on Yom Kippur?

"Those who have been taken out of the ghetto have never returned, because all roads that lead from the Gestapo end at Ponary, and Ponary means death.

"Ponary is not a camp. There everyone is shot. Hitler intends to slaughter all the Jews of Europe. We are among his first victims.

"We shall not allow ourselves to be led as sheep to the slaughter! True, we are weak, and we cannot count on any help from outside, but the only reply we can give to the enemy is resistance!

"Brothers! It is better to die as free fighters than to bow down and live at the mercy of the murderers. We shall resist to our dying breath!"

1 January 1942, Vilna Ghetto

Thus read the text of the first call to action.[38] It was like a bolt of lightning flashing in the darkness of the ghetto. It was read at a meeting of people being initiated into the organization, where a deposition by a teacher named T. Kats, a woman who only a short while before had been saved from the mass graves at Ponary, was also presented. Wounded by several bullets, she crawled out of the pit at night and, half-naked, slipped back into the city.

The bloodied teacher was known to all as a rational and just woman; she was brought here in order to reinforce in everyone a thirst for revenge and a will to fight.

From the very beginning the ghetto group was urged to take up armed resistance.

The first opportunity for active resistance came during the mass slaughter that took place on 21 December 1941. Twenty people were hidden in a cellar on Gospitalnaya Street. With their axes and bloodhounds the police discovered this malina and ordered everyone to come out of the cellar. The people refused to obey the order. Then Schweinberger and a band of policemen broke into the cellar. Two young men, Gaus and Goldshtein, rushed at the bandits.

After a struggle that lasted about an hour, all twenty of the people died a heroic death. The Germans paid for their deaths with several maimed and seriously wounded policemen.

The next day fliers were posted on the walls of the buildings in the ghetto:

"Eternal glory to Gaus and Goldshtein. Eternal glory to the fallen!"

On 21 January 1942 representatives of all the parties gathered in the attic of a building on Rudnitskaya Street. At that gathering the foundations were laid for a future ghetto partisan organization.

After discussing basic organizational matters, participants at the meeting selected a group of leaders to head up the struggle; the commanders were Isaak Vitenberg (code name "Leon"), Abba Kovner (code name "Uri"), and Iosif Glazman (code name "Abram").[39] Four other people were later included among the commanders.

The primary task of the United Partisan Organization (UPO) was the preparation for armed resistance in the ghetto, with the aim of defending the life and the dignity of the surviving Jewish population. They were to carry out acts of sabotage and subversion in the German workshops and institutions; they were also to establish contact with partisan groups operating in the forests.

They set about the task of preparing weapons and recruiting fighters. A UPO fighter could be any reliable young man or woman.

The leaders worked out the instructions for battle... . The organization was set up on purely military grounds. The basic fighting unit consisted of five people: four fighters and a group commander. Four groups of five made a division, which had its own commander; the entire organization was divided into two battalions.

The first group commanders were Edek Boraks[40] (who later organized a partisan group in Bialystok, where he fell in battle) and Isaak Matskevich (who perished while breaking out of the ghetto with a fighting unit). A. Kovner and I. Glazman commanded the two battalions.

In addition to these basic fighting units there were special groups of grenade launchers and machine gunners, as well as specialists in intelligence, subversive activities, and laying mines. The UPO's instructions outlined the order of assembly for all units in the event of a military emergency, as well as tactics for fighting with the Gestapo and for street fighting in the ghetto.

The password "Liza calls" was the signal for general action (Liza was the name of a resistance who died heroically in a skirmish with the Germans). Upon hearing this signal, each fighter was to report to a previously designated point, bringing along a portion of the unorganized population. Individual badges—red tin triangles—were made for the fighters, so that they could be recognized.

Weapons

In the winter of 1942 Soviet parachutists landed in the forests near Vilna. Vitenberg made contact with them. As a result, a communist partisan organization was formed in the ghetto; it became part of the general Lithuanian partisan movement. The first secretary of the communist organization in Vilna was Boris Shereshnevsky.

Boris Goldshtein was the first youth to obtain a revolver for the ghetto partisan organization.

That was at the end of January 1942. Goldshtein was sent to the German military depot in Burbishki for forced labor. He was assigned to a column of eighty people. Goldshtein and his comrades hauled military supplies and loaded train cars under the armed SS guard. At noon they were allowed a half-hour to rest. The workers tried to make use of that time: unnoticed by the guards, they would slip through the barbed wire fence and go buy food from the peasants in the countryside, so that they would have something to take back to the ghetto at night. Goldshtein was looking for something else: guns and ammunition. He used cunning; he went to work a couple of days in a row with his left hand bandaged with a rag, so that the gendarmes at the ghetto gate and the SS at Burbishki would get used to seeing it. On the third day Goldshtein slipped a revolver that he had stolen from the German military depot under the bandage on his "disabled" hand.

That evening, a notorious Gestapo specialist, whom the Jews nicknamed "the Master," conducted a search at the ghetto gate. The Master stepped up to Goldshtein and frisked him; he hardly touched the bandaged hand, when Goldshtein cried out in pain. They let Goldshtein through.

From that moment on a day did not go by that Goldshtein did not smuggle a weapon into the ghetto. Here he would come, limping along. His anxious comrades were waiting for him inside the ghetto, near the gate. Today the gate was guarded by storm troopers. They are very thorough with their searches. Goldshtein is ninth in line. Of the first group that passed by to the tune of whiplashes, half were arrested. Some had a potato, others a piece of bread. Women on whom they discovered some bit of food were stripped naked and whipped in front of everyone. Now only two people stood in front of Goldshtein. If a weapon should be found on him, hundreds of people would be punished. Goldshtein knew it. To his good fortune, they detained someone with a flour "compress." Goldshtein took advantage of the delay and quickly slipped inside the gate.

The UPO had half of a machine gun in their arsenal. The next day Goldshtein brought in the other half. Risking their lives at every moment, within a short time the members of the partisan group had obtained from the German warehouses five machine guns, fifty grenades, thirty revolvers, several rifles, and a good supply of ammunition.

Getting weapons past the gate, which was heavily guarded, was very dangerous both for the participants who were directly involved and for the entire ghetto. It was necessary to resort to various schemes for camouflaging the weapon being brought in. It would be smuggled in a box of utensils with a false bottom, in a coffin sent to the ghetto for someone who had died, and in other ways.

In May 1942 division commander Samuil Kaplinsky (a technician) and another UPO fighter changed into overalls worn by sewer workers; then they picked up some red barriers that were being used to block off the street for sewer repairs and pretended to take them to a repair shop. They set up the markers opposite the guarded gate to the ghetto, thus bringing street traffic to a halt. They lifted up the sewer cover and lowered two boxes into the manhole. That night several of our comrades infiltrated the sewer's night crew, made their way underground to the water hole, and hauled the weapons away in a wheelbarrow.

The grenades that they smuggled into the ghetto did not have blasting caps. Kaplinsky made excellent blasting caps in the ghetto, and in September 1943 the grenades were successfully used against the Germans.

Sometimes the gendarmes at the gate could be bribed. For ten thousand rubles they would allow some potatoes and salt into the ghetto for the starving population. Instead of salt, the Gordon brothers got a bag of gunpowder into the ghetto. In addition, eight hundred grenades were made from small lamps stuffed with explosive materials that were secretly brought into the ghetto.

I. Pilovsky's First Battalion also demonstrated courage and resourcefulness in obtaining weapons for battle. Sometimes revolvers he purchased from a well-known shoemaker on Lipuvka Street. With a weapon bound to his body, he was once getting ready to leave the shoemaker's apartment, when a Gestapo agent suddenly burst in to conduct a search. Pilovsky did not lose his head; he removed a windowpane and slipped out with the weapon.

Members of the partisan organization had to hide their activities not only from the outside world but also from the ghetto. Knowledge of their underground operations had to be kept from large numbers of people right up to the time when they went into action. The transfer of weapons was carried out only at night, when movement about the ghetto came to a halt.

The UPO's arsenal was scattered throughout the ghetto in underground apartments, cellars, and hollowed-out beams. Revolvers were hidden in buckets with false bottoms. Filled with water, these buckets stood out in the open in the "people's" cafeteria at 12 Strashun Street.

In the spacious cellars of the buildings at 3 Karmelitskaya Street, 31 Nemetskaya Street, and in the Library for the Promotion of the Enlightenment on Strashun Street preparations for battle and the training of the UPO fighters were conducted. The organization's instructors were people who had previously been trained and had completed their own military instruction.

Although he had never served in the army, I. Vitenberg became an excellent military specialist; he was an expert at all weapons systems and gave lectures to the commanders on ghetto fighting tactics.

Some non-Jewish partisans were part of the UPO.

A Polish woman named Irena Adamovich, who knew Yiddish very well, had obtained weapons for the Warsaw Ghetto over a period of several months. She helped us in every way she could. Our leaders assigned her to organize partisan groups in Kaunas and Siauliai.

Yazdya Dudets, who also belonged to a Polish democratic circle, spent an extended period of time in the ghetto preparing false Polish and Lithuanian documents for members of the UPO. He hid Jews in his apartment on the outskirts of town. Later, when our group was dispersed into the forest, Dudets' apartment became an underground contact point for the partisans.

A Russian comrade known by the code name "Vanya" lived in the ghetto for a long time and worked with the partisan organization. He was a member of the underground communist organization and later became a liaison to the partisan headquarters in the forest and the partisan committee in the city.

The sixteen-year-old Yanek lived in Vilna. He was born on Yatkovaya Street, and Yiddish was practically his native language. When the war broke out Yanek left the city and headed east to the Soviet home front. He was wounded near Minsk by a shell fragment. Two of his comrades were also wounded. They decided to return to Vilna, where all three of them ended up in the ghetto wearing the yellow six-pointed star.

Yanek was captured during one of the Germans' night raids and taken with hundreds of others to Ponary. He managed to escape along the way. He hid in the city for a whole month, but he never ceased worrying about his friends. Were they still alive? If they survived, then they were probably looking for him. So Yanek returned to the ghetto. Of all his friends he found only one left alive: Z. Tiktin. They found a place together and became active members of the partisan group.

One of the foremost tasks of the UPO was to pick up radio broadcasts from the Soviet Union. It was necessary to know what was happening in the homeland and to follow developments on the war front. To this end we set up a secret receiver at 3 Karmelitskaya Street. We recorded the political news and reprinted it in pamphlets, which we distributed among members of the organization and the general population.

The winter of 1942 passed, the winter of the great Soviet offensive. The news pamphlets were an inspiration to the partisans; the news strengthened their resolve and their faith in victory.

When we set up the radio receiver, we also tried to set up a transmitter to tell the world of the monstrous evils perpetrated by the German invaders.

The Struggle Has Begun

In the summer of 1942 the Germans began an offensive on the Eastern Front. A shipment of fascist tanks rolled along the Burbishki railway. An engineer named Isaak Ratner constructed a miniature chemical device that, when placed in a gasoline tank, would blow up the vehicle after a period of eight hours. Fourteen German tanks headed for the front met with such a surprise.

Goldshtein, who had brought the first machine gun into the ghetto, was now working at the military depot at Burbishki. He put 145 anti-aircraft weapons out of action and removed the locks from ninety machine guns bound for the front.

When the Germans ordered the Jews consigned to forced labor to blow up military goods unfit for use, the Jews would also slip brand new German weapons into the pit and blow them up as well.

In the spring of 1943 an inexperienced German reservist arrived at the depot. He knew very little about handling grenades. When the opportunity came engineer Ratner calmly said to the confused German: "Throw that grenade over there, or it will blow up in your hands." Ratner purposely pointed in the direction of the depot's camouflaged ammunition dump. A huge explosion followed; about a million and a half cartridges were destroyed.

T. Gelperin worked in the German military post office. After picking up the mail at the train station, he would burn and destroy thousands of letters and military packages on the way back. He contrived a way of diverting German food packages to the ghetto, where they were distributed among the hungry.

Seventeen-year-old Lev Distel, a member of the partisan group and a skilled mechanic, quickly figured out the anti-aircraft guns stored in the German depot. Between April and July 1942 he put forty-three anti-aircraft guns out of commission.

At the height of the German offensive summer 1942 in the summer of 1942, when dozens of transports were passing through the Vilna junction every day, Isaak Matskevich used forged documents identifying him as a Tartar to get into the train station as a railroad worker. He diligently misdirected the movements of military cargo and submitted a report to the partisan headquarters.

A German colonel simply could not understand why full tanks of gasoline were running dry so rapidly. He did not know that the Jewish partisans had nine of their comrades involved in this subversive activity.

At the Bezdana station forty kilometers from Vilna there was a concentration camp containing men and women from the Vilna Ghetto. They were all digging peat near the railroad. Three members of the partisan organization who were in the camp worked out a plan to destroy the railroad tracks and asked partisan headquarters for permission to carry out their plan. The organization sent Girsh Levin to help them, and on 20 February 1942 more than a hundred meters of track on the Vilna-Ignalin line were put out of commission.

One of the partisan members most active in the area of sabotage was Z. Goldberg, formerly a designer at the Vilna Jewish Technical School. He worked in a hangar at the Porubanek airfield, where he figured out ways to steal valuable parts and poke holes into the gasoline tanks of fifty German airplanes sent there for repairs.

Two large fires set at German establishments must be recorded in the annals of the UPO. At the Kailis fur factory workers who were members of the UPO joined with their Polish and Lithuanian comrades and in January 1942 and set fire to the right side of the building's roof; at the time the factory had sixty thousand sheepskin coats ready to be sent to the front. All the coats were destroyed in the fire; in addition, the other side of the building also caught fire, and factory equipment and machinery were seriously damaged.

At the Benzinuvka, where gasoline was stored, a worker named Fridman stepped into a guard booth while the guard was napping on duty. The guard woke up just as the flames were engulfing his small wooden hut. The flames spread to the gasoline depot, where three hundred barrels of combustible fuel blew up. Since the fire started in the guard booth, the Gestapo did suspect sabotage.

The UPO's massive agitation among Jews assigned to forced labor in German establishments led to widespread acts of sabotage.

Every inhabitant of the ghetto, whether part of the partisan organization or not, considered it a duty to do damage to the Germans wherever possible.

In addition to systematically obtaining weapons from German military depots, the organization would purchase them. A great deal of money was needed to do this. We took up the task of raising half a million rubles in a month's time.

The Fourth Partisan Division, commanded by Matskevich, undertook a very risky operation. Every day, the fighters penetrated the German military depot with the help of comrades working there; they took out bales of German overcoats, fur-lined raincoats, and underwear and turned it all over to a trusted peasant, who sold the goods. Thus we raised forty thousand rubles.

A typesetter named Isaak Kovalsky proposed an original plan to the partisan leaders. He would print false bread ration cards and sell them; the proceeds would go toward the money needed to purchase weapons. The proposal was approved, and a special group was given the assignment of exchanging the false cards for food. Thus bread and other food were sold in the ghetto; the partisan headquarters brought in about a hundred thousand rubles.

David Vidutsky stole a packet of money containing 35,000 rubles from a German officer and gave it to the partisan headquarters.

Funds were also raised from the ghetto population. When asked for a donation people sacrificed everything they had. Many gave up their valuables that were often all they had left to the memory of loved ones slaughtered by the Germans. The partisan Rotkin donated a gold watch that had belonged to his recently murdered wife, crying out, "Avenge the loss of the one dearest to me!" I myself gave the only possession of any value to me, left to me by my mother when she was slaughtered by the Hitlerites. It was her wedding ring; she gave it to me the day they executed her.

The fundraising proceeded with such energy that instead of raising five hundred thousand rubles, they raised a million.

Sabotage

Isaak Vitenberg, commander of the ghetto's partisan organization, invited me over to see him. We were supposed to discuss arrangements for helping a friend of mine, a Soviet officer, who had slipped into the ghetto and was looking for a way of making contact with the partisans.

It was already evening. When we finished our talk, Abba came into the room with an arms expert named Borukh.

"Listen, Borukh," the commander turned to him, "I know you to be a dedicated, steadfast man. I also know that you are good with weapons. All the playthings that you have repaired fire beautifully. Right now it is important for us to know just one thing: can you make a mine that will blow up a train? This is to be our first act of sabotage. We shall send our finest comrades. They are putting their lives on the line. A failure will cost us many victims, and afterward the railway will be so heavily guarded that it will be extremely difficult to try it a second time. I ask you again: are you certain that a mine can destroy a transport?"

"Yes, I am certain," Borukh answered.

Abba added: "If Borukh say so, then I am certain too. We must take subversive action as soon as possible. We have learned from intelligence sources that tomorrow night cargo transports will moving all night through Novo-Vileika. We cannot let this chance slip by."

Suddenly we heard screams outside. We threw open the window. Women were running up and down the alleys and screaming:

"Children, our children!"

We understood the incoherent howls that penetrated into our garret: the women were weeping for their sons. Every day, their boys were herded off to forced labor in Novo-Vileika. Today they did not return to the ghetto. Murer had detained them along the road as he was passing by in his car and ordered them to be searched. The Germans discovered a potato and a liter of milk. Murer ordered all of them to be taken to the prison, where they were condemned to death.

"So, we'll have to give some thought to Novo-Vileika," said Vitenberg, "but for now..."

"Now," Borukh interrupted him, "I ask you to allow me to take part in this sabotage. After all, I have made a mine and know very well how to handle it."

A messenger named Vitka Kempner entered the room; she was maintaining contact with the partisan organization in the city. She was a tall, well-built young woman with her hair cut short and freckles on her plump cheeks. She delivered Vitenberg a report on news obtained over the secret radio receivers in the ghetto and then said to the commander:

"I know what you are arguing about; I got the hint. I haven't closed my eyes all night. To make it brief: I am going to be involved this sabotage as sure as my name is Vitka."

The comrades burst out laughing. Vitenberg was serious:

"Very well, I agree. But who do you need to help you?"

Abba decided:

"Matskevich and Brauze."

It was a May night in 1942. A young man and woman crawled through a hole in the fence surrounding the Vilna Ghetto and entered the city. Without their yellow badges they took broad strides. The young man confidently took his companion by the hand; they spoke loudly, in German, so as to divert any suspicion from passersby.

They had to hurry. It was already 8:30, and it was permitted to be on the streets only until 9:00. They passed Polotskaya Street and headed toward the highway—that was the way they had to go.

Now they were walking on a footpath, so that cars passing by would not see them and stop. They had arranged to meet Brauze at 11:30 next to an old oak tree near the paper mill. Brauze had arrived at dawn with workers from the Vilna Ghetto; they were paving the road and hauling stones. Brauze had the mine in safekeeping. They moved silently. They went into the woods. Matskevich and the girl crawled toward the rails. Brauze stopped in case he might have to cover them. Matskevich dug under the rails with his bare hands. Into the small pit he placed some stones that Vitka had given him. That was how Borukh said to do it, so that the mine would not sink down into the earth when the train came. Having laid the mine, they covered it with sand and headed for Vileika. They waded across a stream and stopped on a hill under the branches of a willow tree.

It was quiet. There was a sound in the trees behind them, coming closer and closer.

"The train!"

Now the steam engine could be clearly seen emerging from the depths of the woods; behind it came a chain of rumbling train cars. Ten, twenty, thirty... . Even from here they could hear German songs. It seemed to Vitka that the steam engine had already rolled over the mine, and it did not go off. She closed her eyes to keep her doubts from her friends. Matskevich was cool and confident. His eyes were focused on a single point. He remembered precisely where the mine was buried. The steam engine had not yet reached it. But it was getting close. It would happen soon.

Railroad ties, people, and iron went flying into the air... .

Twelve train cars loaded with weapons and Germans rushing to Polotsk were blown to bits.

Three young people from the Vilna Ghetto did this, with the help of a mine made by Borukh Goldshtein in a secret cellar on Karmelitskaya Street.

The peasants who were forced to take away the bodies the next morning told us that they counted two hundred dead Germans. The peasants later collected and hid away a number of weapons that had been scattered in the blast—revolvers, submachine guns, rifles.

A year and a half later, when our partisan organization broke out of the ghetto and went into the woods, we remembered the machine guns and weapons that the Vilna peasants had picked up after the subversive action.

We collected the weapons from the peasants, and with those very weapons we took up the fight against the Germans.

Ties with Other Cities

Once our partisan organization had grown a bit stronger, it was decided to send reliable people to other cities that had significant Jewish populations, so as to strengthen their resistance movements. About forty thousand Jews were languishing in the Bialystok Ghetto. In the Warsaw Ghetto there were about half a million. The Jews in Bialystok did not believe the news of the mass shootings that took place in Vilna. In Warsaw they were convinced that it was impossible to destroy a half million people.

In February 1942 we managed to establish contact with Anton Schmidt,[41] who had been drafted into the German army. He drove three of our comrades to Bialystok and Warsaw: Boraks, Kempner, and Entin. They brought to Bialystok and Warsaw the truth of the monstrous slaughter of the Lithuanian Jews.

When Boraks returned to Vilna and described the disbelief that he met with in Bialystok and Warsaw, the leaders decided to convince our brothers with the help of hard facts. A proclamation was issued to all Jews living under German occupation; it outlined the details of the systematic slaughter of the Jewish people of Lithuania and Belorussia, with all the figures from the bloody statistics on Vilna, Vileika, Kaunas, and Minsk.

"A single fate," the proclamation stated, "awaits all Jews suffering under the yoke of German oppression. They are doomed. And nothing can save them, no matter what economic profit the Germans might derive from the free labor of the residents of the ghettos... .

"Everywhere that Jews have been oppressed by Hitler's yoke Ponarys have appeared!

"To arms! Organize your resistance!"

The sisters Sarra and Ruzhka Zilber took this proclamation to Bialystok. Its contents were made known to various party groups. The proclamation opened the eyes of many of them.

When they returned to Vilna the sisters fell into the clutches of the Gestapo and were tortured in a death camp.

Next a young schoolteacher named Kh. Grossman was sent to Warsaw; she made contact with representatives of the PLP (Polish Labor Party).

At the same time Z. Boraks was ordered back to Bialystok. Kh. Grossman then left Warsaw to join him, and the two of them worked on setting up an underground resistance group to fight the German invaders. Later they were able to establish contact with partisan units operating in the forests. Grossman and Boraks took an active part in the Bialystok Ghetto Uprising. Boraks fell in that battle; Kh. Grossman was one of the few who survived.

In early 1942 Doctor Wulff, Gebietskommissar for the Vilna district, decided to implement the final liquidation of all the Jews left in the area. They were concentrated in the Oshmyany Ghetto, where the Jewish population from Soll, Mikhalishki, Svir, and other towns had been sent.

In order to hasten the gathering of the Jews in Oshmyany, the Gestapo had issued all of them work certificates.

When we found out about it, it was quite clear to us: everyone in the Oshmyany Ghetto was going to be slaughtered. Our organization sent a partisan fighter named Liza Magun there; her assignment was to arrange to have people sent into the forest.

The Oshmyany Ghetto was surround by police. Liza, however, was still able to get into the ghetto and convince people that their deaths were inevitable, that the Germans handed out the work certificates only to fool those who were doomed, and that their only salvation was to escape and join the partisans. She managed to organize several armed groups that made it into the forest.

When she returned to Vilna Liza continued to carry out the organization's assignments. She had to report to the police commissar, however, to register, using false documents. The Gestapo recognized her and arrested her.

Liza was tortured in the basement of Gestapo headquarters; they burned her with a hot iron, but they got nothing out of her. She managed to send us a note from prison:

> I know very well what awaits me. But I just cannot reconcile myself to the thought that they are going to send me to Ponary. I am calm. Send my regards to all our comrades. Any word from Bialystok?
>
> > Be brave!
> > Liza

In memory of the heroine her friends obtained a revolver and added it to our organization's stockpile. In order to mark the date of her death, partisan Goldshtein stole a submachine gun from a German and donated it to the ghetto's arsenal.

The partisan leaders took the name of the brave young woman and made it into a battle cry. The signal for a general military emergency in the Vilna Ghetto became the password: "Liza calls!"

The Underground Printing Press

The leaders of the partisan organization conceived the idea of setting up a printing press.

In February 1942 our headquarters issued a leaflet printed on a mimeograph; it was an appeal to the population of the city. We realized that the current slaughter of the Jews was part of a general plan that Hitler had worked out for the extermination of all the Jewish people in Europe. The appeal was a call to active resistance.

"Do not be led like sheep to the slaughter. If the enemy has to overcome the resistance of each and every one of us individually, he will never be able to carry out his evil plan.

"Join the ranks of the partisans!

"Hurt the enemy wherever you can! Engage in acts of sabotage!

"Destroy the enemy's roads, transports, and factories! Allow him no peace!

"Death to the invaders!

"Union for the Struggle against the German Invaders

"Vilna. February 1942."

This summons was distributed throughout all the factories and establishments in the city. The task of distributing them fell to Jews who had been herded off to forced labor. Surrounded by the storm troopers' bayonets, every second risking their lives, they found ways to post the summons on many of the city's streets.

Many children from nine to twelve years of age were sent out to forced labor every day. The partisan organization entrusted many of them with very important assignments. And the kids carried out their assignments so conscientiously and with such confidence! The little hands of these bright, courageous children posted hundreds and hundreds of announcements and leaflets throughout the city!

Soon after he had produced that first mimeographed summons to the people, our typesetter I. Kovalsky proposed the daring project of setting up an underground printing press.

The commanding staff approved the project.

This is what Kovalsky himself said about implementing the plan:

"In keeping with orders from our organization's leaders, I began working for the German government's printing office. Most of the workers there knew me from before the war, which enabled me to overcome all difficulties.

"I immediately began to carry out the assignment. I arranged with Sonya Madeisker to have someone waiting for me at the gate at noon the following day, during the lunch break; I was to give that person everything I was able to obtain for the printing press. They told me that the person would be of medium height, wearing glasses and a black coat with an astrakhan collar; he would be holding a copy of the Polish paper *Gonec Tsodzenny*.

"A man did indeed show up at the precise time; he took my package and left. That evening back in the ghetto Sonya told me that the package was received and that tomorrow two more comrades would come to me for more. Those two comrades showed up right on time for a week, and I gave them packages of type and other necessary equipment. Later, in order to avert suspicion, just one of them would come, the one who showed up the first time. I later found out that he was the courageous Polish communist Jan Przewalski.

"We met like that for about a month. During that time an underground printing press equipped with everything it needed—type, paper, ink, printing frame—grew up at 3 Zamkovaya Street. I obtained everything and took it from the government press in the following manner.

"When the printing equipment for the *Gonec Tsodzenny* was disassembled, I had access to all the cases of type, and no one followed me around. As I sorted through the type, I took out everything that we needed. This had to be done in the presence of a hundred and fifty people.

"My meetings with Jan were at four-thirty in the afternoon, before I returned to the ghetto. Once I arranged for him to bring a large briefcase for the frame, cylinder, galley, and composing stick. I put all of these things in a corner at the government press, so that I could quickly take them out of there.

"I strapped the frame to myself with my belt; the rest of it I wrapped up in a sheet of waste paper. At the entrance to the printing press something unexpected happened. The director himself was standing at the gate. He asked me what I was carrying. I answered very coolly: 'Some waste paper for the stove; we have nothing to burn in the ghetto.' The director did not check me and let me go on.

"I'm out on the street. My heart is pounding. I look around—Jan is nowhere to be found.

"Meanwhile it was getting late; Jews were allowed to walk about in the city only until six o'clock. I decided to go back into the printing press, hide my goods in some secluded spot, and then head back to the ghetto. But not everything works out the way you want it to. The director of the printing press was still walking around in the courtyard. There was no way I could go back. I had to think. I turned around and headed for the ghetto with my cargo of iron and lead.

"There was a catastrophe along the way. My belt broke, and I was holding the heavy frame through the pocket in my coat. My only hope was to slip inside the ghetto as quickly as possible... .

"It turned out that Jan could not meet me because someone had been following him the whole day... .

"Since I had secured our printing press in the city, with all the necessary tools and equipment, I decided to set up a printing press in the ghetto itself... ."

Both printing presses turned out underground newspapers, pamphlets, and leaflets in Lithuanian and in German. The newspaper *Sztandar Wolnosci* came out in Polish and contained articles written by members of our organization. Polish authors were added later.

Close Friendships

During the very first days of the terror, when the Germans issued a warning that anyone speaking to Jews would be severely punished, many Jews found shelter with Christian neighbors in the city. The fascist newspapers constantly admonished the peasants: "If you sell food to the Jews, the authorities will show you no mercy." Nevertheless many peasants would take their carts down the footpaths precisely to sell food to any Jew that they might meet along the way.

A Lithuanian peasant woman named Yanova Bartoshevich hid me for a long time at the risk of her own life. I develop a bond with this good woman; it was as if I were her own son.

Yanova once told me that she saw a gallows standing on Sobornaya Square. Three Germans were dragging some old man to the gallows to be publicly hanged. Fastened to the condemned man's chest was a white slate, on which was written in black letters: "For hiding Jews."

"They don't frighten me," said the old woman. I spit on them and their laws. I'll hide you just to spite the Germans."

I fell ill. Yanova took me from the cellar where I was hiding, put me in a bed in a back room, and called a doctor. She told the doctor I was her son, who had escaped from a German jail.

On the eve of New Year's Day 1942 Yanova's husband came down to the cellar and asked me to come upstairs. He had gotten some vodka and some delicacies, but he could not bear to eat them knowing that I was languishing in the cellar.

A guest was sitting at the nicely laid table; he was an elderly relative of theirs. He had come for the holiday from the Lithuanian town of Vidukle. I asked him what news there was from his village; he related the following.

About two hundred Jews lived in the village. For many years they had lived on friendly terms with the Lithuanians, like brothers. When the Germans suddenly came in, they gathered up all the Jews and locked them in the synagogue.

The village priest, Ionas, decided to save the little ones belonging to those unfortunate people. He took thirty children from the synagogue and hid them in the church.

The next day a German commissar named Dietrich showed up; he took a bundle of straw and set the synagogue on fire.

It is impossible to describe the screams and the howls of people being burned alive. Two peasants could not bear the spectacle of this horror and went insane. A third lost his head and shouted at the Germans: "You are animals, you are not human beings!" He was immediately shot and thrown into the flames.

Dietrich found out from an informer that the priest was hiding some children. The priest stood at the entry to the church, blocking the murderers' path. "If you murder these children, then I shall die with them." A shot in the head left him lying where he had stood. Then the Germans took the children and crushed their skulls against the wall of the church.

Many Poles and Lithuanians hid Jews in their homes. Among these brave people were Yanova Bartoshevich, Mariya Abramovich, and Viktoriya Bzhilevskaya. Bzhilevskaya's house on Pogulyanka Street was a refuge for dozens of hunted people. The journalist Shimaite organized a group in the city for the purpose of saving Jews. Mariya Fedetskaya saved Doctor Sedlis and his family, Doctor Kamay and his daughter, and dozens of other Jews; she provided them with Polish documents and sent them to stay with peasants she knew who lived in various villages. Professor Stakauskas hid and saved sixteen Jews, including Doctor Libo and his family and the ninety-year-old painter Samek Bak. Professor Chezhevsky saved Professor Fesel, his wife, and their little boy, as well as the teacher Zlata Kacherginskaya.

According to German law, husbands and wives had to be divorced if only one of them was Jewish or was the descendant of Jews, down to the third generation. The Jewish spouse had to move into the ghetto, while the non-Jew could remain in the city. If the father alone was Jewish, then the children of mixed marriages were considered Jewish and had to move into the ghetto.

A Polish physician named Aksen was married to a Jewish woman. The Gestapo arrested his wife and three children and forced them to move into the ghetto. The doctor went to live with his wife. In the ghetto he learned Yiddish and shared the fate of the ghetto residents.

A Don Cossack also lived in the ghetto with his Jewish wife.

An old woman named Stasya, who had worked as a maid for the Lipkovich family, moved into the ghetto with her employers. When the Germans murdered her mistress, Stasya became like a mother to the orphaned children.

As they were taking the singer Ruzhinsky away to be shot, a passerby recognized him. Ruzhinsky had once been an officer in the Polish army. The passerby had served in his unit. Seeing that Ruzhinsky was being led away to be executed, he started asking the escort leader to release his old commander. The escort leader allowed himself to be persuaded by the gift of a gold watch. He warned, however, that since the Gestapo building was nearby and from there you could see the site where the shootings took place, he would have to give the appearance of carrying out the order. He led the condemned man to the pit and shot over his head. Ruzhinsky was supposed to fall down and lie in the pit until dark. That evening he could crawl out unnoticed.

When night fell the Polish soldier who had served under Ruzhinsky went to the pit and took the man who had been "shot" to his home. When Ruzhinsky rose from the pit his hair had turned completely gray.

He spent about a month with the soldier. When the Germans began rounding up the Jews in the area, he managed, with some difficulty, to get back to Vilna and returned to the ghetto. His wife, a Russian woman, went to live with him in the ghetto. She put on a yellow star and never parted from him.

Along the Vilna-Vileika road, near the Vilna Koloniya railroad station, there is a Benedictine convent surrounded by an iron fence. Sometime before the war seven nuns moved there from Krakow.

Abba Kovner hid in the convent after narrowly escaping death. The Mother Superior—or, as he called her, "Matka Przeorysza"—set up a separate cell for him.

The Mother Superior of the convent was a young socialist. She graduated from the university in Krakow. She went into the convent after some sort of personal tragedy. When the Red Army retreated from Vilna, she hid a wounded Soviet soldier in a convent cell and took care of him.

In addition to Kovner, she provided shelter for other members of the underground movement.

The Germans often conducted general searches at the convent. At critical moments the Mother Superior would dress her guests in nuns' habits.

Once the Mother Superior somehow made her way to the ghetto and brought Kovner four grenades. They were of a new and unknown type, and she showed Kovner how to handle them.

The Mother Superior once said to Kovner:

"I want to move into the ghetto to fight and die, if necessary, along with you. Your struggle is a great and sacred thing. You Marxists reject religion, but it seems to me that you have a god, a great god. Indeed, he will help you."

When the Mother Superior later discovered that a fighting organization had been created in the ghetto, she showed up at the ghetto gates and tried to get inside. The policemen at the gate, however, could see that she was not a Jew, and she barely escaped getting arrested.

Aid to Prisoners of War and the Families of Soviet Soldiers

In Vilna there were two large camps for Soviet prisoners of war and for the families of Soviet officers; one was in the "cheap housing" on Suboch Street, and the other was in the prison on Antokol. Jews who worked nearby tried to help the prisoners in every way possible, even though, according to German rules, they could be shot for talking to a prisoner of war.

A few months after the capture of Vilna, satiated with Jewish blood, the Germans began the slaughter of the prisoners of war. They were no better off than the Jews.

Captured Red Army soldiers were often taken to German workshops for forced labor. Many of them tried to escape. The partisans designated a special group whose task was to provide escapees with documents and clothing and direct them to partisan units.

Prior to the war about a thousand Jews had lived in the "cheap housing" on Suboch Street. During the several days when the Jews were being herded into the ghetto, the Germans surrounded the two buildings and killed all the Jews living there. The buildings stood empty for a short while. They were soon filled with the wives and children of Soviet military officers.

The camp was heavily guarded. It was forbidden for anyone to go in or out. And yet, like a dove, a Russian song rose up from that place. It was written in the camp, and from there it found its way into the ghetto, where it was often sung.

The first time I heard the song was in January 1942.

It was bitterly cold; at that time the Hitlerites were being driven back from Moscow. Jews working on the railroad received the joyous news: many transports of "apples"—frozen Germans—were on their way back from the front.

In Vilna, as in all of Lithuania, the Germans announced that they would take up a collection of various goods for the use of the German army. Every citizen was required to bring warm clothing, shoes, felt boots, sheepskin coats, fur hats, and blankets to the German commissariat. The announcement stated that those who freely gave up their belongings would receive a certificate signed by Oberkommissar Renteln[42] attesting to the honorable fulfillment of their civic duty. The Hitlerites announced a collection of goods in the ghetto as well. But there even the promise of a certificate signed by Renteln did not help: no one showed up to voluntarily hand over their belongings. Then the German resorted to more radical measures. They stopped men and women on the street, stripped their clothing from them, and sent them home naked. They began conducting general searches throughout the city, taking everything they found.

The job of sorting, packing, and shipping these things fell to the Jews from the ghetto. I was among them.

Once, while riding in a truck filled to the brim with sheepskin coats and felt boots, I heard a comrade who was with me singing the Russian song. He told me that the women and children locked in the "cheap housing" were dying from cold and hunger.

"How do you know that?" asked a worker from the ghetto who was riding with us.

"How do I know? I was there not long ago. I got through the wire fence and even spent the night in the camp."

The truck stopped on Poplavy Street, near the disinfection chamber. We were supposed to unload the things plundered by the Germans there.

We got the idea of transferring some of it to the "cheap housing" for the starving children and their mothers.

I proposed a plan. The children would often crawl under the wire fence surrounding the camp and go around neighboring buildings begging for alms. We would have to hook up with some of these children. I called out to a barefoot little boy and quietly said to him: "You and your buddies get together here tomorrow and wait for our truck. We will drive by in the evening and throw out whatever we can."

The next day a crowd of kids was waiting for us. We threw them dozens of sheepskin coats, underwear, felt boots, scarves, sweaters, shoes, and bags of food. We got the food from a peasant along the road in exchange for an astrakhan coat. The German sitting in the cabin with the driver did not notice a thing. The driver knew what we were up to. The German guarding him was not familiar with the streets of Vilna, and the driver was purposely driving in circles around the city. When he got to Suboch Street he slowed down so we could throw the goods off the truck.

The boys quickly gathered up their gifts and buried them in the snow; that night they took them into the camp.

We repeated the operation every evening for a week. The prisoners in the camp were revived.

We received a letter from them. It said:

"We shall not forget this. The day will come when we shall tell the people of our homeland that in 1942 the Jews of Vilna, though tortured and enslaved, did not forget their Soviet duty. At a time when speaking to Jews was punishable by death, the Jews risked their lives and saved others from the cold and hunger, victims of the same barbaric fascist regime."

How We Celebrated May Day 1943

We secretly got together in a café at 6 Shavelskaya Street. Members of the underground partisan organization were there, along with teenagers and children. Everyone was wearing white shirts and blouses with red ribbons pinned to them. The hall was decorated with flowers and greenery. Teenagers who had been sent out to forced labor had brought them into the ghetto; they brought them in secretly, hiding them as the Germans conducted their searches at the gate. The scent of the greenery brought a reminder of freedom to this little corner of the ghetto.

One of our partisans opened the holiday. He invited everyone to stand in order to lend an air of solemnity to the light gathering. He proposed a toast to the heroes of the Warsaw Ghetto Uprising that had begun on 19 April. "At this hour," he said, "as we celebrate the First of May, our brothers are fighting against the enemy in a city awash with blood and fire. The day is near when we shall have to take up arms. Let Warsaw serve as an example of how we must do battle with the fascists."

A bulletin from the ghetto's underground radio was read at the gathering; we sang revolutionary songs, and the violinist Rabinovich played a few tunes. I read my poem "To Arms."

The pamphlet writer Shimaite attended our holiday celebration. He broke into the ghetto just to observe May Day with us.

After the festivities a small group of comrades gathered in a room at Vitenberg's place. He told us about the situation at the front and expressed the hope that soon the Red Army would be approaching Vilna. "Then," he said, "we shall break through the ghetto barriers, raise up the population, and, as we crush the German garrison, we shall bring freedom to our native city."

Isaak Vitenberg

The organizer and inspiration for the partisan organization in the ghetto, its leader and commander, was Isaak Vitenberg. The son of a worker, he was born in 1907 in Vilna; he graduated from the Jewish folk school and then pursued a specialized study of manufacturing. He read a great deal at night to complete his education. Vitenberg's intellectual interests were quite diverse.

Even as a youth he was involved in the labor movement and became a member of the Polish Communist Party. He enjoyed a great popularity among the masses of workers. In 1936 he became a member of the Vilna Soviet of Labor Unions.

In 1940, after the formation of the Lithuanian Soviet Republic, Vitenberg became a representative of the Tanners' Union. When the war broke out, he was unable to get out of the city.

It was a trying time for Vitenberg. As a member of the Communist Party, he was a wanted man. He did not obey the order to report for forced labor, and this placed him in an even more dangerous position. He hid in the narrow confines of the ghetto, obsessed by a single thought: to prepare an armed uprising against the German invaders. Vitenberg was brave and intelligent. He solved every problem—and under the Germans the collisions were dramatic—in a calm manner, with his cool self-confidence.

Vitenberg's deputy once told me: "Isaac is one of the most sincere people I have ever met. What impresses me above all is his ability to come up with a remarkably simple and intelligent analysis of reality."

Vitenberg adopted the position—and the entire leadership shared it—that the partisan organization had to defend the residents of the ghetto from within the ghetto. "If we should leave the ghetto," he said, "then we condemn the people in the ghetto to death."

When the matter of whether we should join a partisan unit in the forest arose, Vitenberg declared:

"When it becomes known that the Germans intend to slaughter everyone in the ghetto, we shall summon everyone to battle and then go into the forest."

Vitenberg worked out a plan for breaking out of the ghetto that included a simultaneous departure from the city and the burning down of all German military facilities. Vitenberg shared this plan with the organization's leadership prior to 16 July 1943.

Several members of the Party's committee in the city were arrested on 9 July 1943. The next day Kittel showed up in the ghetto and demanded that Vitenberg be handed over.[43]   He had discovered that Vitenberg was the leader of five hundred armed Jews in the ghetto.

As proof that Vitenberg alone was required for interrogation, Kittel arrested a man named Averbukh and released him immediately after interrogating him. "Let Vitenberg step forward too," said Kittel, "and we shall release him after an interrogation."

On 15 July 1943, at one A.M., the police broke into a meeting of the Judenrat. Vitenberg was there; they arrested him and put him in handcuffs.

At the ghetto gate, however, when several members of the UPO intervened, Vitenberg managed to break free and escape. At that point a general mobilization of the members of the partisan organization was announced.

At dawn on 16 July the Germans issued an ultimatum to the ghetto: Vitenberg must turn himself in by six o'clock that evening, or else airplanes would be called in from Kaunas to drop incendiary bombs on the entire ghetto.

In his ultimatum Kittel added that if Vitenberg should report to the Gestapo, he would be set free immediately after his interrogation.

A tragic dispute arose in the ghetto. Some of the residents demanded that we reject Kittel's deception and defend Vitenberg no matter what.

The partisan leaders decided: Vitenberg would have to turn himself in to save the ghetto.

Vitenberg made his farewells and named A. Kovner as his successor; then he headed for the ghetto gate. Kittel was waiting there for his victim; he put Vitenberg in his car and drove off to the Gestapo headquarters.

Vitenberg was turned over to an interrogator named Max Gross, a special Gestapo investigator in partisan affairs.

The next day our commander's body was lying in the Gestapo courtyard. The hair on his head was burned, and his eyes were gouged out; his hands, tied behind his back, were broken.

The death of our commander had a most destructive impact on the organization. The leadership's decision that Vitenberg should voluntarily turn himself in to save the twenty thousand Jews living in the ghetto was a fatal mistake.

In response to Kittel's ultimatum, on 16 July there was an immediate call to arms.

"Liza Calls"

The feeling that the liquidation of the ghetto was drawing near became more pronounced with each passing day. On 1 August 1943 all the Jews assigned to the 150 German workshops and establishments were removed from their places of work. Two thousand people were sent to the airfield at Porubanek and roughly the same number were taken to the railroad. When they showed up at their new work site, they were surrounded by Gestapo men and herded into train cars that stood waiting for them. The workers tried to resist, and so began a battle in which approximately three hundred people died. Those who were left were forced into the train cars; on 5 August they were transported to concentration camps in Estonia. Several dozen of them still managed to escape along the way: they sawed through the boards in the floor of the train car and jumped through the opening.

An order was issued in the ghetto: the families of everyone sent to Estonia were to "voluntarily" follow them to the camps. If anyone should refuse or go into hiding, then his neighbors would be taken. And so more Jews were gathered together in their turn and sent to Estonia.

On 1 September 1943 Neugebauer showed up and announced: from this day forward no one may leave the ghetto. All work would be done within the confines of the ghetto. And since sixteen thousand people were not necessary for this work, six thousand would be sent to camps at Vaivari and Riga. Work forces were needed there. In order to avert suspicion, Neugebauer read a few letters ostensibly from Vaivari; written by people who had been sent there already, the letters described the good working conditions.

The UPO leaders immediately mobilized the entire organization. Battalions were formed right away. Machine guns were gathered, and the fighters were issued revolvers and grenades; then they waited for the order to go into action.

The first barricade was to be set up on Gospitalnaya Street, but before they could finish building it, police units rushed in and seized some of the fighters in the group.

Having failed in this first attempt, the organization designated 12 Strashun Street as a defense point and set up a barricade there. When the Germans approached, the ghetto fighters opened fire. Police reinforcements were immediately called in, and hundreds of the bandits bombarded the barricade and the buildings with gunfire. Commander Sheinboim,[44] who was shooting at the Germans from a corner window, died in the arms of his comrades. Partisan fighter Ruzhka Korchak took his place.

Having met with stubborn resistance, the Germans used dynamite on the building at 12 Strashun Street; about one hundred people were killed in the explosion.

Next the Germans started blowing up all the buildings from which there was gunfire. In one fell swoop the Germans captured hundreds of Jews who had been hiding in malinas; they took them down Ross Street to the outskirts of the city, where transports were waiting to take them to Estonia.

Every day people were being taken out of the ghetto. One day the Germans would collect only men, the next day they would take only women. There was no way that Neugebauer would allow the women to go with their men or their loved ones. Many women cut their hair and put on men's clothing, so that they could have the "good fortune" of going with their men to Estonia.

Many of the members of the partisan organization were barricaded in the building at 6 Strashun Street, in the library of the Society for the Advancement of the Enlightenment. They all stood at their posts in full battle readiness, waiting for the order to open fire. But the Gestapo did not even reach the building at 6 Strashun Street. On 4 September, after about eight thousand people had been shipped out of the ghetto over a period of several days, the Gestapo received the order to abandon the ghetto.

On the evening of 12 September 1943 thirty of my comrades and I managed to break out of the ghetto. I headed for an escape route that we had already prepared; we were supposed to meet at the Markuchai farmhouse. The leader of the group was Zelda Treger. She lived in the city and walked the streets without the yellow star; she pointed out the path we should follow so as not to run into gendarmes during our escape. Treger went through the city like a whirlwind. Every two hours she would report to the ghetto with news.

A dozen or so kilometers outside of town, as we were crossing a railroad track, we had our first engagement with the enemy. After losing one of our comrades, we broke through the German defense and went deeper into the woods... .

In the ghetto a small number of survivors were holed up in malinas.

The streets were littered with bodies, and the Germans gave permission to bury them in the cemetery. Our fighters took advantage of the situation and placed machine guns in the coffins that were taken to the Zarechenskoe cemetery; the guns were buried there.

On 23 September 1943 at nine o'clock in the morning Kittel arrived in the ghetto and officially announced that the ghetto had been liquidated. By twelve o'clock noon everyone was ready for deportation to concentration camps in Estonia. There was no escape; the few who were left alive in the ghetto got ready for the journey. The last group of UPO fighters, unable to get out of the city, had come to a dead end; they had no machine guns, and it was impossible for them to break through the police cordon. Two hundred fighters with only a few weapons went into the sewers and from there made their way to the Rudnitsky Woods, which was the center of partisan activity.

The entrance to the sewer pipes was at the factory located at 31 Nemetskaya Street. Underneath a large tile oven there was a hatch leading directly to a sanitation basin that no one except our command staff knew about. One of the sewer workers, who was also a member of the UPO, knew the way very well and led a group of fighters through the hatch. They had to crawl on their hands and knees through the thickest sewage, holding their weapons and their documents in their teeth. They spent four hours crawling around in that underground hell. Through a system of specially arranged signals, they received information as to where the path was clear and where they had to turn aside. At one point, when they had to stop, the liquid in the pipes was up to their necks. As it turned out, a group of people had stopped, and they were holding up the flow of escapees. One of the women in the group had gotten lost along the way and did not know where she was to go. It was difficult to turn back; indeed, in several places it was impossible, since the flow of the sewage would wash over the fighters' heads when they tried to move against the current. People lost consciousness and went out of their minds; one of them even killed himself. All the while it was necessary to maintain complete silence, since the sounds could penetrate through the manholes overhead, and the Germans could hear them.

The fighters finally made their way through the pipes to Ignatevsky Lane. Here the building at Number 5, in the courtyard of the police station, had been designated as the exit to the surface. That was where the partisans were to meet Sonya Madeisker and two Lithuanian policemen with whom we had connections; from there, using false documents, they were to go into the city. Drenched in filth, the partisans had difficulty getting through the narrow camouflaged opening and into the cellar to wash themselves off. The fighters came out in pairs; they were shown the way to Suboch and the old farmhouse. The city was crawling with gendarmes and Gestapo agents. Some of the partisans had skirmishes with the police along the way, but they managed to get out of the city; they broke into the cemetery, where they got the machine guns hidden there. Weapons in hand, they went into the Rudnitsky Woods as a standing partisan unit.

Fallen Heroes

Two members of our command staff, Yankel Kaplan and Abram Khvoinik —as well as our intelligence expert Asya Big—managed to escape through the sewers with the last group of ghetto fighters.

A German patrol stopped them at the corner of Bolshaya and Rudnitskaya Street, near the Kazino movie theater. The gendarmes demanded that they present their papers. In response the partisans pulled out their revolvers and started shooting. Many Germans, including several members of the Gestapo, were swarming around the theater. A bullet from Kaplan's gun killed Max Gross,[45] one of the Gestapo's bloody executioners assigned to investigate the partisans. One of the leaders of the Kaunas Gestapo was killed with him. Kaplan, Khvoinik, and Big emptied all their bullets into the Germans.

In their insatiable thirst for revenge they failed to save a bullet for themselves. All three of them were taken alive.

They were delivered to the Gestapo's backyard.

There Kittel erected a gallows for the teacher Yankel Kaplan, the attorney Abram Khvoinik, and the twenty-year-old student Asya Big.

Kittel personally hanged all three of them: Kaplan and Khvoinik on each side, and the young Big in the middle.[46]

After the ghetto had been liquidated and the partisan organization had been reestablished in the forest, one of the shining heroines of the Vilna Ghetto Uprising continued to live in the city using forged Polish papers: Sonya Madeisker.

During the first days of the occupation, when all normal life in the city had died and the Germans turned their wrath toward the Jews with a special fury, Sonya was one of the few who kept her wits about her. She organized a Komsomol in the ghetto, established contact with the workers in the city, and became one of the most active members of the underground Municipal Party Committee. At the same time she was one of the editors for the illegal newspaper *Sztandar Wolnosci*.

After the fall of the Municipal Party Committee, Sonya became an energetic worker in the underground organization. Under her guidance hundreds of UPO fighters, for whom it would have been impossible to remain in Vilna after the liquidation of the ghetto, went into the forest and joined units in the Lithuanian partisan brigade. Sonya accomplished this task single-handedly and then continued to live in the city as before.

After they shut down the ghetto, the Germans placed about three thousand Jews in concentration camps; Sonya visited one of those camps, Kailis, every Sunday. She organized several partisan groups, provided them with weapons, and sent them with special guides into the forest.

Yankauskas Yulian, the former director of the Plastikas factory, worked with Sonya.

He hid more than one Jew in his apartment and obtained a number of weapons for the partisan organization.

Yulian was gradually drawn into underground activities. He recruited agents from the Lithuanian workers and even brought several policemen over to the partisan side. Yulian altered his appearance: he grew a long beard and moved to Zarechenskaya Street, where Sonya lived in a small camouflaged room. Both of them had a great love for life and for a bright future, in the name of which they fought against the Germans.

Several months before the Red Army liberated Vilna a large Gestapo unit surrounded Zarechenskaya Street; dozens of Germans attacked the building at Number 3, where the daring members of he underground lived.

The Gestapo had long since put a huge price on their heads.

They bravely defended themselves and killed several policemen.

Soon, however, Yulian was hit by a bullet and fell. Sonya saved her last bullet for herself; unfortunately, she only wounded herself. The Gestapo put her in the hospital, revived her, and then tried to get information out of her. When their attempts proved to be futile, they took her to the cellar at Gestapo headquarters and turned her over to the executioner.

The Struggle Continues in the Forest

The ghetto fighters moved into the forest, where they set up two bases: one near Lake Naroch and the other in the Rudnitsky Woods. The Nekome (Revenge) Unit at Lake Naroch did not remain exclusively Jewish for long; the fighters were dispersed among various units of the partisan brigade under the command of Colonel Markov. Naroch is located relatively far from Vilna—more than a hundred kilometers. Naturally the Jewish partisans were drawn to their native city, but dozens of the fighters joined Lithuanian units such as the Vilna Unit.

Many Vilna Jews were also sent from Naroch to the Rudnitsky Woods (forty kilometers from Vilna), where four Jewish units were already fighting.

Two Jewish units, Borba (Struggle) and Smert Fashizmu (Death to the Fascists), also received Lithuanian reinforcements. Only two entirely Jewish partisan units remained: Mstitel (Avenger) and Za Pobedu (For Victory). Abba Kovner was commander of the former.

Samuil Kaplinsky, a former UPO instructor, became commander of the second unit, Za Pobedu. He obtained weapons for the whole unit; the fighters in the unit loved and respected their commander.

There were more than two hundred fighters in the two units. A single command staff organized the operations of both units.

Having secured the weapons they needed within the first three months, both units carried out a series of military operations. They derailed three German troop transports. During the first derailment twelve train cars and the steam engine were sent tumbling down the side of an embankment. The second time six cars full of Germans were destroyed. The derailment on the Vilna-Orany line cost the lives of two hundred Hitlerites. The fighters burned down three bridges at Zhagarin and near Darguchi. They blew up a German factory in Olkeniki and helped destroy a German garrison in the heavily fortified town of Konyukhi.

Once the Mstitel Unit had procured enough tolite and machine guns, the "Rail War" began. According to his own count, partisan Isaak Rudnitsky blew up twelve transports on wide rails and three on narrow rails. He and four of his comrades took part in blowing up the electrical power station at Sventsyany. His group captured four Hitlerites and brought them to command headquarters; they also freed the partisan Semenov, who had been captured by the fascists.

In the forest Vitka Kempner, the heroine of Vilna's first act of sabotage, proved what she could do. In October 1943, with a suitcase full of explosives, she walked forty kilometers in one night, made her way into Vilna, and blew up the electrical power station, including its largest transformer. The next night she broke into the Kailis concentration camp and got out sixty prisoners, whom she took back to the partisan base. Vitka organized a group of intelligence specialists in the Mstitel Unit. She personally took part in the sabotage near the Orany station; together with five of her comrades, she burned down the factory at Olkeniki, blew up two steam engines, and destroyed two bridges. She especially distinguished herself in the battle outside Dainava, where she captured two Gestapo agents and personally brought them to command headquarters.

In November 1943 Vitka Kempner was assigned to deliver some important documents to the Municipal Party Committee. A German patrol stopped her along the way and escorted her under armed guard to the Gestapo. The brave girl kept her head and escaped at an opportune moment.

Another partisan, Grigory Gurevich, ambushed twelve Germans in two trucks. He captured what we regarded as two major trophies, given our means at the time: ten machine guns and a German submachine gun. He kept the submachine gun for himself; he studied its design very carefully and became an outstanding machine gunner. Gurevich's mother, a thirty-nine-year-old woman, fought with him. The two of them went on assignments and carried out ambushes together; between them they slaughtered eighteen Germans. The mother and her son were once surrounded by a large patrol. A lopsided battle ensued. Grisha's mother used up all her seventy-five rounds and managed to toss five grenades in the middle of the oncoming fascists. Now out of ammunition, she fell at her son's side. Shaken by the death of his mother, Grisha sprang at the murderer and broke his skull with the butt of his submachine gun. The wounded Grisha broke through the enclosure. He swam across the river and crawled for a long time through the swamp, until he finally fell unconscious. A passing shepherd noticed him and informed the partisans. They went to get Grisha and brought him back to the base. Once he had recovered, he went out on assignments again with his submachine gun; he blew up two German transports in revenge for the death of his mother.

Khaim Lazar, an active member of our organization, did not shame our honor. In a battle with a German motor unit he personally shot three officers. The entire fascist unit was beaten back and scattered by a small group of partisans. On 23 April 1944, while preparing to sabotage a rail line, a mine blew up in Lazar's hands; it took his right hand off.

Zelda Treger broke through the German cordon eighteen times to maintain contact between the partisan unit and the Party organization in the city. She never returned to base empty-handed. Treger penetrated the concentration camp and took out people otherwise condemned to death. She brought us dozens of rifles from the city. Four times she fell into the enemy's clutches; once she was captured by White Poles who were spying on the partisans in the surrounding forest, especially Jews. She always kept a cool head, and that helped her on this occasion to escape from the jaws of death and carry out her mission.

One of the best liaisons and intelligence experts in our unit was Dina Roizenvald; she was of great service to the partisan movement.

And Roza (Ruzhka) Korchak? This modest, quiet girl was always the first to step forward for the most dangerous assignments, both in the ghetto and in the forest. And how can one fail to recall the leader of the Mstitel Unit's intelligence operation, Khonon Magid, who knew every move the enemy made? Who can forget Nyusya Lubotskaya, Lev Levin, Ruvim Rabinovich, Tevye Galperin, Borya Shereshnevsky, and Isaak Kovalsky? These courageous, steadfast young men and women were a hair's breadth from death dozens of times.

Many brave, pure, and fearless people lie in the forests surrounding Rudnitsky and Naroch. May their names shine with eternal memory and glory!

Two brothers must also be remembered: Danya and Ima Lubotsky, the sons of V. Lubotsky, the famous teacher of Vilna. Danya was captured during the fighting in the ghetto. The Gestapo tortured him for ten days. From his cell he asked his parents to send him poison. I remember how the old Lubotsky, completely crushed, came to me for advice on how to get to his son. "My wife," he said, "wants to give him some poison, so he'll suffer less." But the father could not bring himself to poison his own son!

After a few days Danya showed up in the ghetto. He managed to escape literally at the last minute before they took him to be executed. But his parents did not rejoice for long. When the ghetto was liquidated the whole family fell into Kittel's clutches. Only Danya was able to break free and make his way into the forest. There he met his brother Ima, who had managed to get out through the sewer with the partisans.

Danya became commander of the unit's third group Za Pobedu; he was known for his extraordinary daring. He thirsted for revenge; he literally could not sit still and was constantly going out on assignments.

At the end of December 1943 Danya discovered that one of the Gestapo's top agents was in one of the towns in the area; he got together a group of partisans and set out to hunt down the fascist beast. The German was barricaded in a building that they had under siege; Danya was seriously wounded. He was taken to a camp, where his life came to an end.

Ima returned that day after the bitter battle. His brother was interred in the camp. The young man stood at the side of the grave leaning on his rifle, the hot tears running down his cheeks.

A few days later Ima went out with a group of partisans to destroy an enemy telegraph line. One of the telegraph poles turned out to be mined. There was an explosion; Ima and a handful of the fighters were literally blown to pieces.

Both brothers will sleep forever in peace in the Rudnitsky Woods.

During the liquidation of the ghetto some of our fighters who could not get arms were captured and herded off to a concentration camp; a few were sent to Estonia. In the camp the teacher Lev Opeskin and the actor Yakov Bergolsky organized a partisan group; they obtained some weapons and established contact with the partisan base in the forest.

On 10 July 1944 a special SS commando surrounded the camp and opened fire with their submachine guns on the Jews inside. The partisans started shooting back. Thanks to this unexpected resistance, more than a hundred of the inmates managed to break through the German lines and escape into the city, where they confidently awaited their salvation: the Red Army was already quite close.

Opeskin and Bergolsky fell in that battle.

During the battle for the liberation of Vilna, the ghetto fighters, who later became partisans in the Lithuanian and Belorussian forests, broke through to their native city, along with the leading contingent of the Red Army, and attacked the barricaded Germans.

The Last Act of the Tragedy

When the number of the victims of Ponary exceeded 100,000, an order came from Berlin: all the bodies of those who had been murdered were to be burned. Special secret instructions with details on how the burning of he bodies were to be organized were sent with the order.

The Germans knew that the front was drawing closer; they felt that sooner or later they would be driven out of the city, and they were trying to erase all traces of their horrible crimes.

Weiss had the prisoners from the Vilna prison delivered to Ponary to do the job.

The cellar where they were taken for the night was about twenty meters wide and four meters high. The walls were covered with stones, with each stone laid right next to the other. Inside there were several compartments: one for supplies and two long, narrow chambers with plank beds along the walls. Along its ceiling the underground prison had heavy beams filled in with earth and stones. The Germans had opened only two hatches through which ladders could be lowered. One was designated for the prisoners; the other, which was better and more convenient, was for the German foreman, if it should be necessary for him to go down into the cellar.

There were eighty men in all: seventy Jews, nine Russians, and one young Pole from the village of Leshnik. He had been arrested for hiding a little Jewish girl named Liechka.

The "bunker" was fenced in with barbed wire and surrounded by mine fields; the minefields, in turn, were closed in by another fence. Guards with machine guns were positioned along the perimeter. All the prisoners had their legs shackled in chains. A total of 56,800 bodies were burned; that was only half of the victims of Ponary.

One of the few who survived this hell was Isaak Dogim.[47] He relates the following:

"First we dug up a mass grave in which the victims of the hunters were buried. It was located about 150 meters from the Grodnensky Highway. We guessed that they were from the period of the hunters because of the soap and towels that were buried with each of them. (At that time the Jews who were arrested were ordered to bring soap and a towel, since they were supposedly being transported to work.) All of them who had been shot there were young men; they each wore a yellow star with the letter *J* in the middle. Most of them had their hands tied behind their backs and their eyes blindfolded.

"We counted ten thousand bodies in that grave, including about five hundred prisoners of war; there were also several priests in black cassocks. The bodies were lying next to each other and were covered with blood.

"The second grave was filled with the victims of the massacre of 1 September 1941; it contained men, women, and children. Almost all of them had the keys to their apartments: they had left thinking they would return home. In the grave we counted 9,500 bodies.

"The third mass grave was from the time of the liquidation of the second ghetto in November 1941.

"Here it was noted for the first time that the bandits shot their victims in a precise manner, from behind, in the back of the neck. In this grave we counted 10,400 bodies. Almost none of the children's bodies had a bullet wound. Judging from the way their tongues were sticking out, the children were apparently buried alive.

"The fourth and largest mass grave contained 24,000 bodies. Most of them perished during the time of the 'yellow certificates.' There were non-Jews buried in that grave: priests, nuns, Poles, some uniformed German, and many Soviet prisoners of war.

"In the fifth grave, near the gate, lay 3,500 women and children, all naked, shot in the back of the neck.

"The fifth grave had five thousand bodies, all without clothing.

"Political prisoners from the Lukishki prison were buried in a separate grave. There were fifty-one of them. I recognized my brother-in-law Samuil Shats among them; he was arrested in the ghetto for spreading communist propaganda.

"Those murdered during the Kovno Aktion of 5 April 1943 were buried in two other graves; they were women and children, completely naked.

"Those who had perished after the liquidation of the ghetto, as well as the ones found in the malinas, were buried in fresh graves.

"While we were working at Ponary groups of people were repeatedly brought in to be shot. So it once happened to a group of four hundred Jews from Vaivari; with them were thirty to forty Poles and fifteen gypsies as well.

"Work ceased during these shootings. They drove us into the bunker, where we had to wait until the executions were over.

"The screams and the cries of the people being executed penetrated even through the stone walls of our cellar.

"I once came across my family when we were burning the bodies: my wife, mother, three sisters, and two nephews. I recognized my wife from a locket that I gave her on our wedding day. As my wife's body was burning in the bonfire, I slipped the locket from her neck. The two photographs inside it had already been destroyed by the flames."

Digging Out and Escape

From the first day that the workers found themselves in their underground prison, they knew that their fate was sealed. Escape was unthinkable: their every step was carefully watched, and they were bound in chains. A double barbed wire fence surrounded the underground bunker, and the area between the fences was mined. Only a narrow pathway led out of the cellar, and it was guarded by a sentry with a machine gun. Armed SS guards were position all around the perimeter. On top of that, a patrol came down into the bunker every hour and a half to two hours to see to it that all the prisoners were firmly chained. For the Sturmbannführer it was a matter of looking out for his own hide. He wanted no escapes; he could not afford to have a single witness to what they were doing. Once the eighty workers had finished their job, the Sturmbannführer would shoot them and personally burn their bodies in the bonfire. Then he would return to Berlin. That day was drawing near. On that day he would shoot Oberscharführer Fiedler as well. Fiedler knew too much and was no longer necessary.

In spite of all these seemingly insurmountable obstacles, in the underground bunker were people who never stopped thinking about escaping.

Shleima Goll and Isaak Dogim worked out a plan with a Soviet prisoner of war, an engineer named Yuli Farber; they brought three other prisoners into their circle, and together they set about digging a tunnel thirty to thirty-five meters long.

The tunnel was to lead past the wire fences, underneath the minefield, and out to the edge of the pine forest.

They worked only at night.

They began burrowing through the storeroom. A well about two and a half meters deep had been dug there. The tunnel started at the bottom of the well. The workers had no tools in the cellar. They dug with their bare hands, sharpened sticks, and even spoons. They dug about ten meters of tunnel with spoons! The dirt that they dug out was spread along the plank beds, under the floor, and, as the job was coming to an end, between the boards that sealed in the bunker. The floor level rose higher and higher with each passing day, but fortunately the ceiling of the cellar was several meters high, and no one noticed.

In order to keep the tunnel from caving in, the five conspirators—and later others—installed supports. More than once they ran the risk of being buried alive, but their thirst for life was so strong that they overcame every obstacle. Dogim even managed to run an electric light down into the tunnel. The current came from a German sentry hut; they had secretly hooked up a camouflaged wire to it.

The most difficult part in digging the tunnel was digging it in the right direction, so as not to end up in the same ditch as the dead bodies, the victims of the German Aktions. With some cunning, they managed to steal a compass from the Germans. Engineer Farber devised a carefully conceived plan and with great precision figured out the way out of the bunker and past the ditch. In addition, it was important to construct an exit to the surface that was not too close to the sentry's position.

After three months of intensive work, the tunnel was ready.

On 15 April 1944 at four o'clock in the morning, after the patrol had made its round and had left the cellar, Dogim woke up all the prisoners.

They were divided into groups of ten with a commander for each group. For several days prior to the escape the prisoners had been sawing through the chain links in their fetters with a small file; they had replaced the chain links with wire. The whole project was carried off without the guards' noticing; it made it possible, when necessary, to easily free themselves from their chains. Now the moment had come.

The first one into the tunnel was Dogim himself. Behind him came the groups of ten with their commanders leading them, as well as everyone else. Dogim cut the wire for the light and broke through the exit to the surface.

Fresh air gushed into the tunnel. In the distance they could see the purple flames of the bonfire.

There was a patrol of German guards not far from the opening. At first they did not hear anything because the prisoners were walking barefoot and stepping very lightly. But suddenly there was a crunching sound: one of the escapees had stepped on a dry twig. A guard smelled something fishy and opened fire. Rockets were immediately launched into the sky; they lit up the whole area.

The escapees bolted for the woods. They jumped across the pits and went through the wire fence, bullets flying all around them. Many were killed; only eleven men made it to the partisan unit in the Rudnitsky Woods.[48]

A. Sutskever, translated from the Hebrew by M. Shambadal and B. Chernyak

The Diary of E. Yerushalmi of Siauliai (Shavli)

From the Editors

This document, a significant portion of which follows, represents an exceptional phenomenon. Keeping a diary under ghetto conditions was extremely difficult and dangerous. The author's secret could have been discovered by the Germans at any moment, in which case both he and his sacred notebooks would have been threatened with immediate destruction.

Yerushalmi survived many German Aktions. He managed to preserve his diary.

E. Yerushalmi was a member of the Judenrat. Hence he belonged to a small group of the most informed people in the ghetto; he knew everything that happened in the ghetto and often knew beforehand what the Germans were plotting.

The Germans had barely entered the city, when they introduced racist laws, carried out pogroms against the Jews, created the ghetto, and condemned dozens and hundreds of thousands of people to annihilation, from nursing infants to the most aged of the elderly. Before they annihilated them, however, they wanted to deprive their victims of everything they possibly could. They took all their valuables, all their property. They forced them to do unbearable work. For the sake of their own convenience in plundering and exploiting the Jews, they created the illusion of self-government. The Judenrat, which Germans appointed from the best-known people in the city (rabbis, physicians, jurists, scholars), was responsible for order and sanitary conditions in the ghetto, for the distribution of food to the hungry, for enforcing all the laws, and for accommodating the German authorities. Needless to say, any member of the Judenrat who refused to carry out his duty was threatened with an immediate and cruel death. Working under this constant threat, the members of the Judenrat were forced to aid their executioners and become traitors to their people. On occasion, however, the members of the Judenrat used their position to fight against the German terror; they warned the population about repressive measures the Germans were planning and established contacts with the ghetto underground, as well as with the partisans.

When the Germans demanded that the Siauliai Judenrat deliver fifty Jews to be shot, the members of the Judenrat unanimously refused to turn over a single person, declaring that they would rather be killed themselves.

{From the Editors[49]

This document, a significant portion of which follows, represents an exceptional phenomenon, perhaps even a unique one. Under the conditions of the ghetto, keeping diary and making more or less regular entries was extremely difficult. First of all, the writer exposed himself to enormous danger: if his work should be discovered, both the notes and their author would be immediately destroyed. Often there were neither writing materials nor even a light. There was none of the privacy needed for concentration, no way to take the necessary precautions (there were several families in every dwelling, with plank beds several layers high). There was neither time nor energy (they endured exhausting labor with very little to eat). Deprived of all contact with the outside world, the residents of the ghetto were fed the rumors and the lies of the executioners. Under such conditions a diary was transformed into a death warrant; those who were doomed wanted to forget, even for just a moment, that death was hanging over them. Finally, it was impossible to assume that the diary would be preserved after the author's death; everyone was condemned. They were subject to constant searches, and the ghetto was ultimately blown up. If the author were to find a secluded spot where he could temporarily hide his notes, he would carry the secret of the hiding place to his grave.

That is why we usually deal with memoirs, and not with daily chronicles.

The survival of both the diary and its author was extremely rare. This, however, does not diminish the value of the diary. E. Yerushalmi was a middle school teacher with many years of service. Thanks to his level of sophistication, he was able to discern the underlying facts and describe them with a historian's objectivity, giving in neither to indifference nor to a cry of unbearable pain. He is not an accuser; he is, in fact, a chronicler. Of course, he could not forget that he was himself condemned, along with all his loved ones and fellow Jews. But he understood that facts could stir human conscience more than any words or accusations.

Yet the value of his diary does not lie even in this. E. Yerushalmi was a member of the Judenrat. Therefore he belonged to a small group of the most prominent people in the ghetto; he had direct contact with the Germans and knew everything that transpired in the ghetto, and not just what was happing in one place. Often he knew beforehand what the Germans were plotting, as they distributed secret information not available to others, and so on.

What follows is an explanation of what a Judenrat is.

As soon as they entered the city, the Germans began their pogroms and introduced racist laws. Even prior to the establishment of the ghetto, the Jews who had survived the first pogroms were left in a state of complete isolation in the midst of the rest of the population. They were subjected to a special form of justice—or rather, a special form of arbitrariness. The Germans never said that they were going to annihilate all the Jews; they simply did it, one step at a time. Before they annihilated them, however, they wanted to deprive their victims of everything they possibly could, including their possessions and their labor. Thus for the sake of their greatest convenience in plundering and exploiting the Jews, as well as for administrative reasons, they created the illusion of self-government. They appointed a Judenrat (Jewish Council) consisting of the best known people in the city (rabbis, physicians, jurists, scholars, and so on), and made it responsible for order and sanitary conditions in the ghetto, for the distribution of food to the hungry, for having the designated number of people report for work—in a word, for enforcing all the laws, orders, and whims of the German authorities. Needless to say, any member of the Judenrat who refused to carry out his duty was threatened death; every member of the Judenrat answered with his life for the fulfillment of his duties. Hence they were in a tragic position. Under a constant threat, they were forced to aid their executioners. They were liaisons between the ghetto population and the Germans and the transmitters of the Germans' orders. Their actions deserve a harsh judgment. At the same time, many members of the Judenrat tried every possible means to alleviate the condition of their unfortunate comrades, to save the condemned, to save the women, the children, and the sick. But even when they succeeded, they gained only a respite.

It must not be forgotten that the Germans tortured the Jews not only physically—not only with fear—but also with hope. After every murder, and sometimes beforehand, they announced that it would be the last. The attempted universal annihilation of the Jews was categorically denied, denied with indignation and with threats regarding the "spread of vicious rumors." They were constantly making promises to alleviate the plight of the Jews. At first many of the Jews could not accept the idea that millions of their fellow Jews were doomed to annihilation, even as the Germans were seizing more countries and all the people. And the Shavli Judenrat was compelled to adopt the politics by which the right hand did not know what the left hand was doing: as they were implementing the Germans' decrees, they were trying to protect people from the implementation of those fascist decrees, that is, from death.

The Shavli Judenrat failed in this. Not only did they fail; nothing could shake the Hitlerites in their resolve to annihilate the Jews who fell into their hands.

The members of the Shavli Judenrat were not afraid of death. When the Germans demanded that the Judenrat deliver fifty Jews from the ghetto to be shot, the members of the Judenrat unanimously proposed that they offer up themselves and categorically refused to hand anyone over. E. Yerushalmi was among those who did not hesitate for a moment in this decision.

O. Savich}

A Brief Account of Events that Took Place from 28 June to 23 November 1941

The Ghetto

The day after the German army occupied Siauliai (Shavli) on 28 July 1941, they began herding the Jews off to heavy forced labor.

The Jews were thrown out of food stores, driven off the sidewalks, and savagely beaten.

On Monday, 30 June, and Tuesday, 1 July, The Germans carried out mass arrests of Jews. Like robbers they dragged Jews from their homes and arrested anyone who fell into their hands.

A great deal of plundering took place during the arrests. Thousands of Jews were arrested at that time.[50]

On Saturday, 5 July, there were more mass arrests. Many of those who had previously managed to save themselves were taken that day. This time the Germans took all their valuables and their clothing.

On 15 August 1941 they began resettling Jews in the ghetto.[51]

Several commissions were appointed to oversee the resettlement. Each commission consisted of one representative, several members, and, thanks to the intervention of the Judenrat, one Jewish member. Lithuanian members of the commissions included policemen. There was a commission in charge of the property belonging to those who were being resettled. They were allowed to take with them a limited quantity of provisions. The commission in charge of their belongings issued each family a ticket ordering them to report for resettlement in the Caucasus section of the city within twenty-four hours.

The first to be resettled were those living on Vilenskaya Street, then Tilzitskaya, and so on. Such a huge mass of people was crammed into the Caucasus area that the Jewish administration could not accommodate them. The Caucasus was like a small town during a fire. The streets, courtyards, and alleys were overflowing with all sorts of household goods and with hundreds of people, including many women, the elderly, the sick, and children. Day and night they languished under the open sky; the air was filled with screams and wailing. But no one could help them. Once the Caucasus region could hold no more, Stankus,[52] the Burgermeister in charge, decided to add the Troksky section of the city to the ghetto.

Initially all of the Troksky region was enclosed, with the exception of Ginkunsky, Padirsky, Zhilvichsky, Ezhersky, and a large section of Troksaya Street. The area was later compressed, so that only two buildings on Trokskaya Street remained in the ghetto. Within two days the Troksky sector was also overflowing.

The streets of that region were filled with heartrending scenes, just as in the Caucasus.

The question arose as to whether a new sector should be added to the ghetto. Kalnyukas was to be the new area. The streets were sectioned off, and the residents in the area were informed that they must prepare to be resettled. But the residents of Kalnyukas protested with all their might that they did not want to leave their homes. They sent a delegation to the German municipal authorities who were in charge at the time. On top of all that, there was one more matter: Stankus himself lived in Kalnyukas. Therefore the Lithuanian residents of Kalnyukas wrote to Stankus: "If Kalnyukas is to be turned over to the Jews, then let Stankus give them his house."

On Saturday, 30 August, Stankus promised the Jewish representatives that he would give them Kalnyukas. He asked only that they not divulge his decision to anyone. A notation had already been made on the blue cards: "Resettlement in Kalnyukas." On Monday, 1 September, however, it was announced that Kalnyukas would not be turned over to the Jews. It should be noted that this whole affair irritated the German authorities.

That same day a delegation consisting of the attorney Abramovich, Kartun, and Leibovich[53] went to the Burgermeister. At first the Burgermeister did not want to receive them. He met them at the entrance to his office and said: "What do you want from me? Go to your Judenrat!" The delegation, however, was not daunted by such a reception. They all but forced their way into the Burgermeister's office, whereupon the following conversation ensued:

Delegates: We have come to ask for Kalnyukas.

Burgermeister: That is impossible!

Delegates: Where, then, are we to live?

Burgermeister: You will have to squeeze in a little tighter; move into sheds while it is still warm. Then we will house you in barracks.

But even then the Burgermeister knew that no barracks would be built. He mentioned Zhagor[54] and reproached the delegates for not agreeing immediately to a plan for settling in Zhagor.

The six commissions were working every day now. New powers were granted to their representatives, including the power to designated a place of resettlement for the Jews: either in the ghetto or in the "synagogue." By "synagogue" they referred either to a place of worship or to the old-age home, the residents of which had already been transferred to Zhagor. Of all the commissions, the one known for its brutality was headed by Lyubersky. Lyubersky conscientiously sent many Jews to the "synagogue,"[55] that is, to the next world.

The other commissions also began to treat the Jews much more harshly. Controls were tightened, the Jews' belongings were confiscated indiscriminately, and more than a thousand people were sent to the "synagogue."

Resettlement began on Tuesday, 2 September. The designated chapels and old-age home were full. Men, women, the elderly, and children were crowded into a small, narrow space. There was no place to sit. Those who were arrested were given no food or water; people were fainting from hunger and thirst, but the guards would not let anyone out. On Wednesday, 3 September, M. Leibovich and A. Kats visited the old-age home and were stunned by the scene that confronted them: enervated faces, ridden with panic and agony, outstretched hands, and heartrending cries: "Save us! We don't have a crumb of bread or a drop of water! Save us!"

The members of the Judenrat ran to Stankus and asked him to have mercy on the people who had been arrested. Stankus promised to alleviate their condition. Officials were sent to register the ones who had been arrested according to age, sex, and occupation. They announced that the registration would be conducted in an area designated for that purpose.

The registration was done in great haste; lists were made in duplicate and sent to Stankus' office, where no one was admitted. The members of the Judenrat could see that known executioners were going into Stankus' office and that the lists were being turned over to them. The Judenrat members burst into the office and, pounding on the table, demanded an explanation from Stankus: Where were the Jews in the "synagogue" being sent?[56]

Stankus was drunk; he mumbled:

"Don't ask! I don't know! It was against my will!"

On Thursday Leibovich went to the old-age home. The courtyard was filled with an ominous silence—the people had already been taken away! He tried to get inside, but the guard shouted at him: "Get away from here!"

Leibovich, however, saw the executioners dividing among themselves what was left of the Jews' belongings.

The members of the Judenrat reached an agreement with the Chief of Jewish Affairs that an old-age home and an orphanage would remain in the ghetto. The Chief even agreed to bring back from Zhagor some of the people who had been in the old-age home. A large building on Trokskaya Street was designated to serve as an orphanage. In the city all the arrangements were made for transferring the orphanage to the ghetto. Thus the Judenrat was assured that the orphanage would indeed be transferred; they even advised a woman who had just arrived in Siauliai that, since there was no room in the ghetto, she should place her three children in the orphanage.

The transfer was supposed to take place in September. All that remained were various formalities. The designated day passed, but the formalities had not been completed. At seven o'clock one evening the rumor spread through the ghetto that the children in the orphanage had already been taken away. It turned out that on that day, the 6th of September, at 6:30 A.M. a truck pulled up to the orphanage, and the children, along with their teacher Kats and his housekeeper, were loaded inside. They were not allowed to take their belongings with them; they could not even dress for the journey. The truck was escorted by the security police. The truck left and then quickly returned. Forty-three children, Kats, and his housekeeper all perished. Among them were the three Katsman children from Tsitavian.[57] The unfortunate woman had managed to save herself and her children from their pursuers in Tsitavian with great difficulty. During her first days in the ghetto she could find no shelter, so, on the advice of the Judenrat, she had placed her three children in the orphanage. Her older daughter was a rare beauty, and the scoundrels in Tsitavian had pity on her and wanted to let her live. In Shavli her beauty did not stop the murderers.

On Sunday, 7 September, the commission led by the illustrious Lyubersky (head of the first commission at the time of the resettlement into the ghetto) arrived in the ghetto; they came to register the Jews. The residents of the ghetto—old and young, without regard to their condition—were registered. For many of them the registration process took years off their life.

Several days passed; already the registration had been forgotten in the ghetto. Then suddenly, on Wednesday, 10 September, just after twelve o'clock noon, trucks carrying armed policemen pulled up.[58] First they surrounded the building at 2 Padirsyu Street and removed several families from there. They took away Mrs. Fainshtein and her two children, Mrs. Volkov and her two children, Mrs. Smilg and her baby, the tinsmith Aleksandrovich and his wife (most of the women's husbands were working in the city), and everyone else. Then the police went through the ghetto with a list that they used for gathering up the old men and women; they took them away as well. In many cases they took the young with the old. All of this was a matter of only two or three hours. People were so shocked by it that they did not understand what exactly was happening. There were instances in which children went voluntarily with their parents, even though they were not on the list. The vehicles left filled to capacity and soon returned empty. This led people to suppose that they had been hauled someplace near Shavli. When Fainshtein returned to the ghetto and discovered what had become of his family, he ran to Stabsleiter Schrader. His wife had had a special permit, but she was so confused that she failed to present it. Fainshtein tried catch up to his family. He went several dozen kilometers in the direction of Zhagor, where they had supposedly been taken, but he did not find them. Then it became clear to him that they had been taken to a place from which they would never return. Also taken from the ghetto that day was, among others, the very worthy teacher Eliezer Goldshtein, whose sixtieth birthday had been celebrated at the Shavli's Jewish gymnasium six years earlier. He had worked there with selfless dedication since 1920. He was taken with his wife. Also hauled away was a teacher named Taibele Shneider and her elderly father.

The next day, a Thursday, the trucks began loading at nine in the morning. It was a rainy day. The executioners went from building to building in search of the old people on their list. Many of those who were doomed managed to find a hiding place and were saved. One of them was the writer of these lines. He had been warned in time, so that he and his wife and two children went out the back way and hid in a certain building. Later he was taken off the list. On that sad day they took a music professor who had taught for many years in the old Jewish gymnasium; it was Moishe Kravets and his wife. After several hours the rumor spread through the ghetto that someone who had escaped the Aktion had returned and that he was with his family in the city. Judenrat member M. Leibovich went there and discovered the terrible truth: everyone rounded up was taken to the woods near Bubiai.[59] There they were stood next to previously dug pits and shot. The man who had escaped was wounded but managed to crawl out of the pit. A second escapee showed up later and confirmed the story.

A new registration of the ghetto residents was held on 13 September, and yellow passports were distributed. Once again Lyubersky was in charge of the registration process. Everyone in the ghetto walked past him, as he looked each one over and decided his fate; the elderly either went into hiding or disguised themselves by coloring their hair, smoothing out their wrinkles, and shaving their beards. Never before did the hairdressers and barbers have such a flood of clients, nor had they ever seen such clients: old, sick, and tormented people full of despair. Not everyone was able to fool Lyubersky, and many of them were taken immediately from the registration office to the "synagogue." Judenrat workers did many of the "suspicious" passports. Burgin is especially noteworthy in this regard. He collected the blue passports from the old people and sent them on to the registration table; then he passed them on through the registrar's window, where the documents were finalized. Many were saved in this manner. But the next day Lyubersky realized what was happening and checked everyone more carefully. He tracked down Burgin and threatened to send him to the "synagogue." He gave Burgin a yellow passport only when the distribution of passports was completed. On that day Stankus arrived in the ghetto.

Once he saw what was happening in the ghetto, he became terrified by the hunger and had many of the residents sent to the country.[60] An agreement had been made with the kulaks to hire them out as laborers. The agreement was signed by the Chief of Jewish Affairs, who added onto it a special condition: the employer was responsible for keeping an eye on the Jewish worker, had to place him at the disposal of the police as per the original order, and so on.

The agreement was sent to the Arbeitsamt for confirmation. Once the people were sure that the agreement they hoped for had gone through, they set out with all their belongings to see peasants in the country. Several days later, however, the foreman of their group ordered the *virshaitis* (the village elders) to expel all the Jews from the country. The writer of these lines was one of those who went to the country. He had a contract with a peasant named Ionas Aleksandras and had moved into the country with all his possessions. He left on 18 September, and on the 23rd the order for resettlement came. The sergeant major held the order until the 24th. The author of these lines at first tried to plead for a deferment, even for just a day. But there was nothing to be done. He had to quickly gather his things, leaving most of them with the peasant, and go back to the city. There he had to turn over whatever belongings he had for "inspection." The next day it turned out that everything left with the police for inspection was gone; they stole all of it. Such was the lot that fell to everyone who sought salvation in the country. They all returned "relieved" of their possessions.

From the Diary

4 February 1943. Today the Labor Bureau (Arbeitsamt) demanded that two hundred men be delivered for work tomorrow; they also demanded that the contingent of workers at the airfield be increased.

At a joint meeting of the Judenrat and the Labor Commission we discussed for a long time where we were going to get the people demanded for work, but we came to no decision. Reluctantly the question was posed: what became of the 480 people who were assigned as peat workers last summer? Right now there are a hundred working in the peat bog and a hundred at the airfield; at the camp in Linkaichiai there were eight-five people, fifty working on the railroad, twenty in Strala—a total of 355 people. What has become of more than a hundred workers? It turns out that they have turned into invalids. Most of them suffered from a heart condition; many developed a hernia. The rest came down with furunculosis, gangrene, and other conditions. Half the women stopped menstruating and swelled up.

6 February 1943. Existence races on with cinematographic speed. The day of our deliverance is drawing near. Still, the danger is growing.

The Gebietskommissar asked Idaelis, the Lithuanian member of the Judenrat's Labor Commission, whether the Jews have not grown too insolent lately.

22 February 1943. Yesterday a Jew was walking down the sidewalk, when he was stopped by Sergeant Major Velkshtis at a police post. Velkshtis harassed the Jew, saying, "Do you think the approach of the Russians means you'll just be set free? You are mistaken. You won't live that long; we'll cut you down first."

19 March 1943. There are up to two hundred Jews working at the tannery. An order came from the Gebietskommissariat to discharge some of the workers supposedly for disrupting the workday. With great difficulty we managed to have the order repealed. Labor director Zilel, however, went around all the sections and carefully looked into the faces of the workers, noting down the weakest ones for dismissal from work.

27 March 1943. A man who was present at a shooting in the prison on 23 March related that while being taken to be executed with her son, a Jewish woman put up a strong resistance and refused to allow herself to be murdered. They threw her and her son into the pit, but she crawled out. Again they pushed her into the pit and shot her and her son with their machine guns.

29 April 1943. A folk school was semi-officially opened in the Troksky district in the balcony area of the synagogue in a space of eighteen square meters. The school operates from nine to four.

There are ninety children in the school; they are divided into four groups, with each one studying an hour and a half to two hours per day.

A school opened in the Caucasus area of the ghetto on 5 July, also in a synagogue, in an area of twenty square meters. Classes are held from seven in the morning until eight in the evening. Two hundred children divided into seven groups attend the school.

Judenrat member A. Geller and secretary E. Yerushalmi undertook the initiative to set up the schools.

It is worth noting that, despite their harsh living conditions, the little ones joyfully rush to school, where they study eagerly and attentively. Thirty-five to forty children sit—and some stand—pressed tightly against one another. There is not a sound in the classroom, but in this silence it is as though the ghetto has come to life.

The children's work in the gardens has also been justified. Children organized into several groups planted all the Judenrat's gardens; now they are busy weeding and watching over the gardens. The twelve-year-olds feel like adults and carry out their duties no less than the adults.

4 May 1943. Today was a hard day in the Shavli Ghetto. It was not even lunchtime when a pair of policemen at the ghetto gate indicated that they were under strict orders to check everyone going in and out of the ghetto. At lunchtime a man from the Gebietskommissariat named Papen found Zisel Shvarts in the home of a certain Lithuanian. Papen asked the Jew, "What are you doing here?" To which the Jew replied, "I stopped in for a bite." Papen noted down his named and asked where he was working. Shvarts said that he was working with a small group of Jewish laborers loading potatoes for the camp in Bachyuni.

Then, relishing the sad news from Schreiver and acting in behalf of the Gebietskommissar,[61] Papen showed up in the ghetto. He began inspecting the columns of workers returning to the ghetto. The actual searches were conducted by two policemen, Strupkus and Yurgatavichus. Yurgatavichus derided the male and female workers and behaved in the most insolent manner.

Hundreds of people passed through the gate to the Caucasus Ghetto. All of them were frisked, and fifteen were discovered with contraband: pieces of bread, potatoes, a little meat, a pinch of tobacco, and the like. The "guilty" ones were lined up and taken to the prison. The Gebietskommissar released only two little boys who were found with potatoes and ordered the members of the Judenrat to thoroughly "punish" them. Later the Gebietskommissar did not forget to ask whether they had been thoroughly "punished."

Visitors were sent from the Caucasus to the Troksky Ghetto, where they were summoned to go to work loading potatoes. Then all of them except Shvarts were released.

From the ghetto the police were sent to their "ceremonial reception" of the workers' column returning from the airfield. They discovered food on seven of the 329 people. These too were lined up and taken to the prison. Twenty-three people in all were arrested and sent to prison.

6 May 1943. Early this morning in the Troksky Ghetto it was announced that everyone was required to attend an execution. By ten o'clock in the morning the entire adult population of the Troksky Ghetto was at the ghetto gate. Except for the children, no one was allowed to stay home.

The people stood at the barrier in profound silence. They awaited the arrival of their "guest."

At eleven o'clock a car pulled up. In it were Stabsleiter Bub, Papen, Braun of the gendarmes, the gendarmes' translator Shpakauskas, and Krol of the SD. Behind the car were four policemen with machine guns. In the middle of them, wearing handcuffs, was Betsalel. He walked vigorously, with a smile on his lips. Did he have some hope that they would have mercy on him at the last minute?

The condemned man was led to the gallows, where a doctor and two executioners stood.[62] Mazovetsky asked that the fetters be removed from his hands, but his request was denied. He also asked to say farewell to his wife and little boy, but this too was denied him. Then Mazovetsky said: "Take care of my wife and child; tell her and my mother to be strong." He asked that his coat be given to a poor person. Then, with the rope around his neck, he ascended the platform; still smiling, he bowed to the people and said: "I shall be your worthy intercessor in heaven."

At that moment the hatch was pulled, the rope pulled tight, and Mazovetsky's body shook with its final convulsions. A cry of despair rose from a hundred breasts; dozens of women fainted. The strained cry of the martyr's brother resounded in the distance.

At ten minutes after eleven the doctor climbed the platform, felt Mazovetsky's pulse, listened to his heart, and declared him dead.

The Germans left. Bub ordered the body to be left hanging there until noon; only the gravediggers and the Judenrat were allowed to be present at the burial.

At twelve o'clock the body was removed from the gallows, taken to its grave, and buried in profound silence. The martyr's last smile was frozen on his face.

8 May 1943. An order concerning those who were arrested arrived (their number has grown to twenty-seven). At ten o'clock tomorrow morning they will be brought from the prison to the ghetto and subjected to a public whipping. The men will each receive fifteen lashes and the women ten. This is to be the punishment for anyone who tries to bring a piece of bread, some potatoes, or a couple of meager eggs into the ghetto.

ANNOUNCEMENT

In keeping with a pronouncement from the Gebietskommissar, the following is hereby made known:

On Sunday, 9 May, those who were detained and arrested on the 4th of this month for attempting to smuggle food into the ghetto will be taken out of the prison. At ten o'clock in the morning and in the presence of the authorities they will all be subjected to public corporal punishment on the ghetto square at No. 1 Gelgaud Street (in the garden). The residents of the ghetto are ordered to be present for the execution of the punishment.

8 May 1943

10 May 1943. Yesterday at 10:30 in the morning representatives of the authorities drove up to the prison and ordered the people arrested to be brought out. Among the authorities was Papen, an employee from the Preisüberwachungsstelle;[63] he was standing in for Stabsleiter Gaberman (superintendent of schools in the Shavli district). A police unit escorted the prisoners into the square of the Caucasus Ghetto (in the garden). They were ordered to lie down four in a row; each of them received ten blows from a rubber truncheon. Only at the last moment did the members of the Judenrat manage to get the authorities to exempt the eight women and the sick men from the shameful punishment and to reduce the number of blows given.

12 May 1943. Today police officer Yurgatavichus thoroughly searched everyone passing through the gate; he stopped one woman and made her stand on her knees. She knelt there for a while and then he released her for half a bottle of vodka. Another woman was found with a bottle of milk; he ordered it to be poured out.

19 May 1943. Today there was another hunt for contraband in the ghetto. At 5:30 this morning Gebietskommissar Schreiver and Papen drove up to the Caucasus Ghetto, stopped a short distance from the gate, and began checking the work columns passing by. Schreiver personally searched everyone and examined every centimeter of clothing; the search resulted in the arrest of ten people, including a thirteen-year-old boy. Those who were detained were forced to kneel until the entire search was completed. Finally they were taken to prison. Why were they arrested? For being in possession of the following list of confiscated goods: 2.8 kilograms of peas, 1 kilogram of macaroni, 0.5 kilograms of liver sausage, 0.5 kilograms of butter, 2 eggs, 0.25 kilograms of boiled meat, 1 kilogram of bread, 0.25 kilograms of sorrel greens, 1 kilogram of sugar, and 1.5 kilograms of potatoes.

21 May 1943. Yesterday representatives of the Judenrat went to the Regierungsrat[64] to see Bub and Papen. They presented the list of confiscated food mentioned above and described the torment of the workers. All the men and women have been placed in an utterly impossible position. Workers such as those on whom most of the goods were discovered toil from seven in the morning until twelve o'clock at night. People go to work with one hundred grams of bread. How can they endure such a long day of hard labor without food?

The Regierungsrat promised to release the ones who had been arrested. Stabsleiter Bub said that the main problem was the butter. Had they found no butter, then the ones arrested would have been released immediately. Nevertheless, this time they would be released, but they will be whipped—not as others have been whipped before, however: they will be placed on a bench and "scrupulously" whipped.

Received news from Vilna. Security at the gate has become extremely tight. Now Jews themselves have to check people while a German guard stands and observes. In one instance a German conducted a search after a Jew had finished and discovered some food. For this infraction six Jews who had been searching people were shot.

22 May 1943. Today Judenrat members M. Leibovich and A. Kats were at the Gebietskommissariat. There Papen informed them that on Sunday the 23rd the ones who had been arrested would be taken to the Caucasus Ghetto (since nine of the ten arrested were from that ghetto) and subjected to a public whipping in the garden on Gelgaud Street. He added that this time they would be properly whipped, since the supervisor and his assistant would both be present.

The ghetto representatives asked to see the supervisor in the hope of obtaining a reduction of the sentence.

The supervisor received them and loudly declared, so that all could hear, that the "dog-pigs" who were smuggling lard and sausage into the ghetto must be severely punished. When the ghetto representatives pointed out that among the ten there were some who were found only with bread or a potato, the supervisor said that next time "people like that will just turn up someplace else."

OFFICIAL ORDER

In keeping with a pronouncement from the Gebietskommissar, the following is hereby made known:

On Sunday, the 23rd of this month at 11:00 A.M. those who were arrested on the 19th of this month for attempting to smuggle food into the ghetto will be taken from the prison to the garden at 1 Gelgaud Street in the Caucasus Ghetto and there subjected to corporal punishment. All residents are required to be present at the punishment.
Shavli. 22 May 1943

23 May 1943. At ten o'clock this morning the ten who were arrested were brought to the gates of the Caucasus Ghetto. Velkshtis (the former chief of the ghetto guard) and another policeman accompanied them.

The prisoners waited at the gate for an hour and fifteen minutes. Velkshtis brandished a whip over their heads and shouted, "You're going to get it for smuggling illegal lard and for being Bolsheviks!" Then he walked over to the Jewish guard and harassed and mocked him. Several times he repeated, "If things go well for the Germans, you might be allowed to live, so you can draw out your miserable existence. But if things go badly, then you will be massacred. I and people like me will do it, because if you ever get out of the ghetto, you will do the same to us."

At 11:15 the carriage from the Gebietskommissariat pulled up. Schreiver, Liepker, Braun, and a Lithuanian fascist were in it.

Velkshtis and the other policeman led the prisoners into the garden at 1 Gelgaud Street, where a table was set up in an open area. Around it stood all the people of the ghetto, who were forced to attend.

At the last moment Judenrat members Leibovich and A. Kats pleaded with the officials to exempt the minor L. from the corporal punishment, since he had been arrested simply for trying to smuggle in a piece of candy. The boy was taken out of the group.

The punishment began. As it was happening, A. Kats was forced to face the people of the ghetto and remind them that a ration had been established for the Jews (one hundred grams of bread for those who do not work and two hundred gram for those who do) and that nothing more was permitted inside the ghetto. The prisoners were brought over to the table and made to bend over it (anyone wearing a coat had to remove it). Then the policemen beat them with rubber clubs.

This whipping was not enough for Velkshtis. Several times, with all his might, he gave the victim a blow with an iron club.

26 May 1943. Bachyunai is troubling. Three hundred twenty people work at a peat refinery there. Many of them, however, are weak and sick, people who should never have been sent out to work. About two hundred actually do the labor; the rest are in the administrative office, in the yard, and in the workshops. From the laborers they can form every day a total of six brigades of twenty people each. There are never enough people to form a seventh brigade.

For this reason there is an ongoing misunderstanding between the Judenrat and the director of the peat refinery. The director insists that he should be able to form eight, or at least seven, brigades from the 320 workers, since that is what the rural administration of the Gebietskommissariat expects of him. The Judenrat, on the other hand, insists that the number of brigades be left at six. The simplest thing would be to declare that of the 320 people several dozen were not fit to work the peat and that they would have to be left in the ghetto. But the Judenrat is afraid to speak openly of this. First of all, they could demand that the sick be replaced with healthy workers; where would those people come from? But the main thing is that in the ghetto it is generally dangerous to be sick or weak.

28 May 1943. The following proclamation was spread throughout the Lithuanian population in Kovno:

"Since an Aktion against the Jews in the ghetto is being planned, we summon all true patriots not to take part in it, for such behavior would soil the good name of the Lithuanians." Signed: "Committee for the Establishment of Lithuanian Independence"

A Lithuanian worker passed the proclamation along to a Jewish worker, who in turn gave it to a member of the Judenrat named Liftser.

2 June 1943. The German authorities distributed a lengthy, ten-page statement about the Jews among factions of Lithuanian nationalists. On page five it is noted:

"Tasks that appear to be humiliating for Lithuania and the Lithuanian soldier (shooting Jews and citizens captured in Belorussia) are to be assigned to battalions made up of Lithuanians. When the Lithuanian officers refuse to shoot, they themselves will be threatened with being shot. Only one Lithuanian unit has been photographed and filmed during an execution, while the Germans avoided... ."

20 June 1943. Boyer, the secretary of a fascist organization, spent some time in Germany on furlough; while he was there he experienced bombing raids by American and British airplanes. He was very disturbed by it and has turned against the Jews with a vengeance. He told one Jewish worker that he had lunch with a general who said there were too many Jews in the ghetto and that their number had to be reduced.

30 June 1943. Today two agents from the SD,[65] Kroll and Gef, demanded additional information about the ghetto inhabitants and insisted that they be divided into four categories:

1.   Men and women under thirty years of age.

2.   Those employed in work important to the war effort.

3.   Those living in barracks in the camps.

4.   Those with limited work capability.

Also, the Judenrat was to add one more category, a "reserve column" of those who were incapable of work or who could work very little. These would include the mothers of small children, old people, and people working at the airfield only two or three days per week.

The SD would not agree to include approximately one thousand women in this last column and demanded that another five hundred people be designated for work, including those who could work three to four times per week. This meant that the sick, minors, and mothers with small children would have to work. And it is just as well if everyone should fall into this category, since the SD's visit leads one to a disturbing thought... .

9 July 1943. An article titled "Servants of the Jews" by A. Lenzen, Brigadenführer SA and Gebietskommissar for Kauenland (Kovno district), appeared in issue 154 of the newspaper *Ateitis*.

"Unfortunately," he writes, "traces of the talons of Israel are still noticeable in Kovno and the surrounding areas. All one need do is consider the phenomenon of urban life as columns of Jews are return to the ghetto. Literally incredible things happen here. I myself have recently had the opportunity to observe an elegantly dressed lady, a Lithuanian, approach a column of Jews and offer one of them a greeting; with remarkable courtesy she offered him her hand and engaged him in conversation. How is it that such relationships ever existed here? And how can they continue to exist? I decided to step in and interrupt their chat. The Jew fled with great speed; the woman was taken aback, became very timid, and tried to disappear. Unfortunately, since I did not know Lithuanian, I was unable to give her a serious admonition. But she understood me; her behavior made that clear.

"It may also be noted that the residents of the city and outlying areas have had a longstanding acquaintance with the Jews and provide them with food. Many clear cases of this have been established when columns of Jewish workers have been searched. How is it possible for Jewish workers to stop by a Lithuanian's apartment and address him as an equal? Just to get rid of them, then, the Lithuanians with chat with them and even barter with them. How can people who do not conduct themselves properly deserve our sympathy, like those who set such an ugly example for their countrymen?

"Even more deserving of contempt is the bartering with the peasants in the outlying areas. Whenever you ask a peasant whether he has any produce or other food, he evades the question; to Jews, however, he 'will sell with pleasure.' This is a special friendship. Tell me who your friend is, and I will tell you who you are. I suggest that anyone who enters into any relationship with Jews—who aids them or tries to maintain contact with them—be marked with a star that reads 'Servant of the Jews.'"

17 July 1943. On Saturday, 17 July, two policemen at the ghetto gate got drunk and burst into the ghetto at 12:30 in the morning and started attacking anyone they happened to meet. They dragged one man out of the ghetto, beat him up, and threatened to shoot him. They demanded girls... . The Jewish guard Genekh Raiz tried to intervene, but he was beaten too.

26 July 1943. The news of Mussolini's resignation was received in the ghetto with astonishment and joy, but outwardly people remain calm; they know they must not let their feelings show. We are still faced with something!

28 July 1943. Issue 165 of the newspaper *Ateitis* has a new article titled "Jews and the Servants of Jews."

"... The attorney Vsevolod Kopp is especially sympathetic toward Jews. By seven o'clock in the morning he can be found in the city park, where he chats with Jews. When they part he smiles at them and shakes their hand.

"Large numbers of people have been punished for secretly trading with Jews, including Rozaliya Moltene, who lives at 4/9 Yankovskaya Street in Kovno, and Petronele Rudkauskene from the village of Uzhledzhyu in the Kovno district. For this crime they have been deprived of their freedom. In keeping with the order, the arrest of such people has gone on for more than a month.

31 July 1943. We have received word from the camp at the airfield that the pilots had a dance, which was attended by the Generalkommissar and the Gebietskommissar; they talked about the Jews. They paid particular attention to the fact that (1) Jews are not to greet officers and (2) Jews must work on Sundays.

1 August 1943. Today a foreman at the airfield seized a Jewish boy who on the previous day had been deemed guilty of not working. The boy was forced to run behind two bicycles; whenever he failed to keep up with them, he was beaten. The foreman tied a saw and a box containing four kilograms of nails around the boy's neck and then drove him with a whip for two kilometers. Maimed and exhausted, the boy could hardly crawl home.

5 August 1943. Today was a hard day at the airfield. It seems that two junior officers from the Gestapo attempted to teach the Jewish workers what they call "mind-reason." Early this morning they explained what Jews are required to do whenever they pass by a German military figure, including soldiers. Jews must remove their caps five meters prior to encountering a junior officer and hold it over their heads until the junior officer has gone five meters past. In the case of an officer, they must similarly degrade themselves ten meters before and ten meters after meeting them.

When a column of Jews workers passes by a junior officer or officer, they must remove their caps and quickly run by.

In order to train them, the junior officers began drilling the workers according to the rules they had outlined. Then they decided to see how the work was progressing. They caught one worker sitting idle; as a punishment they forced him to run one and a half kilometers. Another man was sitting and was wearing no shirt; they began strangling him for "failure to wear the prescribed Jewish star." A third man was forced to run without stopping, with two people riding bicycles on either side of him. Briefly stated, they tortured anyone who happened to fall into their clutches.

10 August 1943, the 9th of Av.[66] Today news about a great change spread through the ghetto. Our joy was contained but enormous. Someone in the synagogue suggested that we cut short our prayers of mourning because deliverance is at hand.

31 August 1943. Today there was a joint meeting of the Judenrat and representatives from the ghetto. In attendance were: M. Leibovich, A. Geller, P. Rubinshtein, A. Kats, Sh. Burgin, A. Abramson, A. Kalfenitsky, A. Brelovich, B. Abramovich, P. Vits, D. Gets, M. Rubinshtein, I. Minor, M. Mil, A. Zeigarnik, A. Slezin, Kh. Chernyavsky, A. Gets, A. Gutman, Kh. Zhilinsky, K. Utsven, A. Gens, I. Mordel, Kh. L. Sheskin, Sh. Kats, Doctor Burshtein, Doctor Direktorovich, Doctor Kamber.

Chairman: M. Leibovich
Secretary: A. Kats

Ghetto representatives informed of a decree issued by the Sicherheitspolizei (the Gestapo). Chairman M. Leibovich and Judenrat member A. Kats reported:

Today at 11:00 A.M. Gestapo chief Makk summoned Judenrat members M. Leibovich and A. Kats and announced to them: "In view of the fact that Jews are violating orders strictly forbidding them to bring food into the ghetto, and since on 29 August 1943 a column of laborers working in the fields for the Gebietskommissar was detained and many were found with food strictly forbidden by law, tomorrow, 1 September 1943, at twelve noon the Judenrat must have fifty Jews brought to the prison. The Judenrat will be held responsible if the designated number of people should fail to report."

Knowing what it meant to be turned over to the prison, the Judenrat members announced that they refused to follow the order and that they would turn themselves in precisely at the designated hour and place themselves at the disposal of the authorities.

The Gestapo chief assured them that he was interested in only one thing, namely that fifty Jews be there at the appointed time; exactly who they are was to him a matter of indifference. When asked whether it might be possible to revoke or alter the punishment, the chief answered: "I received the order from the Gebietskommissar, and I must follow it to the letter."

With that the conversation ended. The Judenrat representatives appealed to Doctor Günther,[67] Director of the Arbeitsamt. He promised to "take measures."

The chairman invited those attending the meeting to consider ways of averting this new misfortune.

It was decided to submit the names of the Judenrat members to the Gebietskommissar with an appeal to revoke the decree. The appeal was to be delivered by Judenrat members M. Leibovich, A. Kats, and Sh. Kats.

At six o'clock in the afternoon the same people reconvened.

The chairman informed them that Doctor Günther delivered their appeal for mercy to the Gebietskommissar. The Gebietskommissar was in a very nasty frame of mind. He would not discuss it but rather declared, "We are not Jews, and we do not negotiate. Our order must be followed to the letter."

The chairman asked that everyone express his opinion in view of their great responsibility.

Several old men fainted. There was no electricity. The tragic deliberations proceeded in the fading light.

Physically exhausted, Geller, the oldest member of the Judenrat, spoke with tears in his voice about the long history of the Jewish people and the times when at the last minute "good would arise from evil." Others suggested that we cast lots to determine who would be executed; a list of Jews willing to turn themselves over to death could be drawn up.

Resistance was not even considered. There were no weapons. Instead of fifty, the whole ghetto would perish without inflicting any losses upon their executioners. Time was running out.

Everyone at the meeting unanimously decided to turn themselves in at the prison.

An hour before the appointed time M. Leibovich and A. Kats were at the Gestapo office, where the walls were witnesses to the great suffering of the Jews. The Germans were apparently in a festive mood; they were all in their parade uniforms, fully armed, and ready for the "celebration" that was about to take place.

The chief finally showed up and informed them that the punishment would to be replaced with a fine of twenty thousand marks payable in two installments on 15 September 1943 and on 15 October 1943.

18 September 1943. The new ghetto committee announced that the matter of moving ghetto residents into barracks was being decided in Berlin.

23 September 1943. Our new master Hauptsturmführer Forster has been to see us several times. Every time he is several hours late, and each time we await his arrival with fear. He speaks in a calm monotone and carefully listens to what the Judenrat tells him, but his position does not change. And his position is this: ghetto residents will be transferred into barracks and divided into several work units, and they would comply with 100 percent of all orders. His first demand was that five hundred Jews be moved into barracks at the airfield by six o'clock on 26 September. Adults and children more than ten years of age were to be sent to the airfield. It must be made clear that the barracks there are in ill repair and extremely filthy. Nevertheless he was steadfast. He told us: "My order is for Thursday and no later." The commandant at the airfield declared: "Either you will bring the Jews on the appointed day or you will not have them at all." It is necessary either to tear parents away from their families or to condemn entire families to hard labor. Also, it was impossible to send parents with small children. At the last minute a train had shifted its destination to Riga, so that there were thirty-one workers left at the airfield. Subsequently the commandant allowed only four hundred to be sent on Thursday; the remaining hundred would wait until Friday.

The commandant hissed through his teeth that children over ten would not be allowed to follow their parents to the concentration camp but would be housed in a special children's home that would suffer the same fate as all Jewish children's homes: liquidation.

24 September 1943. At seven o'clock this morning a column of workers set out for the airfield. It was the saddest procession of any that have left the ghetto. People walked as if they were going to a funeral. It was especially sad to see the families with children.

The commandant of the ghetto was there, as well as a guide and one of the officials from the airfield. The street was lined with an entire company of armed soldiers. A total of four hundred people went out. But one ran off.

27 September 1943. Twenty men and sixty women were sent to Linkaichiai today. Despairing parents with small children swept into the city to entrust their little ones to the care of Lithuanians. They even handed them over to priests, but only a few were involved.

30 September 1943. The street running alongside the ghetto is still littered with things that belonged to the people taken to camps in Daugiliai and Pavenchia; no truck has been dispatched to pick them up. The barracks in Daugiliai have no floor, no stove, no pots or pans; they do not even have windows. There are no plank beds. The necessities for living are not provided. People go hungry and naked.

1 October 1943. The situation in Daugiliai is catastrophic. The unfinished barracks was designed to hold sixty prisoners; right now there are 246 people there. Four people share plank beds seventy centimeters wide that have been hurriedly thrown together. There is no straw or hay. Much of the baggage is just lying in the street: there is no room for it. What are they to do with the things that have yet to arrive? But it does no good to worry about it, since the camp commandant, an SS Unteroffizier, has observed that the Jews have too many things and that all of it must be examined. The meaning of this observation is clear... .

The windows of the barracks still have no glass in them. The cold and dampness in the camp are terrible. Already there are cases of people falling ill. There is a danger of epidemic.

The camp has none of the necessities of life. Food has not been distributed. People are starving.

The ghetto commandant was here to see, in his typical fashion, how we were getting "settled"; as for the horrid living conditions, his only remark was: "Everything will be okay." Since it was soon clear that he could not avoid saying something in regard to cleanliness in the camp, he added that any disobedience would be punished by shooting or hanging.

Women and children wander about aimlessly. It is impossible to imagine the despair of these people.

3 October 1943. The school has been closed. Some of the children have been sent off to the camps, others are still wandering around in the ghetto. The teachers have gone off to various places.

The old are obliged to go to work, and the young—from ten to thirteen years of age—try hard to get to work to avoid being counted among those who are incapable of work. There are hundreds of them here. Torn from their parents, many children of school age have to take care of their younger brothers and sisters.

Everyone worries about what to do with the children during the day. To set up a childcare center for them is a terrifying thought: Jewish childcare centers do not last long... .

9 October 1943. It is morning. The buildings on Vilenskaya Street have already been cleaned out.[68] All day Friday a brigade of nearly one hundred men and women worked to clean the buildings and straighten them up. All the garbage was hauled away. They washed and scrubbed every corner and put the dwellings in complete order. About four hundred people were resettled. On Saturday, Yom Kippur, the wire fence marking the ghetto boundary was moved to its new position... .

We are awaiting the order for the separation of the men from the women... .

17 October 1943. Today a second resettlement from the Caucasus area to Troksky began. The Caucasus area is supposed to be cleaned out by the 20th and the people transferred to the vacated parts of Ezhersky and Trokskaya Streets.

There is news from Akmian[69] about a similar situation. Gershon Zhemaitishek was marked for the last transport. He complained of a stomach ailment. Upon arriving in Akmian, the commandant summoned him and asked whether he was sick or healthy. He replied that he was sick. "Can you work?" the commandant asked. Zhemaitishek said no. Then the commandant took out his revolver and shot Zhemaitishek right in front of everyone. Immediately afterward the commandant walked through the camp and began asking about camp affairs as if nothing had happened.

18 October 1943. Yet another victim. On Sunday the 17th an order was issued in Daugiliai that no one was to leave the camp. Nevertheless Kushelevsky and his two boys went out to the countryside to beg for alms. They were picked up on the way back; the children were sent back to the camp, and Kushelevsky was shot. They say the first bullet did not kill him. The camp commandant, a sergeant major, then walked up and fired a second shot. He said: "According to my calculations, fifteen thousand Jews have been removed from Slonim; let there be one more... ."

25 October 1943. The camp at Akmian looks very depressing: the barracks look filthy and miserable; they are falling apart. It is no better inside: the residents of the camp have brought their poverty with them from the ghetto, and they possess only rags. Nevertheless they try to keep it clean as best they can; every day they clean the barracks, but the cramped conditions, with the plank beds shared by everyone, are beyond description. The barracks are illuminated partly by lamps, partly by pine shavings. The commandant, a sergeant major, allows people to go outside the camp to work for peasants for butter and lard. The administration of the chalk quarries does not require heavy work, so that the weak can work too. Not only that, precisely the weak and the elderly are dying to work in the quarries, since everyone is terrified by the murder of Zhemaitishek, who cried out as he was dying. "I am a robust man!" This is how they get their food: those who work with the peasants eat their fill while they work; then they bring the rest of what they could get back to the camp. The children pose the most complicated problem; there are twelve tiny ones and about forty who are a little older. The people living in the camp tremble in fear fore them. According to the camp commandant, the head of all the camps, Hauptsturmführer Forster, has ordered him to gather up all the children and shoot them; he has not, however, carried out the order. Then he said that the Shavli Ghetto is in great danger; it is supposed to be destroyed, but right now the danger is minimal, and nothing is threatening us at the moment. The commandant himself, however, does not belong to the assembly of the righteous: he shamelessly demands bribes, and woe to the one who does not come across. A Jewish girl once caught his eye, and he followed her for six hours; he threatened to shoot her, and it was only by chance that she managed to escape. And yet he pretends to be a strict adherent of morality in the camp and will not allow the men to visit the women's barracks. Since the kitchen is in the women's barracks, however, the men are allowed to go there to eat. But they cannot stay past six in the evening.

30 October 1943. All supervisors and village elders (the virshaitis) have received orders to burn the bodies of the Jews slaughtered two years ago in Shavli and surrounding areas and buried in mass graves.

Friday, 5 November 1943. Today was the darkest day of our unhappy life in the ghetto: they took away the children.

This morning, as everyone was about to leave work, the sentry announced that he had received orders not to allow anyone outside the gates. Assuming that they were to be transported to some distant place, as it had happened in Vilna and Kovno, everyone went home and started getting ready for the trip.

Hauptsturmführer Forster showed up in the Judenrat office at 7:30; the illustrious Schwandt was right behind him. In addition, a special killing unit armed with machine guns had arrived from Kovno. Covered trucks could be seen riding all around the ghetto. Forster turned to the sentry with a pretentious air and asked why he had not let the workers go to work; he then ordered them to be sent to work immediately. Forster's order was announced to the residents of the ghetto, and everyone, young and old, headed for the gate, many with their children. But Commandant Schleef was standing at the gate and would not let the children out.

When the workers left, Forster ordered the gates to be closed.

"I have received an order to remove from the ghetto all children up to thirteen years of age and all adults incapable of work. The children will be sent to Kovno and settled in a children's home, where older ones will look after them. All Jewish children from the camps will be gathered there as well. In order that everyone may remain calm and assured of the truthfulness of my words, two members of the Judenrat—Kartun and A. Kats—will accompany them. Once the children have been settled, the Judenrat members will return and bring you greetings from them."

Representatives of the Judenrat tried to object:

"How can you take little children from their parents?"

To this Forster replied:

"Silence! You must carry out the order! Even now many guards stand ready outside the ghetto."

Forster entered a barracks situated in the Semlin[70] warehouse, where there were about 250 people. He gave them the same order, after which everyone was driven out into the courtyard.

In the courtyard people were divided into groups: the old, the sick, and children in one group—the young and people able to work in another.

Meanwhile the covered trucks had entered the ghetto; about one hundred men armed with machine guns and hand grenades followed behind them. They scattered throughout the side streets, broke into buildings, and forced everyone out into the square. Then, just as in a pogrom, they went through everything and stole whatever was more or less of value. They searched everyone they could find and took their watches, rings, and money; some they stripped naked. Many tried to buy their way out and turned over everything they had. The thieves took it all and then drove them out to the gathering place anyway. Once in a while they would take money and act as though they were going to set the person free; a minute later the person would be turned over to others who were finishing up the "operation." They beat women and children with their gun butts; they reviled them and insulted them with the most foul words. They searched every building, smashed the furniture, tore up and tossed out the clothing. Searching for hidden possessions, they pulled up flooring, broke into attics and walls, and did not leave a corner untouched. They searched for the children, and when they found them, they drove them out into the square naked and barefoot. There they picked up the children by the hair and arms and threw them into the trucks. Whoever happened to be left standing in the streets or in the courtyards, they herded along behind the trucks, shooting at them and grabbing them. The unhappy parents ran after their children, crying out and begging for mercy. Their cries and wails were swallowed up in the empty air.

Two places were left that were more or less safe: the clinic and the shoe factory. Schleef had ordered the people there to be kept working. But the order was not heeded. Everyone in the clinic was taken out into the square; among them was Doctor Rozovsky and a girl named Valova. In addition, they found ten children in an attic and dragged them out. It was the same in the shoe factory. Once again they hunted everyone down, frisked them, and threw the children and the elderly into the trucks. Many mothers got into the trucks and begged to be taken away with their children, but only four women managed to enjoy this "good fortune."

... In the square from which the trucks pulled away with the children stood our representatives: M. Leibovich, Aron Kats, and Kartun. At first they managed to have a few children released, but then the Gestapo put the children who had been "freed" into another truck. The Hauptsturmführer ordered Leibovich to leave. Kats and Kartun stayed. Kats's transgression consisted in the fact that he had the "impertinence" to ask that the children be given food and water. The commandant ordered him to be taken away with the children.

All of this took place between 7:30 in the morning and 4:00 in the afternoon. The parents stood in the square outside the factory and looked on as their children were dragged away, powerless to be of any help to them. It is impossible to imagine their despair.

According to the commandant, a total of 860 people were taken, including people from the camps. It seems, however, that twenty-one trucks carrying more than a thousand people drove off.

The same measures were taken in Daugiliai and Pavenchia. Fifteen children were taken from there along with the elderly; from the camp at the airfield nine people were taken—five children and four old people.

... Among those taken away was Rabbi M. Rubinshtein, the author of a number of books. They took Rudnik, a cripple, but a highly gifted, very promising poet, and the painter Furman, who for many years worked as a designer on the Yiddish stage. He fell ill, but his spirit was never broken; he rose above his suffering and persistently awaited the shining day of our liberation.

Prepared for publication by O. Savich

The Death Forts of Kovno (Kaunas)

At the beginning of the German occupation there were forty thousand Jews in Kovno.

On the night of 25-26 June in the Kovno suburb of Viliampole approximately one thousand Jews were murdered.[71] The bandits found the head of the yeshiva, a gray old man named Rabbi Osovsky, wrapped in his tallis. They chopped off his head and would not allow him to be buried for a week. The villains cut off the tongues and gouged out the eyes of many Jews.

{An inscription was found beneath the window of a building on Aregalos Street: "Jews, avenge yourselves!" Next to it lay the body of the Jew who managed to write the inscription before he died—by dipping his finger in his own blood.}[72]

Fifty Jews were tortured in a garage on Vitauto Avenue. Several were beaten to death with iron crowbars and shovels; many died with the end of a rubber hose shoved down their throat. One of the bandits climbed on top of a pile of bodies and started playing a harmonica while his friends were singing and dancing.

After their "mini" pogrom, the Germans began to introduce "order," that is, a "system" for the complete annihilation of the Jews.

At the end of the nineteenth and beginning of the twentieth century a network of fortresses was set up around Kovno. Above the ground they had blocks for cannons and machine gun nests; below ground there were quarters for troops. Surrounded by a barbed wire fence, they had high embankments and deep pits. Now the forts had become execution sites.

The Ninth Fort became and execution block not only for the residents of Kovno but for the citizens of a number of European countries.

The Seventh Fort

At the end of June 1941 the central prison in Kovno was overflowing. Without regard for sex or age, Jews were driven into the Seventh Fort on the northern edge of the city. Indeed, Jewish refugees captured by the fascists while trying to evacuate when the war started were brought here. Several thousand Jews—including men, women, and children—were driven into the Seventh Fort over a period of several days. The women and children were held in the troop casements without food or water; they were not even allowed access to a facility for alleviating natural needs. The mortality rate in the casements was high; nor were the Jews allowed to bury those who had gone to their rest.

The men and teenage boys were kept outside in the open air; they were in a deep ditch that separated the casements from the outer wall of the fort. Guard posts were positioned along the embankments and on top of the outer wall.

The guards robbed the prisoners, taking watches, money, and rings. All they had to do was see a good pair of boots or a new jacket on someone, and they would take the owner for a "walk" in the woods. There they would strip him and shoot him.

People went four days without food or water. Finally the prisoners issued a categorical demand: either kill them immediately or give them food and water—whereupon dried salted fish was brought in. The starving people greedily threw themselves on it. Of course, they were even more thirsty afterward. The next day a barrel of water was brought in. Five thousand people lined up. The guards announced that some of the people would be given something to drink elsewhere. But it was a ruse: as soon as they were outside the fort, shots could be heard.

In the course of a day Germans would often come from military units and take Jews out to work. But they did not bring them back.

"Now you will receive your reward!" the Germans would say as they shot their unhappy victims.

In early July sports competitions were held in Kovno. As a prize for winning first place, a women's team was awarded the right to have twenty-five Jews taken from the Seventh Fort and personally shoot them. The "athletes" accepted this "prize" and murdered twenty-five people in front of the other prisoners.

On the morning of 7 July it was announced that boys under fifteen years of age were to be removed from the group. That day they were taken from the Seventh Fort, along with the women and small children, and sent to the Ninth Fort. It was a sultry day. Exhausted, starving, barely dragging their feet, the women were led along the Viliya River. They begged for a drink of water, but the executioners refused. Dozens of women fainted. They were shot on the spot.

The men who were left behind that day were shot. Thus ended the tragedy of the Seventh Fort.[73]

The Fourth Fort

The Fourth Fort is situated southeast of Kovno, outside the suburb of Panemune. The site where the Neman River forms a loop between two wooded banks is one of the most beautiful in all Lithuanian. On 18 August 1941, three days after the Kovno Ghetto was shut off from the entire world, 534 members of the Jewish intelligentsia were brought here.[74]

Some time went by before the fate of these people was known. But soon a group of Jews from Kovno was sent to work in the barracks at the fort. In the attic they found a man's coat and a packet of passports with the names of those who had been among the 534.

Yuozas Paulavichyus, who lives near the Fourth Fort, relates that in August 1941 (he has forgotten the date, but he remembers that it was on a Sunday) Jews were shot at the fort. One doomed man fled from the execution site. He was in his underwear. They chased after him and shot him right in front of passersby. Paulavichyus says that just before their retreat from Kovno, the Germans ordered the bodies to be dug up. Apparently, once they had finished their work, the "brenners" were also shot and burned; evidence of this could be seen from two shin bones found shackled together at one of the burning sites.

During "Aktion 534," or the "Intelligentsia Aktion," the writer Ari Glazman, the journalist Mark Volfovich, the conductor of the Lithuanian National Opera and violinist I. Stender, the painter A. Kaplan, and many physicians, attorneys, engineers, and other cultural figures perished. The concept of the Aktion was simple: the Germans wanted to wipe out the most cultivated and involved people and get rid of the men and the youth, so that in the ghetto no resistance movement could arise.

The Sixth Fort

The Sixth Fort is located on the northeast edge of Kovno, near the suburb of Petrashyuniai. When the war broke out the Germans started building a prisoner of war camp here for Soviet prisoners of war. According to figures from the Special State Commission on the Sixth Fort, thirty-five thousand prisoners of war were slaughtered at the Sixth Fort. In the camp yard the Commission discovered sixty-seven standard graves, each measuring 5 x 2.5 meters. From most of the graves it could be confirmed that the systematic slaughter of people continued here right up until the Red Army liberated Kovno.

A large number of residents of the Kovno Ghetto perished at the Sixth Fort. We have specific testimony regarding one case. The Gestapo's chief of Jewish affairs, a man named Stitz,[75] seized several young men and women in the ghetto in June 1943, including a Jewish Swiss emissary named Aleksandr Blyumental, his wife Henrietta, and a Belgian woman from Brussels. Stitz announced that the Swiss consul, who was concerned about the fate of Blyumental, sent a visa for the emissary's return to Switzerland. Blyumental would be allowed to depart right away with fifteen kilograms of luggage, including his valuables; Stitz himself would see to it that Blyumental was taken to the airfield. An airplane was waiting there to take them to Berlin; the Swiss ambassador would arrange for the rest of the trip from there.

When the young couple got into the car, Stitz shouted to the driver:

"To the airfield! To the highway to heaven..."

The day before Blyumental's departure from the ghetto Stitz had summoned the young Belgian woman and suggested that she leave her Jewish husband and get out of the ghetto. She absolutely refused and declared that she wanted to share her husband's fate. According to eyewitnesses of the execution, they both went to their deaths with courage. They embraced and kissed one another until Stitz personally shot them.

The Ninth Fort

1. The Mass Murder of Kovno Residents in the Fall of 1941

The Ninth Fort is situated northwest of Kovno, six kilometers down the Kovno-Klaipeda highway. The people of Kovno called it the "Death Fort"; even the Gestapo referred to it as the "Kaunas Vernichtungsstelle."[76]

The Germans initially turned the fort into a branch of the Kovno Central Prison, where Jews, Lithuanians, and Soviet activists were shot. The Special State Commission determined that Deputy Budzhinskene of the USSR Supreme Soviet, Deputy Zibertas of the Lithuanian Supreme Soviet, and others were shot at the Ninth Fort, including the Kovno Stakhanovite Shcherbakov and his wife and child.

At first the shootings took place in the courtyard of the fort. At the same time, beginning in July 1941, thousands of Soviet prisoners of war[77] were digging pits along the western wall of the fort.

On 26 September at eleven o'clock in the morning the Germans spread the rumor that some people had been shot by order of Kozlowski, the commandant of the ghetto. Immediately after the rumor was started, an entire quarter was surrounded; Jews living in the quarter were sent to the fort. Only those who had certificates were allowed to remain.

More than one thousand people—most of whom were old people, women with small children, and families with many children—were shot that day.[78]

A second major Aktion took place on 4 October 1941. A crowd of two thousand people was herded into the Ninth Fort. Children from the orphanage, people from the poorhouse, and sick people found in private apartments were hauled away in trucks. The ghetto hospital located in the quarter where the Aktion took place—with all the patients, physicians, and medical personnel inside—was set on fire and completely destroyed. Those who tried to leap from the windows of the burning hospital were shot. The exits were boarded up from the outside. Gunfire from rifles and machine guns could be heard at the fort the entire evening.

At six o'clock on the morning of 28 October the Gestapo ordered the entire ghetto population of about thirty thousand people to gather in the square, where they would be examined for their fitness to work. With the assistance of Friedrich Jordan (whom the municipal commissar had appointed as head of Jewish affairs),[79] Gestapo agent Helmut Rauka[80] carted off eleven thousand Jews. He held them until the next morning in the buildings left empty after the liquidation of the "Little Ghetto." At dawn on the morning of 29 October, the entire mass of people was driven into the Ninth Fort, where they were shot that very day.[81]

The following day, 30 October, a ten-year-old boy named Itsik Blokh came running into the ghetto (although he endured terrible tortures in Dachau and Auschwitz, he survived the war). Splattered with blood, all he had on was a shirt. He related the following:

On the day of the "examination" he and his parents were sent to the Little Ghetto. From the Little Ghetto they were taken to the Ninth Fort. There the men were ordered to undress and were left standing in their underwear; it was the same for the women. Groups of people wearing only their underclothes were driven out into a field where pits had been dug. The people were forced to jump into the pits; there they were murdered. Small children were lifted up on the ends of bayonets and flung into the pits. Itsik Blokh's mother cried out to her son and told him to try to save himself. He started running, and they shot at him. He fell into the bushes, but the bullets missed him. When it got dark and the shooting and screaming had fallen silent, he got up and ran away. At dawn he made his way back to the Little Ghetto. There everything was deserted and demolished. He stayed in a cellar the whole day; that evening he reached the Large Ghetto, where there were still people.

When Itsik told his story, people did not want to believe him. They thought that the little boy had lost his mind.

2. The Mass Murder of People Transported from Germany and Other West European Countries

In early December 1941 a large group of men, women, and children filed past the ghetto under an armed escort.

That day the Gestapo sent a brigade of Jewish workers from the ghetto to the train station to load baggage into trucks. The luggage was taken to the Gestapo building, where its contents were unpacked and sorted. It was clear that the baggage belonged to the people who had been taken to the fort. They were Jews from various cities (Berlin, Frankfurt-am-Main, Breslau, Hannover, Hamburg, Vienna, and others). They had received a special notice to be transported to the East ("*nach Osten*") for work. The notice specifically indicated what they were to bring with them and how much they could bring. Each bag bore the name and the address of its owner. Many documents were discovered as the bags were unpacked.

Among the new arrivals were physicians, attorneys, engineers, and artisans; many of them had been officers in the German army under Wilhelm II and had been decorated for their service in World War I. Religious books belonging to rabbis were discovered in the luggage. Everything had been neatly placed in the suitcases and carefully packed for the long journey. In nearly every bag there were work clothes: overalls, tarpaulin trousers, and the like.

The former supervisor of the Ninth Fort, Yu. Naudzhyunas, informed the Special Commission that there were four thousand people in this first group of foreign Jews. On 10 December the shootings began. On 16 December a second group of three thousand people arrived at the fort. They too were annihilated down to the last man.

Several other groups of Jews—from Germany, Austria, Czechoslovakia, and other lands occupied by the Hitlerite government—were brought to the Ninth Fort during the winter of 1941 – 1942.[82]

On 4 February 1943, after their unprecedented defeat at Stalingrad, the Hitlerites vented their anger on the Jews.

They gathered together a group of "guilty ones" (people who had purchased a newspaper or a piece of bread), took them to the Ninth Fort, and shot them; among them were women and children.

The terror against the citizens of Kovno increased. People under the slightest suspicion of dealing with the partisans were arrested and taken to the Ninth Fort. Hundreds of anti-fascist workers and people from the intelligentsia met their death there.

3. The Destruction of Mass Graves

Soon after their defeat at Stalingrad the Germans formed a special commando whose job was to dig up the mass graves at the Ninth Fort, extract the bodies, and burn them in bonfires. After working for two months, the commando managed to escape from the fort. Some of those who escaped made their way to partisan bases. From several of those who survived— Alter Faitelson, Isroel Gitlin, Pinkhos Krakinovsky, Aron Vilenchuk, Berel Gempel, Vladislav Blyum—the author of these lines learned the details of what they saw and lived through at the Ninth Fort. The author has also used ghetto notes compiled on the basis of reports from the partisan Aron Maneiskin (he too escaped from the fort).

In the autumn of 1943 peasants delivered to the fort about five hundred kilograms of firewood, a large quantity of gasoline, and various chemical fuels and explosives. The area outside the western wall, where the mass graves were, was partitioned off with a tarpaulin 2.5 meters high. An excavator was brought in. Shields were set up around the fort for several meters. The inscription on them announced that anyone who tried to get near the fort would be shot without warning.

In mid-November 1943 the commando whose job was to extract and burn the bodies consisted of about seventy-two people. Among them were:

1. Thirty-four Soviet prisoners of war;

2. Fourteen Jews seized while on their way to join the partisans (Shimen Eidelson, Berel Gempel, Mikhl Gelbtrunk, Moishe Gerber, Mendl Deich, Aba Diskant, Aron Vilenchuk, Moishe Zimelevich, Shmuel Khonovich, Aron Maneiskin, Alter Faitelson, Pinkhos Krakinovsky, Shepsel Shmit);

3. Nine Jews taken from the ghetto, including Moishe Levin, Lakhnitsky, Maister, Tevye Fridman, Mendel Khas, Isroel Gitlin, and others;

4. Eight Jews picked up in Kovno for various reasons (for being without a yellow star, for buying food from Lithuanians, for hiding among the Lithuanians). Among them were Doctor Portnoy, Girsh Shalit, Vitkin, Rabbi Shusterman from Poland, Vladislav Blyum (a lawyer from Warsaw), and others;

5. Three Russian brothers who had been doing sabotage work for the partisans in the Kovno area;

6. One Polish girl suspected of being a Jew;

7. Three Jewish women arrested in the ghetto.

Among the Soviet prisoners of war were Doctor Neimenov, age sixty-two, a major in the medical corps; a man from Moscow named I. L. Vasilenko-Veselnitsky, who was a captain in the corps of engineers; a young lieutenant named Herman Rubinfeld; Shakhov, a blacksmith from the Caucasus; Doctor Aron, a captain in the medical corps; a pharmacist named Barukh; Latyshin, who operated a tank radio; Anatoly Gran of Odessa; and others.

The commandant of the Gestapo's Sonderkommando in charge of destroying the mass graves at the Ninth Fort was Obersturmführer Radif. Ridle, a man know to the Gestapo for his savagery, was in charge of the fort; he would often visit the Kovno Ghetto. The cook was also a Gestapo agent. The guards consisted of Germans serving in the Kovno police force. Apel and Litschauer were in charge of the guards. After a short time Litschauer became commandant of the Kovno Ghetto.

Before fleeing to partisan bases the group of fugitives went to the ghetto. There they drew up a report on the horrors enacted at the Ninth Fort. Here is the text of that report:

Report. Kovno. 26 December 1943

We the undersigned escaped from the Ninth Fort on the night of 25 – 26 December of this year. Our names are I. L. Veselnitsky (Vasilenko), A. Diskant, A. Faitelson, B. Gempel, Sh. Eidelson, and A. Maneiskin. We hereby present this report on the following matters:

1. In 1941 – 1942 the German command used the area surrounding the Ninth Fort for mass shootings.

2. In order to hide this crime, the German command, under the leadership of the Kovno Gestapo, organized the excavation of pits in which the victims of the shootings were buried; their bodies were subsequently exhumed and burned.

3. In order to carry out the work of burning the bodies, the Gestapo brought 72 people to the fort at the end of October and the beginning of November:

> 34 Soviet prisoners of war
>
> 14 partisans

3 Russians

4 women

17 Jews from the Kovno Ghetto

4. The work was arranged in such a way that no one from the surrounding population would know what was taking place around the Ninth Fort. In a two-kilometer radius announcements were posted forbidding any approach to the fort under the threat of being shot. Tents enclosed a work area of five to seven acres. People sent out to do the work would not leave the fort alive. This was confirmed by the fact that a Jew from the ghetto who came down with appendicitis was shot on 1 November; seven prisoners of war who were sick and elderly were shot on 13 November. Thus there were 64 people left to do the work.

5. In the course of the work—that is, from 1 November to 25 December (the day of our escape)—4.5 pits were dug up, each one 100 to 200 meters long, 3 meters wide, and 1.5 meters deep; more than 12,000 bodies of men, women, and children were extracted from them. The bodies were stacked on huge piles of wood about 300 at a time and burned. What was left of the fires (the charcoal and bones) was ground into dust. The dust was mixed in with the soil, so that no trace would remain.

6. In order to prevent them from escaping, the workers were chained together while they did their work. Machine gun towers were set up. The guards were armed with submachine guns and pistols.

7. Among the 12,000 bodies that were burned, approximately 5,000 were Jews brought here from Vienna, Frankfurt-am-Main, Düsseldorf, Hamburg, and other German cities; another 150 were Jewish Soviet prisoners of war, and about 7,000 were Jews from Kovno. The Jews from Germany were shot and buried in their clothing; the rest were forced to strip to their underwear before they were shot.

8. The position of the bodies indicated that the people were herded into the pits in groups, forced to lie down, and then were shot. It was evident that many of those who were buried were either lightly wounded or not wounded at all.

9. At the time of our escape there were still 9.5 pits left to be dug up. The overseer from the Gestapo estimated that the job would not be finished until 1 February 1944.

10. Judging from the fact that there were 12,000 bodies in 4.5 pits and that 9.5 pits remained, it may be assumed that in the area surrounding the Ninth Fort there were approximately 40,000 victims of the savage terror that the Germans inflicted upon the civilian population. Forty thousand is also the figure mentioned in conversations by the representatives of the Gestapo.[83]

(Eleven signatures appear at the end of the report.)

This is what survivors of the Ninth Fort related:

Every morning the prisoners' legs were bound in chains. At night the chains were removed. In order to prevent the possibility of escape, the Germans initially chained the prisoners together in pairs. When it became evident that this interfered with their work, the Germans ordered that each one be chained separately.

The process of digging up the bodies was as follows: A steam shovel would remove the upper layer of earth. Then a team of workers cleared the bodies from any earth that was sticking to it. Next a team of "extractors" dragged the bodies from the pits with iron hooks. The bodies were examined once they were brought up to the surface of the ground. A specially designated person was supposed to extract their gold teeth. They also had to check the pockets of the German Jews, who were buried in their clothing. Any valuables that were found had to be turned over to the German on duty, under pain of being shot.

After the "extractors" came the "porters." They carried the bodies on litters to the piles of wood.

The wood for burning the bodies was arranged like this: a bottom layer of kindling was spread over an area 4 x 4 meters in size. Underneath the kindling they dug a canal that was filled with flammable liquid. The bodies were then stacked on top of the kindling. Normally there were three hundred bodies in a single pile. To ignite the wood, several incendiary grenades were set off in the canal of combustible liquid underneath. The bonfire burned for days on end. Its flames could be seen ten kilometers away.

A special person was supposed to collect pieces of bodies that fell from the flaming pile and thrown them back into the fire. He was responsible for seeing to it that everything was consumed in the fire.

On one of the bodies Moishe Gerber discovered a photograph of his bride's parents (their name was Fish).

A prisoner of war named Rubinfeld found a wedding ring with "Rubinfeld" engraved in it; the inscription was the same as the one engraved in his brother's wedding ring.

Isroel Gitlin recognized his friend Yankel Shavelsky among the bodies; Shavelsky lived in Kovno on Benedictine Street and was killed during the "Big Aktion."

The children from the orphanage and the old people from the poorhouse, who were taken during the Aktion in the Little Ghetto, were found in one of the pits.

Once a stack of wood had burned down, there remained a pile of charred bones, half-burned coals, and little pieces of metal. The metal objects had to be given to the Germans. They were buttons, buckles, hooks, and so on and were sent to the tailor shop. The bones and coals were placed in a metal basin and ground into powder.

At first the Germans established a quota of three hundred bodies per day. In order to meet such a quota, the work had to be intensified. The Germans drove the workers, shouting:

"Come on, come on! Get some more dolls up here. The wood is burning!..."

The quota was then raised to six hundred per day.[84]

{As the bodies burned, they would start to move in various ways; they curled up and stretched out... . It was as though the dead were saying that all goodness was lost, that this world might be transformed into the finest soap... .

Everyone who got away spoke about a terrible incident that took place while the bodies were being burned. A woman's body tumbled from the top layer. It hit the ground so hard that her belly split open, and an eight- to ninth-month-old infant fell out.}

The condition of the bodies was not the same in all the pits. Those that were buried in clay soil were better preserved than those buried in sandy soil; fat ones were preserved better than thin ones. Clothing was also preserved in the clay soil. But the faces of all the bodies were disfigured to the point of being unrecognizable. The upper layer of bodies in all the pits was covered with lime.

Mikhl Gelbtrunk tried not to touch the dead with his bare hands. This irritated the German guard, who yanked the shovel from Gelbtrunk's hands and started beating him. Gelbtrunk lost some of his hearing as a result of the beating.

Gelbtrunk was a singer from Poland; he had come to Kovno when the war broke out between Germany and Poland. He would constantly be singing these refrains while he worked:

> Whole rivers run red with blood,
> Another twenty thousand dead...
> Buy a paper,
> Read a paper.
> There you have news of the whole world:
> Plunder, murder, devastation,
> Catastrophe, scandal...
> Whole rivers run red with blood,
> Another thirty thousand dead...

And so on. Those who were standing around Gelbtrunk would join in with him. They swayed like drunkards; their chains clanked, and their lips whispered:

"Whole rivers run red with blood..."

From time to time commissions from the Gestapo or the SS would come to check on how the work was going. In one group there was a general visiting from Berlin. The general ordered the dead to be dug up and burned without filling in the pits. That would take too much time; the important thing now was to burn the bodies as quickly as possible... .

A group of Gestapo agents once came in from Vilna. Aron Maneiskin overheard them talking: the guests said that the bonfires in Kovno burn better than the ones in Vilna...

4. The Escape of Prisoners from the Ninth Fort

The prisoners were certain that once the work was completed, all of them, without exception, would be shot. The old Doctor Neimenov would beg the Germans to shoot him, but every time they gave him the same cynical reply:

"No, Jew. You can still be of use... . You must work."

Fourteen young men and women were summoned to organize an active resistance; they had been members of the underground anti-fascist organization and were arrested while on their way to join the partisans.[85]

The prisoners put together a commission of three men: two prisoners of war (Shakhov and Captain Vasilenko) and a representative from the partisan group (Faitelson).[86] First they tried to tunnel their way out. In one of the cells in the bunker they discovered a shallow dried up well.

The prisoners started digging the tunnel at night in the direction of the fort's outer wall ten to twelve meters from the bunker. After digging out about a meter of dirt, they ran into a layer of rock that was impossible to penetrate. They had to give up on trying to tunnel their way out; they needed a new plan that would make it possible for all the prisoners to escape.

At night the prisoners were kept in the cells of one of the underground bunkers. An iron ladder at the end of the hall led up to a dark chamber filled with old junk. Beyond the iron door overhead was a ditch where a guard always stood watch. On the opposite side of the ditch (about twenty meters away) was the entrance to a tunnel that led to the north side of the fort. The tunnel was filled with firewood. Thus the prisoners were faced with (1) securing a way to get out of their cells, (2) getting past the overhead iron door, (3) removing the firewood from the tunnel, and (4) making a ladder to get over the northern wall of the fort, which was six meters high.

The cells were sealed off from the general hallway by an iron partition and massive iron doors that closed from the outside. The locksmiths Pinkhus Krakinovsky and Alter Faitelson often stayed in the bunker to do various odd jobs. Although they were kept in chains, they could move about the bunker more or less freely during the day.

First they made keys to the doors of the cells in the bunker. It was necessary to find a way to break out of one of the cells; then it would be easy to open the other doors. To accomplish this, Krakinovsky loosened a rivet from the iron doorjamb in his cell. With the rivet removed, it was possible to get into the hallway and from there to open up all the other doors.

Each day two prisoners would pretend to be sick and stay in from work. Both locksmiths would always stay in the bunker with the two "sick" prisoners (the Germans watched over only those who went out to work).

It was necessary to make a hole in the iron door big enough for a man to crawl through. The locksmiths smuggled in a small drill from the locksmith shop; it was used to bore holes, one next to the other, along an outline of the opening. The iron between the little holes was filed through with the blade of a pocketknife that had been made into a small file. While one prisoner worked on filing the hole in the door overhead, another stayed below and sat by the stove drying out *portyanki*.[87] If a German should show up in the bunker, the one left below would start coughing or singing loudly as a signal to the prisoner working above.

The work continued into the evening, when the prisoners returned to their cells. In order to drown out the sound of drilling and filing, the prisoners would sing and dance in their cells. The Germans did not interfere. On the contrary, they were pleased that the prisoners were in such a good frame of mind and seemed devoted to their work.

The boring through the overhead iron door was almost finished. Now the tunnel had to be cleared of the firewood. The elderly prisoner of war, Doctor Neimanov, had the job of seeing to it that the bonfires burned as they were supposed to (the Germans gave him the title of "Brigade Chief"). He informed Police Chief Apel that it would be possible to burn more than six hundred bodies per day if the wood were drier. And dry wood could be found in the tunnel... . That day men were mobilized to clean out the tunnel and move the firewood from the tunnel to the burning site... .

A carpenter named M. Khas, who worked in the carpenters' workshop, prepared the parts that would be used to make a strong six-meter ladder.[88]

With the preparations now complete, the escape was planned for the night of 25 – 26 December 1943.

Not all the prisoners were involved in the preparations for the escape. Only on the afternoon of 25 December did the organizers make the announcement to everyone. The people were divided into several groups. A group of fourteen from the underground anti-fascist organization in the ghetto decided to try to make contact with the organization, so that they could then be directed to a partisan base. Twenty-three people—six of whom were Jews from the ghetto and the rest prisoners of war—chose a route leading to the partisans in the Iben Woods. Moishe Zimelevich, a brave anti-fascist activist from the Kovno Ghetto, was designated leader of that group. Twelve wanted to head for the Babtai Woods in the Kovno district; thirteen, including the women, were supposed to scatter in various directions according to their own discretion.

The snow in the courtyard was deep, so that the guard could easily spot the escapees. The prisoners sewed together two sheets; four people camouflaged in white gowns sewn from nightshirts and underwear would take hold of the corners of the sheets. Under the cover of the sheets, the prisoners were to cross the area in groups of eight. The leaders of the escape had collected a supply of knives that could serve as side arms if the need should arise.

On Saturday, 25 December, at about ten o'clock in the evening the daring plan went into effect. After removing a loosened rivet from his door, one of the locksmiths went out into the corridor and opened the doors of all the cells, using the keys prepared beforehand. Strictly adhering to the plan, people came out of their cells in a very disciplined manner. The iron ladder leading to the exit was covered with blankets and rags, so as to muffle their footsteps. They used cigarette lighters and matches to light their way. The guards were getting drunk for the holiday occasion, and the singing and shouting of the drunken Germans drowned out the sounds made by the escapees.

When the prisoners emerged from the tunnel, they found themselves on the edge of a steep precipice many meters high; they had to climb down that to get to the outer wall on the north side of the fort. With the help of the ladder they had made, they scaled the six-meter wall. They cut through the barbed wire along the top of the wall with specially prepared wire cutters. Beyond the wire, the vast winter expanse opened up...

Four hours went by before the administrators noticed that the prisoners had escaped. All the police in Kovno, the SS, the Gestapo, and several military units were called out to apprehend the escapees. But in vain.

Some of the escapees managed to get into the ghetto. There they were received by the underground anti-fascist organization.

The group of escapees arriving in the ghetto supplied the underground organization with several gold teeth that the executioners had forced them to remove from the dead; they also turned over two drawings made by Soviet prisoner of war Anatoly Gran. One drawing showed two prisoners hauling bodies to the bonfires on stretchers and a guard looking on. The other drawing was a portrait, a caricature; just one example of the drawings that Anatoly Gran had hanging on the door of his cell prior to his escape, it showed a Gestapo agent getting the finger... (the teeth and both drawings are now in the European Museum in Vilna).[89]

They also brought out a notebook containing the minutes from the meetings of a Komsomol group that was formed in the fort. Members of the group included Tevye Pilovnik, Aron Vilenchuk, Alter Faitelson, Moishe Zimelevich,[90] and others. One cannot read about Aba Diskant's admission into the Komsomol without a feeling of profound respect. "With regard for his readiness for battle, his seriousness, and the sense of camaraderie that he has shown under the terrible conditions of imprisonment... ." In the minutes it says that he was "prepared to die for the Komsomol."

Unfortunately the protocols were destroyed when the Germans burned down the Kovno Ghetto on 13 – 15 July 1944.

Those who escaped to the ghetto were provided with clothing, provisions, and shelter. Five days later their departure for partisan bases in the Rudnitsky Woods near Vilna was set up.[91] The leader and organizer of the partisan movement in the Kovno Ghetto, Khaim Elin, personally accompanied them.

5. The Ninth Fort After the Prisoners' Escape

After the prisoners escaped, the Germans gathered together fifty men from various Jewish labor camps and sent them to the fort to continue the work of destroying the mass graves. Among them were Jews from the Kovno prison.

Among the prisoners was a group of young men who were captured while on their way to join the partisans (Moishe Rozhansky, Leo Ziman, Itsik Krikel, Khone Meshkul, Iosel Khodosh). "Criminals" arrested in the city for failing to wear the yellow badge or for buying food from Lithuanians included Daniel Rybak, Genakh Segalovich, Mendelevich, and others.

The Jews were kept in chains day and night; they received neither shaves nor haircuts. Once again the flames rose into the night over the Ninth Fort; once again a northwest wind carried the smell of burning human flesh into the ghetto.

On 28 March 1944 the Germans carried out an Aktion in the ghetto against the children, the elderly, the invalids, and those incapable of working. They rounded up 1,500 people and loaded them into freight cars. It is now known that these people were taken to Auschwitz, where they were sent to the gas chambers. The Aktion continued on 29 March. People were hauled away in covered trucks to the Ninth Fort, where they were immediately shot, taken to the bonfires, and burned. That day one thousand people perished at the fort.[92]

6. The Last Traces of the Crimes

After the Red Army liberated Kovno, they found in the yard at the Ninth Fort a large quantity of firewood, barrels of gasoline and combustible fuel, traces of charred human bones, and many metal buttons, hooks, and the like. On the walls of the fort they found dozens of inscriptions written by the hands of the doomed.

One inscription written in Yiddish says:

"I was arrested on 12 February in Saint-Étienne (France). I arrived in Kovno on 18 May 1944. We were 850 young men. I shall write down what will become of us at the last minute."

Of course, the poor soul did not write another word.

On the sides of bowls and on the plank beds in the bunkers one could find hundreds of inscriptions such as these:

"18/V 1944. Willi Grinwald. Nice."

"Khaim Tvoretsky."

"S. Kool, Amsterdam. 18/V 44."

"Vidze, Breslov district. 15/V 44."

"Khatskel Tsukerman, Vilna."

"Wolf Zalekstein of Brussels, deported from Drancy 18/V 44."

The following were written in Lithuanian:

"I am dying innocent at the hands of the German executioners. Stasis Velichko."

"Girsh Burshtein, brought here 7/VII – 44. We burn bodies and await death. Brothers, avenge us!"

"Bravely we die for the Jewish people!"

"Sologub, Prokofev, tell Murava."[93]

"Leonas Shlyamovsky perished here."

"1944 – VII – 7, Antanas Dirginchyus. Tell my brother; he lives in the Taurog district, Erzhvilk sector, village of Atabanniu."

"900 of us Frenchmen."

"Morris Grade, Nice, 18. 5. 1944, one of the 900."

"Written before being shot for political reasons. Vladas Yakshtas."

"8/VI – 44. Russian prisoner of war—for escaping from slavery. Andrei Vasilevich Vyalkin. Tell my wife Mariya Vyalkina."

The Germans erased many inscriptions.

Detailed information about the mass executions that were carried out at the fort was obtained from the peasants living in the area.

Yu. Naudzhyunas, the former head of the Ninth Fort, says that three Catholic priests were shot there.

Naudzhyunas also relates that in November 1941 he saw one hundred men brought to the fort and then herded into the pit; then they were doused with gasoline and set on fire. Heartrending screams could be heard rising up from the flames. The Hitlerites threw grenades at the burning people and shot them with machine guns.

A civilian named A. B. Schesno says that people were forced to strip naked in a garden near the fort. From there they were taken in groups of three hundred to the pits. The poor people had to stand in the cold for a long time and wait their turn.... Many were forced into the pits alive. The screams and weeping of women and children could be heard coming from the pits.

Those who escaped from the fort said that in one of the pits they found documents bearing the name of Vatslovas Sinitskas, a Lithuanian worker from the Dobre Textile Factory in Kovno. This pit was where a large group of antifascists perished; the Germans arrested them in the summer of 1943. The escapees say that they discovered the bodies of the three anti-fascist activists in a beat-up box buried in the ground; the Germans had publicly hanged them in the autumn of 1941.[94]

Inscriptions made by Stasis Velichko and Vladas Yakshtas were dated 8 July 1944. In these inscriptions the final tragedy played out at the Ninth Fort on 5 June 1944 opens up before our eyes. The central prison on Mickiewicz Street was liquidated. The Germans set the convicts free but took the political prisoners away to the Ninth Fort in covered trucks. There, on 7 and 8 July, the Germans slaughtered many citizens of Kovno and the surrounding area whom they regarded as sympathetic toward the Soviet Union.

The Commission for the Investigation of Crimes Committed by the German Invaders in Kovno determined that here the Hitlerites massacred approximately seventy thousand peaceful residents.

Meir Elin

The Kovno Ghetto Fighters

One autumn day in 1941 32,000 Jews—grown men and women, old people, and children—were driven into the square. Dressed like dandies, their whips in hand, the German officers sharply and abruptly barked their orders: "To the right! To the left!" A father would be sent to one side, a mother to the other; a brother would go to the left, a sister to the right. An infant would be torn from its mother's arms, and the officer would point with his whip: "To the left, to the left!" It was all absurd and incomprehensible, as in a nightmare. The long hours dragged on endlessly.

A subdued murmur went through the crowd; people offered their speculations and propositions. Some said that "these" would remain in the Kovno Ghetto, while "those" would be sent to peat factory at Keidany. Twenty thousand people had been sent to the right and twelve thousand to the left.[95] The crowd of twenty thousand was driven back into the ghetto; the others were locked out. They were never seen in the ghetto again. Each day, in groups of several hundred, they were taken to the Ninth Fort and shot.

So went the first Aktion.

Several months passed, and then there was a second Aktion, on a somewhat smaller scale.

Another six months went by, and the Germans conducted a third Aktion.

People went around depressed and hungry. The youth persistently contemplated resistance.

{Those who went outside the ghetto to work every day would return and relate how the Germans were exulting over the fact that the loudspeakers in the streets were shouting about an imminent "victory." ... The old people would shake their head and say, "It doesn't matter.... . All is lost!" Mothers sobbed convulsively while their terrified children hid in corners, sitting motionless and staring silently into space for hours on end.}

To bring a newspaper into the ghetto—much less read one—was strictly forbidden on pain of death. But for the youth, knowing nothing was like being dead. Disregarding the danger, they hoarded scraps of Lithuanian and German newspapers, in which they could read a great deal between the lines. The German papers tried to conceal the first blow they received outside of Moscow, but the young men and women in the ghetto were not fooled. Then the headlines began to appear: "Military Transport Tumbles Down an Embankment" and "Bandits Attack Garrison." Everyone in the ghetto understood perfectly well that this was not about "bandits" but about patriots.[96]

{Several more months went by, and people were no longer guessing; they were convinced that there was a partisan movement in Lithuania. In whispers, with burning eyes full of hope, the young men and women told each other about the courageous partisans who were hiding in the woods and waging an armed struggle against the German invaders.}

The regime of terror the ruled the over the ghetto was intensified daily; from time to time it became known that one group or another taken away supposedly to work in Keidany or Geizhuny was actually hauled off to the Ninth Fort and shot. Once again the news from the front was not good: the Germans were approaching Stalingrad and had penetrated deep into the Caucasus.

At that point a small group of five men decided to leave the ghetto and head east. They dreamt of breaking through the front line, seeking out the partisans, and joining up with them. They passed through the ghetto gates with a column of laborers on their way to "work" and never returned. Several days later an elderly woman named Milshtein complained to her neighbors that her son Isroel had disappeared. A young woman named Davydova said the same thing about her husband. There was also a man named Ioffe who had gone out with the workers; his large family had perished during the first Aktion.

It was an exit into the unknown. They left without weapons or provisions.[97]

All five of them were lost. After a short time the people in the ghetto found out about their tragic end: they were captured not far from Kovno and shot.

This initial failure, however, did not discourage the young. The decision to escape from the ghetto remained a difficult one. Now, however, they were getting ready for their escape in an organized manner. Among them was the future leader and organizer of the Kovno Jewish Partisan movement, a young Jewish writer name Khaim Elin.[98] Early on he was known in Lithuania as one of the foremost activists in Jewish culture; later, when the Soviet authorities took over, he emerged as a talented writer for the Kovno Yiddish newspaper *Der Emes (The*

Truth). Several times Khaim Elin managed to slip out of the ghetto unnoticed and make contact with the communist organization, which was then building up its illicit activities in Kovno.

The first cells to prepare for working with the partisans were formed in the ghetto as a result of Khaim Elin's initiative. Each of these cells consisted of five young men and women, {including the leader of the group.}

At first plans were made secretly, so that the cells did not know anything about each other. Secrecy were necessary, since whenever someone escaped from the ghetto, his family, his work brigade, and the residents of the building where he lived were held accountable with their lives.

A love for life, a thirst for revenge, and a profound faith in the ultimate triumph of our just cause—even in the darkness of the ghetto, on the edge of death—inspired the small groups that would meet from time to time in attics and cellars. It would happen that after a special Aktion, four would be left instead of five, and then three instead of four. But those who were left alive diligently continued their work.

Khaim Elin would go outside the ghetto to work as part of a labor brigade. No one knew where or how he did it, but almost every day he brought the leaders of the cells handwritten pages from the *Political News* and the *Report from the Front*, which reported the military situation not at all the way that the fascist papers reported it.

Future partisans passed a course that prepared them not only politically; they also did a thorough study of the use of weapons. One person had an old pistol; his gun would go from cell to cell and from hand to hand, so that everyone could carefully examine it. Several grenades were carved from wood and used for practice; following standard military procedures, people learned how to gather intelligence, mine an area, and blow up bridges. In order to cross the ghetto's threshold, however, and begin real partisan actions, they first needed weapons, which were impossible to procure in the ghetto. But then it was decided to send out a partisan group without weapons.

Khaim Elin led the way out of the city.

A plan for an escape route was worked out in the summer of 1942. It was decided to move in small groups of four or five people dressed in worn out, patch-covered peasant clothes. Each group would proceed separately and be careful to keep a distance between themselves and the others for as far as they could see. They would move only during the day.[99]

Professor Volsonok, a well-known scholar, drew up a special map showing the route. After days of exhausting physical labor, to which he was unaccustomed, he spent nights on end going over every detail of the map's route with tireless patience. He set about memorizing every alley, bush, and stream, every path winding around every little village and town. If they wanted to escape from the ghetto, they would have to cover more than two hundred kilometers, and it was impossible to take a map with them.

The first thirty people were ready to set out. Some small difficulties, however, still had to be overcome. It was necessary to get past the ghetto gates in such a way that relatives and loved ones left behind would not suffer.

The Gestapo carefully guarded the ghetto day and night. A sentry from the German command headquarters stood guard at the gate with a representative from the Jewish "self-government" (the Jewish police). The number of people in the workers' columns going out and returning from work had to be checked several times. If thirty men should go out to work, then any shortage in the returning column would be easily detected; the consequences could be fatal. Khaim Elin realized that without the help of the Judenrat he would not be able to lead a group out of the ghetto; so he decided to reveal his secret.

Doctor Elkes, a well-known physician in Kovno, was the designated elder (Oberjude) in charge of the Judenrat; he decided to cooperate with the young men and women in their undertaking in every way he could. The Judenrat answered with its head for every Jew in the ghetto, and they knew very well the risks involved. {The members of the Judenrat, however, preferred to assist the initial attempt at resistance rather than passively await the inevitable inglorious death at the hands of the fascists.}

One morning in the autumn of 1942 the German guard at the gate was shown a list bearing a pretentious German signature and seal indicating that the thirty "specialists" listed here were being sent to N. to "work." The ruse of the list worked, and soon all thirty people had passed through the gate with their bundles in their arms.[100]

Each one had peasant's clothing in his bundle.

They had to conceal themselves in doorways and hide in trash bins and broken down sheds in order to remove the yellow star from their clothing.... It was understood that none of them "knew" each other. If anyone should be stopped, the rest of them were to keep on moving. Such an arrangement, of course, could be maintained only during the first days of the escape. For various reasons, this stipulation was soon broken.

Less than half of those who left the ghetto safely reached the thick Augustus Woods, where only after wandering about for a long time did they finally meet up with the partisans. Many fell into the hands of the Gestapo along the way and were tortured; some "lost the thread" and strayed from the route. The twenty-year-old Faingold and his comrade wandered around in the forest for six days. They penetrated the heart of the thicket, ate roots, grew faint, and were completely exhausted; but they did not run into anyone. They returned in despair. Two more later came back to the ghetto: Nekhemiya Endlin and Shmuel Mortkovsky. Their return made a painful impression.[101]

Meanwhile the anti-fascist center in the city took upon itself the direct leadership of the movement. Khaim Elin strengthened his connections with the anti-fascist center. The time came for sending out the young men and women disguised as poor peasants, when they would have to go deep into the thick of the forest without weapons, whether they meet up with the partisans or not. It was clear that the people in the ghetto itself had to be armed first, and only then could those being sent into the forest have weapons. It all came down to one fundamental question: where to get weapons. In the city they could be had for a great deal of money. When the money ran out, mothers sold their wedding rings and watches; everything of greater or lesser value was sold from their homes. Thus some of the young men and women were furnished with revolvers.

After a short time nine young people left the ghetto. They were armed and had a clearly defined route into the Rudnitsky Woods west of Vilna.

The Judenrat knew about the departure of these people and helped them.

Among those who left were Aron Vilenchuk, a former student of the Sholom Aleichem Gymnasium in Kovno (his parents were shot during one of the first Aktions); a worker named Yudel Sherman; and a clerk named Moishe Upnitsky. This time five of the nine were fortunate enough to reach their destination and join up with partisan units. Two of them were captured and taken to the Ninth Fort in Kovno; a third was shot in a one-sided battle with the

Gestapo; and the last one, Moishe Upnitsky, hid with a Lithuanian peasant, where he died from wounds received in the battle.[102]

But more than half of these fearless people reached their destination! Back in the ghetto Khaim Elin found out about their success.

The youth were full of hope and courage; instead of sitting and waiting for their inevitable death, they chose another way: they took up arms to actively resist and fight against the enemy. The partisan movement in the ghetto attracted more and more followers.

Khaim Elin knew no rest. He covered hundreds of kilometers on foot in order to reach the partisans and establish personal contacts with them. His energy was inexhaustible. No sooner would he return than once again he would set out into the forest. He held secret conferences with the anti-fascist center in Kovno and set up meetings with the Judenrat. With the young men and women he worked out plans for obtaining weapons. He consulted with the Jewish tailors in regard to outfitting people who were preparing to go into the forest with the proper costumes. He met with the Jewish locksmiths to consider the matter of setting up a secret workshop in the ghetto for repairing broken guns.... Where to get guns for the young men and women? That was a constant concern for Khaim Elin. Ultimately the weapons were obtained.

Khaim Elin organized an armed fighting unit in the ghetto itself and gave them an assignment: to obtain weapons by force. The fighting unit was to leave the ghetto from time to time and return with weapons.

In the spring of 1943 a young man named Yankel Birger took his group and attacked a military repair shop in broad daylight.[103] As a result of the attack, they obtained eleven rifles. Another group, led by Itskhok Miklishansky, obtained twenty-three rifles in the same way. Khaim Elin began to expand the network of fighting units.

Khaim Elin was faced with a difficult task: he had to select the people most suited for battle. At first he picked only those who were single, that is, who had no family or loved ones in the ghetto. It turned out, however, that there were too many of them; the many Aktions had destroyed some part of every family. A husband had lost his wife, a son his father, a sister her brother.... People had to wait their turn to go into the forest. By mid-1943 the partisan movement in Lithuania had gained considerable strength. The partisans would engage in open battle with sections of German garrisons and disarm them, destroy them, or simply drive them away.[104] Of course, such skirmishes did not always end successfully. There were more than a few victims among the partisans. When they had to retreat, they were not always able to take with them those who had fallen in battle. There were many Jews among the ones who fell, so that the Germans began asking themselves a question: "Where are these Jews coming from? Aren't the Jews locked up in the ghetto?"

The Germans realized that there were connections between the Jews locked inside the ghetto and the partisans in the forest.

Subsequently the terror in the ghetto was intensified. More guards were posted. Everyone entering and leaving was checked more carefully at the gate. Beatings were very frequent. Under the pretense of searching for weapons, Gestapo units would burst into the ghetto, destroy homes, and take people away. But it was all in vain; the dispatching of armed youth into the forest was not curtailed.

One morning a truck pulled up to the ghetto gates. A Gestapo man—a Sturmbannführer in full uniform, holding official documents in his hand—went into the Judenrat building and came out with a group of Jews. The German guards standing at the gate smirked: "Those Jews will never return to the ghetto... ." In a sense they were right, since the truck in fact took these people from the ghetto—to the partisans. The "Gestapo man," of course, was a Jewish partisan, a guide, who knew his business very well.

The Germans once gathered together everyone in the Jewish police force, accused them of aiding the partisan movement, and shot them.[105]

The Germans appointed others to take their place. They were not intimidated, however, by the fate of their predecessors. They too did their duty and helped the prisoners of the ghetto in their struggle against the enemy.

During a search a revolver was found on a young Jew named Mek. A gallows was immediately erected on one of the ghetto streets; everyone in the ghetto, young and old, was forced to come out for the hanging. Mek was hanged, and his family—his mother and two sisters—were shot on the steps of the gallows.[106]

But in response even to this, the Jews sent more parties of young men and women into the forest.

The struggle grew more and more bitter.

At the end of 1943 control over the ghetto was transferred from the German civil authorities to the direct management of the Gestapo. Obersturmführer Geke was named as the new commandant. Aktions became more frequent. Fifteen hundred people were transferred to work in the suburb of Aleksotas. Thirty-five hundred Jews were deported to Estonia. But many managed to escape. People hid in the deep trenches along the road and disappeared into the forest. They jumped out the windows of the train cars at the small-town stations where the trains would stop for a few minutes. All of them went to join the partisans.

A group of eighty people was sent to the peat refinery in the region between the villages of Kaishedoris and Keidany. One night the entire group escaped and went to join the partisans. Lithuanian partisans operating in the area helped them to get away into the forest. Even before their escape the Jews received weapons from them.[107]

The daring escape of a group of Jews from the Ninth Fort, the Death Fort, took place at that time.[108] In the group there were a relatively large number of young Jews who had been captured by the Gestapo while trying to escape from the ghetto. Among them was the aforementioned Aron Vilenchuk, the former student from the Sholom Aleichem Gymnasium, who was in the first group to escape from the ghetto.

One of the organizers of the escape was a Jewish prisoner of war, a captain, who later distinguished himself in partisan battles.[109]

The savagery of the Germans grew worse. The Aktions were renewed. The guards surrounding the ghetto were doubled and tripled. People could pass through the gates now only under unusual circumstances and with a special pass. Throughout the streets of Kovno there were special agents who were supposed to stop any passerby who looked at all suspicious. Once again a thorough registration was held in the ghetto. But despite all these measures, the escape of several dozen young men and women was arranged. This time Rakhmiel Berman, a former actor in the Jewish State Theater in Kovno, served as their leader.

A workers' brigade left the ghetto in a truck one morning. The German driver had been bribed. Every member of the brigade was carrying a hidden revolver. The vehicle was supposed to turn off onto a side street and from there head for the Vilkomir Highway. The driver, however, unexpectedly drove the truck down a main thoroughfare. As he was approaching a restaurant, he stopped the truck and got out of the cab.

"Where are you going?" several voices came from the rear of the truck.

"I just stopped for a minute to have some breakfast," the driver replied.

"Get your guns!" Berman quietly ordered, realizing that the driver had betrayed them.

A moment later the truck was surrounded by the Gestapo. The first shots rang out. The men in the truck fired back. The Gestapo were not expecting that.

"Fire!" one of the Germans ordered.

A brief but fierce battle followed. In an instant the street was empty. The sound of breaking glass could be heard coming from somewhere. The Jews had barricaded themselves behind the truck, and the Germans ran to hide in a doorway. But the Jews knew that their firepower was limited.

Berman gave an order:

"Four will stay here to hold off the enemy. The rest have to get out of here!"

They turned the truck over on its side. Using it as cover, some of them were able to reach a neighboring courtyard. They went over the fence and down a familiar side road, until they finally managed to get out of the city. The four who stayed behind kept fighting so as not to allow the Germans past the courtyard gates; thus they gained some time for their comrades. The Gestapo received reinforcements; in an uneven battle the four men armed only with revolvers fell under a hail of bullets that came from every window and doorway.

Within a few days their companions, led by Rakhmiel Berman, had made it to a partisan base in the forest.[110]

In the spring of 1944, several months before the Red Army liberated Lithuania, the hero Khaim Elin succumbed to death. He fought to his last bullet. The Gestapo wanted to take him alive at all costs, but every attempt the Germans made to get near him cost them dearly. Having spent his last cartridge, Khaim Elin tried to cut the veins on his left wrist with a penknife. He died under torture.[111]

On 27 April 1944 the Germans carried out one of the most monstrous of all their Aktions: the slaughter of children and old people.[112]

A special group of officers was selected to conduct this Aktion.

The officers gathered in the ghetto on the designated day. They were in full parade uniform, with their crosses on their chests and their swastikas on their sleeves, with their motley ribbons and their gold buttons. Each officer had a revolver at his side, a submachine gun over his shoulder, and an ax in his right hand. Presenting such an image, they made their appearance in the ghetto and moved about the narrow byways of the "Jewish Quarter." Immediately heartrending screams and wails could be heard.

It is difficult to convey in words what took place during those terrible, nightmarish hours. Babies were torn from their mothers' arms and tossed into the back of trucks. Fathers were savagely beaten; their children were forcibly taken from them and thrown onto the truck beds. Teenagers tried to run away, but bullets cut them down. The ones firing at them aimed for their legs, since only living children were supposed to be thrown into the trucks. If a mother tried to shield her children, they set dogs on her. If, in the madness that overwhelmed them, any mothers should try to get into the trucks with their unfortunate children, they were hacked with axes. The order required that the children be taken to the Ninth Fort alive.

Thus 350 children and old people were taken away to be shot.

After this horrible massacre, four more youths managed to get out of the ghetto. Among them were Shie Verzhgovsky and Shmuel Razin, whose parents and younger brothers and sisters had perished.

"Blood for blood!" was the Jewish partisans' slogan. Their son Aron, who was one of the first to escape from the ghetto, avenged the brutal shooting of the Vilenchuk family.

Their relative Isroel Milner avenged the annihilation of the Ioffe family. For taking his family away to the Ninth Fort and for two hundred other families the partisan and former student Girsh Smolyakov took revenge. The partisan Peisakh Shtein ruthlessly took revenge on the Germans.

On that spring day in 1943, when under the pretense of sending them off to work the Germans hauled away 620 Jews to the Ninth Fort and shot them, Yankel Birger and a group of partisans attacked a military transport and blew it up. Hundreds of Hitlerites went flying into the air.[113]

Yankel Birger was killed in another sabotage operation. But a Jewish girl named Eira Pilovnik took revenge for him, his fallen brother, and their mother.

The Germans, who had shown such "bravery" when they fought against unarmed Jewish mothers, were afraid to go out alone at night.

Partisans were lying in wait for them everywhere. The Volbe brothers, both master sharpshooters, lay in wait for them along the Vilna-Grodno highway. One night an unseen hand would blow up a bridge, and the next night another unseen hand would set a warehouse on fire.

David Teper, Alter Faitelson, Leya Port, Shmuel Mortkovsky, and dozens of other partisans were the native children of the powerless mothers and the helpless old people of the ghetto. They avenged their blood and tears. Borukh Lopyansky, Shimen Blokh, and Tsodikov were fearless saboteurs.

The Jewish partisan unit was called "Death to the Invaders!" The unit spread. One became three.

The Jews fought shoulder to shoulder with the Lithuanians and the Russians. They became as brothers and fought as single family against the enemy, calling him to account in a single act of vengeance.

I. Iosade[114]

Doctor Elena Buividaite-Kutorgene

Elena Buividaite-Kutorgene was a popular physician among her patients in Kovno.[115] Doctor Kutorgene was a Lithuanian by nationality. She graduated from Moscow University thirty-two years ago. In 1922 she arrived in Lithuania and began working as a doctor in the "OZE,"[116] where poor Jews were the primary patients.

In June and July 1941, during the first dark days of the German occupation, Jews who were being hunted began to turn to Doctor Kutorgene for help.

Not only did her friends go to her but also people completely unknown to her.

The cruel German decree forbade any contact between Jews and non-Jews, under the threat of all sorts of punishments, including the death penalty. Holding such cannibalistic orders in contempt, day by day Doctor Kutorgene expanded her contacts with the Jews. As long as the ghetto was open, she went there daily. She brought food and provided people with all kinds of medical assistance.

When the entrance to the ghetto was closed, Doctor Kutorgene went up to the fence and passed over packages of provisions. More than once the fascist guards caught her "at the scene of the crime."

When the systematic slaughter of the Jewish population began, Doctor Kutorgene would allow seven or eight Jews to spend the night in her office.

Exercising extreme caution, they would go to her in the evening disguised as patients and then stay until morning.

On the eve of the Big Aktion of 28 October 1941, twelve people spent the night in her office. Doctor Kutorgene was taking a huge risk: a German officer lived in her apartment. The slightest noise or carelessness could have cost this courageous woman her life.

Some neighbors once saw a person all bundled up coming out of her apartment at dawn. From that day on she began receiving anonymous letters warning her that if she did not break off her contact with the Jews, she could expect to be killed. But these letters did not frighten her.

Before long her place was searched. Fortunately, at the time there were no strangers in her apartment.

Doctor Kutorgene kept a diary. This diary contains the astounding history of the Germans' persecution and slaughter of the Jewish population. "The situation in the ghetto is horrible," she wrote. "I simply cannot bear to live while knowing that right next to me people are enduring such suffering and are being subjected to such terrible humiliation."

Doctor Kutorgene and her son Viktor sent out a huge appeal to the American public in which they described in sharp and angry words the monstrous persecution of the Jews. The appeal was sent to America through some friends.

Doctor Kutorgene performed a tremendous service in her efforts to save Jewish children. She displayed a great deal of maternal resourcefulness, care, and love in saving Jewish children from the executioners.

Many Lithuanian women, both from the intelligentsia and from the peasantry, helped her to hide children.

In 1942 Doctor Kutorgene met with the leaders and organizers of the Jewish underground organization for fighting and resistance: the writer Khaim Elin and Glezerite (Albina).

In spite of her age, Doctor Kutorgene raised money with a youthful ardor; she helped to purchase weapons for the partisans and to have them sent to partisan units.

Overcoming many obstacles both large and small and having no regard for danger, Doctor Kutorgene distributed underground pamphlets and circulars.

Her physician's office, which was a "salvation station" for the Jews, also served as a hide-out for partisans and for many, many workers from the Jewish and Lithuanian centers for the struggle against the fascists.

Having engaged in such selfless actions, Doctor Kutorgene is a noble daughter of the Lithuanian people.

Reported by G. Osherovich,[117]
prepared for publication by R. Kovnator

From the Diary of Doctor Elena Buividaite-Kutorgene (June – December 1941)

22 June 1941. A clear, bright, beaming morning. Haven't been able to sleep since four o'clock this morning because of the airplanes. My tenant, a sister of charity, came running in to me wearing only her nightgown; terribly frightened, she said: "War." This seemed so crazy to me that I laughed at her and sent her back to bed. She did as I said. At six o'clock I went to the hairdresser's. The streets were quiet and empty. I thought with a chuckle about how easily people panic. Somehow, sneaking from gate to gate, I reached the building. I still could not believe it. I could hear Hitler's speech about the invasion on the radio. He accused the Bolsheviks of violating a treaty. The Bolsheviks and the English were aiding the Serbs, and so on.

Right now Molotov is speaking.

Only now am I starting to believe it. D. B. called and said that he would send a car for me to take me to the USSR. I told him that my daughter is in the hospital with typhus, and I cannot leave her; I asked him to let me have the car to take her home. He agreed and said good-bye.

I brought Lilya home from the hospital. She is weak; we carried her in our arms. They say the airplanes flying overhead are German. The shooting sounds like it is quite near... .

I moved Lilya into the room where the sister of charity had stayed; she packed her things into one large bundle and left. I feel strange and uneasy. On the radio the Germans speak of nothing but their victories. We are silent. Vitya is upset... .

23 June. Troops were moving all night long. The streets were empty this morning. People are fleeing with their suitcases. To where? {No authorities, no orders or explanations. Everyone is lost. Individual soldiers pass by... .} Everyone is lost... . The situation is terrible for the Jews... . The son from a Jewish family living nearby, a charming young man, left carrying a rucksack. The father also intends to leave. He came by to ask me to look after his family. He says that the Germans probably will not kill the women and children. His apartment was turned completely upside down, with their things scattered everywhere... . At first they stuck together, but then the husband and wife left; all she had in her hands was a small bag. The Jews are leaving with baskets, baby carriages... . Frightened faces... . Pale... .

A single soldier rode past the square. At six o'clock this morning you could hear powerful explosions; then the warehouses on the other side of the Neman were burning. Columns of black smoke and tongues of fire ascended into the clear, burning sky—uncanny. The explosions have shattered the windowpanes in three rooms. I went out to buy some morphine around two (just in case). {I saw whole crowds of Russian soldiers with and without their weapons wandering along the riverbank... . Countless vehicles... . They are retreating in disarray, without any order. Gunfire here and there continues.} The streets are empty, desolate. Suddenly there is a terrible quaking; the building started to shake. They blew up the Zeleny Bridge... . {It is now five in the afternoon, and the shooting and explosions can still be heard... . A temporary Lithuanian government has been formed; they have been ordered to take down the Lithuanian flag. They sing the Lithuanian anthem and promise an independent Lithuania united with the "New Europe" under the guidance of the "great" Hitler. A minister has already been appointed, and the radio plays Lithuanian songs constantly. There was an announcement on the radio this evening at nine: the order has been given for the German military government to organize the destruction of the Red Army unit retreating along the Vilkomir Highway and trying to join up with a Red Army column, which is moving out of Vilkomir and hurrying toward Kaunas. The order was for airplanes to strafe these troops. (I do not understand: it is possible that there is already a German military government in Kaunas?!) On top of that, Lithuanian radio said and repeated many times that the water had been poisoned by the "Red bandits and barbarians."}

At about eleven in the morning we heard loud machine gun and rifle fire near our corner building. Through our window we could see a military unit (about one hundred men) hurriedly but with complete order running across Kanto Street with their arms tilted. We could hear their commander giving them orders.

{Two small cannons were moving along behind them; it was obvious that this unit, though retreating in an orderly manner, was in a hurry... . Following the order to kill the Russian soldiers, it seemed, Lithuanian volunteers were after them. A little girl says she saw a dead Russian soldier, murdered, it seems, around the corner... . Isolated Russian soldiers moving around in the street shoot back at people shooting at them from the windows and rooftops of the "Lithuanian patriots." This patriotic savagery is horrible. Shots ring out for another long night; even now, at four in the morning, the gunfire does not cease. Whom are they shooting at? Why? Perhaps out of fear, for their own reassurance, to shore up their "patriotic courage?" I am seeing war with my own eyes and hearing it with my own ears. God! What a senseless, blind, disgusting thing! Victory hangs on so much luck.}

24 June. Five A.M. Loud gunfire is very close... . I sat down at the radio; they are singing "Rose Marie" in German and playing some sort of melodic music. For whom? Why? I don't understand anything.

The railroad is packed with refugees. Our building has been emptied. {All the Jews have fled:} the landlady has left with her daughter, and a young lawyer has taken off with his wife (they helped me bring Lilya up the stairs when I brought her from the hospital). My downstairs neighbor, a Russian woman, broke out a window and left through it with her things... . The window had been covered with strips of paper; the streets are desolate. Everyone is still going, {the Jews} are fleeing with their bundles, carts, suitcases. {Since ten o'clock in the morning on the first day of the war the Russians having been hauling off their families and business.

Lithuanian songs, marches, and promises are playing constantly on the Lithuanian radio. I now see that my contemporaries understand nothing of what is going on. The historians cannot know; even the facts will be recorded with dubious accuracy... . Everything is generally like some fantastic, terrible dream. We have not eaten for nearly two days; I have slept about two hours. I am filled with the most strenuous anxiety and anguish: Lilya lies there with typhus, and then there is all this shooting, cannon fire, murder. So much sorrow and suffering all around. People have thrown away their lives; in the space of ten minutes they tear themselves from their past and flee from Hitler as if they were fleeing from the plague... . It is interesting: where does Hitler's doubtlessly pathological, completely maniacal hatred toward the Jews come form? What psychiatrist could explain it? It is filled with so much emotion, which turns it over to the unconscious; that means that the reason may lie in the depths, hidden, perhaps, in some injury from his childhood, in some sexual trauma.... I doubt that he could explain it to himself....

Once again speeches can be heard on the radio about "world Jewry now uniting the English plutocracy with the Red bandits in the Kremlin." How absurd, crazy, and persistent it all is: beginning with the Great War, the whole of European culture and morality has collapsed before my eyes. Where now is the aristocratic soul? We, the older generation, feel pity for this intellectual and spiritual aristocracy; but in the time of the Revolution it had no place in a world made simple and coarse.... }

... Vitya has a talent for seeing injustice and suffering and cares very much about people. He is helping our Jewish friends; he takes them to the train station, consoles, them, disappears somewhere or other for days, tries to oppose chaos, cruelty, and savagery with humanity and reason.

{On 25 June at 6:00 A.M. the Kovno radio reported in the name of the "partisans" that thieves, robbers, and recidivists would be shot on sight, so that the old police force could be reinstated and contact with the temporary government could be maintained.... The radio is on all the time.... banal, pompous, strumming marches interrupted by various exclamations, appeals, and orders. It has become loathsome and irritating.... I heard two loud, shaking volleys of artillery fire just now....

The Russians have destroyed three hundred tanks and seventy-six airplanes and have taken five thousand prisoners.... "Whenever I start to speak about culture," said Goebbels, according to Russian radio, "I involuntarily place a finger on the trigger of my revolver. To return history to the Middle Ages." (It has already reverted back, I can assure you.)

They say all the counter-revolutionary officers have been released from prison.... The radio issued a warning that Jews are firing submachine guns from windows and that for every German wounded one hundred Jews would be shot. Although the radio announced that everyone could come out and enthusiastically greet the German troops as they enter the city, suddenly an order has been issued to close all the windows and draw the shutters. They warn that they will shoot at the windows; I myself have seen them shooting at the wall. At five this afternoon the city is completely dead. Lithuanians are walking around the streets, and there is shooting all the time. The ominous, somehow evil-sounding noise of the gunfire is very oppressive.... It gets on the nerves.

It is terrible.... They keep leading more and more old and young Jews past my window on their way to the prison. Now and then an ambulance or a truck with a huge red cross and the white figures of nurses and orderlies will pass through the empty streets; they are collecting bodies (whose?).... }

The Red Army came a year ago; their tanks and vehicles drove by endlessly, and people came running out to see them. A new life had begun. We have lived through so much over this past year. I was a believer fascinated by the wonderful Soviet dream....

25 June. A bright, clear, hot day. The Germans are in the city. It has begun.... {Today the city is lavishly decorated with Lithuanian national flags.... There are masses of armed people wearing nationalistic ribbons in the streets. People are very insensitive, savage, walking around with their guns ready.} They are taking Jews away one at a time and in groups with looks of anguish on their faces.... A tall, elegant, elderly Jews with a pale face, peaceful and full of resolve, cuts into my memory; then there is the group of women and old people.

A husband and wife were walking at the head of one such group; an elderly couple, they were gently supporting each other. I was struck by the face of a young Jew in a long frock coat, walking with a proud, defiant look. I cannot forget the short, thin youth in that crowd; he read a book as he walked and paid no attention to anything going on around him. On his face was an expression of cold disdain {and defiance. The crowd surrounding Laisves Avenue was jeering, gloating, guffawing, and making fun of those who were passing by.} A young lady came up to me and, with tears in her eyes, said, "How horrible {that people can find joy in something like this.}" I was shaken, crushed, by everything I saw. Many curious onlookers were standing outside the prison. A blue, dust-covered bus from the provinces pulled up; thirty Jews were roughly herded out of it. They went past the line of armed men, who were rudely and cruelly yelling at them: "Faster!" People were standing around and gloating. Where does this maliciousness, this cruelty, come from? {These "partisans" were behaving with a certain voluptuousness, ecstatic, it seemed, with their power; they rushed around with their weapons ready, their faces filled with the look of victory.}

The German soldiers were well dressed, well fed, and well groomed. {They create an impression quite different from that of the Red Army when they came in last year, worn out, ragged, and thin. The cars, trucks, and transports are all first-rate, powerful, and practical; the horses are good, strong breeds, but thin. The Lithuanians greeted them much more enthusiastically than they did the Russians a year ago; they gave them flowers and joyously unfurled their flags. Efficiently, obsequiously, ingratiatingly the "partisans" cringed before the Germans, especially when it came to showing their contempt for the "Jewish Front."} They persisted in their claims that Jews were firing from windows, sometimes even with machine guns, but it was obvious that not a single Jew was doing that.

{Some unpleasant moments at the counter in the hospital: a nurse attacked me with such rudeness and maliciousness that it shocked me; I had done absolutely nothing wrong. She tore down the portrait of Stalin that I had put on the wall and trampled it with her feet. All the glass exhibit cases throughout the city has been smashed; they've thrown out and destroyed all the Soviet emblems, portraits, books, busts, statues. It is especially sad to see the bookcases and the piles of broken glass mixed in with pages torn from the books. The Lithuanian people obediently comply but secretly think otherwise, keeping their anger to themselves; and the more they keep it to themselves, the more it comes out when they no longer have to hold it in. How I would love to flee from this damned city, from these alien people! Today was such a hard day... . The human depravity, the anger, the futility, the murder of the Jews, the plundering of their possessions... run, terror, tragedies... .

The partisans (what a stupid, phony name) murdered the frightened, fleeing, retreating Red Army soldiers, who were unarmed, exhausted, and broken... . Nowhere, nowhere do I see any humanity or humaneness.}

Germans are occupying two large rooms in my apartment. Lilya and I have settled into my small bedroom on the sunny side of the apartment; the air in the room heats up so much during the day that we cannot breathe at night. I hang wet towels along a cord, but they quickly dry out and do not cool it off at all. A bunch of trucks stand in the yard; day and night you can hear the sound of their engines, wheels, and horns. They've mercilessly destroyed the flowerbed. I spoke with two of the Germans; they are exulting in their victory, satisfied with themselves, obtuse and contemptuous of the whole world... . It is sinister, terrible, ominous. It seems that all my life I have had nothing but bad experiences. The gunfire fire in the distance is getting closer and becoming more frequent. What does it mean? I haven't slept at all... .

26 June. At two o'clock this morning, at dawn, I heard the sound of a vehicle. I went over to the window. A truck pulled up to the gray wooden building at 13 Kanto Street diagonally across from my apartment (the watchman at that building was the first to hang pout a national flag). Several men got out. First they broke down the door, went in and turned on the electric light in the entry way... . I heard a woman's loud, heartrending screams full of indescribable horror... . She kept screaming for several minutes; then a man's voice was shouting in Yiddish, begging for something, babbling some words or other. But it didn't matter... . Then there were three or four shots, and everything immediately became quiet... . A man's voice said in Lithuanian, "You are not to shoot without my permission." Then you could hear the pitiful crying of a child; it sounded like two children. Again there were shots, and silence immediately returned... . They murdered four innocent people... . The truck was parked at the building for a long time, until a group of about six men came out of the apartment. {"Let's keep going" (in Lithuanian). They came toward my entryway: "This is our place" (in Lithuanian). Then they turned the corner onto Kanto Street. Again I heard an engine.} A short time went by, then again came the muffled screams, followed by three shots (from a revolver). Seven or eight people were murdered in the course of two hours, quickly, efficiently, methodically! The gunshots faded into the distance... . Now I know what they mean! {The engines rumble, the city keeps silent, and the police are not heard. The Germans allow shooting at night, when it is forbidden to walked around, in the very city they have conquered! It is clear that the murderers are acting with the permission and the approval of our new masters!} They closed the door to Number 13, but the electric light burned for another twenty-four hours; I looked at it several times with a shudder. My first reaction was to go out, scream, and cry for help. But to whom? Who would come? Who would help? I am noting it down; let it stand... .

I believe there will be a judgment, retribution, punishment for the murderers! Truth will triumph, evil will be punished! ... At 3:20 a white van with a red cross went by. I thought it was headed for that small building, but no: it turned toward the Neman. A column of smoke appeared over Laisves Avenue and then quickly disappeared. And the morning is such a bright, gentle, wondrous summer morning! Anxiety, despair, and sorrow weigh on my soul... . They calmly murdered innocent, helpless women and children simply because they were Jews. And these are people!!!

27 June. A four in the morning, again the sound of engines, again six shots ring out from nearby. Horror overwhelms me... . It is forbidden to go out before 6:00 A.M., so that they can commit their murders without witnesses. At six this morning I went out to see what had happened during the night. An old Jewish man, covered with blood, lay dead in the doorway to the Meirovich home on Kanto Street; he had been struck in the head. When I asked the yard keeper (a dark-haired man with a brutal face) what happened, who killed him and why, he said, "What, are you curious? If you go around talking about it, you'll get the same... ." A group of German soldiers and some pedestrians walked by. No one paid any attention to the murdered man lying in a pool of blood... . {I went up to the building at Number 13, where, as I had found out, there were four people last night. A woman in a green jacket was sitting in the doorway and was apparently waiting for someone; I asked her who was murdered in the night. Obviously lying, she replied, "They came and did a search; nobody was murdered... . What do you want from me? ..." And so I accomplished nothing... . All the yard keepers are murderers and thieves; they betray the Jews, call in the partisans, and plunder the Jews' apartments themselves. My soul is torn apart... . Something even more oppressive is hanging over me. Today is such a bright day, amazingly clear, not a cloud in the sky... it weighs even more heavily on the soul. Suddenly the phone rang, and a woman's voice, somehow unpleasant and malicious (I can guess who it was), said, "Aren't you filled with sorrow, now that your Bolsheviks had left? ..." I grew terrified and felt that I was surrounded only by enemies... . I have become physically weak from lack of sleep and food... . The sadistic, patriotic frenzy has continued all day long: with the permission and approval of the government they are torturing and murdering the Jews... . All the Lithuanians, with very few exceptions, are of one mind in their hatred for the Jews, especially the intelligentsia, who under the Soviet authorities suddenly lost everything. Since they were inclined toward nationalism and felt they had been usurped by the Jews, the intelligentsia did not actively set out to work; moreover, they suffered materially from the nationalization of their homes and their capital. Now they are taking revenge for their suffering and humiliation. Although he condemns the way the "partisans" murder the Jews at night without a trial, one physician I know is seeking an explanation and a justification for Jewish "dominance."... All day long people wearing national Lithuanian bands saunter about the streets with an air of victory; in broad daylight they break into Jewish homes and load their goods into carts, without the slightest compunction about grabbing the every last pitiful thing. It is a kind of epidemic, a debauchery of greed... . Everyone is carrying a gun. Unfortunately, they dare to "fight" only with the permission of the government (red or black, it's all the same; I remember that when the Soviets came, all the hoodlums were also wearing red sashes during the first days).

Everywhere you see either the national colors or white bands with a red cross.} The ambulances are assigned the task of gathering the bodies of murdered Russians and Jews. From the window of the clinic I observed how a truck full of "nurses" was getting ready to leave on one of these jobs: screeching, guffawing, rude flirtation, dirty jokes... . Only one health worker—a simple, uneducated woman—spoke with sorrow about the killing of the Red Army soldiers, about the crowds taking Jews with shovels to be shot, and about their being forced to dig their own graves while singing "If Tomorrow There Should Be War." One patient told how he himself had seen the Germans force the Jews out of the prison, harness them to a tank, and make them pull the tank up to a high riverbank; then for fun they would have them take it around city hall... . I did not verify it, and I asked him about it again several times. He assured me he had seen it with his own eyes. The Jews murdered on Kanto Street were hauled away in trucks. {Jews were also summoned from the prison; I saw them myself. With pale, frightened faces they crawled out of the truck, roughly prodded along by the "partisans." Black terror is made all the more terrible by the fact that the Jews are doomed to death because of race, because of blood, that is, because of something over which no human being has any control... their fate... . It is horrible... inhuman... . Using the pretense that they are "communists," the "partisans" murder people who were perhaps enemies of the Soviet regime... hypocrites... .}

An announcement has been posted on the doors of Outpatient Clinic Number 1, where I work: "Not a single Jew will be served in this establishment."

Everything nationalistic is disgusting to me; it makes me nauseous. I have seen blood and suffering all because of nationalistic hatred. {The partisans attract either stupid boys who have been deceived by slogans about an "independent" Lithuania or the dregs of society drawn to plunder and murder without being answerable to anyone. The yard keeper at the building on Kanto Street, where the old Jew lay dead in the doorway, is a swarthy man with dark, fearsome eyes (they have a trace of insanity about them)—the one who said, "If you go around talking about it, you'll get the same"—suddenly came into my kitchen and asked where Apartment 6 was located. I shuddered: he was looking for Jews into order to murder them.... He saw blood on the floor and was startled by it; he asked where it came from, and we explained that we had slaughtered a chicken. Then, taking on an air of authority, as if he were in charge, he said, "Clean it up." It was obvious that he did not like the sight of blood, so much of which had been shed these last several days; it frightened him.... He left to look for Jews. I purposely followed him, first to our house watchman, who I knew was friendly toward the Jews in our building. In fact, he sheltered a little boy and his whole family; they were not killed during those first terrible days....

During those days the fate of us all was in the hands of the yard keepers, and woe to anyone who had any personal grudges with them....

Oh, horror! His harassment is tiring, exhausting.... And these Lithuanian emblems adorning everything, they're a form of defense, of self-defense for the faint-hearted....}

The Germans have been conducting searches all day. They look fresh, vigorous, elegant; a select people: developed, handsome.... Exemplary order; the higher ranking ones ride by in their limousines, with their monocles and their "Prussian" look of contempt. Placards are posted on the walls.

Today I saw a crowd of about two hundred Jews being very roughly herded through the prison gates. The people were worn out, ragged, filthy, exhausted, pitiful.... {With hatred and disgust I looked upon the crowd of people staring at them, at that mob making fun of those poor people, with its malevolent laughter.

In the outpatient clinic there was immediately the cleanliness and the order that I tried to establish for a whole year, but in vain. The reason for this failure was clear to me: it was not how the Soviets had set it up (as I assured their enemies), but rather it was the stubborn, passive resistance of a people hostile toward a regime that is alien to them.

Yesterday church bells were ringing. Today they broadcast a church service over the radio. I think the Bolsheviks should not have forbidden such broadcasts. I love church music, especially the organ. Music in general can take you out of the hideous realm of bloody reality and into the peaceful, gracious world of divine harmony. Christianity is the last refuge for the exhaustion, weakness, and disillusionment brought on by earthly lies. In the meantime we have some breathing space. Soon we shall have a sense of what sort of German protectorate this is. In vain have our patriots imagined that the Germans are interested in Lithuanian independence. Instead of the bitter truth of their overthrow, Russian radio is broadcasting news of only various isolated military actions, only news of bravery and victory, but not a word about the fact that whole units have surrendered and that the entire Baltic region has already been taken.... The Finnish president said that the Germans are fighting not against the Russian people but only against Bolshevism.... It's a lie! ... The Russians bombed Helsinki, Turku. Sweden has allowed troops to cross its territory, and Spain has sided with Germany to take revenge for the Civil War.}

It is a hot, clear summer day. I am working around the house, cooking, baking. Every noise and knock now frightens me... . What happened to N. I do not know; I am worried. There are no patients; the stores are closed, locked up. The windows are broken out. The Germans now occupy the entire city. The windows are sealed with strips of paper. The city is dead. There is no shooting in our area today; they are not murdering anyone... . I did not know that gunfire could be so loud... . People are talking about all kinds of humiliations that have been inflicted upon the Jews; they are forced to haul excrement with their bare hands. I saw a group of Jews who had been arrested being driven along carrying shovels. Yesterday a patient (Morkunaite) told me that she saw them using boards to beat Jews who were digging graves at the cemetery. {People point out that they are arresting communists.}

28 June. A horrible night! It is hot and stuffy. I left the window in my office open; I forgot about the order to keep all windows facing the street closed. At around midnight they started shooting at my window and at the wall surrounding it. The shots were loud; at first they came one at a time, then in volleys. Then they shot at the door and the other windows. A bullet flew through the window and hit the wall plaster in my office; another came right through the door. At first I did not realize that they were firing at my apartment. Lilya and I lay down on the floor in the hall, but the chatter of gunfire kept on. Thinking they were shooting at the open window, I ran to the watchman so that he could go out to the gate with me and ask for permission to close the unfortunate window. But the watchman had locked himself in the cellar and would not talk to me. Then I crawled over to the window and, at the risk of being killed, closed it. The windowpanes and the shutters where shot full of holes. We hid in the bathroom. Then I heard the sound of many footsteps, machinegun fire, Germans shouting, running around; a large number of vehicles drove by. Two hours later there were loud gunshots outside again; they could be heard on Kanto Street for two or three minutes, and then it was quiet again... . And so it went for the entire sleepless night. {At five o'clock in the morning the doorbell rang. At the door were men—mostly boys, actually—in Lithuanian uniforms; they were quiet and tired, but they mostly had an evil, nervous, somewhat degenerate look. They were searching for the ones who had been doing the shooting—Jews with machine guns (!) who had supposedly been hiding in the attic of our building. They found nothing, of course, and left.} At nine this morning a luxurious limousine {with the national flag} pulled up to our building; out of it climbed the guardians of order, all armed with revolvers... . Their leader, a retired military man—or so he seemed—with a handsome but unremarkable face, announced that he was the one who shot out our windows and that he "saw" a submachine gun firing from my neighbors' window (a Jewish apartment). I pointed to my office with its broken window and explained that the neighboring apartment had been empty for a week now (the Jews had fled). I guaranteed him that there was no one there and that the thick layer of dust in front of the shutters had not even been touched... . But, apparently afraid, they started knocking on door with their revolvers ready. They cautiously entered the apartment, which had been completely ransacked. Everything had been torn out of the cabinets; of course, they found no one, least of all any Jews. After discovering a Finnish knife and an old holster without a gun among some underwear, they started checking to see if these objects too might be weapons. After the search they stuffed their pockets and bags with various small (but valuable) things from the cabinets and grabbed some sausage and preserves. Then they sealed the apartment and left.

Shots rang out again this afternoon... .

29 June. A hot, wondrous day... . Patients came today and told about how Jews were being forced to carry excrement with their bare hands, dig pits with hand spades, and drink water from the canal; about how they were forced to lie down in rows and were randomly beaten with crowbars; about how they were beaten over the head with boards (this was in a garage on Vitovt Avenue behind the cemetery); about how the ones who were killed were thrown into a truck and hauled off somewhere to be buried. {Lithuanians did all of this; the Germans did not take part in it but just stood around.} Several Germans were taking photographs. The simple, poor people—peasants—were grieved and horrified; they felt sorry for the Jews... .

{Throughout the city there are rumors that the Russians and Jews are tormenting Christians and children; that they cut out their tongues, torture them, and so on; that the Jews are shooting from the windows of buildings and killing people. I now know who has spread these absurd, lying rumors and why. The Lithuanian rabble, with the full permission of the intelligentsia (or better: with their tacit approval), has exhibited such a savage, wild fanaticism that compared with them, the Russian pogroms against the Jews look like a philanthropic endeavor... .}

This afternoon we went downtown; it is overflowing with German troops... . Soldiers are everywhere: in the cafes and the stores, on the streets. Early this morning the Germans occupied the apartment next door; the courtyard is filled with vehicles, cars, trucks, officers' aides. Someone is playing the piano in the apartment below. The sound of iron-tipped boots can be heard on the stairs.

30 June. Nightmarish days... . Crowds of people who have been arrested walk by... {Jews}. Fear reigns among the Jews; indeed, I too tremble all the time in the face of such horrible suffering, cruelty, savagery, atrocities. {I think the main reason for the cruelty is fear: they are torturing and murdering out of a zealous, cringing desire to convince their new masters they that are ready to serve them to the best of their ability, that they will stop at nothing... .} I am tormented physically and spiritually. I go to the cellar to cook, since there is no kerosene and very little firewood... . The apartment is full of dust, filth, and ruin... . Countless numbers of trucks, monstrously huge, long, and heavy, are parked along Mickiewicz and Kestuchio Streets... . {Everything is orderly, clean and shiny... . People are healthy, vigorous, and quietly busy. A large number of Russian prisoners passed by in trucks yesterday; they looked very pale... . At the intersections there are German soldiers and signs showing the way. There are very many of these nameplates... . They are working in a very methodical and calculated manner... . You cannot help but be amazed at the organization. In eight days the city has been transformed: the victors have arrived triumphant, while the Russians were nothing but quiet, unnoticed, tolerated guests. They are rapidly buying up our goods (one mark is equal to ten rubles); boots sell for six marks (in Germany they cost more than twenty), but now!

The newspapers are printing selections from *Mein Kampf* with racist quotes. The German papers are reporting huge advances of German troops. They have taken Minsk, Lvov... . The Russians are putting up a bitter fight... .

{I am seeing war: the murder of innocent people, destruction, death, hatred, fear, savagery, destitution, plundering, cruelty, the ruin of everything spiritual, fires, bodies, stench... . For our part, I think we could have been better, since this war was nearly avoided; there was just the murder of the Jews at the hands of an organized mob, the terror that literally paralyzed everyone... I cannot believe my own eyes and ears! I tremble before the power of this blind hatred for a single people, maintained and propagated from obviously base and avaricious motives. In the papers much is written about the victims who have been hauled away—the Lithuanians...but not a word about the fact that the Jews have been hauled away, much less that the Jews have suffered materially, and even less about the savagery and the mass murders... I shall never forget what I have seen over these last several days... When, like a "hero" in the night, the cowardly Lithuanian captain shot at our building and then assured the German SS officer, who had come to requisition my neighbors' possessions, that the children in the Jews' apartment had been shooting from the window in their room, I abruptly declared that it was not true and that no one could prove any of it. Then the German SS said that the Bolshevik-Jews, the enemy, had to be destroyed, that "a struggle is a struggle." The cruel abruptness and lack of compassion in his voice was terrible, inhuman.}

Doctor Ipp—a quiet, modest man and a wonderful physician—took poison and died. Another doctor took poison, along with his entire family. My colleague, an eye doctor, asked me to work the evening shift for him, since he was afraid. Indeed, it is terrifying to sit in the empty clinic, {on whose doors an announcement is posted: "We do not treat Jews"}, terrifying to see Jews arrested and taken to prison, to see the German soldiers and know that to them you are not a human being...

1 July. Clear summer days... The rumble of trucks, the rattle of iron, the noise of engines, propellers, the stomping of iron-tipped boots... War! I tremble inside, I am afraid but, really, of what? Not death, which I calmly await, but the violence, the ruthlessness, the inhumanity. Soldiers make noise in the apartment day and night; there is no rest, no peace. I suffer. I am trying to gather my courage; I summon memories of beauty, of nature, of the Good, of Love, of humanity's finest people...

Huge black bombers are flying very low overhead. The day drags on endlessly. I have less and less strength.

2 July. A long, hard day. Tormented, frightened Jewish faces are everywhere. Mothers wander around outside the prison... Three trucks full of prisoners drive by. Where were they taking them? No one knows. Friends of mine drop in. We weep together... There is no comfort. At night there is shooting and more shooting. I am afraid of everyone and everything. How weary I am...

3 July. This morning L. informed me that I have been discharged from the clinic; they are unhappy with my political activity... My enemies there occupy the highest positions.

The Germans are bombing Smolensk; they have taken Riga and are marching onward... The trucks outside my window are hauling gasoline drums. In the courtyard they are cleaning, washing, and repairing the vehicles. Large airplanes are flying overhead; everything is humming, rumbling, shaking, grinding. Everywhere the hard work of destruction.

4 July. A hard night; I scarcely slept. My heart aches... I am a complete stranger in my own apartment. The doors open and close all day long, with crowds of soldiers going in and out. Everywhere people are talking about the horrible {German-Lithuanian} savagery and cruelty... Homeless and without any rights, the Jews await death. My old patient lost her mother; her father was murdered, and her little boy was left in a Young Pioneer camp. Her husband disappeared without a trace. He was probably murdered too. She is completely petrified with grief. I wept with her. I know of no way to console her. Again the physical pain in my heart. Several thousand Jews have been shot. In Slobodka every third home has been ransacked. Truckloads of Jewish women are headed somewhere...

5 July. My manicurist Goldochka came; from a charming young girl she has suddenly turned into an ugly old woman with a weather-beaten face. She got married just two months ago. I was at their wedding. A sweet young couple beaming with happiness... She and her husband fled from Germans to rural areas, but she fell, as they say, from the frying pan into the fire. They were robbed along the way, and her husband was taken to the Seventh Fort. She is pregnant; she cries and begs for someone to save her husband. But who can save him?

The Jews are thrown out of lines; they won't give them any food. They have been fired from all business establishments; they are even forbidden to ride in cabs and to sit on park benches. {I am amazed at their courageous submission to their fate, with neither protest nor revolt.}

An. has returned... He says that with great difficulty and all sorts of adventures, after being locked up and detained many times by German troops, after travelling on foot and on a passing cart, he finally reached Kaunas. He met many Jewish refugees along the way; they were rushing about in all directions like hunted animals.

7 July. I slept badly last night. The German lodgers kept disturbing me.

I went down to the Aleksot Bridge; it was blown up in the middle and is all torn up. The windows of the buildings along the riverbank are broken out... stones scattered all over, twisted iron bars... There are Russian prisoners on the riverbank; filthy and worn out, they are loading barges... German soldiers are wandering about...

{There is a story of how a certain doctor was murdered at the Seventh Fort, where Jews have been murdered in large groups at a time. In this case, however, the bullet intended for the doctor hit a twelve-year-old boy next to him, and he was only wounded. He asked to be killed, and a pharmacist nearby gave him morphine; after that he calmed down.}

Masses of people—tormented, miserable, and afraid—are coming this way. A pharmacist's wife released from prison is worried about her husband, who is still there... Goldochka came; she is still hoping to have her husband released from the Seventh Fort. An elderly lady, from whom I bought some dishes, came by to ask about her husband... I signed a document stating that he is a peaceful merchant... Outside L. saw the mutilated corpse of a Jew. {The "partisans" are going around to the Jewish apartments and taking away their belongings.}

People are becoming unrecognizable from grief... Just now a trachoma patient, an old friend, was here... She lost her son; yesterday her apartment was robbed. The hoodlums are completely unaccountable to anyone. {The intelligentsia remain silent. They say the clergy have submitted a petition for the cessation of the savagery... The Red Cross is distributing leaflets that say, "We do not help Jews"... a disgrace... I cannot believe it... it's simply unthinkable. The Lithuanian children have already arrived from the Young Pioneer camp, but not the Jewish children. They are starving; they are begging for their mothers and for bread! Humans are worse than animals! My head reels... Nightmarish days of horror and despair...

Individual Germans take pity and hand out medicine and potatoes and offer some comfort... An old woman attending to the graves at the cemetery did not want to go very far into the cemetery; she was convinced that there the Germans would violate her... A kind of delirium...} One may walk around until ten in the evening. There are huge lines everywhere for food rations... It is very hard to find something to eat, but my patients help—some have milk, others have groats.

There is terrible fighting at the front.

10 July. It was announced that the Jews must wear a yellow six-pointed star and that they can be outside only until eight o'clock. The streets are frighteningly empty. The city is dead...I stopped in to see a colleague, a surgeon, in her charming apartment. She sent her things off to friends; some of her things, especially the pretty vases, were still standing on the emptied shelves... Destruction... The two of us wept. I comforted her, suggesting that she spend the days with me and go to the ghetto only at night... I feel utterly crushed; I cannot sleep...

12 July. Jews walk about with the yellow star; they are allowed to walk only on the pavement, not on the sidewalks. They may walk only in single file, not together, and they have to remove their hats for every passing German.

My German lodgers are leaving today to move closer to the advancing front... {Last night they invited Lilya and me to have a farewell coffee... They spoke about a Europe of the future, in which there will be no more war, no more economic wars or nationalistic wars. One of them—a short, thin man—is a painter, a jeweler, and an architect, a German from the Sudet family. He showed us some wonderful work he had done with color photographs. Another one—older, tall, and homely, with sad eyes—was a driver and a family man. More than any of the others, he showed some pity toward my sick Lilya, with her cropped hair; when we said good-bye he brought her some eggs, milk, lemons, and kerosene, for which I gave him three small bars of soap (they had no soap at all). A third German was handsome, young, tall, and muscular—a regular Don Juan; he was a driver for a big truck. A native of Cologne, he was a coarse, uncultured man. A little later some high-ranking guest arrived; he was short and heavy-set and had a hard face marked with jagged scars. Without any show of servility, they seated him at the table with everyone else and continued their conversation about the wealth and wide-open spaces of Russia and about the absence of any real talent or culture there. I tried, although carefully, to stand up for Russia. Covered trucks are parked along Kestuchio Street. My lodgers left precisely at two.} They are headed east... always east. They hope to take Moscow by October or November, so that they can go home for the New Year...

14 July. I am working around the house all day, seeing patients in my filthy, demolished apartment, with the crumbling plaster, the filthy walls, the bugs and the fleas. At night there is shooting and more shooting; I am expecting something even more horrible... {The Lithuanian patients come in, all satisfied and happy, looking forward to an independent Lithuania... Meanwhile no Lithuanian government has been formed.} The mail is not operating; there is neither safety nor order; all commerce is paralyzed...

{The Jews meekly bear their misfortune without protest or indignation.} My neighbor came back for her things; I did not recognize her. Her face had changed so much; she looked so exhausted, and she had aged a great deal. Her husband, an attorney, had been shot. {A polite and good-natured German officer allowed her to collect from her ransacked, devastated apartment the worst articles of clothing she had left; she took two items. But then our building manager arrived. Still going around labeling people as Bolsheviks, he is a young Lithuanian with shifty eyes and a handsome but evil face; he said Jews are not allowed to take anything...} At her request, Lilya and I dragged a sewing machine, a divan, and some other things over to our apartment right under the Germans' noses... I stayed by myself; somehow large rooms frighten me. I am afraid of sleepless nights; I am constantly expecting horror and cruelty... {There is no law; animal instincts are getting drunk on vengeance. It is terrifying to live under the rule of a mob that has no work and that gives itself over to instincts of murder and plunder with impunity.

They have taken Vitebsk and are approaching Petersburg. Horrible fighting. England has signed a military agreement with Soviet Russia not to make a separate peace; America is promising to help. The Germans write, "The plutocratic English reconcile themselves even with communism simply in order to win." In the German newspapers there are terrible photographs of the destruction in Russia, the prisoners of war. I don't think I can stand it... The sleepless nights are so agonizing. Suddenly the bell rings... My heart skipped a beat: "They've come!" I unlocked the door, and there stood a German officer with his swastika, a young man with a stern, harsh face, authoritative, distrustful, hostile... He seems very unhappy about something, an inexorable type: he has rung the wrong bell by mistake. When I explained the mistake to him, he turned without excusing himself and started knocking angrily on the neighbors' door. Vitya came over and tried to comfort me.}

15 July. A night of terror has passed, and once again it is stuffy, oppressive. Something is wrong with my heart; I cannot sleep... There was shooting all night long (were they murdering someone?). I weep from exhaustion and sadness... To die, to no longer see anything.

17 July. Nightmarish days. Jews are being resettled in Slobodka; 25,000 people are housed in places designed for 5,000. They are handing over their belongings and selling them. They brought some furniture to me and put it in rooms that have suddenly become strange to me. {The *Arkhiepiskop* published a call to help compatriots who have suffered from the war.

In a state of ecstasy, and with the permission of the authorities, everyone is humiliating, debasing and insulting, slandering, making up lies about defenseless people who are being victimized... I find it disgusting and nauseating. It is some sort of psychosis of hatred and bestiality.}

Carts of all sorts of baggage and dejected figures with yellow stars plod incessantly along the streets.

The Jews are going into a terrible exile from society, and we are returning to a humdrum life. People come to pick up their glasses, to get a check up, and to ask for something to eat. We talk about ration cards and food... Today it is cold and damp. I am spiritually exhausted.

18 July. A cold, gray day... The city is beginning to assume a "normal look." Movement has returned to the empty streets; but the people with the yellow badges walking on the street pavement somehow grate painfully on the nerves and conscience. Jews fleeing from their apartments are hauling away their things... The manager of the building where my dressmaker lives came and announced that I could go by her apartment and pick up the material that I had left for her to sew. The seamstress was a quiet, gentle creature. The old woman lived alone and sewed all day long; in the evenings she would read... I have often seen volumes of Tolstoy and Chekhov on her table. Her wretched little apartment in the wooden annex in the narrow courtyard was always neat and tidy. She herself was the image of order and efficiency. She ended up on a train while fleeing from the Germans; the Germans bombed the train, and she was burned alive... One of her relatives who had returned on foot told me about it... The explosion had thrown several people's bodies into the wires overhead; they were left hanging there... Fate is whimsical; its victims perish senselessly and at random...

After fierce street fighting, Smolensk has been taken.

Our lodger said they will take Moscow in October; in November or December they will occupy England, and by January the war will be over. The Germans will go home... What madness.

20 July. I am very sad in the evenings. I was at the cemetery; sweet briars, roses, and violets are in bloom. The days are cool. The city is deserted; {the unemployed have been invited} to work in Germany.

Life is in a shambles. {Not a single name of anyone in the government is known; they are all somehow anonymous. There is no police force; people are simply shot for stealing, looting, and plundering (without permission).} Fewer and fewer Germans soldiers are to be seen; instead there are many officers, very important, very arrogant. Most of the stores are closed; there is very little food to be had, and the lines are huge, especially for Jews. It is painful to look at their anguished, tormented faces...

22 July. Moscow has been bombed for the first time. The German radio said that the force of destruction in the bombing was comparable to the most terrible bombing of London, that the Kremlin has been transformed into a sea of flames... It is terrible, shocking, to think of what our people are living through...

23 July. A gray day... low, cold storm clouds... Fog. Heavy aircraft have been roaring through the sky since morning, but you cannot see them. I slept badly, troubled sleep... Many misfortunes come every day. I comfort, I help...

They have bombed Moscow for three nights in a row now. {We have been ordered to obtain German flags and forbidden to fly our national flags.} The paper ran the most stupid article about Roosevelt being a Mason... The most vapid, anti-Semitic articles. {My patients are glad to be free of the Soviet yoke, but they find that the cruelty inflicted upon the Jews has become too severe...}

24 July. I am barely alive... I would like to fade into oblivion, but it is impossible... Huge concern over meals, food, searching for something to eat... I do not have the strength to leave the house; the buses are not running, there is no mail, and the telephone does not work. There is a great deal of sorrow all around. {First they took away the Bolsheviks, then a son is murdered in the street, then a mother is denounced and arrested, maybe for espionage, then a son is beaten unmercifully, and on and on.} There is no rule of law; chaos is everywhere, stores are closed, food is plundered... Everything has come unraveled; everything is disorderly. I am sad most of all in the evenings, to the point of terror... There were many shootings at the prison today, so much so that single shots could be heard constantly. I am afraid: everyone with a gun or some kind of headband looks like a murderer to me. The only ones I am not afraid of are the Jews with their yellow stars.

25 July. It is foggy this morning. You cannot see the Neman, so the airplanes are not flying; I slept seven hours for the first time.

{Lithuania is really of one mind in its hatred for the Jews, and I cannot understand the reasons for this hatred: is it economic (competition)? Envy? Racial hatred? Propaganda? Dissatisfaction with the fact that Jews have supported the communists and the Russians?} A patient from Mazheiek told me that all the Jewish men there have been shot during the last few weeks {and that he approved of it.} In other places all of them have been taken to forced labor, including the doctors.

27 July. I spent a wonderful summer day at the cottage. The fragrance of the pine forest, the earth, the fresh morning dew, the greenery, the river, the quiet... At night the dark sky with its twinkling constellations... {It would all be so nice, but people—with their ignorance and narrow-mindedness, their mixture of malevolence and stupidity and the general superficiality of their judgments—ruin everything. I was speaking with a young doctor, a typical Lithuanian nationalist, who cannot see anything past his own nose. For him, Lithuania is the universe, the German victory is forever and unconditional, and Lithuanian independence is his one desire.} The city is hot and deserted; there is an atmosphere of evil and suffering...

Again they are saying that four hundred Jews have been shot.

28 July. I have many patients today, but nothing serious. After standing in line for three hours, a girl brought me a piece of bone with meat on it; it would have to last for seven days. They worry about me, as I have so little. There is no butter, no eggs. Today is my birthday. I am fifty-three. I had completely forgotten the date. "There is no peace in my soul." M. brought me two wonderful tea roses; I was deeply moved.

{Today the German authorities issued Compulsory Order No. 1 forbidding Jews to walk on the sidewalk and allowing them to walk only on the street pavement one behind the other; prohibiting Jews from using any means of conveyance; requiring cars and carts to post in a conspicuous place a sign that says "No Jews Allowed"; prohibiting Jews from sitting on park benches and from using parks or gardens. No telephone, no radio, no air, no source of information, no work, no dwelling, utterly without rights, cruelty to the point of absurdity, horrible, terrible, fearsome. I dropped by to see one of my friends, a surgeon named K. Her face could serve as a model for an artist painting a portrait of suffering. It has been days since she moved into the "ghetto." I comforted her, suggested that she spend her days with me and just go to the ghetto for the night; she said she doubts that the Germans will allow it.}

29 July. Shooting again in the night... Killing...
Today I went to get my money at the clinic where they fired me.

30 July. The Jews keep moving along with their pitiful belongings... They walk in single file along the pavement, with their yellow stars. It is crazy. Shameful! My colleague, a surgeon, has already moved into the ghetto. At the last minute she brought me her favorite glass cabinet with the beautiful statues.

Reichskommissar [Heinrich] Lohse has been named General Governor of the entire Eastern region; [Doctor] von Renteln has been appointed Generalkommissar of the former territory of the Lithuanian Republic; and Kramer has been made Commissar of the City of Kaunas.[118] "The German authorities in the cities and rural areas will cooperate with your representatives; in cases of need, the German government offices will invite agents of your people to submit reports on your situation to the local general commissars and to the government commissars." There is nothing left of the Lithuanian Republic but table scraps. {So much for the proud hopes of our rah-rah patriots!}

31 July. I am watching the plundering of the belongings in my Jewish neighbors' apartment. First huge military vans came and took away the best things, the expensive furniture for the "General"; then some men in other uniforms came and carted away the dishes, paintings, crystal, and various household goods. At first prisoners of war carried these things off. Then a number of Jews were brought in and forced to haul away the goods.

Jews still move along the streets with carts full of their pitiful possessions; old people and children... They say that Jews will be allowed to take along their possessions only until 1 August; and so they hurry.

1 August. I looked out my window this morning and saw a physician friend of mine and his wife riding in a long peasant's cart; they were hugging their two small children and sitting in the middle of some wretched tables, chairs, and mattresses. Carts full of Jewish goods continue to move along; {Lithuanian *muzhiks* and cabbies extort huge sums of money from the Jews to haul their belongings...} The Jews walk in the street in single file—think of it!—with their yellow stars.

{The 31 July edition of a Vilna newspaper (No. 29)[119] published a reply to the question "What is democracy?" They wrote: "Democracy is an irresponsible association of the rich Jews of the world. And nothing more! The word itself is noble, the idea beautiful. All our unhappiness, however, is the result of world Jewry's having manipulated democracy to its own ends and transforming all of humanity into its slave labor." How ignorant, how impudently stupid! It shames the paper it is written on... but now paper will tolerate everything...

English and Soviet airplanes bombed Finland, as well as ports in northern Norway. A representative from America has arrived in Moscow. Moscow has been bombed for the eighth time and Orel for the third time; the fighting near Smolensk continues, with huge losses on both sides.}

I sit at home in a state of hopelessness; I try not to even look out the window. Today there were heavy rains with thunder. The air is filled with the refreshing aroma of pine trees. Somewhere flowers are blooming; somewhere the sounds of the forests can be heard... fields are turning gold... How my heart aches! Contempt, loathing, dejection, sorrow! I do not know how, but somehow I must fight; it is not enough to suffer, complain, feel pity, and mourn. Still, I help a lot... But it is only a drop in the sea.

I am reading Tolstoy's *War and Peace* and *Sevastopol Tales.*

3 August. Today a patient told me that 1,200 Jews have been shot at the Seventh Fort. After digging deep pits, they were forced to undress and then shot with machine guns. They shoot anyone left stirring and then fill in the pits with lime. Another patient says that on 26 July they dug out a huge pit, the size of a foundation for a large building. All day long {Russian prisoners of war} carried bodies into it. He estimates that approximately 2,000 Jews were murdered, including forty young girls. {The Lithuanian "partisans" murdered them under the supervision of the Germans.} They say the Germans are filming it.

In Pluge every single Jews was shot, including all the women and nursing infants.[120] In the village where Valaitis lives the Jews were first made to carry heavy stones from one end of the street to the other just for fun; then all the men were murdered. My heart is filled with anger toward all these criminals, {these bloodthirsty beasts who hypocritically take refuge in phrases about the salvation of European culture,} who murder in order to cleanse a place that they alone want to possess. {Hypocrisy, lies, deception, and the foulest demagoguery are aimed at the mob, so that with the mob's help they may destroy everything noble and then be finished with it. The Lithuanian mob is now their obedient and contented instrument. I feel that I am alone among enemies. I am more afraid of people than of wild beasts; all around there is such cruelty, blindness, enslavement of thought, and nothingness. "Are you asleep, Justice, or have you been murdered?" asked Michelangelo. "There is no truth on earth, and yet there is nothing higher," said Pushkin.}

6 August. A heavy, dark day... The shooting continues; crowds of Jews are being seized in the streets and led away from their apartments.

They are bombing Moscow every day.

7 August. Days without a ray of hope... I see a doctor with a yellow star walking along the pavement. Jews can shop at the bazaar after ten in the morning, when almost everything has already been sold. The arrests continue. An elderly Lithuanian who was married to a Jew was hanged. The city makes a severe impression. The stores are closed, and the shop windows are empty of their wares; they fill up the empty space in them with wine glasses, some sort of other glasses, rose tea, and surrogate coffee in nondescript packages. It has the look of devastation and destitution.

11 August. The shooting continues. A huge number of Jews have been murdered. {People quickly get used to it, so that such numbers disturb them very little. Everyone thinks, "Just so they leave me alone."} Today a certain worker told me about a mystical eagle that, according to predictions from some ancient volume, would be vanquished by the Good, and then evil would be destroyed forever. An obscure, muddled, laughable belief, but there is a practical intuition in it.

12 August. I was in the ghetto today. The streets are fenced off with barbed wire. A wooden viaduct has been built across a "Christian" street, so that the Jews can cross without "profaning" the Christian street. Pitiful wretched hovels on the outskirts of town, tormented faces... Vacant lots are littered with every sort of pitiful household object; the courtyards are filled with furniture, since there is no room for it in the unbelievably crowded apartments. In the suburb, where about five thousand people had lived, there are now twenty-five to thirty thousand.

I was at the home of a friend of mine, a physician; two families live in one small room {eight square meters in size}. They have all changed a great deal... They understand that they are doomed. Today their electricity was turned off... They are allowed one hundred grams of bread per day... There is one bathroom with endless lines...There is no work, no food, no light, no fuel, no books... And the expectation of an inevitable death!...

At the front: the Russians are bombing Berlin, and the English are bombing other German cities. The Germans are ruthlessly bombing Moscow.

15 August. Today the Germans finally cleaned out my neighbors' apartment. They shot the owner at the Seventh Fort. His wife and daughter have disappeared without a trace. Yesterday huge German vans came and hauled away the best furniture. Today they took the rest. Prisoners carried the things out under the supervision of officers and soldiers. Today I managed to get permission from the guard—a coarse, tall, heavy-set German—to feed the prisoners. We gave them some bread and butter, milk, and cigarettes. I was taken by their intelligence, which was characteristic only of a Russian, and by their openness, their wise patience, and their evident simplicity. The Germans ranted for a long time, with savage hatred, about the Jews and their persecution; they said that Hitler is a socialist and that Germany was not a capitalist state, that in Russia all the officers are Jews. And they asked me to relate all of this to the Russian prisoners... With a note of irony and mockery, the Russian prisoners said, "Well, go out and campaign for him." The Germans boasted about how they would soon conquer everyone.

The Russians were blatantly making fun of them. Their faces had an earthy, scorbutic tint; several of them already had swollen, distended legs. They are fed only once a day, and they receive very little. They haul things very cleverly and quickly, and give away items to whoever wants them right under he noses of the Germans.

18 August. They have taken Nikolaev... I was in the Botanical Garden on Sunday... It was the culmination of summer...lilies were blossoming on the pond, roses, asters, verbenas, peas, wonderful dahlias... I recalled a Swiss alpine meadow, lying in the grass and gazing up at the sky; but there was no joy in my soul, for I could not forget... The city plundered and laid waste...

Carts of goods are moving back and forth throughout the city. {People are moving into the apartments left vacant by the Jews who were driven out. Everyone who took part in the liberation from the Bolsheviks and various robbers and "lumpen" scoundrels in general obtained good lodgings. The Germans, in fact, serve these "proletarians" better than the Bolsheviks did, who, of course, did not know how to take such heroic measures as resettling thirty thousand residents (Jews) in Slobodka.} In Slobodka {the "partisans"} shot a little boy for going around without the star. They murdered two men and women for failing to walk on the street pavement. {The Lithuanian "partisans" behave so disgracefully that even the Germans have arrested several of them for their "zeal."}

Today I saw four armed Germans on bicycles prodding along a tall Soviet officer who had been captured... Where were they taking him? A young Lithuanian was gloating over it. After all, most Lithuanians do in fact hate the Bolsheviks.

The newspapers are anonymous, mediocre, and sycophantic in the extreme. The Lithuanian patriots should be sick when they see how their nationalist sentiments are trampled on, but they are not sick; everyone triumphantly and pompously offers thanks for their "liberation from the Bolshevist yoke."

19 August. I was at the movie theatre. It is hard to imagine a film more mediocre in its production and more wretched in its content. It shows some boys committing acts of vandalism on Rybatsky Avenue, when their teacher with a swastika on his sleeve drives up; he outfits them in a full uniform, complete with swastikas, and they marched off, having turned over a new leaf. The newsreel featured ravaged Russian cities, crowds of prisoners of war... Guns and more guns shooting in the air, on land, and at sea. They showed Spanish, French, and Italian volunteers passing by with flowers as they leave for the Russian front; it is a pity they did not show them dying on the snowy plains of the USSR. They showed Pskov after it was bombed: all that remained were the stone frames. When you see it, it looks as though it came from the hands of madmen.

Life is not returning to normal. All living things are under restraint. Certain people unknown to everyone have been designated as representatives of the authorities to deal with the fact that there is no mail, no railway communication, no buses, no stores, no trade, no libraries, no schools, no universities. Complete destruction. On the post office doors an announcement is posted in German: "Post Office, No Admittance to Lithuanians." ...Lack of character, adoration of power, bowing down before it, and cringing servility do convincing performances.

21 August. I am reading Tolstoy, Shakespeare, Turgenev,[121] *Peter I* by Aleksei Tolstoy.[122] I seek oblivion. {They say the Lithuanian partisans serving in the special units assigned to murder Jews receive six hundred rubles and soldiers' rations. Masses of them want it.}

Two thousand people, among them women, were killed at the front this week. In the Slobodka Ghetto they are taking people's things away, robbing them, and murdering them. I had a dream about a world of Joy all around me... But "it was just a dream," and I awoke with such sorrow...

22 August. They have taken Kherson, Novgorod, Narva, and Kingisepp... Voroshilov[123] has called upon the people of Leningrad to defend their city... The human mind does not have the power to imagine what is now happening on the unfortunate Russian soil...

As for us, we have a life of daily concern over bread and butter. The expectation of hunger and cold... Only scoundrels are prospering; everyone else lives under oppression. Yesterday there was a rumor going around that the attorney Belyatskin and the physician Berman had been shot, along with two thousand other people!...

A patient told me that as she was walking past a synagogue, she saw the following scene: intelligent-looking Jews were hauling some furniture, while a German lashed them with a whip from time to time...

The dead city torments me. You walk past empty buildings, and you remember: this is where so-and-so lived and worked. The lives of tens of millions of people have been crushed.

I am reading Turgenev... In his *Correspondence* I read: "I shall never cease to think that all things in God's creation are honest, good, truly fit, and will sooner or later be fulfilled; not only will they be fulfilled, they are fulfilled." Such wonderful words.

I shall never forget the crimes and the cruelty I have seen; I shall never forgive, never be reconciled with them. I feel a resolve within myself; if necessary, I would die for this feeling. We must work for the victory of justice—that is our task.

Today was a clear, warm day... I went for a stroll in the grove... Green, lush grass, the sound of grasshoppers, flowerbeds... The old oaks, sunset, twilight. So gratifying, but it is impossible for me to forget... I ran into masses of German soldiers; the city is full of them. Someone told me that the Germans opened up a magnificent house of indulgence, complete with all the facilities to meet the demands of hygiene.

25 August. I was at the home of some friends of mine; both of them have changed; they have grown old, and they are depressed.

This afternoon a student told me the following: He was arrested during the first days of the war and taken to a police station; they stood him facing the wall along with several others. They were ordered to hold their hands up and stand there without looking around; otherwise they would be shot. The drunken policemen had also hauled in several Jewish girls, who were frantically screaming and crying... {The soldiers raped them all night long, and} in the morning they took them away somewhere. The shooting continues. Thorough searches are being conducted in the ghetto; people's belongings are being hauled away in three hundred carts.

It is hard to live when people right next to you are suffering.

26 August. I have been very anxious for days, but today I feel brave... One must live and always take the side of justice and truth; we must bear all things with honor, no matter what awaits us.

27 August. This morning I saw a troop of stout, healthy German soldiers marching along in orderly fashion; behind was a string of carts pulled by big, strong, well-fed horses. But the Germans' singing was dull and monotonous, without a spark of merriment or boldness.

Today I saw a truckload of Jews parked on Passazh. One young tormented face, its eyes filled with madness (from eternal fear), is agonizingly etched in my memory and tears me apart.

I am constantly thinking about the ghetto; there is no way I can forget those people suffering so close to me. The Jews, the people arrested and imprisoned, all of them wound me.

Today the sun is shining; it is a charming autumn day. I try to find a moment of oblivion by reading about travels in Asia.

An old professor, and idealist and a humanist, brought me his manuscript to read.

30 August. I spent the whole day with patients. Work is my one consolation and support.

I went out to buy a small stove, since there is no central heating; along the way I saw this scene: Several Jews were walking along with small bags of vegetables. A tall, healthy German in an SS uniform crawled out of a car that happened to be passing by and started beating the Jews with a whip. The Jews threw down their bags and ran away from him; he scattered their bags with his feet and laughed. {A crowd was also hooting but with far less zeal than they had before.}

The Russian prisoners are starving; many people feel sorry for them. Everyday, at various locations, I managed to get them some bread, potatoes, and suet that my friends bring to me for this purpose.

2 September. All the Jewish men in the rural areas have already been destroyed. Now they are murdering the women and children. Here comes a truck full of people with those terrible yellow stars, as if it had emerged from another world. People tell about how Jews are struck across the face with whips, about how prisoners are severely beaten. The situation of those who are in mixed marriages is tragic. One Lithuanian who was married to a Jewish woman shot his wife and their two daughters and then shot himself. There are examples of fidelity and steadfastness.

They are registering those who have no work and know German. Many are being mobilized to be sent to Germany and to the areas in the East under German occupation. The Germans are making intense preparations for a winter campaign. They are putting up prefabricated barracks along the bank of the Viliya. Hundreds of portable stoves have been ordered from the shops, they are making clothing, and so on.

I spend my days working, worrying about food, getting ready for winter, struggling against filth and fleas, washing underwear (there is absolutely no soap)...

{I received the medical journal *Lithuanian Medicine* instead of *Soviet Medicine*. They published a list of the Bolshevik doctors who have been taken away, but the names of the Jewish doctors are absent from the list; after all, one does not speak of them in "proper society." I read an article about racial "purity." It said that the "strongest" should not be mixed with the "weakest." ...It is a new variation of "gambling," of creating castes...}

Today I received a bouquet of heather as a gift... It blooms somewhere in the woods, in the quiet. Around a small cottage on the outskirts of the city I saw a charming little garden. It had dark rose-colored dahlias, tea roses, other dahlias of various shades, a huge bush of violet phloxes... There are many of them this year. The beauty of the colors, the forms...the eternal beauty of nature... I walked past an enchanting little house that used to belong to a Jewish doctor... They say he and another doctor killed themselves, and a third was shot...

3 September. It is 4° C this morning. Since it is cold in my office, I have fled to the bedroom... I am reading a book about the intelligence service in the French trenches during the siege of Verdun.

5 September. Today it was announced that anyone giving aid to prisoners would be arrested; anyone attempting to escape would be shot! {It was signed by the Lithuanian commandant... Someone does not like the sympathy and compassion shown toward the Russian prisoners.} These tortured, starving, tormented men are harnessed to carts like horses and forced to haul cement, lumber, stones, furniture... It is terrible to watch these people dying... People here, especially the women, try to help them... Sympathy for the Russians is growing, as is the revolt against German cruelty...

I am reading Marco Polo's book about his travels (thirteenth century) through China, India, the Pamirs, Asia Minor, Africa...

Jews were expelled from various places during the Middle Ages. But they have never known this cruelty that we have witnessed, when the complete slaughter of all the Jewish people, down to the last one, is presented as a government policy. {There are many stories about the mass murder of women and children; in the rural areas all the Jewish men have been slaughtered.}

Several physicians have killed themselves.

8 September. They are murdering people every day in the ghetto...

Obstinate rumors are going around that in October all the Jews will be annihilated; they have already murdered all the women and children in the countryside. It is terrible!

They have issued a decree forbidding us to give the Russian prisoners food, cigarettes, and the like. The Germans kick the prisoners in the stomach right in the street, like kulaks...they have no shame.

In the provinces the Jews are derided even worse than they are here. They are forced to jump after things that have been thrown into the water and to beat each other with sticks.

9 September. Leningrad is surround on all sides and is cut off from the rest of the country...

They have taken Shlisselburg!...

Life is a nightmare... I shall never forget what I have seen... On the other hand, I am becoming braver; I am rising to the heights of revolt and renouncing all worldly considerations, calculations, and profit... And I am ready to transform my feelings into flesh. There is much that I do not write... I mustn't...

12 September. In Mariyampol (one of my patients who saw it herself relates this story) they dug a deep pit and forced women and children into it (they were screaming and crying). They shot them with machine guns, and then ordered the next group to lie down on top of their warm, trembling bodies—some of whom were still alive—and murdered them; and so on until the pit was full... Moaning, wailing, sobbing. {(Even the Lithuanian guards fainted; an ambulance was called for them.)} Women were left in their slips and corsets and the men in their underwear. The rest of their clothing was gathered into a pile. This morning they shot a crowd of Jews that had supposedly been taken off to work. They were exhausted, pale, with featureless faces, like the faces of the dead... It is terrible to see a crowd of doomed people... Those idiotic yellow badges! The soldiers prod them, force them to walk more lively, in a "march," and they have to remove their hats for every German who passes by.

Various tragic fates unfold before my eyes. I am astonished at human adaptability, endurance, steadfastness, faith in the future...

There are people who dare to actually help... {partly for profit, but there are some who risk their lives out of a genuine love for humanity... "The salt of the earth." ...On the other hand, lots of people with coarse, bestial features, have suddenly appeared on the streets... Life has been stripped bare; legality has disappeared... Everyone is relying on "acquaintances," theft, speculation, deception.}

13 September. I dropped in to see a (Jewish) hairdresser I know. Of course, her apartment was plundered and all her furniture hauled away; she fled with her children. When she returned a few days later to get her things, the building superintendent gave her an old coat out of the "kindness" of his heart... She wept bitterly. Her daughter was in a Young Pioneer camp; the Lithuanian children have already returned from the camp, but no one seems to care about the Jewish children. {It must be said that the building superintendents, who steal with impunity, have exploited Jewish suffering more than anyone else... Many of them have grown rich, which explains the way they welcome the German occupation; even though some of them may not have an easy conscience, they are thinking about the future. And yet "all these crimes will not go undetected; someone will be held responsible for them." Hence there is a deep, hidden, secret, and at times even overt desire for every single Jew to be wiped out once and for all.}

Leningrad is making a heroic stand. It is cold and damp; many of the leaves have turned yellow...

14 September. Today it is sunny and warm; it is damp in my apartment... Everyone is expecting some sort of catastrophe... The savagery is growing worse; the university, gymnasiums, and schools have been closed; German placards are everywhere. We have become the property of the Germans... In the newspapers there are articles on race theory, on the necessity of purifying humanity of the contamination from non-Aryan peoples, who should be annihilated.

In the press there is nothing about real life; the bestial cruelty and the merciless fury are hidden from view. It unfolds undetected right in front of everyone, but they do not like to write about it or talk about it.

16 September. I saw a crowd of tortured, tattered Jews {escorted by Lithuanian volunteers with weapons.} They were weighed down by sacks of vegetables, firewood, and some kind of bowls; they were silent, muted shadows of people. There is no getting used to them. These figures with their filthy yellow stars have become a common feature of our reality.

I was at the movies; as always, it was a vapid, hackneyed German film, very shallow: restaurants, sleeping cars, extravagant parlors, rows of beautiful women, luxurious limousines, irreproachable lackeys, the carefree life of the wealthy, romantic subjects. A splendid performance by the actors was not enough to redeem the emptiness of the content; it was sheer, deadly boredom. Other films come to mind, Russian films full of humanity and ideas that raise up and enrich the soul.

The newsreel showed the destruction of train stations, piles of demolished weapons, burned and devastated cities, endless crowds of prisoners and refugees. It is dark and frightening outside. I think about my friends, so dear to me, locked {in the ghetto} and doomed. They are such kind, gentle, good people. There is no way to save them!...

19 September. On Tuesday everyone in the ghetto was gathered into the square: old people, women, children. They were surrounded by machine guns. After they stood for several hours awaiting their inevitable deaths, a car pulled up at the last minute. A soldier got out and handed the commandant a piece of paper; he read it, turned to the Jews, and told they should be thankful to the German army, who has spared their lives. Why the sham? It is unintelligible...

Trainloads of Russian prisoners of war are coming in from the Leningrad front. The cars are filled to overflowing. Many die along the way; many of the dead are borne by the dying. Hundreds of people have been shot near the station, since the Germans finish off the weak ones. One railroad worker personally saw piles of the dead bodies of Russian prisoners near the Kaunas railroad station.

In the suburb of Shanchiai a young man was shot for giving an apple to a prisoner of war. A German patrol killed a little girl on Lukshio Street for being out at 10:10 P.M. A girl from the ghetto told me that a young German walked into her apartment and ordered her to stand against the wall; he said that he was now going to shoot her... She stood there trembling with horror, while he kissed her for a long time... Then he laughed and said he was joking...

Twenty to thirty people are murdered in the ghetto every day; the Germans shoot into buildings, through windows, and at people walking down the street. The Jew is completely outside the protection of the law; anyone may kill or rob a Jew with impunity.

The day after tomorrow I shall "treat" a "patient" who is seriously ill; I want to save her life... I must "lay down my life for my friends,"[124] but we are forever afraid for ourselves and our loved ones; I too shall be careful. Perhaps I must do more... The eternal tension, waiting for the inevitable troubles, the danger surrounding the "patients" who stay the night with me...

I shall never forget my duty. The lower egotistical "urges" rising to consciousness are destroyed by the higher sentiments of responsibility and the longing to help. And once you have started going good, it is impossible to stop. You keep going, even though you are terrified...

20 September. Taking long back streets and side streets, going through backyard gardens, and past the wire fence, I went into the ghetto yesterday. I had to deliver some food.

A young policeman with a gun was walking down the street. I gave him some money, and he looked the other way. I threw a package of food over the fence.

I saw young, intelligent Jews hauled away in ten to twelve trucks... They had pale, anguished faces, but they were clam and quiet.

Germans were running up and down the street screaming and yelling at people to sit down as quickly as possible... They seemed to be irritated at the crowd of people who had gathered on the corner and were watching the scene. One of the armed escorts, a young man with a cruel face, suddenly turned on us and started driving us away with a whip. The women among the spectators had compassion and felt sorry for the Jews. When I asked where they were being taken, one guard said, "To Lublin," and pointed his finger toward the earth in a suggestive manner. "They are all going to be killed," another guard explained...

I returned exhausted and crushed... Gestapo men were drinking on the other side of the wall all night long. The main staircase smelled of vodka and beer.

21 September. Today is Sunday. It is sunny and warm. After yesterday's trip to the ghetto, I feel a great weariness: the faces of the young people condemned to death— serious, gloomy, calm, scarcely confused or frightened—stand before my eyes, and I cannot forget them.

It is cold in the apartment. They brought a small stove; it smokes. The bent pipes soil the room. Vitya stopped by. He is working in the surgery department and going to school. I read some poetry by Pushkin. It possesses a great beauty that transfigures life, that purifies and enlightens it. No one can find any comfort; one must fight... Once, when I was reading about knights who would select mottoes for themselves, I composed one for me: "Increase the sum of good on earth." I am true to that motto; I know that many of us are and that we shall be victorious.

22 September. Yesterday a patient told me about a Jewish worker from the ghetto who was purchasing some vegetables at the bazaar, when a car pulled up and a handsome, important-looking German with his swastika got out and started shooting at the Jew. He fell, but he was still alive; then the German killed him... People started running around, and the German shot into the crowd; he wounded a Lithuanian woman. He ordered the Jews to take the murdered man away and bury him near the market on the other side of the wire fence... There is shooting in the ghetto at night... Yesterday they took away 1,500 Jews between the ages of 15 and 50... The hardest thing to bear is the constant expectation of reprisal and derision, the utter injustice, the hopelessness.

They led out the Russian prisoners; boys too young to shave kicked them...and all this right on the street, in front of all passersby! ...

27 September. Yesterday they hauled away 1,400 people—none of whom returned... {They say the Germans ordered the Lithuanians to beat and murder the Jews while they, the Germans, photographed and filmed it for movie theaters.}[125]

I ran into some friends of mine today on the street, a doctor and an engineer... How they have changed! Grayish-white faces, sad and tortured, and those horrible yellow stars!

Yesterday I saw one of the men from a crowd of Russian prisoners bend down and pick up a cigarette butt from the pavement; then a kid (he was supposedly SS) started kicking the prisoner in the stomach with his boots and stabbing him with a bayonet. I could not stand it, and, shaking with revulsion, I told him how shameful it was for him to act as he did. With rude and malicious words (his face was wild) he ordered me to shut up: "Or you'll get the same..."

The prisoners gazed at the man who was now dying; they were not men but shadows of men, staggering from weakness... Some two hundred men were carrying chairs on their shoulders, and even that load was too much for them... Words cannot express how painful it was for me to look upon those devastated soldiers!

28 September. I sit here alone...in the evening. Today many Jews were herded past my windows. Row after row, they looked the same, backs bent, the faces of martyrs. The abominably hideous stars on their backs and chests. Those yellow stains are driving me out of my mind! Yesterday in the ghetto (say those who have come running to me) and entire quarter of the ghetto was taken away; women and children were murdered. In their homes windows and doors were left wide open. One child, covered with blood came running back... Yesterday was Friday, the eve of a Jewish holy day. Can it be that the massacre was calculated to correspond with it?

It is quiet in the apartment... An autumn day... The pink asters, violet phloxes, and late roses are so fragile and beautiful. The Beethoven recordings lining the walls, the bust of Pushkin on the cabinet, the Michelangelo hanging over the table will say to me: "Take comfort, all this will pass, it cannot last for long, humanity will discover the truth, it will celebrate..."

1 October. I am nervous, angry, I hate people's indifference and resignation. Only this suffering humanity, only them do I wish to help; I feel pity for all of them, I am wasting so much time and energy...

Leningrad is putting up a heroic resistance.

2 October. The rumor that the children are about to be murdered is growing more and more persistent. Many mothers have come to me. People are running around seeking salvation; we are exploring every possibility for fighting against these inhuman, savage laws.

On the streets you often run into a peasant taking prisoners to work for him; people are glad to see it and say, "Well, at least these won't die."

I saw two Russian prisoners staggering from weakness carrying one of their dying comrades in a wheelbarrow. His small, incredibly exhausted face with tears in his eyes, wide open yet seeing nothing, horribly tattered made a terrible impression on me. Many women were weeping.

Every day, morning and night, dejected crowds of Jews with their stars are driven from the ghetto to work and back. Many are beginning to sympathize with them. {The population is now overwhelmed with anger, and the sight of people so degraded and oppressed summons feelings of compassion.}

It is now 4:00 A.M.... The sound of their iron-tipped boots in the quiet of the night strikes the ears like the sound of ironclad ruthlessness and inhumanity... Terrible scenes unfold before the eyes, like a horrible nightmare...

Now, "according to plan," they are herding people driven to the extremes of despair, exhausted people who have lost all hope and all strength. Women with nursing infants in their arms, children clinging to their mothers, aged and elderly men, all of them weak and sick, who are of absolutely no use... They are being herded to the pits that have already been dug, into the pits, on the bottoms of which the cold autumn water already stands. People living in the area confirm that the next day, after the mass execution, the earth was still slightly undulating, trembling, moaning.

4 October. The Germans burned down the ghetto hospital, with the patients and the personnel inside, {under the pretense that it was spreading infection.} They brought in gasoline and sprayed it through the windows. They loaded the children from the children's ward into a truck and hauled them away somewhere. The weak patients, people who had been operated on, women who had given birth, the paralyzed could not be saved, since it was all done so fast, without warning. From among my friends, an old doctor stricken with paralysis perished in the fire. People were burned alive...

I managed to find an apartment belonging to a trusted friend, where one of my "patients" can stay for a week. Another has been living with me for two weeks... Yes, fear is a powerful weapon, and not everyone can overcome it within himself... But all you have to do is begin, and then it disappears. A person gets used to the constant danger and acts fearlessly; and when you firmly believe in the righteousness and the truth of what you are doing, even death does not frighten you.

{*6 October.* It is a clear, warm day of an Indian summer, with the sun shining in the blue sky, but I feel no joy. I stopped by to see two attorneys who are known for their humanitarianism; I also went to see an old doctor known as a social activist. My aim was to persuade them to join in an organized protest against the terrible persecution of the Jewish doctors and lawyers. After all, we cannot remain silent! But I met only with indifference on their part, even hostility!... They had but one desire: to mind their own business and live out whatever time they had left! It made me so sad that I could easily fall into despair and lose all faith, but I am still trying, still hoping.}

7 October. Vitya has written down in English everything that has happened to us. I went to see a singer who has an important Lithuanian friend abroad. Perhaps world society does not know what is happening here. The world must be informed, protests must be organized; we must seek ways of fighting back in every way possible... We spoke, and she agreed to help us.[126]

I went by a certain cellar where Jews were working. Here in the home of a good, brave (yes, even this requires bravery!) woman they were preparing a pitiful lunch for themselves. On the surface the apartment appears quite ordinary, but what a tragedy it harbors: doctors, engineers, and musicians, ragged and filthy, doing hard physical labor so that they might secure for themselves the right to live for a while, to breathe, so that they might not be murdered in the pit.

Again there are persistent rumors about preparations for mass murder... They have begun registering Poles and Russians. For what?

10 October. Hard, restless days... The daily worry about food... Some of my friends who are suffering a great deal, as well as others whom I do not know, are coming. They are all terrified; they wait for death and run from one place to the next seeking help... I visit various apartments, go down back alleys to secret meetings, always in danger, always terrified, waiting to get caught... I'm very tired...

German proclamations (they are posted on fences, pillars, and walls) announce their huge successes and promise a quick and decisive victory. They emphasize their successes so much it is as though they were trying to constantly reassure someone—perhaps themselves...

15 October. Announcements are posted everywhere in Lithuanian:

"Although the vast majority of sane Lithuanians avoid all contact with the Jews, it has nevertheless been determined that nearly every day Jews leaving the ghetto to go to work have managed to establish contact with individual Lithuanian citizens. Therefore it is announced: (1) all citizens of non-Jewish nationality are forbidden to have any relations with Jews; they are forbidden even to speak to Jews; (2) it is forbidden to sell, barter, or give to Jews food or any other goods; it is forbidden to enter into any kind of commerce with Jews; (3) the German police and the Lithuanian auxiliary police are ordered to take firm measures to abolish all social contact between the general population and the Jews. Failure to comply with these orders will be severely punished."

{It is terrible to think about the savage inhumanity and vindictive rage that runs throughout this order: in the midst of a revived city, with thousands of people, Jews alone stand outside all human society, reviled, without rights, beyond the protection of the law, deprived of every defense...worse than animals... and all because they are of a different blood... Insanity! ...}

In a state of rapture the Germans report on the destruction of Russian cities: Bryansk, Vyazma, Orel...

16 October. The Romanians have taken Odessa... The battle continues in Leningrad—a heroic city.

17 October. It snowed. Winter is early. The leaves are still on the trees...gold and green... Sometimes I manage to get some bread, suet, and cigarettes to our prisoners (it helps that I know German).

25 October. Anxious days... Many shortages... The soul is a little worried... One woman told me that she is afraid to even turn on a light in her apartment or to speak in a loud voice; she trembles at the coming of each day, even though she herself is not under any threat... That is how terror acts on everyone.

Today there was an article, shocking in its hideousness, about the criminal nature of helping prisoners and Jews, about how we must take revenge on them for their "Bolshevik crimes." And this is called the "New Europe!" Terrible...

28 October. I believe firmly in my truth and serve it with all my might and all my means. I would like to live to see it victorious.

30 October. Today ten thousand people were taken from the ghetto to their deaths.[127] They took the weak, the old, mothers with children, people who could not work... There are many tragedies: a husband who was in the city and returned to find his wife and children gone; or a wife who was left, while the husband was taken away... They separated brothers, sisters, fathers, and mothers from small children. On the previous day it was announced that, with the exception of skilled workers who were assigned to various specialties and workshops, the people were to gather in the large ghetto square at 6:00 A.M. and line up in columns. In the first row were the members of the Judenrat and their families; then came the administrative officials, followed by the various brigades, according to their jobs. The manager of the airfield and other German supervisors carefully looked over the rows of people as they slowly filed by. Some of the people were sent to the right, which meant death, and others to the left. All the weak, the old, and families with many children were sent to their death. From six in the morning until dark ten thousand people were gathered together and sent to spend the night in the "Little Ghetto," which in recent months had been "purified" of its Jews. The square was surrounded by guards and men with machine guns. It was a cold day. The people went the whole day without eating; children were crying in their mothers' arms. At dawn the rumor went around that prisoners of war had dug deep pits at the Ninth Forth (the Death Fort); once the crowd was driven into the Ninth Fort, they all realized that this meant death... They started wailing and crying out... Many tried to run away and were killed; many bodies were left lying in the fields. The Germans loaded some of the people into trucks. At the fort the Germans made them undress and herded them three hundred at a time into the open pits, where they murdered them with machine guns, rifles, and submachine guns. The doomed people stood shivering in the freezing cold for hours. At the pits the children were thrown in before the others. All the murderers were drunk. One German soldier, an eyewitness, told my friend that yesterday he wrote to his wife, who is Catholic, saying, "Yesterday I became convinced that there is no God; because if there were a God, He would not allow what happened to happen."

The next day the clothing that had belonged to the ones murdered was hauled away in trucks.

31 October. With regard to the events taking place, I have many cares and much work to do, masses of "patients," especially children. I am busy finding shelter for one, sending another to the monastery, another to a village, busy filling out various papers and certificates for their departure, and so on. Someone is with me every night, and in the daytime they crowd in... Only late at night do I find a moment of relief... Today a remarkable woman came to me, a woman of rare courage and character. Her husband—a veteran of the Great War (he won a cross)—died during the first days of the war, when they were seizing Jews in the street and hauling them off to their deaths. Her daughter, a young girl of seventeen, was shot in prison; a second daughter was forced into the ghetto as a half-Jew... This mother lives in constant danger, and yet she offers a great deal of help to others. She obtained poison from me in order to kill herself if she should be arrested. She bears her profound mother's sorrow with such steadfastness and pride... I am amazed and humbled by the greatness of her heart.

2 November. Anxious days... My lodger left. She spent six weeks with me. I did not have a single night's rest, {expecting all the while that one of the building attendants would turn us both in to the police.} Her husband, a Lithuanian, reassured her and set her up legally in his apartment; the Germans let her go, but with the provision that she be sterilized. There is so much sorrow that it is impossible to describe it; terror reigns everywhere, and death runs rampant all around.

All the finest Jewish apartments are occupied by Germans; their furnishings have been plundered and hauled away. Many stores have signs saying, "For Germans Only"; they are always full of customers. The Germans send thousands of packages back to their homeland.

It is cold in my apartment, just like at the front! Vitya is growing thin; he studies a lot... He tries to help even where there is neither hope nor possibility.

They have taken Simferopol; they are bombing Sevastopol; they have taken Feodosiya...

8 November. Once again in the movie theater they are showing pictures of the war in Finland and the Ukraine and Russian prisoners. Will I ever see any other prisoners? Ah, living is so hard! How long the autumn nights are! It is cold in the apartment. I dry my underwear on the little stove in my office and eat on a filthy tablecloth; I dry the firewood in the apartment and secretly wash my underwear in the bathroom. In order to get a chance to use the bathroom, I stand in line in the freezing cold for two to three hours. Everywhere there is an atmosphere of savagery and primitiveness. I receive threatening letters written anonymously; they warn me against continuing with my Jew-loving activities, or else it will be bad...

10 November. An elderly woman, who was a dentist and a friend of mine, died in the Ninth Fort. Today I saw a group of ragged, tormented, limping prisoners of war. They were hauling bricks under the supervision of a bunch of fat, coarse policemen. A peasant wanted to give one of the prisoners a cigarette, but the policemen would not allow it. When I remarked that it was not good to be so evil, a German bawled me out and threatened to arrest me. I saw four Germans with weapons ready escorting a Russian prisoner. Calm and confident, he was walking fast. They are shooting all the commissars and communists. I looked at him with pain in my heart... A crowd of prisoners was walking down a street (formerly Krasnaya Armiya Avenue). One fell down, and a German started beating him; but he could not get up. Then the German started kicking him, insulting him and yelling at him. A woman stepped out from the crowd and started to protest; the police stopped her. She took out her passport and said, "I am a human being."

12 November. Human sorrow flows from every quarter. I stopped by to see a doctor; they took his wife and four children while he was away. He wanted to find them just so that they could die together. I know they have already been murdered, but I comforted him and promised to look for them.

The Germans have taken Yasnaya Polyana... It is horrible to imagine how deeply the war has penetrated into the land...

{*16 November.* Hard, nightmarish days... First they threaten you with arrest, then they take your apartment, then they haul you away... My heart is starting to bother me; I have a pain on the left side, like a stone is weighing down on me... Falsehood, treachery, stupidity, and hypocrisy... I have few friends, or they are very far away... I am so tired...

Goebbels' article in the 16 November issue of *Das Reich* is called "The Jews Are Guilty" and begins like this: "The historical guilt of world Jewry for starting and continuing the war is so evident that there is no need to even speak of the matter. The Jews wanted to have their war. Well, now they have it. The prophecy made by the Führer on 30 January 1939 in the German Reichstag is being fulfilled: if the Jewish imperialist financiers should once again plunge the people into a world war, the result will not be the bolshevization of the globe and the triumph of the Jews, but the destruction of the Jewish race in Europe. We are now living through the fulfillment of this prophecy. The fate befalling the Jews, though harsh, is deserved." He goes on to praise the introduction of the yellow star (that marks the Jews), which makes it possible to immediately identify the Jew as the enemy; it is a "hygienic prophylactic," a "humane prescription." "The fact that the Jew still lives among us is not proof that he is one of us; just as fleas may still be in your house, it does not mean that they members of your household." "Every German soldier who dies in the war adds to the guilt of the Jews; he is on their conscience, and they must pay for it." "Whoever helps them has gone over to the enemy camp in time of war." And so on, and so on. How one must despise his people to feed them such wretched, ignorant ideas...}

25 November. A German, a tall Prussian, has moved into a requisitioned room (the dining room). He is a pharmacist, polite and punctual, but rather gray, dull, and impersonal. Where are my merry, kind-hearted Soviet pilots who were living in that room last year? Are they alive? I saw the destruction of Kaluga and Kharkov at the movies...

Today it is ten degrees below freezing; the sky is clear. It is cold in the apartment. At times things are very complicated in my work and various other concerns; the days go by quickly, but the nights drag on endlessly.

4 December. Ten thousand foreign Jews have arrived here. I saw them walking with their suitcases. They were told that they were being taken to work and were ordered to bring along all their valuables and their finest possessions; then they were murdered at the Ninth Fort. They say that the young men and women, suspecting nothing, were even dancing the evening they arrived. The next morning they were taken to their deaths fifty at a time. {The Lithuanians call it the cemetery for the Jews of Europe.}

6 December. I tore a photograph of the completely destroyed city of Vyazma from a German newspaper. The caption reads: "This was once a Russian city. The photo is worth paying attention to. The chimneys from towns burned to the ground protrude like tombstones from a winter landscape. Massive stone walls spared by the flames rise up like phantoms in the infinite distance." This "poetic" description pertains to a terrible photograph of a city completely destroyed and covered with snow. Only ruins rise up from beneath the snow. The Germans generally describe in detail their destruction and devastation of the world's cities with overt joy, rapture, and sadistic delight.

Today it is cold, minus 16° C. They rumor is going around that they are confiscating warm clothing. Women are afraid to go out after eight in the evening, since the Germans attack them and take them away somewhere.

9 December. In the infirmary for the prisoners of war people are dying from scurvy, exhaustion, and hunger. Sometimes I can get something to them, but it is difficult to get the one who can do it to help. You beg as if you were asking for a huge personal favor.

In villages that are snowed in live simple, good people who help the unfortunate without any beautiful words or intellectual half-measures. How terrible life is! When the gloom dissipates, the forces of darkness will be destroyed. But now it is better to perish than to ever give up… Viktor traveled far through the winter forest; for long hours he wandered among the villages at night, from hut to hut, looking for his childhood friend Tolya Shvarts, who, now here with his family, is hiding from a cruel fate… They found each other… Viktor brought them much joy and comfort; he gave them encouragement and the light of hope; he brought them whatever he could. People are hiding in haylofts, barns, and empty cowsheds. Their lives depend on chance, kindness, compassion, or base greed. How hard such a life is! And yet Viktor's friend Tolya still contrives to read some poetry by Pushkin, to study and to write about his faith in the bright future of a humanity that will conquer evil and will create at last a just, peaceful, and happy life! Indeed, he is a man who stirs feelings of pride. I am proud too of Vitya's goodness and courage. I give him my blessing and my help. But I so afraid for him. I tremble before visions of tragedy whenever I think about all the danger that awaits my son as he follows the only acceptable path—the path of struggle… For myself I have no fear at all.

12 December. In the evenings the city is empty, dark, and fearsome; young women are afraid to go out, since it is said that they are picked up and taken to brothels. Such establishments of various sorts have been very carefully organized, for the commanders and for the soldiers. Women who come down with venereal diseases are not treated but are simply shot; after all, they belong to "inferior races"—Jews, Poles, and Russians.

Rain is pouring down; it is warm and dark, but we are afraid that a cold winter is already setting in.

15 December. Yesterday three communists were publicly hanged.[128]

I dropped in to see a colleague today; she has a warm, cozy place with a lovely tea table where guests can sit. It was so peaceful, like the happy times of old… It became awkward, dull, strange to me. I left as though I had suffered some kind of insult: millions of people are dying in trenches and on snow-covered plains, millions of hearts are weighed down with terrible troubles, illness, and suffering, and here we were chatting about fashions, sewing, hairstyles, and so on, as if none of it were happening.

18 December. The Germans are attributing their failures to the bad weather, which had temporarily halted the attack on Moscow.

20 December. On a street next to the banks of the Neman, near my place, the Germans have set up a prisoner of war camp. A long fence wrapped in barbed wire. Several towers for the guards, wooden summer barracks, with pipes sticking up here and there. In the morning the prisoners are taken out to work. They look horrible; they are dressed in summer clothing, and many of them are barefoot. A silent suffering oozes from them. They wander past us, staggering, like phantoms from another world. We must follow them with our eyes without saying a word. After asking the sentry for permission, several times I was able to pass them some bread through the gate. Today the sentry sent me to the officer in charge of the guards to get permission. I went into the barracks where the administrative offices were located… It was warm; a radio was playing. I politely asked for permission to give something to the prisoners. I got a rude remark in reply, asking my why I crawled in here; they sent me to the sentry box next door, where a guard was on duty. There were many drunken soldiers; they surrounded me and started examining my briefcase, which contained loaves of bread. One of them took the briefcase and said he would buy it for ten marks; I took it back and said that just the day before I had paid fifty marks for it. Another one, with an evil face and a kind of carnivorous smile, his arm bent and extended as if he were offering it to a lady, said. "If you have a seventeen-year-old daughter, but no older, then send her to us." They took the bread and put it in the cupboard… I did not go any more, since I could see that they were not going to let me give anything to the prisoners.

The mortality rate among the prisoners is horrible; they are dying of typhoid fever…

Due to the threat of typhus, our churches, movie houses, and theaters have been closed.

22 December. Pushing his generals aside, Hitler has taken the military command into his own hands. It is rumored that the Germans are retreating and that the Russians have taken back many cities. The official word is that the front is "evening out." They are collecting warm clothing for the front. Young men and women who are cooperating go around to the apartments; the newspapers print lists of the most severe casualties. The winter is cold. The German soldiers are poorly dressed, as if it were summer; often they do not even have an overcoat.

24 December. The German lodger says that the troops have moved back to new positions and that in the spring the war will be over… Today it is seven degrees below freezing. We are not celebrating Christmas Eve. I gave the children all the modest gifts I have, all but pitiful gifts; I put a vase with some green pine branches in my office…

27 December. I wish I could live many lives and dedicate each one to the struggle… I do no want to die… I want to live, so that I may think and work; I believe in humanity… If it can raise itself up from an orangutan to Tolstoy, Beethoven, Pushkin, Mendeleev, creating arts and sciences—if it can "fly around the world on the wings of an idea and discover its limit in a single infinity"—then it can defeat all the forces of darkness that now oppress Europe… .

28 December. Vitya decided to go to work in Belorussia, for several reasons; the main reason is that he thinks he is more needed there, since he will be closer to the people and to the front.

29 December. Many French, Hungarian, and Romanian Jews have been shipped in. They were well dressed, with suitcases. They walked from the train station full of vitality, almost cheerfully; they thought they were being brought here to work. In a few days they would no longer be alive… They were murdered at the Ninth Fort. It is called the "Death Fort."

Today a stranger came to me; he looked like a laborer. He told me I must be careful, and then he left with a mysterious air about him. Was he some sort of provocateur?

30 December. A joyous day today. I managed to get some bread and cigarettes to some prisoners on the street. The Lithuanian escorting them said, "Go ahead," in a good-hearted way, and the prisoners cried out in Lithuanian, *"Duok,"* that is, "Yes, please!"

This afternoon an engineer from the ghetto came to see me; he was once a prominent social activist. He had run off from his job, even though such a thing was dangerous to both of us. He had two sisters who were killed during the Big Aktion. He wept as he remembered them. I gave him some of his things that he had left in my keeping, as well as some money, butter, and bread. He told me his strength was running out.

Once everyone had left, I stoked the oven… I lay down alone, tired and sad. I thought about Russia, about her suffering, about the Russian people, millions of whom have had their blood shed and have experienced the loss of thousands… Yet they are with their own people; they are fighting, working, creating. How much more difficult it is for those in occupied territories, who have been torn from their homeland, who are defenseless and have no rights; who are in the grip of cruel, ruthless, merciless killers…

There is a photo of Russian prisoners on the cover page of a German magazine. In the midst of those tortured faces worn out with suffering, there is one that is brave, proud, even mocking…

The year 1941 will go down in history for all time as a testimony to the Germans' treacherous, vile attack and the heroic Russian defense. No matter what happens, no matter how long the struggle continues, we firmly believe that light will triumph over darkness...

31 December. Vitya has come to see me. We drank a toast to victory, to freedom, to our peace, to all those who are fighting against evil, to youth, to heroism, to the future.

On the other side of the wall drunken Germans are carousing, screaming, yelling, singing in their coarse voices… They believe in their triumph…they believe they are the master race, chosen to create a "New Europe."

It is so touching, so sweet, the way the modest little bouquet of primroses that I got for New Year's blooms on the table. The room used to be filled with flowers… My patients and friends were always giving me azaleas, roses, carnations, hyacinths… Darkness! War! Typhoid fever! Death! The occupation!

Still, spring is not far away, and these modest flowers are its first messengers.

The Fate of the Jews of Telshiai: The Story of Galina Masyulis and Susanna Kogan

There were about 3,500 Jews in our city. After the expulsion of the Germans there were four men, about sixty women, and eight children left. We two women, who were saved by a miracle, would like to tell the story of the torments of our brothers and sisters.

When the Germans occupied Telshiai they ordered all the Jews to come out of their homes without any of their possessions. A huge crowd gathered. Everyone was led to the lake. People thought they were going to be murdered because men with submachine guns were standing all around them. [To those who were weeping, Rabbi Blokh said, "Trust in God…"] We stood around the lake for several hours. Then the men were separated from the women and children. The women were allowed to return home, and the men were taken away somewhere. We subsequently found out that they were sent to the camps at Rainiai, Veshveniai, and Giruliai, where they were shot.[129]

The women found their homes in complete disarray; everything had been plundered and smashed to bits.

The next day they resettled us in the ghetto. It was set up on the shore of Lake Mastis ("Meditation") and in several apartments on Maschio and Zhuves Streets. The lake was on one side and barbed wire was on another; on a third side was the office of the prison commandant.

The women and children lived in small houses without any furniture, with twenty to thirty people to a house. Neither firewood nor food was provided. On the very first day the commandant of the ghetto demanded that all our money, gold, and valuables be turned over to him. In exchange he promised to spare our lives. In the autumn the weaker ones started dying from cold and exhaustion. Those who were still alive knew that just such a death awaited them—or that they would be shot, since the Germans were shooting people in groups at a time.

It turned out, however, that the Germans had decided to use us for the time being to work on the farms. We were sent out to farms and to agricultural collectives under the supervision and responsibility of the heads of the farms. The farm owners paid three rubles per worker, supposedly for the upkeep of the ghetto. In fact the Germans pocketed the money.

Several women were sent to camps where the men were. One of these camps, Rainiai, was located near the estate of a popular Lithuanian opera singer named Petrauskas. The woods near the estate became a mass murder site. Prior to almost every mass shooting the camp commandant proposed that he be paid a tribute, in exchange for which he promised to have mercy on the condemned. In fact this only postponed their deaths, and not for long: just one day.

The ones doomed to death dug the pits themselves. Vodka was brought to the forest, and the executioners got drunk while the ones condemned to death did the digging. This is what we found out about one shooting: The first one to be shot was a worker from the forest training enter named Fogelman, then an American bookkeeper named Joseph Bai. He had come from America to visit his sisters. The physician Zaks was sick; the executioners carried him to the pit with their own hands; he was murdered along with his wife, child, little boys, and father, an elderly man ninety years of age. Then they shot our neighbor Tallis, a bank director named Levin, an old man named Vollert, and the family of the electrician Gilis, which consisted of the husband, wife, and two children. The Krenkel family was also murdered, as were the family of the painter Shavel, one of our own families—the Maslyulises—and dozens of others whose names we do not know.

That is how it was. It started raining very hard while the fourth group was being shot. The Germans did not want to get wet, so they postponed shooting their victims until the next day.

One of the Jews (unfortunately we do not know his name) cried out to the executioners: "Our blood is spilled on these trees, while your blood will flood the streets of your cursed German cities!"

There were up to nine thousand Jews in the entire district, not counting the ones living in the city. After they murdered all the Jews in the city, the Germans concentrated on the ones who lived and worked in the villages. The degradation that took place during the shootings became more and more terrible. People were forced to strip naked and lie down in the pits they had dug; then grenades were thrown into the pits. Children were flung into the pits with bayonets, or they were knock in with a rifle butt or kicked in. The Germans invented a "merry dance." They would line up some of the doomed people, front to back, and force them to run in a circle for hours while they others prodded them with sticks. The people were ordered not only to run, but to fall down, get up, and run again.

The last mass murder took place on Christmas Eve 1943. By then the camps and the ghettos were empty; everyone there had been murdered. After killing the Jews in the camps and ghettos, the Germans started gathering the ones on the farm under the pretense of holding inspections. Many women with nursing infants were brought to Rainiai on 24 December; the others had already been murdered. Everyone knew what to expect. Several tried to escape by crawling under the wire fence surrounding the camp.

But not everyone who got out managed to survive. Mothers wandered around in the forests with their children, lost their way, and froze to death. Many bodies of women clinging to their dead children were found in the forests that spring.

A peasant family gave us shelter on their farm; we stayed with them and awaited the arrival of the Red Army.

Prepared for publication by O. Savich

Notes

1.   The first order requiring Jews to wear the yellow star was issued by Von Osten, the military commandant of the city, on 3 July 1941; on 4 July the Lithuanian administration issued the decree. A few days later a new military commandant, Colonel Zenpfenning, gave the order requiring the badge to be worn on the sleeve.

2.   SA Sturmbaumführer Hans Khingst was Gebietskommissar of Vilna and head of the municipal administration of the occupying forces.

3.   SS Oberscharführer Horst Schweinberger was in charge of the shootings at Ponary until 1942. In January 1942 he was called back to Berlin.

4.   SS Hauptscharführer Martin Weiss was chief of all the prisons in Vilna. Beginning in June 1942 he was in

charge of a Sonderkommando unit at Ponary and was known as the "Master of Ponary." In 1943 he worked in the Jewish Section of the Gestapo. In February 1950 at a trial held in Wurzburg he was given a life sentence for crimes committed at Ponary.

5.   *Ipatingas Buris* is a Lithuanian term referring to the special SD Sonderkommando unit in Vilna, a sub-unit of Einsatzgruppe A and later known as the Vilna SD. The number of men in the unit ranged from 40 to 150. During the first year of the occupation the unit was commanded by Yuozas Shidlauskas, a senior lieutenant in the Lithuanian army; he was followed by Lieutenant Balis Norvaisha. They, of course, took their orders from the SS.

6.   The Germans set up two ghettos in Vilna; they were separated by Nemetskaya Street. The first one, which was centered primarily around Rudnitskaya Street, was known as the *Facharbeiter* Ghetto, or the Skilled Workers' Ghetto; the second ghetto was for old people and others who were not working.

7.   The first Aktion in Vilna was the "Yellow Schein" or "Yellow Pass" Aktion. The Germans issued three thousand passes to the artisans and skilled workers. On each Schein a worker could enter the names of his wife and two children. After those three thousand passes were issued, twelve thousand people were allowed to enter the Vilna Ghetto. Between the 25th and 27th of October 1941, 3,781 people who did not get a yellow pass were shot at Ponary.

8.   August Göring was a Lithuanian-born SS agent from the Jewish section of the Gestapo. He was chief of the Sonderkommando from January to June 1942. In 1950, at the same trial in which Martin Weiss was convicted, he was found guilty of the crimes he committed at Ponary and was given a life sentence.

9.   The Jews were accused of wounding a German soldier. According to an Einsatzkommando report, 3,700 of them were shot on 2 September. On 6 September two ghettos were set up in the areas left vacant after the arrest of the Jews; in the larger ghetto there were 29,000 people, in the smaller 11,000. The executions by firing squad, however, continued. On 12 September 3,334 were murdered, on 17 September 1,271, and on 4 October 1,983 (those who were arrested during the Yom Kippur Aktion).

10.   *Shema Yisroel* is the opening of one of the most basic prayers and teachings of Judaism: "Hear, O Israel, the Lord our God, the Lord is One!"

11.   Young Vilna was a group of artists and writers that was formed after an article appeared in the Yiddish newspaper *The Vilna Tor* on 11 October 1929. It said, "Young Vilna is stepping into Yiddish literature." Members of the group included Chaim Grade, Abraham Sutzkever, S. Kacherginsky, G. Glink, R. Sutzkever, Bentsion Mikhtom, S. Efron, and others.

12.   According to partisan reports, in April 1943 the Germans killed all the Jews in the area along the border between Lithuania and Belorussia. Four thousand Jews from Sventsyan, Oshmyan, Sviri, Eishishkes, Yashyunai, Turgyalyai, Onushkis, Aukshtadvarisa, other towns were sent to Ponary in the "Kovno-Ponary Aktion." Realizing that they were being taken to Ponary instead of the Kovno Ghetto, the Jews tried to run away; about six hundred were killed. Two members of the Sonderkommando were also wounded.

13.   Franz Murer organized, set up, and ruled over the Vilna Ghetto. In 1947 the British captured him and charged him with war crimes; in 1948 a Soviet tribunal sentenced him to a prison term of twenty-five years. In 1949 he was turned over to Austria. He was tried once again in Graz in 1963 and was acquitted.

14.   Known as the "Father of the Jews of Vilna," Yakov Vygodsky (1857 – 1941) was a physician and social activist. A longstanding leader of Vilna society, he served as the Minister of Jewish Affairs in Lithuania's first independent government, as well as in the Polish parliament.

15.   Jacob Gens assumed the job of Chief of the Jewish Police in the hope that in such a position he could help the Jews in the ghetto. After the Vilna Judenrat was officially dissolved in July 1942, Gens became the sole Jewish authority in the ghetto. While Gens was a controversial figure and an apparent accomplice to Nazi murders, he was a supporter of the partisans. As a result of that support, on 9 September 1943 he was summoned to Gestapo headquarters and was shot.

16.   Established in 1918, the Vilna Technical School was one of the first middle schools to conduct classes in Yiddish; the Judenrat was housed in the school building.

17.   Bruno Kittel was the Director of the Gestapo's Jewish Section in Vilna after June 1943. Prior to the war he was a film actor and singer. During the war he was a specialist in Jewish affairs in France and in Riga. He oversaw the liquidation of the ghettos in Riga, Vilna, and Kovno.

18.   Maier was the director of the department of Jewish affairs in Vilna until June 1943, when he was sent to the front.

19.   A factory for manufacturing fur clothing for the German army was located in Kailis. In October 1941 a number of Jews and their families (eight hundred to a thousand people in all) were transferred there to work in the factory; a concentration camp was set up to house them. When the Vilna Ghetto was liquidated in September 1943 there were approximately 1,250 people in the camp. On 2 – 3 July 1944 the camp was liquidated.

20. HKP stands for "Heereskraftpark," a labor camp for Jews from the ghetto. In September 1943, 350 workers and their families (800 people in all) were moved into two large buildings at 37 Subachaus Street. Known as the "low-rent buildings," they were made into a concentration camp. Jews from the HKP Camp, as well as from Kailis, were shot ten days before the city was liberated on the 2 and 3 June 1944.

21. Zelig Girsh Kalmanovich (1881 – 1944) was a famous Jewish scholar and philologist. He was one of the founding members of YIVO (see Note 27) and served as its director in 1939 and 1940; he was also the Editor-in-Chief of the *YIVO Blatter*. His diary from the Vilna Ghetto was published in the *YIVO Blatter* in New York in 1951.

22. Stefan Zweig (1881 – 1942) was an Austrian playwright, essayist, and biographer. Forever addressing the plight of the human spirit in a violent world, he authored scholarly studies on a wide range of literary figures. Although he was not active in the Jewish community, several of his short stories deal with Jewish themes.

23. Mendele Mokher Seforim was the penname for Shalom Jacob Abramowitsch (1835 – 1917), one of the great masters of literary Yiddish. Born in the Belorussian town of Kapuli, Mendele wrote fiction and drama in Hebrew and Yiddish. In his works he explores the issues, ideas, and tribulations that characterized East European Jewish life in the late nineteenth century.

24. Isaac Leib Peretz (1852 – 1915) was a poet, novelist, playwright and folklorist who wrote in Polish, Hebrew, and Yiddish. Residing in Warsaw, he viewed Yiddish as the national language of the Jewish people.

25. Sholom Aleichem (1859 – 1916) was born Shalom Rabinovitz in Pereyaslav, Ukraine. With Mendele Mokher Seforim and Isaac Leib Peretz, he is considered one of the great founders of modern Yiddish literature. He is most famous for his Tevye tales, which deal with the collisions between tradition and modernity that led to many upheavals in East European Jewish life.

26. Born in Radi, near Zhitomir (Volhynia), Chaim Nachman Bialik (1873 – 1934) is generally regarded as the greatest Hebrew poet of modern times. A resident of Odessa and Warsaw, he was able to leave the Soviet Union and emigrate to Palestine in 1924, thanks to the help of the "originator of Soviet literature," Maxim Gorky (1868 – 1936). There he was one of the first residents of the newly created city of Tel Aviv.

27. Herman Kruk (1897 – 1944) was the director of the Grosser Library in Warsaw. He fled to Vilna in the second week of September 1939. He was murdered in Estonia on 18 or 19 September 1944. His diary from the Vilna Ghetto was published in the 1965 edition of the *YIVO Annual of Jewish Social Studies*.

28. In his *Diary of the Vilna Ghetto* Yitskhok Rudashevski (1927 – 1943) writes the following in an entry dated 13 December 1942: "Today the ghetto celebrated the circulation of the 100,000th book in the ghetto library.... Hundreds of people read in the ghetto. The reading of books in the ghetto is the greatest pleasure for me. The book unites us with the future, the book unites us with the world." (tr. Percy Matenko. Tel Aviv: Ghetto Fighters' House and Hakibbutz Hameuchad, 1973, p. 106).

29. YIVO is an abbreviation for Yidisher Visenshaftlikher Institut, the principal world organization for conducting research in Yiddish. The organization was founded at a conference of scholars held in Berlin in August 1925. At the conference it was decided that the institute would be located in Vilna. After the war what was left of the institute was moved to New York City. Most of the material sent from the Vilna Institute to Berlin was recovered and transferred to New York.

30. Mark Antokolsky (1843 – 1902) was born in Vilna, where his artistic talent was first discovered when he served as an apprentice to a woodcarver. Although his subjects came primarily from Russian and Christian history, he was attacked during the wave of pogroms in the 1880s for being a Jew unworthy of such themes.

31. Vladimir Solovev (1853 – 1900) was a religious thinker who influenced numerous Russian authors; the character Alyosha in Dostoevsky's *The Brothers Karamazov* is modeled after him. French author Romain Rolland (1866 – 1944) was a music professor at the Sorbonne; known for his biographies of composers, he won the Nobel for Literature in 1915. Ilya Repin (1844 – 1930) was Russia's greatest naturalist painter. Theodor Herzl (1860 – 1904) was the organizer of the modern Zionist movement and Father of the State of Israel. The Vilna Gaon is Rabbi Elijah ben Shlomo Zalman Kremer of Vilna (1720 – 1797); a major opponent of Chasidism, he was one of the greatest Jewish scholars and thinkers of the eighteenth century. Marc Chagall (1887 – 1985) was born in Vitebsk but moved to Paris in 1922, where he became known as one of the first great surrealist painters.

32. Peter I (1672 – 1725), also known as Peter the Great, was the first tsar to attempt to Westernize Russia. He founded the city of St. Petersburg as a gateway to Europe and Russia's new capital.

33. Isaak Levitan (1860 – 1900) was a famous Lithuanian painter of landscapes.

34. Born in Poland, Tadeusz Kosciuszko (1746 – 1817) fought in the American Revolution, after which he returned to Poland in 1794 to lead an unsuccessful attempt to win Polish independence from Russia.

35. Kazys Boruta (1905 – 1965), poet and novelist, attended the University of Kaunas and became well known for his romantic lyrical poetry.

36.   Ona Shimaite (1894 – 1970) was a librarian and journalist. She worked in the University of Vilna library during the Nazi occupation and helped the Jews in the ghetto. She set up an underground organization to help save Jewish children and cultural treasures. She was arrested by the Gestapo and sent to Dachau. In 1966 at a ceremony in Paris Yad Vashem recognized her as one of the Righteous among the Nations.

37.   This organization was formed on 21 January 1942. It was known in Yiddish and the Vareinigte Partizaner Organizatsie.

38.   This text was written by Abba Kovner (1918 – 1987), who later became commander of the United Partisan Organization. When the ghetto was liquidated on 23 September 1943 he led a group of fighters from the UPO into the forest, where they formed a Jewish partisan brigade. In 1970, after immigrating to Israel, he was awarded the Israel Prize for his poetry. He was also one of the founders of the Diaspora Museum in Tel-Aviv.

39.   Iosef Glazman (1913 – 1943) served on the Jewish police force in the ghetto before he left to become one of the founders and the first commander of the UPO. When he left to join the partisans, he became the head of the Jewish partisan unit known as "Vengeance." He was killed in battle in October 1943.

40.   Edek Boraks (1918 – 1943) was one of the leaders of Hashomer Hatsair (The Young Watchman) in Vilna, a left-wing socialist Zionist group founded in Galicia in 1915. At the end of 1941 the organization gave him the assignment of going to Warsaw. After that he was involved in the formation of the Jewish Fighting Organization in Bialystok. In his first skirmish with the Germans, on 5 February 1943, he was captured and sent to Treblinka. The exact date of his death is unknown.

41.   Austrian-born Anton Schmidt (1900 – 1942) was a sergeant major in the German army; he was very helpful to the Jews of Vilna. He drove people from the Vilna Ghetto to Bialystok and Warsaw in early 1942. He also took a large group of people in the Zionist youth organization Dror (Freedom) to Bialystok; the group was led by Mordecai Tennenbaum. Schmidt was arrested and shot in April 1942 for helping the Jews.

42.   Theodore Adrian von Renteln was the General Commissar of Lithuania from 1941 to 1944.

43.   Kittel demanded the arrest of Vitenberg on 8 July 1943, after Yu. Vitas, secretary of the city committee, had been arrested, along with V. Kazlauskas, a member of the committee who had divulged Vitenberg's name under torture.

44.   Yekhiel (Ilya) Sheinboin (1914 – 1943) was active in the Young Socialist Movement. In the ghetto he organized a separate fighting organization called Yekhiel's Fighting Group; their primary aim was to form a partisan group to go into the forest. The first group of fighters to leave to ghetto and join up with the partisans was from this organization. In the spring of 1943 they merged with the UPO as their first fighting battalion.

45.   According to some accounts, Gros was not killed but only wounded; he is said to have lived in East Germany after the war.

46.   Yankel Kaplan (1907 – 1943) and Abram Khvoinik (1907 – 1943) were members of the UPO's command staff; Asya Big (1922 – 1943) was their associate. On 23 September they were hanged, along with a watchmaker named Girsh Levin.

47.   Isaak Dogim went to live in Israel and appeared in Claude Lanzmann's film *Shoah*; in the film he and Mota Zaidel talk about Ponary.

48.   A total of thirteen people survived Ponary. Eleven of them joined the partisans, and the other two made it through the front lines.

49.   Irina Ehrenburg notes that the original text "From the Editors" was subjected to major ideological revision; therefore she includes this original version in its entirety.

50.   Many of those who were arrested were shot in the forest near Kuzhiai.

51.   The resettlement of the Jews in the Siauliai (Shavli) Ghetto took place between 25 July and 15 August 1941.

52.   Antanas Stankus was a captain in the Lithuanian army up to 1940. In 1941 – 1943 he was the chief person in charge Burgermeister of Jewish affairs in Siauliai.

53.   Mendel Leibovich was the head of the Judenrat in the Siauliai Ghetto. He died in the ghetto during the bombardment of Siauliai on 22 July 1944.

54.   Zhagor is a village about sixty-five kilometers from Siauliai.

55.   Jews were gathered into three of these "synagogues": the main synagogue on Varnya Street, the one attended by rural tradesmen on Vilnyaus Street, and the old-age home on Vilnyaus Street.

56.   All the Jews in these so-called synagogues were sent to Kuzhiai and shot.

57.   Tsitavian, or Tituvenai, is a small town about forty-five kilometers from Siauliai.

58.   This Aktion was carried out by secret police under military command.

59.   In September 1941 five hundred Jews were shot near Bubiai, fourteen kilometers from Siauliai.

60.   In keeping with an order issued by Stankus and District Chief Noreiki, Jews were sent to the country to work for the peasants.

61. The Gebietskommissar was Hans Heweke, a barber by trade. In 1969 he was sentenced to four and a half years in prison for his role in the murder of Betsalel Mazovetsky. Mazovetsky attempted to smuggle cigarettes into the ghetto, for which he was sentenced to death. It was absolutely forbidden to bring anything into the ghetto. The Jews had to live on whatever rations were allotted to them. Of course, the men who worked outside the ghetto did everything they could to help the women and children who never left the ghetto.

62. The two executioners were Jews named Davidovich and Kerbel. Gebietskommissar Heweke forced the Judenrat to assign Jews to carry out executions; otherwise all twenty members of the Judenrat would be shot. Davidovich and Kerbel received several thousand marks for their work.

63. The Preisüberwachungsstelle was the office in charge of controlling the delivery and distribution of food.

64. The Regierungsrat was where local government offices were located.

65. On 1 July 1943 authority over the ghetto was transferred from the Lithuanian civil authority to the SS.

66. A day of mourning for Jews, the 9th of Av commemorates the destruction of the First Temple in 586 B.C.E. and of the Second Temple in 70 C.E.

67. Günther wanted to preserve the Jewish work force.

68. Here Yerushalmi is commenting on the reduction in the size of the Caucasus Ghetto in Shavli.

69. Akmian is a city in northern Lithuania about seventy-five kilometers from Shavli.

70. A flax refinery located next to the ghetto.

71. A report filed by Einsatzgruppe A on 15 October 1941 states: "It is important for the sake of the future to have proof that the liberated population, on its own initiative, took active and energetic measures against the enemy—the Bolsheviks and the Jews—so that the German authorities did not have to expose themselves... . During the first pogrom, on the night of 25 – 26 June, Lithuanian partisans killed more than 1,500 Jews; they burned and destroyed several synagogues and completely burned down more than 60 buildings in the Jewish quarter. On the following night approximately 2,300 Jews were killed."

72. According to D. B. Gelpern, a former prisoner of the Kovno Ghetto, the inscription was written by Akiva Pukhert on the doors of the Dobre lock factory.

73. On 1 December 1941 Einsatzkommando III reported that 463 Jews were killed at the Seventh Fort on 1 July of that year; on 6 July 2,514 were killed. In accordance with an order from SD and security police headquarters, the action was carried out by Lithuanian partisans.

74. According to records kept at the Fourth Fort, on 18 August the Germans shot 698 Jewish men, 402 Jewish women, 711 members of the Jewish intelligentsia, and 1 Pole, for a total of 1,812 people.

75. One of the cruelest governors of the ghetto, Hauptscharführer SS Ernst Stitz served as head of the Gestapo's Jewish Affairs section for the SD and chief of the security police from the middle of 1942.

76. A *Vernichtungsstelle* is an "annihilation center."

77. There were actually six hundred Soviet prisoners of war digging pits in July 1941 at the Ninth Fort; only ten of them survived until the winter of 1943, when they were put to work digging up and burning bodies.

78. On 26 September 1941 Willi Kozlowski, the German police officer in charge of the ghetto, ordered 1,608 people to be shot at the Fourth Fort.

79. Hauptsturmführer SA Friedrich Jordan organized a series of Aktions in the ghetto. In early 1942 he was sent to the Eastern Front, where he was killed.

80. Hauptscharführer SS Helmut Rauka was in charge of the Gestapo's Jewish section from 1941 to mid-1942. He conducted all the major Aktions in the Kovno Ghetto. After the war he went to live in Canada. In 1986 a court in Toronto convicted him of murdering more than 11,500 Jews. He was extradited to Germany, where he died in prison.

81. According to German records kept on the elimination of "unnecessary" Jews, a total of 9,200 Jews were murdered at the Ninth Fort on 29 October: 2,007 men, 2,920 women, and 4,273 children.

82. Ten to fifteen thousand Jews from Germany and other countries were murdered in Kovno.

83. The text of the report was significantly edited in order to raise the number of the victims reported. In the original report, which is preserved in the museum at the Ninth Fort, the following figures appear: "We dug up 6.5 pits, which left 7.5. We estimate the number of victims at 25,000 to 30,000 people, a figure that was also mentioned by representatives of the Gestapo."

84. According to an account written in the ghetto by Veselnitsky several days after his escape from the fort, the Jews themselves raised the quota to five hundred bodies per day to weaken the guards. After the war Veselnitsky said that initially it took two days to prepare one bonfire of 250 bodies. Later, in order to wear out the guards, they would prepare three bonfires of 250 bodies each in a single day.

85. Leading the group was a prisoner of war from Leningrad named Aleksandr Podolsky. He had been in the Ninth Fort since 1941 and worked as an electrician. He sometimes had the opportunity to walk freely about the fort and was therefore able to study it thoroughly.

86. The exact composition of the committee is not certain. Other sources mention A. Podolsky, I. Veselnitsky, T. Pilovnik, A. Diskant, M. Zimelevich, R. Shakhov, T. Fridman, and A. Faitelson.

87. *Portyanki* are pieces of coarse cloth wrapped around one's feet in place of stockings.

88. Khas made wooden steps for a rope ladder, which the cook, V. Sankin, smuggled into his quarters under his clothing.

89. What is referred to here is the European Museum that was open in Vilna (Vilnius) from 1944 to 1949.

90. Moishe Zimelevich was actually too old to be a member of the Komsomol (the Communist Youth Organization).

91. The escapees were sent out of the ghetto on 6 January 1944, which means that they spent about two weeks there.

92. This Aktion was known as the Children's Aktion; it took place on 27 – 28 March 1944. Nine hundred people were arrested on the first day and about two hundred on the second day.

93. Murava is a suburb of Kovno (Kaunas).

94. These were the partisans A. Slapshis, A. Vilimas, and B. Baronas, hanged in 13 December 1941 in Kovno.

95. This was the so-called Big Aktion of 28 – 29 October 1941.

96. At that time, 1941 – 1942, the partisan movement in the ghetto was just getting started; it developed to its fullest throughout the second half of 1943.

97. The group referred to here left the ghetto on 5 August 1943. It consisted of Israel Milshtein (the leader), Tsalel Ioffe, Yasha Davydov, Moshe Slavyansky, and Meir Teitl. The resistance organization in the ghetto assigned them to seek out partisans in Eastern Lithuania. They were armed with revolvers and grenades; they also had maps and compasses and were completely prepared for their mission.

98. Khaim Elin led the underground movement in the Kovno Ghetto from the beginning of 1942.

99. This was the march into the Augustus Woods that took place in the summer of 1943.

100. Led by Leizer Podikov, this group left the ghetto in three carts in the autumn of 1943. There were twenty people in the group.

101. About one hundred insufficiently armed fighters would go on partisan raids in the Augustus Woods (prior to 31 October 1943). This was due to apprehensions over new Aktions in the ghetto. On 23 October 1943 three thousand Jews were sent to concentration camps in Estonia. Only Nekhemiya Endlin and Shmuel Mortkovsky made it to the designated site near Burzhany Lake. More than forty fighters were captured and killed by the Germans. Endlin and Mortkovsky subsequently became guides for other groups.

102. Led by Eliya Olkin and Moishe Upnitsky, this group set out on 23 November; they had three partisan guides with them. Having to cover 150 to 160 kilometers, they suffered heavy losses: E. Olkin died, and M. Upnitsky was severely wounded in the arm. He was taken back to the ghetto and survived the war. He later moved to Israel.

103. The first major operation for obtaining weapons was carried out in January 1944 at a warehouse for a German military hospital. Itsik Miklishansky, Mendl Moscowicz, and M. Geguzhinsky conducted the operation. Ya. Levi, I. Miklishansky, M. Moscowicz, and two partisans from the forest—Sh. Mortkovsky and B. Lopyansky—carried out a second operation at a military depot. Both operations were conducted at night.

104. This is an exaggeration. In 1943 the partisans in Lithuania engaged in acts of sabotage and minor skirmishes. They were still too weak to disarm any garrisons.

105. All of this happened in early 1944. Thirty-four Jewish policemen were shot during the Children's Aktion on 27 – 28 March 1944. The Germans said it was to avenge the murder of an underground Gestapo agent named Fain and for the policemen's refusal to hand over members of the underground movement. A "service unit" was organized to take the place of the police force; it was headed by a Gestapo agent, who fervently carried out the Germans' orders.

106. On the night of 15 November 1942 the Jew Mek was arrested while trying to escape. On 18 November he was hanged in front of the Jewish elders, and they were not allowed to take his body down for twenty-four hours. His mother and sister were shot at the Ninth Fort on 19 November.

107. There were labor camps at Kaishedoris and Keidany. In April 1944 more than forty prisoners managed to escape from Kaishedoris and reach the partisans. Only ten Jews escaped from Keidany. The rest were captured and tortured.

108. The escape from the Ninth Fort took place on 25 December 1943.

109. The man referred to here is Captain I. L. Vasilenko-Veselnitsky.

110. This took place on 14 April 1944. Rakhmil Berman, one of the ghetto's activists, was the leader of the group; Aba Diskant was their guide. Of the group, about ten died; the rest, including A. Diskant and R. Berman, managed to get to a partisan base and then return to the ghetto.

111. This happened on 6 April 1944.

112. This is the Children's Aktion, which actually took place on 27 March 1944.
113. The details of this partisan action are unclear, since partisan acts of sabotage against the Germans began in the fall of 1943.
114. During the war the author Iokubas Iosade was on the front with the 16th Lithuanian Division; he arrived in Kovno only after its liberation. His account of the events in Kovno is based on the stories of a few survivors who had fought as partisans in Lithuania. Therefore the account contains a number of inaccuracies and errors in chronology.
115. A physician and social activist, Doctor Elena Buividaite-Kutorgene (1888 – 1963) was acknowledged by Yad Vashem in 1982 as one of the Righteous among the Nations.
116. Jewish Health Organization.
117. Girsh Osherovich (b. 1908) was a Yiddish poet; during the war he was a correspondent and was active in the Jewish Anti-Fascist Committee.
118. Von Renteln was appointed Generalkommissar of Lithuania on 17 July 1941 (see Note 42). After arriving in Lithuania on 28 July, he appointed his Gebietskommissars. The Gebietskommissar of Kaunas (Kovno) was Hans Kramer, Oberführer SA; it is his order that Kutorgene refers to in her entry for 28 July.
119. The *Naujoji Lietuva* (*New Lithuania*) was the Lithuanian newspaper published in occupied Vilna.
120. All 1,800 Jews of Pluge were shot on 15 – 16 July 1941 near the village of Kaushenai.
121. Ivan Sergeevich Turgenev (1818 – 1883) is one of the greatest authors in Russian literature. Associated with the Westerinzers—those who wanted Russia to adopt the best of European culture—he is most famous for his novel *Fathers and Sons* (1862), a book that explores the dangerous dimensions of nihilism.
122. Aleksei Nikolaevich Tolstoy (1883 – 1945) was a member of the aristocracy who became a devout Stalinist. He was one of the most prominent writers of the early Soviet period.
123. Kliment Efremovich Voroshilov (1881 – 1969) served as Soviet commissar of defense from 1925 to 1940. After a number of military failures, he was removed from his position as commander of the northern front during World War II. When Stalin died in 1953, he was made head of state, a position he held until 1960.
124. This is clearly a reference to St. John 15:13: "Greater love has no man than this, that he may lay down his life for his friends."
125. According to a report submitted by the Third Einsatzkommando, on 26 September 1941 1,608 Jews who were either ill or thought to be ill were killed at the Fourth Fort.
126. Viktor Kutorga (1920 – 1991) and his mother wrote the letter in the fall of 1941. Lithuanian opera singer V. Ionushkaite-Zaunene took the letter with her on a trip to Berlin and delivered it to the American embassy.
127. This was the so-called Big Aktion.
128. See note 94.
129. On 30 July 1941 840 Jews were murdered in the Rainiai Forest about five kilometers from Telshiai. Between 1 September and 15 September 1941 1,580 people were shot near the village of Giruliai ten kilometers from Telshiai; forty families were shot near the village of Veshveniai in that same time period. Two hundred people were murdered near the Telshiai – Plunge railway that runs north of Telshiai.

Part 5

Latvia

Riga

1. The Germans Enter the City

The rumbling of bombs at the crossings near the Western Dvina River and the train station announced the Germans' approach to Riga. From the very first hours of the war dozens of Junker and Heinkel fighter-bombers roared over the streets and squares of Riga. They dropped their bombs from high altitudes and then swooped down to turn their machine guns on people in the streets. More machine guns and automatic rifles joined them from attics and rooftops— these were German paratroopers and saboteurs who had penetrated into the city. Hitler's secret agents who had remained in Lithuania, Latvia, and Estonia also made their presence known: the fascists tried to blow up bridges, seize government buildings, and paralyze movement along the most important lines of military communication.

[A sinister threat hung over the Jews of Riga. Tens of thousands of leaflets dropped from German airplanes painted a detailed picture of what would be done with the Jews. The Russians and Latvians were categorically warned that they would be severely punished if they should help the Jews to evacuate. The Jews crowded into the railroad stations, filled the freight cars to overflowing, and sat on the railroad platforms for days waiting for the trains to pull out for the East. The railroad workers did everything in their power; with bullets whistling and bombs thundering overhead, they worked the railways and sent the trains on their way. Many people who had lost all hope of leaving by train threw their bundles onto carts and began their long journey on foot. All roads were crowded with refugees. Women and children became targets for the German pilots.

With each hour the evacuation grew more complicated.]

There were jams at the railroad stations between troop transports and trains leaving with evacuees. It became more and more difficult for people trying to get out of the city to get past the all the ambushes set up by German paratroopers; the brazen Hitlerites even bombed the city's main boulevard, Brivibas Street. The Germans had the advantage in terms of men, tanks, and especially air power. Many times Soviet troops fell back and then fought and then fought again at a new battle line. [About eleven thousand Jews were finally evacuated from Riga.]

By the morning of 1 July the Germans were in Riga. They took the first Jewish men they met, tied them to their tanks, and dragged their bloody bodies through the city streets for hours. By noon they were seizing Jews in the streets and herding them into the synagogues.

[Many did not make it to the synagogues: they were shot on the way there.

When the Germans decided that they had crowded a sufficient number of Jews into the synagogues, they began to invite the people of Riga to gather at the synagogues for an interesting show. But here] the Hitlerites ran into their first surprise: the Jewish houses of prayer became strongholds that resounded with the heated firing of rifles and submachine guns. It was clear that the people holed up inside were doomed; by that time there was already a large concentration of German infantry and tanks in Riga. In several instances the Germans had to storm the synagogues with tanks. The uneven battle lasted for several hours; by the end of the day all the synagogues of Riga were engulfed in glaring flames. In some cases the Germans burned the synagogues down; in others the Jews themselves set the buildings on fire, preferring to die rather than surrender to the Hitlerites. The screams of women and children rose up from the burning buildings. In the great choral synagogue Rabbi Kilov loudly chants prayers, as bursts of machine gun fire came from the basement portals. A sawmill worker named Abel took an old hunting rifle and shot two Germans who were trying to break into his house. A German officer called out a whole platoon to take Abel alive. But Abel would not surrender; he died fighting. Two companies of German soldiers stormed the synagogue on Gogol Street.

In several Jewish apartments people involved in the pogrom met with gunfire.

The school director Elkishek, who had a Ph.D. from the University of Vienna, died with a gun in his hands.

Many memories of the courage with which the Jews of Riga met their executioners have been preserved. Two SS men were taking a woman named Ganshtein, who worked at the textile factory, to a synagogue; along the way they beat her with their rifle butts and jabbed her with their bayonets. For a long time she walked in silence, wiping the blood from her face from time to time. At an intersection where a group of Latvians were standing Ganshtein suddenly broke away and cried:

"People, remember these beasts! The Soviet authorities will never forgive them for this. Our people will come; tell them how they tortured us here…"

The Germans did not let Ganshtein finish; they shot her [point-blank. Then they fired several rounds from their machine guns into the air and ordered the crowd to disperse.]

That same day a group of Jews undertook a desperate attempt to break through the lines and join the Red Army troops. A student from the University of Riga named Abram Epshtein led the group. This was the plan: they would go into the forest outside the city, find a weak spot in the line, penetrate across the front, and join their people. Three hundred women and children were stretched out in a long column. Armed students accompanied them. This mass of people managed to get past the guards, through the woods, and into the suburbs. Someone, however, betrayed them to the Germans: several tanks and an infantry battalion rushed off in pursuit of the fugitives.

The Germans overtook the column fifteen kilometers outside of the city. Abram Epshtein ordered his unit (about sixty armed young men and women) to cover the women and children. They selected the Maza-Yugla Creek, which flows east of Riga, as their battle line. Here the brigade of Riga students fought off the advancing Germans for several hours. They enabled the women and children to hide in the forest and find their way along inconspicuous paths to the Madonskoe Highway, where Red Army troops were fighting. Almost everyone in Abram Epshtein's unit was killed, including their commander; but in the heavy fighting on the Maza-

Yugla they slaughtered more than one hundred Germans and made it possible for several hundred women and children to reach Soviet troops.

Latvians and Russians made a number of attempts to save Jews from the inevitable violence. A student named Ilya Abel hid several of his Jewish comrades for many days in his apartment. During the first days of the pogrom Father Anthony hid several dozen Jews in the Catholic church. Another priest helped an engineer named Likhter to escape from the city. But these attempts were of little help to these poor people. Most of them subsequently fell into the hands of the Gestapo and suffered the fate of the Jews of Riga.

Night over Riga

The first night under German occupation set in. Hitler's secret agents came out of the attics, down from the roofs, and up from the cellars. German "repatriates" who had emigrated from Latvia in 1940 turned up in the city. The Germans sent them in by train to work as informers, undercover agents, future commandants of prisons and camps, [and just plain executioners.] The Baltic Germans did not let their hosts down. Of all the Hitlerite scoundrels they were the most notorious; they were the cruelest the executioners and the meanest investigators and interrogators.

With each passing hour the pogrom against the Jews became more and more unbridled and spread out farther and farther.[1] The indiscriminate plundering of Jewish apartments began. Then came mass arrests. They seized everyone they could get their hands on and took them to the prison, to the prefecture, or directly to the Bikernieki Forest.[2] Six thousand Jews were arrested in a single night.

The Bikernieki Forest has an unforgettable, horribly infamous place in the history of Latvia. In 1905 hundreds of participants in the revolutionary movement were shot in the Bikernieki Forest. During the Civil War mass executions of fighters for a Soviet Latvia were carried out here. The bones of fighters and martyrs of two generations lie buried in this forest in layers one on top of the other, like geological strata. This was the place the Hitlerites chose for the mass slaughter of thousands of Jews, both from Riga and from Western Europe.

The Germans tried to outdo each other in the refinement of various means of slaughtering defenseless people. Sturmbannführer Kraus of the Sicherheitspolizei, for example, worked out his own favorite method. He would line up groups of Jews on the streets of the Moscow Vorstadt and cover their faces with portraits of Lenin and Stalin; then he would arm Latvian boys with rifles and order them: "Shoot the Bolsheviks!" Whenever they refused, he would grab one or two of them, put the portrait masks on their faces, and force them to join the crowd of Jews. Then the SS commando would shoot the entire column of condemned people. Untersturmführer Bruns would force the Jews to dig their own graves and lie down in them; then, carefully measuring their height, he would spend a long time meticulously checking to see that each pit had the proper geometric form. Only after he had thoroughly enjoyed himself would he then shoot the doomed people.

Jews were constantly being taken to the prefecture building to "register for work." Filling out some sort of forms, the Germans measured the Jews' noses, foreheads, and cheekbones and then spent a long time making notes. Then they would burst out laughing, burn the documents they had just completed in the stove, and finally come to a "decision":

"To the Bikernieki Forest."

[Once at midnight an SS man gave an order to fetch a barber. He then ordered the barber to shave off half the beard of every elderly Jew assembled there. Next he had the Jews tear off one sleeve of their suit and remove one shoe; then he made them dance. Half an hour later the commander of the SS unit showed up completely drunk; he announced that he would now make a political report. He spoke for a long time in an incoherent manner, but one thing was clear: he, the Sturmbannführer, would have no mercy on the Jews. Once they had fallen into his hands, they could consider themselves dead and prepare to meet their forefathers in the next world. To prove that he meant what he said, the Sturmbannführer took out his pistol and shot several men on the spot.]

That night about three thousand men underwent a "re-registration" at the prefecture. More than a thousand were immediately sent to the Bikernieki Forest and shot. The rest were locked up in the city prison.

In the courtyard of the Central Committee of the IOAR³ the Germans discovered a number of posters, placards, and several banners. The Hitlerites ordered the Jews to take the banners and the posters, hold a "demonstration," and sing the *Internationale* and other songs of the revolution. The butchers took the "demonstrators" out to the streets, where they tried to provoke the population against them. But the Hitlerites' provocation failed. The Latvians and the Russians were disgusted by it all and refused to take part in the atrocity. Then the Germans opened fire with their automatic rifles and machine guns, and all the "demonstrators" were shot right there in the street.

That night in the building at 10 Mariinskaya Street officers of the Württemburg-Baden Grenadier Regiment were having a drinking bout. They brought in dozens of young Jewish girls to join them in their orgy, forced them to strip naked, drink, and sing songs. Many of the poor girls were raped and then taken into the courtyard and shot. Captain Bach surpassed them all in his creativity. He broke the seat cushions off two chairs and replaced them with sheets of tin. Two female students from the University of Riga were tied to the chairs, facing each other. The officers' aides then lit two Primus stoves and placed them underneath the chairs. The officers were very pleased with this form of entertainment. They joined hands, danced around the two martyrs, and sang. The girls writhed in torment, but their arms and legs were bound tightly to the chairs. When they tried to cry out, their mouths were gagged with filthy rags.

3. The First Days of the Occupation

For the most part, Jewish affairs were turned over to the Baltic German fascists who had returned to Riga. These scoundrels had long since been obsessed with a loathing for the Latvians and a savage hatred for the Jews.

Now they had returned as storm troopers with unlimited rights and authority. In his day a certain Hans Mannskeit was known around the police stations of Riga as a notorious hoodlum. When he was repatriated to Germany in 1940, the people of Riga heaved a sigh of relief. He returned with the German troops as a Gestapo investigator of Jewish affairs. A number of Baltic Germans began to play prominent roles in the Gestapo: an accountant named Lorenzen, Doctor Bernsdorf, and the accountants Schultz and Brasch. Although they did not hold official positions with the Gestapo, other Baltic Germans who had returned to Riga were no less sophisticated than the Gestapo in their torment of the city's defenseless Jewish population.

{Plundering and mass arrests proceeded at a growing rate. Fascists yet to be unmasked, local quislings, and two-faced nationalists played more than a small role in these activities. Over the course of several years there existed in Latvia an organization known as "Penkokrust."[4] Coming together with the encouragement of nationalists and proto-Nazis, they borrowed heavily from the ideological arsenal of fascist German anti-Semitic slogans. This wretched organization was dissolved in 1940, but its disciples managed to hide their true faces. The Germans recruited most of the instigators of the pogroms from these scoundrels, who faithfully served their masters.}

A special order prohibited Jews from purchasing food in stores where Germans and Latvians shopped. [They were also forbidden to engage in "voluntary" labor: all Jews were to be enlisted in forced labor.] Jews were required to wear a six-pointed star—the "Shield of David"— on their chests and were forbidden to walk on the sidewalks; they were allowed to walk only on the street pavement.

The arrests, mass shootings, and sadistic tortures continued unabated. On Gertrude Street a group of storm troopers went up to the roof of a six-story building and from there threw Jewish children to the ground. Some official was about to order them to stop these executions. From the roof they answered him:

"We are conducting scientific work here. We are testing the accuracy of the law of universal gravity."

["Donnerwetter! Well said! Continue, gentlemen. Science requires sacrifices."]

An old Jewish tailor was walking down Lacplesa Street, bent under the weight of a sewing machine. Some German officers who were driving by tried to run him down with their car, but the old man managed to jump to one side and get behind a telegraph pole. The Germans turned the car around and went hunting for him; when they had him pressed up against a newspaper stand, he jumped onto the sidewalk.

"What? How dare you violate the laws of the German Empire by stepping on the sidewalk?" the Hitlerites shouted.

They dragged the old man into the street and started beating him with iron bars. When he fell unconscious and covered with blood, the Germans went over to their car, lit a cigarette, and began merrily chatting. A Latvian woman named Petrunya Salazas, who had been a witness to the savage scene, took a cup of water over to the old man to wash off his face and give him a drink. A German tore the cup from the woman's hands and violently threw it at her face; then he beat her with his whip, threatened her with his pistol, and chased her away. The old man died right there on Lacplesa Street next to the newspaper stand.

In those days cruel violence was done not only to the Jews but also to everyone whom the Germans suspected of being sympathetic toward the Soviet authorities. [Jews were shot for being Jews. Latvians were found guilty mainly of one thing: good relations with the Soviet authorities. This made both nationalities the same in the eyes of the executioners.] On 3 July fifty pairs of people bound back to back were brought out into the courtyard of the Riga prison; each pair had one Jew and one Latvian. The Latvian Elvira Damber and the Jew Yakov Abesgauz were in the first pair.

"You wanted equality," said the Untersturmführer who was conducting the execution. "Now you will have it."

One hundred people bound in pairs—Jews and Latvians—were shot. Every bullet passed through two bodies, and the blood of the murdered Latvians and Jews mixed together in the prison courtyard.

The martyr's death of nineteen-year-old Lina Gotshalk is preserved in the memory of many citizens of Riga. She was seized on the street and taken to an apartment on Elizavetinskaya Street, where some drunken German officers were carousing. The Hitlerites began considering how they were going to kill their victim. The girl knew German and silently listened to the discussion that would decide her fate. The Germans finally came to a decision: they would transform her into a creature without bones. They stuffed her into a sack and beat her all over her body with ramrods. The beating lasted two hours. The girl was already dead, and all her bones were broken. Then the officers' aides threw the bloody lump of flesh into the boulevard in front of the opera theater.

A few days later the Germans began implementing the order regarding the conscription of Jews for forced labor. The Generalkommissar of Latvia Obergruppenführer Drechsler and Gebietskommissar Witroch ordered all hard and dirty labor to be done by Jewish hands. Jobs that were completely unnecessary were set up.

Lieutenant Kraus and Sonderführer Drawe were in charge of the Jewish section of the labor exchange. They were especially sadistic in the torture of their victims. Initially a large group of Jews, mostly young adults, was assigned to clean up the buildings that were half destroyed in military actions. The tasks they were given were beyond their strength. On stretchers normally handled by two people the Germans ordered them to carry four to five hundred pounds of bricks. [Those who fell from exhaustion were beaten—often to death—with clubs.]

The workday generally began with beatings and usually ended with murders. People were most often punished for failing to follow the order to wear the six-pointed star. At first the star was to be worn on the left side of the chest. Then they issued an order that it was to be worn on the right side. Then the order was to wear it on the back. A short while after that came the order that the star was to be worn on the chest and on the back. Then, after the rule was changed several more times, the Germans went back to the first variant, then to the second, and so on endlessly. Every morning people would ask themselves where they should attach the star, and every morning the Hitlerites found "violators." And a mass beating would begin.

The Germans forced people to remove bricks from the foundations of demolished walls, so that the buildings would come down faster. Almost every day walls would collapse, burying dozens of people under the debris.

Hundreds of the Jews of Riga perished at the peat factory near Olaine.

The Gebietskommissar of the Elgava (Mitava) district was Baron Emden, a Baltic German. He was nicknamed the "King of Zemgale" because he used to own property in the Mitava area. In the district under his command Emden behaved like a tyrant; he had an insatiable thirst for power. There is evidence that he organized several "hunts" and "roundups" of Jews. The list of his accomplices for one of these "hunts" is also known: Captain Cukurs, Major Arajs, the prefect of Riga Stiglitz, Untersturmführer Jäger, and some Baltic Germans—the Bruns brothers and Gruppenführer Kopitz.

This group once went to the director of the peat factory and demanded that he turn over two hundred Jews to them. The director tried to object that the loss of so many workers would result in an interruption in the peat deliveries, but the Gebietskommissar would not budge. True, he too had to make some "concessions": he was given only women and children. Soon the "hunt" began. They chased groups of ten to fifteen of those poor people in a field and told them that if they could run across the field and hide in the woods within eight minutes, then they might have a chance to save themselves. Otherwise they would be shot as worthless subjects. At the sound of a whistle the women and children ran for the woods. They had to run, jump over canals and hillocks, and make their way through overgrown thickets. Timing them with a stopwatch, the Germans restrained the pack of hunting dogs. Every eight minutes they released some of the dogs. The dogs overtook most of the unfortunate people in the open field or in the short bushes. Specially trained dogs would rip out people's throats and then take off after the others. Some of the dogs would bring their victims down to the ground and wait for their masters to come. The master would shoot the person lying on the ground, and then the dog would run on ahead in search of new "game."

When they were done with the bloody murders in the open field, the roundup in the woods would begin. It was conducted in accordance with all the rules of the art of hunting: wide encirclement, chase, and ambush. The dogs would bound through the woods and herd the women, who had now gone out of their minds, to a spot that the "King of Zemgale" and his friends had prepared. As soon as the women ran out into the small clearing, they were gunned down.

Jews were murdered every day in Riga. [Hundreds of people were shot while returning from work or just walking down the street. Many preferred to stay put in the cellars and go hungry, rather than risk being seen by some fascist.] Especially memorable dates are 15 July, when a thousand people were shot, and 23 July, the anniversary of Latvia's incorporation into the Soviet Union; on that day more than two thousand people were murdered. The Germans persecuted even the dead among the Jews: they issued a special order not to accept Jewish bodies in the morgue. For seven days the streets of Riga were littered with the bodies of Jews.

Soon the Germans eagerly began their preparations for the complete slaughter of the Jews. In order to do this, they had to gather all the Jews into one place and isolate them from the rest of the population. The site selected for the resettlement of the Jews was the Vorstadt (suburb) of Moscow, where the Jewish ghetto had been located during the Middle Ages. The Germans were not guided by historical sensitivities; it was simply that the Moscow Vorstadt was best suited for their purposes: [it was situated close to the Bikernieki Forest, the traditional site of mass shootings.]

A governing board for the Riga Jewish Community was formed; they were answerable to the German authorities. Doctor Shleter, a Viennese Jew and former state advisor in Austria, was appointed head of the board. Members of the board include the attorneys Mikhail Ilyashev and Mints, the physician Rudolf Blyumenfeld, a former director of the textile factory named Kaufer, the bookkeeper Blumenau, and others.

[In the first days it became clear that the appointment of the board would create no opportunities for the improvement of living conditions. Food rations were cut: the Jews received one hundred grams of ersatz bread per day, which was half of what the rest of the population got. Jews were strictly forbidden to go into the village to purchase provisions. The Jewish population began to starve. Cut off from the entire world—correspondence by mail was forbidden—the Jews of Riga anxiously awaited the events to come.]

4. The Ghetto

The Hitlerites hastened the resettlement of the Jews into the Moscow Vorstadt. [Sometimes the Jews were given only two or three hours' notice before they had to leave.] The furniture and possessions of the ones being resettled the Germans confiscated for themselves.

[The area designated for the ghetto was very small, and people kept coming in. On 21 October the Generalkommissar issued the order to create the ghetto and to introduce new, more severe restrictions. From that time onward the Jews were subject to the misanthropic Nuremberg Laws and the "Goebbels Novella" that was issued as an elaboration on them. According to the creators of these "laws," Jews were no longer subjects of society but objects of racial policy.]

An order issued by the Generalkommissar forbade the Jews to go outside the barbed wire.[5] The establishments where the prisoners of the ghetto worked were responsible for getting their workers to the job site and back to the ghetto under armed escort. The population in the city was strictly forbidden to have any dealings with the Jews or to even go near the boundaries of the ghetto.

A double barbed wire fence sealed off the Moscow Vorstadt. On the evening of 24 October the German guard posted at the entrance to the ghetto [admitted the last of the Jews through the hastily erected gates. The Jews of Riga had been herded into an enormous trap.]

Days filled with anxiety dragged by. Every morning the gates of the ghetto were thrown open and thousands of people went out to work under an armed escort. Business managers, contractors, and German military commanders made extensive use of the slave labor provided by the inhabitants of the ghetto. Lieutenant Kraus, the head of the Jewish section at the labor exchange, never turned down anyone who requested workers. A poster hanging on the ghetto gates read: "Jews provided for a fee. This applies to military units."

Every day the Jews returning from work were searched at the ghetto gates. Once they found a sandwich on a student named Kremer; the boy was shot on the spot. [Meanwhile hunger was spreading throughout the ghetto, and many were collapsing from malnutrition. The community council took local measures for improving living conditions.]

Given the debilitated state of the population and the unsanitary living conditions (the Germans would not allow the removal of sewage from the ghetto), the doctors did everything in their power to prevent the spread of epidemics. Outpatient clinics, an orphans' shelter, and a cafeteria for the elderly and invalids were operating in the ghetto.

On 27 November the community council was informed that, by order of the authorities, male "specialists" would be separated from the general population, [including their families]. On 28 November they began building a fence inside the ghetto. Thus the "Little Ghetto" was formed; only men capable of working were housed there, about three thousand in all. Fenced off from the others by barbed wire, they could not see their wives and children. The ghetto guards were smirking in an ominous fashion. Everyone sensed the approach of a catastrophe.

[On 29 November Sturmbannführer Brasch summoned the entire community council to his office. He was more insolent than usual and flaunted his candor. He announced that, by order of the authorities, some of the Jews of Riga were to be annihilated, since the ghetto was overcrowded. The community council was to take part in this action by helping the Germans select the people to be shot. To this end they were to immediately draw up a list of old men, sick people, criminals, and other persons whose presence in the ghetto was considered unde-sirable by the council.

The members of the council quietly listened to what the executioner had to say; then they looked at one anther and hung their heads. To argue with him or try to persuade him of anything was pointless. The members of the community council knew each other very well, and that is why, remaining silent, they exchanged glances and came to a decision. Doctor Blyumenfeld gave Brausch their answer:

"The council will not hand over anyone to be shot. I am a physician and have devoted my entire adult life to healing sick people, not killing them. Your view on the value of a human being is too different from ours. So is your view on the matter of who should be regarded as a criminal. In our opinion, the criminals should be sought outside the ghetto…"

Brasch cut Blyumenfeld short and ordered the council to leave.

In spite of how hard the council members tried to hide what Brasch had told them, the ghetto found out about the execution that the Germans were preparing.]

On 29 November the commander-in-chief of the police forces in Ostland, Obergruppenführer Jeckeln,[6] informed all the business offices and establishments that no Jews would be sent out to work until a special order was issued. On 30 November the gates of the ghetto were not opened; the armed escorts were sent away. From all the preparations, it was evident that something extraordinary was about to happen.

5. Aktion

The Riga Ghetto Aktion took place on 30 November and 1 December 1941, five weeks after the establishment of the ghetto. It began with an order for all men to line up on Ludzas Street. No one knew what to expect; all sorts of rumors were floating around. [Fearing that they would be shot, some men hid with their families. Some women, on the other hand, dressed themselves in men's clothing and tried to get into a column of men in the hope of finding salvation there.] Soon the men were led away, some to the Little Ghetto, others to the Salaspils concentration camp. Toward six o'clock in the evening the women, children, and old men were forced out of their apartments. The police tore through the quarter in the Mos-cow Vorstadt. They finished off the sick on the spot. Mothers burdened with large families were left with no more than two children; the rest were shot right there. Every last one of the three hundred old men from the old age home was murdered. All the patients in the ghetto hospital were murdered. Death cries could be heard everywhere. Groups of women and chil-dren driven from their homes were standing in the streets. They were forced to wait there until the next morning. Numb and shivering from the cold, they watched the bloodbath in horror. Toward morning the Germans began forming columns of two to three hundred people; under the armed guard of an equal number of policemen, they were sent eastward.

{Outside the building where the community council was housed all the council mem-bers—including the Chief Rabbi of Riga, Rabbi Zak—stood surrounded by Hitlerites. Doctor Blyumenfeld managed to whisper to a man passing by named Abram Rozental:

"Our minutes are numbered. Perhaps you will live to see brighter days; tell our loved ones that we died in the firm belief that our people cannot be destroyed. We are waiting here to be shot—that much is quite clear. But there, next door, by the light of a kerosene lamp, Professor

Dubnow is writing the last lines of his memoirs, like a chronicler of old.[7] He is convinced that his words will reach his readers."}

One of the commandants of the ghetto was a German named Johann Siebert, a butcher educated at the University of Heidelberg. Semen Markovich Dubnow would periodically do a lecture series at Heidelberg on the history of the ancient East and the general history of the Jews. And here student and professor met in the Riga Ghetto—one an all-powerful boss and cruel butcher, the other a prisoner doomed to death. Siebert recognized his former professor and at every opportunity tried to insult and taunt the eighty-year-old man.

{"Professor, I was once so stupid as to listen to your lectures at the university," Siebert told Dubnow on one occasion. "You spent a long time explaining to us how the ideas of humanism would triumph over all the world. I remember how you criticized the anti-Semites and prophesied that the twentieth century would see the complete emancipation of the Jews. Yesterday I was in the Bikernieki Forest; 480 Russian prisoners of war were shot there along with—just imagine—an equal number of Jews. You may celebrate, Dubnow. You have already attained equality with the Russians."

"How many Jews did you say were shot?"

"Four hundred eighty."

"Thank you for the information. You see, I am continuing my work, and this is important for me to know."}

Up until his last day the author of *The General History of the Jews* kept a diary in which he recounted the history of the Riga Ghetto in detail. Notebooks containing his writings were secretly taken out of the ghetto and placed in the care of Latvian friends in the city. Those notes have not yet been recovered: the Germans drove out the people who had taken care of his diaries.

Dubnow came out of his building under the prodding of two Germans. He had the look of a man who had fulfilled his duty to his people to the very end. He glanced around. It was snowing, and hundreds of women and children herded along by the SS were on their way to their deaths. Johann Siebert bared his teeth in a smirk. Dubnow wanted to say something to him. But the automatic rifles started firing.... Dubnow fell dead.

Witnesses of the mass murders in the Riga Ghetto unanimously confirm that everything that happened took place according to a calculated, predetermined plan worked out to the last detail.

[No one cleared away the bodies inside the ghetto; but once the column had passed the barbed wire, carts and wheelbarrows immediately joined up with it. Without giving it a second thought, the guards shot crying children and people who lagged behind; their bodies were tossed onto a cart or wheelbarrow.

Brasch stood at the ghetto gate with his pistol drawn and shot into the moving column. He did it calmly, methodically taking aim. Izidor Berel, a member of the "order commando" made up of Jews from the ghetto, went up to Brasch and asked:

"What are you doing, Mr. Brasch? Do you call this German culture, willfully shooting defenseless people?"

During the dictatorship of the Ulmanis Izidor Berel served in the Latvian police force and rose to a high rank. Therefore when he was enlisted in the "order commando" in the ghetto, he was required to wear a police uniform with the badge of distinction that he had earned. Brasch was lower than Berel in rank, and, like a proper German functionary, thought it necessary to give him an explanation:

"We are acting in complete accordance with the instructions we have received. We must adhere strictly to the schedule for moving the column to its designated site; therefore we are culling from its ranks everyone who might slow the pace. Judge for yourself, do you really think that old woman over there in the purple housecoat will be able to keep up?" And, taking aim, he shot the old woman.

All the executioners acted just as calmly and methodically. The only thing that upset them was the danger of a delay in their precise schedule for moving the column and completing the "operation" in a timely fashion. Only once did Brasch lose his self-control. An engineer named Volf jumped out of the column and gave the butcher a slap in the face. Brasch emptied his pistol into the engineer. In other instances he was more frugal with his bullets.]

The leaders of the Aktion were somewhat surprised to find so many orphans in the ghetto. A special children's battalion of six hundred boys and girls was formed. Two hundred policemen from the Ordnungspolizei escorted them. Along the way they tossed children into the air and shot them.

As the column was going past and Old Believers church, several dozen Russian Old Believers led by a priest fell to their knees on the side of the road and began singing hymns. The police tried to disperse them, but the priest replied:

"Do not interfere with our prayers to God. You are not leading simple people here but holy martyrs. [They will soon stand before the Most High and tell Him what is happening in our sinful land. Let our prayers go with them to God."]

The mass executions stirred up a deeply rooted revolt among the workers at the Quadrat Rubber Factory. They ceased work as a sign of protest. The gendarmes were called in. The affair developed into an armed skirmish, and many of the workers perished in the uneven battle.

Eight huge pits had already been dug in the Bikernieki Forest. As soon as the columns entered the forest, the people were ordered to undress. Boots had to be placed in one pile, galoshes in another. The SS herded the unclothed people to the edge of the pit with the rifle butts; there stood the Baltic German Baron Sievers firing his submachine gun in short bursts. His two assistants changed the cartridge clips for the submachine gun and took turns handing them to Sievers. He stood there completely splattered with blood, but for a long time he did not want anyone else to take his place. He later boasted that on 1 December he personally shot three thousand Jews. [Cameramen furiously cranked the handles on their movie cameras. Photographers bustled about, and many of the SS took amateur photographs, clicking away with their "Leicas."]

The Germans devised various means of humiliating their victims. They selected old men with long beards. They ordered them to undress. Then they divided them into two groups, gave them a ball, and order them to play soccer in the snow. Cameramen and photographers photographed the horrible scene.

The poor victims were overcome with numbness from the cold. Someone's nerves cracked, and a loud cry of despair echoed through the woods; women went into hysterics. Malkina jumped on top of a tree stump and shouted:

"Why are you crying, Jews? Do you really think these monsters will be moved by your tears? Let us be silent! Let us be proud! [We are Jews!… We are Soviet Jews!…]

And everything in the forest grew quiet; only the sound of automatic weapons disturbed the silence.

[One of the SS men walked up to the column and mocked them:

"Why have you fallen silent? You have only a few minutes to live, so make the most of the time you have left. Sing something."

In reply,] an old man's voice could be heard singing the *Internationale*. At first people joined him individually, here and there; then everyone burst into a single voice singing the hymn. The seamstress Frida Frid related this episode; she was the only Jew to live through that day in the Bikernieki Forest. The story of her survival and her three years of wandering about the farms of Latvia could fill a book.[8]

"Our column was broken up into sections," Frida Frid relates, "and everyone was ordered to undress. I undressed to my underwear, and then I felt ashamed; there were men standing around, and all I had on was a slip. I grabbed my cotton work smock and put it on. I was very cold. I stuck my hands in the pockets of the smock to get warm, and I felt something: it was a piece of paper. I looked at it: it was my diploma showing that I graduated from seamstress school with distinction. I had kept it for fifteen years. Lord, I thought, maybe this piece of paper will save me. I ran out of the column and went up to one of the Germans. He looked like an officer to me.

"'Officer, sir,' I said to him in German. 'Why do they want to kill me? I want to work. There is no need to kill me. Look, I'm not lying: I have a diploma. Here's the document.'

"He pushed me away, and I fell down. When I started to get up, he kicked me again and yelled:

"'Don't bother me and don't come crawling to me with your papers. Take your documents to Stalin.'

"I was back in the column. I started tearing at my hair. I grabbed a tuft of hair and yanked it out; it was there in my hand, and I did not even feel any pain. The Germans were herding us closer and closer to the pit with their rifle butts. Again I turned to a policeman and told him that I was a seamstress and that I wanted to work; I showed him my diploma, but no one would listen to me. I approached the pit. There were tall trees growing on either side of us, and beyond the pit was a narrow path. People were already walking one at a time toward the precipice and tumbling over the edge; the only thing that could be heard was the sound of automatic weapons: rat-tat-tat-tat-tat.

"'Can this really be the end?' I thought. 'In a few minutes I shall be dead. No more shall I see the sun or breathe the air. How can it be? After all, my papers are in order, I have done honest work all my life, my customers have never been angry with me, but the Germans pay no attention to any of it. I don't want to die! I don't want to!' I ran over to the officer in charge of the shooting and cried out in a voice not my own:

"'What are you doing to me? I am a specialist. Here are my documents... I am a specialist....'

"He hit me in the head with his pistol, and I fell right next to the pit. I pressed against the ground and tried not to move. Half an hour later I heard something: someone was shouting in German, 'Pile the shoes up here!' By that time I had crawled back a little. I opened one eye just slightly and saw a shoe lying next to my face. They were covering me with shoes. My gray cotton smock must have blended in with the color of the shoes, and they did not notice me. I felt a little warmer; a whole mountain of shoes was lying on top of me. Only my right side was frozen through. I could have placed several shoes underneath myself, but I was afraid that the pile would move and they would find me. So I lay there until it got dark, frozen to the icy ground.

"I could hear gun shots very close to me. I clearly heard people's last cries and the moaning of those who were wounded and thrown into the mass grave alive. Some died cursing their executioners, some perished remembering their children and parents; others chanted prayers out loud... Still others asked at the last minute if they could dress their children, so that they would not catch cold. I had to lie there and listen to all of it. Several times I thought I heard my brother's voice, then my roommate's voice... At those moments I thought I was going insane.

"By evening the shooting subsided. The Germans left a small guard unit next to the mountain of clothing and went off to rest. Several Germans were standing just three paces from me. They were smoking cigarettes and talking among themselves. I listened to their smug, cheerful voices: 'The work went well today.' 'Yes, it was a great day.' 'There are still a lot of them left. There's more work to be done.' 'Well, see you tomorrow.' 'Pleasant dreams.' 'Oh, I always have pleasant dreams.'

"I decided to crawl out from under the pile of shoes. The first thing I had to do was put some clothes on. I crawled over to another pile; it was men's clothing. There was no time to think about it; I put on someone's pants and jacket and tied a large kerchief over my head. Just then I heard the faint voice of a weeping child coming from the pit, where the ones who had been murdered were lying: 'Mama, I'm cold... Why are you just lying there, Mama?' Well, I thought, what will be will be. I'll try to save the child. But the Germans beat me to it. They went up to the pit, poked around for the little boy with their bayonets, and stabbed him. One of the Germans said, 'No one gets away from us alive.'

"I realized that I had to get as far away as possible from that terrible place while it was still night. But there were guards all around, and they could see me in the white snow. Then I remembered the film *War in Finland*, where soldiers who were dressed in white were well camouflaged in the snow. Not far from where I was I saw a pile of sheets that mothers had used to wrap their infants....

"I came across a blanket cover, wrapped myself in it, and crawled away... "

Those who were left in the ghetto waited for the pogrom to resume, but for the time being it was quiet. Only now and then could the moaning of a wounded person be heard, followed by the sound of a policeman's rapid footsteps... A lone shot could be heard coming from between the buildings, and then silence once again. No one took away the bodies. No new orders were issued, except one: to inform the police of any wounded. The Germans invariably finished off the wounded.

Only on the fifth day did the order come to bury those who were murdered. A single huge grave was dug in the old Jewish cemetery, which was located in the ghetto zone. A certain doctor carried his wife and two children to the grave; a number of people buried all their relatives, both close and distant.

6. "Deportation" from the Ghetto

A week after the first Aktion it was announced that the Big Ghetto would be "deported" from Riga. What that word meant exactly, no one knew. The Germans explained that "deportation" was essentially different from "evacuation." If by "evacuation" they understood being settled in a new place, then "deportation" meant being evicted... Whether those being "deported" would settle somewhere, nobody knew...

On the evening of 9 December, in weather twenty degrees below zero Celsius, the inhabitants of the ghetto were ordered to get ready for "deportation." From seven in the evening until the next morning people crowded together in the freezing cold. By this time the Germans had already managed to plunder the ghetto of all it warm things. Many old men and old women froze to death that night. At dawn they started leading the columns out under armed escort. Not far from the Shkirotava Station on a dead-end track stood several trains without steam engines. The "deportees" were herded into the freight cars. In those freight cars people were hauled off by the hundreds to the Bikernieki Forest; there the Germans shot them with machine guns. Approximately twelve thousand people perished that day.

Several days later the authorities put out a general announcement that they would soon celebrate the liquidation of the Big Ghetto in Riga. Many German soldiers wielding all kinds of weapons took part in the festivities; there were Germans in civilian clothes, policemen and gendarmes, the dregs of Riga's criminals, and fascist scoundrels from among the Latvian nationalists. The debauchery went on for a long time. Little children were thrown into the air. Naked girls were forced to play volleyball, and the losing team was shot; then a new game began with new players. The entire holiday was directed by Untersturmführer Jäger. Jäger was known for having long been a member of the Nazi Party; he had been part of Hitler's Munich Putsch.[9]

By the time the celebration was over there were only 3,800 people left in the ghetto; among them were 300 women and several dozen children. Within a day, however, the Riga Ghetto had begun to fill up again: the first transport of Jews from Germany had arrived.

7. The Jews from Germany

It is difficult to explain exactly why Riga was selected as a site for the murder of German Jews. Once when he was very drunk, the adjutant to the ghetto commander, Untersturmführer Migge, explained in very blunt terms why the Jews had been brought from Germany to Latvia: the Germans did not want to murder them at home, because every executioner was well known to a large circle of people.

{Secondly, entrusting some of the shootings to the traitors among the Latvian nationalists, the Germans had generally become accomplices to the crimes of the Latvians upon whom they had extensively relied.}

The Hitlerites arranged the deportation of these Jews to their deaths in such a way that the poor victims did not know until the last minute what fate awaited them. They were told that the resettlement was for purposes of German colonization in the East and that Germany, as always, regarded German Jews as its citizens; they found it more expedient, however, for the Jews to settle in Ostland. It was recommended that they take along everything they would need in their new location. In the pocket of one of the German Jews murdered in the Riga Ghetto the following order concerning the evacuation from Berlin was found:

Berlin No. 4, 11 January 1942

To Mr. Albert Israel Unger and spouse:

By order of the authorities, your departure has been scheduled for 19 January 1942. This order pertains to you, your wife, and the unmarried members of your family included in your property declaration.

At noon on 17 January 1942 an official will seal the premises of your residence. You must therefore have your large luggage and your hand baggage ready by the time designated. You are to hand over to the official the keys to your apartment and its rooms. Then you must accompany the official to the police station in the district where your apartment is located; take your large luggage and hand bags with you. You will check the large luggage at the police station. From there our baggage department will have it sent by truck to the assembly point at 7/8 Lowetzov Street. Once your large luggage has been transported to the police station, you are to take your handbags to the assembly point at the synagogue on Lowetzov Street (at the Jagow Street entrance). You may go there by the usual means of transportation.

We shall take charge of your belongings at the assembly point and during the train ride. Be sure to take provisions for your new residence, especially something for your supper, in your hand baggage. Medical and food services will be available both at the assembly point and along the way.

Enclosed is a memorandum with all the necessary instructions. You must follow these instructions very carefully and prepare for your trip calmly and thoughtfully.

… The train pulled up to the platform at the Riga station. Obersturmführer Krause or one of the higher officials from the Generalkommissar's office met the train. The German smiled politely and in the most carefully selected phrases congratulated the elder in the transport on their safe arrival at their new home. After an exchange of pleasantries, the German reported in an apologetic tone that, due to unforeseen circumstances, there had been a slight misunderstanding with regard to transportation: not all the buses had arrived. Therefore he asked the elder to separate out the men and the healthiest women, who could walk the three to four kilometers; the old men, children, and the rest of the women would take the buses.

The boarding of the buses was very highly organized. With jokes and courteous smiles on their faces, the police and gendarmes helped the women and the old men to their seats, and the children were gently picked up and handed to their mothers.

The men went on foot to the apartments previously occupied by the Jews of Riga in the Moscow Vorstadt; the women, old men, and children were taken to the Bikernieki Forest. There was an amazingly sudden change in the way they were treated. The doors of the bus opened, and the police and gendarmes were lined up, just as they had been at the train station. Here, however, they were not smiling and made no attempts at gallantry. [They beat everyone they could with their rifle butts; they shot some people on the spot.] Then came the order to undress, pile up their clothes, and proceed to the precipice, where huge pits had already been dug… .

From some transports everyone was taken directly to the Bikernieki Forest, from others everyone except those who were most fit for work. Soon the Big Ghetto was once again populated by Jews—from Berlin, Cologne, Düsseldorf, Prague, Vienna, and other European cities.[10]

The Riga Ghetto continued to exist for a year after the arrival of the German Jews. It consisted of two parts: the Big Ghetto and the Little Ghetto. German Jews lived in the Big Ghetto and Riga Jews in the Little Ghetto. A barbed wire fence separated the two. The commandant of the ghetto was Obersturmführer Krause; he had the right to personally judge and execute people. The one who was generally in charge of the slaughter of the Jews, however, was Standartenführer Lange, commander of the Latvian police; in Germany he had the official title "Doctor of Anti-Semitism."[11]

The restrictions and prohibitions placed upon the ghetto included a prohibition against giving birth to children. When Krause found out that Klara Kaufmann, a new arrival from Germany, was about to have a baby, he ordered her to be brought to the hospital. An hour after she gave birth, several hundred people were led to the hospital. Krause stood on the balcony in full dress uniform and gave the signal to the police to go into action. Wachmeister Kabnello brought out the baby and lifted it high over his head to show it everyone who was gathered there. Then, holding the baby by the legs, he swung it around and crushed its head against the porch steps. Blood gushed out. Kabnello wiped off his face and hands with a clean white towel and then brought out the mother and her husband. They were both shot on the spot, right next to the body of their firstborn. Thus the birth of a child was announced in the ghetto. [Beyond the boundaries of the ghetto the Germans unleashed a zealous campaign for the "preservation of racial purity." No matter how hard the Hitlerites tried, however, they had to make several concessions in one area. Wanting to attract former officers from the Latvian army and the most powerful functionaries from the bourgeois Ulmani government to their side, they allowed them to take Jewish women from the ghetto to be their wives. But they all soon receive a notice to report to the commissariat for registration. There, they were received by Frits Steiniger, the man who reviewed racial issues. He interrogated each woman for a long time about her genealogy, her state of health, and other matters. Each one of them received a notice to report to Doctor Krastyn at the infirmary and to bring enough money to pay for a two-week stay. They were all sterilized. The sterilization was conducted under the supervision of German doctors in full compliance with the Nuremberg Laws.]

8. The Salaspils Concentration Camp[12]

After a year had gone by the Germans transferred the ghetto from the capital of Ostland to the Salaspils concentration camp. The camp at Kaiserwald[13] served as the original transit point for people being sent to Salaspils. No one could escape from this terrible place. Sturmbannführer Sauer, a notorious criminal from Germany, was appointed head of the camp. [Sauer perfected searches. Everyone who came to Kaiserwald was put on a two-day "diet": they were fed only castor oil to see whether any of them had swallowed any jewels or gold coins.]

"Level III Criminals" were brought from Germany and placed in charge of the Jewish barracks; these were criminals who had served half their prison terms and had demonstrated a devotion to National Socialism.

In Salaspils the Germans carried out a ruthless and consistent agenda of extermination. Several "disinfections" of the barracks were conducted, after which hundreds of people who had been gassed were taken out to nearby ravines. Thousands of people were tortured with unbearable forced labor.

Many people were slaughtered in two German "scientific" establishments operating in Riga: the Institute for Hygiene and the Institute of Medical Zoology. In these institutes licensed butchers cultivated and perfected the science of death. The Germans took one group of Jews—which included Associate Professor Schneider of the Sorbonne—and cut open their veins to study how hormones and iron from the endocrine glands act when someone is bleeding to death. One of the scientific workers prepared a dissertation on the historical development of methods of hanging people. He carefully examined the types of ropes and the knots that produced the most effective results. This "dissertation" cost the lives of thirty-five Jews.

The year 1944 came. The front line was moving closer and closer to the Baltic. The Hitlerites rushed to complete the work of their terrible slaughter. One Aktion followed another. Finally the last inhabitants of the concentration camps were loaded into a steamer and sent to Zemgale, where they were shot.

Here is an excerpt from a German newspaper published in Riga on 28 August 1944. It is a report on the apprehension of some Jews who by some miracle survived the period of the mass Aktions.

Jewish Gang Rendered Harmless

The security police and SD command headquarters in Latvia made the

following report. As the result of investigations that have recently been conducted, on 24 August a band of Jews consisting of six men and one woman was rendered harmless. They were all hiding in one of the apartments at 15 Plovuchaya Street in Riga. The men had revolvers and began shooting at members of the security police as they were being arrested. One of the policemen was fatally wounded. Two of the Jews tried to resist and were killed by the police; the rest tried to escape to the building next door. By now a heavy guard of police units and field gendarmes, as well as SS patrols, had surrounded the buildings on the block. All the buildings were searched from roof to cellar. All the Jews in the gang who were hiding were arrested. Once again a skirmish between the police and the Jews broke out.

Also arrested was a Latvian woman named Anna Polis, the owner of the apartment; she had hidden the Jews and had provided them with food. She will get the punishment she deserves. In addition, all the residents of the building at 15 Plovuchaya Street were detained.

The Jews who were arrested and those who hid them will be brought to justice as soon as an investigation has been completed.

Doctor Lipmanovich, Gruntman, Manke, Blyum, Berkovich, and others perished that day on Plovuchaya Street... . Anna Polis, the woman who had hidden them, was shot two days later. On the next street, however, a teacher named Elvira Ronis and her mother, the seventy-year-old Mariya Veninzh, hid a group of Jews for half a year and managed to keep them alive until the Red Army arrived. The Latvian Jan Lipke[14] hid more than thirty Jews on his farm for several months and then led them across the front line.

On the third day after the Germans had been driven out of Riga a spontaneous demonstration involving many people arose. That morning the people of Riga found out that at two in the afternoon a unit from the Latvian army's sharpshooter corps, which was being transferred to a different front, would march through the streets of the city. Thousands of the residents of Riga came out to Brivibas, the city's main street, with flowers in their arms.

The military band could be heard playing. Everyone eagerly awaited the appearance of the troops. Just then the people who were gathered there saw a small column of about sixty to seventy demonstrators coming from the direction of the Western Dvina. The standard bearer, his assistants, and many others in the column were dressed in striped prisoner's uniforms; all of them had yellow stars on their chests and large black numbers printed on their backs. They were deathly pale; it looked as though these people had not seen the light of day for a long time. The faces of some them were bruised and scratched; several walked with a heavy limp. For a minute it seemed as though these were not people treading the asphalt of Brivibas Street; it seemed, rather, that they were the ghosts of those who had been tortured and shot, risen from their terrible graves to come out and meet the Red Army.

And in fact there were people in that column who had lain in mass graves, people who had crawled out from under the bodies of their fathers and children and had spent three terrible years fighting for their lives as they were persecuted and hunted.

Among them were former residents of the Riga Ghetto.

They were the remnants of the 45,000 Jews of Riga murdered by the Hitlerites.[15]

When they saw the column of Jews, the residents of Riga lowered their heads. Generals and admirals standing at the foot of the Obelisk of Freedom conferred military honors upon the demonstrators. And in the square now overflowing with people it quickly became unusually quiet.

Soon the ordered ranks of the Latvian army corps marched past. The people showered the soldiers and officers with flowers. [Suddenly a voice from the crowd could be heard speaking Yiddish:

"Meyer, is that you?"

"Yes!"]

A young pale girl and an old man with a long, gray beard ran out from the row of spectators, threw themselves on Sergeant Moren, and started hugging and kissing him. With two medals on his chest, the sergeant who had covered a trail of fighting that stretched from Narofominsk to Riga now found his father and sister! Together they walked through the festive streets of Riga in the ranks of Red Army soldiers.

An hour later I met with some people wearing the striped prisoner's uniforms in one of the empty apartments on Gertrude Street. From them I heard the tale of the deaths of tens of thousands of their brothers.

Riga Jews with rifles and automatic weapons strapped to their shoulders came marching down Gertrude Street—soldiers, sergeants, and officers in the Red Army. They came to ask about their relatives and loved ones. Almost all of them received the same sad replies: "Shot during the first Aktion," "Committed suicide," "Tortured to death by the Gestapo." The soldiers tightened the straps on their automatic weapons and left, saying:

"We shall make them pay in full for everything."

Captain E. Gekhtman

From the Notebook of the Sculptor Elik Rivosh (Riga)

They are beginning to fence in several blocks in the Moscow Vorstadt to construct a ghetto. They Middle Ages have come to life before our very eyes.

Jews are forbidden to shop in stores, read newspapers, and… smoke.

A so-called Judenrat has been organized; [it consists of representatives of the local Jews. The Jewish Council is supposed to take care of medical needs, find housing for Jews, and so on.] Its members included G. Minsker, the engineer Blumenau, Kaufer, and M. Mints. On their sleeves they wear a blue band with a six-pointed star; of course, there is also a star on their chests and backs. In a word, they are adorned all over. The Judenrat is housed on Lacplesa Street, near the intersection with Moscow Street, in a former schoolhouse.

There have been many suicides in the city, primarily among the physicians.

My little boy Dimochka has grown nervous and afraid. As soon as a German soldier turns up in the street, he immediately runs inside the building. The poor child is frightened; he does not even understand what a Jew is. Our little girl is well; completely ignorant, she knows neither sorrow nor fear.

Mama brought us something to eat from the Moscow Vorstadt. Jewish rations, of course, are much smaller than the normal rations, and the food is of the lowest quality. Mama is shattered by what she sees and hears.

They are rapidly putting up the fence around the ghetto; there are already stretches of barbed wire in some places.

In the Moscow Vorstadt yellow stars pierce the eyes. Men are almost nowhere to be seen, only old women and children—but not a single child playing. All of them just sit in the gateways or cling to their mothers like hunted animals.

Everywhere you turn there are Jews dragging carts filled with all sorts of junk. The large schoolyard is overflowing with people. Here too there are very few men, and all the women have sad faces, their eyes full of tears. There are mountains of furniture along the fence, the junk they were allowed to take with them after they were evicted. The rain has caused some of the furniture to come apart.

We run into acquaintances; there is not one among them who has not lost a close relative. We met Noemi Bag. She wants to do away with herself and speaks constantly of her husband, who was burned to death in the synagogue. She gives the impression that she is not altogether in her right mind.

I ran into Fenya Falk; her husband and brother have been taken away. She has a sick mother on her hands, her little boy Felix, and a sister-in-law with two tiny children. It was painful for me to see how thin she had grown and how she had aged.

She and I were once riding bicycles down the highway, when she started fooling around and headed straight for the oncoming cars. I got angry with her and yelled at her, but she assured me that nothing bad could ever happen to her; she said she would die a very old woman.... .

Who can know his fate? Now death has raised it terrible Hitlerite paw over her.

Betty Markovna told me about an incident with her stepdaughter Heidi. A perfect picture of a beautiful northern girl, Heidi is tall with bright blonde hair, cornflower blue eyes, and a straight nose. She grew up in Vienna and, of course, speaks excellent German. A German officer once stopped her in the street and abruptly accused her of provocation: what was she doing with a Jewish star pinned to her, he wanted to know. Heidi calmly informed him that there was no reason to get excited, since she had a perfect right to wear such a "badge of honor." The officer flew into a rage.

It is a psychological riddle. During the last months before the war I worked in a shop with three other men: Noy Karlis, the foreman L., and a fellow named Anravs, whose profession was unknown. I had heard all sorts of unflattering stories about him, and everyone generally disliked him. I had no dealings with him, neither good nor bad. When I found myself outside the protection of the law, all the Christians who had been my childhood friends and all my friends at work disappeared. And here A. shows up, like a miracle. He came to my house and simply announced that he would like to help my family and me and that he would do anything he could. He said that he had decided to go to work repairing buildings damaged in the war and that he would give me a job. He started coming over to see us; he would bring Dima presents and play with him. In a word, he had taken a profound interest in our fate. This took great spiritual fortitude and nobility. It is a great joy for a person to have friends in times of need.... .

The resettlement of the Jews into the ghetto proceeded by districts. People in the central areas were the first to be sent there. There were many who had moved to streets in the Moscow Vorstadt that were not part of the ghetto, so they had to move again.

Dima's nanny Melanya arrived from Dimbazhi crying and pleading with us to let her take the little boy. I was ready to agree, but Alya declared that if we are all fated to perish, she did not want to leave an orphan behind. It is a mother's right to determine the care of her children: we did not give Dimochka to Melanya.

Evening. The wind is blowing, and an autumn rain is pouring down. There is something peaceful about such weather; you know you will have no unexpected guests. I sit on the bed with Alya and Dimochka, and as I get lost in thought I start singing a Soviet song. Dimochka climbs onto his mother's lap. Suddenly I hear her exclaim, "Dimochka, what's the matter, sweetie, why are you crying?" Dimochka does not answer, but he is all red. Through his tears he says in a soft voice, "Papa was singing a Soviet song that I haven't heard for a long time. [Mommy, I just hope the Germans didn't hear it."] Tears run down Alya's cheeks. I roll a cigarette. Such a tiny creature, and his little heart is broken.

It is our turn to move into the ghetto. I went with Alya to look for a place to live. I try in every way I can to calm her down and remove all her dark thoughts; I paint a picture of how we will get settled and promise her that I will even build a pigeon coop in the attic. We kiss and joke, trying to deceive one another. When it gets dark we head for the other side of the Dvina; it may be the last time we make this trip.

Tomorrow we must vacate our beloved nest, the home we have known for so long. I walk about the rooms with inexpressible anguish; I am choking with anger and despair. Dimochka is also terribly upset; he is constantly reminding us that we mustn't forget to bring along his toys. [He itemizes his favorites: the plaster dogs and elephants, his blocks and trains and trucks.] He anxiously asks, "Mommy, what if the Germans won't let me take my airplane? Can you hide it?" Then, like an adult, he comforts his mother: "If they take may bed, Mommy, don't worry—I can sleep with you."

Morning comes. There is an autumn wind.

A couple of policemen with briefcases and a business-like look show up in the courtyard with the janitor. They walk by with an air of importance and disdainfully look over our apartment.

I go to look for a cart.

Jews are not allowed to ride in a cart with Aryan horses and an Aryan driver; this is apparently regarded as an insult to the master race. But we decide to ignore that order.

We start loading the cart. The pile grows bigger. We tighten the ropes holding it on. Time to say good-bye... .

Slowly but surely the cart makes its way toward its destination. Already the bridge is behind us, and we are getting closer and closer to the barbed wire. The cart turns off Moscow Street and onto Lacplesa. The fence is to the right of us; a few minutes later were enter the gates of the ghetto. Sadovnikovskaya Street. The cobblestones are rough, and the cart shakes and rocks back and forth. There are carts ahead of us and behind us. The street is full of people. We arrive at our "apartment": Maza Kalnu Street, No. 11/9/7, Apartment 5. Taking a running start, the horse huffs and puffs through the gate. Hurriedly we struggle to unload our things, drag them into a shed, and lock them up for the time being. I go to the Gutmans to drag in the old people's things. On Ludzas Street, near a small building, someone calls out to me. I see my friend, a tinsmith named Markushevich, in a window. He really wants me to drop in for a few minutes; he wants to have a smoke and chat for a bit. Markushevich has a large family, including several grown daughters—one with children—and they all live in one room.

His wife, though not more than forty, looks like an old woman. I ask him where he works and how he's getting along. He does not complain. He has been poor all his life; he knows poverty as well as he knows his own mother. He works for the Germans. I thought that, as a highly skilled worker, he would get better treatment and that his living conditions would be better. When I told him so, he was taken aback: "What are you talking about, how can you say that? I should start working for them as a specialist and have them profit from my work? They have no idea that I even know how to cut tin. I work for them as a Jew who knows nothing about anything. Even if I were starving to death, I still would not let them know that I am a tin-smith." This meeting remained a bright spot for me. A small man noticed by no one, he is nonetheless brave and had a strong spirit! After that I never saw him again in the ghetto; most likely he was shot.

The last cart arrived with our small items and a load of firewood. The driver was in a hurry, and so he just dumped the firewood in the courtyard. It started to rain, and the firewood could not be left out in the open, so, keeping our spirits up, we went to work. Although she is tired Alya hauls the logs and keeps up with me. Tsapkikh runs out into the courtyard. Alya is agitated. I am glad she is still able to worry about the cat; it means she is still "alive." We are seriously concerned about our daughter. We left her with Mimi, and the ghetto could be closed any minute. After all, we receive no warning with regard to measures taken or orders issued; rather, they are presented to us as established facts. In a matter of minutes people are evicted, seized for work, or shot.

I personally believe that our daughter is better off there. Mimi will not throw her out, and since she is a girl, and not a boy, it is easier to conceal her Jewish origin. True, Mimi is old, but even if she dies, the neighbors will take our little girl in. If we survive, then we shall find her. If we perish, she will grow up and live without us. But I am afraid to even speak to Alya about it.

Mama arrived. Her "friends," the Romms, offered her nothing but a chair in which to spend the night—and she spent the whole night in the chair. Poor Mama: she probably envies Papa for having died a long time ago. When I look at her, I feel terrible. How quickly people fade away in their grief.

Alya and Mama argued all evening about what to put where. I don't really care, so I don't interfere. We are starting to get used to our new place. Dima's favorite pictures are hanging over his bed. The rug on the floor is folded in four, so that our little girl will not catch cold; after all, we are living in a shack.

Children run, play, and fight in the courtyard, but Dimochka is afraid to leave the building. He won't move a step away from Alya or me.

Our building is set back from the street, and so it is very quiet. In the central part of the ghetto they are hunting down people to send them off to work. Three parties are involved in this: the German Lieutenant Stanke, Sergeant Major Puchel, and a local German named Dralle. The Jews are ruthlessly beaten as they leave the ghetto and return from work. The Germans beat anyone they want to, with fists, sticks, or their boots.

Alya brought Lidochka over after lunch. Alya is tired and upset; it was hard for her to say good-bye to Mimi. Mimi and our janitor promised to pass food through the wire fence.

The ghetto has finally been closed. It has been officially announced that all contact with the outside world is forbidden. The guards at the gate thoroughly search everyone, especially the young women. With cold, filthy, crude hands, as everyone leers and jeers, the guards grope their clothing and fondle their naked bodies. The men are searched superficially, but to make up for it they are severely beaten. On the day after the ghetto was closed they caught a Jewish lad who had spent the night with his [Christian] girlfriend. They brought him to the ghetto and shot him in the yard next to the sentries; they left his body there as a deterrent.... .

Everyone is in a state of depression; you feel like you are in a mousetrap. The hunt for people has increased. Now they come looking for people in their apartments at night. It is like going fishing in an aquarium or hunting in a zoo. In the forest an animal can run away, hide, or fight back. But what can a person do in the ghetto? Surrounded by a fence with guards on the other side, we are like livestock in a pen.

I went to Antokol, a civil engineer who worked for the city council for twenty years. Antokol said there is not a single stove maker in the entire ghetto and that if I should try to become one, it would be a blessing for the ghetto.

The news that the Judenrat had found a stove maker spread throughout the ghetto. That very evening my first customer came to see me.

The next morning I did not even have a chance to have a bite to eat, when there was a knock at my door. Some man wanted to see me. About what? He tells me that he has rented what used to be a shop not far from here, and his mother and sister are living there. But the shop does not have a stove; he needs to have just a small stove built. No sooner did this customer leave than my cousin Roza Girshberg showed up.

There is a new unpleasant surprise: the distribution of milk has been curtailed. Such a luxury does not belong to Jewish children. The hospital is also denied milk.

Since instances of food being passed over the wire fence have been noted, a second fence has been erected—cutting off not the street, of course, but the sidewalk. In some places—on Gersikas, Lazdonas, and other streets—the sidewalk is so narrow that you can only pass sideways to avoid getting your clothes caught on the barbed wire. A fat person cannot get by at all. In order to avoid difficulties, the Judenrat had ordered that all courtyards adjacent to streets along the periphery of the ghetto be connected to one another; that way pedestrian traffic can move through the courtyards. Our courtyard has become a thoroughfare, and people are constantly scurrying past our window.

This is what happened to our former neighbor from Sassenhof, a boy named B. Zaks. He was walking down Bolshaya Gornaya Street. A guard yelled out to him: "Hey, Yid, what time is it?" The boy folded back his glove, looked at his watch, and answered the question. The soldier pointed his rifle at him and said, "And now, while you're still in one piece, toss the watch in the snow, if you want to stay alive!"

... In the evening we bathe our little girl. Sitting in the bathtub, splashing around like a duck and happily playing, she does not have a care in the world. She is as plump and healthy as ever, and it is a joy to hold her in my arms. Dimochka dries off her feet and kisses her rosy little heels. She squeals with laughter and pulls at his hair. Alya and Mama are filled with joy at this idyllic scene.... . They say that people show their true feelings toward one another only in times of need. Never before have Alya and I shown each other so much tenderness, care, and attention.

After Lidochka was done, Alya "bathed" in the same water. She has grown so thin that the children's tub was almost big enough for her. The soapy water was not poured out but was used to wash her underwear. That's economizing!

It is seven o'clock in the morning. Mama is already up; she has lit the stove, cooked some potatoes, and poured the tea. Fridman's son Izka and his friend arrive while we are eating breakfast; they are my "apprentices." I grab my briefcase full of tools, the boys load a box of materials on the sleigh, and we set out for Gertsmark's place. On Gersikas Street we walk down sidewalks so narrow that I have trouble passing. Next to us were Russians and Latvians on their way to work, laborers like us. But the barbed wire is between us, [and it creates an abyss. I try not to see or notice the people on the other side.... .]

The building at No. 5. Heavy old gates, a rickety fence. To the right there is a large building, to the left a half-demolished shack. There is a steep, narrow wooden flight of worn-out steps. I lean against a door with a small window half boarded up with plywood. I knock once, then twice; no one answers. Finally my efforts pay off, and the door opens. I go in. There is a garret, an average-sized room, with black walls. It is as cold as it is out in the yard. Like a worn road, the floor is full of dents and holes; bottles plug up the rat holes along the baseboards. In the middle of the room there is a table with a stool; next to it is a big old axe. Next to the wall stands an iron bed buried under a pile of rags. Having let me in, the lady of the "house" goes back to the bed and pulls the rags over herself. Only then does she ask who I am and why I have come. I thought she would be glad, but I am deeply mistaken. I look at her with curiosity. She is an old woman of sixty or seventy. Her face has an expression of such indifference toward everything that I am taken aback. I go to work dismantling the heater and "examining" the stove; both are in terrible condition. Like a "specialist," I have to strain my brain as to how I am going to fix everything. My clay for repairing stoves is as hard as a rock; I need hot water, and I ask the old woman to help me. With the same expressionless face she crawls out of her lair and goes to ask a neighbor for some hot water. She comes back and says the water would be ready soon.

Working warmed me up. I took off my coat and saw a nail in the wall. I asked her: "Tell me, ma'am, are there any bedbugs or lice on the wall? Is it okay for me to hang up my coat?" "Of course, dear, we have everything, bedbugs and lice, but you don't have to worry about hanging up your coat—they don't crawl out of their holes when it's so cold." I did not want to bother the old woman and went to fetch the water myself; I wanted to get a look at the neighbors anyway. Next to her door was another door covered with an old blanket. A little girl let me in. The room and the kitchen were in approximately the same condition as the old woman's, only they were full of old junk. A large family lived there: several small children, a teenager, adults, and an old woman.... . A little girl was sitting on a pot in the middle of the room and playing with a rag.

My hands grew numb from the cold clay, and from time to time I dipped them into the hot water. I was hurrying, since it was nearly four o'clock, and I still had a "special" order to fill, for which I expected to receive riches—two eggs and a pack of tobacco.

I was as dirty as a chimney sweep, but I was in a good mood. It gives you great pleasure when your work is useful not only to yourself but to others as well. I am convinced that in the ghetto, a stove maker in the winter is no less important than a doctor in an epidemic.

After washing up and eating some supper, I went over to Fridman's. I did not want to remain in debt to him. He once gave me a matchbox full of tobacco; now that I was rich, I could give him a treat. Fridman has a relatively nice apartment: a room and a small kitchen. It is impossible to sleep there, but it is still a lodging. His wife is a charming woman with a deep sense of warmth and kindness. Like most families, they have their cross to bear. Besides their two sons—my assistant Izka and a younger boy of sixteen—they have a little girl. She is twelve, but she is the size of Dima, a cripple with what they call "withered feet." She sits for days on end cutting things out of paper, stringing beads, or sewing rags together. She speaks intelligently, like an adult, and is always sad. She loves to have children come see her, but how she must suffer when she sees them running around. The poor girl worships her parents and brothers. The younger brother tries to cheer her up. I did not expect such tenderness from a boy his age. While Fridman and I were smoking and exchanging news and hopes, a neighbor from another apartment came in. He said that he was working somewhere in the Bikernieki Forest today. They were digging long, deep pits in the woods. "Without a doubt," he said, "these are future fortifications, which means they are expecting a Soviet offensive."

We optimists have developed the ability to see the good side of everything. I do not know whether it is smart or stupid, but in any case it is easier to live that way. I have made it my obligation whenever I am around others, friends or strangers, to joke and try to cheer them up in times of unhappiness and failure. I know that they are not digging these pits for fortifications but for some other purpose. Can it be? I drive away the insane thoughts.

The number of beggars in the ghetto increases every day. They wander about the apartments trying to get something to eat. They get a few potatoes, some turnips, a bowl of soup. There is another type of beggar, one who does not live by begging. In a courtyard on Sarkanu Street I saw a little old man busily searching for potato peelings and breadcrumbs in a garbage dump. They way he was so careful to avoid being noticed made it clear that he was no professional. He saw me only after I had walked by; he tried to act like he was doing something else entirely.

An anthill in the forest does not make any special impression on a passerby; it is just a pile of ants, that's all. That is how our ghetto is; outwardly everyone here is gray, bustling, frightened, and half-starved. But, in fact, life within the ghetto is full of tension.

Professor Dubnow is living in a shelter on Sadovnikovskaya Street, where he is writing his *History of Europe*. In the hospital on Ludzas Street doctors are operating on patients.

There are several funerals every day in the ghetto. All day long, simple sleds with a black box and two or three people walking behind make their way down Ludzas Street to the cemetery. Sometimes the sleds move more rapidly, which means there were no relatives.

Another young fellow was recently shot near the wire.

Orders have been posted on the buildings: the Jews have one week to turn over all their gold, silver, valuables, and rugs. When the week is up there will be a search. Anyone holding back will be severely punished. We know only one punishment: to be shot.

Alya and I have only our thin wedding rings; Alya has two or three other rings, and that is all.

The order affected me in another way. My friends came to me and asked me to hide their valuables. I have gone to many of my friends' homes to make "safes," in a door for this one, in the corner of a cupboard for that one, under the floor for this one, in a heel for that one. I advised them to throw their silver into the toilet or bury it; just don't give it to the Germans.

The lack of food is having an effect on Alya. The other day she stood in line for a long time. When she finally had her turn and was about to leave, her head started spinning, and she fainted—for the first time in her life.

I go to a job. I open the door. The first thing I see is a bed. A woman is lying there exhausted; next to her is a little boy under a blanket with his neck bundled up. At the foot of the bed are three more children wearing little coats, huddled together like animals. Along the opposite wall is a door resting flat on some bricks; it is covered with a blanket and some gray pillows. An earthenware pot, a bucket, and a chair are the only furnishings. "Who are you? What are you doing here?" I explain that the Judenrat sent me to repair the heater and stove. I ask whether there is anything I can do to help her. "How can you help? I have gallstones and probably cancer. We have no heating fuel and nothing to eat."

A disheveled man is standing in the kitchen; his name is Khaim. He is the owner of this wealth. I start working. Khaim started fidgeting around; he ran to get some hot water—in a word, he came to life. I could see that it was terrible for him to be left alone with his family; he is glad to be around other people. The kitchen is in half-darkness; part of the window is covered with paper. On the floor are several pots, some dirty dishes, a basket of frozen potatoes, a box—that is all. It is terribly cold. Again a pitiful, tormented voice can be heard coming from behind the door: "My poor, poor Khaim. Who will take care of you when I'm gone? What will you do with these little ones?"

There is a knock at the door. Khaim lets in a young man who is speaking German with a foreign accent. He is a Czech immigrant. He has no one in the ghetto; he has not eaten for three days. He wants to know if Khaim might have something for him to eat. Without saying a word, Khaim takes out an earthen pot of boiled potato skins that were still warm. From somewhere he pulls out a small cup of salt. "Eat right out of the pot; that way it won't get cold so quickly. Eat as much as you want; we have plenty of potatoes. Don't be shy." Khaim expresses his regret that he has nothing more to offer. The fellow is hungry, but he sees that he is getting food from another beggar, one who is telling him not to be shy! Next Khaim stuffs several potatoes into the man's pocket.

The days fly by; there is more and more work to be done. Rumors fly through the ghetto, each more fantastic than the other. I try not to pay any attention to them or think about them.

A new announcement has been issued in the ghetto: all Jews must immediately inform the police of any non-Jews who are hiding in the ghetto. If there should be any infraction of the order, the entire ghetto will suffer. [They say German deserters are hiding in the ghetto. I found out from a friend that there had been a search and that two people were caught. Judging from the description, one of them was the beggar I met in the building on Daugavpils Street, the one who was posing as a Czech. The poor fellow: now instead of potatoes he will get a bullet.]

I do not work for the Judenrat on Saturdays; it is my "day off."

This Saturday I decided to rest and go nowhere.

Dima and I wanted to make a snowman, but the snow was too dry. We stayed in; he sat in my lap, and I read him Pushkin's "Tale of the Priest and His Worker Balda." Dima loves this fairy tale, and he can listen to it over and over again. Lidochka was playing around on the floor.

Rumors, endless rumors.

They say that only able-bodied men will be allowed to remain in the ghetto; women and children will be sent to a camp, perhaps in Lublin. The ghetto itself will serve another purpose. All of this is very troubling; people are lost in apprehensions and suppositions. Just the other day the Judenrat received an order to build a bathhouse, and an entire building was designated for setting up various workshops. If the ghetto has been set up for only a few months, then why were non-Jews moved out, and why are we doing all this "construction?"

Jewish doctors have apparently received an order to take the lives of all patients who are critically ill. According to the rumors, in the hospitals in Germany all patients who are seriously ill and even the patients who are too weak to live a normal life are poisoned with a sweetener added to their coffee.

People in the ghetto are extremely agitated. But there is not a sound, not a cry, not a single lively conversation. On the contrary, it is as quiet as a funeral. Everyone is expecting something terrible; everyone senses that a storm of blood and tears will soon burst forth.

From minute to minute we await a new order. The word *Aktion* flashes by. At first it went right past us; we did not understand it.

We did not have long to wait. Two orders came immediately:

Order No. 1: [On 28 November 1941 (I many be mistaken about the date, since I do not remember exactly what it was)] at 7:00 A.M. all men aged seventeen and older are to assemble on Sadovnikovskaya Street.

Order No. 2: All men incapable of working and all women and children are to prepare for resettlement in a camp. Every person may take along up to twenty kilograms of luggage. The day and hour of the resettlement will be announced separately.

After the second order came, the first one somehow faded into the background. All the old men, without exception, realized that they had been sentenced to death. It was hard to look at them, men condemned to death without knowing what they were guilty of. Alya's Aunt Sofya Osipovna, a very reserved old woman, came to see her. She seemed to be sitting there calmly, but tears were flowing down her cheeks. She has a son in America; no one else. She asks Alya and me to give him her regards when times are better but not to tell him how she died. "Why should my son suffer any unnecessary grief?"

All the neighbors are providing each other with whatever they can. Warm things, shoes, food—everything has become common property. Today everyone is generous and is sincerely sharing everything. Today there is no more "mine" and "yours"; today there is only "ours."

I dropped in to see Magarik along the way. His wife and I kiss like brother and sister. All the women have become dear and beloved to me; I feel so sorry for all of them, they behave so heroically. I am convinced that women are better able to endure serious upheavals. The children instinctively sense their ruin; they are quiet and dejected; they show no capriciousness, no tears, no anxiety. Mine too have hidden somewhere, like mice. Mama goes around with a stone-like face. Alya is putting aside some warm things for me. It is evening now; I am to leave tomorrow at first light. Will I ever return? Will I ever see my dear ones again?

We know it is our last night together. Will I ever see Alya again? I will never again spend a night under the same roof with Mama, of that I am certain. Poor, dear Mama, forgive me for being powerless to watch over you in your old age.

The alarm clock calmly ticks away, its hands unmercifully tracing their path. The hours pass. My shirt has grown wet where Alya is resting her head is on my shoulder. Heavy, silent tears. What is happening in her soul, what is happening in the souls of thousands of women, no one knows; indeed it is impossible for words to convey. And the alarm clock continues to tick.

People are already bustling about in the courtyard. They stand in bunches, in small groups. It is dark; their faces are not visible.

Already the street is full of people. I step out of the ranks and go up on the porch of a building to see how long the column is. It is a strange and terrifying sight. It reminds me of a grandiose funeral. Young men are leading many of the old men by the hand. The column slowly moves forward and stops on Sadovnikovskaya Street. It seems that the authorities are afraid of a "slave uprising," because there are four or five fascists armed to the teeth every few feet.

It is freezing cold. Most of the people are jumping up and down to keep from freezing. If you were looking only at their feet, and not at their faces, you might think they were happy. The column gradually loses its shape and turns into a large crowd. People are trading places, looking for friends. I see my teacher Grigory Yakovlevich in the distance. He is standing there, leaning on a stick. His eyes are swollen with tears and frost; the cold has transformed them into slits that are barely visible. He looks at me, and his lips start to tremble. He is so overwhelmed that for a long time he is unable to say a word. He takes my hand and shakes it convulsively: "Farewell, Elik. This is the last time I shall ever see you. It is difficult knowing that soon I shall be destroyed like an old, useless rag. My Fanny will be destroyed too. See to it that you do not lose heart. You are still young; you will still live to see brighter days. Think of your old teacher and friend from time to time. Let me kiss you good-bye."

At that moment a policeman walked by and shouted an order that all invalids and people over sixty may go home.

The crowd came alive and was abuzz. Loud German voices could be heard barking commands in the distance. With rapid steps, Puchel, Stanke, and others came running down the sidewalk.

Stanke went up to the front of our group as if he were leading a parade. His speech and his order are laconic: "It is now two o'clock. Run home, pack your things, and gather at the gate of the Little Ghetto at 2:30. March!"

I stumble into my house all out of breath. It is already ten after two. I have to be at the gate in twenty minutes. All the necessary items fly into the suitcase; I put my tools in a sack and bundle up a pillow and blanket. I can sit "quietly" for ten minutes. I hear some news: Liza L. has had a baby. The birth was difficult, but both she and the baby are "out of danger."

Alya and I agree that no matter where we may be sent and no matter what might happen to us, we shall let our friends in Sassenhof know the first chance we get.

That way we shall always be able to find each other. We make no such arrangement with Mama; it is superfluous. Mama's lips are cold, her face like stone. Our little girl is sleeping, lying on her tummy; her rosy heel is sticking out from under the blanket. I lean over and tickle her heel with my moustache; her little foot disappears back under the blanket. I hugged Dima so very tight. But he did not cry out. What will happen to him? What will they do with him? Why? For what? Hatred, despair, and hope blend into one lump that chokes and squeezes my throat. Our greatest suffering comes not from our own pain but from that of our closest friends and loved ones.

There is a crowd at the gate of the Little Ghetto. The guards keep order, sometime using their rifle butts. Near the gates stands a handsome officer, like a statue; he is the new assistant to the commandant of the ghetto. He is good looking, with eyes the likes of which you have rarely seen. They are not human eyes; they are simply organs for seeing. They are like bright, transparent glass, like dead, beautiful stone. They contain neither boredom nor love nor hate; they see but express nothing. To look for pity or mercy in those eyes is just as hopeless as trying to make them laugh.

Gertsmark met his friend S. Finkelshtein. He lives at 26 Liksnas Street and was trying to get into his apartment. He suggested that we do the same. We hurry, so as to get there before the others. Finkelshtein and his family have lived in this apartment since yesterday. He has a wife and a two-year-old daughter. In every little thing, in every object, he sees the image of his wife and daughter. For a few minutes he tries to give the appearance of being brave, but he is suddenly overwhelmed by a wave of despair; he falls to the floor, sobbing and shaking.

Vilyanu Street runs between Bolshaya Gornaya and Ludzas; it is short and wide, like a square. On Bolshaya Gornaya there is a new gate leading from the ghetto to "freedom." The entire street is full of people. Here and there they are forming columns. The Germans are walking up and down gathering people together.

My column is called the "Cable" column. Knowing what this word signifies and what hard labor awaits us, several of my comrades in misfortune look for a way out. Finally a column of 120 men is selected. We turn off Moscow Street down a narrow side street, go past the Braun Factory, and come out on the Dvina River. There is a sawmill on the island, and the island is connected to the riverbank by a dam. The dam is 200 to 250 meters long; there they are laying the famous cable. It is not a comfortable work site in the winter; the wind howls, and it is freezing cold.

Under the awning overhanging the factory office are picks, shovels, and crowbars. Pits are being dug approximately three and a half meters apart; then the bottoms of the pits are connected by tunnels. They can be dug only by lying on your side or on your stomach. The most unpleasant and most difficult thing is digging through to soft sand. Not knowing how to do earthwork or how to work with frozen ground, it is like trying to dig a pit in a rock. I have often had to dig holes for fence posts in the winter, and I dug trenches when I was in the army, so I am not afraid of this work. For a man who is physically weak, of course, the work is more than he can take; it is torture for him.

We have three foremen. The chief engineer is a German. He is a big man with a red, wind-blown face, cold, tiny eyes, thin lips, and a broad chin. They say that in his youth he was an amateur boxer and that when talking to people he likes to use his fists and sometimes his feet to drive home his point. We work in pairs on each pit. One of us chops up pieces of frozen earth with a crowbar, and the other tosses them to the side. You cannot work on an empty stomach; you will freeze. So the cold drives us to work hard. In the afternoon we are allowed to stand in small groups for thirty minutes; that is considered our lunch break. We are not allowed inside where the factory workers are, and we are forbidden to talk to them. Some of the workers leave the factory to go home for lunch. One of them is a good friend of mine. We were very close when we worked at the factory, and we served together on various commissions for the IOAR. Unnoticed by the others, I go over to him on the path, and we walk together for a few minutes. He slips a pack of cigarettes into my pocket. "... the front is getting closer, here is my address... it may come in handy." We inconspicuously give each other a firm handshake.

The second half of the day passes like the first, only it is harder to work; it is very cold, and we are hungry. It is getting dark. The Germans quickly count us, and we head out. There is the ghetto fence, and we can see the gates. A moment later the word *Aktion* passes through the column. There has been an Aktion in the ghetto!

We do not walk the last few dozen meters—we run. The guards at the gate do not count us; there is no search. The sentry does not look at us; can it be that something in his conscience has stirred? As I run I find out that some of the people in the Big Ghetto were taken away in the wee hours of the morning and that many were murdered; workers in the commando for removing bodies labored all day long. I run for the gates. The guard turns his back to us and looks the other way; none of them now can look us in the eyes. Finally I am through the gates and in the Big Ghetto. The street is empty, the shutters are closed, and many windows are darkened. There are horseshoe tracks, piles of dung, and puddles of blood all over the sidewalk. Puddles, stains, trails, and drops of blood. It appears that the street has been cleaned, but in places there are gloves and children's galoshes trampled down into the snow. Here and there you step on small copper tubes: spent cartridges from revolvers. Without noticing, I step in some blood. Strange: it is freezing, but the blood is still sticky.

Nothing has changed in our courtyard. It is still light out, but the windows in our little building are dark. I knock twice on the window; it is our prearranged signal. Mama and Alya open the door for me. Their faces are blank. The apartment is in a state of unusual disorder; the dishes are unwashed, the beds unmade. They did not sleep all night; they sat without getting undressed and waited for the Germans to come for them. The children went to bed in their clothes. That evening they found out that on Katolicheskaya, Sadovnikovskaya, and Moscow Streets "it had already begun."

The street is littered with the bodies of old men. For the sake of economy and convenience they were shot right in the ghetto.

Many killed themselves that night, including several physicians. Alya's cousin Lelya Bordo slit her wrists and those of her five-year-old son Zhorzhik. They were found the next morning in their beds, covered with blood. Zhorzhik was already dead; his mother is in the hospital. They have given her blood transfusions, and she will live. But why save Lelya? Try to grasp it, to understand for a moment, what must take place in the soul of such a mother, when she has taken a razor and slit her little boy's wrists... .

On this day puddles of blood have become a common sight. We walk past them and step in them. We stop by a building on the corner of Daugavpilskaya and Ludzas. The first thing we see is that the front door has been broken down with an axe. The first apartment is wide open. The beds are smashed, pillows and clothing are all over the floor; everything is in a state of chaos. On the table lie bits of uneaten food and unfinished tea. It looks as though the people were driven away unexpectedly and in a hurry. The door to the apartment on the left in half open, and there is a strong draft. We pass through the kitchen and into a room; its window is broken, and the wind is blowing in. Someone is lying in the bed. We walk up and gaze into the face of a dead man. He is an old man with a short, gray beard; his eyes are fixed on the ceiling in a glassy stare.

I do no know why, but I cover him up again; I am even careful to leave no part of him uncovered—after all, the window is broken. That was enough for first impressions.

When I return home, Mama lets me in and gives me a sign to make no noise. In the disordered room on an unmade bed, covered with a coat, Alya is sleeping. The children have also gone to sleep, even though it is only seven o'clock. Mama will kiss Alya and the children for me; I must hurry.

Those who have lost their loved ones, whose families have been driven away, are certain that the ones remaining will also be taken. They have lost all hope and see things clearly; they are in despair, but they are sober. Those of us whose relatives are still "at home" are poisoned by hope. We are still asleep. We still do not understand all the cruel consistency of the Aktions.

Two residents from our apartment building worked on the removal and burial of bodies. The number of people murdered inside the ghetto was five or six hundred. Generally only the old and the sick were shot; perhaps several young people and children also happened to be murdered. They were shot in the head—the famous *Kopfschuss*.

At first light the next morning we set out for the assembly place. I spent the day working at the harbor, loading coal. I was at the "Cable" again, and it was horribly cold. These [days] they no longer allow us into the Big Ghetto to see our families, but the police assure us that everything is quiet there. As for what happened to the first group that was taken away, no one knows exactly. The wildest rumors are circulating, including the most fantastic one of all, namely that no one was sent to a camp, but they were taken in groups to a nearby forest and all shot with machine guns. At the police station they told us that we would be able to visit our families two or three times a week.

Today on the way back from work I found out that people are being allowed into the Big Ghetto; I have not seen my family for six days, and in our situation six days are an eternity. Without going first to my place, I ran to the gates. The guard was warming himself next to a fire and was not interested in anything; I walked unhindered onto Ludzas Street. Snow had fallen in the last few days, and a carpet of white covered the street, hiding all traces of the recent tragedy. The emptiness of the ghetto is striking. After all, no one has been moved out of this area; the buildings are full of people. But what an empty street, what an ominous silence! I hurry so as not to lose a single precious minute. Our courtyard is covered with snow; only a narrow path leads from building to building... .

We say almost nothing. We just sit very close together and gaze at one another's hands.

I chopped wood for the week, cleaned the stove pipe, and ate some potatoes with salt. Then it was time once again to say good-bye. Good-bye, Mama; good-bye, children; good-bye, my beloved Alya. Perhaps I shall come again in a week; perhaps we are saying good-bye forever... .

The door closed behind me. The first stars are in the sky; the snow crunches under my feet. I feel like filling my chest with a deep breath of the winter air, but something inexpressible is pressing against my breast.

During my absence the number of people in our apartment grew larger. Some complete strangers have shown up. They have carefully shaved their beards, and even their heads, so that no gray hair can be seen. With all their might they want to look young and capable of working.

Gradually they begin to settle down to rest. It is dark in our rooms. You can hear the sound of whispering, individual words, and then an oppressive silence sets in. But what is that? It sounds like someone is knocking somewhere very close by, and suddenly wild shouting tears through the nocturnal silence: *Aufmachen, Schweinhunde, oder wir schiessen!*[16] We are at the window in seconds. Thanks to the snow and the moon, we can see everything. There is a group of armed people banging at the door of the two-story building across from us; along our fence there is a heavy guard of soldiers. The word *Aktion* shoots through the apartment is a matter of seconds. We can hear shouting and cursing. A gunshot rings out, an axe flashes, [and the doors to a cellar are smashed;] there is a light in the cellar. A soldier crawls through a window, and a few minutes later the front doors are open. A woman with a travel bag on her back darts past a window. Individual gunshots can be heard coming from the Big Ghetto. [The same thing is happening there.] Figures appear as they are driven out of the building across from us. They are lined up in pairs; many women have bags on their backs and children in their arms. Soldiers pace back and forth with cigarettes in their teeth. It is freezing outside, and the women go on standing and standing there with their children. Soon it is 1:00 A.M. Finally, after 1:30, the command is given, and, to the sound of cheerful chat and abusive language, the column moves toward Ludzas Street. Shots can be heard more and more frequently. Every shot means that someone's life has been ended. I lie on the bed. I feel nothing, neither in my body nor in my soul—I am like a piece of wood... .

Is it possible that Mama, Alya, Dima, and my little girl have been driven out of their building? Why? For what? No, it cannot be true, I am only dreaming.

There is now movement in the building; it is morning, but it is still dark out. I shall not go to work today; I must know what happened during the Aktion. To avoid being caught by one of the slave hunters, I walk with Gertsmark to the technical section. They already know everything there. Early this morning all the people who were left in the ghetto were hauled away. There is rampant disorder in the streets; a work detail is supposed to assemble around nine o'clock to clean up. The technical section is to assign people to work... at the cemetery. I join them. We drag out shovels, picks, and crowbars from a storehouse. The traces of a sleepless night can be seen on the faces of all. All are silent and gray.

The sun has risen, and the morning has set in unnoticed. The streets in the Big Ghetto are unrecognizable. Where is yesterday's snow? It has disappeared; it has been ground up, pressed down, and dirtied. I have seen streets after the retreat of an army, with broken equipment and vehicles, the bodies of people and horses, and all kinds of military debris; but those were the traces of a battle. These were the traces of a slaughter. The street is filled with blood; over night the white snow has turned gray with streaks of red. The bodies... they are old men, women, and children! Trampled carriages, children's sleds, purses, gloves, and galoshes, bags of food, baby bottles with frozen oatmeal in them, baby shoes. The bodies are still warm and supple. The faces are covered with blood, the eyes wide open.

We are to take the bodies to the cemetery. We put them the on sleds and carts two at a time. When we haul them in a cart they move back and forth as if they were alive, and blood falls into the snow in lumps.

For the time being we take the bodies just inside the cemetery gates, where we lay them out in rows, men and women separately. Members of the council search the murder victims for documents. We brought in a little boy of about twelve. He is a lovely, handsome child in a gray coat with a fur collar and new boots. He lies on his back with his blue eyes wide open. A bullet from a revolver hit him in the back of the head, and only part of his collar is splattered with blood. He lies there like a doll; it is hard to believe that just a short while ago he was a living and probably a happy child.

Others replace us, and now we go to dig the graves. We dig a pit next to the synagogue's burned-out cemetery. The earth is so frozen that we have to chip away pieces of it as if we were chipping stone. You do not notice the blood flowing from the lip you have bitten. There are no clear thoughts, just fragments. I am outwardly calm; I light a cigarette, spit blood, and continue biting my lip. Finally we have broken through the frozen layer of earth; we cut away roots, and the pit becomes noticeably deeper. It is a large grave, about two meters by five. We are already chest deep in the ground; we dig out another meter and then start burying them. Some of the bodies have already been brought in; for the time being they have been laid along the walls of the synagogue that are still standing. Some of them are in a half-sitting position.

A policeman comes up and warns us that no one is to leave the cemetery or even go up to the fence. It seems that some streets—the outermost ones—did not get cleaned out during the night; now they are leading the last column through the ghetto. The policeman warns us that the curious will be shot. We obey and wait. We do not have to wait long before we can hear the familiar shouting. The heads and shoulders of mounted guards appear above the fence; from beyond the fence comes the sound of the treading of many feet. The iron gates of the cemetery are twenty-five to thirty centimeters above the ground. Standing in the pit, you can see an endless number of feet. The feet move carefully, taking small steps, as though they were afraid of slipping. They are all the feet of women, with the little feet of children flashing among them; one of them is fumbling along with a walking stick. In the little building opposite the cemetery, in a garret window, a curtain is open; through it you can see the faces of several women. They have an expression of horror, of mute reproach and sympathy. The feet of the victims and the heads of the horsemen. These feet bespeak so much horror and these heads and shoulders so much insolence and self-satisfaction. We have no weapons, only hatred and a thirst for revenge, but this is no help to our sorrow. Beyond the fence there is an amazing silence; from time to time we hear a child crying or the shout of a guard. We can no longer see the feet; the horsemen slowly move into the distance. One of the women in the window raises a handkerchief to her eyes. The curtain is pulled shut. Before us lie the half-sitting bodies. Their faces have not changed.... .

The pit is ready, but a different shift will do the burying; hey have already shown up, and we can go rest. For some reason I take the wedding ring off my finger and bury it in the bottom of the grave. With it I bury my past and my hope.

We go to the first gate to take a look at the bodies that have just been brought in; there may be loved ones among them. We walk along a narrow, snow-covered path between the old graves. The sun is already low and casts a long, uneven shadow. My father is buried in this cemetery. The cemetery is old, and no one has been buried in it for many years. It did not expect such a flood of the dead. The rows of bodies next to the gate do not get any smaller. I go over and take a look. There are several familiar faces, old men. Behind the bushes, about seventy meters to the left of the gates, the bodies are quickly being carried to the grave. The stretchers are so saturated with blood that they look as though they have been painted red.

The sun is sinking lower. They must hasten their work. The pit quickly fills up with frozen sand. The large, light yellow mound is getting bigger. Everything is quiet. Only beyond the fence is there movement; you can hear the scraping of sleds and carriages on their way to the cemetery. And behold, as if by some silent agreement, forty to fifty Jews stand around the grave in a semicircle, facing east. Those who have just buried their dead mothers and fathers step forward. I do not pray, but I stand there as though in a trance, without feeling my body, only my heart is ready to burst out of my chest; I have goose pimples all over the nape of my neck.

I did not understand the words of the prayer, and its meaning was incomprehensible to me; I only know that that this scene has been burned into my memory with a red-hot iron.

Twilight. The street along which we are walking has not been cleaned up yet; there are no bodies, but stains have been left in their place.

Our apartment is full of people. We try not to speak about what has happened, at least not now.

I lay down and immediately fell asleep without dreams or nightmares. I woke up around ten. I slowly come to my senses. Gertsmark is sitting across from me, his head buried in his hands. His eyes are full of tears, but his face is dry. His lips repeat over and over: "Poor people, poor people." His words cut into my heart like a knife. In an instant everything appeared in bright, living colors. I saw the doors to our little home fly open; I saw people with green armbands break in. Alya hurriedly wraps Dima and snatches our sleeping little girl from her bed. Mama helps with trembling hands. With a bag slung over her shoulder, Alya pushes the carriage with our little girl in it. With a bag on her back too, Mama is leading Dima by the hand. They join up with the column; they wait, freeze, and wait. What was happening in their souls, what did they experience? They took that secret with them...

Prepared for publication by Vasily Grossman and R. Kovnator

The Story of Sema Shpungin (Dvinsk)

I am sixteen years old. When the Germans came, I was twelve. I was in the fifth grade at the time. We lived in Dvinsk, at 83/85 Rainis Street. My father, Ilya Shpungin, was a photographer. I had a mother and a six-year-old sister named Roza.

When the Germans came, my whole family and many friends left Dvinsk on foot. We walked during the bombing. We got all the way to Belorussia; there the Germans caught up with us and cut off our path. We realized we could go no further and turned back to our hometown.

They were seizing Jews in the streets of Dvinsk and taking them to the prison, where they were severely tormented. They were forced to endlessly lie down on the ground and jump up again; those who could not do it fast enough were shot. We did not make it to our building; our building had been burned down, so we stayed with Grandma for a while; then we were moved into the ghetto. [This was "fortunate," because many people were being shot in the prison. They were murdered in the yard and in the garden outside the railroad station.]

By 20 July all the Jews who were still alive were in the ghetto. It was set up on the opposite bank of the Dvina, across from the fort, in an old building. The Germans themselves said that it was not fit for horses. Doctor Gurevich was with us. He said that the children would not stay alive here for more than two months. But the children lived longer than that.

It was very crowded and dirty. And very cold: we lived without glass in the windows, and the building was made of stone. After about two weeks the Germans ordered all the old men to assemble in the courtyard and said that they would be taken to a "second camp." Instead the old men were shot. At the same time they shot everyone who had come to Dvinsk from other places. The executioners took for themselves the things that had belonged to the ones who were murdered.

Later the "selection" began. This was done almost every day. People were assembled and divided into two groups. No one knew why he was in one or the other group or what would happen to his group: whether they would be taken out to work or to be shot.

The executioners were very often drunk.

It was very cold. The Germans suddenly announced a "quarantine." During the quarantine it was forbidden to leave the city even to go to work. Each of us received 125 grams of horrible bread and water with rotten cabbage. People began to swell up from hunger. One woman named Meyerovich, who had seven children, secretly tried to get bread from the workers who were working outside the ghetto. They caught her and shot her right in front of everyone. Her children were murdered on 1 May 1942.

I came down with typhus and was hidden inside the ghetto itself so that the Germans would not kill me. I recovered.

Our family stayed alive until 6 November. We were even surprised that all four of us had survived. Papa was working; he secretly got us a little food. He did not eat what they gave him at work but secretly brought it into the ghetto.

On 6 November a big selection was held. One woman who was standing near us made a run for it. They did not catch her, and the Germans announced that because of her ten others would be shot. They had already selected my mother and sister, and they stepped out of the ranks. I was supposed to go too. But I grabbed hold of Mama's hand; she was holding my sister, and I pulled them back into the crowd. It was a thick crowd, and the Germans did not notice.

On 6 November the men who were working for the Germans, including my father, left. After their departure everyone was forced into the courtyard. First they gave an order that the members of the "committee" that the Germans had appointed were to step out; then medical workers and their families were ordered to line up separately. I do not know how I guessed that the ones left would be murdered. I went over to the medical workers and started begging someone, anyone, to tell them that we were their relatives. A dentist named Magid, who had a small daughter, said to me, "Okay." Then I went to get my mother and sister. But I could not find them. I ran everywhere shouting, "Mama! Roza!" No one answered. It turned out that the Germans had already taken away one group. Mama and Roza were probably in that group. But I remembered that when they took us out into the yard I kept asking Mama, "Where are we to go?" Roza also asked her where to go. After all, we understood—Roza too—that some would be killed and others would be left alone. And Mama said, "I don't know." [I wanted to take Roza and then Mama over to the group of medical workers and beg someone to take them in as members of their family.] But I was too late.

Papa and the men working with him returned that evening. Papa already knew something. Immediately he asked me, "Is Mama here? Is Roza here?" There was horrible weeping in the ghetto. Very many men found no one left in their families. Papa cried horribly. The Germans said they would be shot if the crying did not stop.

The killing continued the whole winter. Papa and I were left by ourselves. In the event of a new selection, we agreed that we would hide in the same place. [Once I failed to hide there and spent the whole day in the outhouse up to my neck in excrement. They came into the outhouse but did not find me.]

That winter a woman named Gitelson was hanged in the courtyard in front of everyone. They caught her in the city. She had the right to be there, but she was not wearing the Jewish badge and was walking on the sidewalk, not on the street pavement, as Jews were ordered to do. We did not have the right to walk on the sidewalk. A girl was hanged too; I do not know her last name, but she was called Masha; she had tried to hide the fact that she was a Jew. [They tried to force a Jewish man, whose name I do not know, to hang her. He refused, and they beat him. The Germans themselves finally put the noose around her neck, but, with an automatic weapon pointed at him, the man was forced to kick the bench out from under Masha's feet. Several Germans photographed it.]

I remember too one evening when some policemen came running and said that their car had broken down and that they needed a rope. They were given a chain, but they said the chain would not do. Then everyone realized that they did not need the rope for their car, and we told them that we had no rope. They cursed for a long time and then left. Later it turned out that they had taken someone to be executed; they had decided to hang him, but they did not have a rope.

The next big selection that the murderers conducted was on 1 May 1942. There were very few of us left by then—maybe fifteen hundred. After 1 May there were 375 people left, not counting the ones who were working [for the Germans]. People would often say, "How are we better than our parents, our wives, our brothers, sisters, and children? Can it be that we are to live while they are murdered?" There was nowhere to run; our town is small, and it was impossible to hide. As for where the partisans were, we did not know. Nevertheless, some people had weapons. They got the weapons from German warehouses in the fort, where many of our people worked. I asked Papa whether this was stealing. But Papa said that the Germans had taken everything away from us, had murdered our loved ones and would murder the entire the Jewish people. That means that everything we do against the Germans is not a crime but is war. The invaders are not soldiers—they are criminals. [The young men and women ran off to join the partisans. It was hard for Papa and me to do that. We had no weapons, and it was hard for Papa to leave the place where Mama and Roza died. And he was afraid for me. I was thirteen at the time.]

In the wee hours of the morning of 23 September[17] sentries that we had secretly posted came running to us and cried, "Jews! It looks very bad! The Gestapo are here!"

It turned out that the Gestapo were already in the courtyard. They could have come for only one reason: to murder. I cried out to Papa: "Papa, I'm going to our old place!"—that is, the place we had agreed upon. I started running, thinking that Papa was running right behind me. And he probably was running behind me. But it was already impossible to get through: the path was cut off. I bolted down the stairs and jumped through a window onto the street. It was very dark. I waited a moment—Papa was not there.... Gunfire broke out between our people and the Gestapo. Later survivors told me that on that night many people, anticipating death, poisoned themselves and hanged themselves so as not to be taken alive by the Gestapo. They say that Feigin had hidden away a very long rope and gave a piece to anyone who wanted to hang himself. He would even help people to hang themselves; in the end he hanged himself. Some of those who were saved saw it with their own eyes.

In the dark I bumped into two adults and a boy my age; they were running away, like me. We headed down the road. Soon the two adults lagged behind; walking in a group of four, we ran too great a risk of being noticed. By evening the other little boy and I had covered twenty-five kilometers (all I remember is that he was from Kreslavka and his name was Nosya). My feet were killing me. Whenever we met some people, I would cry, "Vanya, where is Papa?" or I would loudly sing Russian songs. Nosya was very frightened. We spent the night in a burned-out building. The next morning we realized that we would not reach Belorussia; I decided to go to Poland. I told a woman straight out that we are fleeing from the Germans, and she fed us. Nosya kept saying that we should surrender, that we could not hide anyway, but I encouraged him. A truck was driving down the road. I decided to pay no attention to it, but Nosya stopped. I heard shouting in German. Then I turned off the road onto a path. Soon a bicyclist caught up with me and told me that the Gestapo were in the truck and that they had ordered me to go to them. I said, "I'm not going." The bicyclist said, "That's up to you. You're the one who'll answer for it." But he went on down the path, and not back to the Germans. I hid in the bushes. I heard whistling and the Germans asking someone if he had seen a boy. That's when they caught Nosya.

So I was left completely alone. Once everything was quiet I continued on. I decided to pass myself off as someone whom the Germans had transported out of the central regions of the USSR. But I still had not figured out what to say by the time I was arrested. [While they taking me down the road to headquarters, I managed to throw away the little red star I had in my pocket; I had kept it while I was in the ghetto. During the interrogation I announced that my name was Ivan Ostrovsky, that my father was a Tartar, and that my mother was Russian. I thought it was necessary to explain why I have thick black eyebrows, so I added that my grandmother was a gypsy. I did not know that the Germans were exterminating all the gypsies. I knew that Muslim boys underwent a rite of circumcision at the age of thirteen, and that is just how old I was at that time. I also said that my father had died when I was one year old, and that was why I did not understand a word of Tartar. Fortunately for me, the Germans were as ignorant of these things as I was. I made up a story about my mother being a laundress who worked at the Collective Forest Department in Bryansk. All of it was the first thing that came into my head. I knew absolutely nothing about Bryansk, and when they asked me where my mother and I lived, I replied, "Outside of town, in a settlement. We had no address, so people just wrote us at 'Bryansk, CFD.'" I was unable to escape, and the next morning they sent me to Dvinsk. My feet were hurting terribly, but on the way I still tried to escape, because I knew that in Dvinsk everything would come out or I would simply be recognized. But they caught me, beat me, and took me to Dvinsk.

I was beaten at the Dvinsk police station. They kept saying, "Tell the truth that you are a Jew, and nothing will happen to you. Otherwise we'll kill you." But I stuck to my story. I was very lucky. First of all, my papers were not sent from the village where I was arrested; I had torn the word *Jew* from them, but now they would have given me away, since my real family name was on them. Secondly, the doctor who was supposed to come and attest to whether I was a Muslim or a Jew never showed up. Finally, the document sent with me from the village stated that a suspicious boy going by the name of Ivan Ostrovsky was on his way to Dvinsk. And I was still using that name.]

I was severely beaten at the police station. One policeman hit me in the face so hard that he sent me rolling head over heels; I did not get up when he walked into my cell. I already thought that I was going to die, but I decided to hold out until the end. And suddenly they sent me to the Arbeitsamt (Labor Bureau). [The paper sent along with me had said that "the boy going by the name of Ivan Ostrovsky" should be put to work. Obviously, they believed me.] The Arbeitsamt issued me a pass to go to a village. [It simply said: Ivan Ostrovsky.] I spent almost nine months in the village, until the arrival of the Red Army. I told no one there that I was a Jew. Only once in my sleep did I cry out something in Yiddish. The landlord started questioning me about it, but I convinced him that I was shouting in German. After that I slept very uneasily, afraid that I would cry out again in my sleep.

When I returned to Dvinsk, the Jews whom I had met and who had escaped from the ghetto told me that my father had hidden for three weeks in the city, but the Germans found him and murdered him.

I cannot say exactly how many of us were in the ghetto. More than thirty thousand Jews perished in Dvinsk, but I think there were around twenty thousand in the ghetto.[18] These are the names of the ones who survived: the two Pokerman brothers, Motl Krom and his wife and child, the tailor Antikol, Lyak and his wife and child, Muler, Gallerman, and two women: Olim and Zelikman. There were eighteen in all, but I do not remember the names of the others. I left Dvinsk and did not want to go back, for it was painful for me to walk the streets where my loved ones had walked and where so many friends had died; it hurt me to walk past our burned-out house. More than anything I want to go to school and find people whom I might come to love and who will love me, so that I do not feel so alone in the world.

Prepared for publication by O. Savich

Notes

1. According to a report submitted by Einsatzgruppe A on 15 October 1941, "with a little pressure, the auxiliary Latvian police managed to organize a pogrom against the Jews in Riga. All the synagogues were destroyed during the pogrom and approximately four hundred Jews were killed."

2. According to testimony given at a war crimes trial in Riga in 1946, more than 46,000 Jews were murdered in the Bikernieki Forest. Another site of mass executions was Rumbuli, a suburb of Riga. During the last days of November 1941 alone about four thousand Jews from Riga (some place the figure at 10,600) and one thousand German Jews were murdered there. Another 25,000 were shot between 7 and 9 December. According to transcripts from the trial, a total of 38,000 Jews were murdered at Rumbuli.

3. The International Organization of Aid to Revolutionaries was founded in 1922. When the Second World War broke out, they were active in seventy different countries. They remained active in the USSR until 1947.

4. Penkokrust was a Latvian nationalist party founded in 1930. They came out against Jews and Masons and promoted a totalitarian government.

5. On 23 October 1941 the Gebietskommissar gave the order establishing the ghetto and forbidding all contact with the Jews. The order from the Generalkommissar outlining special rules for the Jews was issued on 1 September 1941. Those rules pertained to wearing the yellow star, the prohibition against using the sidewalks and public transportation, the prohibition against attending schools, and so on.

6. After 15 November Obergruppenführer SS Friedrich Jeckeln was in charge of the SS and the police in Ostland, which included Lithuania, Latvia, Estonia, and part of Belorussia. Prior to taking that position, he was in charge of mass executions of Jews in Kiev, Berdichev, and Old Constantinople. On 3 February 1946 he was hanged in Riga on the Pobeda Square.

7. Semen (Simon) Markovich Dubnow (1860 – 1941) was a renowned Jewish historian and essayist, most famous for his groundbreaking histories of East European Jewry. The Nazis destroyed all but one copy of his three-volume memoir *The Book of Life*; the English edition of that copy was published in New York in 1957.

8. Indeed, Frida Frid's story has filled a book. In 1973 her Holocaust memoir *I Survived Rumbuli* was published in Israel under her married name Frida Michelson. Judging from the account in her book, it seems certain that this mass execution took place at Rumbuli, rather than in the Bikernieki Forest.

9. The Munich Putsch was Hitler's failed attempt to take over the Bavarian government in November 1923. He was arrested, tried, and sentenced to five years in prison but was released by Christmas 1924. During his imprisonment he wrote his infamous manifesto *Mein Kampf.*

10. Between 27 November 1941 and 16 February 1942 approximately 25,000 Jews were deported to Riga from Berlin, Nuremberg, Stuttgart, Hamburg, Cologne, Düsseldorf, Hannover, Leipzig, Dortmund, Theresienstadt, and other cities.

11. Sturmbannführer SS Rudolf Lange was in charge of the security police and the SD in Latvia. He was a participant in the Wannsee Conference that was convened by Heydrich on 20 January 1942 to work out the logistics of murdering all the Jews of Europe. As the one in charge of the slaughter of the German Jews sent to Riga, Lange personally greeted the trains arriving from Germany.

12. The Salaspils concentration camp was one of the most notorious in the Soviet territories. It was in operation from October 1941 to October 1944. According to information gathered by the Soviet commission investigating war crimes in the republics, 53,700 people were murdered there.

13. Located near Riga, the camp at Kaiserwald was in operation in 1943 and 1944. Jews capable of working were sent there from the Vilna Ghetto and from the Riga Ghetto in September 1943; those who could not work were murdered. In August 1944 the Jews in Kaiserwald were transferred to Stutthof.

14. Jan Lipke took Jews out of the Riga Ghetto from the very beginning and hid them. With the help of his family and a group of friends, Lipke hid Jews in various places and saved forty-two lives over the three

years of the occupation. Yad Vashem acknowledged him as one of the Righteous among the Nations in 1977; he died in Riga in 1987.

15. In June 1941 approximately five thousand Jewish men were murdered by the Nazis. According to German records, there were 29,602 people in the Riga Ghetto. In the course of two Aktions held on 30 November and 7 – 9 December 1941, 27,800 Jews were murdered. The remaining 2,500 were deemed capable of work and remained in the Riga Ghetto until 1943.

16. "Open up, dogs, pigs! Or we'll shoot!"

17. The year was 1943.

18. There were fourteen to sixteen thousand Jews in the Dvinsk Ghetto; they came from the city and from neighboring villages. According to German documents, after the Aktions of 8 August and 18 – 19 August 1941, there were about seven thousand left. On 9 November 1941 it appears that another 1,134 Jews were murdered; some documents indicate 1,034, while the records kept by Einsatzkommando II show 11,034. By the beginning of 1942, 950 able-bodied workers were left in the ghetto.

Part 6

The Soviet People are United

A Letter from Officers Levchenko, Borisov, and Chesnokov (Lopavshi, Rovno District)

We drove the Germans from their command position and cut through the enemy until we broke through to a populated area. The Germans fled in panic.

The residents met us with joy and took turns telling us about the savagery of the fascists. Citizen Vera Iosifovna Krasova came up to us and invited us to her home. We were met with a horrible scene. There were six people sitting in a room—no, it was impossible to recognize them as people. They were mere shadows.

Vera Iosifovna began telling her tale with tears in her eyes:

"I hid these people from the Germans for a year and a half. When the Germans came, [they started rounding up the Jews; every Jew had to wear an armband. Then the commandant was replaced, and an order was issued that they had to wear a larger armband, so that it could be seen from a distance. The next commandant changed it from an armband to a wide ribbon worn on the chest.

"Soon] the mass destruction of the Jews of Dubno was underway. They drove them into the square, where they committed monstrous atrocities. Jews were forced to run a gauntlet, and old men's beards were torn out; then they were forced to dance, sing, and pray. After that the Jews were forced to dig graves and lie down in them in rows; they were shot, and many of them were buried alive. There were ninety people in the first group to be shot. Children were picked up by the feet and their skulls were crushed; they were drowned in bathtubs, [and this was done by German women who were as savage as their animal-like husbands.] Then the annihilation of the Jews took on a more massive character... .

"In the village of Demiduvka they set up a special camp surrounded by barbed wire; they herded up to 3,700 Jews in there each day and murdered them. I had the opportunity to observe this horror many times. Once I ran into a doctor I know named Abram Emmanuilovich Grintsvaig, who treated me at one time. I offered to help save his life. But he told me that he was not alone. That night I took them all in a cart to my farmhouse, where I hid them. It was difficult to keep them hidden, however, so I decided to make an underground shelter. I spent the whole night secretly digging the shelter; there I hid everyone I had brought out of the death camp. No one knew about it except my little girl Irina. The Germans conducted round-ups and even searches several times, but they did not discover my secret. It was very hard for me. I would bring them food at night and let some fresh air into the shelter. All of it entailed great danger. But my daughter Irina and I kept our secret. We were hoping that soon our people would come and wipe the Germans off the face of the earth. The lives of our Soviet people are very dear to us. And now you have come. These people are seeing the 'light of God' for the first time in a year and a half."

There are six people sitting in the room: the two Goryngot sisters, Mariya, twenty-one, and Anna, eighteen. Thin and black, they can hardly speak; their eyes are filled with tears of joy. They still cannot believe that they have been saved. The Goryngot sisters have no parents; the Germans shot them.

There is twenty-year-old Mikhel Sel and his sisters: Ita, fourteen, and Etl, fifteen, as well as his brother Yakov, who is ten. The Germans shot their parents. At the age of twenty, Mikhel looks like an old man. He pronounces his words with difficulty. Little Yakov cannot walk. He looks at us with a confused expression.

After seeing this, our hearts were filled with even more hatred for the thrice-cursed enemy. Vera Iosifovna said:

"Comrades! These are not all the people whose lives I saved. There are four more in another shelter."

And the woman took us there. At the entrance we went down a narrow well, passed through the darkness of a winding corridor, and in the dim light saw four more people. They were Doctor Abram Emmanuilovich Grintsvaig of the Dubno Hospital, his seventy-year-old father Emmanuil, his mother Anna Yakovlevna, and Anna Lvovna Oleinik, the wife of a Dubno pharmacist.

We helped them crawl out of their shelter. Their joy was limitless; they took turns thanking us and the woman who saved them.

Comrade Ehrenburg! We decided to write to you about this so that you would write about the heroic actions of Vera Iosifovna of the village of Lopavshi in the Demiduvka region of the Rovno District, and her sixteen-year-old daughter Irina, and so that our whole country might know of it.

> With greetings from the front,
> Guards Captain Levchenko
> Guards Captain Borisov
> Guards Lieutenant Chesnokov
> Field Mail 39864
> 23 March 1944

Prepared for publication by Ilya Ehrenburg

The Peasant Woman Zinaida Vashchishina (Dombrovitsy, Rovno District)

Not long ago I was sent to carry out a special assignment. In a populated area where I stayed near the front I was very well received by a certain woman. She told me about everything that peaceful people were forced to endure during the years of the German occupation. While we were talking a girl came into the hut. When she saw me, she ran away. I was surprised and asked who the girl was. The woman started to say it was her daughter, but then she told me the girl's entire story. The girl was a Jew. The Germans shot her parents, sister, and brother. She was saved by a miracle. And [this honest Russian woman hid her, even though the Germans would have killed her and her whole family for doing it. This modest Russian] peasant saved the girl, fed her, and clothed her just like one of her own five children. When I returned to my unit I told the story to my commander and all my comrades. They were moved as they listened to the tale.

The old woman's name is Zinaida Vashchishina. We took the girl into our unit, and she will live with us. Of course, it would be good to send her to the rear so she can go to school; she is only fourteen. Her name is Feiga Fishman. Before the war she lived in the village of Dombrovitsy in the Rovno District. I ask you to please write about the feat performed by Zinaida Vashchishina. Let the world know that the Russian people have never been hostile toward the Jews and that in hard times the Russian people extended to the Jews the hand of brotherly aid.

With greetings from the front,
R. Soltsovsky
9 June 1944

Prepared for publication by Ilya Ehrenburg

Collective Farmer Yuliya Kukhta Saved Jewish Children

When the war broke out a surgeon from the First Soviet Hospital in Minsk named Sarra Borisovna Truskina put her two sons—Mark, age seven, and Alek, age eleven months—into a cart with their nanny Yuliya Kukhta. Truskina herself walked along behind the cart down the Moscow – Minsk highway. During the bombing she lost sight of the cart. It was carried away in a stream of refugees. She reached Chkalov, where she worked and mourned for her children during the entire war.

A week after the liberation of Minsk her brother sent her a postcard he had received from Moscow saying that her children were alive. Now the mother lives with them in Minsk.

This is the story told to Jurisprudence Senior Lieutenant Mayakov by Yuliya Kukhta, a thirty-year-old collective farm worker from the village of Krivoe in the Beshenkovickesky region of the Vitebsk district:

"Beginning in 1934, I lived first as a housekeeper and then as a nanny for the family of Sarra Borisovna Truskina. I was present when both of her sons, Mark and Alek, were born. On 24 June 1941, when we left Minsk, I kept the children next to me in a cart and tried not to lose sight of Sarra Borisovna. But when the bombing started, we lost each other. Sarra Borisovna's sister Anna Borisovna, her husband, and the boys' grandfather Boris Lvovich were also on the cart. After traveling about twenty kilometers outside of Minsk, Felitsian Vladislavovich, Anna Borisovna's husband, said that it was pointless to go any farther; that evening we returned to Minsk.

"At first we lived with Felitsian Vladislavovich's parents. But when the Germans forced the grandfather and Anna Borisovna into the ghetto, Felitsian Vladislavovich's mother, Polina Osipovna, began to insist that I take Mark into the ghetto too because his face had Jewish features.

"'Because of him our entire family could be killed; take him into the ghetto,' she demanded, and once she went with Mark and me to leave him with his grandfather.

"But after turning the boy over to the ghetto, I could find no peace. 'He'll be killed,' I thought. Every day I would go to the ghetto; whenever the police turned their backs, I would pass food through the wire fence. During that time I managed to register Alek in my own name, as my son, and I never parted from him. Once they dragged me down to the police station and tried to find out how I happened to have the child.

"'You probably decided to hide a Jewish kid for a lot of money.'

"I denied everything, even when they started whipping me. 'The child is mine, that's all there is to it.' Fortunately, when they started beating me Alek grew afraid; he clung to my dress and started crying, 'Mama, Mama!' They let me go.

"[But then Polina Osipovna demanded that the boy and I leave.]

"I rented a small room on a distant street, where I was not known. Meanwhile they had started shooting the Jews in the ghetto. I was horribly tormented thinking about Mark. I made a decision: 'Come what may, I have to get the boy.' And once, while I was visiting Anna Borisovna, she got Mark past the policemen and the fence and gave him to me.

"Several times, through the neighbors, Polina Osipovna tried to scare me by saying I would get them and myself killed. But I had resolved that it was better to die with the children than to ever give them up. After all, they had no one left in the world besides me. By then their grandfather and Anna Borisovna were no longer in the ghetto; they had probably been shot, like the others.

"Soon I managed to get Mark registered on my passport.

"From that time onward I never let the children go anywhere without me. When I went to work I locked them in my room with something to eat. Since he was the older one, Mark looked after the baby; he understood that their lives depended on it.

"Several times, as soon as the children aroused suspicion, I had to change jobs. Every day I trembled with fear for their lives.

"But I knew that the Germans would not live among us forever, for sooner or later our people would come. And I kept the children alive and healthy."

Reported by Lieutenant Mayakov,
prepared for publication by Vasily Grossman

I Was Adopted by the Lukinsky Family:
A Report by Polina Ausker-Lukinskaya

I was a second-year student at the Medical Institute in Minsk. On 21 June 1941 I left Minsk for the city of Borisov to see my parents before leaving to work at a Pioneer camp. I was supposed to leave Borisov on 23 July, but I never got out: on 22 June I heard on the radio that the Germans had attacked our homeland.

The Germans entered Borisov during the first days of July. [I did not have time to evacuate. Frightened by stories about the savage Germans, I did not go out for two weeks.] The Germans went around the houses asking about people's nationalities and confiscating all their finest possessions. On 25 July the Germans began setting up the ghetto. The Jews had to abandon their homes and move to the outskirts of the city, into an area fenced off by barbed wire; [it had already been emptied of its Russian population.

We were forbidden to have any contact with the outside world. On all the streets and at the one gate leading into the ghetto the Germans posted signs that read, "Jewish Traffic Restricted." Our every step was controlled by police outside and inside the ghetto. People could leave the ghetto only if they had a special pass.

Everyone in the ghetto was required to wear bright yellow badges on the left side of their chest and on their back. If they did not wear the badge, or if it was covered by a handkerchief, they could be shot.

An order was issued in Russian: "Upon meeting a Jew, you must cross over to the other side of the street; greetings, as well as any exchange of any item, are forbidden." Russians violating this order were subject to the same fate as the Jews.]

This is how a day would go by.... . All able-bodied people would report on the square at 6:00 A.M.; then they were divided into groups and sent to work under an armed escort. When he left for work, not a single Jew knew whether or not he would ever return to the ghetto. Each worker received a ration of 150 grams of bread per day. Due to hunger, hellish labor, and overcrowding, epidemics broke out; many died, as there was no medicine.

The Germans ordered the people in the ghetto to turn over all their warm things: fur coats, felt boots, jumpers, gloves, sweaters, and so on. Then came the order to hand over everything made of gold or silver. The Germans threatened to shoot fifty people if anyone should fail to turn in warm items and twelve hundred for failing to hand over any gold. Next came the order to hand in all silk items: shorts, slips, and stockings. Once everything had been taken away, the Germans levied a tribute of 300,000 rubles.

Then began the mass extermination of the Jewish population.

All Jews in the towns and villages were wiped out. On 20 October at six o'clock in the morning the Borisov Ghetto was surrounded by police. I lived in the center of the ghetto and could hear screams and children crying everywhere; people were seized, loaded into trucks, and hauled off "to work," that is, to be shot. At four in the afternoon that day my mother, father, and other relatives were also taken away. I heard my mother screaming and begging for mercy.... . But what could I do? My two younger brothers (they were fifteen and eleven) and I were hiding in the attic, and from there we saw people led off to be executed. The Germans spent three days shooting Jews. The executioners tried to arrange this mass murder so as to keep it a secret. It was forbidden to walk on the streets near the ghetto; at the tannery located near the ghetto, work was halted for three days. Trucks loaded with people left the ghetto and returned with the belongings of those who had been murdered. It was impossible to escape; police lined the street and would wildly open fire if anyone should try to get away.

Sitting in the attic, I heard the drunken voices of the policemen who were searching our building for loot; they divided it up right there. A girl they were torturing for trying to escape was screaming. [She cried, "I am a Russian! Don't kill me!"]

On the third day the police broke into the attic where we were hiding. They ordered us to lie down with our hands raised and searched us; they took our money and valuables, joined us up with a group of about sixty people, and led us off to be shot. Those who were too sick to walk were shot on the spot.

They took us to Razuvaevka, near the airport, two or three kilometers outside of town. This was the execution site. The earth was freshly filled in; you could even see human heads protruding from the ground. They forced us to undress and tore up all the photographs and documents we had; then they handed out shovels and ordered us to dig a pit. All you had to do was stop for just a moment, and immediately you would receive a blow in the back from a policeman's rifle butt. I lagged behind the others, since I had to dig a pit not only for myself but also for my younger brother. Many times they beat me for stopping; a German was standing nearby, laughing and taking pictures.

When the pits were ready, they lined us up facing them, and I realized that they were going to shoot us in the back. I was standing at the very end of the line, close to a group of Germans. One of them was Austrian; I had worked in his unit as a cleaning woman. I looked at him, and he recognized me; he waved at me, and, paying no attention to the policemen, I ran over to him. Police Chief Kovalevsky demanded to know my name, but the Austrian [said that he knew I was a Russian. He] took me aside, put me in his car, and drove me to Minsk. As we were driving away, I heard the machine guns firing; they were shooting people who were guilty of nothing. In three days they murdered more than ten thousand people.[1]

About twenty kilometers outside of Minsk they let me out of the car and told me, "Save yourself any way you can." I spent the night under the open sky, startled at every sound. "Where am I to go?" I thought to myself. The next morning I headed for Minsk, where I had lived for two years; I had friends and relatives there. Minsk was badly destroyed, especially in the downtown area. I had no papers with me, so I went to the Minsk ghetto. There I told people about what had happened in Borisov. After spending a day in the ghetto, I decided to head east, closer to the front, where I could cross over to our soil.

It was the anniversary of the October Revolution; I used every means possible to prepare myself to reach Smolensk. I stood on a bridge crossing the Dnieper, not knowing where to find refuge. The only thing left to do was to spend the night in the Smolensk Ghetto in Sadki. The front had moved far to the east, and I did not have the strength to go any farther. I decided to spend some time in Smolensk. They were checking papers very carefully in the city, so I had to seek shelter in the suburbs. I found out that a Jewish family named Morozov was living in Serebryanka, four kilometers from Smolensk; they had not been sent to the ghetto yet, and I set out to find them. I spent only a day with the Morozovs, however, because a German translator from the flax factory was watching them. They recommended that I go to a Russian family named Lukinsky for help. I told the Lukinskys all about myself, and they let me stay with them.

The Lukinskys risked their lives by offering me refuge, but that did not frighten them; they treated me like their own daughter.

[It was necessary to obtain papers for me. The Lukinskys introduced me to some Russian girls, and one of them—a girl named Pechkurova—agreed to go to the passport table and get a passport for me under the name of her friend Olga Vasilevna Khrapova. Thus began my new life under a new name. Once I had my papers, I got a job. I very quickly got used to my new family; the Lukinskys took the place of my parents, who were shot by the Germans.]

On 10 November the Germans arrested the Morozovs. The Lukinskys managed to keep their children from being arrested and moved them to a safe place. The Germans shot the Morozov family. In the spring of 1942 the same fate befell the Smolensk Ghetto that had befallen the Borisov Ghetto: two thousand people were shot.[2] The Hitlerites tried to find the Jews [hiding under Russian names]; whenever they found them they killed both the Jews and the Russians who were hiding them. The Lukinskys were very much concerned about my fate. The Gestapo were seizing people at random and annihilating them.

I was often depressed, but my new father E. P. Lukinsky kept up my spirits and my faith that the Red Army would come and save us from the fascist servitude. We read the Soviet leaflets dropped from airplanes and found out that the Red Army was penetrating westward. We lived on the hope for a speedy deliverance. The Germans hauled off all the young people to dig trenches or to be sent to Germany. [I was afraid of every policeman who went past our house; fortunately, my turn never came, and we were liberated by the mighty Red Army. The very last days of the German occupation, however, were especially hard. I had just come out of the hospital, when we all had to immediately] go into the woods; the Germans were emptying out the houses and burning them down.

There were many of us in the forest; we spoke in whispers so that the Germans would not find us. On 24 September Soviet artillery shells were flying over our heads, and we applauded them. On 25 September 1943 we saw the first Red Army reconnaissance soldier in the woods; I kissed him all over, with tears of joys in my eyes.

[Olga Evgenevna Lukinskaya
Polina Markovna Ausker]

Prepared for publication by V. Ilenkov

The Teachers Golneva, Terekhova, and Timofeeva

After graduating from the Smolensk Pedagogical Institute, I worked for three years in the Kasplyansky region of the Smolensk district, first in a school in Enkov and then in Kasplya. I offered my students all my knowledge and strength; I had the love of the children and the respect of the parents.

When the Germans occupied the Smolensk district, I was in the village of Kasplya, unable to evacuate. When the Germans started registering the Jewish population, I had to hide. Some teachers I knew, as well as some students, helped me, especially Ekaterina Abramova Golevna and Anna Evseevna Terekhova. For four months I wandered from place to place, spending a day here, a night there. I finally hid with Aleksandra Stepanovna Timofeeva; I had taught with her for two years at the school in Enkov. I moved in with her in a small house in the village of Babintsy; her mother Domna Arsentevna lived there with her married sister, who had two children. They were all threatened with mortal danger, but Timofeevna courageously helped me to hide. They hid me from the eyes of strangers under pillows, above the stove... .

But then the Germans moved into the village, and it was impossible for me to stay in Babintsy. Aleksandra Stepanovna arranged for me to stay with her aunt Ekaterina Efimovna Ksendzova, who lived in a neighboring village with her daughter Nina, a student at the Smolensk Pedagogical Institute. Ksendzova was already hiding a Jew named Sarra Veniaminovna Vints, who was a friend of Ninas from the Institute. They lived in the school where E. E. Ksendzova had taught for a long time. We made an underground passageway beneath the school, and Sarra and I hid there. This is how I lived for six months, now with the Timofeevas, now with the Ksendzovas. There were times when I wanted to die; my situation seemed hopeless. But my friends encouraged me and uplifted my will to live. They also helped local partisans a great deal. The elderly Ekaterina Efimovna Ksendzova could stand guard for hours so that a partisan might get some sleep.

In May 1942 Sarra and I went into the forest to join the partisans. There I met some familiar people: the secretary of the Communist Party in the Kasplya region, Volkova ,who was
commissar of the brigade, and Goldnev, who was in charge of the regional Department of the
People's Education. A short time later Ksendzova and her daughter joined the brigade. From
the partisan brigade I went far behind the Soviet lines.

Soon after the Germans were driven out of the Smolensk district I had the opportunity to
embrace the wonderful Russian women who saved my life.

Reported by Khana Khaimovna Khodos,
prepared for publication by Ilya Ehrenburg

The Bookkeeper Zirchenko

Seven Jewish families who lived in the city of Ordzhonikidze in the Stalino district managed to get out. The refugees went to the village of Blagodatnoe of the Gulyapol settlement in
the Dnepropetrovsk district.

The Germans were shooting people for hiding Jews. The bookkeeper for the collective
farm, Pavel Sergeevich Zirchenko, knew this very well. Nevertheless, he would not hand over
the Jews to the Germans. The Jews worked on the collective farm, and on 22 November 1943
they were freed along with all the residents of the village by the Red Army. Thus were saved
the families of Traiberg, Nukhimovich, Babsky, Kuskovsky, Gontova, Peresedskaya, and
Shabis—thirty people in all.

Prepared for publication by Ilya Ehrenburg

The Story of F. M. Gontova

In October 1941 I lived with my children in Enakievo. My husband was in the Red Army.
When the Germans began to approach our city, my children and I left for the Rostov district.
We stayed there until June 1942. By June the Germans had reached the settlement where I
was living; it turned out that I was in the middle of a combat zone. I left for the steppe along
with several other Jewish families. We had to hide the fact that we were Jews; we moved
along on carts from village to village, under the constant threat of death, until fall came. By
that time we were close to the village of Blagodatnoe, where a woman in our group had a
friend, a veterinarian's assistant named G. I. Volkozub. He greeted her with a very warm
welcome and helped us to find work and lodgings. The bookkeeper for the collective farm, P.
S. Zirchenko, turned out to be a great help to us. We told him everything about ourselves, and,
at the risk of his own life, he helped us to get settled.

We remained in Blagodatnoe until the happy day when the German monsters retreated
under the blows of the Red Army.

Prepared for publication by G. Munblit

One Survived: The Story of Evsey Efimovich Gopstein

On 2 November 1941 the Germans burst into Simferopol. Freshly shaved and in clean clothes, they looked as though they had just come from a military parade, not from Perekop. These were Germans for show, for the psychological effect on the Soviet people, a military unit transferred to the Crimea from behind the German lines. All the shutters, all the front doors and courtyard gates, were closed tight. Only toward the end of the day did some people grow restless and emerge from their homes. Small groups of citizens began to appear on the street corners and in the squares. Among them was the sixty-year-old Evsey Efimovich Gopshtein; an old inhabitant and native of Simferopol, he was an economist for the People's Commissariat of the Municipal Economy. Gopshtein's son, a pilot decorated three times, was at the front. His son's wife, a professor who lived in Simeiz with their daughters, had already been evacuated from the Crimea in August. She had persuaded her mother-in-law, Evsey Efimovich's wife, to go with her and the granddaughters. Old Gopshtein was left in Simferopol alone, but he did not feel lonely prior to the arrival of the Germans. His elderly sister, a chemist with an advanced education, had stayed in Simferopol; she worked in one of the city's laboratories. Evsey Efimovich had many friends of various nationalities who had stayed, too. Gopshtein was saddened by the knowledge that the enemy had burst into the flourishing, fertile Crimea. He says:

"It was a sunny day. The fall weather had not yet set in; it was just a little cool. I walked through the downtown streets and looked up and down Pushkin Street. There, near the theater, in a bright red frame hung the first order in three languages: Russian, Ukrainian, and German. Several people were crowding around the order; someone was reading it aloud in a loud voice. He read clearly, and if I did not get everything, I certainly grasped the general sense of the order. It made a cruel, depressing impression. It was as though our former Soviet life had been hacked off with an axe. There were many nationalities among the residents of Simferopol. People lived as brothers, in friendship. Half of the order was directed toward the Jews. The word *Jew*, however, was not used in it. Instead the word *kike* appeared at every turn. The order stated that the filling in of trenches, the disposal of German and Russian bodies, the collection of garbage and all sorts of sewage was to be done by 'kikes.' The responsibility for assigning the Jewish population to do these jobs fell to the Jewish elders, who were appointed by the German command and, in part, elected by the people. [I stopped listening and started looking into the faces in the crowd. It was a mixed group. There were Armenians, Tartars, Jews, and Russians. And I am not mistaken, for I remember very clearly: not on a single face did I see any sign of approval regarding the German order.] People stood with bowed heads and wrinkled brows. In silence they listened, and in silence they walked off in different directions."

Over the next few days German orders poured out on the residents of the city one after the other.

1. Jews and Krimchaks[3] must report for registration. Those found in violation will be shot.

2. Jews and Krimchaks must wear distinguishing badges and six-pointed stars. Those found in violation will be shot.

3. Russians, Tartars, and other residents of the city are to report for registration. Those found in violation will be shot.

4. It is forbidden to walk about the city after five o'clock in the afternoon. Those found in violation will be shot.

Simferopol was transformed into an utter torture chamber, into a hideous human slaughterhouse. On 9 December 1941 the Germans exterminated the most ancient inhabitants of the Crimea: the Krimchaks. On 11, 12, and 13 December they shot all the Jews. The Germans registered fourteen thousand Jews in Simferopol, including a thousand who were half Krimchak. These Jews had not been living in Simferopol prior to the war. A large number of Simferopol's Jews were evacuated during the war with various enterprises and establishments; a few left on their own. Later, however, Jews fleeing from Kherson and Dnepropetrovsk settled in. Jews from the villages in the Fraidorf, Larindorf, and Evpatoria regions also came pouring into Simferopol. Here, in the thick of a large Jewish community, people thought they could find salvation; but they found only death. The Hitlerites annihilated the Krimchaks on 9 November; next they began killing Jews in various places by various means. For three days their death cries could be heard in Simferopol and the surrounding area. D. Davydov, a Russian worker from the Simferopol mechanical plant, relates the following:

"I lived at No. 78 Pushkin Street, not far from the stadium. I could see everything from the window of my three-story building. Beginning early in the morning, thousands of families were crowded into the square. The poor people were herded down Salgirnaya, Gogol, Pushkin, and Kooperativnaya Streets; all those streets were lined with SS men. The Germans were not sure that all the Jews had shown up, so they began searching the city. They conducted an especially thorough search in the Tartar area of Subri and around the cannery on Karl Marx Street. Many workers had taken in Jewish workers and Jewish patients from the hospital. Those seized by German soldiers were beaten with rifle butts and kicked with boots. Toward evening a thousand Jews were herded into the area of the large municipal garden. The garden was brightly lit, and there was music playing. German officers and soldiers were amusing themselves. At about ten the Germans set to a monstrous slaughter. The old men were separated into a special group: they were hanged along the surrounding streets—Lenin, Salgirnaya, Kirov, and Pochtov Lane. The rest were led into a deep pit near the new bathhouse, where they were shot with machine guns. That night the renowned [Jewish] psychiatrist Balaban and the Honored Actor of the Republic, the Jew Smolensky, were murdered. Later citizens in the surrounding areas told me that the Germans threw children into the pits alive and that they cut off the breasts of young women."

Comrade Davydov ended his story with the words: "Not a single Jew was left in Simferopol." Davydov was mistaken. [One survived. One out of fourteen thousand people. It was] Evsey Efimovich Gopshtein, who heard the first German order on Pushkin Street and decided not to register. But it was impossible to hide from the rumors that were running rampant. Here are some variants of those rumors:

1. The Jewish population would be sent out in front of the German army to act as a shield, as the army advances on Sevastopol.

2. They would be sent to work in Bessarabia.

3. They would be sent to colonies in the Fraidorf and Larindorf regions, where they would do agricultural work in the fields that had not been sown yet.

4. All the Jews would be sent to the Russian front. And finally,

5. They would all be annihilated.

Not a single Soviet could believe the last one. Gopshtein's sister was killed when she reported to the designated registration point. All his Jewish friends were shot as well, [from infants to senile old men.] Then they wiped out the Russians who were in mixed marriages, along with their offspring. It seemed as though the air itself had changed and was saturated with horror and blood. In January 1942 the mass roundups began. The Germans conducted their searches from street to street, building to building, apartment to apartment. When the registrations began many Jews hid with friends and relatives. By December 1942 nearly all the shelters had been uncovered; people were caught like animals cornered in a hunt. Gopshtein lived in the same building for twenty-eight years. Twenty apartments faced the courtyard. Russians, Jews, and Tartars lived in them. No one betrayed Gopshtein. A Russian teacher, an old friend of the Gopshtein family, hid him in her room. Terrible days set in for him and for the woman who saved him. [No one in the apartment knew that a Jew was hiding in the room of this single Russian teacher.] Whenever she left, she would lock him in. Under no circumstances was Gopshtein to give away his presence in the locked room; otherwise both he and his savior would die. [Once, while the Russian woman was gone, the Germans tried to get into the room.] The door was massive and had a strong American lock. It would not immediately yield to the shoves and blows. Suddenly Gopshtein heard a dog scratching at the door. He froze. The conversation outside the door confirmed that the German officer had brought along a German shepherd. It was impossible to hide from the dog the fact that a man was hiding behind the door. But at that moment a dog belonging to one of the residents of the building ran into the hall and sprang at the German officer's dog. The Germans tried to pull them apart. Fearing for the safety of his dog, the German officer pulled the dog away from the door and led it down the hall.

The Germans set up a dining room for their anti-aircraft gunners right next to the room where Gopshtein was hiding. German soldiers were constantly scurrying up and down the hallway. The schoolteacher had to move her lodger into the closet and then, a few hours later, back into her room. At dawn, after hearing that a roundup was beginning, the teacher led Gopshtein back into the closet, which was crammed with cupboards and cluttered with geographical maps, suitcases, and books. She locked the door and put the key in her pocket. But when the Germans conducting the search demanded that the closet be opened, the landlord produced a second key. Evsey Efimovich stood in a narrow recess between two cupboards. When the Germans entered the closet, Gopshtein no longer felt any fear in his soul. "I had reconciled myself with the thought," as he tells it, "that this time I would not escape. I had to gather all my strength to meet death with dignity, without humiliation."

But in the half-darkness of the closet cluttered with so many things the Germans did not even see the man who was hiding there. They left and took the key with them, promising to come back soon to pick up a few things. After they went away, the teacher knew to seize the moment to get Gopshtein back into the room that had already been searched. No one in the building knew that she had a second key to the closet door.

Gopshtein spent twenty-eight months in his shelter, until 13 April 1944. He was afraid that he would go out of his mind. He read and wrote. Everything he did he had to do without making a sound. There was cold and hunger—for the population in general but especially for the woman who saved him. She divided her meager provisions into two parts. All they had was sixteen kilograms of flour, twenty-four kilograms of potatoes, a bottle of vegetable oil, a few kilograms of groats, and a jar of lard that had already been opened. A Russian carpenter whom Gopshtein knew gave them the jar in early December 1942. At that time Evsey Efimovich would still step out for a bit; one day he met his carpenter friend on the Feodosia Bridge. They spoke for a few moments. The carpenter simply said: "There is a way I can help you. I have just slaughtered a wild boar; I can bring you some of the lard." That evening, in fact, he brought some meat and some lard. The carpenter could not find Gopshtein himself in his old apartment, so he gave the gift that was all he could give to some friends, who got it to Gopshtein. The two people lived for three months on these goods; then the teacher had to share her meager ration with Gopshtein. That is how Evsey Efimovich Gopshtein came to be the sole survivor [from fourteen thousand Jews.]

Prepared for publication by L. Seifullina[4]

The Orthodox Priest Glagolev

German troops entered Kiev on 19 September 1941. [A terrible date! The next day we had to walk across Kreshchatik. This street known to me since I was a child seemed ominously strange. A reinforced German guard stood alongside several buildings (the post office and others). Here I was a witness to how a German beat a woman with a whip for daring to go near one of the guarded buildings.]

On 28 September (that is, nine days after the fascist horde had seized Kiev) an order was posted at the city's intersections, on fences and walls. It declared that all Jews living in Kiev must show up on the morning of 29 September on Degtyarevskaya Street in the vicinity of the Jewish cemetery.

They were to bring warm clothing, money, and valuables. The order threatened that any Jew who did not show up and any non-Jew who dared to hide a Jew would be shot.

Not only the Jews but all who harbored a human feeling were seized by a terrible anxiety. {Everyone tried to figure out what lay hidden in the evil decree. On Shevchenko Boulevard I spoke with two German officers who were coming from the train station. They were quite amiable. Regarding the question of what the order concerning the Jews meant, they said they had just arrived in the city and knew nothing about the order; they thought it might be about registering Jews and handing out armbands to them. When they found out that I was a Jew, they hurriedly mumbled, "Aufwiedersehen," assumed a bombastic air, and abruptly left. So no one knew exactly what was in store for the Jews; there was no doubt, however, that it was something terrible.} Tormented by the foreboding of something horrible, people either fell into utter despair or, like a drowning man, would grab at any straw—at the flimsy hope that the Jews would be taken somewhere outside the city (to a place where they would present their passports, such as the train station). [The thought of a violent impending death, the death of their relatives and loved ones—especially of the little children—was so nightmarish that everyone tried to drive it out of his mind.] The screams of people in their death agony could be heard from one end of the city to the other. A horrible night was replaced by an even more horrible morning. An uninterrupted flow of tens of thousands of Jews moved slowly toward the site specified in the order. This sea of humanity contained people of all ages: teenage boys and girls in the blossom of youth, full grown men, decrepit old people, mothers with children, even nursing infants.

There were professors, physicians, attorneys, office workers, artisans, and laborers. Flowing in separate streams, all these people crowded together from various parts of the city to form one endless river. The street was teeming with life as it never had before; at the same time, the cold horror of death was closing in from all around... .

On the morning of 29 September my relatives walked their last mile. I went with them for several blocks; then, at their insistence, I went to see whether my daughter and I had to register. My husband was a Russian. My relatives and I agreed that they would wait for me in one of the squares near Dorogomilovskaya Street.

{I went into various offices to get permission, as the wife of a Russian, to stay in Kiev and to find out where they were taking the Jews. Of course, I received no permission and found out nothing. The Germans everywhere, with their dark, threatening faces, said: "Go to the cemetery."}

I took my daughter Ira, who is ten, to her grandmother's (my husband's mother) and took some of my things as well.

At about five in the afternoon I headed for the Jewish cemetery. There was no one in the small square where we had agreed to meet. [They were gone forever. It was impossible for me to go home.]

I went to m y husband's relatives and hid with them in a shed behind the stacks of firewood for about a week.

Very soon it became known that at Babi Yar more than seventy thousand Jews had been savagely killed.

My relatives on my husband's side turned to a priest named Aleksey Aleksandrovich Glagolev for advice and help.

Glagolev was the son of a well-known professor of Hebraic studies at the Kiev Spiritual Academy; his name was Aleksandr Aleksandrovich Glagolev, [and he was the former Father Superior of the Church of Nikola Dobry in Podol.] In his day, Professor Glagolev had defended Beilis at the famous trial [and proved that there was no ritual murder.]

[Father Aleksey went to consult with Professor Ogloblin, the former mayor of the city, about me.

Ogloblin knew our family. He, in turn, took the problem to the German commandant. Ogloblin left the commandant's office very disturbed and pale. It turned out that the commandant had told him that the matter concerning the Jews was under the exclusive authority of the Germans and that they would use any means they deemed suitable in order to resolve it.]

There was no way out for me. To hide with my husband's relatives meant subjecting them to the threat of being shot.

[Father Aleksey Glagolev's wife Tatyana Glagoleva came up with a desperate idea: to give her passport and baptism certificate to me, Izabella Naumovna Egorycheva-Minkina. With these documents in hand,] I was told I should go to some peasants I knew living in a village.

[Left without papers in such a trying time, T. P. Glagoleva had placed herself in great danger.

T. P. Glagoleva's photograph in the passport, moreover, had to be replaced by a photograph of me. Fortunately this task was made easier by the fact that edges of the passport had been burned and soaked with water from a fire that had broken out and was extinguished in the Glagolevs' apartment. The print on it was faded and smudged. We successfully switched the photographs. Toward evening on that very day, with T. P. Glagoleva's passport and birth certificate in hand, I headed for the suburb of Stalinka (Demeevka); from there I went on to the village of Zlodievka (today it is known as Ukrainka). Using the name of T. P. Glagoleva, I spent eight months in that village with a peasant friend of mine.

While searching the apartments for booty, the Gestapo very nearly took T. P. Glagoleva in as a suspicious person, since she had no papers. She just barely managed to get away, thanks to the testimony of witnesses.

As I have already said,] I did not spend a long time in Zlodievka. The local village authorities started eyeing me with suspicion. The problem was that partisans began showing up, and anyone who was "foreign" to the area aroused suspicion. In the end I was summoned before the village authorities to prove my identity. I somehow got out of that trouble and hurriedly fled to Kiev. I arrived at the Glagolevs' home late in the evening of 29 November. From that time onward and for a bit longer my ten-year-old daughter Ira and I stayed with the priest's family, posing as relatives. For two years we did not leave their side and went everywhere with them.

[We hid in the Glagolevs' apartment and in the church's bell tower. It was a very difficult task, since I had to hide not only as a Jew but also as a woman of an age subject to mobilization for various jobs, including jobs that would entail being sent to Germany. Many people in the city knew me and could give me away even without wanting to.] The Glagolevs saved several other Jews besides my daughter and me. Among them were Polina Davidovna Sheveleva and her mother Evgeniya Akimova Sheveleva. P. D. Sheveleva was twenty-eight years old and married to a Ukrainian named D. L. Pasichny. They lived in the large building at 63 Saksaganskaya Street.

When the fateful order of 28 September 1941 was published, D. L. Pasichny locked his wife in their apartment and went off to do some "intelligence work."

He showed up on Lukyanovka Street at the time appointed for the Jews. He was stopped and narrowly escaped being killed along with the Jews; he barely managed to get away. It was quite obvious that for P. D. and E. A. Sheveleva, going to the cemetery would mean going to their eternal ruin. Death also threatened them if they should stay in the apartment. What was to be done? As he was wandering through the city, Pasichny ran into the singer Egorycheva, with whom he used to work. She advised him to turn to the priest Glagolev for help. Among the papers belonging to his late father Father Aleksey found several blank baptismal certificates that had long since been superseded by a local ordinance. On one of those blank certificates they wrote in, "Polina Danilovna Sheveleva, born 1913 to a Russian Orthodox family." Pasichny himself got the official stamp for the certificate; he peeled it off some old document. With this document Polina Davidovna and her mother were secretly brought to the church grounds and placed in a little house at 6 Pokrovskaya Street; the house was under the jurisdiction of the church congregation. In all these matters, the priest Glagolev received active assistance from a scholar of the Academy of Sciences named Aleksandr Grigorevich Gorbovsky. He did not want to continue his work under the Germans and became a manager for the buildings belonging to the Kiev-Podol-Pokrov Church. He hid Jews on "his property," as well as many Russian teenagers who were threatened with being shipped off to Germany. He even contrived to obtain bread tickets for his "tenants."

Many who were hiding in the church buildings received papers stating that they were singers in the choir, church officials, sextons, and the like. If the Germans had paid attention to the fact that this poor little church had a such a large staff and had figured out what was going on, the authors of those papers would have been shot immediately.

The Pasichny family I mentioned hid in the church's little house for about ten months.

The Glagolevs went to great lengths to save the family of Nikolay Georgievich Germaize.

This family of Jewish descent was baptized in pre-revolutionary times. [According to their passports, they were all Ukrainians.] N. G. Germaize was a mathematics teacher. His wife Lyudmila Borisovna was a housewife. Their adopted son Yura, an extraordinarily gifted seventeen-year-old boy, was a student at the pedagogical institute. [While from his outward appearance Yura could pass for a Ukrainian, his parents clearly had Semitic features. That was their ruin.]

A few days after the events at Babi Yar a general registration of all men was announced. Yura reported for registration. As he was being registered, his surname drew some attention. They asked if he was of German descent. They were not satisfied with the boy's answer and asked him to call his father. The outward appearance of his father aroused suspicion; in the end the father and son were taken to the cemetery after receiving a terrible beating. As soon as Yura had been ordered to bring over his father, one of his comrades who knew the Glagolevs went to them and told them about everything. The Glagolevs rushed to the school where Germaize taught [in order to obtain evidence that Germaize was not a Jew.] Before they could put together the necessary papers, the tragedy had already taken place.

Lyumila Borisovna had to be saved. The poor, grief-ridden wife and mother had lived through terrible times. The Glagolevs often visited her, even though they had not been friends with the Germaize family. Once Lyumila Borisovna's neighbors came running to the Glagolevs and told them that she had been arrested and taken to Gestapo headquarters [as a Jew.] T. P. Glagoleva rushed to the Gestapo with a letter from Father Aleksey [stating that L. B. Germaize was not a Jew], but they treated her very roughly and would not even listen to her. Later it was discovered that they starved Lyumila Borisovna for five days; on the sixth day they prepared to take her to Babi Yar, along with other Jews who had been arrested. Among those arrested were several children who had tried to hide with Russian relatives and neighbors.

The Gestapo held L. B. Germaize; after a short while an investigator went to see T. P. Glagoleva to determine whether or not Lyumila Borisovna was a Ukrainian. T. P. Glagoleva was forced to sign a statement asserting the truth of her testimony and stipulating that if Lyumila Borisovna should prove to be a Jew, then Glagoleva would be shot along with Germaize. [Glagoleva declared that she had known the Germaize family for a long time as members of the church where her father and husband served and that there could be no doubt as to the nationality of Germaize.] Only then was Germaize released.

When she got home, Lyumila Borisovna met with a new blow. She discovered that her seventy-year-old mother had been seized by the Germans and sent to Babi Yar. Three months later Lyumila Borisovna once again fell into the hands of the Gestapo; this time she perished.

In the fall of 1942 and the winter of 1942 – 1943 I lived with the Glagolev family in different villages beyond the Dnieper; at first we stayed in Tarasovichi and then in Nizhnaya Dubechnya. By that time—that is, by the fall of 1942—partisan activity on the other side of the Dnieper was on the rise, especially in the wooded areas. The partisans operated at night and sometimes even in broad daylight. They made short work of the oppressors and their lackey police forces.

Being in no position to deal directly with the partisans, the Germans chose another means of fighting them. They sent killing units to the villages that had "committed offenses"; those units would burn the villages to the ground, as they shot and hanged the peaceful inhabitants, or forced them into the flames. Many settlements that had been flourishing were reduced to ashes. Thus many of the villages near Kiev were burned down: Piski, Novaya Basan, Novoselitsa, then later Oshitki, Dneprovskie Novoselki, Zhukin, Chernin, and others.

The Glagolevs were once summoned to the village authorities to have their passports checked. They were rudely informed that the priest, his wife, and his children, as well as the deacon, would be allowed to live there for the time being, but as they put it in Ukrainian, "the relative and the girl [that is, my daughter Irochka and I] have no business here and could go to work in Kiev."

With great difficulty my daughter and I returned to Kiev and hid once again in the bell tower of the Pokrov Church. That was on the 10th of January; at the end of January the Glagolev family also returned to Kiev. Glagolev himself stayed in Nizhnaya Dubechnya. On 31 January a killing unit showed up in the village to carry out reprisals against the people there because partisans had been passing through. The newly arrived Hitlerites drank and caroused with the police all night. At dawn they locked three men, a woman, and a five-year-old boy into a hut, doused the hut with kerosene, and set it on fire.

When Father Glagolev found out about what had happened, he hurried to the site where the killing had taken place; all that was left, however, was a heap of burned out ruins. The next day, a Sunday, he announced in church that following services there would be a requiem for the ones who had been tortured to death.

He buried the charred human remains in the cemetery. After that it was impossible for him to remain in the village, so he returned to the city.

All this time I was receiving certificates indicating that I worked as a cleaning woman and that I had a young daughter as a dependent. Ration cards for bread were obtained for me. At that time all sorts of inspectors were out looking for victims to send to forced labor for the Germans. Fortunately these investigators never penetrated into our "quiet abode." The certificates that I mentioned and the clever manipulations of A. G. Gorbovsky saved us.

As the Red Army drew closer in the fall of 1943, the Germans announced the evacuation of Podol; we decided to sit tight in the Glagolevs' apartment.

Ten days after Podol (part of Kiev) was designated a "restricted zone," German gendarmes broke into the apartment and dragged all of us, half dressed, out to a nearby public garden; then they herded us off to Lukyanovka. After that we were moved three times, [all the while hoping to stay in Kiev. The last place we were quartered was a church in the basement of the Pokrov women's monastery (on Artem Street). From there the gendarmes moved us to a concentration camp on Lvov Street (it was once a military registration and enlistment office). Here they starved us and forced us to clean latrines.] Soon after dividing the men and women into two separate groups, the Germans herded the prisoners to the railroad station. We got separated from Father Aleksey's family in the process and lost each other.

My daughter and I, A. G. Gorbovsky and his mother, and a mass of other people were transported to Kazatin in sealed train cars; there we were released (which happened purely by chance). In Kazatin we awaited the arrival of the Red Army. After returning to Kiev we found out that Glagolev was seriously ill. He had been severely beaten by the Germans for refusing to leave Kiev. He suffered a brain concussion from the beating and was in the hospital for a long time.

{His physical state was such that he required rest, but, after the unjust reallocation of apartment space, his living conditions were very bad. Five people shared one room of twenty square meters. Among them were the ailing Father Aleksey and a little boy two and a half years old. Even according to the lowest standards, his family should be allotted more living space. I believe that Father Aleksey and his family deserved to live under more humane conditions.

This family is suffering from serious material need, and their living conditions should be improved immediately.}

All of us who were saved by Glagolev will be eternally grateful to him!

Reported by I. Minkina-Egorycheva,
prepared for publication by R. Kovnator

[The Roman Catholic Priest Bronyus Paukshtis

A tall, heavy-set man of about forty, Paukshtis invited us into his study—the oldest study in Kovno's Trinity Parish—and told us various details about his efforts to rescue and save the Jews during the German occupation.

Paukshtis established contact with a certain monk named Brolyukas,[5] who was obtaining passports to save Jews. Paukshtis would often have to pay five hundred marks from his own pocket to cover all the expenses for obtaining a false passport.

As a priest, Paukshtis himself would fill out birth certificates for children who were kidnapped and saved from the ghetto; then he would personally help find them a place to live. After he had found a home for the fourth little Jewish girl he rescued, a child named Vizgardinskaya, he was informed that the Gestapo was interested in him... .

"What else could I do?" says Paukshtis. "I got on the train and, having announced upon my arrival that I was going to visit some priest colleagues, I went to see some peasants with whom one of my little Jewish 'daughters' was staying. Thinking that I was traveling around to see various colleagues, the Gestapo was no longer interested in me."

Paukshtis issued a total of 120 birth certificates to Jewish children.

But Paukshtis did not help only children. He hid twenty-five adults in his church. Among the ones he saved or helped to save we find the names of Doctor Taft, the attorney Levitan, the daughters of the head of the Slobodsky Yeshiva, Rashel Rozentsveig, Kisensky, the lawyer Avram Golub and his family, Kapit, and others.

Whenever someone he had saved would fall into the hands of the authorities, Paukshtis looked for ways to bribe the Gestapo agents, and he often succeeded.

"You believe," says the priest Paukshtis, "that I helped a lot. But it saddens me when I think of how much more I could have done if I had been gifted with a great understanding of concrete matters."

Paukshtis showed us a letter from the Jewish girl Rashel Rozentsveig, whom he helped to save and who is now studying at the Kovno University.

The letter is written in Lithuanian. I shall translate the first few lines.

"Dear Father! Please allow me to call you that. Aren't you, indeed, related to me as a father is to a daughter? Didn't you give me shelter when I came to you in such a miserable state after all I had lived through? Without asking any questions and demanding nothing of me, as if everything were perfectly clear, you said: 'You will find rest here, my child; come stay with me for a while...'"

It is a long letter. It is written with love and respect, and all of it attests to the fact that amidst the cruel conditions that the Hitlerites imposed upon Soviet Lithuania there were good, honorable people who calmly did their human duty, as if it were a completely natural thing to do.[6]

Girsh Osherovich,
translated from the Yiddish by M. A. Shambadal]

Notes

1.   At this time there were eight thousand people in the Borisov Ghetto. On 20 October 6,500 were murdered. About 1,500 skilled workers whom the Germans needed were temporarily allowed to live. The shooting was organized and carried out by the Russian Security Police under the supervision of a German named Echow.
2.   The Smolensk Ghetto was liquidated on 15 July 1942. All the residents of the ghetto—two thousand Jews—were shot in the Tantsov Grove.
3.   Among the oldest inhabitants of the Crimea, the Krimchaks were a small group of Crimean Jews whose native language is Tartar.
4.   Lidia Nikolaevna Seifullin (1889 – 1954) was a prose writer and playwright who worked in newspapers and radio during the war.
5.   Meaning "little brother" is Lithuanian, Brolyukas was a nickname for Bronyus Gotautas (1901 – 1973). Until his arrest in 1944 he provided aid to the Jews of the Kovno Ghetto by supplying them with documents, food, and hiding places. He died in West Germany in 1973.
6.   After the war the Soviets arrested Father Paukshtis and placed him in solitary confinement for ten years.

Part 7

The Annihilation Camps

Ponary: The Story of Engineer Yu. Farber

I am an electrical engineer by profession. Prior to the war I lived in Moscow, where I worked in communications at a scientific research institute while finishing graduate school.

I spent the first days of the war in the ranks of the Red Army.

In the fall of 1941 we were surrounded; after wandering around in the woods, trying to rejoin my unit, I was captured by the Germans.

One of the Germans looked at me and said, "This one won't have to suffer captivity—he's a Jew; he won't live long enough to see the sun set." Since I know German, I understood everything, but I did not let on that I knew what they were saying.

{One thing I managed to do was destroy all papers and documents that had anything to do with me. Just as I had destroyed them, a large group of prisoners came walking down the road. I was placed in their ranks and led away under an armed guard.... An SS patrol stopped us along the road; without offering any explanation, they started pulling individual prisoners from the ranks. If a man had a long, hooked nose, they would pull him out; or they would open his shirt, and if he had a hairy chest, they would pull him out. But they did not bother me. It must be said that when I am not wearing my glasses, I do not look particularly Jewish, and I have a nearly perfect Russian pronunciation.}

I was led with the large group of prisoners to a small hill surrounded by a barbed wire fence. We lay on the ground under the open sky; men with machine guns stood all around us. Three days later they locked us into freight cars and hauled us away; they gave us no food, no water, and did not open the doors.... One the sixth day we arrived in Vilnius. Many dead bodies were left behind in the train cars. Eight thousand prisoners were installed in the camp at Novo-Vileika near Vilnius.[1] People lived in what used to be stables, without windows and doors and with huge cracks in the walls. Winter was setting in.

The food ration consisted of one kilogram of bread for seven men, but often the bread was not handed out. The Germans would bring in potatoes frozen into a block of ice with dirt, peels, and straw. It was thrown into a cauldron and boiled into a starchy ooze; the prisoners received half a liter of this slop.

Every morning the dead were dragged out of the barracks. The bodies were towed to a pit, where they were lightly sprinkled with lime chloride. They were not covered with dirt, however, since the next day a new load of bodies would be thrown into the same pit. On some days there were more than 150 bodies; it was not unusual for people who were still alive to be thrown in with the corpses.

439

The Germans called us *Untermenschen*—the dregs of humanity. Once, because of some trivial offense, the Germans ordered two prisoners to lie face down in a puddle that was covered with a thin sheet of ice.

They were left there over night; since they were lying there naked, they froze to death.

Two dates are fixed in my memory: the nights of 5 December and 6 December 1941. I had a comrade, a young fellow of twenty; he was a Ukrainian named Pavel Kirpolyansky. It was cold in our barracks. In order to keep warm, we would lie down on one overcoat and cover ourselves with another; then we would sleep with our arms around each other. We were infested with parasites. Typhus was cutting people down left and right. That night Pavel and I were lying with our arms around each other. Suddenly I was awakened: I could feel him trying to break free from me. I felt his forehead and immediately knew what was wrong. Pavel was burning up with fever; in his delirium he did not recognize me. There was no way I could leave him there without an overcoat, so I grabbed hold of him and held him firmly in my arms until morning... . By morning he was dead; they dragged him off to the pit... . However, I did not come down with typhus.

On the night of 6 December two of my comrades, a couple of Ukrainians, were lying on either side of me. We had our arms around each other; I was warm and slept soundly. The whistle blew at down, and I tried to awaken my neighbor Andrey. He did not move: he was dead. Then I started to wake up my other neighbor, Mikhailichenko. He was dead too. That night I had slept between two dead men.

The thought of staying alive and returning to Moscow never abandoned me.

I forced myself to wash and even to shave. There was a barber in the barracks. He would shave the prisoners of war from time to time and would charge one potato as his fee. On that day, the 7th of December, luck was with me: I got a whole potato in my soup. I decided to get a shave. When I handed the barber the potato I had fished out of the soup, he looked at me and said, "No need..." I asked, "Why not?" He replied, "You are going to die this week anyway; eat it yourself."

A week went by, and once again I went to get a shave. The barber was amazed to see me: "How can you still be alive? Well, okay, I'll shave you again for free, since you'll soon be dead anyway." When I went to him a third time, however, the barber said, "I will shave you for free until you die."

{At that time nobody had a number, and nobody was registered anywhere. They were not making a huge to hunt down Jews. But it was enough for someone to point a finger at a man and say "Jude" or "kike," and the man would be shot immediately. There did not have to be any proof.}

By New Years I could no longer walk; I was swollen from hunger. My toes were starting to turn black; then the flesh fell off, and you could see the bones.

There was a prisoner who had been selected as an interpreter, a student from Leningrad named Igor Demenev, who later killed some German guards and escaped with some of his comrades. He helped me to get into the camp infirmary. The interpreter and several doctors from the prisoners of war had set up an infirmary among several wooden barracks and the ruins of a small brick house. My treatment went well.

The chief physician's assistant was Doctor Evgeny Mikhailovich, from Stalingrad. He treated me with brotherly compassion and care. By May I could walk, and by June I could climb the stairs to the second floor. The infirmary was the one place in the camp that the

Germans would not enter because they were afraid of typhus and tuberculosis. They did not force me to leave the infirmary—they made me the janitor. The mortality rate was astronomical.

I stayed in the infirmary until the end of 1943. The number of prisoners of war was diminishing. Of the eight thousand who had been brought there only a small handful was still alive.

The Germans used the prisoners for work outside the camp. Local residents would give the prisoners food.

An army doctor named Sergey Fedorovich Martyshev took great risks to save as many people as possible. He used every excuse he could think of to keep people in the infirmary, and he showed them every consideration.

When we found out about Stalingrad there was a huge turnabout in the morale of the prisoners and the civilian population; we all knew that the Germans had lost the war.

Although we were cut off from the whole world, our little group also joined in the fight against the German invaders.

We wrote leaflets for the Germans; I wrote some of them in German myself. In one leaflet I wrote, "The Lord God gave the Germans three qualities: intelligence, decency, and Nazism. But none of them has more than two of these qualities. If a German is intelligent and a Nazi, then he is indecent. If he is intelligent and decent, then he is not a Nazi."

On another leaflet I simply wrote, "Hitler kaput."

We wrote as many as twenty leaflets and made successful use of them. We grew more and more bold. Often, as soon as the lights would go out at midnight, we would start singing the *Internationale*. The Germans were furious and took all sorts of repressive measures, but they could not find the "guilty" parties. There were German underlings among us; them we killed.

{Once I threw a piece of paper out a window in the direction of a German guard at the fence. The guard saw it, but, fortunately for me, the note fell on my side of the fence. He called a prisoner named Vanya Nizhny over to pick it up and hand it to him. Vanya quickly grabbed the slip of paper and put it in his pocket; then he took out another piece of paper and gave it to the German. On this piece of paper it said: "Save us from the kikes. Jews are masquerading in the hospital. They are working for the NKVD and are awaiting the arrival of the Soviet authorities.}

Little by little my health improved; Sergey Fedorovich considered it a miracle. I think the main thing was my inner determination to stay alive until victory came. I gathered together all my physical and spiritual strength. I subjected myself to the strictest discipline. I cut the bread ration of 150 grams into twenty slices; later I learned how to cut it into forty. These were small oval-shared loaves of German bread. The bread was made from a special flour that contained a lot of sawdust. One small loaf was divided among seven men, and from my own portion I cut forty slices that were as thin as cigarette paper. They brought us the bread at five in the afternoon, and I made my share last for five hours. I would take a slice and put it on a small wooden stick; then I would take it over to the stove, toast it, and eat it.

There was a small garden next to the infirmary. You could not find a single blade of grass or the smallest leaf of a tree there. Even the bark had been eaten off the trees.

They took us to the bathhouse from time to time. In the bathhouse they would try to detect the Jews and capture them. Once a German started harassing one prisoner and said to him: "You're a Jew." The German wrote down the prisoner's number to take it to his supervisor. The prisoner Vanya Nizhny decided to save his comrade. He seized a moment when the German was not looking and in a split second changed the number on the list.

It was late in the evening when we bathed in the bathhouse, and the next morning the informer met with some embarrassment. The fellow whom they had summoned turned out to be a Russian, and they could find no fault with him.

At the end of 1943 they renewed their efforts to catch the Jews. Everyone was lined up and forced to undress; our doctors were told to serve as the experts.

Sergey Fedorovich categorically stated, "Kill me, do what you want to me, but I will not use my expertise for this." They threatened him with every kind of reprisal. Seeing his example, the other doctors also refused.

In the camp I was known as a Ukrainian named Yuri Dmitrievich Firsov.

Nevertheless the Germans found out that I was a Jew. They caught six Jews, one of whom was a Russian from Kazan named Kostya Potanin, who never in his life even had a Jewish friend. But the Germans determined that he had a big nose.

A memorable day came: 29 January 1944. A covered truck known as a "Black Raven" pulled into the prisoner of war camp. The commandant summoned all the Jews who had been arrested (including Kostya Potanin). They took us away. Suddenly the truck stopped; as we later found out, it was outside the Lukishki Prison. Two Jews were brought out from the prison. They had escaped from the ghetto and gone into hiding, only to be caught and thrown into prison.

A few minutes went by. As soon as the truck started to move, the two prisoners started crying. We asked one of them, a young fellow named David Kantorovich, why he was crying. He said that the truck was headed in the direction of Ponary and that no road led back from Ponary.

They brought us to Ponary. The place was surrounded by a barbed wire fence. At the gate there was a sign that said: "Entrance strictly forbidden, danger to life, mines." The truck passed through the gate and drove about three hundred meters, until it came to a second gate, with guards. A second group of guards came out the gate; neither the guards who were with us nor the guards posted outside the gate were allowed inside. Order was strictly observed: no one could penetrate into Ponary.

The guards were tall and stout, with broad shoulders. The truck carrying the new guard unit entered the camp. There were two barbed wire fences; as we found out later, the space between them was mined.

There was another small, narrow opening in the fence. They led through this passageway to the edge of a huge pit. It had once formed the bottom of an oil reservoir and was about twenty-four meters in diameter. The pit had a depth of about four meters. It walls were lined with concrete. Two thirds of the pit were covered with wooden logs, and one third was open. I saw a woman at the bottom of the pit and realized that people were living there. There were two ladders leading into the pit. One of them was considered "clean" and was used only by Germans. They had us climb down the "unclean" ladder; the guard stayed up on the surface. They summoned an old worker from somewhere; he was a Jew named Abram Hamburg, from Vilnius. The Germans called him Franz. They called out another worker named Motl; the Germans called him Max. He was wearing shackles and was ordered to put us in chains as well.

The chains were made of links just a little less than the thickness of a finger. They were attached to the leg just below the knee, about where your boots would end. The chain dragged along on the ground; we were allowed to fix half the length of it to our belts, so that it would not interfere with our walking.

Once all the new arrivals were in irons, the foreman, a Sturmbannführer appeared.

He was a refined sadist of about thirty. He was dressed like a dandy, with white gloves that went up to his elbows. His boots were as shiny as mirrors. He smelled strongly of perfume. He conducted himself in a very arrogant manner, not only around us but also around the German guards, who were incredibly afraid of him.

They lined us up, and he asked each of us where we were from. Kostya Potanin and I said that we could not understand him (I hid the fact that I knew German the whole time). The senior worker Franz translated. The Sturmbannführer spoke Yiddish and Polish and could make himself somewhat understood in Russian.

When my turn came he asked, "Where are you from?" I told him I was from Moscow.

In a mocking voice the Sturmbannführer said, "Moscow is a luxurious city," looking me right in the face. I replied, "What's the matter, don't you like Moscow?" Franz, the translator, started to tremble; he translated my words in a very watered down form. The Sturmbannführer raised his hand, but he did not touch me.

He said that we would be working on an important project of great significance to the State. "Do not try to remove your chains, because they will be checked several times a day; if you make the slightest attempt to escape, you will be shot. Don't even think about escape, for no one has ever left Ponary, and no one ever will." Then they started counting us off; the slightest attempt to escape, and we will be shot. We must obey the foremen's every order; the slightest infraction, and we will be shot. We must follow the rules for keeping order, otherwise we will be shot. We must work diligently; anyone found to be lazy will be shot. He spoke for a very long time, and it became clear to me: it was not hard to die here... .

After giving his edifying speech, he left. We stood at the bottom of the pit; we saw one woman, and out of the depths a second woman emerged. We started a conversation with them.

Right away we asked them if we were going to be fed. They replied, "Don't worry, they'll feed you. But you'll never get out of here alive."

We went under a canopy; there was a wooden structure that they referred to as a bunker, with a small kitchen. The women said that Jews from Vilnius and surrounding areas were living here. They were hiding in the ghetto but were found, sent to prison, and brought here. Kantorovich, whom I have already mentioned (he was from Vilnius), exchanged a few words with the women. They opened up and said that this was Ponary, where not only the Jews of Vilnius had been shot but also Jews from Czechoslovakia and France. Our job would be to burn the bodies. All this was held in the strictest secrecy. The Germans thought the women knew nothing, and we should never say anything about it. Whenever the Germans were around we were to say that we cut timber. No sooner did we hear this than a whistle sounded, and we had to go up the ladder. We were lined up in pairs and led away.

The first thing that hit us was the odor.

The SD overseer said:

"Grab your shovels and dig up the sand. If you see a bone, toss it up to the surface."

I took a shovel and started digging in the sand; right away I hit something hard. I scooped away the sand and saw a corpse. The overseer said, "It's nothing. That's the way it has to be."

It was a large, circular pit that they had started filling in as early as 1941. People were not systematically buried and were not even covered with lime; they just moved along a conveyor belt that operated unceasingly. The bodies just fell in, without any order, in various poses and positions. People who were murdered in 1941 were dressed in their outer clothing. In 1942 and 1943, however, came the so-called winter aid campaign to "voluntarily" give up warm clothing for the German army. Beginning in 1942, people were herded in and forced to undress to their underwear; their clothes went into a "fund" to be voluntarily donated to the German army.

In order to burn the bodies: a small bonfire consisting of a scaffold of pine logs 7 x 7 meters was set up along the edge of the pit; one row of tree trunks was stacked on top of another, with a flue made of pine logs in the middle. First the sand was dug up until a "figure" was found (the Germans ordered us to call the bodies "figures").

The "hook men" carried out the second operation; that is what they called the workers who would drag the bodies out of the pit with iron hooks. The bodies lay close together. Two hook men, who were usually the strongest members of the work detail, would cast their hooks into the pit and drag out a corpse. Most of the time the bodies were torn apart in the process.

The bearers, or the "*Trägers*," carried out the third operation. They had to lay a corpse onto a stretcher, whereupon the Germans made sure that there was actually a whole body on the stretcher, that is, two legs, two arms, a head, and a torso.

The Germans kept a careful count of how many bodies were taken out. Our assignment was to burn eight hundred bodies per day; we worked from dawn to dusk. The Trägers carried the bodies to the bonfire. There the "figures" were laid out in rows, piled one on top of the other. Once one layer had been stacked, fir branches were piled on; a special worker known as a *Häufenmeister* attended to the fuel and fed dry logs into the fire.

Each time the logs and branches were piled on, they were covered with black fuel oil; then a second layer would be added, then a third, and so on. Thus they would stack a pyramid up to four meters high and sometimes even higher. A pyramid was considered ready once it had 3,500 bodies in it. It was soaked through with fuel oil, not only from above but also from the sides; special dry logs were stacked along the sides and saturated with gasoline. Then one or two thermite bombs were inserted, and the whole pyramid was ignited. The Germans would stand around these fires with a very triumphant air.

The pyramid usually burned for three days. It had a characteristically low flame; heavy, thick, black clouds of smoke would rise up, as though reluctantly. The smoke was filled with large flakes of black soot.

A *Feuermeister* stood next to the bonfire with a shovel; he was supposed to see to it that the fire did not die out.

Three days later all that was left was a pile of ashes with bits of bone that had not burned up.

Those who were very old or physically weak worked with the crushing device. The charred bones were scooped onto a huge sheet of iron, where they were crushed so that not a single bit of bone would be left.

The next operation consisted of shoveling the crushed bones onto a finely meshed metal screen and sifting them. This operation had a dual purpose. First, if nothing was left on the screen, then the bones were sufficiently pulverized. Secondly, when the crushed bones were sifted through, valuable items such as gold coins would be left on the screen.

One other operation should be pointed out. As a corpse was being dragged out of the pit, a special person was assigned to insert a metal hook into the corpse's mouth; if he should find any crowns or gold bridges, he was to rip them out and put them into a special box.[2]

Some pits contained as many as twenty thousand bodies. The stench literally wrenched your insides out and made your head spin.

The work pace was such that we were not allowed to stop even for a second.

There were sixty SS guards. These well-fed wolfhounds were responsible for seeing to it that we did not escape. They formed a chain around the pit and would move from one spot to the next every fifteen minutes. They had an abundance of everything: meat, wine, chocolate. But they were not allowed to step beyond the boundaries of Ponary. When they were not standing guard, they were in their quarters.

More terrible than even the SS were the SD; they were concerned about keeping production on schedule. They stood around with clubs and often made use of them. We were under their constant supervision. Their vocabulary was very simple. They would shout either "*Renn, renn, renn!*" which in Germans means "Run, run, run!" or "*Prendzej!*" which in Polish means "Faster!" They also used Russian curse words. They assumed their positions at vantage points from which they could see every part of the pit. They frequently used their clubs at the drop of a hat. When we were carrying the bodies, the SS would shout, "Carry them, carry them, or soon you'll be carried too."

The first day the Sturmbannführer was there; he looked over the pit and shouted, "Why is this Muscovite working with a shovel, why isn't he carrying bodies?" Immediately one of the SD men ran up to me and ordered me to grab a stretcher.

We picked up a body and laid it on the stretcher. It was very heavy, and my knees buckled. Suddenly the Sturmbannführer shouted at the top of his lungs, "He can carry one figure when he is in Moscow; here let him carry two." We had to take another body. Fortunately for me, I had a partner who was physically strong. We carried two bodies. Once again the Sturmbannführer shouted: "They have a very light stretcher. Have a third body placed on top of it."

At the end of the workday they counted us again, checked our shackles, and ordered us to climb down into the bunker. Once everyone had climbed down, they pulled the ladder up. [When we had come here, it was necessary to build a second bunker.]

We could not complain about the darkness; there was electric lighting in the pit.

When we came back from work, basins filled with a solution of manganese were waiting for us; we diligently washed our hands in it.

There were eighty of us in all: seventy-six men and four women. The men were in irons. The women were not. They had the job of cleaning the living area, fetching water and firewood, and preparing food. The oldest of the women, Basa, was thirty. She was an experienced woman and very influential, for she held total sway over the senior worker, Franz. The others were young girls of eighteen, nineteen, and twenty. One of them, Susanna Bekker, was from one of the famous wealthy families of Vilnius. Typically, even in Ponary some of the old men would remove their hats before her and say, "That is Bekker's daughter. He had so many stone buildings!"

A third girl was named Genya, the daughter of an artisan from Vilnius.

The fourth girl was Sonya Sheindl. From a poor family, she was exceptionally hard working and friendly. She tried in every way she could to make our existence a little easier. Even tough it was not her job, for example, to wash our underwear, she would often do it for us.

Most of the men were from Vilnius.

Among those from Vilnius, there was not a single man who did not find some of his own family members among the bodies.

A second group of workers was made up of about fifteen Soviet prisoners of war.

A third group of men was from Vevis, a small town between Vilnius and Kaunas.

The Vilnius group was the largest, and it included people of a variety of ages and from a variety of social classes. Although they had known each other for many years, there was often no friendship or unity among them. People would remind each other of offenses committed ten years ago. Isaak Dogim and David Kantorovich stand out among them. Born in 1914, Dogim was a young, energetic worker; a printer and an electrician, he was an extremely unsociable person.

Kantorovich's lot was unlike anyone else's. Born in 1918, he was spry and very active. Before the war he worked as a clerk in a bookstore. The Germans murdered his wife. He joined the partisans but was captured.

Motl Zaidel was the son of a poor couple from Sventsyany. His mother and father perished; he lived in the ghetto. A good-looking youth of nineteen, he had a wonderful voice and loved to sing. Since 1941 he had constantly gone from prison to prison; it was terrible to hear the tale of his endless wandering.

We called him "Little Motl," or "Ingele," to distinguish him from the Motl with the "vonses," or the moustache.

Leizer Ber Ovseichik from Oshmyan and Matskin from Sventsyany were inseparable friends. Matskin was thirty-five. He had been a wealthy man, a storeowner. Ovseichik used to be a craftsman.

Despite their social inequality, these two men had formed a close friendship. Ovseichik would not eat without giving something to his friend, and the same went for Matskin.

Shlema Gol was an interesting personality. He was a middle-aged man, extraordinarily kind, but had a very weak constitution. His wife had been a member of the Polish Communist Party since 1933; subjected to a great deal of persecution, she had been in the concentration camp at Bereza-Kartusska. During the Soviet period they both had managerial positions in Barannovichi. He never uttered a foul word when speaking to his neighbors and was amazingly dedicated to the business of escaping. But that is another matter.

Abram Zinger was a relatively well-known composer; prior to the war he was an orchestra conductor. He was an intelligent, educated man. He knew Yiddish, Russian, Polish, and German quite well.

Our senior worker Franz acted as the interpreter for the Sturmbannführer, but whenever the Sturmbannführer gave an especially triumphant speech, Zinger was the interpreter. Even under the terrible conditions of the pit, Zinger composed songs. He once composed a nice song in German. And we started singing it in our pit. Unfortunately, the Sturmbannführer heard the song. He wrote it down, put his name to it, and in exchange gave Zinger a cigarette and a hundred grams of jam. Zinger was terribly upset by all this and poured out his heart to me. He regarded it as the greatest insult against his soul and said, "I do not sing songs for the Germans."

There were several men in the pit who had a spiritual calling. From time to time they would hold prayers for the dead, tragic liturgies, that were conducted with a solemn and sorrowful air.... Everyone would carefully wash and prepare for these prayer services. Ovseichik prayed twice a day for two hours at a stretch, with great passion and sincerity.

I shall say something about the prisoners of war. In addition to myself there was Petya Zinin from Moldavia, a Russian and a paramedic by profession, born in 1922. After his escape he joined the partisans, where his very best qualities came out.

Miron Kalnitsky, a Jew from Odessa, proved to be very useful, since he had worked near Ponary in a prisoner of war camp (not in a death camp) and knew the area very well. Veniamin Yulevich Yakobson of Leningrad was also the prisoners there; he was fifty-four and a pharmacist by profession. Yakobson was an extraordinarily kindhearted man who took care of the prisoners like a father. He always had some ointment, bandages, or powders in his pocket. There was an air of authority about him. Whenever an argument arose, he always made peace between the ones who were arguing. But he was a little "screwball" and constantly maintained that they would never shoot us. "We are not guilty of anything. What should they shoot us?"

The Sturmbannführer was a threat and a terror. Whenever he made an appearance at the edge of the pit, everyone knew that it could not end well. People would labor to the point of exhaustion, and then the Sturmbannführer would stand there with his hands behind his back and look around; he would turn to someone (he gave some of the men contemptuous nicknames) and say, "Why are you walking around so slowly? Are you sick?" The man would reply that he was well and that he had no complaints. But the Sturmbannführer was not satisfied with that: "No, you are not well." There was an old man of sixty-five among us; we called him "Feter" or "Uncle." The Sturmbannführer told him, "Tomorrow you will go to the infirmary." Everyone knew that this meant he would be shot. It was a terribly hard night for us that night in the bunker. We were afraid and ashamed that the old man was going to his death and there was nothing we could do about it. Were tried to comfort Feter. "Why do you try to console me? I've lived my life."

Once we were approaching the pit on our way back from work, when the Sturmbannführer suddenly showed up in a very bad mood. He wanted to know: "Who is sick?" It turned out, of course, that no one was sick. The Sturmbannführer lined up everyone into two columns and said, "Now I will find out who is sick." He went up to each man and looked intensely into his eyes, literally staring right through the person. "You are sick: step to one side," he would say to one and then to another.

But that was not enough for him. He went up to a young, healthy fellow and asked, "Are you familiar with metalwork?" He replied, "Yes." He too was taken our of the ranks, and his irons were removed. It was quite clear that any man who had had his shackles removed was going to be shot.

The Sturmbannführer went up to a fourth man and said, "Are you familiar with metalwork?" This one answered, "No, I am not." "Well, it doesn't matter. You will be." And so the fourth man's chains were removed, and he was brought up to the surface.

A few minutes later we heard four shots. The Sturmbannführer reprimanded our foreman: "How disgusting! Can't these people wash themselves? They get sent to the infirmary, and they're full of lice!" The Sturmbannführer stooped to such a method. He would walk around a group of men lined up in a row, look into their eyes, and ask which of them did not like the work. All of them had to answer in chorus that they liked it just fine. The Sturmbannführer would turn to Zinger: "You are a musician; perhaps you find this work unpleasant?" The Sturmbannführer would then go on to ask, "Perhaps one of the guards has been rude to you and treated you badly?" We would answer all together that the guards were treating us well. Then he ordered us: "Sing!" After a hard day we could hardly stand on our feet, but we had to sing. More often than not, he would order us to sing the "Suliko" arias from the operetta "The Gypsy Baron," as well as a few other songs.

He would listen for a while and then give an order to the sentry: "I am leaving now, but have them sing until I get back." There was no limit to the filthy humiliations those wretches would inflict upon us.

Everything inside of me revolted against all this; it seemed to me a disgrace to go to our deaths like "sheep to the slaughter." I was not the only one who felt that way. The thought of escape "hovered" in the air.

Soon that thought assumed a concrete form.

It fell to me to play a prominent role in all this. The fact that I was a Muscovite immediately won for me a reputation as an intelligent man and strengthened my authority a great deal.

I was brought to Ponary on 29 January, and by 1 February we were already digging a tunnel.

Among those who played the most active part were Petya Zinin, Isaak Dogim, and David Kantorovich. Shlema Gol was also a tireless worker. If necessary, he would rise at 4:00 A.M.

Ovseichik's golden hands were also of great use; whether there was sawing to be done or adjustments to be made, he was always there. A baker from Vilnius named Iosif Belits was an illiterate, unsophisticated man, but when it came to working in the tunnel, he proved to be very useful, since he had some experience along those lines.

With regard to the tunnel, I must say a few words about two other inhabitants of the pit.

Iosif Kagan (his real name was Blazer) had spent some time in prison for crimes he committed.[3] Kagan-Blazer held the distinction of having escaped from Ponary twice. He was picked up in 1941 and sent to Ponary; he was placed at the edge of the pit and "shot." He showed an amazing presence of mind and self-control. Seeing that the line of machine gun fire was approaching him, he fell into the pit at the last second. He was alive. Bodies fell on top of him, and they were covered over with sand. He lay there until evening. When it grew dark, he crawled out of the pit and went back to the city. He hid in a malina, but they found him and sent him to Ponary a second time. He took part in the digging of the tunnel and thus was delivered from Ponary a second time.

Franz (Abram) Hamburg was also in Ponary twice. The first time they found him hiding in a malina along with seventeen other people. They were all sent to Ponary; they were forced to strip naked and were led to the edge of the pit. Contrary to their custom, the Germans started shooting them one at a time. Hamburg was seventeenth in line. He saw the Germans shooting people in the back of the head point blank; he saw people falling one after another. Thus sixteen people were shot. When his turn came, he turned around and said that he had a great deal of gold. "If you do not shoot me, I'll give it all to you." The German wanted to know: "Where's the gold?" "Hidden in the city." They let him get dressed; then they put him in a car and took him to Vilnius. He knew of a cellar in Vilnius where there were two thousand tons of potatoes hidden. He led the Germans to the cellar and said that the gold was there, right in the corner, under the potatoes. The Germans organized a large group of workers, who spent several days digging out the potatoes and uncovering the corner that Hamburg had indicated. He told them they had to dig deep, as the gold was buried under the ground. They dug but found nothing. The Germans beat him savagely, but he insisted that the gold was right there. To his surprise, they did not shoot him but returned him to Ponary and put him in charge of the "Brenners."

On 17 February 1941 a new group of prisoners arrived. Among them were two of my friends from the camp.

Prior to the war Yuri Gudkin was an electrical engineer who lived in Elektrostal, near Moshe. He had a wife and a three-year-old daughter in Moscow. In the prisoner of war camp he assumed an active role in the distribution of leaflets, in setting up contacts with the partisans, and other areas. A second prisoner of war, Kostya Zharkov, a student from Leningrad, was with me in the hospital and helped me out a great deal. He was in a state of depression. I tried to cheer him up. That same night I had shown Yuri our tunnel. He admired it and offered some good advice. I valued his opinion very much. The next morning we "old timers" were sent to work, while the newcomers were left in the pit. Later the women told us that the Sturmbannführer had come and lined everyone up; the Sturmbannführer scrutinized the newcomers. If he asked us where we were from, he asked them what their profession was. I do not know how it happened that Yuri Gudkin, a man with experience in tight spots, could have been so careless as to say that he was a civil engineer. It should be pointed out that the Germans slaughtered the intelligentsia first. The Sturmbannführer was suddenly in an unusually cheerful mood. He rubbed his hands together with pleasure: "Why were you sent here? We'll give you a job more in keeping with your specialty. Remove his irons." They took him out of the pit. Kostya Zharkov and one other prisoner said they were students. The Sturmbannführer was delighted. Announcing that the Germans had the highest regard for learning, he ordered their chains to be removed. They were all taken out of the pit and shot. The rest were sent to join us.

The provocation, sadism, and cynicism of the Hitlerites was truly incredible.

Here is a story told by one of our workers; he name was Kozlovsky.

On 6 April 1943 a transport of women pulled into Ponary. The Germans started a provocative rumor that the ghetto in Vilnius was to be liquidated, while the Kaunas Ghetto would be left alone. Then the Germans selected 2,500 of the prettiest and healthiest women and told them that in a few days they would be going to Kaunas. The women were issued tags, which they took to be their right to life. People would trade everything they owned for one of those tags. The train pulled into Ponary. The Germans entered the train cars and ordered all the women to strip naked. The women refused and were severely beaten. Then they were led to the pits under a reinforced armed escort. The men supervising the operation saw to it that they were left with not a single shred of fabric, not a single thread. And, indeed, when we dug up that pit we found the naked, well-preserved bodies of 2,500 women.

The man who gave the order for this slaughter was Weiss.

Kozlovsky, who was in the unit that gathered up the clothing, related the following episode to me:

Weiss was rushing everyone; all you could hear was, "Faster, faster!" The doors of a train car opened (Kozlovsky was standing right there); a woman who was getting out stumbled and fell. Then Weiss gave the signal for everyone to stop; he gathered together the men and women and gave them a speech: "How could this have happened, that a woman stepping out of a train car could have stumbled and fallen, and no one came to help her up? Where is your gallantry, your gentility? After all, this woman may be a mother one day." He held forth like that for ten minutes and then gave the signal for all the women, including the one who had fallen, to be taken away and shot.

There was a boy of sixteen among us named Benya Vulf. A car once drove by, and Benya Vulf ran across the road in front of it. The Sturmbannführer was standing in the distance and saw the whole thing. He was beside himself; he blew his whistle and ordered all the workers to be assembled at once. We stood there, filthy, holding our shovels, while he repri-manded Benya Vulf: "How could you be so careless? You might have hurt your hand, and that would be most unfortunate. Though it's terrible to even think it, you could have been killed, and that would have been an irreparable catastrophe. Life is a gift from God; no one has a right to infringe upon life. You're only sixteen; you have your whole life ahead of you."

In one pit Isaak Dogim found the bodies of his wife, mother, and two sisters. He was so shaken by it that he nearly went insane. But he was a melancholy and quiet man even prior to that. The Germans taunted him and mocked him.... Motl found the body of his son in one pit. That was the hardest day. When we returned "home" to our pit, Isaak Dogim said that he had a knife, that he was going to stab and kill the Sturmbannführer. For a long time I pleaded with him not to do it; I told him he would get everyone killed. Meanwhile the tunnel was almost ready. I gave him my word that he would be the first to emerge to freedom.

How did we make the tunnel? We had a small storeroom for our provisions. In the little storeroom we put up a false wall. It had two boards hanging on loose nails that would come out with a good tug, making it possible to pass through. We got all our tools from the burial pits; the dead helped us.

The soil was sandy, and it was easy to dig, but we had to make wooden supports to keep it from falling in. We needed boards. Ovseichik and Kantorovich were assigned to that job. When we were brought to Ponary, a second bunker had to be built, since the one bunker was to small to hold all of us. The prisoners who built it secretly removed some boards.

In the pit we once found a saw-edged knife used for cutting bread. It became our primary instrument; we tempered it with fire. We also found a package of small files; thus we were abe to make a real hand saw.

We dug the tunnel every day after work.

People would come back from work; they would eat and start singing. They sang loudly, and the Germans were pleased with their merriment. Although I am a Soviet citizen, I did not know as many Soviet songs as the Vilnius Jews did. They knew all the Soviet films and the names of all the Soviet actors; the songs from the films they knew by heart. They especially liked the song "Soviet Rifle"; it went "Shoot, rifle, true and sure."

As our foreman, Abram assisted us by making sure there was something left for us to eat. We ate later than the others. While they rested and sang we immediately went to work digging the tunnel in the storeroom. At first the work went rather slowly. During the first half of February Kagan and I were the only ones digging. Kostya and Ovseichik were busy preparing the boards. Matskin helped with dragging the sand out of the tunnel and spreading it over the grounds. The pit we lived in was four meters deep; by the time we finished our work, it was three meters, ninety centimeters deep—we had removed enough sand to create a layer ten centimeters deep over the bottom of our pit. First we dug out the shaft, and then we started digging the tunnel, the gallery. We made the passage seventy centimeters wide and sixty-five centimeters high.

The work became more complicated and more intensive. At the time we had two bunkers. We had the most reliable and most active participants involved in the digging moved to our bunker, while those who were more passive stayed in the other bunker.

This was our system: first we set up two posts and supports; this part of the work required two men.

One would dig out the earth and set the posts, and the other would hand him the boards and remove the sand. It was the hardest job; two men would work for an hour and a half to two hours and emerge from the tunnel completely exhausted. During that period of an hour and a half to two hours they would install four boards. The main difficulty was that there was not enough air for matches and cigarette lighters to burn. The problem of running electricity into the tunnel arose.

When two workers would crawl out (Kagan and I, or Belits and Kantorovich, or Shlema and his partner, whose name I forget), a team would crawl into the tunnel to throw out the sand. The men would lie in there with their chains to the side, scoop up a handful of sand next to their head, and throw it to their feet. It was extremely hard work.

We managed to run electricity into the tunnel; the switch was in the girls' room, in their bed. We posted a sentry in the kitchen; he would look up above the pit, and if there were no Germans, we could work. As soon as the Germans showed up, he would run to the switch and give the signal; we had to crawl out immediately. We would lie down and cover ourselves with our overcoats. One time, literally three seconds after we jumped out of the tunnel and got the boards back in place, an SS man appeared.

Many of the men refused to work in the tunnel because they did not think we could make it; the main reason, however, was that they were utterly exhausted after a day of forced labor. There were even some who did not want to leave Ponary. They would say: "My murdered wife, my murdered family, are here; where am I to go?" That is how the older men talked, including the rabbi.

On 9 April we came to the roots of some tree stumps that were laid out in the shape of a triangle. We tried to dig the tunnel so that it would come out in the middle of these tree stumps. When we reached the roots I realized that we were in the right spot and that we were close to the surface. We used an iron hook to poke through the earth a little ways above us. We felt the flow of fresh air. My comrades and I rejoiced; as an engineer, I was proud of having correctly solved a technical problem.

I had a compass and a ruler; we made a level ourselves. I gave the orders and was responsible for deciding which direction we should dig. Here it must be pointed out that by the beginning of April the people working in the tunnel had reached the end of their strength. They would say, "We've been digging for two months, but it's no use." We took a sample of the earth, and it turned out that right next to the tunnel there was a pit full of corpses. There was a danger of our running into the bodies. Several of the men started cursing me for having us dig in the wrong direction. The last days were literally critical days; there remained only a small group of men who still had faith in me. I had to demonstrate my resolve and determination; my triumph was all the greater when on 9 April I reached the roots and saw that we had made it to where we wanted to go. Now an extremely crucial question arose: how to organize our exit. We knew that the Germans guards were all around; other than that we knew nothing. No one had the slightest notion of whether there were partisans nearby.

Zinger knew the area. He told me that the famous Rudnitsky Woods, a large forest, was fourteen kilometers from Ponary and that there was supposed to be a river somewhere nearby.

The Germans posted an unusually tight guard on Ponary. Once a serious concern suddenly arose for us: an SS man, dead drunk, got lost and wandered into our area. The Sturmbannführer shot him on the spot. No one was supposed to penetrate into the secret of Ponary.

We decided to all go together in a predetermined direction.

We divided all the prisoners into eight groups of ten. A commander was appointed for each group. He knew who was in his group and gave his men their instructions. I put the problem this way: it would be possible to escape only if we exercised ironclad discipline. I said, "Choose anyone you wish for your commander; I shall follow his orders without question."

I was told to make up lists. I combined the first two groups of ten. Among them I included the men who had done the most work on the tunnel, as well as those who would be of use to the partisans.

This is the order in which the first group set out: (1) Dogim, (2) Farber, (3) Kostya Potachin, (4) Blita, (5) M. Zaidel, (6) Petya Zinin, (7) Ovseichik, (8) M. Kalnitsky, (9) Shlema Gol, (10) Kantorovich.

I wanted to leave on 12 April, since it was a significant date in my life: it was my brother's birthday.

Unfortunately, however, there was a bright moon on 12 April; at that point the rabbi gave us some helpful advice. Ovseichik went to him. The rabbi told him that in three days, on 15 April, it would be the darkest night of the month.

On 12 April Belits and I went down into the tunnel. We had a small, graduated copper tube with us, and we made sure that it was only ten centimeters to the surface. We could already see the stars; we could feel the fresh April air, and it gave us strength. We saw with our own eyes that freedom was near.

On 15 April we worked the whole day. That day a German whom we had nicknamed "the monkey" took a stick and hit me hard across the shoulders for no reason.

At eleven o'clock that night Dogim and I gathered everyone together.

The first group of ten had two knives and a large flask of vinegar extract that they poured into two bottles. We took all of this from the corpses. Everything we had we generally got from the corpses. Before we escaped I said, "Remember that there is no going back under any circumstances. If we are caught, they will shoot us all anyway. It is better to die fighting, so just keep moving forward."

We started crawling. Dogim removed the last layer of earth; already we were breathing deeply of the air. The night really was very dark; there was absolute silence all around. Once everything was ready, Dogim and I removed our chains. We sent Volf to give the signal that all was ready, and the first twenty men climbed down into the tunnel one at a time. Kostya removed the chains from everyone, and they started crawling. They started coming out of the tunnel. We had to remain absolutely quiet; even if there should be gunfire, we would have to keep order and stay quiet. We had to crawl 200 to 250 meters from our pit, where there was a small wood. When we got to the wire fence, we would cut it with a pair of pliers. We were to tie two pieces of white cloth to the spot where we cut through, so that the people behind us could see where to go. I proposed that we cover fourteen kilometers that one night. The first one to crawl out was Dogim, and I was second. As we were crawling along I was holding on to his foot, when suddenly I saw Dogim turn to the right. To the left, against the background of the sky, I saw the silhouette of a sentry. We crawled another twenty to thirty paces, but there too we could see the figure of a sentry. He was slowly walking along. Once again we had to turn aside. When I was crawling over the ground, I had an utterly indescribable feeling. I was breathing with all the pores of my body.

I felt that our labor had not been in vain, and I exulted. Suddenly a shot rang out. Apparently a twig had snapped under someone's hand. As soon as the first shot rang out, there was shooting from all directions. I looked around: our entire path was filled with people crawling. Some jumped up and started running in various directions. But we reached the wire fence and cut through it with the pliers; the shooting was getting louder and closer.

We went two kilometers and came to another fence; we cut through that one, and I saw that there were only five men left with me. And the Germans were firing mortars. That was the alarm signal for the entire garrison. We ran into the woods but had not taken into account the fact that there were gun emplacements situated all around us. They fired at us from all sides. We made it to the river and faced a new problem: none of my five companions knew how to swim. I had to take each one of them individually across the river. We walked all night long; during the day we hid in the woods.

It took us a week to cover fourteen kilometers; by 22 April we were deep in the Rudnitsky Woods and had arrived at the forest village of Zhagariny. We ran into a peasant, and I asked, "Are there Germans around here?" He gave me a surprised look and said, "There are no Germans, no Poles." "What about Soviets?" "That I don't know, *prosze pana*." That evening we met three partisans. They were Soviet officers; one of them turned out to be Captain Vasilenko. I started kissing him. He asked, "Where did you come from?"

"From the other world" "Where's that?" "Ponary." "Ponary? Come with me."

I told him I was from Moscow. It turned out that he too was from Moscow. Our conversation was suddenly interrupted by gunfire. The shooting was heavy, but the men who had escaped from Ponary did not run for cover. Surprised, Captain Vasilenko asked, "Aren't you afraid?" They replied, "We are not afraid."

They took us to the partisan base; the Jewish partisan units "Death to the Fascists" and "For Victory" had their base right next to it. My comrades from Vilnius had many friends in the Jewish units. Isaak Dogim's cousin Abba Kovner was in command of "Death to the Fascists." The Jewish partisans knew very well what Ponary was. None of them could believe that we had gotten out of there alive; it made a tremendous impression on them. We were literally torn apart with questions from all sides. The order went out to all the partisan units to be on the lookout for escapees. That very day a partisan reconnaissance unit found five more men from our party.

Prepared for publication by R. Kovnator

In the Khorol Concentration Camp

I am Abram Reznichenko, an artist; under the German occupation I hid under the name of Arkady Ilich Rezenko.

During the retreat in the fall of 1941 I ended up being surrounded on the left bank of the Dnieper.

Wounded and separated from my own people, I circled around Piryatin; for two weeks I wandered about in the forest and hid in the ravines. I was afraid to go into the city. Exhausted, hungry, weak, and lice-infested, I finally fell into the hands of the Germans. They sent me to the Khorol concentration camp.

Sixty thousand people languished in this small area fenced off with barbed wire. There were people of all ages and professions, military and civilian, old and young, of various nationalities.

I had spent all my adult life in the Soviet government. Naturally, I never had to hide from the Soviet government the fact that I was a Jew.

During the first days of October 1941, right in from of many prisoners of war, a German soldier lashed an innocent man across the face with his whip; as the man stood there covered with blood, the German shouted at him, "You must die, Jew!" They lined us all up; speaking through an interpreter, the German ordered all the Jews to step forward.

Thousands of people stood there in silence, and no one moved.

The interpreter, a German from the Volga region, walked along the ranks, carefully examining everyone's face.

"Jews, step forward," he said. "Nothing will happen to you."

Several people believed his words.

No sooner did they step forward than they were surround by an armed escort and taken to the other side of a hill. Soon we heard several volleys of gunfire.

After those first victims had been murdered, the terror of the Khorol camp showed up: the camp commandant.

The commandant turned to us and gave a speech.

"Prisoners of war," he said, "the war is finally at an end. A line of demarcation has been established; it runs along the ridge of the Urals... . On one side of the ridge is mighty Germany, on the other side mighty Japan. {The Jewish commissars, as might have been expected, have run away to America. In keeping with the will of the Führer, you prisoners of war will be allowed to go home. First we shall release the Ukrainians, then the Russians and Belorussians.}"

Built on the grounds of what used to be a brick factory, the Khorol camp had only one barracks; it was half-rotten and rested on posts that were leaning to one side. It was the only shelter from the autumn rains and storms.

Only a few of the sixty thousand prisoners managed to cram in there.

The rest had no barracks.

In the barracks people stood pressed tightly against each other. They were gasping from the stench and the vapors and were drenched with sweat. Within a few minutes I realized that it was better out in the rain, better to turn numb in the autumn wind, than to stay there. But how to get out? Crying out, I began struggling to get to the only exit over the backs and shoulders of my neighbors. I was shoved and tossed to one side. Blind with perseverance, I crawled and crawled forward, toward the ones who were trying to get into the barracks, no matter what... .

They woke us for breakfast at five in the morning. Thousands of people immediately lined up one behind the other. The putrid liquid slop (compared to which the thin soup seemed tasty) was doled out slowly. Hence many had to eat their "breakfast" late at night.

Almost every day, and sometimes twice a day, the camp commandant would show up for the distribution of food. He would spur his horse and break into the line. Many people were killed under his horse's hooves!

The German cooks, the Gestapo, and their trusted assistants the *Volksdeutsche* would stand around the cauldron of hot swill.

"*Jude?*"

"No, no!"

"Kike!"

And the poor person was dragged out of the line.

It once happened that a half-naked, shivering, filthy man covered with scabs, whom the Gestapo suspected of being a Jew, was lifted up above the crowd, swung around, and thrown headfirst into the hot swill.

They held him by the legs for a few minutes. Then, when the poor man stopped moving, the cooks dumped out the swill. {Ignoring the shouting and the gunfire, the crowd rushed to the dead man. Having lost every trace of their humanity, people greedily lapped up the slop dripping from his clothing; then they scooped up the puddles of the soup from the ground with their bare hands.}

Groups of Jews were often brought the to Khorol camp. Escorted by a heavily armed guard, they had the identifying badges, the six-pointed stars, sewn on their arms and backs. The Jews were oppressed throughout the camp; they were sent to do the most degrading work, and at the end of the day they were annihilated right in front of everyone.

Various forms of execution were used in the camp at Khorol; the Germans did not limit themselves to shooting and hanging.

They set their German shepherds on the {Jews.} The dogs would chase people down as they scattered in all directions; the dogs would pounce on them, tear their throats out, {and drag the dead or dying people to the commandant's feet...}.

A soldier patrolling the grounds walked up to a young Jewish doctor and with a shout of "Jew!" shot him point blank. The doctor fell down bleeding; the bullet had shattered his jaw. The Germans picked him up by the arms and legs and threw him into a pit. They started filling in the pit immediately. The doctor was still breathing, and the earth over his body moved.

A dysentery epidemic broke out in the camp. Thousands died every day.

The fortunate ones among us were those who still had a pot; they could let a neighbor use it in exchange for a portion of his daily ration. People who did not have a pot had to hold out an army cap or an undershirt to the cook... .

Residents of the surrounding area would try to slip something to the prisoners for them to eat.

One fellow's wife from Zolotonosha once brought him a bag of produce. She managed to toss the bag over the wire fence.

People gathered around the lucky one. He looked at them with frightened eyes.

"Brothers, there are thousands of you, and I am only one man,' he whispered. "All I have is this one little sack... . How can I possible feed you all?" Then he seized a loaf of bread in his hands and clutched it to his chest, like a child.

I spent three and a half months in that camp; December was already coming to an end.

From time to time village elders from various regions would visit the Khorol camp. They made arrangements with the camp authorities for the release of people from their villages.

I would look on with envy as they let the people go. I knew that no one would come for me. I watched how the fortunate ones conducted themselves. Once (when the people from Lokhvista had been summoned), I decided to tempt fate.

"Which of you are from Lokhvista?" the elder asked. "People from Lokhvista, identify yourselves!"

One fellow shouted out, and two more went up to the elder. I decided that I would be the fourth. I was lucky: the village "elder" recognized me as a fellow villager... .

Thus I left the Khorol concentration camp.

We went to Lokhvista on foot. It was a freezing cold December. With an open wound on my leg, it was painfully difficult for me to move. Nevertheless I walked; I was afraid of being separated from my "fellow" villagers from Lokhvista.

On the second day I came down with dysentery.

They left me alone in the snow. Several hours went by. I got up and started to drag myself along. Toward evening I came to a village and knocked on the door of a large hut. It turned out to be a school. They gave me refuge and allowed me to spend the night.

I lived there with a watchman's wife. I ate and warmed myself up. It was impossible, however, to stay with her for long; I had no papers… [and I could be spotted as a Jew…].

I decided to go to my hometown, to Kremenchug.

On the way to Kremenchug I stopped in the village of Pirogi and spent the night with a peasant woman. I told her I was a prisoner of war who had been released from a camp, and she gave me refuge.

The next morning a German unexpectedly showed up at the hut. Just before he stepped inside, my trusted new friends, the woman and her children, hid me on the stove.

The German acted like he was the master of the hut. He sat down at the table, gave out orders, and ate everything that the woman had prepared for herself and her children.

He finally left, and I continued on my way.

I reached Kremenchug at last, after a long and tortuous journey. There I entered the municipal hospital; the wound on my leg continued to fester.

I saw a great deal of suffering in the Kremenchug hospital. I saw a mobile gas unit take away the sick and wounded Jews. I witnessed the death of Doctor Makson, a prominent specialist respected by all; he was a gentle, compassionate old man. Despite his age, the doctor continued to work in the hospital; he stayed at his post on the ward with the sick—until one day, when a German patrol entered the hospital building.

"Makson is a Jew. Give us the Jew!"

Thousands of people from Kremenchug interceded on behalf of Doctor Makson.

The Germans backed down. The eighty-year-old man left the commandant's building and went home surrounded by people.

The next morning the Germans burst into Makson's apartment. They threw the old man into a cart and took him outside of town. There they shot him. One of the patients, a Jewish shoemaker, heard about what happened to Makson and tried to run away.

They caught the shoemaker and mercilessly beat him; then they tied him up and brought him back to the hospital. That night he took a razor and slit his own throat.

The next morning a Gestapo agent came into the ward and went over to the bed where the shoemaker lay in agony. The Gestapo man had put on a smock and a white physician's cap.

"You poor man," he said, sitting down on the edge of the bed. "Look at what your fear has driven you to do."

He patted the shoemaker and repeated:

"You poor man, you poor thing!

Suddenly the German jumped up, raised his fist, and hit the shoemaker in the face: "Oh, you Jew!"

The shoemaker was shot outside the gates of the hospital.

The same Gestapo agent shot him; he didn't take off the smock and the white physician's cap.

Reported by A. Reznichenko,
prepared for publication by Vasily Grossman

The Camp at Klooga (Estonia)

From the Editors

The Red Army occupied the Estonian town of Klooga with such a swift attack that the bonfires of the bodies of Jews shot by the Germans were still ablaze when they arrived. The Germans did not even have time to light one of the fires. Foreign correspondents who were with the advance units saw the bonfires. Their descriptions and photographs have been circulated throughout the world.

The speed of the Soviet offensive took the Germans by surprise; otherwise they would certainly have finished off their prisoners earlier and would have tried to conceal all traces of the shootings. But the element of surprise saved he lives of only a few dozen prisoners in the camp. These fortunate ones managed to hide well enough, so that the Germans could not find them.

The stories of some of the survivors appear below.

Zaintraub, a Student from the Vilnius University

I was in the Vilnius Ghetto. On 23 September 1943 they woke us up and ordered us to prepare for evacuation. By 5:00 A.M. we were lined up five in a row and marched out of the ghetto under the guard of a large detachment of storm troopers.

Forty to fifty people stood around the ghetto boundary with their faces toward the wall. They were selected for execution. Exactly why they were selected I do not know.

They took us to the Suboch region (four kilometers from the ghetto). Both the ghetto and the streets along which they led us were heavily guarded by storm troopers.

Once we got to Suboch, we men were separated from the women and children. Later we found out that the women were sent to Majdanek.[4]

The "selections" continued until ten o'clock in the morning. During this operation the Germans called out Palevsky's name. He was not there; he was hiding in the ghetto. Then they called Levin's name; Palevsky worked in Levin's ten-man unit. They took Levin away, along with Khvoinik, Big, and a teacher named Kaplan.[5] We found out later that they were shot.

It was four in the afternoon by the time we were loaded into the warmth of the boxcars. The windows and exits were covered with barbed wire. The cars were locked, and the train pulled out under a storm trooper guard.

After traveling for four days, we arrived at the Vaivari concentration camp. From there they sent us to Klooga.

At that time there were four hundred men and a hundred and fifty women in Klooga.

First they carefully searched us and took away everything that appeared to be of any value. A storm trooper found twenty rubles in Soviet money on one prisoner and shot him on the spot.

They put us in a demolished barracks. We had to sleep on a cement floor. They divided us up into brigades and sent us out to work. While we were on a job, we were under the supervision of the Todt organization.[6] In the camp the storm troopers and the SS were in charge of us. They all treated us the same way.

I was in a group of three hundred men who had to carry fifty-kilograms sacks of cement from the factory to the train station (one hundred fifty meters). The overseers kept a close eye on us porters. They took a thick club and beat anyone over the head who did not show enough zeal. [Faced with such a threat, we did not walk but had to run.]

The rest of the men worked in the cement factory, at the sawmill, in the mines, and in workshops. The women worked in the quarries. They dragged huge rocks from one place to another. Their quota was four tons per day.

This was the daily routine: We got up at 5:00 A.M., drank some tasteless ersatz coffee, and went out for *Appell* (role call). At six we set out for work; from noon to 12:45 we had lunch and then went back to work until six. After that came the evening Appell. Lunch consisted only of watery soup. There was no supper.

During the Appell we lined up a hundred men to a row and had to wait until the overseer sent us off to work in the morning or back to the camp in the evening. Sometimes we had to stand there for hours; those who did not stand at attention were punished.

Each group of a hundred men had its own torturer. Especially savage were Steinberger, Karol, and Dybovsky; Steinberger would hit people over the head with a shovel or a club. Dybovsky once broke the leg of a worker named Levi. In addition, there was an SS man in the camp, whose name I do not know. The prisoners called him "Six Legs": he always had a large wolfhound with him. The dog would hunt down "criminals," that is, anyone who had hidden a piece of bread or sat down to rest for a moment. The dog would pounce on the "criminal," tear his clothing apart, and bite him, often leaving serious wounds. Then Six Legs would personally give the offender twenty-five lashes with his whip.

There was another overseer named Lauya. He shot Vainshtein for no reason.

The matter of bowing caused us a lot of grief. According to orders, Jews did not have the right to bow to Germans. When we did not bow, however, we were beaten for being rude. When we did bow, we were beaten "for violation of an order."

We were deprived of our names: each of us received a number that was written on our clothing on the shoulder and the knee. Whenever someone committed some infraction, a German would write down his number; during Appell the guilty party would be called out for corporal punishment.

They had a curved bench about a meter in length. They tied the offender to it by his arms and legs. One of the butchers would sit on the victim's head, while another beat him. The man being punished had to count out the blows himself. If he should lose count, the punishment would start all over again. If he lost consciousness, they poured water over him and continued the flogging. [They started by beating him with a birch rod, and then they beat him with a bull's penis with a steel wire running through it.] The punishment was carried out in the presence of all the prisoners.

There were other forms of punishment. They would tie a man to a tree and leave him there in the sun or in the freezing cold for hours; they would deprive people of food, and so on. The work was hard and the living conditions severe. Since we received nothing besides ersatz coffee, watery soup, and [340 grams] of bread mixed with a little sand, many people got sick and swelled up. The number of people who were sick grew larger each day. The Germans, however, had a simple method for getting rid of those who were seriously ill: they poisoned them and then cremated them. There was no medical treatment.

Doctor Bodman was the senior "sanitation officer." He was the one who decided who had to be poisoned; he would prepare the poison and prescribe it for the patient. Whenever he appeared before the patients, he would shout, "Achtung!" (Attention!). All the patients had to instantly fold their hands across their blankets. The doctor would beat anyone who was slow about it with a stick.

We secretly organized get-togethers in the evening. Artists such as Blyakher, Rotshtein, Rozental, Dumarkin, Fin, Poznansky, Motek, Krengel, and others would perform at them. We had conversations about politics, the situation at the front, and other topics. Despite all the prohibitions, we managed to get our hands on some newspapers and would discuss them. It took more than a little insight to detect even a grain of truth in the German papers. We also learned how to shoot in the secrecy of the cellar.

The women were separated from us. Their situation was even worse than ours. They worked beyond the limits of their strength and were beaten more often than we were. One of them tried to escape. It turned out to be impossible to pull it off; the camp was too well guarded. They caught her. It was not enough for them to beat her unmercifully; they forced the poor woman to wear a sign on her chest that said, "Hurrah! Hurrah! I'm back!"

Several children were born in the camp. They were thrown into the oven by order of the Lagerführer.

In August 1944 many of the camps in Estonia were liquidated; among them were Kivioli, Ereda, and Fililoki. We found out about it from labels on the cement bags that were shipped from those places. That was how prisoners communicated with each other.

We knew that the Red Army was getting closer, and we held our breath awaiting its arrival. On the morning of 19 September they took us out to the area where they held Appell. The men were lined up separately from the women. They called out the numbers of three hundred of the healthiest men and announced that everyone was to be evacuated; the three hundred men were needed to carry firewood out of the camp. With the approach of the Red Army and the evacuation of the other camps, all of this seemed plausible to us. Besides, the Germans ordered lunch to be prepared for everyone, including the three hundred men who were sent to carry the wood.

But at 1:30 in the afternoon we heard gunshots. At first we thought it was the SS practicing their shooting, as they had done a number of times before. Soon, however, thirty armed SS appeared in the camp, selected thirty people, and took them away. When we heard more shooting a short while later, we realized that everyone was going to be murdered. Many bolted and ran. I hid in the cellar with twenty other people. A short while later we heard the Germans talking to each other: "Quick! Quick! The Soviets are closing in!"

A few days later we heard the voices of Red Army soldiers... .

Anolik[7]

Altogether there were twenty-three camps in Estonia. They held about twenty thousand people, including ten thousand Lithuanians. Most of the camps were located in Eastern Estonia. There was a concentration camp at Vaivari; people from various ghettos were sent there, and from there they were sent to other camps.

The camp at Klooga was surrounded by two rows of barbed wire. Between the rows were balls of woven barbed wire. Tall watchtowers stood along the fence, and guards were posted there day and night.

Everyone was shaved. The women were shaved bald, and the men were left with just a strip of hair on their head.

We were allowed to have only one shirt. Anyone found wearing a second shirt was whipped. If anyone was found with more bread than was allowed, they would punish the entire cell. After 1 April we had to turn in our outer clothing and work without a coat. For long hours we stood for Appell, also without a coat.

In several of the camps conditions were even worse. The camp at Viivikonna was lit up with powerful reflectors. The prisoners were huddled together in barracks built over a swamp. In order to get to the camp on foot, it was necessary to walk through water up to your knees. They had a special form of punishment in that camp: the overseers would tie up prisoners and thrown them in the swamp for several hours. Several people in Viivikonna were whipped to death. In the camp at Vaivari six hundred out of a thousand prisoners died within a very short period of time.

In December of 1943 a typhus epidemic broke out in the camps. A huge number of those who came down with it died. The ones who were recovering were sent back to work within fourteen days. Of course, they could not stand up under the strain; they would collapse, and then they were murdered. Then they started burning the bodies of the dead and the murdered in large bonfires.

In the camp at Kivioli the prisoners worked in slate pits. At Ereda there was a camp full of sick people. I was there. On 1 February 1944 the camp was evacuated. The sick had to cover 180 kilometers on foot. Twenty-three prisoners were so weak that they could not walk. The doctor who accompanied us ordered them to be thrown into the sea. That was near Iekhvi. We flatly refused to carry out the order. Then the SS and the doctor himself threw those poor people into the sea.

In July 1944 all the old and the sick in Kivioli were slaughtered. They called it an "Aktion." Two doctors from Vilnoius named Volkovysky and Rudik perished during the Aktion. By that time the camp at Leezi had already been evacuated; there too the old and the sick were shot. They removed the dresses from the women and led them off half-naked.

It was May 1944 when I arrived in Klooga, so I was not there for long. When they started slaughtering the prisoners, I hid in the barracks; there I lay under some blankets and did not moved until the Red Army came.

[E. Yerushalmi

As a former member of the Juderat in the Shavli (Shiauliai) Ghetto, I can relate the following. In early February 1944 a transport of women, children, and people unable to work passed through Shavli on its way from Estonia. It took them five days just to reach Shavli; they were given no food or water the whole time they were riding in the sealed cars wrapped in barbed wire. A seventeen-year-old boy named Beker was on the transport. He came down with typhus; as soon as his temperature went down, he was sent to work sixteen kilometers from the camp. He feet were frostbitten; he caught a cold in his kidneys and became an invalid—that is how he ended up on the transport. At the Meshkuichai station he got permission from the guard to get off the train for a drink of water. Meanwhile the train left, and he was arrested at the station.

Since he could hardly walk, he was sent to our ghetto and locked up. The commandant of the ghetto, Obersturmführer Schlef, asked Gekke, the man in charge of all the Jewish camps, about it, and Gekke can to a decision: Sonderkommando. This meant that Beker was to be turned over to the Sonderkommando, that is, to the SS in charge of exterminating the Jews. The Judenrat found out about it and petitioned Schlef for permission to poison Beker right in the ghetto. Schlef agreed, and Beker was transferred to the hospital, where the sentence was postponed for a month under all sorts of pretenses, both genuine and false. In the meantime one of the ghetto inhabitants died and was entered into the hospital records under the name of Beker; Beker took the names of the dead man and was sent to another camp. We later found out that the transport that Beker had originally been on left for Majdanek.]

Vatsnik

I was among the three hundred men whom the Germans first led out of the camp to their deaths under the pretext of having them haul firewood. I was one of the first thirty taken into the forest to get the firewood. We loaded the wood onto carts, and the carts drove off. When the last cart had gone, we were ordered to lie down on the ground. We lay there until 4:30 in the afternoon. Then they led us back to the barracks. Armed SS lined the way back. We were ordered to walk with our "heads lowered" and our arms behind our back. They left us outside one of the barracks. An SS man came up to me and ordered me to gone on ahead to the barracks. I realized that death awaited me and started trembling as I passed through the entrance. A German asked me very tenderly, "Why are you trembling, boy?" At that very instant he shot me twice, in the neck and in the back. One bullet went right through me, and the other lodged in my body. But I did not lose consciousness. I fell down and pretended to be dead. I heard the German leave the barracks, and I wanted to get up. But at that moment the German brought in two more prisoners. Again I pretended to be dead. He forced these two to lie down on the floor, and he shot them. Then they brought in more prisoners, forced them all to lie in a pile, and murdered them. They brought in a child; I could hear him crying out, "Mama," and then a shot rang out. The ones who were not dead but dying moaned and gasped. Finally the shooting stopped.

I started to drag myself out from under the bodies. I finally managed to do get free with great difficulty. I had to step over bodies to get to the exit. Suddenly I saw that my friend Lipengolts was still alive. I helped him to his feet. Yankel Libman was also still alive. He asked, "Help me stretch out my legs." We pulled on him as much as we could, but we had no strength left; we were both wounded. Libman soon grew still... .

We smelled gasoline. We rushed for the doors, the windows—they were bolted shut! I pounded on a window with all my might; I broke it and jumped out, with Lipengolts behind me. We fell to the grass, jumped up, and made a run for it. Without realizing it, we started running toward the bonfires where the Germans were burning bodies. They shot at us. But we ran without looking back, and, fortunately, the bullets missed us. We ran seven kilometers, until we reached the Russian prisoner of war camp. There they hid us in the hospital, where we awaited the arrival of the Red Army.

Benyamin Anolik, Junior [8]

The first one we saw was a Red Army captain. We asked for permission to touch him, since we could not believe that we were free, that a soldier from the Red Army was standing before us. The captain embraced us and congratulated us on our liberation. As for us, we wept; and each of us just wanted to touch the star on the captain's cap.

We took our liberators around the camp. There was the bench where they whipped us. [A bloody whip made from a bull's penis lay on the ground.] There were the trees they tied us to. And there was the barracks where people lived. The captain took out his handkerchief; it was difficult to breathe. Here lay the ones whom the Germans did not manage to carry off to the bonfires and burn. There was a three-month-old infant, dead. His arms were stretched out toward his dead mother. I look at the captain. Tears are flowing from his eyes, and he does not try to hide them. On his chest he has medals and decorations for wounds he has received. He is a Russian. He knows death and suffering. He weeps. Right now his tears are more dear to us than anything in the world... .

Over here there used to be an eight-room house overflowing with prisoners. All that was left of it were two chimneys and a pile of charred bones. And here are the bonfires. Things are scattered around them, dresses and skirts. There were four bonfires; three of them were still smoking; the bodies were smoldering. The Germans failed to burn one of them. A layer of firewood, a layer of the murdered, a layer of firewood, a layer of the murdered.... As the men were dying, they covered their eyes with their caps; the women covered their eyes with their hands. Here are two lying in each other's embrace; they are brothers. One bonfire has no bodies, just wood. It was being prepared for us. If the Red Army had arrived a few hours later, we survivors would probably have been lying there burning. There are eighty-two of us who survived by some miracle. In the bonfires there are 2,500... .

We beg the captain: "Take us with you! Take us into the army! We must be avenged!"

Again the captain has tears in his eyes. "You are all sick," he says. "Wait a while. You must rest. [We shall avenge you. We shall go to Berlin and there call the Germans to account for you."]

Nevertheless, one of us immediately enlisted in the army. He was healthier than the rest of us. He was a poet whose name was on the lips of every Jew: Beilis, the same name as the Jew whom the tsarist regime put on trial under the accusation of ritual murder and who was later acquitted. They also told him to wait a while and to rest. But he pointed to the star on the captain's cap and said, "This is my only rest." Then he pointed toward the west: "This is my only path." And, pointing to the Red Army soldiers, he said, "These are my brothers."

Prepared for publication by O. Savich

Treblinka

East of Warsaw, along the Western Bug River, there are stretches of sand and swamp, of thick evergreen and deciduous forests. The area is empty and gloomy, and villages are rare. People traveling on foot and in carts try to avoid the narrow sandy paths, where one's feet stick and wheels sink into the sand up to the axles.

Here, on the Siedlce railroad line stands the lone Treblinka train station sixty kilometers from Warsaw, not far from Malkinia, where the lines leading to Warsaw, Bialystok, Siedlce, and Lomza meet.

Many of those who were brought here in 1942 may very well have passed through here during a more peaceful time, their eyes tracing the monotonous landscape of pines and sand, sand and pines, brush and heather, ugly stationhouses and railroad crossings.... And perhaps the passenger's bored gaze may have fallen on a single spur of track going from the train station into the middle of the pine thickets that surrounded it. The spur led to a sandpit, where white sand was extracted for industrial and municipal construction projects.

The sandpit was located four miles from the station, in a wilderness surrounded on all sides by a pine forest. The soil here is stingy and sterile, and the peasants do not cultivate it. So the barren stretch of land remained barren. Here and there the ground is covered with moss; here and there a scraggly pine protrudes. Now and then a jackdaw or a brightly crested bird flies by. This wretched wilderness was selected and approved by the German Reichsführer SS Heinrich Himmler for the construction of an all-embracing execution block, the likes of which humanity has never known, from the time of primitive barbarism to our own cruel days.

There were two camps at Treblinka: Camp No. 1, where prisoners of various nationalities—mostly Poles—worked, and the Jewish camp, Camp No. 2.

Camp No. 1, a labor or punishment camp, was located right next to the sand pits not far from the edge of the woods. It was an ordinary camp, like hundreds and thousands of others that the Gestapo had built throughout the occupied Eastern territories. It was set up in 1941.

Thrift, efficiency, accuracy, and pedantic cleanliness—characteristic of many Germans—are not bad traits in themselves. When applied to agriculture or industry, they can produce good results. Hitlerism applied these traits to their crimes against humanity, and the Reich SS operated the labor camps in Poland just as if they were raising cauliflower or potatoes.

The camp was laid out in uniform, rectangular sections, and the barracks were arranged in neat rows; the paths were lined with birch trees and covered with sand. They built concrete ponds for domestic fowl and pools for washing out underwear, with steps conveniently leading down into them; they installed services for German personnel, such as a modern bakery, a barbershop, a garage, a gas station, and storage units. The Majdanek camp at Lublin and dozens of labor camps in East Poland, where the Gestapo and SS intended to settle in for along time, were built according to the same principle, with gardens, water fountains, and concrete paths. The traits of German efficiency, the attention to details, the pedantic obsession for order, and the German love for schedules and timetables showed in the construction of these camps, down to the most minute detail.

People were brought into the camp for various periods of time, sometimes for a very brief period—four, five, or six months. They were Poles who had violated the laws of the General Government—minor violations, as a rule, since any significant violations would mean immediate death, not the concentration camp. Denunciations, a slip of the tongue, a chance word overheard by a passerby, the failure to make a delivery, a refusal to hand over a cart or a horse to a German, a young's girl's audacity to refuse the advances of an SS man, the suspicion of involvement in some possible sabotage (not sabotage itself)—all of these offenses landed hundreds and thousands of Polish workers, peasants, intellectuals, men, girls, elders, and teenagers in this penal camp. A total of fifty thousand people passed through its gates.[9] Jews were sent to this camp only if they happened to be highly skilled workers—bakers, shoemakers, carpenters, stone masons, tailors. The Germans had set up all sorts of workshops there, including a substantial furniture factory that supplied German army headquarters with armchairs, tables, and chairs.

Camp No. 1 was in operation from autumn of 1941 until 23 July 1944. As it was being liquidated, the prisoners could hear the muffled rumble of Soviet artillery.... Early on the morning of 23 July the guards and the SS men downed a stiff shot of schnapps and set about the business of liquidating the camp. By evening all the prisoners in the camp had been murdered and buried.[10] A carpenter from Warsaw named Max Levit managed to survive; he lay wounded beneath the bodies of his comrades until nightfall and then crawled off into the woods. He said that as he lay in the pit he could hear a group of thirty boys who had been in the camp singing "Vast Is My Homeland" before they were shot. He heard one boy cry out, "Stalin will avenge us!" After the first volley he heard the boys' leader Leib, the camp favorite, shout, "Mister Guards, you missed! Please, sirs, shoot again, again!"

It is now possible to relate the details of the regimen that the Germans set up in this labor camp. Dozens of witnesses, Polish men and women, either escaped or were released from Camp No. 1 at one time or another, and they have offered a detailed account of the rules governing the labor camp. We know about the work in the sandpits, about how they took people who did not meet their quotas and pushed them over a cliff into a ravine. We know that the daily food ration was 170 to 200 grams of bread and a liter of some slop that passed for soup. We know about people who starved to death and about those who, swollen from hunger, were hauled away in carts to be shot. We know about the wild orgies that the Germans held; about how they raped girls and then shot them; about how they threw people from a tower six meters high; about how a group of drunken Germans would snatch ten or fifteen prisoners from the barracks at night and calmly demonstrate their killing methods by shooting them in the heart, the back of the head, the eye, the mouth, and the temple. We know the names of the SS who were in the camp, their personalities and peculiarities. We know that the head of the camp was a Dutch German named Van Eupen, an insatiable murderer and sex pervert who loved good horses and fast riding. We know about the huge young man named Stumpfe, who broke out into uncontrollable fits of laughter every time he murdered one of the prisoners or when one of them was executed in his presence. They dubbed him "Laughing Death." Max Levit was the last one to hear him laughing, when the guards shot the boys on Stumpfe's orders. All the while Levit lay at the bottom of the pit, only wounded.

We know about the one-eyed German from Odessa, a man named Svidersky who was known as "the master of the hammer." He was considered a consummate expert in "cold" murder—murder without firearms; in the course of a few minutes he took a hammer and murdered fifteen children from eight to thirteen years of age, who had been deemed unfit for work. We know about the sullen and quiet SS man named Preifi, a skinny man who looked like a gypsy and was known as the "Old One." He would alleviate his melancholy by sitting at the camp garbage dump and shooting at prisoners who would sneak in to eat potato peelings; he forced them to open their mouths and then would shoot them in the mouth.

We know the names of the professional murderers Schwarz and Ledecke. They amused themselves by shooting prisoners returning from work each day, killing twenty, thirty, and forty people at a time.

Such was existence in this camp that resembled a little Majdanek, and one might suppose that there could be nothing in the world more terrible. But those who lived in Camp No. 1

knew very well that there was something more horrible still, a hundred times more horrible than their camp.

In May 1942 the Germans began construction of a slaughterhouse for Jews three kilometers from the labor camp. The construction proceeded at a rapid pace; more than a thousand laborers worked on it. Nothing in this camp had anything to do with life; it was entirely for the purpose of death. According to Himmler's conception of the camp, its existence was to be kept an absolute secret. Anyone who happened to come within a kilometer of the camp was shot without warning. German aircraft were forbidden to fly anywhere near this area. Brought in on transports along special railway lines, the victims knew nothing of the fate that awaited them until the last moment. The guards who escorted the transport were not allowed inside the boundaries of the camp. When the trains arrived, the SS from the camp took over. Normally consisting of sixty train cars, the transports would be divided into three sections outside the woods; then the locomotive would haul twenty cars at a time up to the camp platform. Pulling the cars behind it, the engine would stop at the barbed wire, so that neither the engineer nor the fireman ever crossed over into the camp area. Once the cars were unloaded, the SS non-commissioned officer on duty would signal the next twenty cars, which were waiting two hundred meters up the line. After all sixty cars had been unloaded, the camp command headquarters would phone the train station to send another transport. The empty train would go on up the line to the sand pit, where it picked up a load of sand and then went back to Treblinka and Malkinia.

This was a good location for Treblinka. Transports of victims came here from the four corners of the world, from north, south, east, and west. Transports came from the Polish cities of Warsaw, Miedzyrzecz, Czestochowa, Siedlce, and Radom; from Lomza, Bialystok, Grodno, and many Belorussian towns; from Germany, Czechoslovakia, Austria, Bulgaria, and Bessarabia.

For thirteen months transports rolled into Treblinka, with sixty cars per transport; on the sides of the cars written in chalk were the numbers 150, 180, and 200, indicating the number of people in each car. Railroad workers and peasants secretly recorded the number of transports that pulled into the camp. A sixty-eight-year-old peasant from Wulka (the village closest to the camp) named Kazimiersz Skarsynski told me that on some days six trains would pass by on the Siedlce line alone; he said that in the course of those thirteen months there was almost not a single day that a transport did not pull in from Siedlce. And the Siedlce line was only one of four lines that led to Treblinka. A railroad worker named Lucian Zukov, whom the Germans enlisted to work for them on the line from Treblinka to Camp No. 2, said that he worked from 15 June 1942 to August 1943 and that one to three trains were sent to Treblinka every day that he was on the job.[11] Each train had sixty cars, and each car held at least 150 people. We have dozens of testimonies to this effect... .

The area fenced off inside the camp itself—with the warehouses for the things that had belonged to the murdered people, the platform, and auxiliary premises—occupied a small area 780 x 600 meters. If you were to doubt for an instant the fate of the millions who were brought here and if in that instant you were to suppose that the Germans did not murder them immediately upon their arrival, then you must ask: where are they, all these people who could comprise the population of a small state or a large European capital? After all, the area of the camp is so small that within a few days it would be overflowing with the people coming in; within ten days there would be no room at all for the streams of humanity flowing in from the ends of Western Europe, Poland, and Belorussia. For thirteen months—395 days—the trains left either empty or with a load of sand; not one person sent to Camp No. 2 ever left.

Everything recorded below has been compiled from the accounts of living witnesses, from the testimony of people who worked at Treblinka from the first day of its existence until 2 August 1943, when the doomed rose up, burned down the camp, and escaped into the woods. It comes from the accounts of camp guards who were arrested and who confirmed the witnesses' stories word for word and often filled them out. I have seen these people myself and have spoken with them in detail about what happened; their written statements are here on this table before me. These many testimonies converging from a variety of sources are consistent in every detail, from their descriptions of the commandant's dog Bari to their account of the technology used to murder the victims and to construct the conveyor system for the dead.

Let us proceed through the circles of hell known as Treblinka.

Who were these people transported on the trains to Treblinka? In the spring of 1942 the Jewish population of Poland, Germany, and the western regions of Belorussia were driven into the ghettos. Millions of Jewish people—including workers, artisans, physicians, professors, architects, engineers, teachers, artists, and other people of various professions, along with their families, their wives, daughters, sons, mother, and fathers—were herded into the ghettos of Warsaw, Czestochowa, Lublin, Bialystok, Grodno, and dozens of others in smaller towns. There were approximately 500,000 people in the Warsaw Ghetto alone. [Apparently] confinement in the ghetto was the first stage in the premeditated Hitlerite plan to exterminate the Jews. The summer of 1942, during the time of the fascists' great military victories, was deemed to be the most opportune time for carrying out the second stage of the plan: the physical annihilation of the Jews. It is known that at this time Himmler went to Warsaw to issue the appropriate orders. Work for the preparation of the slaughterhouse at Treblinka proceeded day and night. In July the first transport set out from Warsaw and Czestochowa for Treblinka.[12] The victims were told that they were being taken to the Ukraine to work on farms. They were allowed to take along twenty kilograms of luggage and some food provisions. In many cases the Germans forced the victims o purchase train tickets for Ober-Majden; that was their code name for Treblinka. Soon throughout Poland the name of Treblinka was heard with such horror that the SS quit using it in front of the people they were loading onto the transports. The treatment of the people loaded onto the trains, however, was such that they were left with little doubt as to the fate that awaited them. Each train car was loaded with no less than 150 people; usually there were 180 to 200. Throughout the trip, which sometimes lasted two to three days, the prisoners were given nothing to drink. People were suffering from thirst so much that they would drink their own urine. The guards would offer them a drink of water for one hundred zloty and then pocket the money, usually without giving the victim a drink. The people were packed so tight in the cars that sometimes they only had room to stand; in every instance some had died by the time they reached the end of the line, especially during the hot, humid days of summer, when a number of old people and people with heart trouble would die in transit. Since the doors to the train cars were not opened until the end of the trip, the bodies would start to decompose and foul the air inside the cars. No sooner would one of the prisoners light a match during the night than a guard would open fire, shooting through the walls of the train car. A barber named Abram Kon relates that in his car five people were killed and many were wounded when the guard started firing at the sides of their car.

The conditions on the trains arriving in Treblinka from the Western European countries—from France, Bulgaria, Austria, and other countries—were completely different. People there had never heard of Treblinka; up until the last minute they believed they were being sent off to work, and the Germans painted all sorts of pictures of the new life of ease and comfort that awaited them. The people on some of these transports believed that they were being sent to neutral countries, as they had paid the German authorities a lot of money for their visas.

A train once arrived in Treblinka carrying English, Canadian, American, and Australian citizens who had been stranded in Western Europe and Poland during the war. After prolonged negotiations involving huge bribes, they were allowed to leave for neutral countries. All the trains from European countries came without guards and had all the usual services, including sleepers and dining cars. The passengers brought along large trunks and suitcases and ample supplies of food. Their children ran out at the train stops to ask whether it was much farther to Ober-Majden.

From time to time a transport of Gypsies would arrive from Bessarabia and other regions. Several times transports pulled in carrying young Polish peasants and workers who had been involved in uprisings and partisan activities.

It is difficult to say which is more terrible: to go to your death in a horrible state of agony, knowing what awaits you or to gaze out the window of a comfortable coach, suspecting nothing, at the very moment when a call is being placed from your train station to Treblinka to let them know when your train will arrive and how many people it is carrying.

In order to maintain the deception of the people coming from Europe until the very last moment, the railhead at the death camp was set up to look like a passenger train station. At the platform where groups of twenty cars were unloaded there was a train station complete with a ticket window, a place for storing baggage, and a restaurant; there were signs pointing the way to Bialystok, Baranowicze, Wolkowysk, and other towns. An orchestra played to greet the arrivals, and all the musicians were well dressed. A porter wearing a railroad uniform collected the tickets from the passengers and led them out to a square. Three or four thousand people loaded down with bags and suitcases, supporting the aged and the sick, found themselves standing on this square. Mothers holding children in their arms and older children clinging to their parents looked about the square. There was something unsettling and terrifying about this place that had been trampled down by millions of human feet. With a growing realization the people looked around at the disturbing details of the scene surrounding them: they saw the objects hastily cast aside by other groups taken away, items littering the ground, piles of clothing, open suitcases, shaving utensils, enamel kitchenware. How did all these things happen to get tossed aside here? And why did the tracks come to a halt at the railway station? Where were the railways to Bialystok, Siedlce, Warsaw, and Wolkowysk. Why was that yellow grass growing here, and why this barbed wire fence three meters high? And why are these guards chuckling in such a strange manner, as they looked at the men straightening their ties, the nicely dressed old ladies, the little boys in their sailor suits, the slim girls who somehow had managed to keep up their tidy appearance during the journey, and the young mothers who were tenderly adjusting their infants' blankets? All of these guards decked out in the black uniforms of SS Unteroffizieren acted like cattle drivers at the entrance to a slaughterhouse. For them the newly arrived cargo did not consist of human beings, and so despite themselves they smirked at the expressions of embarrassment, love, fear, concern for loved ones, for possessions; they found it amusing that mothers would chase after their children who had started to run off and scold them, that men were taking out clean handkerchiefs to wipe their brows and then lighting a cigarette, and that girls were fixing their hair and worried about holding down their skirts when a gust of wind rose up. They thought it was funny whenever old men tried to squat down on their suitcases, that some of them had piles of books with them, and that the sick would wrap their scarves around their necks. Each day as many as twenty thousand people passed through Treblinka. Days when only six or seven thousand were hauled away from the station were considered wasted. Four and fives times a day the square filled up with people. And all of these thousands of people—these tens and hundreds of thousands of people, with their young and old faces, their dark-haired and golden-haired beauties, their bent and bald-headed elders, their timid teens—all of them merged into a single deluge that swallowed up all reason, all the sublime human sciences, all maidenly love and childish wonder, all the coughing of old men and the beating of the human heart.

And so the new arrivals trembled as they sensed the strangeness of the reserved, satiated smirk of superiority on the faces of the ones who looked upon them as an animal might gaze upon a dead man.

Once again, in a manner of moments, the ones who had just arrived on the square latched onto those incomprehensible details that stirred their anxiety.

What was behind that huge six-meter wall covered with blankets and yellow pine branches? The blankets in particular frightened them: they were quilted from colored silk and covered with embroidery, just like the ones packed in the travelers' bedrolls. How did they get here? Who brought them here? And where were their owners? Why did they not need their blankets any longer? And who were these people with the blue bands on their arms? They began to recall all the warnings they had heard, all the fears, all the rumors spread in whispers. No, no, it cannot be. To a man they drove away the terrifying thought. The anxiety on the square persisted for a few moments—for maybe two or three minutes, until everyone had filed into the area. There was always a delay at this juncture, since in every group there were the crippled, the lame, the sick, and the elderly, who could hardly move their legs. And now everyone was gathered in the square. An Unterscharführer (an SS non-commissioned officer) loudly instructed the new arrivals to leave their possessions in the square and proceed to the bathhouse; he told them to keep only their papers, their valuables, and whatever toiletries they might need. The people standing there had dozens of questions: could they take their underwear, should they undo their bundles, would their belongings not get mixed up lying in the square, might they not lose them? But some strange force impelled them to silently and quickly move on without asking any questions, without looking back, toward the opening in the six-meter wall camouflaged with branches. They went past the barbed wire fence three times a man's height, past anti-tank trenches three meters wide, past thin coils of steel wire designed to trap the legs of the escapee like a fly in a spider web, then past another barbed wire fence several meters high. A terrible feeling, a feeling of doom, a feeling of helplessness would take hold of them. There was no escape, no turning back, no fighting back: from low wooden towers the muzzles of heavy machine guns were aimed at them. How to cry out for help? They were surrounded by SS and guards with submachine guns, hand grenades, and pistols.

Meanwhile in the square outside the train station two hundred workers wearing sky-blue armbands (the "blue group") quickly, quietly, deftly untie bundles, open suitcases and baskets, and remove the strap from bedrolls.[13] The things belonging to the group that just arrived were sorted and appraised. Neatly packed sewing kits, spools of thread, children's underwear, shirts, blouses, jumpers, shaving sets, bundles of letters, photographs, thimbles, flasks of perfume, mirrors, nightcaps, slippers, felt boots sewn with wadded material in case of freezing weather, women's slippers, stockings, lace, pajamas, packets of butter, coffee, cans of cocoa, prayer shawls, candlesticks, books, biscuits, violins, and children's blocks went flying to the ground. It required a certain skill to sort through these thousands of objects and appraise them in a matter of minutes—some to be sent to Germany, the old and shabby items to be set aside for burning. Woe to the worker who might mistakenly put an old wicker suitcase in a pile of leather valises set aside for shipment to Germany, or who might toss a pair of Parisian stockings with a fashion label onto a pile of old worn-out socks. The worker would make the mistake only once. They were not allowed a second chance. Forty SS men and sixty guards worked at the "transport" site, as this first stage we have been describing was called; they met the trains and escorted the arriving party into the "station" and out to the square; they also supervised the workers who sorted through and appraised the passengers' belongings. While they were working, the men with the sky-blue armbands would often pop into their mouths a piece of bread, sugar, or candy that they had found in the food bundles when the guards were not looking. It was forbidden. After they finished their job, however, they were allowed to wash their face and hands with eau de cologne and perfume, since there was a water shortage at Treblinka, and only the Germans and the guards were allowed to use it. While the people who were still alive were being prepared for the "showers," the work on their belongings was nearing an end. The valuables were sent off to the warehouse; their letters, baby pictures, photos of brothers and brides, wedding announcements—all the thousands of precious items infinitely dear to their owners that were so much rubbish to the lords of Treblinka—were gathered into a pile and hauled off to huge pits. At the bottom of the pits lay hundreds of thousands of similar letters, postcards, calling cards, bits of paper with children's scrawls and their first awkward drawings in crayon. The square was then quickly cleaned up and made ready for a new group of condemned people. The reception of a group did not always go as I have just described it. There were times when the prisoners knew where they were going and resisted. The peasant Skarsynski twice saw people break through the doors, jump out, overpower the guards, and bolt for the forest. In both instances every last one of the prisoners was shot down with machine guns. Four of the men who were murdered were carrying children in their arms. The children were murdered too. A peasant woman named Maryana Kobus has described similar struggles between the prisoners and the guards. Once, when she was working in a field, sixty people who had broken away from the train and were headed toward the forest were murdered right before her eyes.

By this time the group of arrivals have gone into a second camp and onto another square. There is a huge barracks on the square; to the right there are three more barracks—two for sorting and storing clothing and a third for shoes. Further ahead, on the west side of the camp, were the SS barracks, the barracks for the guards, food stores, a cow shed, cars, trucks, and armored vehicles. It looked like a regular concentration camp, like Camp No. 1.

In the southeast corner of the camp grounds was an area fenced off with tree branches; at the entrance to the area was a booth with a sign on it that said "Infirmary." All those who were decrepit and seriously ill were separated out from the crowd waiting for their "shower" and taken on stretchers to the infirmary. A doctor wearing a white smock and an armband with a red cross on his left sleeve stepped out of the booth to greet them. What took place in the infirmary will be described in detail below.

The second phase of the initiation process was designed to break the will of the new arrivals by constantly barking short, abrupt orders at them. The orders were given in that well known tone of voice that is the pride of the German army, a tone calculated to demonstrate that the Germans belong to the master race. The letter *R*, at once rolling and hard, sounded like a whiplash.

"Achtung!" the command rings out over the crowd, and in the leaden silence the voice of the Scharführer repeats the instructions that would be repeated several times a day for months on end:

"The men are to remain where they are. Women and children go to the barracks on the left and undress."

According to the accounts of eyewitness, at this point terrible scenes would unfold. The great sense of their maternal, marital, and filial love told them that they were seeing each other for the last time. Handshakes, kisses, blessing, tears, and brief words of farewell were exchanged, filled with all these people's love and anguish, all their tenderness and despair... . The SS death psychiatrists knew that these emotions had to be instantly crushed and extinguished. The death psychiatrists were familiar with the laws that ruled in the slaughterhouses of the world, laws that in Treblinka the animals forced upon the humans. This was one of the most critical moments: the separation of daughters from fathers, of mothers from sons, of grandparents from grandchildren, of husbands from wives.

Again the command rings over the square: "Achtung! Achtung!" That was precisely the moment when they had to shake the people's reason again, when they had to tantalize them with a glimmer of hope, switching the principle of death and the principle of life. Thus, word for word, the voice hacked away:

"Women and children remove your shoes at the entrance to the barracks. Place your stockings in your shoes. Children's socks are to be placed in their sandals, boots, or slippers. Be orderly."

Immediately the words were repeated:

"Proceed to the showers. Take your valuables, your papers, money, towels, and soap.... I repeat..."

Inside the women's barracks was a barber who sheared the naked women; the old ones had their wigs taken away from them. A strange moment, psychologically: according to the testimony of the barbers, more than anything this shearing before death convinced the women that they were actually going to a shower. Teenage girls would sometimes feel their heads and ask, "Could you please even it up in this spot?" The women usually calmed down after the shearing; nearly every one of them came out of the barracks carrying a piece of soap and a towel folded over her arm. Some of the younger ones would cry over the loss of their beautiful locks. Why did they shave the women's heads? To deceive them? No, their hair was needed in Germany. It was raw material.... I have asked many people what the Germans did with the hair that they had shorn from the heads of the living dead. All the witnesses testified that huge piles of black, golden, and auburn hair—straight, curly, and braided—were disinfected, packed into bags, and shipped off to Germany. All the witness confirm that the hair was packed into bags with German addresses on them. How was the hair used? According to a written deposition from a man named Kohn, the German navy used the hair to stuff mattresses and for things such as making ropes for submarines. Other witnesses claim that the hair was used to pad saddles for the cavalry.

The men undressed in the courtyard. From the first group of arrivals that day 150 to 300 men of great physical strength were selected to bury the bodies; they were usually murdered the following day. The men had to undress very quickly but in an orderly manner, placing their shoes, socks, underwear, jackets, and pants in neat piles. A second work detail sorted through their belongings; they were the "reds," distinguished from the workers at the train station by their red armbands. Anything deemed worth sending to Germany was sent off to the warehouse. All metal and clothing labels were carefully removed. The rest of the items were either burned or buried in the pits. The feeling of anxiety was increasing at every moment. There was a terrible stench in the air, mixed with the smell of lime chloride. It seemed that there was an inexplicably huge number of fat, irritating flies in the area. How did they get here, with all the pine trees and paved ground? The men were finding it difficult to breathe now; they jumped at every little detail, looking for some sort of an explanation, for some hint of the mysterious fate that awaited them, the doomed. And why were those gigantic excavators over there, toward the southern part of the camp?

Then a new procedure began. The naked people were lined up in front of a window, where they were told to turn over their papers and their valuables. Again the terrible, hypnotic voice cried out: "Achtung! Achtung! The penalty for concealing valuables is death!... Achtung!"

The Scharführer sat in a small wooden booth. SS men and guards stood around him. Next to the booth were wooden boxes into which the prisoners were to throw their valuables: one for paper money, another for coins, a third for watches and rings, for earrings and brooches with precious gems, for bracelets. Their papers were tossed to the ground, since no one on earth had any use for these documents belonging to the living dead, who in an hour would be lying stiff in the pit. The gold and other valuables, however, were carefully sorted; dozens of jewelers worked to ascertain the purity of the metals, the value of the stones, the purity of the diamonds.

Here, at the "window," the illusion came undone. Here the attempts at lying that had held the people in a trance of uncertainty—all the efforts to keep them wavering between hope and despair, between visions of life and visions of death—to an end. The torture by means of lies was one of the methods used in concentration camps; it helped the SS to do their work. Once the process of plundering the living dead had reached its final stage, the Germans abruptly altered the way they treated the victims. The Germans broke women's fingers as they tore off their rings, and ripped their earlobes, as they yanked the earrings from their ears.

The final stage of this conveyor-belt system of execution required speed if it was to function properly; hence the word "Achtung" was replaced by the disturbing, hissing sounds of *"Schneller! Schneller!"* Faster, faster, faster!

The cruel practices of recent years have shown that a naked man immediately loses his powers of resistance and no longer struggles against his fate; when his clothing is lost, so is his instinct for survival, and he accepts the inevitability of his fate. The very one who had just been filled with an insatiable thirst for life has now become passive and indifferent. Just to make sure, however, the SS took an additional, monstrous measure in this final stage of the conveyor-belt system of execution, one that sent them into a state of psychic, spiritual shock.

How did they do it?

Through the swift and sudden use of unthinkable cruelty. These naked people who had been stripped of everything but who stubbornly persisted in their humanity—a thousand times more so than the creatures surrounding them in the uniform of the German army—continued to breathe, to see, and to think, their hearts beating all the while. The soap and towels were knocked out of their hands. They were lined up in rows of five.

"*Hände hoch! Marsch! Schneller, schneller!*"[14]

They started walking down a lane lined with flowers and pine trees, about 120 meters long and two meters wide; it led to the execution site. Both sides of the path were lined with barbed wire and guards in black uniforms standing shoulder to shoulder; the SS wore gray. The path was covered with white sand, and as the ones in front marched forward with their hands in the air, they could see in the sand the fresh imprints of bare feet: small women's feet, the tiny feet of children, the heavy footprints of old men. This faint trace in the sand was all that remained of thousands of people who had recently passed this way, who had passed by just as this new group of four thousand was walking by, just as another four thousand would pass after these in two hours, and then thousands more waiting their turn at the railway station in the woods. And so they passed by, as they had the day before and tens days ago and a hundred days ago, as they would pass by tomorrow and fifty days from now, as they did throughout the thirteen months of the existence of the hell at Treblinka.

The Germans referred to this path as the "road with no return."

A humanoid by the name of Sukhomil, his face twisted into a grimace, would shout in a deliberately distorted German:

"Come on, kids, schneller, schneller, your bath water is getting cold. Schneller, kids, schneller!" Then he would laugh out loud, take a bow, and dance with delight.

Their hands in the air, the people walked silently between the two rows of guards, who beat them with their rifle butts and rubber clubs. The children ran, barely able to keep up with the adults. Everyone who witnessed this final, sorrowful procession has commented on the savagery of one of the human-like SS men: Zepf. He specialized in the murder of children. Possessing immense strength, this creature would suddenly grab a child from the crowd and either swing him around like a stick and smash his head against the ground or simply rip him in two.

It took three or four minutes to go from the "window" to the execution site. Hurried along with blows and deafened by shouts, the people came out onto a third square, where for an instant they halted in astonishment.

Before them stood a red brick building surrounded by trees, built in the style of an ancient temple. Five broad, concrete steps led down to wide, massive, beautifully decorated doors. At the entrance there were flowers growing in planters. Chaos reigned everywhere; everywhere there were mounds of freshly dug earth. A huge excavator clanked away as it dug up tons of yellow sandy soil with its steel jaws; the dust that rose into the air from its work hovered between the earth and the sun. The roar of the colossal machinery digging the huge mass graves from morning till night mixed with the savage barking of dozens of German shepherds.

Small rail lines ran along both sides of the death building; people in large overalls pushed small dumpster cars up and down the rails.

The wide doors leading into the death building slowly opened, and two of Schmidt's assistants (Schmidt was in charge of the operation) appeared in the entrance. They were sadists and maniacs. One was a tall man of about thirty, with broad shoulders, black hair, and a tawny, laughing face that beamed with excitement; a bit younger, the other was short, with brown hair and pale yellow cheeks, as if he had just taken a strong dose of quinine. The names of these men who betrayed humanity, [their homeland, and their oaths] are known.

The tall one held a massive pipe about a meter long in one hand and a whip in the other; the short one was armed with a saber.

At that moment the SS released their dogs, who were trained to pounce upon the crowd and tear the flesh of the doomed people with their teeth. The SS men brutally shouted at the women, who stood petrified with fear, and beat them with their rifle butts.

Inside the building itself Schmidt's men drove the people through the open doors leading into the gas chambers.

At that moment Kurt Franz, one of the commandants of Treblinka,[15] would show up with his dog Bari at his side. He had specially trained the dog to pounce on the doomed people and tear out their genitals. Kurt Franz made a fine career for himself in the camp; he started out as a junior non-commissioned officer in the SS and rose to the relatively high rank of Untersturmführer. This tall, thin, thirty-year-old SS man not only displayed his skill in the organization of the conveyor-belt system of execution—not only did he adore his work and could not imagine himself outside of Treblinka, where everything operated under his tireless supervision—but he was something of a theoretician who liked to elaborate on the general meaning and significance of his work.

The stories of how the living dead of Treblinka preserved their human dignity until the last minute shake you to the depths of your soul, rob you of your sleep, and deprive you of your peace. There are tales of women who tried to save their sons and performed heroic but hope-less feats for their sake, of young mothers who hid their infants in a pile of blankets and protected them with their own bodies. No one knows, nor will anyone ever know, the names of these mothers. There are tales of ten-year-old little girls who consoled their sobbing parents and of a little boy who cried out at the entrance to the gas chamber, "Don't cry, Mama, the Russians will avenge us." No one knows, nor will anyone ever know, the names of these children. Tales are told of dozens of doomed people who rose up against huge contingents of SS men armed with machine guns and grenades, [of how they died on their feet, their chests riddled with bullets.] There is the story of the young man who attacked an SS officer with a knife and of the youth who had been in the Warsaw Ghetto Uprising and by some miracle had managed to hide a grenade from the Germans; as he stood naked, he tossed it into a group of executioners. There is the story about a battle that was fought all night between a group of condemned men and a detachment of guards and SS men. The sounds of gunfire and hand grenades could be heard until morning; when the sun came up the entire square was covered with the bodies of the fighters, their weapons lying beside them: sticks torn from the fence, knives, razors. For as long as the earth shall endure, no one will ever know the names of those who perished that night. The story is told of a tall girl on the "road with no return" who tore a carbine from the hands of one of the guards and turned it on dozens of SS men. Two of the animals were killed in the fight, and a third lost his arm. He returned to Treblinka as a one-armed man. The girl was subjected to terrible torture and execution. No one will ever know her name.

Hitlerism deprived these people of their homes and their lives; the Nazis wanted to erase the memory of their names from the world. But all of them—the mothers who shielded their children with their bodies, the little ones who wiped the tears from their fathers' eyes, those who fought through the night with knives and grenades and fell in battle, and the naked girl who fought alone against dozens—all of them, having departed from being, have preserved forever the dearest name, one that the Hitlerites and Himmlerites could not trample into the ground: the name of the Human Being. On their memorial it shall be written: "Here Lies a Human Being."

The people who lived in Wulka, the village closest to Treblinka, relate that sometimes the screams of the women being murdered were so horrible that the entire village would be driven out of its mind and run off into the forest, so as not to hear the piercing shrieks that penetrated through the trees, through heaven and earth. Then the screaming would suddenly subside only to erupt again just as horrible, just as piercing, penetrating into the bones, the skull, the soul…. And so it was repeated three or four times a day.

I asked one of the captured executioners about those screams. He explained that the women screamed at the moment when the dogs were released and the group of condemned people was driven into the death building. "They saw death; besides, it was very crowded in there. They were beaten terribly, and the dogs tore at them."

The sudden silence set in when the doors to the gas chamber were closed. When a new group was brought to the gas chamber, the screams would erupt again. And so it was repeated two, three, four, sometimes five times every day. After all, the executions at Treblinka were not just executions. They were executions by conveyor system, based on methods of mass production used by the major modern industries.

And, like a genuine industrial enterprise, Treblinka did not start out operating in the manner we have described. It gradually grew and developed as it introduced new techniques. The first three gas chambers they built were small. During the time when the gas chambers were under construction and were not yet ready, several transports came in, and the arrivals were murdered with axes, hammers, and clubs. The SS did not want the people in the area surrounding Treblinka to know about their work, so they avoided any gunfire. The first three concrete chambers were small—5 x 5 meters—so that each had an area of 25 square meters. The ceiling was 190 centimeters high. Each gas chamber had two doors: one to let living people in, and one for dragging out the dead bodies of the people who had been gassed. The second door was quite wide, and 2.5 meters high. The gas chambers were all built on one foundation.

These three gas chambers did not satisfy the demands of the authorities in Berlin who ruled over the conveyor system of execution.

The construction of the building described above began right away. The men in charge of Treblinka were proud of the fact that in terms of production capacity and manufacturing area, their gas chambers far surpassed all the others in the Gestapo's death factories, including Majdanek, Sobibór, and Belzec.

Seven hundred prisoners worked for five weeks on the construction of the new death facility. When the work was at its peak an expert came with a whole crew from Germany to install the equipment. The new gas chambers—there were ten in all—were symmetrically arranged along each side of a wide concrete corridor. Like the original three gas chambers, each of these had two doors: one through which living people entered from the corridor, and another one right across from it in the opposite wall, through which the bodies of the people who had been gassed were dragged out. These doors led to special platforms that stood along each side of the building. Narrow-gauged rails ran up to the platforms. Thus the bodies were dragged out onto the platforms, immediately loaded into dumpster cars, and hauled off to the mass graves that the huge excavators were digging day and night.

The floors of the gas chambers were built with a large incline slanting from the corridor to the platforms, so that the job of cleaning out the gas chambers could be done much faster (in the old gas chambers the bodies had to be carried out on stretchers or dragged out with straps). Each gas chamber was 7 x 8 meters, for an area of 56 square meters. The ten new gas chambers covered an overall area of 560 square meters; counting the size of the three old gas chambers, which continued to operate when there were smaller groups to be gassed, the total floor space area devoted to the death factory at Treblinka was 635 square meters. Between 400 and 500 people could be packed into a single gas chamber at one time.[16] Thus when the ten gas chambers were all operating at the same time, an average of 4,500 people were destroyed in a single gassing.

It took twenty to twenty-five minutes for the people to perish in the gas chamber. Early on, when the gas chambers were still new and the executioners were not able to immediately determine the ideal amount of gas to administer, they experimented with various poisons, and the victims were subjected to horribly torturous deaths that would drag on for two to three hours. During the first days of operation the intake and exhaust systems worked so badly that the poor people writhed in agony for eight to ten hours. Various methods were used in the killing operation. One was to pump into the chambers the exhaust fumes from a heavy tank engine that ran the Treblinka power station. These gas fumes consisted of two to three percent carbon monoxide, which combines with the hemoglobin in the blood to form a stable compound known as carboxyhemoglobin. Carboxyhemoglobin is much more stable than the compound formed from the combination of oxygen and hemoglobin in he respiratory process, when the blood circulates through the lungs. Within fifteen minutes human blood becomes so saturated with carbon monoxide that the hemoglobin no longer carries any oxygen. The victim gasps, breathing "emptiness," but the oxygen no longer reaches the organism, resulting in oxygen deprivation: the heart races to pump blood into the lungs, but the carbon-monoxide-saturated blood is unable to draw oxygen from the air. Breathing becomes labored, the agonizing symptoms of suffocation appear, consciousness blurs, and the human being perishes just as though he had been strangled.

A second method—and the one most widely employed at Treblinka—entailed the use of special pumps to pump the air out of the chambers, so that, as in the first method, the victim died of oxygen deprivation. And finally the third method, used less often but used nevertheless, was to murder the victims with steam; this method also entailed depriving the organism of oxygen, since the steam was used to drive the air out of the chambers. They made use of a variety of poisonous substances, but this was entirely experimental; the first two methods were the ones used for mass murder on an industrial scale.

How can we find the strength to imagine what the people in those gas chambers experienced during the last minutes of their lives? It is known that they fell silent.... .

Packed in so tightly that their bones cracked, their crushed lungs could not breathe; they stood next to each other covered with the last drops of mortal sweat in a single mass of humanity. Someone, perhaps a wise old man, musters the strength to say, "Be comforted: this is the end." Someone cries out in a terrible scream of execration.... . And must that sacred curse not be fulfilled?... With the last ounce of her human strength a mother tries to make more room for her child, so that his last mortal breath might be made easier by one millionth of a fraction through his mother's care. A young girl asks, her tongue petrified, "Why are they suffocating me? Why can't I live to love and have children?" The head turns, the throat contracts. Were such images reflected in the eyes of those who were dying? Consciousness reels in the last moments of terrible agony... No, we cannot imagine what transpired in the gas chamber... The dead bodies stood pressed together, growing cold. Witnesses maintain that the children clung to the last breaths of life longer than anyone else.

After twenty to twenty-five minutes Schmidt's assistants would peek through the peep holes. It was time to open the doors to the platform. Driven by the shouting of SS men, prisoners in overalls started the unloading process. Since the floor was slanted toward the platform, many of the bodies rolled out on their own. People who unloaded the gas chamber have told me that the faces of the dead had turned yellow and that about 70 percent of those murdered were bleeding slightly from the nose and mouth. Physiologists can explain this. The SS men examined the bodies while chatting among themselves. If someone appeared to be alive, groaning or moving, they finished him off with a bullet from their pistols. Then a team armed with dental pliers came in to extract all the gold and platinum teeth from the bodies lying on the platform waiting to be shipped out. The teeth were sorted according to their value; then they were placed in boxes and sent to Germany. Had it suited the SS to pull the teeth out of living people, they, of course, would not have hesitated to do so; to them it would be like cutting the hair off living women. Apparently, however, it was easier and more convenient to remove the teeth form the dead.

The bodies were loaded into small wagons on rails and hauled off to huge mass graves. There they were laid out in rows, one packed tightly against another. The grave was not filled in yet, however; instead, they waited for a new batch of bodies. As soon as the gas chamber was emptied out, the Scharführer working at the "transport" site received a phone call and a brief order. The Scharführer blew his whistle as a signal to the engineer, and another twenty cars slowly pulled up to the platform at the station with the phony placard that read "Ober-Majden." A new batch of three or four thousand people carrying suitcases, bundles, and packages of food moved into the station square. Mothers carried babies in their arms, children held their parents tight, and all were curiously looking around. There was something foreboding and terrible about this square that had been trampled down by millions of feet. Why did the railway suddenly end just beyond the station platform, where the yellow grass was growing; why the barbed wire fence three meters high?...

Thus, in keeping with the strict procedure, the new group of the doomed was led down the "road with no return" just as the last of the bodies were being dragged from the gas chambers and sent off to the pits. And the pits stood yawning wide and waiting.

After a short time the Scharführer's whistle sounded again; another twenty train cars emerged from the woods and slowly pulled up to the platform. Thousands more people carrying suitcases, bundles, and packages of food moved into the square and looked around. There was something foreboding and terrible about this square that had been trampled down by millions of feet...

Sitting in his office amidst piles of papers and charts, the camp commandant would phone the Treblinka station, and roaring down a side track between the pine trees came another transport of sixty cars under an escort of SS men armed with machine guns and automatic weapons.

The huge excavators rumbled and labored day and night, digging huge new graves hundreds of meters long and many meters deep. And the graves stood yawning. Waiting. They did not have to wait long.

Himmler went to Treblinka with a group of Gestapo chiefs at the end of the winter of 1942 – 1943. Himmler's group flew to a landing strip near the camp; from there they took a light truck and entered through the main gates. Most of them wore military uniforms, but some—perhaps the specialists among them—were in civilian clothes, with overcoats and fur hats. Himmler personally inspected the camp; one of the people who saw him told us that the minister of death walked up to a huge pit and silently stared into it for a long time. Those who accompanied him stood back at a distance and waited while Heinrich Himmler contemplated the colossal grave that was already half full of bodies.

Treblinka was the largest factory in Himmler's industry. The SS Reichsführer's airplane left that same day. As he was leaving Treblinka, Himmler gave and order to the camp commandant that disturbed Hauptsturmführer Baron von Fein, his assistant Karol, and Captain Franz—all of them. The order was to immediately dig up the bodies of everyone who had been burned and burn every one of them; their ashes were then to be taken out of the camp and scattered over the fields and roads. There were already millions of bodies buried in the earth,[17] and this assigned seemed remarkably complicated and difficult. In addition, the bodies of those who had jus been gassed were not to be buried at all but burned immediately. At first the task of burning the bodies did not go well at all: the bodies would not burn. True, it was noticed that women's bodies burned better than men's, so they tried to use them to burn the men's bodies. The bodies were doused with large quantities of gasoline and fuel oil, but the process was expensive, and it did not produce results. It looked like they had come to a dead end. But they found a way out. An SS agent arrived from Germany, a heavy-set man of about fifty who was a master of his trade.

Under his supervision, they set about building ovens. These were special furnaces; neither the furnaces at Lublin nor those in the world's largest crematorium could have handled such a gigantic number of corpses as they had to burn at Treblinka. The excavator dug a pit 250 to 300 meters long, 20 to 25 meters wide, and 5 meters deep. Three rows of reinforced concrete pillars 100 to 120 centimeters in height were installed along the bottom of the pit. These pillars supported steel beams that ran along the entire length of the pit. Rails were laid across the steel beams every five to seven centimeters. Thus the grating for a gigantic oven was constructed. Soon and second oven and then a third were built with the same dimensions. Each of these ovens could hold 3,500 to 4,000 bodies at a time.

A second huge excavator was brought in and then a third. The work went on day and night. The men who participated in the burning of the bodies have said that the ovens reminded them of gigantic volcanoes. The terrible heat burned the workers' faces, with flames leaping eight to ten meters into the sky; columns of thick, black, greasy smoke filled the heavens and hung in the air like a heavy, motionless shroud. At night people in the surrounding villages could see the flames from thirty to forty kilometers away, as they rose above the pine forests surrounding the camp. The entire area was filled with the terrible smell of burning human flesh. Whenever the wind blew in the direction of the Polish camp three kilometers away, the people there gagged from the awful stench. More than eight hundred prisoners were forced to do the work of burning bodies—more than the number of workers employed in the blast furnace and open-hearth area in large steel plants. This monstrous work unit labored day and night, without interruption, for eight months and could not handle the millions of human bodies exhumed from the earth. True, new groups of people continued to arrive to be gasses, and that also put a strain on the work unit.

Transports from Bulgaria pulled in. The SS and the guards were very happy about their arrival; deceived both by the Germans and the Bulgarian fascist government, these people had no idea of their fate and brought along large quantities of valuables, many delicious foods, and white bread. Then came the transports from Grodno and Bialystok, then from the rebellious Warsaw Ghetto, then transports of Polish rebels—peasants, workers, and soldiers. A group of Gypsies arrived from Bessarabia; there were about two hundred men and eight hundred women and children. The Gypsies came on foot, their caravans trailing behind them; they had been so fooled that this convoy of a thousand people was escorted by only two guards, although even the guards did not know n that they were leading these people to their death. It is said that the Gypsy women clapped heir hands in excitement when they saw the beautiful building that housed the gas chambers; until the very last moment, they did not know what fate awaited them. The Germans were especially amused by it. The ones who arrived from the Warsaw Ghetto Uprising were cruelly tortured by the SS; they took the women and children from the group and led them not to the gas chambers but to the site where the bodies were being burned. Insane with horror, the mother were forced to lead their children between the red-hot bars along which thousands of dead bodies writhed in the smoke and flames; there, as if they were still alive, the bodies twisted and turned. The bellies of women who had been pregnant burst open from the heat, and the bodies of stillborn infants burned in their mothers' opened wombs. Such a spectacle could rob even the most hardened man of his reason; it had a hundred times the impact on these mothers, who were trying to cover their children's eyes, as the crazed children screamed out to them: "Mama, what's going to happen to us? Are they going to burn us?"

The "infirmary" was also rearranged. A round pit was dug, and iron bars, upon which the bodies would be burned, were placed in the bottom of the pit. Around the pit, as around a sports stadium, were low benches that were so close to the pit that anyone sitting on them would be hanging over the edge. Sick and feeble old men were brought to the "infirmary," where the "nurse aides" would seat them on the benches facing a bonfire of human bodies. Once they had enjoyed the sight for a while, the cannibals shot them in the back of their gray heads and their bent spines; then the murdered and the wounded tumbled into the flames.

Can any living human being on earth imagine the SS humor of Treblinka, the SS amusements, the SS jokes?

The SS set up soccer games for the condemned, forced them to play tag, and organized a choir of the doomed. There was a menagerie built near the Germans' dormitory; in the cages were the harmless beasts of the forest—wolves and foxes—while the most terrible, most savage beasts of prey on earth freely walked around, sat on birch benches, and listened to music. They even wrote a special hymn for the doomed people; titled "Treblinka," here are a few lines from it:

> Für uns gibt heute nur Treblinka
> Das unser Schicksal ist...[18]

A few minutes prior to their death the bloodied people were forced to stand as a choir and were taught to sing idiotic, sentimental German songs:

> ... Ich brach das Blümelein
> Und schenkte es dem Schönsten
> Geliebsten Mädelein...[19]

The chief camp commandant selected several children from one group; he murdered their parents and dressed the children in the finest clothes, gave them candy and played with them. Then, after a few days, he became bored with them and ordered the children to be murdered.

The Germans posted an old man in a prayer shawl and phylacteries next to the outhouse and ordered him to allow people no more than three minutes inside. He had an alarm clock hanging from his chest. The Germans would look at his prayer shawl and laugh. Sometimes the Germans would force elderly Jewish men to hold prayer services or to arrange funerals for individuals who had been murdered, observing all the religious rites and rituals. They would bring in gravestones, and then after a while they would dig up the graves, toss out the bodies, and destroy the gravestones.

Among their favorite amusements were the orgies of violence and humiliation perpetrated against young, beautiful women and girls, who were selected from every group of the doomed people. The next morning the rapists would personally escort their victims to the gas chambers. That is how the SS at Treblinka—the mainstay of the Hitler regime, the prize of fascist Germany—amused themselves.

Here it must be emphasized that these creatures did not mechanically or blindly carry out the will of others. All the witnesses attest to a trait they held in common: a love for theoretical reflection, for philosophy. They all had a weakness for delivering speeches to the doomed, for boasting to them and explaining the great meaning and significance for the future of everything that was transpiring at Treblinka.

The summer of 1943 was unusually hot in this area. For many weeks there was no rain, no clouds, no wind. The work of burning the bodies proceeded at full speed. For six months the ovens had been going day and night, but little more than half of those who were murdered had been cremated.

The prisoners who had the assignment of burning the bodies could not endure the horrible moral and physical torment; every day fifteen to twenty of them committed suicide. Many sought death by intentionally violating the disciplinary rules.

"To get a bullet was a luxury," a baker from Kosow told me; he escaped from the camp. People would say that in Treblinka being doomed to live was many times worse than being doomed to die.

Charred boned and ashes were hauled outside the camp compound. The Germans mobilized groups of peasants from the village of Wulka to load the bones and ashes into carts and scatter them along the road from the death camp to the Polish penal camp. Imprisoned children would take shovels and toss the ashes along the road. Sometimes they would find melted gold coins or gold crowns. These children were known as the "children from the black." The road turned black from the ashes, like a black mourner's band. Automobile tires make a strange sound when they travel over this road. When I ride along the road, all the while from under the wheels I hear a sad whispering sound, like a timid lament.

This black mourner's band made of ashes, running through the woods and fields from the death camp to the Polish camp, was a tragic symbol of the terrible fate that united the peoples who had fallen under the axe of Hitler's Germany.

The peasants hauled the charred bones and ashes from the spring of 1943 to the summer of 1944. Twenty carts went out every day, and each of them made six to eight trips per day, with a load of 100 to 125 kilograms each time.

In the song "Treblinka" that the Germans forced the eight hundred men burning bodies to sing, there were words that summoned the prisoners to submissiveness and obedience; in exchange they were promised "just a little bit of happiness" that would "flash by in an instant." Surprisingly enough in the living hell of Treblinka there actually was one happy day. The Germans, however, were mistaken: those doomed to death in Treblinka were neither submissive nor obedient that day. Reckless bravery gave birth to that day. The prisoners conceived a plan to revolt. They had nothing to lose. They were all doomed to death, and every day of their lives was a day of suffering and torment. The Germans would not spare a single witness of their terrible crimes; the gas chamber awaited them all. Indeed, many of them were sent to the gas chamber after working for several days; then they were replaced in their turn by a new group of arrivals. Only a few dozen men survived not for hours or days but for weeks and months; they were skilled laborers, carpenters and stone masons, bakers, tailors, and barbers who served the Germans. It was they who put together a committee for the uprising. Of course, only those condemned to death—only men possessed by a fierce thirst for revenge and an all-consuming hatred—could have devised such a mad and courageous plan of revolt. They did not want to escape until they had destroyed Treblinka. And they destroyed it. Weapons started to turn up in the workers' barracks: axes, knives, clubs. At what a price, what an insane risk was every axe and every knife obtained! And what tireless patience, skill, and cunning were required to hide all this from the searches conducted in the barracks! Stores of gasoline were created for dousing and setting fire to the camp buildings. How was this gasoline accumulated, and how did it disappear without a trace, as if it had evaporated? All of this required superhuman strength, a focused mind, a determined will, and a terrible audacity. A tunnel was finally dug beneath the barracks where the Germans kept their arsenal. Here their audacity came to the aid of these men; the god of courage stood by them. Twenty hand grenades, a machine gun, rifles and pistols were taken from the arsenal. All of it disappeared into secret hiding places that the conspirators unearthed. The participants in the conspiracy divided themselves into groups of five. The immense, complex plan for the uprising was worked out down to the minutest detail. Each group of five had a specific assignment. One group was to storm the watchtowers where the guards stood watch with their machine guns. A second group was to launch a sudden attack upon the sentries who patrolled the path between the camp squares. A third would attack the armored cars. A fourth would cut the telephone lines. A fifth would take the barracks, and a sixth would cut a passageway through the barbed wire. A seventh group was to build bridges across the antitank ditches. An eighth was to douse the camp building with gasoline and set them on fire. A ninth group would destroy everything that could easily be destroyed.

There was even plan to provide the escapees with money. The Warsaw physician who collected the money nearly gave the whole thing away. One day the Scharführer notice a thick wad of banknotes sticking out of his pants; it was the money he had collected at the time, and he was on his way to stash it in a hiding place. The Scharführer acted like he did not notice anything and then reported the matter to Franz. It was, of course, something extraordinary. Franz decided to question the doctor personally. He immediately suspected that something was amiss: what was a doomed man doing with money? Franz began the interrogation in a calm and calculated manner; after all, no man on earth was so adept at torture as he was. He was convinced that not a single human being on earth could stand up to the torture meted out by Hauptmann Kurt Franz. In the hell of Treblinka there were great academicians of torture.

But the doctor from Warsaw outsmarted the SS Hauptmann. He took poison. One of the participants in the uprising told me that never before in Treblinka had they tried so hard to save a man's life. Apparently Franz realized that the dying physician harbored an important secret. But the German poison worked very well, and the secret remained a secret.

Toward the end of July a stifling heat wave set in. When they opened up the mass graves, steam rose up out of them as from out of gigantic boilers. People were killed by the horrible stench and heat from the ovens; exhausted men dragging out the dead themselves fell dead into the burning ovens. The ground was thick with fat-bellied flies crawling around, and the air hummed with them. The last hundred thousand bodies were being burned.

The uprising was planned for 2 August. It was signaled by a gunshot. A portent for success favored the sacred cause. New flames appeared in the sky—not the flames producing the heavy, thick smoke of burring human bodies but the bright, hot dancing flames of a conflagration. The camp buildings were on fire, and to the rebels it seemed that the sun itself had been torn from the heavens to blaze over Treblinka, announcing a triumphant freedom and honor. Shots rang out, and the blasts of machine guns resounded from captured towers. The explosions of hand grenades reverberated like a clarion of truth. The air vibrated with explosions and rumbled with the sound of buildings crashing down; the whistling of bullets drowned out the buzz of carrion flies. Axes dripping with blood flashed in the clear, pure air. On the 2nd of August the evil blood of the SS flowed into the ground of the hell of Treblinka, and the bright blue sky was aglow with the triumph and celebration of payback time. Here it happened as it had since times of yore: creatures strutting around like beings from a superior race, with roars of *"Achtung, Mützen ab"*[20]—who called the people of Warsaw out of their homes with the thundering voices of conquerors, shouting, *"Alle r-r-r-raus, unter-r"*[21]—these people so smug in their power when it came to executing millions of women and children turned out to be despicable cowards—pitiful, whining worms crawling around on the bellies—when it came to a genuine fight to the death. They lost their heads and ran around like rats; they forgot all about the diabolically contrived defense systems of Treblinka, about the flaming ovens they had prepared, about their weapons. Need one say anything more about this; is anyone surprised at it?

Treblinka was awash in flames. As the rebels bid a silent farewell to the ashes of their people and crossed the barbed wire boundary, SS and police units were in hot pursuit of them. Hundreds of police dogs were set on their trail. The Germans mobilized aircraft. Battles were fought in the swamps and forests, and very few of the people involved in the uprising are still alive. But those who fell fell in battle, with guns in their hands.

After the 2nd of August Treblinka ceased to exist. The Germans finished burning what bodies were left; then they tore down the brick buildings, took down the barbed wire fence, and burned the wooden barracks that had survived the uprising. The equipment used in the death factory was blown up, taken apart, and shipped out; the ovens were destroyed, the excavators removed, and the huge pits filled in with earth. The building at the train station was dismantled down to the last brick; even the rails and railroad ties were finally hauled off. Lupine was planted on the site of the camp, and a settler named Streben built a small house there. That little house is no longer there; it was burned down. What did the Germans want from all this? Were they trying to hide the traces of the murder of millions of people in the hell of Treblinka? Did they really think they could do that? Did they think they could silence the thousands of people who had seen the transports of doomed people arriving at the death factory from all over Europe? Did they think they could hide the deadly flames and the thick smoke that lingered in the sky for eight months and could be seen by people in dozens of surrounding villages? Did they really think they could force the peasants of Wulka to forget the horrible screams of women and children that went on for thirteen months and that continue to ring in their ears to this day? Did they think they could silence the living witnesses who had seen the slaughterhouse Treblinka from its first day of operation until 2 August, the last day of its existence—witnesses whose stories of the SS and the policemen agree down to the finest detail, witnesses whose step-by-step, hour-by-hour account of the daily events in Treblinka have formed a kind of diary of Treblinka? No longer are the words *"Mützen ab"* shouted at them; no more are they herded into the gas chamber. And Himmler no longer has any power over his minions, who now timidly bow their heads and nervously play with the fringes of their jackets; speaking in dull, atonal voices, they relate the seemingly insane and delusional story of their crimes.

We arrived at Treblinka in early September 1944, thirteen months after the uprising. For thirteen months the slaughterhouse was in operation. For thirteen months the Germans tried to hide every trace of their work. It is quiet. The pine needles on the trees lining the railroad hardly moved. The eyes of millions of people peering out of train cars slowly pulling up to the platform looked upon these pines, this sand, and this old tree stump. Now covered with white pebbles neatly arranged in German fashion, the ashes and crushed slag along the black road quietly stir. We enter the camp and tread the Treblinka earth. With a faint popping sound, the lupine pods burst open at the slightest touch; millions of seeds scatter over the earth. The sound of falling seeds and the soft popping of bursting pods blend together to form a sad, lingering, quiet melody. It seems as though a funeral dirge of little bells is rising up from the earth itself; barely audible, it is mournful, deep, and peaceful. The earth moves under our feet; full and rich, as though it had been saturated with linseed oil, it is the bottomless earth of Treblinka, as unsteady as the sea floor. This stretch of land fenced off with barbed wire has swallowed up more human lives than all the earth's oceans and all the earth's seas since the existence of humankind.

The earth ejects from itself crushed bones, teeth, various objects, bits of paper; it does not want to keep the secret.

These things ooze from the earth's unhealed wounds. They lie there: the half-rotten shirts that belonged to the ones murdered, their trousers and slippers, moldy cigarette cases, cogwheels from watches, penknives, shaving kits, candlesticks, children's shoes with red tassels, towels with Ukrainian embroidery, lace underwear, scissors, thimbles, corsets, and trusses. Further along, emerging from another crack in the earth, are piles of kitchenware: frying pans, aluminum mugs, cups, pots and pans, pottery, cans, dishes, plastic children's cups.... Further on—as if someone's hand had forced them from the depths of the bottomless, swollen earth up into the light—are half-rotten Soviet passports, notebooks with Bulgarian writing, photographs of children from Warsaw and Vienna, letters scribbled by children, books of poetry, a prayer jotted down on a yellow slip of paper, food ration cards from Germany.... And everywhere there were hundreds of perfume bottles of various shapes and sizes, green, pink, blue.... Hovering over everything is the horrible stench of decay; nothing can overcome it, neither fire nor sun nor rain or snow nor wind. And hundreds of tiny forest flies swarm around the rotting objects, the bits of paper, the photographs.

We walk on, treading the bottomless, undulating Treblinka earth, and suddenly we stop. There before our eyes is a yellow lock of hair gleaming like burnished copper, the fine, light, lovely hair of a young girl, trampled down into the earth; next to it is a lock of light blonde hair, and further on we see a thick black braid lying in the brightly-colored sand, and on and on and more and more. These are apparently the contents of one—and only one—of the sacks of hair that the Germans had failed to ship out. It is all true. The last hope that it was all a dream is crushed. The lupine pods pop open, and the seeds make the sound of countless little bells ringing out a funeral dirge from deep within the earth. And it seems that the heart will come to a halt under the weight of such sadness, such sorrow, such anguish, beyond all human endurance.

Vasily Grossman

The Children from the Black Road

We were walking through a field densely overgrown with lupine. The sun was blazing; the rustle of dry leaves and the crackling of seedpods blended to form a sad, almost musical sound. The old man who was our guide uncovered his gray, quivering head, crossed himself, and said:

"You are treading over graves."

We were walking along the earth of the Treblinka death camp, where the Germans had gathered Jews from all over Europe and the occupied territories of the USSR.

Here the Germans murdered millions of people. The terrible black road cuts through the field of Treblinka; it is black because it is strewn with human ashes for three kilometers.

Tons of ashes were hauled out to the road in carts. Children between the ages of eleven and thirteen were selected to spread the ashes over the road with shovels. They are known as "the children from the black road."

One freezing February day in 1943 a freight train delivered sixty boys to the Treblinka death camp, along with its usual load of "passengers." They were Jewish children from Warsaw, Vilnius, Grodno, Bialystok, and Brest. As soon as the transport was unloaded, they were separated from their families; the adults were sent to the death camp, and the boys were taken to the "labor camp."

The chief or Hauptsturmführer of this camp was a Dutch German named Van Eupen. He decided that there would always be time to kill the boys; in the meantime they could be put to work. He instructed Untersturmführer Fritz Preifi to take charge of the children.

{Preifi selected sixteen of the most weakened, emaciated boys turned blue from the cold and sent them to the one-eyed Svidersky.

The one-eyed Svidersky used to live in Odessa, where he was involved in some shady business. In the camp he was known as an "expert with a hammer."

Svidersky lined the boys up and pulled the hammer from his belt; his spit on his hands like a carpenter getting ready to drive a nail and started beating the children on the bridge of the nose. Their frail bodies tumbled to the frozen ground. The children's lives were quickly and easily snuffed out. The boys were quietly sobbing. And then a terrible, loud moan went up. Adult prisoners who had seen thousands of people die covered their faces with their hands. A small red-haired boy with curls the color of gold and copper and deep blue eyes started to protest:

"This is not a good way to die. It would be better if you were to shoot us.'

"Shoot you?" Svidersky retorted, pointing at his blind right eye. "I can't shoot you; I'm no good with a rifle."

He raised the hammer to kill the red-haired boy, but Preifi stopped him.

And the red-haired boy walked off.}

The children who were left to work were placed in barracks. There were three tiers of planks to serve as beds for them. Preifi told them to sleep on the boards. He named the tallest of the boys, a fourteen-year-old named Leib, as ["kapo"] or leader.

The children's unit went to work at five in the morning. All day long they could hear the cries of men, women, and children being murdered by the Germans. The screams would die out and then start up again. They were cries of sorrow and torment. They made the blood run cold and filled the boys' souls with unspeakable suffering.

The adults in the barracks took in the boys with a tenderness that could be shown only by fathers who had lost their own children. They were highly skilled Jewish workers who had been spared in order to work; their families had been exterminated. Among them was an elderly foreman from a meatpacking plant in Grodno. His name was Aron, and he befriended the boys; no one knew his last name (in the camp people went by first names or by nicknames). They referred to affectionately as Arli.

Arli was a good singer; he even wrote songs. In order to distract the boys from their dark thoughts, he would teach them songs at night. The redheaded boy was nicknamed "Red." He had a soft soprano voice and sang well. Whenever Red sang, each of the grow-ups thought of his own children. Aron wept and stroked the boy's head.

The Germans took everything away from the children who came from the Soviet territories. They took away their relatives, their homes, their schools, and their books; they took away their dreams and their childhood. But there was one thing the Germans did not know how to take away: their songs. They sang about their homeland, about Moscow. Often in the darkness and gloom of the barracks one could hear the song "Vast Is My Homeland."

The children's work unit attended to the geese and cows, cleaned potatoes in the kitchen, and sawed wood. The whole camp knew the children. Preifi ordered the boys to be dressed in blue linen jackets with buttons of iron. Preifi forced the boys to march for hours and tried to have them attain the strict military step of soldiers on parade. He played with the boys as if they were living toys that he would break whenever he felt like it. He liked to show off his marching "toys" to his supervisor Van Eupen.

Arli once decided to see if he could arouse in the German some feeling of compassion for the children. He had the boys sing the saddest song he knew. The children's voices reverberated with endless bitterness.

Just then a little boy walked in with a pitiful little turnip for his Arli. The German summoned a carpenter from Warsaw named Max Levit; he handed the carpenter a stick and ordered him to give the boy twenty-five blows. Levit gave the boy one light blow. Preifi tore the stick from his hands and started to furiously beat the boy. The last five blows were given to a dead body. After breaking his "toy," Preifi said, "That's the way to beat them."

Among the children was a little boy named Izak. He was a good dancer. Preifi ordered Izak to dance on the table, since all wind-up toys dance on tables. And Izak danced on a table one meter square with amazing speed, with a dead, mechanical rhythm, and with a sad, waxen face that really did resemble a wind-up toy.

485 The Annihilation Camps

There was another boy named Yasha; he was an artist. He drew the sad pictures of camp life on pieces of plywood. Sometimes he would draw a picture of a tank with a five-pointed star on it, tearing through the barbed wire barrier and crushing the Wachmänner (guards). Then he would quickly erase the drawing.

Yasha and Red slept in the same bunk. On cold nights the little singer and the little artist kept each other warm.

Preifi was called away on military business to the camp at Krakow. The camp foreman Van Eupen named Untersturmführer Stumpfe as the "guardian" of the children. He was a young, heavy SS man as tall as a giant. According to the testimony of Jewish and Polish witness, Stumpfe would laugh the whole time they were executing the prisoners; he was nicknamed "Laughing Death."

This "guardian" came up with a new job for the children. He ordered their work unit to take up shovels and spread along the road human ashes that had been carted in from the death camp.

July came. The sun was beating down relentlessly. The air was so heavy that one could not draw a breath. Suffocating from the heat and the stench and driven by the whips of the Wachmänner, the children fell exhausted upon the ashes of their mothers and fathers.

During an evening inspection Stumpfe discovered that five boys were missing. Red's absence was particularly conspicuous.

"Where is Red?" the "guardian" roared.

"Here I am," a timid voice sounded out. Stumpfe caught sight of a boy with black curly hair. I was Red, his hair covered with black ashes. Stumpfe walked up to him, grabbed a fistful of the boy's thick curls, and with his strong hand lifted him up by the hair.

"Negrito," he said, his voice full of contempt; then he let Red go.

There were still four missing. It turned out that two of them were dead; they had been unable to withstand the inhuman torment. Their little bodies lay on the black road among the ashes. Two others had disappeared: the quiet Misha and handsome Polyutek. The boys had run away.

A few days later the escapees were captured at a railroad station and were brought to the camp.

The children's work unit was lined up in front of the gallows. Misha and Polyutek were brought out. Their hands were not tied. Untersturnführer Lanz said:

"So much the better. If their hands are free, they will wave them about like birds flying straight up to heaven."

"Laughing Death"—Stumpfe—burst out laughing. They hanged the boys. Polyutek died quickly, with almost no convulsions. Misha's rope turned out to be too long, and his toes touched the ground. He gasped for a long time, his eyes rolling in his head. Lanz cut the end of the rope from the beam, and the little boy lay on the ground still alive; pulling the noose tight, Lanz easily lifted the Misha's thin body into the air and hanged him again.

For the first time the boys started crying. Their comrades' torment had penetrated their hardened hearts. Stasik became ill. The [kapo] Leib held him up and said:

"Don't cry. Misha and Polyutek are fine now, for they are no longer alive."

Hauptsturmführer Van Eupen and Untersturmführer Lanz, as well as with Hagen and Ledeke, got on their bicycles, rode around the gallows in a big circle, and {had their photographs taken} as they merrily chatted about something.

That evening the children sang a song called "We Have Lost." Arli wrote it. A long and mournful tune, it portrayed life in the camp and lamented the lot of the boys who were still alive.

The song ends like this:

> A bonfire roars in the field of death
> The ashes of brothers and sisters burn the heart
> We shall live no more in this world,
> We have lived our short life.

No one could go to sleep the night after the execution of the two children. The singer and the artist held one another and wept.

On 22 July 1944 the children's work detachment was sent with their shovels not to the black road but to the edge of the forest. They had to dig pits "for anti-aircraft emplacements," Stumpfe explained to them. But the kapo noticed that the pit they were digging did not look like an anti-aircraft emplacement. Soon they all could hear the distant rumble of gunfire: the front was drawing near. Red listened to the sound and said:

"The Germans are fleeing, and we are going to be left here." And he struck the bottom of the pit with his shovel.

The children realized that they were digging their own grave. It had to happen sooner or later. They were doomed, and they had no fear of death. It had become their companion during their short life in the camp. And red calmly said to his inseparable friend Yasha:

"When they kill us, let's lie down next to each other."

"We'll fall into the pit at random. How can the dead lie next to each other?"

"They can. We'll stand at the edge of the grave and embrace each other as we fall. That's all there is to it."

And the two of them neatly evened out the edges of the grave.

Morning came. In the distance, beyond the boundary of the camp, the peasants were harvesting grain and storing up hay for the winter. They sound of gunfire was growing louder. Nervously whistling, German steam engines were heading out somewhere. The Germans had hurriedly liquidated the "labor camp" at Treblinka (the death camp had already been liquidated). The Haupt-, Unter-, and other Führers, as well as the Wachmänner, drank up what was left of the wine reserves. Shooting broke out at 7:00 A.M. Only ten people at a time were led out to the mass graves for security reasons. The "work" continued until evening. The next group of ten was brought out in its turn; in it were Arli and the carpenter Max Levit. As he walked past the boys, who were waiting their turn, Arli cried out

"Farewell, my children!"

"Farewell!" the boys answered.

"So long, Arli," said Leib. "We'll soon join you."

Red slipped past a Wachmann and hugged Arli tightly, pressing himself close to him. Arli embraced his favorite.

"When was the last time we sang? Was it Wednesday? Remember? It was Wednesday," he said to the boy.

Arli knew he was going to be shot. He knew that the little singer was going to be murdered. Why did he tell him to remember? The Wachmann shoved Red to the side before he could ask. Arli started weeping.

When the Wachmann counted off ten boys, the entire work unit rose up.

"We all want to die together."

There were thirty of them. Since they were in a hurry, the Wachmänner gave in. Leib lined up his detachment and, with head held high, led them to the graves that they themselves had dug.

Max Levit was already lying in the pit. The drunken Wachmänner had a bad aim. Unharmed, Max Levit was only pretending to be dead. He could hear the harmonious voices of the children. They were singing as they walked to their death. The little ones doomed to death were singing a song about Soviet Moscow.

Closer, louder, closer. Levit heard their friendly footsteps and the shout of the German Schwartz:

"Quiet!"

"Long live Stalin!" the work detachment answered. "He will avenge us!" The singer and the artist held each other tightly. A volley of shots rang out. Yasha was struck dead and fell into the pit, taking Red with him; Red was only wounded. Red began to move, trying to hold his friend closer; he caught sight of Arli's terrified face lying dead right next to him. The boy closed his eyes, pressed his head against Yasha's shoulder, and for a minute did not budge. The Red lifted up his head and said:

"Mr. Wachmann, you missed, once more, please, once more."

The Wachmann cursed. "Laughing Death"—Stumpfe—started laughing. The Wachmann fired again. [The head covered with curls of copper and gold fell and did not rise up again.] Twilight came. The weary Wachmänner decided to fill in the pits the next day and left (on that day, 23 July 1944, they shot seven hundred Poles and Jews).

Max Levit crawled out from under the children's bodies and went off into the forest.

We met with Levit in the village of Wulka-Okronglik, two kilometers from the former camp at Treblinka. A sixty-year-old Pole came to see us from the same village; his name was Kazimiersz Skarsynski, and he had worked with the children spreading the ashes along the black road. Max Levit and the peasant Kazimiersz Skarsynski told us about the children and the black road.

V. Apresyan

The Uprising at Sobibor

1

Like the camps at Majdanek, Treblinka, Belzec, and Auschwitz, the death camp at Sobibir was created by the Germans for the purpose of the systematic, mass destruction of the Jews of Europe. It was situated in the forest, next to the train station at Sobibor. There the railroad line came to a dead end, which was supposed to keep the place a secret. As always, the Germans kept it carefully guarded from the surrounding population—all criminals are afraid of witnesses.

The camp was surrounded by four rows of barbed wire three meters high. The area between the third and fourth rows was mined. Guards patrolled the area between the second and third rows. Sentries were stationed in towers, form which they could see the entire compound.

The camp was divided into three basic sections or subdivisions, each of which had its own clearly defined purpose. In the first camp were the barracks, the wood shop, the shoemaker, the tailor, and two officers' homes. In the second camp were the barber shop, stores, and warehouses. In the third camp stood a brick building known as the "bathhouse."

The camp at Sobibor went into operation on 15 May 1942.[22] The first groups of prisoners camp from France, Holland, and western Poland. This is what one prisoner, a Jewish woman from Holland named Selma Weinberg, has to say about her arrival in the camp:

"I was born in 1922 in the town of Svolle (Holland). In Holland there was no animosity between the Dutch and the Jews; we lived together in peace and had no sense that we were segregated from one another. But when the Germans arrived, the persecution began. A camp for displaced Jews from Germany was set up at Westerbork in 1941. When the oppression of the Jews in the land began and they were forced to wear special badges, the Dutch welcomes the people who were wearing such badges. When the German started deporting the Jews to Poland (in 1941), the Dutch called for a strike in Amsterdam. Life in the city came to a halt for three days. The Dutch hid the Jews from the Nazis. Of the two thousand Jews in Utrecht, only two hundred were deported to Poland; the rest were hidden by the local population. A special organization was operating in the country to save Jewish lives; it provided people with a great deal of food and money. The organization known as 'A Free Holland' saved many Jews.

"My entire family and I were sent to the camp; Westerbork was expanded in 1942. There were eight thousand people in the camp, but the inmates were changing constantly, since a transport of one thousand people set out for Poland every Tuesday. Many went of their own free will, taking along clothing, shoes, and provisions. In fact, letters were arriving from Wlodawa stating that life in Poland was good. Later I found out that it was all a ruse used by the Germans. People were forced to signed postcards printed by the Germans. Sobibor was never mentioned in the postcards.

"I did not want to leave Holland; I escaped from Westerbork. A Dutch family took me in. All of my relatives had been shipped off to Poland. A Dutch German (the Volksdeutsche) turned me in. Spent two months in prison in Amsterdam and then was sent to the camp at Fichte, where there were political prisoners and Jews. I worked in the laundry there.

They took us to Poland in March 1943. Many hoped that they would be reunited with their relatives. After all, the Jews who were sick had even been treated in the hospitals in Holland before being sent to Poland. It created the impression that people had nothing to fear. As we passed through Germany, German nurses came on board and offered medical assistance to people who had fallen ill along the way.

I arrived in Sobibor on 9 April 1943. The men were ordered to undress and move on to the third camp. The women went between two rows of pine trees to a barracks, where they had their hair shaved off. A German officer selected twenty-eight girls to work in the second camp. I spent five months in Sobibor.

The enterprise of mass extermination at Sobibor required a carefully thought out plan, a constant care for details, and the skill of thoroughly experienced executioners. People went to their deaths completely naked. Their possessions, their clothes, and their shoes were sorted and sent to Germany. The women were completely shaved. Human hair was used to make mattresses and saddles; a furniture shop was located right in the camp, so that the hair from the people who were executed could be put to immediate use. Finally, the construction of the "bathhouse" itself—that is, of the centerpiece of this monstrous death factory—was quite complicated and required the attention, care, and skills of technicians, stokers, guards, gas suppliers, coffin makers, and grave diggers.

The prisoners themselves had to perform this work at its various stages under the threat of immediate death.

In his testimony given on 10 August 1944 one of the few surviving inmates of Sobibor, a barber from Warsaw named Ber (Dov) Moiseevich Fainberg, claims that approximately 100 people worked in the first "subcamp" and around 120 men and 80 women in the second.

"I worked in the second camp," he writes, "where there were stores and warehouse. When the people doomed to death undressed, we gathered up all their things and sent them off to the stores; the shoes went to one store, the outer garments to another, and so on. There their things were sorted, packed, and sent to Germany. Every day a train pulled out from Sobibor with dozens of cars full of things. We burned documents, photographs, and semi-precious goods in the bonfire. Whenever we had an opportune moment, we also threw money and valuables from the prisoners' clothing and pockets into the fire, so that it would not fall into the hands of the Germans.

"After a while I was transferred to another job. They were building three barracks designed especially for women in the second camp. In the first barracks the women had their shoes removed, in the second their clothes, and in the third their hair. I was assigned to work as a barber in the third barracks. There were twenty barbers. We cut off their hair with scissors and put it into bags. The Germans told the women that their hair was being cut for the sake of cleanliness, 'to prevent lice.'

"While I was working in the second camp in 1943, I inadvertently witnesses scenes of terribly inhumane treatment of innocent people. I saw a transport arrive from Bialystok crammed full of completely naked people. The Germans were obviously afraid that the prisoners might escape. Those who were half-alive on that transport were mixed in among the dead. The people were given nothing to eat or drink along the way. Those who were still alive were doused with lime chloride.

"The Gestapo in the camp often kicked the children and split open their skulls. They set dogs on defenseless people, and the dogs were trained to tear people apart. Many could not take it and committed suicide. Those who were sick the Germans exterminated immediately."

What took place in the third camp, in the brick building known as the "bathhouse?" According to all the witnesses, the 'bathhouse' area was itself surrounded by barbed wire. Entrance into this area from the first two camps was strictly forbidden on pain of immediate death.

"Once a group of eight hundred people entered the "bathhouse," writes Ber Fainberg, "the doors were closed tight."

In a separate building there was a machine designed to release the deadly gas. Once it was released, the gas was fed into tanks, and from the tanks it went through pipes into the gas chamber. It normally took fifteen minutes for everyone in the gas chamber to be asphyxiated. There were no windows. Only in the ceiling was the a small glass portal; a German assigned to the third camp peered through the portal to see when the death process was complete. On his signal the gas flow was cut off, the floor was mechanically open up, and the bodies fell below. Carts were waiting in the basement area, and a group of doomed men piled the bodies into them. The carts then were taken off to the forest to be buried in a huge pit. The people who delivered and disposed of the bodies were immediately shot.

On one occasion a group of people was already in the "bathhouse," when the machine that was to pump the gas inside broke down. The poor people broke down the doors and tried to escape. The Gestapo killed many of them and drove the ones who were left back into the gas chamber. Mechanics quickly repaired the machine, and everything proceeded according to plan.

A woman assigned to take care of some rabbits that the Germans were raising saw a line of naked women and children through the cracks in the rabbit hutch. They suspected nothing and were calmly talking among themselves.

The opposite also happened. As she was going to her death one summer day, an eighteen-year-old girl from Wlodawa cried out to all who could hear her:

"Avenge us! The Soviets will come and will show you criminals no mercy!"

They beat her to death with their rifle butts.

Among the Germans who worked in the third camp was a boxer from Berlin named Gomersky who was especially feared; he boasted that he could kill a man with a single blow. On the other hand he was a sentimental German who went around to all the naked children doomed to death, patted them on the head, and gave them candy. He would mutter:

"Hello, little one. Don't worry, don't be afraid, everything will be all right."

An especially terrible scream once went up from the third camp: women and children were being thrown into raging flames alive. That was how the Gestapo amused themselves.

The reality of the camp abounded in fantastic dramas before which anything that could be imagined pales. A certain young man from Holland whose job was sorting through the possessions of new arrivals unexpectedly came across his parents' things. Beside himself, he ran out of the warehouse and into the line of people on their way to their deaths, where he saw his parents. Another youth found his father's body among the people who had been gassed. He tried to bury his poor father's body with his own hands. The Germans murdered the son too. None of the details of these stories differs from the stories told of what happened at Majdanek or Treblinka. Perhaps the one way in which the butchers of Sobibor showed any personal imagination and initiative lay in how they hid what they were doing from the local population. In the area surrounding the camp they raised geese; whenever the slaughter was in progress, they stirred up the geese and made them cry out. That was how the Germans muffled the screams and the cries of their victims.

Wanting to hide all traces of their crimes, the Germans built ovens in the third camp in the summer of 1943. A special vehicle for moving earth was delivered to Sobibor. A mass grave was dug up. The vehicle moved the bodies unearthed onto bonfires near the railroad tracks. On such days the air in the entire area was filled with the smell of corpses.

No matter how well documented the reality of this terrible place might be, it still seems like the wild invention of a sick mind; and yet on that piece of earth defiled by the Germans there occurred an uprising that ended in victory for the prisoners on 14 October 1943. Twelve of the most highly placed officers of the German guards, as well as four regulars, were killed during the uprising. After the uprising the camp at Sobibor was destroyed.

How did it happen? Who had the human strength, who was organized enough, to stand up against the German hardware aimed at those unarmed people? Who in that terrible atmosphere of death and destruction had the will, the intelligence, and the foresight? On 22 September 1943 six hundred prisoners of war arrived in Sobibor from Minsk. Eighty of them were assigned to work in the second camp. The Germans gassed and burned the rest. Among those who were left was an officer named Aleksandr Aronovich Pechersky.

2

Pechersky was born in 1909 in Kremenchug. After 1915 he lived in Rostov-on-the-Don. During the years just before the war he worked mainly as a director of amateur artistic performances. On the first day of the Great Patriotic War Pechersky was drafted into the army; in September 1941 he was certified as a technician-quartermaster second class. In October he and his unit were surrounded in the Smolensk area and captured. While in captivity he came down with typhus and lay sick for seven months under horrible conditions. Pechersky survived by a sheer miracle. [The Germans shot people who contracted typhus. He managed to hide his illness.] Pechersky escaped in May 1942 but was caught on the same day, along with four other escapees. The captured prisoners were sent to a "penal" unit in Borisov; from there they were sent to Minsk. They arrived in Minsk in the fall of 1942. Here the new arrivals were subjected to a medical examination. That is how they discovered that Pechersky was a Jew.

[He was taken away for interrogation.

"Do you admit to being a Jew?"

Pechersky admitted it. If he had not admitted it, he would have been savagely beaten with a whip.]

He and some others were placed in the "Jewish" camp, where he remained for about ten days. There was total darkness in the cellar where he was kept, and he had no means of escape. They were fed every day: one hundred grams of bread and a cup of water.

On 20 August Pechersky was sent to the SS labor camp in Minsk (on Shirokaya Street). They kept him there until mid-September. In the camp there were approximately five hundred Jewish specialists from the Minsk Ghetto, as well as Jewish prisoners of war; two to three hundred of the inmates were Russians. The Russians were sent there for their involvement with the partisans, for failing to report for work, and so on—in a word, they were the ones whom the Germans regarded as "incorrigible." The inmates were only half-starved, mainly because they managed to steal from the Germans. They labored from dawn till dusk.

"Camp Commandant Wachs," says Pechersky, "could not go a day without murdering somebody. You had to look him in the face, the sadist, with his fat, trembling upper lip and his left eye all bloodshot. He always had a foul, drunken hangover. What he wouldn't dream up! Someone went out to urinate one night. Wachs shot him from his window; the next morning, in a state of ecstasy, he showed the body of the murdered man to his lady friend and beamed: 'This is my work!'

"People would get in line for bread. Wachs would come out and command them to stand at attention; then he would rest his automatic pistol on the shoulder of the man standing first in line and fire a shot. Woe to anyone who was even slightly out of line: he would get a bullet in the head or shoulder. Wachs's usual means of amusing himself was to set his dogs on the prisoners, who were forbidden to defend themselves. Wachs loved his dogs more than anything.

"Whenever women were brought from a ghetto to the bathhouse, Wachs was always there to personally conduct a search of the naked women."

There was once an attempt at a mass escape from the camp. Next to the camp's food warehouse was the Schutzpolizei[23] dormitory. Sometimes prisoners managed to sneak in there and steal weapons. Thus a group of fifty men working in the warehouse plotted to get their hands on some grenades, pistols, and ammunition. Their scheme was discovered the day before their escape. A driver who had agreed to take them outside the camp area for twenty thousand marks betrayed them.

The Germans herded the men who had been betrayed into the cellar of a burned out house, surrounded it with a heavy guard, and let the dogs loose. Then the entire group of bloodied prisoners was led through the town with their hands over their heads. Back in the camp it all started up again: the savage beatings with whips, the dog attacks. All the Germans who felt like it participated. Each man was taken separately into the bathhouse, which had been heated to a very high temperature. In the bathhouse there was a tub filled with hot water. The victim was dipped into the tub, taken out, and doused with cold water. Then he was taken out into the freezing cold; two hours later he was shot.

[All fifty men in the group were Jewish prisoners of war. Pechersky knew two of them personally: Boris Kagan of Tula and Arkady Orlov from Kiev.]

In September 1943 they started scaling down the camp. On 18 September Pechersky was on a transport headed for Sobibor.

Wachs, the commandant of the camp in Minsk, told the prisoners that they were going "to work in Germany." For four days they traveled in sealed cars without bread or water. On the fifth day the transport pulled into the small station at Sobibor. The train was switched to a side track and put into reverse; the steam engine backed the cars through the gates, over which there hung a sign with the word "Sonderkommando" inscribed upon it. Pechersky arrived in Sobibor after spending two years as a prisoner in German camps; through cruel and terrifying experience he had grown wise enough—he had seen enough and endured enough—to quickly orient himself to the conditions of the new camp that rose up before his eyes.

This is what Pechersky said about his first day in the camp:

"I was sitting on some logs outside the barracks with Shleima Leitman, who was later to be my chief assistant in organizing the uprising. A man of about forty, whom neither of us knew, walked up to us. I asked him what was burning in the distance, about five hundred meters away, and what that foul odor was that seemed to be everywhere in the camp.

"'Don't look over there,' the stranger replied. 'It is forbidden. They are burning the bodies of your comrades, the ones who arrived on the train with you.'

"I did not believe him. But he continued:

"'This camp has been here for more than a year. There are five hundred Jews here from Poland, France, Holland, Czechoslovakia. This is the first time they brought in Russian Jews. The transports arrive every day, and each one carries two thousand new victims. They are exterminated within an hour, no more. Here on this little piece of land of twenty-five acres more than five hundred thousand men, women, and children have been murdered.'"

The appearance of the prisoners of war from the East, of the Red Army soldiers and officers, made a huge impression on the camp. Avid, inquisitive eyes waiting for something, hoping for something, were fixed on the new arrivals.

From the day of his arrival in Sobibor Pechersky was preoccupied with the future: what could be done? Should he try to save himself from death, which here was inevitable? Should he escape on his own or with him just a small group of his comrades, leaving the rest to torture and death? He rejected that idea.

For Pechersky, the thought of escape was bound up with the idea of revenge from the very beginning. To take revenge upon the killers, to annihilate them, to set the whole camp free and seek out the partisans—that was the plan for future action that he envisioned. Nor did the incredible difficulty of the task stop Pechersky.

First of all he had to learn the layout of the camp and the daily routine of the prisoners and the officers of the guard. It was clear to Pechersky that everyone wanted to escape from the camp. But how was he to find people he could depend on in that mass of strangers who were physically and perhaps morally exhausted? Indeed, could he find anyone?

Five days after his arrival in Sobibor Pechersky was unexpectedly invited to the women's barracks. There he was greeted by a group of prisoners from various nations, most of whom did not know Russian. They questioned him. The conversation turned into a kind of political consultation. The situation was complicated by the fact that Pechersky had no idea of whom he was dealing with. Among those present was a kapo, that is, a prisoner who worked for the Germans—an informer. Pechersky spoke in Russian. The volunteer interpreters explained what they could gather from his evasive answers.

Pechersky told them about how the Germans were beaten outside of Moscow, about how they were surrounded and destroyed at Stalingrad, about how the Red Army was approaching the Dnieper, and about how the liberators of the Red Army would soon march across the German border.

Pechersky also spoke about partisan activities in the German-occupied territories of the Soviet Union. Even while he was still in Minsk he had heard rumors of partisans derailing German trains and of partisan terrorist activities in the city itself.

"Everyone listened very closely, trying not to miss a word. Those who understood a little Russian translated what they could for their neighbors. These people doomed to death were truly excited by the stories of Soviet fighting and heroism.

"'Tell me,' a timid voice spoke, 'if there are so many partisans, why don't they attack the camp?'

"'To what end? To free you, me, or him? The partisans have their own business to attend to. No one is going to do our work for us.'"

Pechersky abruptly turned and slammed the door behind him as he left the barracks. No one translated his last words. They were understood without being translated.

Pechersky had made such a great impression on them that, in one way or another, all the prisoners were now thinking about how to escape from the camp. Pechersky was now faced with an important task: to stop and reason with those who were most impatient and show them that the preparations for escape had to be carefully thought out before they could act.

Pechersky, however, was approached by his comrades, among whom was Shleima Leitman.

"Sasha, we've decided to escape," he said. "There are not many guards. We'll kill them and escape into the forest."

"That is easier said than done. While you are taking care of one guard, another will open fire on you with his submachine gun. And what if you do manage to take out every guard? How are you going to cut through the barbed wire? How are you going to get across the minefield? What are you going to do about our comrades who will be left behind? Do we have the right to forget all about them? Escape if you wish. I won't stand in your way; as for me, I won't go."

And Pechersky walked off with a comrade who called himself Kalimali. The escape was cancelled.

At about that time something else happened that greatly influenced Pechersky's decision. The elderly man with whom he had spoken on his first day in Sobibor came to see him again. The old man's name was Borukh; as it turned out, he was a tailor. Borukh had been in the women's barracks where Pechersky had met with the camp inmates. The old man warned Pechersky that they had begun to follow him.

"You may have noticed a tall, thin man standing next to me yesterday in the barracks. He is a kapo named Bzhetsky, a notorious scoundrel. He understood everything."

"Wait a minute. What are you talking about? Why are you worried? He has no reason to follow me around. I'm not planning to do anything. Escape is hopeless."

Borukh fell silent. Then he said:

"You are afraid of me, and you are right to be afraid of me. It has been only a few days since we first laid eyes on one another. But we have no other way out. You could suddenly take off on your own, but then it would be all over for us. Understand me"—and he grabbed Pechersky by the arm—"there are many like me who would like to escape. But we need someone who can lead us and show us what to do. Trust us. We know a lot here, and we can help you."

Pechersky looked into his good, sincere face and thought: "Traitor or not, I'll have to risk it!"

"How is the field beyond the barbed wire mined? Do you understand my question?"

"Not entirely."

"Mines are usually placed in a pattern like a chessboard."

"Ah, now I understand. Yes, that is how it mined. The mines are one and a half to two meters apart."

"Thank you. And now I have a request to make of you. Will you introduce me to a certain girl?"

Borukh was surprised:

"A girl?"

"Yes. Yesterday a young girl was standing on your right; she looked like a Dutch girl, with short, chestnut-colored hair. You remember: she was smoking. She would be perfect. She doesn't speak Russian, which, for once, is a good thing. There is no reason for you to meet with me again. Leitman and I sleep in the same bunk; he will pass on to you everything you need to know. Now let's go to the women's barracks and meet the girl."

A few days went by. Every night Pechersky met with Lyuka, his new young friend from Holland. The two of them sat on board benches outside the barracks. First one and then another prisoner would walk up to Pechersky and have a word with him, seemingly about very ordinary things.

Whenever the kapo Bzhetsky, who understood some Russian, would come up to him, Pechersky would immediately become affectionate with the girl. Lyuka guessed from the start that she had been drawn into a serious game. She quietly went along with the conspiracy. Pechersky was a Soviet—that alone was enough to inspire hope in Lyuka. She wanted to believe in him.

Pechersky was twice as old as the eighteen-year-old girl. But he became close to her. Lyuka told him her story. In the camp she had to hide the fact that she was the daughter of a German communist who had escaped from Germany to Holland when Hitler came to power.

When the Germans occupied Holland, her father was forced to go into hiding a second time. The Germans arrested her with her mother. The mother and daughter were sent to Sobibor.

Pechersky and Lyuka remained on friendly terms throughout those tragic days. Lyuka understood the meaning and the aim of their friendship. Having grown used to conspiracies from her childhood, she asked no questions and knew that Pechersky had his reasons for not sharing his plans with her.

Thus, without arousing any suspicion, Pechersky gained the confidence of many people he did not know and learned a great deal about the layout of the camp, about what people were thinking, and about the extent of the security.

Soon he met with Borukh again.

"This is the first plan," Pechersky began. "It is complicated and hardly worked out, but listen anyway. The carpentry shop is five meters from the barbed wire fence. There are four meters between the rows of barbed wire. The field is mined for another fifteen meters. Add to that the seven meters to the carpentry shop, and you have thirty-one meters. We have to dig a tunnel. I figure we'll have to hide about twenty cubic meters of earth under the floor and in the attic. We'll have to dig only at night. This plan has two downsides. Six hundred people can hardly crawl thirty-five meters in single file in the course of one night; besides that, if we leave this way, we leave without destroying the Germans. Speak to your people about this plan. For now I won't say anything about the second plan."

"Why?"

"I need more information. In the meantime, do you think your could get hold of about seventy knives and razors? I'll pass them out to the fellows."

"It will be done," Borukh answered. "And now I must give you some advice about an important matter. Monya has become part of our group; you know him—he's one of the young fellows building the barracks. Yesterday the kapo Bzhetsky went up to him and announced that he knew about the escape that was being planned. Of course, Monya tried to convince him otherwise. The kapo heard him out and told him that he wanted to join us and escape with us."

"I thought it over," writes Pechersky. "Although it looked like a trap, the thought of having a kapo helping us was extraordinarily tempting to me."

"Monya thinks that no matter how much of a scoundrel Bzhetsky is," Borukh continued, "he could be of use. Bzhetsky knows very well that ultimately the Germans will kill the kapos too: they cannot leave behind a single living witness to their crimes."

"What did you tell Monya?"

"That I could not decide anything without you."

"We'll think about the kapos. Right now it's time to go."

Raiman the blacksmith secretly filled Pechersky's order: he made the knives. The blacksmith shop was located right next to the metal works. One evening several people met in the blacksmith's shop; Bzhetsky was among them. A German guard had sent a gramophone to the metal works to be repaired. Pechersky and Leitman were invited to "listen to gramophone records."

The conversation picked up slowly. They started playing the gramophone. The blacksmith fried pancakes.

"I turned down the pancakes," says Pechersky, "and started talking about the records. Bzhetsky kept trying to bring the conversation back to the topic of escape. Using various pretexts, I avoided it. He finally signaled to the blacksmith, who took the record and went out to the metal shop. Everyone followed him. Bzhetsky and I were left alone face to face.

"'I wanted to have a word with you,' he began. 'Can you guess about what?'

"'I don't understand German very well.'

"'Very well, then we'll speak Russian. True, my Russian is bad, but we can manage if you like. All I ask is that you hear me out. I know that you are planning an escape.'

"'Nonsense! It is impossible to escape from Sobibor.'

"'You are being very careful. You stay away from the barracks. You never talk with anyone other than Lyuka. But is only a cover. Sasha, if I wanted to turn you in, I could have down it a long time ago. I know you think I'm a lowlife. Right now I have neither the time nor the desire to convince you otherwise. So be it. But I want to live. I don't believe Wagner [the camp boss] when he says the kapos won't be killed. They'll kill us all right. When the Germans liquidate the camp, they'll kill us along with everyone else.'

"'It's a good thing you realize that. But why tell me about it?'

"'I can't help seeing what is going on. All the others are simply following your instructions. Shleima Leitman speaks with people on your behalf. Sasha, understand me: if the kapos are on your side, it will be much easier for you. The Germans trust us.... All of us can move freely around the camp. In short, we are offering you an alliance.'

"'Who is we?'

"'Chepik and I. He's a kapo in the bathhouse unit....'

"I got up and paced several times from corner to corner in the blacksmith shop.

"'Bzhetsky,' I began, looking him in the face, 'could you kill a German?'

"He did not answer right away.

"'If it were necessary for our cause, I could.'

"'And if it were not necessary? Just the way they have exterminated thousands of our brothers?'

"'I never thought about it that way....'

"'Thank you for your openness. We must part now.'

"'All right. But I ask you again: think about what I have said.'

"I told him there was nothing for me to think about, said good-bye, and left. The fact, however, that Bzhetsky had to think before answering whether he would kill a German led me to suppose that perhaps this time he was not playing the provocateur. A provocateur would have agreed immediately."

The next day, 11 October, we heard screams and machine gun fire while we were working on the construction of a barracks in the north camp. Immediately the Germans herded people into one area; they forbade anyone and everyone to leave the workshops in the first camp; then they locked the gates and posted an additional guard. It was not until five o'clock that the reason for these extraordinary measures became clear. A routine transport of victims doomed to death had arrived. When they undressed and were led away, however, they realized what was happening and bolted in all directions. Completely naked, the poor people only got as far as the barbed wire; the Germans opened fire on them with their rifles and machine guns.

The meeting at which they agreed upon the final plan for escape took place on the following day, 12 October, in the carpentry shop. Borukh, Leitman, a senior carpenter named Yanek, Monya, Pechersky, and a few other "Easterners" were at the meeting. Two men were quietly talking in the yard outside the shop; there were two others at the gate to the first camp. They were the lookouts.

The meeting opened with the question of what to do about Bzhetsky. They decided to invite him to join them. Monya left and then returned a few minutes later with Bzhetsky. This is how Pechersky tells the story:

"'We've decided to invite you to join us, Bzhetsky,' I began, 'but by making a friend of someone like you we risk the fate of the entire camp. Therefore understand this: if the slightest thing should go wrong, you will be the first to die.'

"'I know.'

"'All right, comrades, here is the one plan that I think might work. We must kill all the German officers. One at a time, of course, but within a very short time. The whole thing should take no more than an hour. Only the prisoners of war whom I know personally and can rely on will kill the Germans. After lunch, at half past three, Bzhetsky will make up some excuse to take three men to the second camp. These men will kill the four officers. At four o'clock the electricians will cut the telephone lines that run from the second camp to the reserve units. At that same time we'll start killing the Gestapo men in our camp. We have to see to it that we take them one by one, at different times. Everything should be over in our camp within half an hour. At four-thirty Bzhetsky and Chepik will line up the whole camp into a column, like we're going out on a work detail, and the column will head for the exit. The Easterners will be in the first rows. On the way to the main gates they will have to take the weapons depot, without making any noise if possible. Keep in mind that while the column is moving, it will be very easy to create a panic. If that happens, all is lost; the Germans will realize that this is an escape. If we can take the weapons depot, then we can fight them. If not, then we shall have to press on. The officers' building is near the carpentry shop, next to the barbed wire. We can be sure that the Germans were afraid to place a minefield right next to it, but they may have planted a mine or two here and there. That is the place where we must cut through the wire fence. There you have it: that is the plan. Think it over until tomorrow. Any objections?'

"Borukh answered for everyone that there were no objections."

3

This incredibly bold and daring plan was devised by a man who burned with a thirst for freedom and revenge. It goes without saying that the plan could be carried out only under conditions of extreme precision and extreme secrecy.

It is no wonder that every hour of the following day, 14 October, Pechersky noted down an entry in his diary.

He worked in one of the barracks all morning; from a window in the barracks he could see the entire camp. The seven men who were working with him in the barracks that morning knew nothing about the escape. In the neighboring barracks there were twenty Easterners selected from a special list; they were building plank beds under Leitman's supervision. At ten o'clock Leitman called Pechersky and gave him the following report:

"At four o'clock Untersturmführer Ernst Berg will be invited to the tailor shop to be fitted for a coat. At four-fifteen Oberscharführer Gettsinger (the chief of the third camp, that is, the death camp) will arrive there. Unterscharführer Emil Schumacher is supposed to be at the shoe shop at four o'clock. I'll attend to Unterscharführer Friedrich Gaulstich personally. The four Germans will be killed in the second camp; the men will lure the rest of them into the workshops as best they can."

"Good. Send me each of the comrades whom you've selected to kill the Germans."

"Five minutes later," says Pechersky, "Kalimali stopped by the barracks where I was working.

"'Today at three o'clock,' I told him, 'you will go to the tailor shop. Take along a plane, a chisel, and an axe. Be careful, Kalimali: if you miss, we're dead. Understood?'

"'Yes.'

"'Very well. Go. And good luck.'

"I gave him a firm handshake.

"Half an hour later Boris Tsibulsky came to see me; he was to kill the Gestapo men in the second camp.

"'Boris,' I said to him, 'the time has come. I'm sending you to the most dangerous area. Mikhail and Benya will go with you. Take two axes. Bzhetsky will take you to the second camp. Remember, Boris, you will be the first to begin. The blow you strike will inspire everyone else. If the comrades who are to go with you grow afraid, replace them. We mustn't force anyone.'

"'Don't worry, Sasha. They're just waiting for the signal.'

"At two o'clock one of the Gestapo men showed up unexpectedly in the first camp; he grabbed Bzhetsky and three other men and took them off somewhere. The terrifying thought that everything had been discovered cut through us.

"Two hours later we found out that Bzhetsky had been taken to the north camp to stack wood. The kapo Chepik took on the job that had been assigned to Bzhetsky: he took the men to the second camp to kill the Gestapo men.

"The tension in the camp was rising. The conspiracy among the rebels had come to completion. Very few of the camp inmates knew about the impending escape, but many of them felt a vague sense of anxiety. And almost all of them believed that they could trust these silent, clever, melancholy men who had recently arrived in the camp and who were always quietly talking among themselves."

Two days before the escape it had been Yom Kippur. Among the inmates in the camp were some devout worshippers. One of the prisoners put a question to the cantor:

"Why do you pray to God? What does He do to help you? You should address your prayers to Sashka (that is, to Pechersky)."

This was the answer he received:

"We pray to God for Sashka's success."

Hope seeped through the silence and through the wall of despair. The way was paved for the events that erupted on 14 October.

The first one to be killed was Untersturmführer Ernst Berg; he showed up at the tailor shop twenty minutes earlier than expected. The moment Berg took off his belt with his pistol and holster and started to try on the coat, Kalimali hit him over the head with the ax. They threw the German's body onto a bunk and covered it with some clothes. It is impossible to read Pechersky's diary without being moved:

"It was not yet four o'clock when Kalimali ran into our barracks and set the pistol down in front of me. We embraced.

"'It is done,' I said. 'It is too late for anyone to back out now. Thank you, my friend.'

"Kalimali left. Suddenly the Dutchman, grown deathly pale, got up and tried to follow after Kalimali.

"'Where are you going?'

"'I need to take a leak.'

"'Get back. Wait a minute. Comrades,' I turned to everyone in the barracks, 'you know what is happening. Watch this character; don't let him out of here.'"

At 4:10 Semen Mazurkevich killed Michel, chief of the guards for the whole camp, in the same tailor shop. At the same time Arkady Vaispapir killed the head of the death camp, Oberscharführer Gettsinger in the shoe shop. At 4:15 Tsibulsky reported to Pechersky that he had completed his assignment (to kill the Gestapo men in the second camp). Four Gestapo men were dead, the telephone line was cut, and the exits were closed.

It was time to line the people up in a column.

But Pechersky hesitated. He was hoping he could cut down just one more German. At that moment Shleima Leitman killed one more German (it was Friedrich Gaulstich).

Bzhetsky returned at 4:30. His return was very timely: only a kapo could line up a column without arousing suspicion.

The rebels had just a few weapons in their hands: eleven pistols taken from the Germans they had killed and six rifles that the tinsmiths had hid away earlier in some drainage pipes. They had to manage with what they had.

At a quarter to five Bzhetsky gave the signal to line up the column. He gave a sharp whistle, and people came running from all directions.

The chief of the guards (a German from the Volga region) tried to force the people back into the barracks, but he was killed.

The crowd bolted for the weapons depot. Heavy machine gun fire cut them off. Pechersky realized that he would not be able to get to the weapons. He cried out:

"Comrades, forward!"

The people hurried behind him toward the officers' building. Many of them rushed over toward the other side, toward the main gates.

They took the guard posts. People set out across the minefield toward the forest, which they could see in the distance. Many of them were blown apart by the mines. Of the six hundred who headed for the forest, four hundred made it.

A carpenter from Chelm named Khaim Povroznik, a Polish soldier who was captured by the Germans in 1939, tells about that day:

"A large group of people had gathered in the camp. In the center stood our glorious leader Sashka. [Earlier Povroznik had referred to Pechersky as 'the glorious lad from Rostov.'] Sashka cried out:

"'For Stalin! Hurrah!'

"After dividing up into small groups, we scattered throughout the forest. The Germans tried to hunt us down. Airplanes fired on us with their machine guns. Many were killed. No more than fifty were left alive. I managed to reach Chelm, where I hid until the Red Army arrived. On that day life returned to me, a prisoner of Sobibor."

The Dutch girl named Zelma Weinberg relates:

"When the uprising broke out in the camp, I managed to escape. Two other girls, Ketti Khokes from the Hague and Ursula Stern of Germany, escaped with me. Ketti joined a partisan unit and died there of typhus. Ursula also fought with a partisan unit. She is now in

Wlodawa. Ursula and I were in Westerbork and in the Fichte prison together. Together we survived Sobibor; together we escaped; together we were saved."

The fate of Pechersky's Dutch girlfriend Lyuka is unknown, as is her real name.

After wandering the back roads of Poland for a long time, Aleksandr Pechersky and several of his comrades joined up with a partisan unit on 22 October. [He now holds the rank of captain in the Red Army.][24]

... The wind howls through the rusty barbed wire where the Sobibor annihilation camp stood on twenty-five acres of Polish earth. After the uprising the Germans burned down the camp, plowed up the ground, and planted it with cabbages and potatoes.

[The cabbage or potato field that the Germans planted here to hide the traces of their monstrous crimes has been dug up once again. Beneath the surface were found pieces of human bones, the pitiful debris of camp existence, unmatched shoes of all sizes and styles, and a multitude of bottles with labels from Warsaw, Prague, and Berlin. There were baby bottles and false teeth, Jewish prayer books and Polish novels, postcards with scenes of European cities, documents, and photographs. There were prayer shawls lying next to faded knit rags, cases for canned preserves and cases for eyeglasses, and a little girl's doll with twisted hands. These were the mute witnesses to the murder of hundreds of thousands of people sent to this death camp from every corner of Europe.]

The sufferings of the people who perished here, their tears and their horror in the face of death, are over. These people are no more.

But a few survived to tell the tale of what they knew and saw.

P. Antokolsky[25] *and V. Kaverin*[26]

The Report of the Special State Commission for the Verification and Investigation of Atrocities Committed by the German Fascist Invaders and Their Accomplices in the Monstrous Crimes of the German Government in Auschwitz

Even before the Red Army liberated the Polish territory in Upper Silesia the Special State Commission had received many reports regarding the existence of a huge camp that the German government had set up in the vicinity of the town of Auschwitz for the annihilation of Soviet prisoners. After Soviet troops had liberated Polish Silesia a Red Army detachment discovered this camp.

By order of the Special State Commission's Procurator of the First Ukrainian Front, and in conjunction with representatives of the Special State Commission D. I. Kudryavtsev and S. T. Kuzmin, a thorough investigation of the German atrocities committed at Auschwitz was conducted in February and March of 1945.

A special commission of specialists took part in the investigation; they were led by forensic medicine experts F. F. Bryzhin of the First Ukrainian Front and M. G. Chursanov of the Red Army, therapist I. I. Pertsov, chief army pathologist N. A. Lebedev, army gynecologist G. A. Kolegaev, psychiatrist N. R. Vannovsky, and criminologist N. I. Gerasimov. Former prisoners were also on the commission: professor of pediatrics and director of the clinic at the

University of Prague B. V. Epstein, professor of pathological anatomy and experimental medicine in Clermont-Ferrand (France) H. H. Limousin, and Dean of Medicine in Zagreb (Yugoslavia) M. Ya. Grossman. Among the technical experts were Krakow professors Roman Dawidowski and Jaroslav Dolinski, as well as two doctoral candidates in chemical engineering: V. F. Lavrushin and A. M. Shuer.

The 2,819 Auschwitz prisoners rescued by the Red Army were questioned and given medical examinations. German documents obtained in the camp and fragments of the crematoria and gas chambers that the Germans blew up upon their retreat were also studied. In addition, the commission examined bodies found in the vicinity of the camp, as well as objects and papers found in warehouses and barracks; they had belonged to people from the various countries of Europe slaughtered in the camp. As a result, it was determined that:

1. By means of shooting, starvation, poisoning, and monstrous tortures, the Germans exterminated at Auschwitz more than four million citizens of the Soviet Union, Poland, France, Belgium, Holland, Czechoslovakia, Yugoslavia, Romania, Hungary, and other countries.[27]

2. German professors and physicians in the camp performed so-called medical experiments on living human beings—men, women, and children.

3. With regard to the levels of calculation and technical organization, with regard to the massiveness and cruelty of the extermination, Auschwitz far exceeds all the other known German "death camps."

Auschwitz contained gas chambers and crematoria, chemical facilities and laboratories, all designated for the monstrous extermination of human beings. The Germans referred to the gas chambers as "baths for special purposes." Over the entrance to these "baths" was a sign that said "For Disinfection"; over the exit was a sign that said "Entrance to the Bath." Thus the people marked for annihilation suspected nothing as they filed into the "disinfection" area and undressed; from there they were forced into the "bath for special purposes"—that is, into the gas chamber, where they were exterminated by means of the poisonous substance known as "Zyklon."

In the camp the Germans set up special hospitals, surgical blocks, histology labs, and other facilities—not, however, for treating people but for slaughtering them. In these facilities German professors and physicians conducted mass experiments on completely healthy men, women, and children. They experimented with the sterilization of women and the castration of men; they artificially infected children with cancerous tumors, typhus, and malaria and then stood back and observed them. They performed experiments on the effects of poisonous substances on living people.

Reichsführer SS Himmler, Organizer of the Auschwitz Annihilation Camp

Auschwitz specially was built in 1939 by order of Reichsführer SS Himmler for the annihilation of the enslaved citizens of the occupied countries of Europe.[28] The camp was situated in a large area near the town of Auschwitz and consisted of an entire system of camps: Auschwitz, Birkenau, Monowitz, Golleschau, Jawichowitz, Neu Dachs, Blechhammer, and others. The main camps—Auschwitz and Birkenau—covered an area of 467.5 hectares[29] and had more than 620 barracks and office buildings. Auschwitz continuously held between 180,000 to 250,000 prisoners. All the camps were surrounded by deep trenches and were cordoned off by thick webs of barbed wire charged with a high-voltage electrical current.

In 1941 the first crematorium was built in Auschwitz for burning the bodies of people who had perished there; it had three ovens. Adjacent to the crematorium was a so-called "bath for special purposes," that is, a gas chamber for suffocating people. This first crematorium existed until mid-1943. In the summer of 1942 Reichsführer SS Himmler conducted an inspection of Auschwitz and arranged to have it technologically improved and expanded into gigantic proportions. The construction of the new high-capacity crematoria was undertaken by the German business firm Topf and Sons of Erfurt; they immediately started building the four high-capacity crematoria and gas chambers in Birkenau. Berlin impatiently insisted that they speed up construction and that all work be completed by the beginning of 1943. An extensive correspondence between camp administrators and Topf and Sons was found in the administrative offices at Auschwitz, including these two letters:

Date: 12 February 1943, Erfurt

To: The Central Building Administration of the SS and Police, Auschwitz
Re: Crematoria II and III in the prisoner-of-war camp

This is to confirm the receipt of your telegram of 10 February stating the following: "Once again we confirm receipt of your order for five three-muffle ovens, including two electric lifts for the removal of corpses and one temporary lift. You also ordered a device for feeding coal into the ovens, as well as a device for the removal of ashes. You are to deliver complete the installation for Crematorium III. We expect you to take all measures for the immediate dispatch of all machinery and parts. The installation absolutely must go into operation by 10 April 1943."

I. A. Topf and Sons

No. 121 15/42/Er Na

Point 2

With regard to the installation of two three-muffle ovens next to each of the "baths for special purposes," engineer Prüfer has recommended that they be taken from the ovens ready for dispatch to Mogilev. The Director of the SS Office of Economic Administration in Berlin was immediately informed of this and has been asked for further instructions.

SS Untersturmführer (S)   Auschwitz, 21 August 1942

The four new crematoria had twelve ovens with forty-six retorts. Each retort could hold three to five bodies; the cremation process took twenty to thirty minutes.

"Baths for special purposes"—gas chambers for killing people—were built near the crematoria; they were above ground, underground, or in special structures next to the crematoria. The camp also had two separate "baths," from which bodies were taken and burned in special bonfires. The "baths" were designed for killing the people driven into them with blows from clubs, gun butts, and dogs. The doors to the gas chambers were hermetically sealed, and the people inside were poisoned with "Zyklon." Death occurred within three to five minutes; twenty to thirty minutes later the bodies were dragged out and sent to the ovens of the crematoria. Dentists removed gold teeth and crowns from the bodies before they were burned.

The "production levels" of the "baths" significantly exceeded the oven capacity in the crematoria; therefore the Germans burned the bodies in huge bonfires. They dug special trenches for these fires; the trenches were twenty-five to thirty meters long, four to six meters wide, and two meters deep. Special channels ran along the bottom of the trenches to serve as vents. The bodies were hauled out to the fires in narrow-gauge railcars, arranged in the trenches between layers of firewood, doused in oil, and set on fire. The ashes were either buried in large pits or were dumped into the Sola and Vistula Rivers. In 1943, with the aim of making industrial use of the bones that were not burned up, the Germans started grinding up the bones and selling them to the Strem Company, where they were processed into superphosphate. Documents found in the camp show that 112 metric tons and six hundred kilograms of bone meal from human beings were to be shipped to the Strem Company. The Germans also made industrial use of the hair cut from the women marked for extermination.

The Germans murdered and burned ten to twelve thousand people per day in Auschwitz; eight to ten thousand of the victims were from transports arriving in the camp, and two to three thousand were from prisoners already there.

Former prisoners Shlema Dragon, a Warsaw Ghetto fighter from Zirowny, and Heinrich Tauber of Krzanow (Poland) worked in the Sonderkommando, a special unit assigned to the crematoria and gas chambers. They were questioned as witnesses, and this is what they affirmed: "... When the camp first went into operation the Germans had two gas chambers located three kilometers from each other. There were two wooden barracks. People arriving on the transports were led into the barracks, where they undressed; then they were taken to the gas chamber.... Fifteen to seventeen hundred people would be driven into the gas chamber; then SS men in gas masks would dump in the 'Zyklon' through a hatch. The gassing took fifteen to twenty minutes, after which the bodies were dragged out, loaded into carts, and hauled off to the pits where they were burned.... Later there were four more crematoria operating in Birkenau; each one had a gas chamber. Crematoria II and III were built in an identical manner and had fifteen ovens each. Crematoria IV and V were constructed differently. They were inferior in their design and technology; each one had eight ovens. These crematoria burned ten to twelve thousand bodies in a twenty-four-hour period."

German Fascist Professors and Physicians: Murderers of the Prisoners in Auschwitz

At Auschwitz German fascist professors and physicians performed many "medical" experiments on living people that showed monstrous ingenuity.

Among the prisoners rescued by the Red Army were several physicians: Steinberg of Paris, Gordon of Vilnius, Professor Grossman of Yugoslavia, Doctor Erwin Walentin of Berlin, Anna Keppich of Hungary, Eduard DeWind of Holland, and Albert Flechner of Paris. They report being witness to a huge number of "medical" experiments performed by the German fascist professors and physicians on camp prisoners.

Doctors arbitrarily performed operations simply to improve their surgical skills. A young German physician named König would select prisoners whose arms and legs had become inflamed with sores and practice amputation procedures on them. German physicians Tillo and Fischer assembled large groups of prisoners who showed no symptoms and performed hernia operations on them. At the slightest complaint Doctor Entress, the chief physician at the hospital, would perform stomach operations to practice surgical techniques for treating stomach ulcers.

Experiments were conducted on women at the medical facilities in Auschwitz. Block 10 contained up to four hundred female prisoners at a time. They were used for experiments on sterilization through the use of x-rays and the removal of the ovaries; on vaccinations against cancer of the cervix; on inducing labor; and on the use of various substances for taking x-rays of the uterus. They used prisoners from Block 28 for experiments that involved artificially infecting the skin with kerosene, various salts, pastes, and powders; they also used acridine to study artificially induced jaundice. The German physician Emil Kaschub was involved in these experiments. In Block 21 they conducted massive experiments on the castration of men in order to study the possibilities for sterilization through the use of x-rays; the castration was performed at a designated time after irradiation. Professor Schumann and Doctor Dering were involved in the castration and radiation experiments. Often the procedure entailed the removal of one or both testicles for examination after exposure to the x-rays.

All of these facts have been confirmed by the testimony of former camp inmates, including Yudita Klein, Klara Ausen, Minna Gerbman, Nona Sonders, Yakov Skurnik, David Sures, and many others upon whom the German physicians performed these and other experiments.

By order of the chief German physician Entress, from 1941 to 1944 prisoners in the camp hospitals were killed by injecting phenol into the heart. Dering performed the first injections; then nurses' aides did them. A former German shoemaker named Kler particularly distinguished himself in this operation; he killed thousands of victims by injection. A certain Polish prisoner by the name of Panszik killed twelve thousand people by injection (he was later killed by Polish prisoners). A German named Stessel exterminated ten thousand people with the needle.

These facts pertaining to the inhuman experiments performed on the prisoners are confirmed by documents found in the camp administrative offices. In reports filed by the camp hospital section it was indicated that during the three months from October to December 1943 the operations performed included the following: eighty-nine testicle amputations (castrations), five sterilizations, and the removal of five sets of ovaries. In telegram No. 2678 dated 28 April 1943 Obersturmführer SS Colonel Sommer instructed the office of the camp commandant to designate 128 women as "prisoners to be used in experiments." There is a "statistical survey conducted by the camp commandant on the number and distribution of women prisoners in various categories"; it is signed by Sella, a representative of the camp commandant. There is one category that always appears on the list: "prisoners designated for various experiments." The groups of women designated for experimentation included 400 on 15 May 1944, 413 on 5 June 1944, 348 on 19 June 1944, 349 on 30 July 1944, and so on.

The German physicians played a major role in the so-called selections, that is in the selection of prisoners to be gassed and cremated. Selections were held everywhere: near the crematoria, in the hospitals, and in the barracks. The German physicians sent people who were emaciated, sick, and unable to work to the gas chambers. The following German doctors took part in the selection of prisoners to be killed: Wirtz, Mengele, Rode, Fischer, Tillo, Kitt, König, Klein, and many others.

During typhus epidemics entire blocks of people were murdered by poison gas, in accordance with orders from Doctor Wirtz, the German physician in charge of the medical operation in Auschwitz.

The commission of experts in forensic medicine determined that German physicians in Auschwitz performed the following experiments on living people:

1.   The cutting away of large portions or the complete removal of the uterus.

2.   The testing of various unknown substances for x-raying the uterus and ovaries. These substances were injected into the uterine cavity under pressure with special instruments, which often caused excruciating pain to the woman.

3.   The sterilization of women by exposing the pelvic region to x-rays and then removing the ovaries. These experiments were generally done on young women.

4.   The study of human reactions to various chemical substances, as ordered by German business firms. According to the testimony of German physician Doctor Erwin Walentin, on one occasion two representatives of a German chemical company—a gynecologist named Klauberg[30] from Königshütte and a chemist name Gebel—actually purchased 150 women from the camp administration.

5.   The sterilization of men by means of x-rays.

6.   Experiments on men involving the use of chemical irritants to artificially induce the formation of ulcers and inflamed tumors on the leg.

7.   Various other experiments, including artificial infection with malaria, artificial insemination, and so on.

Very many experiments resulted in the rapid, excruciating death of the prisoner used as a test subject. Once the prisoners were no longer useful for experimental purposes, they were murdered and burned. In this way the Germans intended to eliminate the witnesses to their inhuman experiments.

This is the testimony given by former prisoner Samuil Abramovich Stern:

"… In Auschwitz I worked as a surgeon's assistant. Following the orders of Oberfeldwebel Kaschub, I gave prisoners injections and subjected them to other treatments. I know very well that many prisoners had kerosene injected under the skin of their legs… . A second experimental method involved the chemical irritation of the skin. An 80 percent solution of acetous aluminum (alum actinium) was used for these purposes. The entire layer of skin was then removed and sent off to be examined. Those who had a deep skin irritation had the flesh cut out with the skin; this too was then sent out for examination… . Kaschub also artificially infected people with jaundice and gave them malarial blood transfusions."

M. Baligura, one of the prisoners subjected to these experiments, reported the following: "… Several days after my arrival in Birkenau—I think it was in early December 1942—all the young men between the ages of eighteen and thirty were sterilized by means of exposing their scrotum to x-rays. I was one of them. Eleven months after they had sterilized me, on 1 November 1943, I was castrated… . In addition to myself, there were two hundred men sterilized in a single day… ."

David Sures of Salonika (Greece) gave the following testimony: "…Around July 1943 ten other Greeks and myself were registered on some sort of list and sent to Birkenau. There they forced us to undress and subjected us to sterilization by x-rays. A month after we were sterilized they summoned us to the camp's central division, where we underwent an operation: castration."

A former female prisoner named M. Hauser (of 9 Citemilion Street, Paris) gave the following testimony: "…We were in Block 10 in Auschwitz. Why they put us in Block 10 we did not know. A hospital section was located in that block, but we were completely healthy women… . In Block 10 they drew some blood from me; I did not know why they drew the blood. At the end of August 1943 they took me to the operating room; they gave me an anesthetic and performed and operation on my reproductive organs. A prisoner named Doctor Samuel performed the operation under the guidance and by the order of the German Doctor Wirtz. After the operation I lay sick in Block 10 for eleven months. Among those who were subjected to the sterilization procedure was a Greek Jewish woman named Bella; I do not know her last name. After the x-rays came the operation; she had an incision in her abdomen. She recovered from the operation, and the incision in her abdomen healed. Doctor Schumann came to Block 10 to examine her and took her to Block 28; there he made another incision in her abdomen, going sideways. I saw the intersecting incisions in her stomach myself. A few days after the second 'operation' Bella died."

At Auschwitz the German Executioners Murdered Citizens of Every Country in Europe

Evidence has shown that three to five transports of people marked for death arrived in Auschwitz every day; there were 1,500 to 3,000 people on each transport. These doomed people came from every country in Europe. Among the 2,819 prisoners liberated from Auschwitz were the following: 754 from Poland, 542 from Hungary, 36 from France, 315 from Czechoslovakia, 180 from the USSR, 159 from Holland, 143 from Yugoslavia, 91 from Italy, 76 from Greece, 52 from Romania, 41 from Belgium, and a number of people from other countries.

From each of the transports the Germans selected two to three hundred of the most able-bodied people to work in the camps; the rest were sent directly to the gas chambers and the crematoria in Auschwitz and Birkenau.

Stanek Fransiszek, a dispatcher who worked in the Auschwitz station, offered the following testimony: "... In 1942, 1943, and 1944 transports came from Czechoslovakia, Belgium, France, Norway, Greece, Poland, and other countries."

Witness Eduard DeWind testified to the following: "... After the Germans occupied Holland in 1940 they purged the government offices, establishments, and educational institutions. Three of us assistants were expelled from the university. I moved to Amsterdam. They found a Dutch fascist who had been killed in one of the residential quarters. The Germans arrested four hundred hostages in reprisal, and I was one of them. They picked me up on the street and sent me to the camp."

A witness named Yakov Gordon of Vilnius testified to the following: "... I arrived in Auschwitz on 22 January 1943. There were 3,650 people in our transport; of those 265 men and 80 women entered the camp; the rest were sent to the crematoria to be gassed and burned. Among them was my wife Matilda, who was a physician, my four-and-a-half-year-old son, my father of seventy-three, and my mother of sixty-four."

A witness named Emily Dessanti, an Italian woman, testified to the following: "... On 12 September 1944 the Hitlerites took us from Italy to Auschwitz. There were five hundred of us, all from Italy; thirty survived. The rest were brutally tortured and killed in the camp."

The witness David Sures testified to the following: "... I arrived in Auschwitz on a transport from Greece on 3 April 1943. There were more than 2,500 people on the transport, including my mother of fifty-three, my sister, her little boy, and myself. Of the 2,500 approximately three hundred were sent to the camp; the rest—among them my mother, my sister, and her five-year-old son—were sent straight from the train to the crematorium, where they were burned."

The witness Georg Kitman testified: "... In June 1944 my parents and I and three thousand men, old people, woman and children arrived in Auschwitz. As soon as we were unloaded, all the old people and mothers with children were separated from the healthy ones; they were sent to the crematoria and burned. Among those who were burned was my fifty-two-year-old father and my forty-eight-year-old mother. Of the three thousand no more than 350 people were sent to the camp."

The witness Ziska Shleter testified: "... I arrived in the camp along with 1,100 people from France in February 1943. Of those 205 able-bodied workers were sent to the barracks that same day; the other 895—old people, women, and children—were sent to the gas chambers, where they were asphyxiated."

Former prisoner Anna Keppich a Hungarian woman from Cluj, testified: "...I arrived in Auschwitz in June 1944 with three thousand Hungarian prisoners; out of those five hundred able-bodied people were selected for work in the camp; the other 2,500 were sent to the gas chambers to be exterminated."

Professor Berthold Epstein of the University of Prague told the Commission: "... Selected prisoners were sent to the gas chambers to be killed. Over the next few months we saw long lines of people going to their deaths in the crematoria; especially large groups were exterminated in May, June, and July 1944.[31] During that time the crematoria were operating day and night, which was evident from the flames shooting up through the chimneys. We could often smell the stench of burning flesh, hair, and nails. In addition to the flames from the chimneys of the crematoria, during that time we saw two large bonfires whose flames lit up the night. All through the night screams and cries and the barking of SS dogs could be heard in the camp. The poor victims, who due to the overflow in the crematoria were lined up and sent to their deaths in the open fires knew what fate awaited them.... I knew that my closest relatives were marked for such a fate and that I too could not escape it. About every two weeks the camp physician Mengele conducted a selection to send more victims to their deaths in the crematoria. Thus approximately five hundred children were wiped out in a single day. There were heartrending scenes when those children were taken away, since everyone knew where they were going. The SS and their assistants were especially cruel during that operation.... When I arrived in Auschwitz I was separated from my wife; I never saw her again. I later found out that she was not sent to the camp. My wife, no doubt, was murdered in the usual manner. In March 1944 the SS also exterminated my wife's sister and her two children, along with my thirty-eight-year-old niece. In July 1944 my sister also perished."

Auschwitz: The Mass Production of Death

The investigation found that in addition to people designated for experiments, a steady work force of about 200,000 prisoners was exploited for forced labor in the camp. These people were worked to the last ounce of their strength and were then slaughtered. Every week the German doctors conducted a selection of the prisoners to send those who were sick and unable to work to the gas chambers. They were replaced by prisoners arriving on the steady flow of transports. It was a highly organized system of a terrible conveyor belt of death. Some were killed, and others took their places; they would be mercilessly worked to the point of exhaustion and illness and then sent to the gas chambers in their turn.

In 1941 the Germans undertook the construction of a large chemical weapons plant for I.G. Farben-Industrie near Auschwitz, as well as a plant for explosives and trigger devices for bombs and artillery shells. The construction was initially supervised by Krupp, later by Union and other firms. Tens of thousands of prisoners from Auschwitz worked on the project, including prisoners of various nationalities: Russian, Ukrainian, Belorussian, Polish, French, Czech, Yugoslavian, Greek, Belgian, Dutch, Italian. They labored in this construction project—as well as in draining swamps, in mines, and building roads—to the point of complete exhaustion.

It was seven to eight kilometers from the camp barracks to the work site. The SS lined up people by the thousands into columns and led them out to work; they were escorted by armed guards and surrounded by overseers with clubs and dogs. The SS, overseers, and foremen beat the prisoners as they worked; they would beat one for failing to stand up straight, another for shoveling too little dirt, and a third for working too slowly. Others were beaten while being forced to pull earth-laden carts at a run. The foremen would declare: "The firm pays four marks for you; therefore you must work like a horse."

Those who collapsed from exhaustion were shot on the spot. The work site was also an execution site for the mass murder of prisoners. The administration encouraged murder by all sorts of means. Obersturmbannführer Liebehenschel issued an order offering the SS sixty marks for every prisoner murdered "while trying to escape." In order to get their reward, the guards murdered people with impunity.

A former Belgian prisoner named Maurice Stasman gave testimony on the slaughter of prisoners at the work sites: "...I worked at the I. G. Farben-Industrie installation in August 1943. One day the SS brought four hundred prisoners to the site; among them were Yugoslavians, Greeks, Frenchmen, and Belgians. They forced the prisoners into a ditch and started to bury them alive. The ones condemned to death cried out for mercy in various languages. The SS men standing next to us turned to us and said, 'See to it that you worker harder, or the same will happen to you.' Two weeks later we were transferred to prepare a site for one of the buildings in Auschwitz. An SS man named Lossmann, along with some other SS men, selected thirty men from our group, took them out to a pit, and buried them up to their shoulders. Then they got on their horses and started galloping around the area; all thirty were trampled to death."

A huge section of the swamps around Auschwitz became a grave for many thousands of people of various nationalities. More than 300 commandos of 50 to 1,200 men each worked there. Due to the inhumane working conditions in the swamp all year round—due to the beatings, the murder, and the violence—people working there did not live more than two to three months. They died in the swamps, or they were murdered when they were no longer able to work, either by phenol injection or in the gas chamber.

A sixty-year-old land reclamation engineer from Hungary named Yakov Koenig worked in the swamps as a simple laborer. He testified to the following: "...I was in a commando of four hundred men draining the swamp.... The overseers, among whom were German criminals, beat people unconscious with clubs and shovels. Men and women of all ages worked in our group. Many were professionals—physicians, academicians, professors. There were fourteen engineers from Yugoslavia alone working as laborers."

A former Belgian prisoner named Simon Meiselier testified: "Every day for three months in 1944 we brought back the bodies of 100 to 200 people who had been worked to death in our commando of 1,200; they were replaced by new victims."

The German executioners were especially brutal toward the Soviet prisoners, who were generally wiped out upon their arrival at the camp; only the most able-bodied of them were selected to work.

The following order regarding Soviet citizens was found in the camp administrative offices:

Oranienburg, 15 November 1941

Top Secret

Reichsführer SS, Inspector of Concentration Camps

Police (Auschwitz 14 F 14 L)

Re: The execution of Russian prisoners of war

To: Concentration Camp Commandants

Cc: Camp physicians and leaders of prisoners under special guard

The Reichsführer SS and Chief of the German Police has in principle agreed to suspend the execution of Russian prisoners of war sent to concentration camps (especially the commissars) if their physical condition would enable them to work in the stone quarry. In order to take such measures, however, it is necessary to obtain the approval of the SD and the Chief of the Security Police. I therefore issue the following order:

When transports carrying people marked for execution arrive in the camp, the camp superintendent (E) and the chief camp physician are to select physically healthy Russians who can work in the concentration camp quarry. A list of the names of the Russians selected is to be sent to us in duplicate. On the list the camp physician must make a note that he has no medical objection to sending these men to do hard physical labor.

Once the approval of the SD and the Chief of the Security Police has been obtained, we shall issue an order for the transfer of the Soviet Russians to the stone quarry.

Signed: Brigadeführer and Major-General SS Glücks

As a result of this order, some of the Soviet prisoners were designated for the most difficult, most exhausting labor; from the standpoint of the SS and the overseers, these prisoners faced an fate much more cruel and inhuman than those who were executed.

A resident of Auschwitz named Marina Gandzlik testified: "… In the winter of 1941, when it was -33° C, the Russian prisoners were driven like cattle, with whips and clubs, from Auschwitz to the village of Babicz every day for two weeks. Many of them had nothing on their heads, just their field shirts, trousers, and ragged boots. Every evening several carts carrying the bodies of dead Russian prisoners would head back from Babicz. On top of each cart sat two or three of their comrades. Their faces, hands, and feet were frozen; they were utterly exhausted."

The Hitlerites were constantly demanding more and more murders from their subordinates. On 14 February 1944 Obersturmbannführer Liebehenschel, chief of the Auschwitz garrison, issued the following order:

"…From extensive personal observations I have determined that, with the exception of the armaments factories, all work sites have too many prisoners and that the work force is not being utilized to its full capacity. They loaf around…. We know that closer supervision on the part of the junior SS officers would be necessary in order to increase the prisoners' production levels; we also know, however, that there are no additional personnel available for this purpose, since they are either at the front or are serving in other important capacities. Hence we shall help ourselves…. It is clear that we must act quickly, and I hope that each one of us will do what is necessary…."

As a result of this order, every evening terrible processions of workers trudged back to Auschwitz from every direction, back from the factories, the swamps, and the mines. Surrounded by SS men, overseers, and huge packs of dogs, the bloodied, exhausted prisoners bore the bodies of their comrades on stretchers. At the evening role call the prisoners lined up, with the bodies of those who had been tortured to death that day were laid out in front of them. Then the overseers reported to their supervisors on the execution of Liebehenschel's order. The administration showed its gratitude to the work teams that brought back the largest number of bodies. Then, right in front of everyone, prisoners accused of various infractions were beaten with clubs.

Added to the terrible working conditions were the nightmarish living conditions in the barracks. The Germans would cram 1,000 to 1,500 prisoners into barracks designed to house 400 to 500. Hunger, sickness, torture, unsanitary conditions—all of it was created for the expressed and calculated purpose of exterminating the prisoners as quickly as possible.

After examining 2,819 prisoners of Auschwitz who were rescued by the Red Army, the forensic medical commission determined that 2,189 or 91 percent suffered from total exhaustion and that 223 had pulmonary tuberculosis. The experts also established that the Germans had subjected the prisoners to torture resulting in broken ribs, fractured vertebrae, broken bones in the face, various wounds, ulcers, and frozen hands and feet. Many of those who were liberated suffered from nervous and psychological disorders.

The forensic medical commission examined 526 corpses found in various places on the camp grounds. It was determined that in 474 instances (83.3 percent) the cause of death was exhaustion.

Murderers of Children

Hundreds of thousands of children, from infants to sixteen-year-olds, were exterminated by the Hitlerite criminals at Auschwitz. As a rule, the Germans sent the children arriving in the camp from the trains to the gas chambers, where they were murdered. Only a small number of healthy teenagers were sent to the labor camps.

The investigation determined that the Germans drove children between the ages of eight and sixteen to exhaustion by forcing them to perform the same physical labor as the adults. Through the use of torture and beatings each child was forced to do work that was beyond his strength, driven to the point of exhaustion, and then murdered.

Yakov Gordon of Vilnius, a former prisoner, testified: "…In early 1943 at Birkenau 164 boys were selected to be sent to the hospital, where they were all murdered by means of injections of carbolic acid into their hearts."

Former prisoner Bakasch Weldtraut of Düsseldorf (Germany) testified: "In 1943, when we were building a fence around Crematorium V, I personally saw SS men throw children into bonfires alive."

This is what the children saved by the Red Army themselves attested to, regarding the tortures inflicted upon them by the fascist beasts:

A boy named Sami Mundianov, born in 1930 in Rod (Italy): "…Working in groups of fifteen to twenty, we were forced to pull carts loaded with various kinds of cargo, but mostly with the bodies of victims. We took them to a special block, where they were piled up; from there they were taken to the crematoria. We worked from four in the morning until night. At the end of October 1944 the Germans held an inspection and gave us a 'punishment' because our block was not clean enough. They lined up 150 of us outside the block and took us to a bathhouse, where we were stripped naked, doused in cold water, and driven naked back to the block. Many of us fell ill afterwards."

A nine-year-old boy named Andras Lerinciakos from Klez (Hungary) gave the following testimony: "…When we were driven into Block 22 in the camp we were beaten, particularly by the German women who were in charge of us. They beat us with sticks. During my stay in the camp Doctor Mengele took a great deal of blood from me… . In November 1944 all the children were taken into Camp A, the gypsy camp; during a roll call they found that one of us was missing. Brandem, who was in charge of the women's camp, and her assistant Mandel herded us outside at one o'clock in the morning and made us stand in the freezing cold until twelve o'clock the next day… ."

The SS took children born in the camp and murdered them along with their mothers. Women who arrived at the camp pregnant were immediately taken to a special barracks, where birth was prematurely induced. Pregnant women who resisted were sent to the gas chambers.

Former prisoner Sofya Isaakovna Flyaks testified: "…Many women who arrived in the camp in August 1944 had children between the ages of five and twelve. All the children were sent with their mothers to the crematoria. I was seven months pregnant when I arrived. When SS Doctor König saw that I was pregnant, he sent me to Barracks V-3 in Birkenau. In the barracks were sixty-five women in a similar condition. Three days later they gave me an injection in the pelvic region to induce premature birth. The injections continued over a period of four days. On the fifth day I gave birth to a baby boy; they took the baby away from me. I saw fourteen such cases in the barracks where I was staying. Newborns and babies born prematurely were taken away. Where we did not know."

Among the prisoners liberated at Auschwitz doctors examined 180 children. There were 52 of them up to the age of 8 and 128 between 8 and 15. All of them arrived in Auschwitz during the second half of 1944; that is, they had been in the camp for three to six months. All 180 children were given medical examinations, which established that 72 of them suffered from pulmonary or glandular tuberculosis. Forty-nine suffered from malnutrition (and from severe exhaustion), 31 had frostbite, and so on.

The Extermination of the Intelligentsia

In Auschwitz the Germans exterminated thousands of scientists, scholars, and other members of the intelligentsia of various countries.

André Foudri of Samot Dipuenne told the commission the following: "…Out of the six hundred Frenchmen who arrived in the camp with me, most perished within a few months. Among them were the economist Émile Boreau, the gifted Professor Jean Compienne, department deputy Haron Philippe Leaudi, Mayor Lebigus Wilwife, the academicians Godeau and Brus, the architectural engineer Moline, and others."

Henri Limousin, a professor from the University of Clermont-Ferrand, testified: "…In November 1944 I was transferred from Dachau to Auschwitz as a specialist in pathology. I spent nearly a month in the quarantine block, where I was forced to clean latrines, scrub floors, and take food to inmates of the prison."

Those who were murdered at Auschwitz included Professor Freida, the well-known Dutch economist; Doctor Lavoslav; the engineer Kimar; a doctor of engineering named Enkodlyan from Yugoslavia; the Polish engineer Wisnewski; a pharmacist from Warsaw named Teichert;

Polish Professors Geszczikewicz and Riubarski; Czech Professors Otto Sitik in neuropathology, Leo Tausik in psychiatry, and Jan Levit in surgery; Kraus, the famous attorney from Vienna; the general and physician from the French army, Zhob; and many, many others. They were all either worked to death or suffocated in the gas chambers.

The Special State Commission received "An Appeal to the International Community" written in three languages—German, Hungarian, and French—and signed by twenty-seven former inmates of Auschwitz. Among them were professors, doctors, engineers, attorneys, students, and other representatives of the intelligentsia of various countries. The appeal opens with the following words: "We the undersigned, liberated by the great Red Army from the bloody Nazi persecution, stand before the international community and charge the German government under the leadership of Adolf Hitler with the greatest mass murder, brutality, and kidnapping into German slavery ever committed in the history of humanity... ."

The Appeal ends with the following words: "We turn to the international community with a request to clear up the fate of millions of people of all nationalities who have disappeared and to employ every means of saving the millions of prisoners from all countries who continue to suffer in Hitlerite Germany. We were saved by a miracle when the Nazis were withdrawing from Auschwitz. Although the Hitlerites retreated in a panic, they took with them about 58,000 prisoners from Auschwitz and its satellite camps. These people, worn out from hunger, were forced to go on foot; most of them could not have made it for more than a few kilometers... . We believe that as the front advances deeper into Germany, the same fate will befall the people who are still in the hands of the bloodthirsty Nazis. We the undersigned appeal to the international community, to countries at war and to the neutral countries, and ask in the name of humanity that they do everything possible to prevent the brutality and the crimes of the Nazis from ever being repeated, so that the blood of millions of innocent victims might not have been spilled in vain.

"Together with some ten thousand prisoners rescued from the Nazis, we ask that the crimes and the unbelievable atrocities committed by the Hitlerites not go unavenged.

"The former prisoners are indebted to the courageous Red Army for saving their lives and ask the international community and all governments to consider this and to express their gratitude in our name... ."

The Hitlerite Plunderers

In Auschwitz the Hitlerites revealed themselves to the world not only as bloodthirsty murderers of defenseless people but also as greedy plunderers of their victims. Millions of people who were brought to Auschwitz from various countries were subjected to the organized plundering of their possessions within an hour of their arrival. The SS took all of their belongings—suitcases, clothing, bedding, even their underwear and shoes—and sent them to special camp warehouses to be sorted out and shipped to Germany. Some of the people who were able to work and were selected for forced labor had their own clothing replaced by a striped outfit.

At Auschwitz there were thirty-five special warehouses for sorting and packing objects and clothing; twenty-nine of them were burned down, along with everything in them, prior to the Germans' retreat in the face of the advancing Red Army. The following items were found in the six warehouses that remained standing:

1. Men's outerwear and underclothing	348,820 sets
2. Women's outerwear and underclothing	836,255 sets
3. Women's shoes	5,525 pairs
4. Men's shoes	38,000 pairs
5. Carpets	13,964

Large quantities of toothbrushes, shaving brushes, eyeglasses, dentures, and all sorts of dishware that had belonged to the prisoners were also discovered in the warehouses. A large quantity of children's clothing was found: shirts, baby tops, pants, coats, caps. With their bloody hands the Hitlerite child murderers carefully sorted through these things that had belonged to the children they slaughtered and sent them off to Germany.

An examination of the items found in the warehouses revealed that all of it had belonged to people of various nationalities who had been tortured and murdered. On the clothing, footwear and other articles were labels from France, Belgium, Holland, Yugoslavia, Czechoslovakia, and other countries. On the suitcases were stickers from the various hotels of the cities of Europe.

On the camp grounds the commission found seven train cars loaded with clothing and bedding ready to be shipped out to Germany. From papers found in the camp containing orders signed by Oberscharführer Reichsenbach, it is evident that in a period of only forty-seven days—from 1 July 1944 to 15 January 1945—the following items were prepared for shipment to Germany:

1. Children's clothes and underwear	99,922 sets
2. Women's clothes and underwear	192,652 sets
3. Men's clothes and underwear	222,269 sets
TOTAL	514,843 sets

On 7 March 1945 the commission found 293 bales of women's hair weighing a total of 7,000 kilograms at the Auschwitz tannery factory. Experts on the commission determined that the hair had been cut off the heads of 140,000 women.

The Hitlerite Thugs Murdered More than Four Million People in Auschwitz

Prior to their retreat the Germans diligently destroyed all the documents that would prove to the world how many people they annihilated at Auschwitz, thus carefully erasing the traces of the monstrous crimes they committed in Auschwitz. But the massive techniques that the Germans created for murdering people, the testimony of Auschwitz prisoners liberated by the Red Army, the evidence presented by two hundred witnesses, documents discovered, and other substantial proof are enough to convict the German executioners of the extermination, gassing, and cremation of millions of people.

Considering that the Germans used a large number of bonfires to burn the bodies, the general capacity for murdering people at Auschwitz must be set significantly higher than what might previously have been thought.

Allowing, however, for the fact that not all the crematoria were working at full capacity, experts on the commission have established that at Auschwitz the German butchers exterminated no lees than four million citizens of the USSR, Poland, France, Yugoslavia, Czechoslovakia, Romania, Hungary, Bulgaria, Holland, and other countries.

Calling the German-Fascists to a Serious Accounting

The monstrous crimes perpetrated by the Germans at Auschwitz were committed by the order of the Hitlerite government and under the supervision of Reichsführer SS Himmler. Among the people directly responsible for committing these heinous crimes are: chief of the camps in Germany, Lieutenant-General SS Glücks; chief of the Main Sanitation Administration for the concentration camps General SS Pohl; chief of concentration camp construction Major-General SS Kammler; and the representative of the firm Topf and Sons, senior engineer Prüfer. In addition there were the camp chiefs: Obersturmbannführer Polliachek, Sturmbannführer Hess,[32] Sturmbannführer Baer, and Sturmbannführer Schwartz. There were the camp commandants: Obersturmbannführer Liebehenschel (he was the chief of the garrison), Sturmbannführer Kraus, Hauptsturmführer Aumier, Obersturmführer Hoffmann, Obersturmführer Höss, Obersturmführer Jostan, and Obersturmführer Schwarzhuber. There were the men in charge of the crematoria at Auschwitz: Oberscharführer Moll, Oberscharführer Boger, Unterscharführer Scheter, and Rotenführer Schulz. There were also: the man in charge of the work commandos, Obersturmführer Sell, and chief of the construction office, Sturmbannführer Bischof; Unterscharführer Schumacher, Oberscharführer Klermann, Unterscharführer Lachmann, Oberscharführer Emerich, Unterscharführer Stibitz, Oberscharführer Klausen, Oberscharführer Khartwik, Unterscharführer Kaduk, Oberscharführer Palitsch,[33] and Obersturmführer SS Sommer. The camp physicians included the director of experiments Major Doctor Schmidt, Obersturmführer Doctor Mengele, Untersturmführer Doctor König, Rotenführer Rode, Obersturmführer Doctor Fischer, Obersturmführer Doctor Klein, Doctor Dering, Hauptsturmführer Doctor Wirtz, Obersturmführer Doctor Tillo, Sturmbannführer Doctor Klauberg, Professor Schumann, Doctor Baber, Oberfeldwebel Emil Kaschub, Obersturmführer Entress, Hauptsturmführer Doctor Geotmermann, Hauptsturmführer Doctor Kitt, Hauptsturmführer Doctor Horstmann, and Hauptsturmführer Doctor Kraus.

Like all Germans who personally took part in the torture and murder of the prisoners of Auschwitz, these men must all be brought before the people to stand trial and bear the harsh punishment they deserve.

A Girl from Auschwitz (No. 74233)

On 16 August 1943 the Germans finally liquidated the Bialystok Ghetto. Everyone who was still alive was assembled and taken to the prison in Grodno. We spent two days there; then we moved on. There were approximately eighty people in each vehicle. My father died along the way; we—my relatives and I—took some morphine that I had long since prepared for us. My brother gave his son, a thirteen-month-old baby, an appropriate dose of a sedative called luminal. Because the ride was so bumpy, the morphine did not work on us, and we arrived at Lomza prison in a state of exhaustion. My brother's baby was dead. {I was in a horrible state: I felt that he died because of my advice. The eyes of my brother and mother were saying, "You murdered him!" Now that I have emerged from the fascist bandits' hell, I know that in Auschwitz they would have murdered the baby anyway; then they would have burned him.}

They held us in the prison for three months. On 18 November 1943 they led us out into the yard, took down our names and occupations, and hauled us off to the train station.

We arrived someplace near Danzig. They unloaded us from the train cars in a wooded area, where the SS were waiting for us. Reflectors lit up the path to the camp. They were herding us onward with shouts. The men walked separately from the women. In the camp they handed us over to the camp's "senior" woman, a kapo. As we approached the barracks, I detected the strong odor of sulfur. I realized that here we would meet our end. Nothing mattered any more. The threat of death had hung over our heads so many times that all I thought was: "Let's just get it over with!" The next morning, however, they took us to the showers. They took all our belongings away from us and dressed us in camp outfits; then they gave us numbers and took us back to the barracks. We received bread twice a day. A few began to hope that they might decide to let us live. It should be noted that at this time they were not burning people alive in Stutthof. Later, in Auschwitz, I found out from a prisoner who arrived from Stutthof six months after me that indeed they were burning prisoners alive.

Soon there was talk that we would be taken to another place, most likely to Auschwitz. Once again we endured some hard days.

On 10 January 1944 they loaded us into an open train car. From time to time I looked over to the men's side to see if I could spot my brother. We rode for three hours. We pulled into some station; there they loaded us into passenger cars. We arrived in Auschwitz on 12 January.

As we approached Auschwitz, we saw many people working on the road. [This elevated our mood a bit; it meant that this was not a death factory, and that people were alive here. At the time we did not know that the Germans used prisoners for especially hard labor, creating working conditions that were unbearable so that the prisoners would die more rapidly.] As I got off the train, I took one last look at my brother, who was being driven away with the other men. After an hour's walk we came to the gates. Divided by wire fences into several fields, the huge camp looked like an entire city. {Girls were walking past us singing songs. Again the hope stirred that perhaps the rumors about Auschwitz being a death camp were exaggerated: how could there be a death camp with singing?}

In a wooden building near the gates was an office of some sort. They registered us, and the gates closed behind us—forever. They took us to a barracks for the night. It had no beds, no chairs. We had to sit on the damp earth. That evening camp commandant Höss and his right-hand man Tauber showed up. We were ordered to line up by fives; they carefully examined each one of us and asked us about our professions. In some cases, including mine, they wrote down the profession. The next day the camp's chief executioner, Tauber, returned; girls, senior prisoners, tattooed numbers on our left arm. We were no longer human be-ings—we had become numbers. Toward evening we were taken to the "sauna"—the bath-house—undressed, and herded into the showers to wash. Prior to this they shaved our hair off. The lucky ones were those whose numbers Höss had noted down the previous day. [Everyone else looked horrible.] Girls who were left with no hair were crying. One of the camp personnel pointed at the huge flames rising into the sky and said, "Do you know what that is? You will go there too. There you won't need your hair or anything else that has been taken away from you."

After bathing we were given old, filthy underwear and wooden shoes. A red stripe was painted down the length of our outer clothing, and our number was sewn on. Then they sent us to a room—the Schreibstube—located near the bathhouse. On an index card each of us was given the name Sarah in addition to our own name. I did not understand what was going on and said that my name was not Sarah; the person taking down the names smiled ironically and said that was how Hitler wanted it. Again we were lined up by fives and herded into the so-called quarantine block. The block was divided into "Stuben," and each Stube has a "Stubowa" in charge of keeping order. We slept five or six together on plank beds in horrible darkness; whenever one of us pointed to an empty bed and started to ask if we could use it, they answered us with curses and beatings. They got us up at four in the morning and herded us to the kitchen for tea; then they took roll for everyone in the block. The roll call was called "Appell," and the count was taken twice a day, in the morning and in the evening, when people returned to the camp from work. Each Appell lasted two to three hours, regardless of rain, snow, or cold. We stood absolutely still, exhausted and frozen to the quick. Those who got sick were taken to the hospital block, where they disappeared forever.

On 18 January we suddenly heard whistles out on the camp streets and shouts of "*Blocksperre!*"[34] It was forbidden to leave the block. It had been six days since our arrival in Auschwitz. No one explained to us what all this meant, but from the looks on the bosses' faces we knew it was not good. They lined us up, counted us, and took us to the sauna. There we were ordered to undress, and we had to file past Höss and the doctor. They took down the numbers of some of us, including my mother's. After we returned to the barracks we found out that this had been a "selection." It was the most feared word in the camp; it meant that people who were alive today were doomed to be burned. I was in a terrible situation! I knew that I was going to lose my mother, and there was no way I could help her. My mother tried to comfort me, saying that she had lived out her life and that she was sorry only for us, her children. She knew that the same fate awaited us. Two days after the selection the doomed people were still being held in the block and were fed just like the rest of us; but on 20 January they came for them and took them to the special death block (Block A25a). There these poor people from all the blocks were gathered and then taken in trucks to the crematoria. There were many from our block who were not at the evening Appell. The smoke and the flames told us that on that day, 20 January, many innocent people were burned; my mother was among them. My only consolation was that I would perish too and that they were now free of their suffering.

Hard days set in. We were beaten often. It was no use complaining. These were, at best, new beatings, when we knelt inside the block or outside of it for several hours, regardless of the weather. The Stubowas herded us into the kitchen and forced us to carry heavy cauldrons for them. The work was very difficult even for healthy men. We had no soap or water, and there was no way to maintain any cleanliness. To wash up, we had to go to the so-called "Waschraum"; the whole block was taken there at the same time, and we had only three to five minutes to wash.

People from the quarantine block were usually sent to work after five or six weeks. They took us to work earlier than that. Most of the girls who came in on the same transport that I did went to work at the Union factory; as a pharmacist, I was sent to a different block. From there I would again be called to work. And so we left the quarantine block. But it did not remain empty: every day new victims arrived from Poland, France, Belgium, Holland, and other countries. Meanwhile many people died. The death rate reached 300 to 350 per day. Typhus and dysentery raged.

The same organization was in force in the new block as in the old one: the same signs on the walls, the same demand to observe cleanliness, the same treatment from the Blockowa and Stubowa. When I got there they started asking me how it was that, as a newcomer with such a high number, I was allowed to keep my hair. When I explained that the reason was my profession, they told me ironically: "Well, just wait until they call you to work in your profession." I later realized what was going on: in order to be given such work, you had to have protection, and that meant giving a bribe (a "gift") to the one who was protecting you. To get a "gift" you had to know how to "organize," that is, to steal. I did not know how to do that, and so I had to wait. Resting was not permitted. It became my duty to carry cauldrons in and out and to clean up the block. If I had objected, I would have wound up in the selection line. Since the block had to be "rein" (clean), we would not be allowed inside for days on end and were kept in a small, unheated room. They drove us out of the block even when it was freezing cold. Only after the evening Appell, which lasted one and a half to two hours, were we allowed to go inside. On top of that, to keep the "parquet" cement floor from getting dirty, we had to wash it several times a day with our freezing hands, as we wept biter tears. But even that was not enough: since they wanted to keep us busy, they used us for hard labor. For four to five hours a day we had to walk three kilometers and carry back heavy stones that the other women's work teams would use to pave the camp. From all the blocks they would gather together the women who were not assigned to specific work sites. They counted us at the gate, and a German guard and his dog would join us; then, under a barrage of swear words, they herded us out to the site where the stones were. Everyone tried to find a small a stone. But it did not work; they checked us out and beat us. In addition to the armed escort, female Einweiser watched over us. The Einweiser were German prisoners; most of them were prostitutes. An Einweiser could be bribed—a pack of cigarettes was enough; but to get the pack of cigarettes, again, you had to know how to organize. The work was very hard. I spent five weeks working under such conditions. I simply could not take any more than that; my legs were terribly swollen, and I was in no shape to even walk. It was also impossible to stay in the block, since they came to see that everyone had gone to work. Everyone was required to work; there was no place for the sick. They were sent to a special block, to a block for the sick: the Revier. At that time the Revier meant death; rarely did anyone ever return from there. In the Revier people would become even more ill; they would infect one another, waste away, and die. There was yet another danger in the Revier: selection. Whenever there was a selection, the people in the Revier were the first ones subjected to this danger. But I had no way out. Even though I knew everything that threatened me, I asked the Schreiber in our block to send me to the Revier. New surroundings, new beasts. I had to share a bed with another sick girl. When I saw that her whole body was covered with ulcers and wounds, I burst into sobs. I knew that I would get infected sharing a blanket with her. At that time people were eaten up with mange. Under normal conditions, it could be cured in two or three days, but here it lasted forever. Besides that, during a selection it was enough to have just a trace of this illness to be sent to the ovens. I begged a nurse to let me have another bed. She gave in after I pleaded for a long time. I spent three weeks in the Revier. I used the tea that we were given in the mornings to wash my hands and face. Twice a week I used the bread ration we were given to buy some hot water, so I could wash better. I did this at night. When without bread for two days to keep relatively clean. There is no way I can describe the surprise on the face of my blockmates when they saw me again. {I proudly showed them my clean body and advised everyone who was sick to go to the Revier as long as they were not utterly exhausted and still had the strength to fight the illness. Because the ones who were totally exhausted—the "Muselmänner," as they were called in the camp jargon—were prime candidates for selection.}

After I was released from the Revier, I was taken to the sauna (the bathhouse); there I washed and was given new clothes—rags. I had to deny myself bread, so that I could use it to "buy" clothes. You could buy such things from the ones who worked sorting the baggage from the transports that were endlessly arriving in Auschwitz. [We had been in the very same situation after the "Entlausung" (the disinfecting of the block and of people against lice). Then they took us to the sauna to bathe; they gathered our things and disinfected them in steam boilers. After the disinfection we got back not our own things but rags, so we had to start all over again trying to acquire everything.]

After the Revier they sent me to work in the Weberei.[35] I had to weave plaits from scraps of rags, leather, and rubber. I had to make my quota no matter what, and to do this, I had to have enough raw material. But it was necessary to "organize" even the raw material, that is, to give cigarettes or other things to the Einweiser who worked as the overseer. In addition to the Einweiser, there were SS women—the "Aufseher"—who oversaw our work, and they liked gifts too. A number sewn poorly onto a dress or the absence of a red stripe (a "Streich") on the outside of your clothing was enough for the Aufseher to write down the number of the "guilty party" and the number of the block where she lived. They also wrote down numbers for talking to men or for having letters from men. The next day the ones who were to be punished were sent to a special block. People in that block had a red circle on their back. From there prisoners were sent to do the most backbreaking work.

Here I should describe how it was when we went out to work. We got up at four in the morning. The person on duty for the day went to the kitchen for the tea. After the plank beds were made and the tea distributed, we were herded outside for Appell. There was no time to wash. After Appell people who were to go outside the camp boundaries to work lined up by fives in the camp street (the Lagerstrasse). Once again various kapos would count us and then lead toward the gates. At the gates there was an orchestra. It consisted of women prisoners. The first time I heard the music I started crying like a baby. Music and flames soaring into the sky! Who could have conceived of such a thing? Toward evening, when people were returning from work, they met with the same orchestra. It was forbidden to rest; we had to stand another hour and a half to two hours for Appell. [At that time and afterward] the evening Appell lasted a long time, because almost every day there were escapes by men who worked outside the camp. We knew about the escapes from the howling of the sirens. We rejoiced at the sound; although the roll call lasted an especially long time, we willingly stood for the Appell. I worked at the Weberei for three days and then got a job at the Revier. I ended up there because I was listed in the card file as a medical worker. Without protection or bribery, this was the rarest turn of luck; the hygienic conditions in that job were better, and you did not have to go outside the camp to work—in other words, you did not have to walk sixteen kilometers a day. The main thing was that in the Revier I worked on behalf of the poor prisoners. Every day we had a visit from Mengele, the camp physician. Hundreds of thousand of people were on that cutthroat's conscience. The Revier was located inside the camp but was isolated from the camp by a barbed wire fence. It consisted of fifteen blocks. [It was a kind of state within a state.]

I started working there on 21 April. A few days later the sound of whistles and cries rang out after the evening Appell: "Lagersperre—selection!" A deadly silence set in, the silence before the storm. I knew that I would not see many of the patients in the block the next morning. With remarkable punctuality the trucks pulled up, and they started dragging out the ones who were doomed to death. There was screaming and crying. And suddenly you could hear the old Hebrew song "Hatikvah." Several more trucks pulled up, and then silence reigned. It was horrible to be so close, to hear everything and to be completely helpless! This selection was conducted just like the ones before it; several days beforehand Doctor Mengele had written down the numbers of the unfortunate patients who were marked for the ovens.

After the selection work continued as before. The most difficult says were setting in. Every day large transports of Jews arrived from nearly every part of Europe; at that time most of them were Jews from Hungary. The transports used to stop at the Auschwitz station. They unloaded and the selection was conducted there; the "lucky" ones passed through the gates to the camp, and the rest, marked for death, were taken away in trucks directly to the crematoria. The Germans, however, thought this was inefficient, so they had the prisoners build a rail line that went from the Auschwitz station directly to the ovens. The rails ran parallel to the Revier blocks just 150 to 200 meters from us. We were constantly looking upon the terrifying scene. Eight or nine trains would pull in during the day; they were unloaded, and the baggage was left lying near the rails. The chief executioner, Doctor Mengele, conducted the selection. Mengele had a lot of work to do that summer. The people getting off the train cars had no idea of what awaited them. Beyond the wires they could see girls in white smocks (they saw us, the Revier workers). If they arrived in the morning, they heard the sound of an orchestra; they saw groups of girls going out to work outside the camp ("Aussenkommandos"). [The new arrivals could scarcely comprehend where they were being taken.] Meanwhile the ones who were doomed to annihilation were being led off to the crematorium. There they undressed in a large hall; they were given a piece of soap and a towel and were told that they were going to take a shower. In fact, the poor people were being driven into a gas chamber to be murdered. Their bodies were burned. The task of burning the bodies was done only by male prisoners who belonged to the so-called Sonderkommando. But they did not have to work there for long: after one or two months they too were burned and replaced by others marked for the same fate. How horrible it was to gaze upon the endless lines of men, women, children, and old people walking to the crematoria! They realized so little of what awaited them that they fussed about the baggage that they had left at the train. At that time the transports were arriving so frequently that they did not have time to haul the luggage away; the mountain of things grew larger, but their owners were no longer among the living. When the transports were coming in from Hungary, at the selections Doctor Mengele was sparing the lives of twin children regardless of their age. Mengele also took an interest in families of dwarves; after a while they even enjoyed his sympathy. It should be pointed out that in the Revier we had some abnormal people. Twice a week they were taken to the men's camp at Buna, which was nine kilometers from our camp; there the Germans performed various experiments on them. Doctor König was in charge of it. [Even after the crematoria were no longer in operation and they were piling the bodies between logs in ditches, dousing them with kerosene and burning them], even then the sadists Mengele and König were occupied with their "scientific" experiments. The experiments were performed on prisoners, too, on men and women.

The summer of 1944 was terrible; endless transports arrived every day. At the same time trainloads of men and women prisoners were leaving from Auschwitz to various work sites in Germany. Germany needed the manpower. Our spirits were lifted by the fact that "little birds"— Soviet airplanes—started to visit us every day. They did not bomb the camp, but twice bombs fell on the SS barracks, where, much to our joy, there were many casualties. We sensed that the front was drawing near. Escapes became daily occurrences. On one occasion the evening Appell lasted an especially long time. The sirens went off. At first we thought it was an air raid, but the wailing of the sirens was completely different and drawn out. After a long count of the prisoners, it turned out that one of the women from our camp and a prisoner from the men's camp were missing. Later we found out that a Belgian Jewish woman named Malya had escaped. She held a high position; she was a "Laufer" and assigned jobs to people who came out of the Revier. She was a human being in the truest and highest sense of the word; she did absolutely everything she could to help people. Malya escaped with her Polish boyfriend. Several days later they were captured in Bielsk. They were in SS uniforms and were armed. They were brought to Auschwitz and thrown into a dungeon, the "bunker." They Germans interrogated and tortured them, but they revealed nothing. On 21 August we saw an SS man bring Malya into our camp; she was beaten, exhausted, and dressed in rags. She was to be hanged in front of all the prisoners. And she knew it. She also knew that they were going to hang her friend. She hit the Gestapo man who was escorting her, grabbed the razorblades she had hidden in her hair, and slit open her veins. The Germans did not succeed in executing this heroic girl.

{At that time the Germans were generally in a rage. They searched the prisoners as they returned to camp from work and took everything away from them. There were also some changes in our block. A certain Sonya, the camp commandant's right-hand woman, was known for her extreme cruelty. Not only did she take all the finest things from the prisoners, but she also beat them and humiliated them. She was their right hand.}

As the front drew closer, the Germans grew more nervous. They stopped burning people in the crematoria. More than that, in order to erase the traces of their crimes, the Germans destroyed the death factory. They blew up one crematorium after another. It seemed that the barbarians were mindful of their inevitable day of reckoning. Even our living conditions improved a bit. True, this was not reflected in the food. {We got the same little pot of grass tea at four or five in the morning, the same two hundred grams of bread; three times a week they handed out some margarine (a pack of margarine for twelve people) or a piece of sausage. Lunch and supper—that is, a plate of water with a turnip and a piece of bread—were distributed at the same time....} Our Revier was moved to Field E in Birkenau, where the seventeen thousand gypsies who were burned that summer had been. We were between two men's camps. It was so pleasant and yet so miserable when we would "meet" after work in the evening, separated by the wire fence with the electric current running through it. Even more pleasant was the fact that Soviet aircraft flying overhead began to interfere with our evenings; the lights on the fence would go out, and we would part full of hope.

On 17 January 1945 it became known that they were going to liquidate the camp. That night all the hospital documents were destroyed. At ten in the morning Doctor Kitt showed up and ordered the personnel and the patients who were able to march to get ready. He announced that a train would come for those who were seriously ill. All the other fields of the camp were also evacuated. When Kitt conducted the selection in the Lagerstrasse, he sent me to the group that was leaving the camp; unnoticed, I went back into the barracks and did not come out again, even though those still inside advised me several times to join the march. I lay down on a plank bed and said I was sick. Several thousand patients and personnel remained in the Revier. Since the director of the pharmacy had left on a transport, I got a job in the pharmacy. Over the next few days events unfolded at a rapid pace. On 20 January, after a major air raid, the camp was without water and electricity. As always, the air raid greatly boosted our morale. The camp itself was not bombed a single time. We were afraid that at the last minute the Germans would blow up our Revier camp in order to cover he traces of their crimes. That fear was the reason why most of the women from our camp left on 18 January. They left in the hope that somewhere along the road outside of the camp they could escape. Many of them managed to do so.

By 21 January chaos reigned. There were still a few SS in the camp. Stores of bread, food, and clothing stood open. The warehouses were full of all kinds of good things. [These barbarians had hoarded the best of everything, but to us, the prisoners, they gave out the worst, the filthiest underwear, rags instead of clothes, wooden shoes, and food that was not fit for pigs.] At around three in the afternoon the last of the SS left; they said that anyone who wanted to could go with them, except for the Jews. But no one went. The gates of the camp stood open. In the evening of that same day a fire broke out in a neighboring field of he camp (Birkenau), and later that night the last crematorium was blown up. We were afraid that our camp would get the same treatment as the crematorium. We cut through the fence and joined the men, who, like us, had stayed in their Revier. We felt much safer with them. Many left the camp. The 23rd of January was a very hard day. Several Germans showed up on bicycles. They spent several hours in the camp looking for anything of value and then left. On the morning of 24 January more Germans showed up and shot five Russian prisoners in the men's camp. On 25 January a vehicle pulled up with a group of Gestapo men. They ordered all the Jews who were able to walk to come out of the blocks. They lined up several hundred men and a comparable number of women. Having learned from experience, I decided not to go out. A friend and I made our way into a block that had been completely emptied out. In the block there were bags of underwear and clothing. We hid under the bags and listened for what was happening in the camp. When it got dark we came out of our hiding place. One by one those who had not obeyed the Gestapo's order began to show themselves. Like us, they had hidden and thus were saved. {They said that the whole operation had been carried out by German prisoners who had gone into the blocks and dragged out the Jewish prisoners. The Gestapo simply looked on while it happened and promised to come back the next day for the rest.} All the Jews who had lined up had obviously been taken outside the camp and shot.

We spent that night in the men's camp. We no longer had to hide. My friend and I spent 26 January in the pharmacy in the men's camp, where our non-Jewish comrades had built a shelter for us under the ceiling. If the Gestapo should show up, they would hide us there. That day was especially joyous for us: Soviet artillery and aircraft were going nonstop. The next day we did not hear artillery fire or see any aircraft. We concluded that the front was moving away from us. Our nerves could not take it. The thought that the Gestapo could come back made living impossible. Then suddenly, from the pharmacy window, I saw a silhouette in white and gray clothing on the road near the camp. It was around five in the afternoon. At first we thought it was people from the camp returning. I ran out of the pharmacy to see who it was. How great was our joy when we saw that it was our saviors—Soviet troops! It was a reconnaissance party. There was no end to the kisses and the greetings. They told us that we should leave, explaining that we could not stay here because they had not yet determined where the enemy was. We drew back several paces and then moved toward them again, so as to be closer to our liberators. We stood around the gate almost until dark. Then we went back to the camp; there too we met up with our long-awaited and dear friends.

On 28 January many of the prisoners finally left the camp for freedom. We hosted the commanders and soldiers in the pharmacy. We told them about the terrible life in Auschwitz. On 3 February we set out from Birkenau and went to Auschwitz. There we found many people who, like us, had managed to save themselves. On 4 February we went into the town of Auschwitz. They could not believe that we were free. We looked in amazement at the people on the streets. On 5 February we headed for Krakow. Gigantic factories stretched out along one side of the road; prisoners who had long since perished under the exhausting labor had built them. On the other side of the road was a large camp. We went in and found sick people who, like us, had survived only because they did not go with the Germans on 18 January. From there we moved on. For a long time we followed the electric fence on stone pillars, the symbol of slavery and death that we knew so well. It seemed that we would never break free of the camp. Finally we came to the village of Wloseniuszcza. We spent the night there; the next day, 6 February, we pressed on. A car picked us up and gave us a ride to Krakow. We were free, [but we still did not know how to rejoice. We had endured too much and lost too many.]

Prepared for publication by Osip Cherny

Twenty-Six Months in Auschwitz: The Story of Mordecai Tsirulnitsky, Former Inmate No. 79414

1. In the Village of Ostrino

I was born in 1899 in the small town of Ostrino, now in the Grodno district. I lived there with my family until the Hitlerite invasion. I had a large family: five children. My children were wonderful. They all went to school. My older daughter Galya would have been twenty-two now. When the Soviets came to power she entered the school for technical engineering, and in the spring of 1941 she advanced to the second-year level. My oldest boy, my seventeen-year-old Yakov, was an intern at a printing and publishing plant. The rest of my children were still in school: my sixteen-year-old Yoel was going into the ninth grade, my thirteen-year-old Vigdor was in the eighth grade, and the youngest one Lanya, who was nine, would have been going into the fourth grade.

Ostrino was located near the border. By 23 June 1941 the town was surrounded by Germans; those who tried to escape were forced to turn back. On the 25th the Germans entered Ostrino.

As soon as they entered the town, the Germans started shooting people. The first victims to fall were those who had worked in the Soviet government and who were involved in Soviet activities in our area.

Our town was part of the Shchuchinsky region. In early September a German Gestapo agent was appointed commandant of the region. I do not remember his name; my memory has grown weak since the camp. From the moment of his appointment {the Jews were hunted down and persecuted. First the Jews were forbidden to leave the city limits. Anyone who violated this order was shot. That was how the eighty-year-old Aryeh Tanevitsky got shot; the Hitlerites ran him down just outside of town. The town's rabbi, Rabbi Bezdansky, was also murdered around that time. He was supposedly taken to a concentration camp with a group of other citizens; a few days later we found out that they shot him.

Then came the order forbidding Jews to go outdoors on Sunday afternoons. Again, anyone violating the order would be shot, only this time they would shoot not only the violator but his entire family as well. Zhen Khaim Khlebovsky went out for some water. They caught her and shot her along with her husband and two small children

On 7 November 1941 someone's barn caught fire. The Germans accused the Jews of setting the fire and ordered the entire Jewish population to assemble immediately in the town square "for inspection." Several dozen people, including all who did not report on time or whose papers were not in order, were shot on the spot.}

Shootings became a common and frequent occurrence in our town. Most of the time they took place on market days in order to frighten the peasants living in the area. The commandant lived in Shchuchino, in the center of the region; he often came to Ostrino, and when he did, we knew that the shootings were about to begin. Among others, all the teachers were shot: Miller and his wife, their two daughters, Elin, and others. {The elder of the synagogue, Draznin, fell too.

On one occasion in late November 1941 all the Jews were driven out into the square once more; they were ordered to bring their valuables with them. People assumed that they were going to be resettled somewhere. It turned out, however, that everything they brought to the square with them was confiscated. Their houses were also being plundered while they stood on the square. Later, when I returned to my home, I found out that a German agronomist had even stolen my children's notebooks and pencils. Anyone who tried to put up the least resistance was murdered.}

A listed of the residents living in a given apartment building had to be posted on the building's wall, by order of the commandant. If anyone should be missing from the list, the entire family would be shot. That is how the family of Osher Amstibovsky, a family of eight, perished.

The Ostrino Ghetto was established in December 1941. Jews from all the surrounding villages were driven into our ghetto; all who were weak or sick were murdered along the way. When the ghetto was being set up, another dozen people were shot. Then came new decrees and more shootings. Leib Mikhelevich and his sister Feiga-Sore were shot for sneaking a little grain into the ghetto. Osher Boyarsky was caught grinding some grain, and he was shot. I really cannot remember all of it!

In January 1942 it was announced that the Reich was annexing Ostrino and the entire Grodno region.

Every day the people in the ghetto were herded out to work in the forest. The men cut timber and collected tar. The overseers beat the workers half to death; anyone who lagged behind or became weak was murdered on the spot. More than once people were accused of sabotage and sent to prison; once a Jew landed in prison, he would live no longer than the following Friday. On Fridays prisoners were shot, [including all the Jewish prisoners.]

2. In the Kelbasino Camp

On 2 November 1942 the entire Jewish population of Ostrino was taken to the camp at Kelbasino, near Grodno. Prior to that time it had been a camp for Soviet prisoners of war. By the time we got to Kelbasino there were no more prisoners of war. Jews from all the cities and towns in the Grodno region were gradually sent to the Kelbasino camp. They were crowded into small dugouts with up to three hundred people in each one. There was no room to lie down; at times there was not even any standing room. The crowding, the stench, and the filth were unbelievable. We were driven out to the swamps to do backbreaking work. They gave us one or two frozen potatoes and 150 grams of bread per day, and even that was inedible. Lagerführer Insul would mercilessly beat people with a heavy club for the slightest infraction; he would beat them over the head until they were completely unconscious.

Hunger and typhus raged in the camp. Several people died every day in every dugout; they also died on the job. Now it is terrible to recall the so-called hospital, which was nothing but a dugout where they threw people who had come down with typhus. Hardly any of the sick who wound up there had any hope of getting out alive, despite the efforts of Doctor Gordon, a noble man who did everything he could to save the sick.

We later met Doctor Gordon in Auschwitz. He was one of the active members of our resistance organization. I do not know whether he survived.

At Kelbasino they did not even bury the dead. Near the camp, a short distance from the dugouts, there was a huge pit that always remained uncovered. The dead were thrown into the pit and sprinkled with a thin layer of lime; then more and more bodies were piled on top of them. It is hard even to imagine how many human bodies were swallowed up in that mass grave.

3. The First Months in Auschwitz

We spent a month at Kelbasino. {But in that short time we were reduced to such a state that it did not matter what would become of us.}

On 1 December 1942 we received the order to get ready to leave. We were instructed to pack our things and write down our first and last names on the bundles; they promised to send everything along to our new place of residence. On 2 December all of us, along with our families, were loaded into open train cars. The cars were crammed full of people and closed shut. We rode for three days. We received no bread or water. Most of all people suffered from thirst, especially the children. When the train was moving we tried everything we could think of to gather even a few drops of moisture. We lowered a tin can on a string to try to pick up a little snow so as to moisten the lips of the children; they were pining away with thirst. We lowered rags and pieces of paper; a rag would get wet with snow, and then we could wring out a few drops of water.

Despite being under a heavy guard, I managed lower two of my boys out of the train car: Yakov and Yoel. "Perhaps," I thought, "they will survive somehow." But they did not survive... . Yakov decided to run into the woods to the partisans. Only now, when I got home after the war, did I find out that he never made it to the partisans. Yoel managed to get to Grodno, where my sister was still living in the ghetto. He was brought to Auschwitz a few months later with my sister and her family and sent directly from the train to the gas chamber. My wife Sarra and I arrived in Auschwitz with our three other children on 5 December 1942.

Our transport stopped at a small platform in the middle of a field. As I later found out, the platform was specially built between Auschwitz and Birkenau... . There was some sort of shed nearby. In the distance there were endless lines of barbed wire fences.

Near the platform there was a small group of people in civilian clothes. The first thing I saw was a man bent over as a fat SS man with a club was beating him. I had to witness the same scene many times over, but I shall never forget this cruel first impression during my first few minutes in Auschwitz.

Lagerführer Schwarz[36] pulled up to our group in a car bearing the sign of the Red Cross (by the way, cases of poison for "gassing" people were always brought into camp in cars bearing the sign of the Red Cross). We were surrounded by SS. They started unloading our things from the train. But they did not give them to us. The bodies of the dead were dragged off the cars and lined up next to the road. A team of prisoners in striped outfits showed up; they were directed to our belongings.

The selection began. The sick and the weak were sent over to where the dead bodies were laid out. The healthy men were placed in a special group. All the rest—the women, the elderly, and the children—were loaded into a truck and taken away. Thus I was separated from my wife and children forever. I did not even have a chance to say good-bye to them; I had no idea that they were being taken to their death.

I wound up in a group of 189 men who had gone through the selection. They took us to the central camp, to Auschwitz. At the entrance we saw an arch; over the arch were written the words: *Arbeit Macht Frei*. In the bathhouse each of us had a number and a triangle tattooed on his left arm. As you can see, my number was 79414. Only those prisoners who were allowed a little time to live in order to work were tattooed. All prisoners, moreover, were required to wear an identification badge on their clothing, on the left side of their chests. For Jews it was a red triangle with a yellow triangle over it to form a six-pointed star (this badge was later replaced by a red triangle with a yellow stripe over it). For the Russians it was a black triangle; political prisoners wore a red triangle, and the criminals had a green one.

Anyone found on the camp grounds without his badge or who was not wearing it in the right place would meet with certain death. The first SS man you ran into could stop you, knock you down, kick you in the face with his boots, and send you to the gas chamber.

Our whole group spent the first night together in one of the barracks. The next morning there was another selection. All the men under forty were separated out and sent to Buna, the third largest of the camps, after Auschwitz and Birkenau. There were 140 of them. The remaining forty-nine of us were housed in Block 4 (a barracks). I was on a work detail assigned to level the Sola River (*Solodurchsteig*). Morning roll call (*Appell*) before work took two to three hours; it was the same in the evening when we returned to the barracks. We had to walk three kilometers to the work site. The work was hard, exhausting. A special SS unit accompanied us to guard us—or rather to torment us—while we worked. No words can describe the sadism of the SS; they beat us and tortured us for the slightest reason and often for no reason at all.

A guard might come up to you. The order would ring out: "Bend over!" And right there he would count out twenty-five blows with his stick. In those moments your every thought is focused on one thing: to stay on your feet and do not fall, or else a bullet will be waiting for you.

At the end of December they held a "sanitation" campaign (*Entlausung*). They took all our clothes from us and locked us up completely naked; then they herded us into the bathhouse, still completely naked.

On 2 January 1943 I was assigned to the commando whose job was to sort through the things that belonged to prisoners arriving in the camp. There was a group of Jews from France working with me on this commando. The Jewish actor Blumenson, my cousin Aron Leizerovich, and others were also there. Some of us unpacked the newcomers' baggage, while others sorted out their things; a third group packed the items for shipment to Germany. Seven or eight train cars full of these things would leave every day for various cities in Germany. The old worn out items were sent for handling in Memel[37] and Lodz.

The work went on day and night, without interruption for twenty-four hours a day, and still it was impossible to go through all of it because there were so many things.

Here, in a bundle of children's coats, I once found the coat that had belonged to my younger daughter Lanya.

Soon after I started working on this commando I found out about the gas chambers and the crematoria, where they burned thousands of people everyday; I found out about the fate of everyone who was not fortunate enough to be selected for a work commando. And I realized that such had been the fate of my family. People who were weak, weary, sick, and unable to work were inevitably gassed, and others took their place. Once, when it was freezing cold outside, the SS forced a whole group of people to work with no clothes on. Within two hours the people were completely frozen. The SS beat them with sticks; the ones who could not stand up to the beating and fell were sent to the gas.

To report sick and wind up in the clinic amounted to volunteering to be sent to the gas. We figured that out very quickly. My older brother Mikhl, who was in Auschwitz with me, had swollen legs. He went to the clinic and never returned. That is how others from Ostrino died: Moishe-Yankel Kamionsky, Shloime-Girsh Shilkovsky, Motl Krinsky, and others.

I felt my strength ebbing more and more every day; I could hardly stay on my feet. But my comrades in the commando supported me and helped to hide my sick condition from the guards. If they had not helped me, I would never have escaped the gas. {On the job, in spite of the danger, we tried to harm the Germans whenever we could. We sometimes found valuables, gold, and money among the things we were sorting; we would take it and bury it in the trash or hide it just so the Germans would not get it. We tried to cut up and ruin overcoats or cut a six-pointed star into them.}

On 12 January 1943 our commando was transferred to Birkenau.

The Germans tried to give Auschwitz the appearance of a labor camp. You would seldom see a prisoner's corpse lying in the vicinity of the camp. {Sick people were sent to the clinic on stretchers, as if they were going to be treated. In fact, they were sent from the clinic to the gas chambers. But when I first arrived at Auschwitz, all of this was kept secret.}

The situation was completely different in Birkenau. Here everyone could plainly see that we were in a death factory. Dead and dying people were lying everywhere around the blocks. The filth in the barracks was indescribable. On freezing winter days people were sent to the cold bathhouse and doused with icy water. Anyone who got sick was sent to the gas chambers. At first selections were held once a week; later they became more frequent. The weak, emaciated people could hardly lift their feet from the mud that covered the entire area of the camp. The SS amused themselves by tripping these people with their sticks. If a person fell, he did not get up again. One evening as I was leaving work I saw two trucks with trailers full of bodies.

The overseers in the individual barracks were no less brutal than the SS; most of them were recruited from the criminals. A German overseer in our barracks once murdered fourteen people right before my eyes. The situation was the same if not worse in other barracks.

We got up at four in the morning. Morning and evening Appell lasted about three hours. It was held in the yard. The evening Appell was especially torturous. At that time, in front of the formation, people accused of some offense on the job would be punished. In addition to the beatings they received from the guards while at work, they would receive a beating once again at the Appell. Sometimes a person was sent straight to the gas. The Appell was especially brutal if someone happened to be missing. Then the Appell would go on forever. Everyone who worked with the one who escaped had to pay the price.

I remember once in the summer of 1943 eight Russian prisoners from the agricultural unit drove out of the camp with a load of manure. They spent several hours working outside the camp. Three of them managed to escape. The guard shot the other five prisoners several times in the face. Their bodies were brought back to the camp and laid out on tables at the gates in order to scare the other prisoners. They lay there for two days.

If anyone was in not condition to work, he was sent to Block 7. That is where all the sick were gathered. When the barracks was full, they would all be sent to the gas chambers.

Within two months of our arrival in Auschwitz only four or five men were left out of our group of forty-nine. One by one all the rest were murdered or sent to the gas.

Some of the men from Ostrino worked in the forest on a commando that was cutting wood for the crematoria and the pits. One of them, Fishel Lyubetsky, told me that the SS hanged Leib Bril, Yakov Slatsnik, and Leib Slatsnik in the woods. Lyubetsky himself was covered with bruises from beatings. But he was a strong fellow; he endured, and the two of us made to the last days in the camp.

In February I saw my own nephew among the new arrivals; his name was Yoel Kamionsky, my sister's son from Grodno. From him I learned the fate of my little boy Yoel, whom I had tried to save on the way to Auschwitz. But he did not escape Auschwitz. They brought him there with the rest of my sister's family; out of all of them Yoel Kamionsky was the only one who wound up in a work unit. The fate of the others was now clear to me: the gas!

In the spring of 1943 most of the transports came from the Polish territories that the Hitlerites annexed to the Third Reich; some also came form the "General Government." Then the first transports from Greece, Czechoslovakia, Germany, and France started to arrive.

A transport from Paris once pulled in. When one of the arrivals saw the prisoners in our commando, he asked, "Tell me, what kind of death have they condemned us to?"

I could feel my strength draining away with each passing day. No matter how my comrades in the commando tried to protect me from the guards, I would often fall prey to the blows from their clubs. To this day I can still hear the command ringing in my ears: "Bend over!" Among the items we sorted we would sometimes come across something to eat. We tried to hide it from the guards, but if the SS caught us with some bit of food or saw us eating something, they beat us without mercy. I once received thirty-five blows from a stick for passing a piece of stale bread to my nephew Yoel Kamionsky. Life became unbearable. Still, my comrades tried to bolster my courage and convince me that I should watch out for my life; it might still be useful.

Now I recall my friends Albert (from France) and Kabachnikov with special gratitude. They were sent to Auschwitz before I was; their numbers were in the forty thousands.

Most of the Jews who came from Greece were from Salonika. Prior to their departure from Greece they were told that they were being sent to work in Poland. These people believed it;

they were stunned when upon their arrival at Auschwitz they got off the train and the Germans began separating the healthier men from the women, children, and old people. "*Wie so Frauen separat?*"[38] a young man asked in his astonishment when he was separated from his family.

When the first transports from Greece started arriving, three rabbis were taken to Birkenau and forced to sign a letter saying that everyone was alive and working and that things were going well for them. Then the usual fate befell them.

In the fall of 1943 about four thousand prisoners, mostly from Greece, were singled out in the camp. They were taken to Warsaw to work in the ruins of the ghetto. A fair number of them managed to escape; most of them were sent back to Auschwitz and burned in the ovens of the crematoria.

On one of the transports from Greece were children from an orphanage. At the railroad platform the SS wanted to separate the children from the woman who was their teacher and guardian. She categorically refused to abandon the children, {even though by then it was clear to all the arrivals as to what fate awaited them. Neither the surroundings nor the attempts to frighten her had any effect on her. And so} she went with the children to the gas chamber.

We were once shocked to see several Jewish families from Germany, with wives and children, brought into the men's camp. Our amazement soon dissipated, however. The gas chambers and crematoria could not immediately handle the huge number of victims arriving in Auschwitz. They had to be held here for a short time. After a day or two all these people were sent to the crematoria.

Sometime later a family camp was set up near our barracks; there they housed the Jews arriving from Theresienstadt in Czechoslovakia. This camp was in existence for about six months, at the end of which all the inhabitants were sent to their deaths.

I also saw a family camp for Gypsies. They occupied two large blocks. There were no more than a thousand of them. Every last one of them perished.

And so we lived with death before our eyes every minute. The help of my comrades was the only thing that enabled me to get through those times, in spite of everything. With the coming of spring I started to feel a little better, a little stronger. And in the summer my life in the camp underwent a change.

4. At the Factory

In June 1943 I was assigned to work as a locksmith at a factory located seven or eight kilometers from Auschwitz. Altogether there were 2,600 prisoners working there, of whom about 1,300 were men; the rest were women.

The factory initially belonged to the Krupp firm. Some of the machinery and equipment was relatively new, some was charred and mutilated, apparently damaged from bombings. The sight of the damaged machinery truly brought us a sense of satisfaction. A short time later all the Krupp equipment was hauled away, and the factory was turned over to the Union firm, which brought in equipment stamped with Soviet markings, from Zaporozhe.

The foreman in the workshop where I wound up was a Czech named Kotšeba. He and I quickly went to work making pots and pans and similar items. This pleased the Germans. The demand for pots and pans was growing every day. Sometimes they would give us an extra piece of bread for the pans.

Incidents of people dying in the factory while they were at their machines were fairly frequent. Prisoners in the factory were beaten regularly. Obermeister Stratmann was especially brutal; a disgusting piece of work, he was unlike almost anyone else. He would walk up to his victim very calmly, speaking with a smile on his face, and then the whole thing would end up in a savage beating.

At one time it seemed to us that the gassing and the burning in the camp had subsided a bit. Even the following incident occurred: four hundred people who were selected to go to the gas chambers were taken back to the barracks. Through the senior prisoner in the block (the Blockälteste), Lagerführer Hoffmann[39] announced that no one else, especially non-Jews, would be gassed. But this was only for the sake of appearances. In fact, the gas chambers and crematoria continued to swallow up tens of thousand of victims every day. The day after Hoffmann's "solemn" promise several thousand people were sent to the gas chambers from the smaller camps: Jaworzno, Buna, Janina-Gruben, and others. People worked to the point of exhaustion in these smaller camps used to be taken first to Birkenau or to Auschwitz and from there sent to the gas chambers. Now they had shortened the procedure: they were taken from these camps directly to the crematoria. Often people were also taken from our factory to the gas chambers.

The summer of 1944 was especially horrible with regard to the number of people slaughtered in the Auschwitz camps. During that summer they burned the people brought to the camp from Theresienstadt, as well as the gypsies who for a short time occupied two large blocks in Auschwitz. During the winter of 1943 – 1944 several transports of people arrived from Bialystok; they were the ones who had been involved in the Bialystok Ghetto Uprising. The SS shot many of them as they were getting off the train; it was the first time a mass shooting had taken place on the railroad platform. The rest of them were sent to the gas chambers. Not a single person from those transports reached the camp.

In the summer of 1944 a large group of men and women from Majdanek arrived. A serious dysentery epidemic broke out among them; every morning hundreds of people were sent to the gas chambers.

Toward the end of June and the beginning of July 1944 there was a sense that the Germans were preparing to bring in a large number of people and slaughter them. Despite the fact that the crematoria and ovens were operating constantly, ditch diggers started digging large pits, and woodcutters were preparing firewood. Soon transports of Hungarian Jews started to arrive. In June and August they brought in no fewer than 500,000 people.

The first group of Hungarian Jews arrived at the camp. They were forced to write letters home saying they were in the Waldsee region, near Vienna, and that they were doing fine. Soon, however, the transports started heading straight for the gas chambers. The people were convinced that they were being taken to the bathhouse; they calmly stood outside the chambers waiting their turn.

At that time the gas chambers were "processing" between 20,000 and 26,000 people per day. The crematoria could not handle such a large number of bodies, and soon bonfires were burning around the camp day and night. The whole place seemed to be enveloped in flames, and the smell of burning human flesh was everywhere. Clouds of smoke rolled over the earth. We breathed in this odor, this smoke, and it drove us mad.

At the very height of the slaughter of the Hungarian Jews Lagerführer Hössler decided to have some fun one Sunday afternoon. We were all driven out of the barracks and into the camp yard, where an orchestra played constantly. There was Höss himself in a Tyrolean out-fit, with leather pants and a feather in his hat, strolling about and admiring the crimson colors that the flames produced in the sky.

At about the same time a large group of Jewish women and children arrived from Yugoslavia; then came a group of 65,000 people from the Lodz Ghetto.

In 1944 there was a particularly large number of "medical experiments" performed on people. Even in 1943 children under the age of sixteen were selected from the transports. Some sort of experiments were performed on them over a period of time, and then they were injected with poisoned. Victims for these experiments were subsequently selected from every transport. In the spring of 1944 women designated for the experiments were transferred into a separate barracks (the second barracks in a new building). It was surrounded by a barbed wire fence with a guard posted.

Blocks 8, 9, and 10 were also fenced off; the "experimental" women were kept there too.

One by one, almost all of them were sent to the gas chambers. Those who survived until the camp was liquidated were slaughtered upon evacuation.

Men were castrated; some had one testicle removed, others had both removed.

Isolated incidents of resistance and escape attempts were fairly frequent. As early as the summer of 1943 a Polish engineer escaped and took with him the building plans for the camp. In reprisal for his escape twelve Poles who worked with him were hanged. It was announced that for each subsequent escape one hundred people would be executed. That, however, did not stop people. The escape attempts continued. In the summer of 1944 Henach Gromp and his brother, from Warsaw, and a Czech Jew tried to escape. They were caught. Henach was sent to the camp at Janina-Gruben, and the other two were thrown into the "bunker" (the prison) in Birkenau. In Janina-Gruben Henach tried to dig a tunnel, but he was caught again. They sent him to Birkenau, where he was hanged.

His two comrades tried to escape from the "bunker"; they were also hanged.

The camp prison, or the "bunker," was in Block 11. The fate of people who ended up in the bunker was known beforehand. Every ten days a farce of a trial was held. There was only one sentence: death. The wall where the executions took place was known as the "Black Wall." There were many Polish partisans, both men and women, executed in the bunker. Here they also executed Jews who had escaped from ghettos. They once shot a Jewish woman and her two children at the Black Wall.

In 1944 the shootings at the Black Wall were replaced by a mobile gas unit. The mobile gas unit was in operation up until the last days of the camp.

Often when we were returning from work we would see puddles of fresh blood on the ground. Once, as we were entering a fenced-off area, we passed by a truck; streams of blood were flowing from the bed of the truck. It was loaded with the bodies of people who had been murdered.

As we were returning late one night in the winter of 1944, when the evening Appell should have long been over, we found the entire camp out in the yard. From the general mood we realized that something serious had happened. It turned out, in fact, that something very disturbing to the Hitlerites had taken place. A young Jewish woman had been on one of the transports that had arrived from France. When she was being taken into the gas chamber, already naked, she started to plead with Raportführer Schillinger, who was in charge of the gassing, to let her live. Schillinger stood there with his hands in his pockets and, rocking back on his heels, laughed in her face. With a powerful punch in the nose she knocked Schillinger to the ground, grabbed his revolver, and fired several shots into him; she killed him and one other SS man and wounded a third.

This incident also occurred: a Jew from Yugoslavia who worked on the Sonderkommando threw himself into the flames while he was burning bodies and dragged an SS man along with him.

At the end of 1943 a resistance organization arose in the camp. People of various nationalities were part of both the organization and its leadership. The work was initially carried out separately by each nationality. We knew that there were communists at the head of the organization.

Gutman, one of the participants in the Warsaw Ghetto Uprising, brought me into the organization. Later I brought in other comrades: Alberstat and Robert (he was from Belgium; I do not remember his last name). We were generally organized into units, and each of us knew only the people in his circle: those from whom he received assignments and to whom he gave assignments. We managed to establish contact with the women's barracks, with workers in the Sonderkommando, and even with prisoners in the smaller camps.

At first the organization's primary task was to help the comrades who were most in need. Then the organization transmitted information. With the help of comrades working in the radio shop, we managed to pick up Soviet radio on a more or less regular basis; we received news of the Red Army's victories, which was passed on by word of mouth. It bolstered our courage and gave us faith that for the Hitlerite cannibals the hour of reckoning was drawing near. At the factory we made some shears in preparation for the moment when we would cut through the wire fence surrounding the camp.

Then we turned to acts of sabotage in the factory; we slowed down the work pace and damaged the equipment.

At the suggestion of the organization, in May 1944 I transferred to the night shift to establish contact and introduce the work of the organization to that shift. There was no doubt that our activities bore fruit. Little by little, we started stealing gunpowder from the factory and turning it over to members of the organization in the Sonderkommando.

At the end of August the Hitlerites began to exterminate the Sonderkommando that had burned the bodies of the Hungarian Jews. Several hundred of them were suffocated in the disinfection chambers in Auschwitz. The rest soon found out about it. One hundred twenty men from the Sonderkommando attacked their guards and killed them. They burned the foreman of one of the crematoria in the ovens; then they blew up the crematoria and escaped. A military unit was set out after them, and many of them perished; but according to what we were told, thirty-six of them got away.

Afterward there were random searches and repressive measures taken in the camp. Even Schulz, the German kapo on our night shift, was arrested. A letter was found on a girl from Krakow; it led to the arrest of three other girls. All four were hanged outside the factory building, two on the day shift and two on the night shift. Lagerführer Hössler supervised the executions.

Five members of the organization decided to escape from the camp in order to establish contact with the outside world and to prepare for action on a broader scale. They were put into boxes that were used to haul things out of the camp. All of them were caught and brought back to the camp to be hanged "for attempting to escape and blow up the camp."

The mood in the camp grew extremely tense. Construction began on a road leading from the factory to the camp; there was a barbed-wire fence on either side of the road.

In December 1944 we sensed that the Germans were preparing to liquidate the camp. We heard rumors that all the prisoners would be gathered together and exterminated.

In early January 1945 the Soviet air attacks on Auschwitz assumed an especially interesting character. On the night of 12 January we no sooner started our shift than a loud explosion rang out. The lights went out. Soon we found out that a bomb had fallen in the section of the camp where the SS quarters were located and that they had suffered many losses.

During the bombing people prayed to God that they might die from the bombs and not by the hands of the Germans.

The Hitlerites were in a complete panic. They sensed that the end was near. But what would our end be? It weighed heavily on our souls.

They started evacuating the camp. First they took away all the Poles. On the night of 18 January our factory was still in operation. The next day, however, we were driven westward. There was one SS man for every five prisoners. They drove us onward for seventy kilometers on foot. Those who lagged behind were shot; in two days as many as five hundred people were murdered along the road.

On 20 January we came to some little train station. The bodies of people who had been shot were lying everywhere. They shot anyone who tried to take even a step out of the ranks. There they loaded us into open train cars, and the train set out.

That night, at a small train station fifteen kilometers from the Niesse River, I managed to escape. I hid in the woods for nine days and then tried to find my way out; I was arrested and escaped again. I joined up with a group of German refugees and made it to Falkenburg with them. There I was detained again and sentenced to be shot. I managed to escape yet again, and after many ordeals I crossed the front lines on 3 February. After I was checked out I had the honor of joining the ranks of the Red Army. I was happy to be able to participate in several battles against the Germans. On 7 May I was wounded and spent two months in the hospital.

Now I have been discharged. I went home to Ostrino. Life in the town has been restored. But now it was difficult for me to go on. The wounds in my heart were bleeding. Everything reminded me of my family, my children. I decided to move to a different place. The Soviet motherland has given me this possibility. I am not a bad craftsman; I can work. We must live! We shall live!

Prepared for publication by L. Goldberg

The Story of Former Prisoner of War M. Sheinman

During the first days of the war I became a volunteer in the people's militia and soon tried to enlist in the active army. In early October 1941 my unit I was surrounded outside of Vyazma. Suddenly we found ourselves behind German lines. During an attack on 12 October I was wounded in the leg. The winter of 1941 came early. In addition to being wounded, both of my feet were frostbitten, and I could not walk. A small group of my comrades and I managed to get through the German lines; on 19 October they left me in the village of Levinka in the Temkinsky region of the Smolensk district. The Germans found me there on 27 October.

On that day my ordeal in the fascist camps began.

As a Soviet citizen, a battalion commissar, and a Jew on top of it, I was a prisoner marked for death, a sentence that could have been executed at any moment if the Germans should find out anything about me. In captivity Soviet citizens perished en masse from cold and hunger, the unbearable living conditions in the camp "hospitals," and in the so-called "work commandos." The Germans shot prisoners by the thousands at the train stations from which they transported them. Those wounded in battle were often finished off in the field. The Germans developed and implemented, methodically and persistently, a complete system calculated to exterminate as many of their prisoners as possible.

During the first period of the war the Germans were convinced of their victory and their lack of accountability, so they did not even try to hide the fact that they were intentionally annihilating the prisoners. The extermination of the Soviet prisoners of war continued until the last days of the war. Toward the end, however, the Germans tried harder to conceal it.

I shall offer some facts about the camps that I was in, as well as facts that my comrades in captivity have related to me.

From November 1941 to 12 February 1942 I was in the Vyazma "hospital" for prisoners of war. According to the testimony of the physicians who worked in the hospital and in the camp at that time, up to seventy thousand people died in the Vyazma camp in the winter of 1941 – 1942. People were housed in half-demolished buildings without roofs, windows, or doors. Many of they who fell asleep did not wake up; they froze to death. At Vyazma the Germans forced people who were exhausted, worn out, and could hardly stay on their feet—Soviet prisoners of war—to do work that was beyond their strength. Many wound up in the hospital; most of them perished in the camp.

In February 1942 I was transferred from Vyazma to the camp at Molodechno (in Belorussia). Here, according to the testimony of doctors and nurses, as many as 43,000 people had died, mostly from hunger and typhus, by that time (since the beginning of the war).

From December 1942 to August 1944 I was in the camp at Czestochowa (in Poland). In that camp many tens of thousands of prisoners of war died or were shot by the Germans. Every day the bodies of those who had died of hunger and tuberculosis were hauled out to the cemetery in a covered truck. The medic who took the dead out to bury them told me that in Czestochowa there were several cemeteries where Soviet prisoners of war were buried. They were buried in two or three layers; the bodies were stacked one on top of the other in huge trench-like pits, with up to ten thousand people in each pit. In 1942 – 1943 the Germans systematically shot prisoners of war, political activists, Jews, officers, and members of the intelligentsia in Czestochowa.

The Germans tortured many thousands of Soviet prisoners of war in camps in Germany. Wesuw (near Meppen on the Ems, on the Dutch border) was the last camp I was in; Dalium, a small camp for Russian prisoners of war, was not far from there. After the prisoners were released in June 1945, our comrades who had lived to see the liberation erected a monument in the Dalium cemetery to the 34,000 Russian prisoners of war who had been tortured to death by the Hitlerites. After the liberation of Camp 326, near Padeborn and Bielefeld, they set up a monument for the 65,000 Soviet prisoners of war that the Hitlerites tortured to death in that camp.

M. V. Sutyagin, a former commissar in an infantry unit of the Moscow Guard Division, was captured near Vyazma, as I was. He testified that in the camp at Gomel, where he was, four to five thousand people died every day in December 1941.

My comrade-in-captivity, Colonel A. G. Molev was in the camp at Demblin (Poland). As many as 100,000 of the 106,000 prisoners there died between September 1941 and March 1942.[40] According to the testimony of my comrade-in-captivity Lieutenant D. V. Shuturov (from Dnepropetrovsk), of the 12,000 people in the officers' camp at Zamoste in the winter of 1941 – 1942 only 2,500 were left by the end of March 1942. The rest died of cold and hunger.

According to the testimony of Doctor V. A. Saiko, between 1941 and May 1943 approximately 60,000 people died in the camp at Zhitomir. From the beginning of the war to May 1944 (according to figures from the German commandant's headquarters) 54,000 prisoners of war died in the camp at Suvalki.

Engineer V. V. Fokin was chief of medical services in the camp at Mogilev toward the end of 1941; I was in the camp at Kalvaria with him in 1943. He told me that in the winter of 1941–1942 more than 100,00 people perished in Mogilev from cold and hunger; they were also tortured to death by the fascists. As many as seven hundred died every day. They could not bury all the bodies.

According to the testimony of Doctor S. P. Doroshenko, who worked in a prisoner of war hospital in Minsk, 110,000 people died in the Minsk forest camp between July 1941 and March 1942. Four to five hundred people died every day.

In the fall and winter of 1941–1942 the Germans built prisoner of war camps under the open sky in a number of places. Such camps were in Zamoste, Sukhozhebrovo (near Siedlce), Minsk, and other locations. As a result, almost everyone in those camps died. In a camp for regular soldiers at Zamoste prisoners were living out in the open toward the end of 1941. It snowed in October. Two thousand people froze to death in two days.

During the winter of 1941–1942 the Germans would drive the prisoners out of the barracks and into the yard in the morning and would not allow them any shelter in the camps until late at night. People froze to death. Food distribution also took place in the freezing cold. In order to get "lunch" in Mogilev during the winter of 1941, one had to stand in the bitter cold for three or four hours. Every day several people froze to death while waiting endless hours for food.

Thousands of prisoners of war perished at transit stations and while being transported in trains. Groups of men were often transferred on foot. Anyone who fell behind was shot, a practice that was continued until the end of the war. Often the guards escorting the prisoners would fire into the columns simply to amuse themselves. During the winter of 1941 there were times when six thousand people would leave a camp and only two or three thousand would reach their destination. The rest either froze to death along the way or were murdered by the Germans.

Prisoners were transported by train either in freight cars (without heaters) or on open flatbed cars. There were as many as a hundred people in each car. People froze to death and suffocated from the lack of air. In February 1942 the prisoners of war in the Vyazma "hospital" were transferred to Molodechno. At every stop along the way people who had died of exhaustion or who had frozen to death were taken off the train.

Lieutenant Major D. S. Filkin was in Camp 3 in Grodno. He says that in January 1942 a transport of 1,200 prisoners of war arrived from Bobruisk. When they opened the doors of the cars they found that eight hundred people had frozen to death or suffocated in transit. By July 1942 there were only sixty people from that transport left alive.

In December 1941 the Germans sent a transport of prisoners from the Shakhovskaya station to Vyazma. A Soviet physician who was sent to meet the transport told me that a large number of people had frozen to death along the way. They took the bodies off the train cars and stacked them in piles. Several of them still showed signs of life; they were moaning and trying to raise their hands. The Germans would walk up to those people and shoot them.

In the prisoner of war camps, both in the work commandos and the punishment details, the cruelty and ingenuity of the Germans knew no bounds when it came to murder.

During 1941 – 1943 people were generally given nothing to eat during their first five to seven days of captivity. The Germans cynically asserted that this was done to weaken people so they would be unable to escape. In the Vyazma hospital in January and February 1942 patients were allowed seventy grams of uncooked rye per day. From this grain a "soup" was prepared twice a day, when each person received a ration of half a liter. Bread was not distributed. Not surprisingly, people grew weak and died like flies.

In the summer time during 1941 – 1943 all the grass in the camp yards was eaten; they ate tree leaves, and if a frog happened by they would eat it too. If they could manage to get it, they roasted horsehide over a fire and ate it. Salt was an unobtainable luxury.

[Physicians have estimated that the maximum daily caloric intake for the Soviet prisoners of war in the German camps was 1,300 to 1,400 calories. A person in a state of rest requires 2,400 calories per day, and one who is engaged in physical labor needs 3,400 to 3,600 per day.]

In the prisoner of war camps there were adults whose weight was reduced to thirty or thirty-two kilograms. That is the weight of a boy.

The Hitlerites constantly obstructed all medical treatment in the camps. For the most part, they handed out no medications at all. For weeks on end the prisoners in the hospitals did not have their wounds dressed because there were no bandages; nor did the Germans make any surgical instruments available. Many thousands of Soviet citizens died in the hospitals from their wounds and blood poisoning and even more from exhaustion, dysentery, typhus, and tuberculosis.

I was in camp hospitals for prisoners of war in Vyazma, Molodechno, Kalvaria, Czestochowa, and Ebelsbach. The word *hospital* does not fit these facilities at all. In Vyazma the hospital was on the outskirts of the city in half-demolished houses abandoned by their residents and in the ruins of a creamery. It was always cold and dark in the small houses. The wounded lay on the bare floor. There was not even any straw for bedding. Only toward the end of my stay in Vyazma did they install plank beds in the buildings, but even then the patients lay on the bare boards, with no straw. There were no medications. The lice infestation in the hospital was incredible. In all the three and a half months I spent in Vyazma I did not bathe once.

The Molodechno hospital was the same. In each "ward" eighty people lay squeezed together, four in a row, on the bare floor. Typhus raged. For the whole floor (eight to ten wards) there was only one thermometer. I came down with typhus. During the whole time I was sick the medic was able to take my temperature only once. Part of the required regimen was the removal of lice three or fours times a day. We stripped naked and examined everything. Three to four hundred lice would be collected in a single inspection; the little ones were gathered up by the handful. The Germans did nothing to combat the lice. The doctors told me of instances when the Germans would implement a "cardinal" solution in the fight against typhus: they would set fire to the typhus barracks with all the patients inside.

The Hitlerites developed a system of refined punishments calculated to inflict physical suffering on the prisoners of war and to rob them of their human dignity. Flogging, beating, confinement to cells and bunkers—all of it was used in the camps. People were tortured, hanged, and shot without the slightest provocation.

In the Molodechno camp (and later in Kalvaria) we saw prisoners flogged in the yard many times. The police did the beatings, but German officers often supervised the procedure. In Molodechno I saw a German officer take a whip from a policeman and savagely beat the naked body of a man laid out over a bench. When the beating was over the officer threatened the policeman: if he did not give the prisoners severe beatings, then he himself would be beaten.

Only the twisted mind of a sadist could have devised the system of torture that existed in the camps, especially for the officers, the politicals, and the Jews.

This is what junior political officer Melnikov (from Rogachevo in the Stalingrad district of the Berezov region) told me: He was captured near Kerch in May 1942. He had been betrayed: someone told the Germans that he was a political worker. They sent him to Camp 326 (near Augustdorf, not far from Padeborn and Bielefeld); there they had a special "SS block" where they put political workers, Jews, and others who were particularly suspect.

Comrade Melnikov wound up in that block. During his interrogation they were mainly interested in his lineage and whether there were any Jews among his ancestors. They beat him in the face with a pistol and knocked out his teeth. Then they beat him with a rubber club, trying to get him to confess to being a political instructor. In that block people were beaten until they lost consciousness. When a person fell unconscious, he was doused with cold water until he came around; then they beat him again. They would put a person's fingers into the crack of an open door and then break them by slamming the door shut. They would force a person's head into a bucket of water. Sometimes they held his head under water until the person nearly drowned.

After being tortured for two hours comrade Melnikov was taken out for "tactical maneuvers": he had to crawl on his stomach in a gutter filled with urine from the latrine (half naked) for fifteen to twenty meters. Then he had to do it again, this time on his back.

This was the procedure for getting lunch in that block: the "soup" was poured into mess tins, and the people formed lines twenty to thirty meters long. They had to crawl on their bellies to the mess tins, take them, and quickly eat the "soup." Anyone who lagged behind or tried to crawl ahead was beaten or attacked by dogs. During the day they gave out a half-tin of camp soup (turnips and water) and a hundred grams of bread; in the evening it was boiled water. After lunch, from 12:30 to 2:30, people were taken out for "physical exercise": they had to run around the barracks without a break. Those who lagged behind or fell down were beaten and punished: they had to stand motionless for two hours, with their hands tied behind their backs and a stone hanging around their necks. After running, they had to dig a hole 50 x 50 centimeters in size. One prisoner was to climb into the hole, and then his comrades had to fill it up to his chest. Then they would dig him out and repeat the procedure with another prisoner. Next they had to fill the pit with water using a bucket full of holes; the same bucket would then be used to empty out the pit. When evening fell everyone in the block (at that time there were eighty) had to quickly jump up to the third tier of the bunks, lie down, then jump back to the ground again; they would repeat the drill ten to fifteen times. Those who lagged behind were attacked by dogs. And so it went until seven or eight in the evening. At night the prisoners were forced to use their mess tins to empty the urine from the latrine (they also had to eat from the same tins). Then they were taken to the bathhouse and washed down with a fire hose, first with hot water, then with cold. At nine o'clock they got their boiled water, their "tea." From 9:30 to 11:00 they went out once more for "physical exercise," where the exhausted people were forced to run around the barracks without a rest. For 11:00 to 12:00 they had to "goose step" around the barracks. At midnight the signal was given: back to the barracks. The daily torture began again at three in the morning. Jews were murdered after agonizing torture. A few of the non-Jews, however, stood up under the inhuman torture. Ultimately everyone met the same end.

The Hitlerites tormented and murdered prisoners at hard labor in factories, mines, and quarries. From December 1944 until the end of my captivity I was in the death camp at Wesuw. Soviet prisoners of war who had spent some time working in German factories or who had become invalids were sent there to die. There were many such camps for people who were dying. There were other death camps not far from Wesuw: Dalium, Witmarschen, Aleksis, and others. They were all part of a single camp complex known as Stalag VI-C.

There were 1,500 people in Wesuw, most of whom were dying from tuberculosis. [After our liberation from Wesuw, British and Canadian soldiers and doctors came and asked those who were dying from tuberculosis how they had come to such a state. They heard shocking tales of how] the Germans sent young and healthy people, captured soldiers and officers of the Red Army, to mines and factories; there the prisoners were forced to work fourteen and sixteen hours a day on one or two liters of soup made from grass and turnips and 250 grams of bread. People were subjected to humiliations and tortures never before heard of. Even the healthiest of the men came down with tuberculosis within four to six months; then the Germans sent them to a death camp. Healthy people were brought in from other camps to take their place; in four to six months they too would be worn out. That is how the Hitlerite conveyor system of death worked. But even in the death camps prisoners were not allowed to die peacefully. The butchers tortured them up to the last minutes of their lives with hunger, cold, beatings, and other atrocities.

From the moment of their captivity the Germans removed shoes and clothing from the prisoners and dressed them in rags. Thus they not only turned the prisoners over to the torment of the cold but also robbed them of their human dignity. A group of Red Army officers who had recently been captured arrived in the Vyazma hospital in January 1942. Most of them had frostbitten feet. Instead of shoes they wore some sort of rags on their feet. These comrades said that when they were captured the first thing the Germans did was to take their warm winter boots and clothing away from them; then they forced them to go out in groups into the ice and snow barefoot. In February 1942, on the way from Vyazma to Molodechno, I saw the Germans removing the warm felt boots from prisoners and putting them on their own feet.

It is no wonder that under these conditions and receiving such brutal treatment in German captivity hundreds of thousands of Soviet people perished. They were literally tortured to death by the fascist butchers.

The Hitlerites spared neither Russians, Ukrainians, Belorussians, Armenians, Georgians, Tatars, Jews, Uzbeks, nor Kazakhs. At the same time, they tried to incite nationalistic animosity among the prisoners in order to divide the Soviet peoples and set one national group against the other, so as to facilitate the implementation of their vile schemes. In their newspapers they pitted the Russians against the Ukrainians and the Ukrainians against the Russian and the Belorussians. In newspapers that the Germans published in Ukrainian, they cast Pushkin, Belinsky, and other noted Russians in the crudest light. In the Belorussian papers the Germans ranted against the Russians, Ukrainians, and others. Here and there in the camps the guards were Ukrainians, from the Ukrainian Germans. All kinds of low life, nationalists, and hoodlums were selected to serve as guards. They beat the prisoners—Russians, Ukrainians, Belorussians, Tatars, and others—and they would betray the Jews. These people are now hiding in camps in the British and American zones of occupied Germany posing as "refugees."

The Germans would incite an especially brutal hostility toward the Jews. They carried out an unprecedented campaign of anti-Semitic propaganda.

Every Soviet citizen captured by the fascists was marked for death regardless of his nationality. But the Jews were in the most terrible position of all. The hunt for them and for political activists did not abate for a single day. Jews were captured in the same way that Russians, Ukrainians, Belorussians, Armenians, Georgians, and others were captured: by being either trapped or wounded. Among the few Jews I met in captivity were physicians who had been trapped with their hospital staff and patients. Some Jews were seriously wounded and bleeding profusely on the battlefield when they were captured. [Jews in the army knew of the torturous death that awaited them if they should fall into the hands of the Germans. If they still were captured nevertheless, it was only under highly unusual circumstances.

At the end of 1941 I was in a hospital for prisoners of war in Vyazma. One day in December a medic walked into the ward and announced: "The Germans are looking for Jews." A military doctor named S. Labovsky was lying on a plank bed not far from me; before the war was he was in charge of a railroad outpatient clinic in Kaluga. His unit was surrounded, and when he was trying to get away, his feet became so frostbitten that his toes fell off. Now they were just two bloody stumps. He could not move even on crutches. The Germans found out that he was a Jew. That night six Germans came in and ordered him to get ready to leave immediately. They took him away in serious condition. That same day they took away all the patients whom they suspected of being Jews. Among the Jews they arrested and hauled off were doctors, medics, and nurses. They all knew what awaited them; torture, suffering, and death.

According to prisoners who were in the camp at Roslavl (in the Smolensk district) in 1941, the SS set dogs on the Jewish soldiers; they would take the soldiers out into the camp yard and release the dogs. Deriving great pleasure from the spectacle, the butchers would beat anyone who tried to defend himself or drive the dogs back.

The Germans took Jews and political workers captured in the Vyazma area in October 1941 and threw them alive down wells. When I was in the camps at Vyazma and Molodechno I heard many accounts of this from eyewitnesses. People who were caught were picked up in the streets of villages and delivered to a gathering place. There they picked out the Jews according to their appearance and murdered them. In the Baranovichi penal camp (the so-called Ostlager) they systematically shot Jewish prisoners of war, including women nurses and doctors. [In the camp at Brest-Litovsk they had what was known as an SRU (Severe Regimen Unit) that consisted of politicals and Jews. From time to time people from that unit were taken out and shot.]

In many camps the Hitlerites held general examinations of the prisoners of war to determine whether there were any Jews among them. The German physicians disgraced themselves in their base role as butchers and murderers. In the camp at Slavutsky the Germans lined up all the prisoners of war upon their arrival on a transport and ordered them to uncover their penises. The Gestapo went down the line and culled out everyone they suspected of being Jewish. They took them away to be shot. The same thing went on in Camp 326. Here, in addition to the Jews, the Germans culled out political activists, officers, and members of the intelligentsia.

Captain K. I. Manushin (of Simferopol) told me that in February 1942 in the camp hospital at Bokunya (near Zhitomir) the Germans conducted a general physical examination of all the sick and wounded (four thousand people). The patients who could walk were lined up in the camp yard. A commission consisting of the commandant, the Feldwebel, and two doctors examined each person individually. Thirty-three of them were suspected of being Jewish. They were separated out from the rest of prisoners. The Germans and the policemen started beating them right there. After examining the patients who could walk, the commission went to examine those who were bedridden. The seriously ill and the wounded who were suspected of being Jews were dragged out of their beds, beaten, placed in carts, and sent off to the general camp. At five o'clock the next morning everyone who had been selected—forty in all—was taken in their underwear outside the camp fence and shot. The same thing happened in the camp at Zhitomir.

The Jews were systematically rounded up in the camp at Czestochowa up to the fall of 1943. A "commission" consisting of the commandant, a Feldwebel, and physicians selected everyone who appeared to be a Jew from groups of prisoners arriving in the camp. Those selected were shot.

Colonel V. A. Pshenitsyn, who was captured in September 1941 east of Piryatin, told me that from the first day of his captivity he saw them hunting down Jews at transit points, assembly sites, and in the camps. At a gathering point near the village of Kovali a column of prisoners was lined up, and they picked out everyone who looked like Jewish. Germans from the Volga region and Ukrainian German nationalists—all traitors—helped to identify the Jews. Those who were selected were taken outside the village, forced to dig their own graves, and then shot. At all the subsequent transit points and train stops the Germans would announce: "Jews and political workers step forward." At a stop in Khorol four Jewish doctors stepped forward. The Germans thoroughly humiliated them; later, in Vinnitsa, they shot them. In early October 1941 the Germans shot 378 Jews at Vinnitsa. In Kremenchug V. A. Pshenitsyn saw a group of Jewish prisoners of war as they were taken out to be shot. Those who were wounded and could not move were taken out on stretchers. The Germans perpetrated similar massacres in the Vladimir-Volynsky camp: on 2 March 1942 220 Jews and political workers, including doctors, were taken outside the fence and shot. Prisoners who had typhus and others who were seriously ill were also shot. They were carried out on stretchers, unconscious with fevers of 40° C (104° F). [Among those who perished were Commanders Shilkrot and Zinger, a doctor from Kiev named Grinberg, and others.]

Comrades who wound up in the camp at Czestochowa in 1942 told me that after the new arrivals were installed in the barracks the police would started hunting for Jews and politicals. The Jews were picked out on the basis of their physical features. They were taken out to be shot on 5 October 1942; the politicals were shot ten days later.

In the camp at Zhitomir the invaders first tried to exterminate all the Jews and political workers, so that they could then slowly and methodically exterminate thousands of prisoners of other nationalities. All the new arrivals had to file past a special "commission." The ones identified as Jews were turned over to the SS. They were housed separately from the other prisoners and forced to do the hardest and filthiest work. They were fed only once every three days. Every night the Gestapo and their dogs would go into the prisoners' barracks. The dogs would pounce on people, biting and tearing at them. After being endlessly humiliated, they were taken outside of the town and shot.

Lieutenant D. S. Filkin told me that on 9 July1942 two SS men arrived in Camp 3 at Grodno. In the camp they had a "special" room where they kept 106 wounded men who were Jews and politicals. All night long the Hitlerite animals beat people who were seriously wounded; some had no arms or legs. On 12 January a truck pulling a trailer drove into the camp, and fifty people from the "special" room wearing only their undershorts were loaded into the trailer, taken away, and shot. A short while later the vehicle returned and hauled off another fifty people. Six men were left alive.

Major N. K. Tikhonenko, who was in the prisoner of war camp at Mitava in 1941 and 1942, says that the Hitlerites used their agents to uncover the political workers and Jews, all of whom then disappeared without a trace. [This is what Commander L. B. Berlin told me: In September 1941 a group of prisoners of war was brought into the camp at Zhitomir. They were assembled in the yard, where a German interpreter with a camp officer stood before them and gave the following speech: "Command headquarters has issued an order allowing all Ukrainians to go home tomorrow. We cannot let you go, however, because there are Jews and commissars among you. Turn them over to us, and then you can go home." These exhausted people were offered freedom at the price of betrayal.]

In February 1942 I was taken to the prisoner of war camp at Molodechno. At that time there were more than twenty thousand people in the camp and as many as two thousand in the "hospital." The prisoners lived in barracks made of iron. It was unbearably cold inside them. The amount of food distributed in the camp bordered on starvation levels. In December 1941 the Germans lined up everyone living in the barracks and counted off every tenth person. Thus they selected 150 people. They were led off to one side, and the Germans opened fire on them with machine guns right in front of the entire camp. Only a few managed to save themselves by mixing into the middle of the crowd of prisoners when the first shots were fired.

The camp was on a cruel regimen. People were publicly whipped. People would be kept in a cage in the bitter cold for several hours as punishment.

The Germans did not allow Jewish doctors to work. [There were exceptions, but they were short lived. There was a doctor named Kopylovich working in the camp hospital at Molodechno (he used to be the head of an outpatient clinic in Shakhty). He was allowed to work only because he was an outstanding surgeon. From many of my comrades I heard that even under the severe conditions of German captivity this doctor faithfully carried out his duties as a physician and saved many Soviets from death. He himself was sent from Molodechno to the Baranovichi penal camp known as "Ost," where the Germans sent Jews and politicals. No one ever returned from there.]

Doctor S. P. Doroshenko, who was in the camp at Minsk in 1941, told me that at the end of 1941 the Germans prohibited the Jewish doctors from working in the camp hospital. At one time Doctor Feldman was the head of the hospital (I heard that he used to be in charge of the

Mogilev district hospital). At the end of November he was summoned to the German commandant's office and never seen in the camp again. Jewish women doctors were also taken away; sometimes they were starved to death, and sometimes they were shot. Sick and wounded Jews were placed in the typhus ward even if they did not have typhus. Later they were sent to a special Jewish section of the Minsk forest camp. Here they were subjected to the cruelest of regimens: they were fed only every other day, and the food was of a very poor quality. By spring all the Jews in the camp had been murdered or had died of hunger and illness. According to the testimony of I. K. Deryugin, Jews were also kept in a cellar in the same Minsk camp; from time to time a group of them would be taken out and shot. Typhus was rampant in the cellar. The bodies of the dead were taken out once a week.

In June 1942 all the officers were taken from the Molodechno camp and sent to Kalvaria (Lithuania). I was among the patients who ended up in hospital in this camp. Here too a routine of savage arbitrariness ruled.

Especially difficult was the position of small a group of Jewish doctors (about twelve) who had arrived from Molodechno with a transport of prisoners of war. Among them were Doctors Belenky, Gordon, Krug (from Moscow), Kleiner (from Kaluga), and others. They had lived through many horrors by the time they reached Kalvaria. In Kalvaria they and a small group of political prisoners were isolated from everyone else. No matter what happened in the camp, the Germans would vent their anger on the Jews first. The elderly Doctor Gordon—a surgeon and a highly experienced physician (he claimed to have performed more than ten thousand operations)—was very sick. He was swollen from hunger and had been in the "hospital." By order of the German Doctor Breuer, he was forced out of the hospital because he was a Jew; even though he was seriously ill, he had to stand for hours at roll call and was subjected to unheard-of humiliations.

The person in charge of the hospital was a German medic; a barber by profession, he was young but already a seasoned scoundrel. He treated all the Soviets with a malicious contempt. He once dropped into the barracks. Doctor Gordon was sitting on a plank bed and did not manage to stand up in time. The fascist degenerate beat him. Although he lived under the constant threat of death, oppressed and persecuted, Doctor Gordon somehow found the strength to hold discussions on medicine with his fellow doctors and to help the Soviet doctors in the hospital to treat complicated illnesses.

Another physician, Doctor Belenky, was a specialist in children's diseases; he too suffered beatings at the hands of the German barber-"medic." He perished in the fall of 1942.

The hunt for Jews and political workers in the camps did not subside for even a day. By the spring of 1943 about twenty-five Jews had been discovered among the prisoners who arrived at the camps at various times; they had previously been able to conceal their nationality and by some miracle had escaped death. The Germans ordered them to sew white pieces of cloth in the shape of rectangles on the front and back of their outer clothing as a "sign of disgrace." In the summer of 1943 they were taken out of the camp, along with a group of political workers.

Soviet people who had had the misfortune of being captured by the Germans and who remained faithful to their homeland understood perfectly the aims of the Germans' anti-Semitic politics and struggled to opposed it in every way possible. Many Soviet physicians who worked in the hospitals in the prisoner of war camps hid Jews and political workers, as well as officers and regular soldiers, who were particularly threatened with being torn to pieces. Many thousands of prisoners passed through a transit camp, Camp 326; in that camp the Germans conducted careful examinations of all arrivals in order to find any Jews among them. There was a group of Soviet doctors and medics in the camp who set out to save political workers, Jews, and other prisoners that the Hitlerites were hunting down for various reasons. The doctors would admit them to the hospital, perform fake operations on them, change their names, and have them transferred to a camp for invalids.

I know of instances when our Russian comrades went to physical examinations in the place of the Jews and thus saved their lives.

I was personally saved by Soviet people, by Russian comrades who were officers and doctors.

When I was sick and wounded in Vyazma Doctors Redkin and Sobstel hid me from German police dogs. In Kalvaria the doctors kept me in the hospital at the constant urging from senior officers—often from Lieutenant Colonel S. D. Proskurin, battalion commissar G. S. Bantrovsky, and others. When I was about to be discharged in February 1943 and was in real danger of being discovered by the Germans, Doctor Kuropatenkov (of Leningrad) put me into the hospital's isolation ward. Doctor A. D. Sheklakov (of Moscow) and others later hid me—a number of political workers, Soviet civilians, and military prisoners—in the hospital with the dysentery and tuberculosis patients until the end of 1943. In Czestochowa, where the Gestapo's spies were everywhere, the doctors hid me in the hospital with the tuberculosis patients; Doctor N. M. Tsvetaev (of Kizlyar) and Colonel S. I. Kurinin were especially helpful.

A significant number of the officers and soldiers in the Red Army who had the misfortune of being captured by the Germans due to the uncertainties of war perished in the camps from unheard-of persecutions, starvation, unbearably horrible living conditions, and disease. And if among those who survived there should be even a small number of Jews, it is only thanks to the support of Russian, Ukrainian, Belorussian, and other comrades.

The Warsaw Ghetto Uprising[41]

From the Editors

The Germans held more than 500,000 Jews in the Warsaw Ghetto. Tens of thousands of people died from hunger and epidemics. Starting in the summer of 1942, the Gestapo deported thousands of Jews to Treblinka every day. For a time, the people in the ghetto believed the Germans' lie that the Jews were being transported to the East to do agricultural work. The Germans maintained this deception among the residents of the ghetto by the most cunning and perfidious means. They used the same means of deception on Jewish citizens of the Soviet Union during the fascist occupation of Soviet territories. Even as they were being taken from the cities and towns of the Western Soviet territories to be slaughtered in Auschwitz and Treblinka, the Jews were convinced that they were going to work in factories and on farms.

When the terrible truth about Treblinka penetrated into the Warsaw Ghetto, it led to an uprising. The resistance organization had long since been preparing weapons and military detachments in the ghetto. When they found out about Treblinka, it served as a signal to begin the uprising. Uprisings also took place in Bialystok and other ghettos, led by the people in Soviet and Polish cities.

The Warsaw Ghetto Uprising characterizes the struggle of Soviet and Polish Jews during a time when the truth of the mass murder of the Jews was becoming evident and the executioners could no longer hide their secret. We believe it is necessary to publish in our book this material illustrating the time of their struggle. The Warsaw Ghetto Uprising is without a doubt one of the most heroic and beautiful pages in the history of humanity's fight against fascism. The tragic end of this doomed uprising only underscores its greatness.

In mid-August 1942 a Polish railroad worker went to see his contact in the Polish sector from the Jewish Anti-Fascist Bloc. He brought to the Warsaw Ghetto [the first terrible news about the fate of the Jews who had been deported, the first] information about the gas chambers of Treblinka.

The news flashed through the ghetto like lightning.

A shot rang out in one of the dark alleys of the ghetto. A German gendarme was killed by a Jewish youth named Yisrael Kanal.[42] Soon, several more Germans were killed.

In the time of the fascist terror, the streets of the ghetto became an arena for a most unusual event. The hand of an unknown avenger set fire to German military establishments and warehouses. Enraged prisoners of the ghetto dragged into the streets the valuable furs that the Germans had plundered in the occupied areas and burned them. Residents of the ghetto attacked the German dispatch office and destroyed the building.

Bloody reprisals were immediately inflicted upon the ghetto.

The Germans sent the police into the ghetto. The police opened fire, shooting out windows and murdering passersby. Fascist troops broke into the apartments of Jewish social activists. Armed bands settled accounts with the leaders of the Anti-Fascist Bloc. Levartowski,[43] Sagan,[44] Kaplan,[45] a young cultural activist named Linder,[46] and many others who were dedicated fighters in the underground resistance movement fell at the hands of the murderers.

German newspapers published in the so-called General-Government ran brief notices about these events under the headline "Party Disputes in the Jewish Sector." The German press tried to portray the Jews' first military actions as an episode in an internal struggle among the Jews themselves. Nevertheless, these "party disputes" troubled General Governor Frank enough for him to immediately submit a report on the events to Berlin.

Himmler flew to Warsaw. Luigi Fucco, a Berlin correspondent for the Italian paper *La Tribuna*, reported that at the time a plan of "suppression" for the Warsaw Ghetto had been worked out by Fischer,[47] Governor of Warsaw, with the active participation of Himmler himself. The "suppression" was to take place on 1 September, in honor of the third anniversary of the German occupation of Poland. It took the form of a horribly bloody slaughter that lasted almost the entire day.

The ghetto's Fighting Organization had already existed for some time. The Polish "People's Army" put together a unit in the "Jewish Sector." The head of the unit was Andrzej Schmidt,[48] a former freedom fighter in the Spanish Civil War; having fought battles in Madrid, Somosierra, and on the banks of the Ebro River, he had a great deal of military experience.

The People's Army initially assigned three hundred fighters to the ghetto. The militant group of young workers known as Spartak was also active. As a result of the events of 1942, all the military elements in the ghetto united to form a single Jewish Fighting Organization (JFO). Representatives of all the resistance groups, as well as people from a broad cross-section of unaffiliated fighters, were in the Organization.

The Organization was divided into detachments, and the detachments were divided into groups of five. A command staff was at the head of the Organization. Members of the staff included Mordechai Anilewicz,[49] [an energetic twenty-four-year-old activist in the scouts and a man of courage and ideals]; Michael Roisenfeld,[50] [a communist with a great deal of political experience]; Hersh Berlinski,[51] [an old workers' activist who was once the leader of a Lodz defense group for protection against pogroms in prewar Poland]; Yitzhak Zuckerman,[52] [a member of the Hehalutz Zionist youth organization]; and Marek Edelman,[53] a former member of the socialist youth organization Zukunft.

During the first days of its existence the JFO maintained close contact with the leaders in the Polish fighting underground. At the same time, its influence spread to other ghettos, as they sent representatives to Lodz, Sosnowiec, and Bialystok.

Underground leaflets were distributed. They urged the population of the ghetto not to report to the gathering site, the so-called *Umschlagplatz* (from which people were deported to Treblinka).

The Organization continued to direct people to the partisan units, especially those who were in danger of being arrested. On occasion the Gestapo managed to capture a young man or woman as they were trying to make it to the partisan units. The Germans would torture them without mercy to get information about the underground organization in the ghetto or about the partisan movement. Once the Gestapo caught several Jewish teenagers. They were members of the Jewish Fighting Organization. [The youths were afraid that they would not be able to stand up under the torture; therefore they decided to put up a fight, so that the Germans would kill them on the spot.] As the Germans were leading them through the streets of Warsaw, the prisoners started shouting slogans in honor of the Red Army and loudly abused Hitler. Then the young men attacked their armed escorts. A fight broke out, and the teens died heroic deaths while battling the guards.

After several months of concerted effort, the JFO had together a large underground army.

The creation of the Jewish Fighting Organization was a major event in the inner life of the ghetto.

One member of the JFO was a young woman named Tosia Altman.[54] She describes her spiritual condition at the time when she decided to join the ranks of the JFO in the following words:

"I felt the very foundations that had sustained my life start to crumble and collapse. I felt that once I had made this decision, there was no way I could find the strength to re-establish any connection to my previous life. My life was no longer my own. I knew I was going to meet my death, but I was also conscious of a duty that I could not avoid."

The fighters dug tunnels and built bunkers. They ran electric wiring into the bunkers, installed air vents, and set up radio receivers. They made weapons there.

The tunnels and bunkers were constructed in the strictest secrecy. The tunnels that connected the ghetto to the outside world were especially important.

Soon the Jewish Fighting Organization staged their first massive armed action.

On 17 January 1943 the SS and the "Blue Police"[55] surrounded several streets in the ghetto and began their usual round up of people. Most of those who were captured resisted. The SS shot several of them. Bullets were fired from windows that were closest to the scene.

The SS surrounded the building and dashed up the stairs. But members of the Fighting Organization greeted them.

Meanwhile large groups of fighters armed with revolvers rushed in from neighboring areas. The skirmish did not last long. The fascists retreated. The round up was a failure. Those who had been detained fled.

The underground fighting organization had passed its first test.

The Hitlerites exacted a cruel price on that occasion. The Gestapo murdered one hundred hostages. [Among the hostages hanged were the aged Rabbi Isaac Tenenbaum, the elderly writer and publicist Hillel Zeitlin,[56] the famous historiographer of Polish Jewry Professor Meir Balaban,[57] an activist in the underground cultural organization named Juzef Giterman,[58] and other prominent representatives of the Jewish intelligentsia.]

Our losses were heavy, but we succeeded in achieving our general aim. Between January and April transports to Treblinka all but ceased. A period of relative peace set in. True, everyone knew that this was the calm before the storm. The Hitlerites were secretly preparing a general retaliation. No one was fooled by the German authorities' announcements that the time of mass retaliation had passed.

Contrary to instructions from representatives of the Polish government in London, the Polish underground's anti-fascist fighting organization was systematically using the tunnels to provide the ghetto with weapons; weapons were also obtained from supply transports. It has been documented that rifles, machine guns, grenades, and sticks of dynamite were smuggled in potato shipments sent to the cafeterias in the industrial establishments in the ghetto.

It has also been established that representatives of the ghetto fighters purchased weapons from Italian soldiers who were passing through Warsaw. The soldiers were paid in dollars, gold, and jewelry collected from many residents of the ghetto.

The leaders of the underground movement organized the secret manufacture of weapons in the cellars of the Jewish quarter. An engineer named Michael Klepfisz[59] and a married couple named Fondaminski (Edward[60] and Alya) directed the operation. Polish friends of the Fondaminskis offered to help them to escape from the ghetto, but the couple refused run away, declaring that they wanted to share the fate of their people to the end.

There were electricians who organized the secret production of homemade bombs: they stuffed burned out lamps with dynamite. Grenades and pistols were also perfected in the ghetto underground.

Judging from official reports of the Warsaw Gestapo, German deserters and German civilian merchants who had moved to Warsaw from the West also sold weapons to the Jews.

The underground fighters trained inexperienced novices, prepared nursing teams, and set up units of teenagers who worked in intelligence and radio operation; they also formed fire brigades. Polish instructors from partisan units would often attend the secret training sessions.

At the same time, widespread unrest was unfolding among the population, as they prepared themselves for the impending events.

But the enemy was also getting ready. In the Gestapo headquarters on Szucha Avenue, in the Governor's residence, in the Gestapo operations along the ghetto wall on Leszno Street, in the SS bureau, in the Blue Police headquarters, and in special killing units—everywhere the fascists were feverishly making preparations for the final liquidation of the "Jewish sector."

Remembering the events of January, the Hitlerites decided to use treachery and deception. The Governor entrusted the owners of the ghetto factories with the task of organizing a false provocation of the "peaceful" Germans; among the factory owners were the sophisticated Toebbens,[61] the sentimental Brandt,[62] the "workers' friend" Stegmann.

These "peaceful" Germans went to the Jewish workers with the following proposal: "We are transferring our operations to Trawniki and Poniatow outside of Lublin; those who would like to survive the war in peace should go with us."

Brandt went from factory to factory and, with tears in his eyes, swore on the health of his wife and children that he was speaking the absolute truth. Toebbens painted a picture for the Jews of the life in "paradise" that awaited them in the bosom of nature. But the Jews did not believe the Germans. No one showed up at the assembly point.

Once again the fascists had to resort to open violence.

And then the voice of the ghetto underground cried out:

"Not one more person!"

Under such circumstance the leadership in the ghetto's underground made their final decision, the decision for an armed uprising.

On the eve of the uprising the following message was sent abroad:

"The Jewish Fighting Organization is calling upon the Jewish population to resist the Germans. Indeed, what must be done is destined. Nothing can make us change our decision. Having made the decision, we feel revitalized. We are convinced of the solid ties that bind us together. We have turned a new page in our existence, one that could be torn out at any moment. We are informing you of this because we know that you have an interest in our fate. Be assured that we shall offer up our lives at a very high price."

The organization issued the following summons to the residents of the ghetto:

"Brothers! The decision has been made. We shall fight off the enemy. Fight to the last drop of blood! Let the image of the Maccabees rise up before us. Long live the Jewish people! Long live Poland!"

On the night of 18 April a group of Jewish fighters captured the Jewish policemen who were standing guard inside the ghetto gates. When the police came at dawn to escort the workers out of the ghetto, they could not get in; the Jews had locked the ghetto gates and would not let the police in. A deadly silence reigned throughout the ghetto all day long. The leaders in the Fighting Organization used the moments of calm to make final preparations. The commanders of the JFO settled into the cellars on Nalewki Street. They checked to be sure that the fighting units were ready.

The ghetto territory was divided into three defense zones: the Brush Makers sector, commanded by Marek Edelman; the Central Ghetto, where Yisrael Kanal was in command; and the outlying industrial area, where Eliezer Geller[63] was in command.

Every street had its weapons depot. The sick, the weak, and the children were housed in cellars and bunkers. A network of contacts, both internal and external, was set up to maintain communication with the Polish underground. Every street had its first aid stations and its common kitchen where women worked. Teenagers were assigned to intelligence units. The fire brigades were kept in a state of constant readiness. Traitors and Gestapo agents were killed. The Jewish police force was disbanded. Some of them declared that they were ready to fight alongside the JFO to the end.

Apparently the German authorities realized that the ghetto had decided to fight back. In the wee hours of the morning intelligence sources reported to the headquarters on Nalewki Street that an SS unit was approaching the ghetto. Soon the SS had burst into the ghetto; in small groups they went in various directions down the ghetto streets, probably to search the buildings.

And suddenly something unusual happened in the ghetto. Out of the buildings that had seemed to be empty and dead—from the windows, attics, and rooftops—a hail of bullets came raining down on the Hitlerites. The ghetto had opened fire! The SS were running around the streets looking for a way out. The Jewish fighters had lured them into the depths of the ghetto and had cut off their retreat; having surrounded them on all sides, the Jewish fighters took a heavy toll on the enemy. They wiped out three SS companies. Three hundred SS were captured by their own slaves and held captive in the ghetto![64]

The entire ghetto was on its feet. The JFO headquarters issued the first information about the victory won with Jewish weapons and announced how many Germans had been killed and taken prisoner. The order was given to come out of the buildings. The people came out into the streets, and the fighters took up their assigned positions.

At dawn on the morning of 20 April, when Warsaw, occupied and desecrated, should have been celebrating Hitler's birthday, the Polish flags, red flags, the flags of the Anti-Fascist Coalition, and the flags of the Jewish parties were flying over the ghetto. Governor Fischer had to postpone the festivities honoring the Führer and assume the position of someone in a city under siege.

The next day all of Warsaw resembled a military camp.

Large contingencies of fully armed Germans were marching through the streets. A powerful military corridor separated the Polish sector from the German sector. The authorities made mass arrests and conducted mass searches among the Poles. The invaders were in a panic over the thought that the insurrection might spread and that the fires of rebellion would leap over the ghetto walls. Reinforced patrols appeared in the streets where the Germans lived. The Gestapo issued orders forbidding people from leaving or entering the city.

German units were on the move all day long, gradually surrounding the Jewish area. Gun muzzles and mortars were aimed at the ghetto walls. The siege had begun.

As Gestapo representatives later announced at a press conference, the Germans planned to force the Jews to surrender by depriving them of water. The method that the Gestapo had developed for the suppression of insurrection during its first decade of operation entailed cutting off water lines. The Hitlerites, however, decided against such a measure because it would jeopardize the Zoliboz, Citadel, and Gdansk train stations; the water line leading into those areas ran through the Jewish streets. Besides, the Gestapo had evidence that the Jews had long since dug a number of wells and had secretly installed brand new pumps for them.

At night the streets of Warsaw were filled with the rumbling sound of military vehicles. The ground shook from the movement of tanks into the ghetto. The attack had begun. The gates had been broken down and some of the tanks had broken into the ghetto. At first they met no resistance. The Jews lured the tanks into the depths of the ghetto but blocked the path of the advancing enemy infantry soldiers, who had wanted to penetrate into the ghetto by using the tanks as cover. The Jews set up a reinforced barricade at the entrance to the ghetto. The ghetto fighters drove back the SS infantry; they threw hand grenades and Molotov cocktails at the bursts of fire coming from the tanks. Soon the tanks burst into flames and came to a halt. They tried shift their burning tanks into reverse and escape, but their path of retreat had been cut off. The tracks on all six tanks had either broken off or were on fire. The following day both warring parties reported this fact.

This was the second major victory for the insurgents. The occupying authorities separated the Gestapo from the military leadership and commissioned the army to suppress the revolt.

Preparations for a more effective means of countering the revolt were underway. This required the suspension of military action for several days. Military units were generally under the command of Jürgen Stroop.[65] To help him accomplish this task, Major-General of police Globocnik,[66] a specialist in the destruction of Jewish areas, was summoned.

Meanwhile the insurgents used the time to better organize their forces, strengthen their positions, and store up new weapons. They took over all the German factories and warehouses in the ghetto. Thus they obtained many German military uniforms, helmets, and a significant quantity of provisions. Subsequently the Jews were able to mount their famous assault on the Gestapo arsenal at the Citadel.

They undertook the attack at night. A unit of fighters approached the Gestapo arsenal dressed in German uniforms. The guards let them in. The Jews killed all the guards and seized weapons and ammunition, as well as some trucks that they used to transport their trophies back into the ghetto.

In the course of the first week the fighters not only strengthened their positions and increased their arsenal, but they also expanded the base of their military operations by drawing thousands of new people into the battle.

On the second or third day of the fighting the residents of the so-called Little Ghetto joined the struggle. Once they heard about the uprising, people from the Little Ghetto flooded into the ranks of the fighters in the Big Ghetto. All the residents left their buildings at night. The Little Ghetto was surrounded by flames. Six thousand metal workers, chemists, and tailors turned up in the fighting units of the Big Ghetto. The rest of the residents from the Little Ghetto scattered throughout the city or escaped into the forests to join the partisans.

From the moment the events began to unfold, Warsaw Governor Fischer and the higher administration of the Gestapo repeatedly tried to get the insurgents to lay down their weapons. Suspicious individuals infiltrated the fighters to try to sow panic among them and to persuade them to betray their leaders. A special committee set up to fight against treason, espionage, and sabotage soon destroyed these provocateurs.

On the ninth day of the uprising the commanders of a German military unit charged with crushing the uprising by any means necessary made an appeal to the leaders of the Jewish fighters. The Germans presented the ghetto with an ultimatum that demanded first of all the return of German prisoners. The Germans announced that any Jews who laid down their weapons and voluntarily turned themselves in would be treated not as partisans but as prisoners of war; they would be granted all the rights of prisoners of war of other countries and nationalities. Finally, the German command pledged that, if the Jews should surrender, then the Germans would leave the ghetto alone; but if the Jews should reject the ultimatum, then the ghetto would be destroyed and its residents executed.

The leaders of the ghetto's fighting organization answered:

The fighters were prepared to turn over their German prisoners under the condition that for every German prisoner released, the Germans would release ten Jewish prisoners. As for the other two points of the ultimatum, the ghetto fighters rejected them and announced that they would fight to the last drop of their blood.

Thus the ultimatum was refused. Berlin entrusted the army with the task of suppressing the uprising and ordered the ghetto to be completely destroyed.

In accordance with orders from the German command center in Warsaw, on the eleventh day of the uprising artillery was brought in and positioned in Krasinski Square near the Gdansk

Station. At six o'clock in the evening the Hitlerites started shelling the ghetto; it lasted until the following morning.

In a single night the enemy's artillery destroyed the ghetto's walls and many of its buildings. The German command had adopted the tactics of field warfare by sending in infantry units to attack the ghetto fighters' front positions under cover of artillery fire. The Jews fought off the infantry attack.

It was a memorable night for Warsaw. The residents of the capital compared it to that terrible September night on the eve of the fall of Warsaw, when the German artillery destroyed building after building, street after street. The sound of artillery fire reverberated throughout the city. The air shook with bomb explosions. The cannon fire was so loud and powerful that it shook the foundations of the buildings.

The Germans were convinced that the powerful artillery barrage would be enough to force the Jews to surrender. The "cream" of the German military units were positioned on Krasinski Square and all around the Gdansk Station. Many of the Poles were forced to be present at the destruction of the ghetto and to watch the huge fires raging in the Jewish sector.

But the artillery barrage did not work; the ghetto was not shaken. Early the next morning a delegation from the German civilians of Warsaw appeared at the German command headquarters. The delegates were upset over the fact that the Germans' firing positions were set up in the center of the city, where so many highly placed Germans lived! The delegates pointed out to the commanders that many buildings on Krasinski Square and on nearby streets had developed dangerous cracks and had been damaged by the vibrations. The windows in all the apartments had been blown out by the noise. The buildings in the Old City had been especially damaged, buildings that in many cases were occupied by Germans.

More than the protests of the German residents, however, the Germans' decision to curtail the artillery fire was the result of the unexpected entry of the ghetto's military ally into the fight: the Polish People's Army. One night, when the Nazi dignitaries were admiring the columns of flames over the Jewish sector from the balconies of their plush apartments, a People's Army unit under the command of the famous Major "Richard" (Kowalski) penetrated into the streets leading to Krasinski Square and the Gdansk Station. They shot the German troops that were blocking the way, and, under the cover of night, they struck the enemy several severe blows.[67] At the same time Polish Army units commanded by Jacek, Frenek, and others opened fire on German gun emplacements.

The entry of the People's Army into the fight made it necessary for the German command to refrain from public demonstrations of punishment by means of artillery.

One night, following some gunfire, German bombers appeared in the sky over the ghetto. The bombing lasted all night. Once again the entire Jewish sector was engulfed in flames.

The bombing runs were repeated the following night. Many buildings were destroyed, and many people perished in the rubble. At the same time the Germans were advancing on all fronts and were surrounding the ghetto. That night, with their air support, the Germans won their first victory. They managed to penetrate deep into the ghetto. The Jews, however, were able to retreat to the Central Ghetto with all the provisions that had been stored in the buildings captured by the enemy. The fighters withdrew from portions of Nalewki and Powonzki Streets.

The commanders of the ghetto fighters started planning countermeasures. At dawn the Jews mounted an attack. They managed to retake several of the buildings, since the Germans did not have air support during the day.

After two days of heavy fighting almost no residents were left in the ghetto who were not taking part in the fighting.

The Jews concentrated their forces on Okopowa Street and launched a counterattack. After many hours of bloody fighting the ghetto fighters managed to force the enemy from the positions that they had taken on the first day of the battle; the fighters pushed them back deep into the non-Jewish section of Warsaw.

The Jews quickly fortified the positions they had captured and organized sorties into the side streets.

The German command started calling in reinforcements. The fighting became more intense. The Jews held on to their strategic positions until the end of the day. Only at 2:00 A.M., under the growing pressure exerted by the enemy, were they forced to retreat.

When the uprising broke out, the Jewish Fighting Organization had a total of about one thousand people. On the second day of the fighting several thousand fighters had taken up their positions. Defiance in the face of death and self-sacrifice became a universal phenomenon. Over the heads of the fighters on the field of battle waved a banner with the inscription "We Shall Die with Dignity!" This became their battle cry. Examples of courage multiplied day after day.

For a long time the enemy had regarded the Brush Factory sector as an area of hopeless resistance. Marek Edelman commanded the unit assigned to defend the area; Hersh Berlinski was the group leader. Among those who fought to their last bullet were Eiger,[68] Ratajzer,[69] and Klepfisz. After the enemy flushed them out of the factory yard they went into the building and continued to fight, defending every floor until at last they were on the roof. There several of them died a heroic death, but some managed to break through the ramparts and join up with other units that were still capable of fighting.

Aron Owczinski's detachment of armed workers had 280 fighters. This detachment fought on Pawia Street, a street ridden with Jewish poverty, and showed extraordinary courage. Eliezer Geller's unit distinguished itself in the battle on Okopowa Street; later they fought in the vicinity of the Jewish cemetery.

Young men and women demonstrated a deep devotion to the cause and a contempt for death. Seventeen-year-old Rebecca Peker was the first to engage an SS unit by throwing a Molotov cocktail at them. Sixteen-year-old Shanan Lent, who was happy to have a rifle—a weapon rarely found in rebel units—was wounded; as he lay on the asphalt awash in the heat of the burning buildings, he continued to fire.

The young ghetto fighters lured the fascists into seemingly deserted, apparently undefended buildings and destroyed them; then they would go back and lure more of the enemy into the trap they had prepared for them.

The old also fought fearlessly alongside the young. Natan Smolyar led his students in the fight against the Germans; a Warsaw tram worker named Lent held his post, shoulder to shoulder with his son, to his dying breath. Doctor Pavel Lipstadt fought alongside a worker named Leib Gottom; in his insistence on fighting without surrender, the poet Jozef Kirman did not yield to experienced junior officer Diamant.

Aryeh Wilner[70] was captured by the Nazis; he escaped from the hands of the butchers and went on fighting.

During the first days of the uprising the Germans had nothing but contempt for the forces that opposed them. When the first German motorcycle blew up from a Jewish mine, the

Hitlerite command could not believe that the Jews had made the mine and had planted it.

After the first aerial bombardment the Germans announced that the uprising would be suppressed within two or three days. But it turned out otherwise. The uprising continued to grow in intensity. In the German dispatches were mentions of their own losses.

After the battle on Okopowa Street the German command announced:

"In our efforts to surround the ghetto we have encountered enormous difficulties; in order to suppress the uprising, we must fight from building to building. The Jews are fiercely defending themselves. This assignment is costing us bloody losses and significant effort."

In one of its reports the Gestapo complains that its attempts to put down the uprising are hampered by the existence of underground passageways that the Jews use to maintain contact with Polish patriots from whom the Jews are receiving aid. In another report the Hitlerites note that the Jews do not allow themselves to be captured; they either die with their weapons in their hands or disappear somewhere underground.

That was also how foreign correspondents assessed the situation.

After the battle on Okopowa Street the Warsaw Gestapo invited journalists from the Axis countries to look for this "new front." Several Italians, one Finn, and one Hungarian came. We may read the results of this inspection in the Polish underground paper:

"The inspection was conducted along the streets bordering the ghetto; those streets were destroyed by artillery fire and aerial bombing and then taken over by the German infantry. Smoke swirled above the crumbling buildings. Some of the ruins of the buildings were still engulfed in flames. Among the bricks, the broken beams, and the debris piled in the street were the bodies of Jews and Germans.

"Under such conditions," declared the Gestapo agent who accompanied the journalists, "it is difficult to confer military honors upon the German soldiers who have fallen."

"The battle for these streets," the newspaper goes on to report, "was fierce and desperate. The Germans had to fight for every building. Seizing a single building meant many casualties and took many hours."

The battle cost the Hitlerites dearly. One dispatch that the German command issued a week after the fighting broke out stated that thousands of Germans had died on the "ghetto front."[71]

After two weeks of intense street fighting the insurgents were forced to switch to a new tactic.

The tactic consisted of carrying out quick, sudden attacks, mainly at night.

These attacks continued throughout the third week of the uprising, which the Polish underground press was now referring to as the "great week of the uprising." Storm units took to the streets bordering Warsaw and used dynamite to blow up buildings, warehouses, and establishments occupied by the Hitlerites. In one week the rebels blew up forty-six German establishments, including the Frazhet factory, the Kleiman electrical supply company, and an auto parts factory. It turned out that several factories belonging to the Hermann Göring Werke were also destroyed. [This was a severe blow to German industry.] In addition to buildings, machinery, and people, supplies of raw materials ready for production, manufactured goods, and weapons were destroyed.

After three weeks of fighting the situation in the ghetto deteriorated. The number of buildings destroyed quickly grew. The ghetto fighters took up new positions in the ruins, but the noose surrounding them was growing tighter and tighter.

The leaders of the uprising turned to the Polish underground with a request to assist the Jews not only with military supplies and provisions but also with joint armed resistance from the Poles in the areas surrounding Warsaw. But the Polish anti-fascist groups did not have the means to begin a major resistance movement in Warsaw. The anti-fascist organizations were, however, able to mobilize Polish youth groups who rushed to the aid of the Jews; they broke into the ghetto and fought shoulder to shoulder with the rebels. The anti-fascist groups organized transports to take the wounded out of the ghetto to partisan camps. The fighters in the People's Army were especially selfless in their efforts. The Polish Workers' Party and the Polish Socialist Workers were particularly active in sending reinforcements and supplies and in helping the insurgents with their retreat when they were seriously threatened.

The Polish patriots posted brief appeals on the streets of Warsaw:

"Poles! The Germans are executing a death sentence upon the last thirty thousand Jews in the Warsaw Ghetto. From our homes we can hear the sound of gunfire. Women and children are defending themselves with their bare hands. Rush to their aid!"

On 1 May the workers' organizations issued an appeal to the Jewish rebels. The appeal was mimeographed during the attacks from the German air force.

"This year," the appeal read, "we shall observe the First of May not with street demonstrations. No, we shall greet the workers' holiday with street fighting. This year on the first day of the awakening spring we shall speak not of love but of our boundless hatred for the enemy. This year on the First of May we shall fight and kill."

Even later, after a month of bloody fighting—when the enemy had taken many key positions—the ghetto fighters' spirit remained firm. As late as 23 May the ghetto fighters' commanders issued the following radio broadcast from the ashen ruins of the ghetto:

"Last Friday German airplanes once again bombed the ghetto. The entire ghetto is engulfed in flames. The Germans have also renewed their tank attack. Our units are as united as ever. We are defending ourselves and standing up to the enemy's blows."

In the final stage of the battle the rebels once again changed their tactics. Although the German tanks and aircraft had broken down their lines of defense, the fighters never even considered surrender. Young Jewish men and women showed up at their headquarters on Nalewki Street to volunteer for the "death brigade." This unit would attack the German soldiers, break into their ranks, bombard the enemy with hand grenades, and fight to their last drop of blood. Prior to their operations the fighters in the death brigade took an oath that they would return to their comrades only if not a single German should be left alive.

The death brigade brought devastation to the ranks of the enemy. They carried out attacks on German tanks. Armed with grenades and Molotov cocktails, they threw themselves under the tanks' treads and took out the enemy vehicles while sacrificing their own lives.

Still the enemy pressed forward. His victory over the ghetto cost him dearly. The German losses numbered in the thousands. The Jews transformed every building into a fortress. Reconnaissance men followed the enemy along the rooftops, and shots were fired from the windows. The ghetto held tightly to every meter of earth, to every building. People fought in the ruins and in the ashes.

By the end of May the uprising in the ghetto had been suppressed. The Jewish sector was hit by hunger; since the Germans had seized all the major lines of communication, it became almost impossible to use a secret means of transporting provisions from the Polish sector of Warsaw into the ghetto. The weapon supplies dried up. The finest fighters in the ghetto fell in battle with honor. Yet the struggle continued. Several individual rebel units managed to break through enemy corridors and escape into the forests to join the partisans. The Germans organized search parties. Given the ghetto's hopeless situation, there were times when fighters would break out of the ghetto and blow themselves up along with the Germans who caught them. Only two or three dozen fighters managed to escape their pursuers.

By the forty-second day of the uprising the entire ghetto had fallen into the hands of the Germans. But it was no longer part of Warsaw, for there were no buildings, no streets. Artillery, tanks, and aerial bombing had destroyed every last building. The official German report proclaimed the final victory of the Hitlerite troops; it closed with the following words:

"There was only one way to destroy the essence of the uprising: to exterminate all the inhabitants of the ghetto and to thus root out the very core of this dangerous revolutionary cell."

And yet the uprising was not rooted out! It went underground. The last of the fighting units, led by Mordechai Anilewicz went into the catacombs, where they had some meager supplies of food.

At first the Gestapo did not know where the rebels were hiding. The ghetto fighters suddenly organized a sortie and hit the Germans. The next day the Germans issued the fighters an ultimatum over the radio: lay down your weapons, come out from your hiding places, and we shall spare your lives.

Not a single one of the insurgents, however, would surrender or accept a truce.

A few days later the Gestapo used sound detecting devices and dogs to root out one of the hiding places. A heavily armed German detachment surrounded the exit. The "heroes" of Treblinka, Auschwitz, and Belzec were afraid to break in. They decided not to confront the rebels face to face.

Those who were inside had no way out. They ran out of water, food, and ammunition. In order to avoid having the fascists take them alive, the rebels decided to kill themselves. Among those who shot themselves was Mordechai Anilewicz.

When other fighters saw their provisions running out, they went through the sewer and drainage pipes that led to the Polish sector.

The Polish workers' party formed armed units and sent them to the places where the ghetto fighters would make their escape; the units surrounded the streets to cut off the movements of the German sentries. Thus approximately one hundred were saved and managed to get to partisan units in the forest.

Not all the attempts to save the trapped fighters succeeded.

In many cases the Hitlerites released poisonous gas into the underground canals.

The last defenders of the ghetto stubbornly continued to fight until July 1943. The struggle was led by two of the great chiefs of the uprising, Juzef Farber and Zecharia Artstein. They both fell in battle.

[On the fortieth day of the uprising there was one four-story building left standing. Here the last handful of courageous fighters did battle.

The whole day, from morning till night, they defended the last stronghold in the ghetto. As the flags of the nations flew from the rooftop, the last of the ghetto fighters fired from the windows.

Having decided to take the last of the fighters alive, the Germans fought hard from stairway to stairway, from floor to floor. At the end of the day three rebels were still alive. Exhausted from many hours of fighting, the Germans set the building on fire.

Three men appeared on the roof of the building that was now enveloped in flames. Each one of them was wrapped in a flag. As though moved by a single powerful force, all three of them leapt into the flames at the same time. The last of the ghetto's defenders perished in the fire wrapped in the banners under which they had fought to their last breath.]

Thousands of ghetto fighters fell on the field of honor in the battle for human and national dignity. The Jewish women displayed unparalleled examples of heroism. An elderly woman, the well known social activist Rachel Stein, fought on the front lines and never left her post, even when she took a bullet in the shoulder. Underground fighters Tosia Altman[72] and Hancia Plotnitzka[73] fought bravely and selflessly to their last breath.

The young men and women formed the advanced guard and the soul of the uprising. Luna Rozental, Shmuel Braslaw,[74] Mirsky, Lent, and hundreds of other youths will live forever in the hearts of the people. They turned back enemy troops and gave their lives on the field of battle.

Laborers and intellectuals, free thinkers and religious people, fought shoulder to shoulder in the ranks of the rebels. Let us not forget the name of the elderly writer Aron Zeingorn, who refused to run away and stood fast as a ghetto fighter to the last minute. Many of Warsaw's Jewish literary figures, scientists, and artists perished in the uprising. [Among them were the poets Israel Shtern,[75] Juzef Kirman, and Yehiel Lerer;[76] the writers Solomon Gilbert and Shiya Perle;[77] the essayist Samuel Girshgorn; the sculptor Ostshega; the artists Feliks Friedman,[78] Weintraub, Shliwniak, Gershaft, and others. A galaxy of performing artists known throughout the world perished.]

The blood of Poles also flowed through the streets of the embattled ghetto, mixing with the blood of their Jewish brothers. Among those who gave their lives for the cause of freedom were Streletzki, Waszczina, Piotr Turski, Wolski, Kowalski, and many others.

The Warsaw Ghetto Uprising is at once the most tragic and most glorious page in the thousand-year history of Polish Jewry. This tragic rebellion will go down forever in the annals of humanity's struggle for freedom against the savage forces of fascism. May the memory of the fighters and soldiers of the Warsaw Ghetto endure forever!

B. Mark

Notes

1.   In 1941 and 1942 thirteen thousand people perished at Novo-Vileika. According to evidenced gathered by the Special State Commission, a total of more than sixty thousand were murdered there while the camp was in operation.

2.   Similar projects for digging up mass graves were conducted through Eastern Europe. In 1942 Himmler gave the order for every trace of mass executions to be erased. Sonderkommando 1005 was created to carry out that assignment under the command of Standartenführer SS Paul Blobel (executed for war crimes in 1951). In some places where these operations were carried out—Babi Yar, the Ninth Fort in Kovno, and Ponary, for example—a few Jews who were forced to do this work escaped to tell their tales.

3.   After the war Abram Pinkusovich Blazar provided exhaustive details on the operations of the special units assigned to erase all traces of the Nazis' crimes.

4.   There were about 10,000 Jews left in the Vilna Ghetto when it was liquidated on 23 September 1943. About 8,000 were taken down Suboch Street; about 2,000 were still in the ghetto hiding in malinas. Between 1,500 and 2,000 men were sent to concentration camps in Estonia; 1,400 to 1,700 women were sent to camps in Latvia. The remaining 4,300 to 5,000 women and children were sent to the gas chambers at Majdanek; about 100 of the old and the sick were shot at Ponary.

5.   Abram Khvoinik (1907 – 1943) and Yakov Kaplan (1907 – 1943) were part of the command unit of the United Partisan Organization of the Vilna Ghetto; Asya Big (1922 – 1943) was also one of the ghetto fighters.

6.   The Todt organization consisted of German army engineers; it was named after the man who was in charge of it, Franz Todt.

7.   Nisan Anolik (1921 – 1974); he moved to America after the war.

8.   Benyamin Anolik (b. 1926) was the brother of Nisan Anolik. After the war he settled in Israel, where he became the director of the Ghetto Fighters' Museum.

9.   About two thousand prisoners were kept in the penal camp Treblinka I at any one time. According to Irina Ehrenburg, about ten thousand prisoners actually passed through its gates.

10. This camp was in operation from July 1941 to August 1944. On 23 July 1944 more than five hundred Jewish prisoners were shot; twenty Polish prisoners were shot in early August.

11. The first transport arrived in Treblinka on 23 July 1943. It carried a load of 7,300 people from the Warsaw Ghetto; the next day a load of 7,400 people pulled into the camp. On 6 August 10,085 people arrived, on 7 August 10,672, and on 8 September 13,596.

12. The first transport of about eight thousand people set out from Czestochowa upon the liquidation of the Czestochowa Ghetto on 22 September 1942; others followed on the 22nd, 25th, and 28th of September and on the 1st, 4th, and 7th of October. Altogether approximately forty thousand people were sent to their deaths from Czestochowa.

13. The unit of workers with the sky-blue armbands gathered together the luggage and picked up bodies from the roadside; a unit with red armbands helped with dividing the victims into groups; those with yellow armbands were skilled workers who worked in the shops. About a thousand people were put to work to process the incoming transports; another three to five hundred worked on the disposal of the bodies.

14. "Hands in the air! March! Faster, faster!"

15. Kurt Hubert Franz was the acting commandant of the camp. Appointed in April 1942, the first commandant of the camp was Hauptsturmführer SS Tomala, who had formerly served at Sobibor. In August 1942 Hauptsturmführer SS Franz Paul Stangl was appointed commandant of the camp; prior to his appointment at Treblinka, Stangl was the commandant of the murder camp at Sobibor. Stangl was arrested in Berlin in 1967 and sentenced to life imprisonment in Düsseldorf. He died in prison in 1971.

16. Other sources indicate as many as six hundred people were packed into a single gas chamber.

17. It is estimated that approximately 800,000 Jews were murdered at Treblinka.

18. For us today there is only Treblinka,
     That is our fate.

19. I broke off a blossom
     And sent it to my Most Beautiful,
     My beloved, fair maiden…

20. "Attention! Hats off!"

21. "Everyone out! Get down here!"

22. The first transports of Jews were murdered at Sobibor on 6 – 12 May 1942. Prior to the arrival of the initial transports—on 3 May 1942—the Jews who had worked on the construction of the camp were murdered.

23. Security police.

24. After the partisans joined the Red Army in the summer of 1944, the Soviets sent Aleksandr Pechersky to a penal brigade, since he had been taken as a prisoner of war. Only after he had been seriously wounded was his "guilt washed away with blood." This selection was published in the journal *Znamya* in 1944.

25. Pavel Grigorievich Antokolsky (1896 – 1978) was a poet and translator who worked as a war correspondent during the war years. He wrote works dedicated to the plight and the courage of the Jews, such as *Camp of Destruction* (1945) and *A Non-Eternal Memory* (1946).

26. Veniamin Aleksandrovich Kaverin (1902-1989) was a prose writer and a correspondent for TASS during the war. He wrote several books about Jewish heroism and was an active member of the Jewish Anti-Fascist Committee.

27. Various other sources have lower estimates of 1.8 to 2 million people, including 1.3 to 1.5 million Jews, who were murdered at Auschwitz. Similar figures were introduced into evidence at the trial of Auschwitz commandant Rudolf Hoess, who was executed at Auschwitz on 16 April 1947.

28. Himmler issued the order for the construction of a camp at Auschwitz on 27 April 1940.

29. About 1,155 acres.

30. In accordance with an order from Himmler, Karl Klauberg developed a method of mass sterilization that was to be used against enemies of the Reich, that is, again Jews, Poles, and Russians.

31. Between 15 May and 8 July 1944, 445,000 Hungarian Jews were murdered in Auschwitz.

32. Obersturmbannführer SS Rudolf Hess was the first commandant of Auschwitz; he served from May 1940 to November 1943. His successor was Obersturmbannführer SS Arthur Liebehenschel, who had been stationed at Majdanek.
33. Hauptscharführer SS Gerhard Palitsch was in Auschwitz in May 1940. A notorious sadist, he personally shot prisoners. He was commandant of the family camp for the gypsies.
34. "Lock up!"
35. The weaving shop.
36. Hauptsturmführer SS Henrich Schwarz arrived in Auschwitz in 1941; prior to that he was in Mauthausen. He was in charge of the labor division for the entire camp; he served as Lagerführer for Auschwitz I and as commandant for Auschwitz III (Monowitz).
37. The Germans referred to Memel as Klaypeda.
38. "Why are the women being separated from us?"
39. Obersturmführer SS Franz Johann Hoffmann served as Lagerführer from November 1943 to June 1944.
40. Stalag 307, a prisoner of war camp, operated in Demblin from the fall of 1941 to February 1942. About eighty thousand prisoners died there in 1941 – 1942.
41. This selection was written by Ber Mark, one of the founders of the Jewish Historical Society in Warsaw; it is the first recorded account of the Uprising. An English edition of Mark's book-length history of the Uprising was published in 1979 by Schocken Books (New York) under the title *Uprising in the Warsaw Ghetto*.
42. On 20 August 1942 Yisrael Kanal (ca. 1920 – 1943) shot not a German gendarme but Josef Szczerynski, chief of the Jewish police. The assassination was ordered by the Jewish Fighting Organization in reprisal for Szczerynski's role as an accomplice in the Nazis' murder of the Jews. Although Szczerynski did not die of the gunshot to his face, he committed suicide in January 1943. In October 1943 Kanal was deported to Auschwitz, where he was murdered.
43. Josef Finkelstein-Levartowaki (1899 – 1943) was a member of the Central Communist Party and a founder of the Anti-Fascist Bloc. He was captured during a manhunt in August 1942 and sent to Treblinka.
44. Szachna Efraim Sagan (1892 – 1942) was a prominent social activist in the ghetto. He was a leader in the left-wing Zionist Workers' Party, an essayist, and one of the organizers of the underground in the ghetto. He was murdered in August 1942.
45. Josef Kaplan (1913 – 1942) was one of the founders of the Jewish Fighting Organization. He was arrested by the Gestapo on 3 September 1942 and placed in the Pawiak prison; they hanged him on 11 September.
46. Menachem Linder (1911 – 1942) was very active in YIVO and in social work in Warsaw. One of the founders of the Secret Ghetto Archives, he was murdered by the Gestapo at the entrance to his building on 18 April 1942.
47. Ludwig Fischer, the Nazi Governor of Warsaw, was executed for war crimes in 1947.
48. Andrzej Schmidt was a pseudonym for Pinkus Kartin (1912 – 1942). He fought in the Jaroslaw Dombrowski International Brigade in the Spanish Civil War. One of the founders of the Anti-Fascist Bloc, he was betrayed by a member of the Polish underground and fell into the hands of the Gestapo on 30 May 1942.
49. Mordechai Anilewicz (1919 – 1943) became the commander of the JFO in September 1942. He fell at Mila 18 on 8 May 1943, at the end of the Warsaw Ghetto Uprising. At the time there were about four hundred people in the bunker, of whom about one hundred were ghetto fighters. The Germans surrounded the bunker on 8 May. The people inside the bunker fought back for about two hours; the Germans fire gas canisters into all five of he openings to the bunker. Most of the ghetto fighters—including Mordechai Anilewicz, Arien Vilner (1917 – 1943), and Edward Fondaminski (1910 – 1943)—committed suicide.
50. Michael Roisenfeld (ca. 1913 – 1943) was among those who escaped through the sewers after the Uprising. He joined the partisans in the Lomianski grove and the Wyszkow forests, where he fell in battle with the Germans.
51. Hersh Berlinski (ca. 1909 – 1944) survived the Warsaw Ghetto Uprising and fought with the JFO in the Wyszkow forest. He died in the Polish Uprising of August 1944.
52. Yitzhak Zuckerman (1915 – 1981) joined the leadership of the JFO in July 1942. During the Warsaw Ghetto Uprising he was sent outside of the ghetto as a JFO liaison with the Polish underground organizations. After the war he and his wife Zivia Lubetkin moved to Palestine, where they were among the founders of the Ghetto Fighters' Kibbutz.
53. Marek Edelman (b. 1921) was among those who escaped the Warsaw Ghetto Uprising through the sewers. After the war he remained in Poland, where he became a well-known cardiologist. He is the author of *The Ghetto Fights* (New York: American Representation of the General Workers' Union of Poland, 1946).
54. Tosia Altman (1918 – 1943) was one of the founders of Hashomer Hatzair in the occupied territories. She maintained contact between the Warsaw Ghetto and the ghettos in Bialystok, Vilna, and other places. She

was captured by the Germans while escaping through the sewers after the Warsaw Ghetto Uprising; the Germans tortured her to death.

55. The Polish police force that cooperated with the Germans.

56. One of the most prominent figures in Polish Jewry, Hillel Zeitlin (1871 – 1942) was the author of numerous books and articles on a variety of topics in Judaism. He was the father of the famous Yiddish poet Aharon Zeitlin and a close friend of Yitzhak Katznelson. He was not among the hostages hanged, as indicated in the selection, but died a torturous death on the way to Treblinka. He was taken to the Umschlagplatz wrapped in his prayer shawl.

57. A renowned scholar and historian of Polish Jewry, Meir Balaban (1877 – 1942) served as director of the famous Tachkemoni Rabbinic Seminary from 1920 to 1930. From 1928 until his death he was a professor at the University of Warsaw.

58. Juzef (Yitzhak) Giterman (1888 – 1943) escaped from Warsaw to Vilna when the war broke out but was arrested while trying to get to Sweden. Very active in maintaining underground cultural archives, he worked with the JFO to raise funds for arms. He was murdered on 23 January 1943.

59. An active member of the Bund and the JFO, Michael Klepfisz (ca. 1913 – 1943) acquired the formula for making Molotov cocktails. He fell in a clash with the Germans in April 1943.

60. Edward Fondaminski (1910 – 1943) took the place of Josef Finkelstein-Levartowaki as Communist Party secretary and party representative after the latter's deportation to Treblinka. Fondaminski fell in the bunker at Mila 18.

61. Walther Toebbens was a notorious exploiter of Jewish labor in the Warsaw Ghetto. He served as the civil attaché for the expulsion of Jews to camps in Poniatow and Trawniki, where they were murdered in November 1943. After the war he went underground to avoid punishment. It was rumored that he died in an auto accident.

62. Untersturmführer Karl Brandt was in charge of the section on Jewish affairs in the Gestapo headquarters in Warsaw. He organized the deportation of Jews to murder camps and personally sent approximately 300,000 Jews from the Warsaw Ghetto to their deaths.

63. Eliezer Geller (1918 – 1943) fought in a Dror unit in the January battles. He was among those who managed to escape through the sewers at the end of the April Uprising. He was captured and sent to Bergen Belsen; in October he was sent to Auschwitz, where he was murdered.

64. These figures might be a bit inflated. According to a report submitted by Brigadeführer Jürgen Stroop, the Germans lost twelve men in this attack, with a few more than that taken prisoner.

65. Brigadeführer SS Jürgen Stroop had been in charge of guarding the railways from partisan attacks. In March of 1943 he was sent to command the police in the Galicia area. During his stay in Lvov the actions against the Jews increased significantly. On 17 April he was transferred to Warsaw. In June 1943, after the suppression of the Warsaw Ghetto Uprising, he became director of the SS and of police in the Warsaw region. In 1947 he was sentenced to death in Germany, but he was extradited to Poland; in 1951 he was sentenced to death for a second time.

66. Gruppenführer SS General Odilo Globocnik was head of the SS and the police in the Lublin region in 1939 – 1943. He was in charge of Operation Reinhard, which was the annihilation of the Jews of Poland. One of the bloodiest of the SS murderers, he was sent to Warsaw to gather up machinery, people, and raw materials for slave labor in the Lublin concentration camps. He believed that he should have been in charge of the liquidation of the ghettos and accused Stroop of carrying out his actions with excessive cruelty by razing the ghetto to the ground and wiping it off the face of the earth; it entailed the destruction of property, which should have been carried by Globocnik himself. Himmler, however, supported Stroop, and soon Globocnik left Warsaw. Globocnik committed suicide in 1945.

67. This event occurred on 20 April 1943, when a Home Army unit commanded by Major Boleslaw Kowalski eliminated a group of German guards; their action made it possible for some of the Jews to escape from the ghetto.

68. Abraham Eiger arrived in the Warsaw Ghetto at the end of 1942. According to Zivia Lubetkin, Eiger fought in a unit commanded by Hanoch Gutman. He did indeed fight to his last bullet, whereupon the Germans killed him. He was around twenty.

69. Simha (Kazik) Ratajzer (dates unknown) was one of the organizers to aid the ghetto fighters from the Aryan side of the wall. On 8 May he went back into the ghetto as head of a rescue operation and led a number of ghetto fighters out through the sewers. After the war he moved to Israel, where he changed his name to Rotem.

70. Aryeh Wilner's real name was Chaim Israel. A member of Hashomer Hatzair, he left the Vilna Ghetto in 1941 and went to the Warsaw Ghetto, where he became one of the leaders of the Jewish Fighting Organization. After that he worked on the Aryan side of the wall, where he was arrested and escaped. After his escape, he became one of the leaders of the Warsaw Ghetto Uprising.

71.   According to a report filed by Jürgen Stroop, approximately two thousand German soldiers were lost in the Warsaw Ghetto Uprising. About a thousand of them were from the Waffen SS; the rest came from various police units, including a unit of Lithuanian, Latvian, and Ukrainian recruits. Other estimates place the number of German casualties as high as five thousand men.

72.   Tosia Altman (1918 – 1943) was born in Wloclawek and was one of the founders of Hashomer Hatzair. A member of the JFO delegation on the Aryan side of the wall, she was trapped in the ghetto during the uprising. She got out of the ghetto through the sewers, but on 24 May she was severely burned in a fire that broke out in the ghetto fighters' hiding place in a celluloid factory at 11 Listopad Street in the Warsaw suburb of Praga. The Germans captured her and tortured her to death.

73.   Hancia Plotnitzka (1918 – 1943) was very active in the organization and development of the ghetto underground. She represented the resistance movement in various cities in Poland, but in March 1943 the underground leaders called her back to Warsaw to make arrangements for her to get out of Poland and alert the world to the murder of the Jews. She escaped Warsaw and went to Bendzin to organize a resistance movement in the Bendzin Ghetto; she was killed in the Bendzin Ghetto Uprising on 3 August 1943.

74.   Born in Moscow, Shmuel Braslaw (1920 – 1942) was one of the founders of Hashomer Hatzair, as well as one of the founders of the Jewish Fighting Organization in the Warsaw Ghetto. An operative in the Radom district, he was killed on 3 September 1942 while trying to obtain information on the fate of Josef Kaplan.

75.   Israel Shtern (1894 – 1942) was born in Russian and moved to Warsaw in 1917. Recognized as one of the major Yiddish poets of the period between the wars, he frequently associated with Hasidim and wrote about ways in which God reveals Himself among the poor and downtrodden.

76.   Yiddish poet Yehiel Lerer (1900 – 1943) was born in the Polish town of Mrozy and was active in the Yiddish culture organization YIKOR. He was killed in January 1943.

77.   Born in Radom, Joshua (Shiya) Perle (c. 1888 – 1943) was a Yiddish novelists know for his portrayal of the everyday life of the Polish Jew. He and his son were sent from the Warsaw Ghetto to Bergen-Belsen. They were both taken from Bergen-Belsen to an unknown destination. Nothing more was ever heard from them.

78.   Feliks Friedman (1897 – 1942) studied in Paris and was known for his drawings of life in the Warsaw Ghetto.

Part 8

Executioners

The Racial Politics of Hitlerism and Anti-Semitism

The history of civilized peoples has never known a war more barbaric, more savage, than the war that the Hitlerites waged against the peoples of the Soviet countries.

From the very first days of its inception Hitler's state machinery was determined not only to instill in the consciousness of the Germans the "right" to their rule over other peoples but also to "train" them to achieve that aim.

The Jewish population of Germany was the initial target of that "training." The German soil had already been prepared for that.

Beginning in the last quarter of the nineteenth century, long before Hitler, the most reactionary elements in Germany—figures such as Treitschke, Wilhelm's court pastor Stöcker, and various Junker circles—had used anti-Semitism to distract the disconcerted masses from the real reasons for their miserable condition.

Although they made up less than 1 percent of the population, the Jews were blamed for all the ills of the mass population. Social problems were cast in terms of religion, race, and nationality. Anti-Semitism was embellished with the "social" nuances concocted by "true Germans" and "Christian socialism." Even then August Bebel referred to German anti-Semitism as the "socialism of fools."

From the moment the Hitlerites came to power, they began their "racial training" with pogroms, beatings, murders, and pillaging perpetrated against the Jewish population. Hitler's Storm Troopers and the police apparatus, which was overflowing with Hitlerites, carried out the pogroms.

The Jewish people were forced "outside the law." The Jews were expelled from civil, public, and other institutions. They were stripped of their German citizenship, a move that was formalized with the Nuremberg Laws of 1935.

The criminal code of civilized states usually makes provisions for the severe punishment of murderers and robbers, as well as those who incite them or aid them. But when the Hitlerites came to power in Germany, it was openly preached—in schools and universities, in books and in the press—that everything was permitted to the German "master race." Thus they could build their own happiness and well being on the bones of other peoples.

This was not a state apparatus in the usual sense. It was a weapon in the hands of political hoodlums who used the authority of state (the police, government officials, and the army) for pillage and plunder that is punishable under the legal codes of all civilized governments.

Hitler taught: "If we want to create our great German empire, then we must first expel and exterminate the Slavic peoples—the Russians, Poles, Czechs, Slovaks, Bulgarians, Ukrainians, and Belorussians."

This teaching was fundamental to Hitler's plan. Several years before the war, at a congress of the fascist rabble held in Nuremberg, Hitler stirred up their instinct for plunder by saying: "Once the Urals with their immeasurable wealth, Siberia with its boundless forests, and the Ukraine with its endless fields are in our hands, then our people will be guaranteed everything they need."

In the first year of their assault on Soviet land the greedy and presumptuous Germans thought that from now on Ukrainian wheat, Ukrainian lard, and Donets coal would be in their hands. Hitler's henchman Erich Koch, Reich Commissar of the Ukraine, wrote that the Ukraine must "support and provide the German military command with the extraordinarily large sources of raw materials and provisions in that country, so that Germany and Europe could wage war for as long as it suited them."

The Hitlerites thought that by setting the Soviet peoples against one another, they could facilitate their aim of creating the "new order." Goering's "Green Folder," which contained instructions for German agents upon their occupation of Soviet territories, clearly stated that it was necessary to sow enmity and hostility among the people of the USSR in order to weaken their resistance.

Thus the Hitlerites ingratiated themselves with a group of Ukrainian nationalists (the Bendera group and others), with whose help they enslaved the Ukrainian people and set the Ukrainians against the Russian and Jews. At the same time in a secret memo from German army commander Kinzinger dated 18 July 1942 (No. 5771/564/42—Secret) it was emphasized: "The Ukrainian has been and continues to be alien to us. The simplest expression of trust or interest in the Ukrainians and their cultural life is harmful and weakens those fundamental traits to which Germany is committed in all its might and glory."

The ringleaders created a system in which it was possible to serve and ascend the fascist hierarchical ladder only by becoming adept at the murder and torture of peaceful populations in the occupied regions and unarmed people in the concentration camps.

In their instructions the ringleaders constantly reminded their subordinates of the necessity of creating strife among people of various nationalities.

In accordance with directives outlined in Goering's "Green Folder," the German commandant of Borisov reported to his superiors: "I am striving to sow antagonism between the Belorussians and the Russians and to pit both of them against the Jews."

Everywhere the German army went there was a nightmare of blood and plunder, the victims of which were primarily Jews. Following behind the army were the Gestapo and their "specialists" on policies in the occupied territories.

A special "Apparatus" was created specifically for the plunder and murder of the Jews. The Hitlerites threatened death to any Russian, Ukrainian, Belorussian, and so on who was hiding Jews.

Like many other cities in the Soviet nations, the cities of Lvov, Kiev, Zharkov, Minsk, and Riga witnessed the total annihilation of Jewish workers and their families.

The closer the war came to reaching an end, the greater the madness of the Hitlerite monsters. Hitler's henchmen introduced "racial legislation" to all of their vassal governments (Italy, Romania, and Hungary). Jews were transported from every corner of the occupied area to Majdanek and Auschwitz to be exterminated.

In December 1942 the governments of Belgium, Great Britain, Holland, Greece, Luxemburg, Norway, Poland, the United States, the USSR, Czechoslovakia, Yugoslavia, and the French National Committee issued a statement indicating that the German fascist invaders were "implementing Hitler's often stated intention of slaughtering the Jewish people of Europe."

The governments again affirmed their "solemn obligation to join the United Nations in their assurance that the people responsible for these crimes would not escape the punishment they deserve."

Titled "On the Implementation of the Nazi Plan to Exterminate the Jewish Population of Europe" (published in *Izvestiya*, 19 December 1942), a subsequent report by the Information Bureau of the People's Commissariat of Foreign Affairs of the USSR introduced concrete evidence of Hitler's politics of extermination. This report, incidentally, noted: "Through their brutality against the Jews and vicious anti-Semitic propaganda, the Hitlerites are attempting to divert the attention of the German people from the catastrophe approaching fascist Germany, the imminence of which is increasingly obvious. Only the reckless few in Hitler's inner circle, now doomed to perish, could be so conceited as to think they could submerge in the blood of many hundreds of thousands of innocent Jews countless crimes against the peoples of Europe, who were plunged into war by the insatiable German Imperialists."

Now it is all over. Hitler's armies have been crushed and his plundering machine dismantled.

Now the main perpetrators of these atrocities, those who inspired and carried out mass murders and tortures, stand before the International Military Tribunal. Among them is the "specialist" on anti-Semitism, Hitler's close friend and associate Julius Streicher. He was the editor-in-chief of the despicable newspaper *Der Stürmer*, which combined pornographic amusement with anti-Semitism as it pandered to obscurantists and sadists. Streicher held the title of SS Troop General and became the Gauleiter of Franconia. Others who are being held accountable before the International Military Tribunal are lined up ahead of him: Goering, Ribbentrop, Hess, Kaltenbrunner, Rosenberg, Frank, and others who were in charge of the governmental and military pillaging.

In a Europe now liberated from the German fascist invaders all racial and nationalistic discrimination has been eliminated, including discrimination against the Jewish people.

But can it be said that, with the elimination of Hitler's political gangsterism and the Hitlerite state, the struggle against fascism and its misanthropic "ideology" has come to an end even if anti-Semitism has ended?

Of course not! This is evident from the serious struggle that continues against Hitler's lackeys in the liberated countries, against the neo-fascists who for the time being have gone underground but who slip to the surface at every opportunity to once again take up their fanaticism.

Even in England it was possible for a reactionary (conservative) member of Parliament—Captain Ramsey (held in prison under the Law for State Security from May 1940 to September 1944)—to openly introduce from the rostrum of the Parliament a proposal demanding that the English government "reinstate the Jewish statute and again enforce its articles."[1]

General Radescu is now head of the government of Romania; waging a struggle against the democratic reforms, in February 1945 he attempted to incite a civil war. In order to achieve his goal, he made anti-Semitic attacks on individuals in the Democratic Front.

In Poland, now free from the German fascist invaders, anti-Semitism is a weapon in the arsenal of the former "government in exile," which even now has joined with former Gestapo men to stir up nationalistic resentment. As early as August 1945 former Gestapo agents in Krakow tried to incite a pogrom against the Jews but were beaten back by military force and by an organized democratic public.[2]

The fight against anti-Semitism, therefore, cannot succeed without an active struggle for democracy and for a close alliance of the democratic elements of all countries. The stronger and more consistent the development of democracy, the firmer the unity and cooperation of all nations and races, and the sooner the end to anti-Semitism.

The USSR stands as an example of a country, where, in keeping with the Soviet Constitution, any encroachment on the equality of nations and races or any incitement to nationalistic persecution is punished with all the severity of Soviet criminal law.

I. P. Trainin[3]

Himmler's Order (From *Freies Deutschland*, No. 23, 19 December 1943)

Carrying out the order in the Central Army Group in November 1941, the head of the group's intelligence division expressed an urgent desire to speak privately with my general. For reasons already mentioned, I took park in the conversation. On the instructions of Field Marshall Von Bock, the head of the intelligence division informed us of the following: At the head of every army group is a high-ranking SS Führer. Three days ago Reichsführer SS Himmler visited the SS Führer of a certain army group and happened to ask how many Jews were being shot each day as per his order. After hearing the number, Himmler shouted: "What swinish cowardice! Follow the example of your colleague in the Nord Army Group, where they are shooting five times as many as you are!"

Major Berhhard Bechler
Member of the Board of the Union of German Officers

Text of a German Dispatch Found in the Region of Rossoshi among Staff Documents of the 15th German Police Regiment,[4] Concluding Report

After the order to march immediately was cancelled, the company received another order on 27 October 1942: to reach Kobrin by 21:00 on 28 October 1942. The company arrived in Kobrin as ordered and from there was sent to Pinsk. The company showed up at the western entrance to Pinsk at 04:00 on 29 October.

At a conference held with the regiment commander on 28 October 1942 in Pinsk it was decided that two battalions—the Second Battalion of the 15th Police Regiment and the 2nd Cavalry Division—would form and outer cordon. The 10th Company of the 15th Police Regiment and the 11th Company of the 11th Police Regiment, less two platoons, would be assigned to comb the ghetto. The 11ᵗʰ Company of the 11ᵗʰ Police Regiment (less their 1ˢᵗ Platoon), which had been relieved from combing the ghetto that evening, was assigned to guard the assembly point and the individual transports to the execution site four kilometers outside of Pinsk. They were also to form a cordon around the execution site. At times cavalry were later used for the latter assignment. This proved to be a brilliant move, because when 150 Jews once tried to escape they were all caught, even though some of them managed to go a few kilometers.

The cordon was to be set up at 04:30; it turned out that, thanks to the leaders' personal reconnaissance beforehand and to the maintenance of secrecy, the cordon was completed in the shortest time, and none of the Jews could get away. According to the order, the combing of the ghetto was to have begun at 06:00, but the operation was delayed half an hour due to darkness. Soon the Jews were gathered at the checkpoint. Due to the unexpectedly massive size of the crowd gathered at the checkpoint, there was no roll call (they had estimated that they would have only one to two thousand on the first day). The initial combing of the ghetto ended at 17:00 without incident. About ten thousand people were executed on the first day. That night the company was ready to unwind at the soldiers' club.

On 30 October 1942 they combed the ghetto a second time, on 31 October a third time, and on 1 November a fourth time. A total of approximately fifteen thousand Jews were herded into the assembly point. Jews who were sick and children who were left in the buildings were executed right there, in the ghetto. Approximately twelve hundred Jews were executed in the ghetto itself. There were no incidents, with one exception. The Jews were promised that anyone who revealed where they had hidden their gold would be spared; one Jew stepped up and said that he had hidden a huge amount of gold. A cavalry sergeant was sent with him to find the gold. The Jew kept stalling and asked the sergeant to go up to the attic with him; then the sergeant brought the Jew back to the assembly point. There the Jew refused to sit on the ground like everyone else. Suddenly he rushed one of the cavalry troopers, grabbed his rifle [and stick], and started beating the trooper. In the ensuing struggle the Jew was hit over the head with an axe; he fell and did not get up.

At 17:00 on 1 November the company was assigned to the outer cordon, and a second cavalry unit was sent to its post. Nothing out of the ordinary took place.

At 8:00 on 2 November 1942 the company was released from Pinsk and started the march to its post. The company reached Kobrin at 13:00; by 17:00 it had returned to its base.[5]

Conclusions:

1. Units assigned to combing should definitely have axes and other such instruments, since almost all the doors were locked [or bolted] and could be opened only through the use of force.

2. Even in instances where no internal exits into the attic can be seen, it should be assumed nevertheless that people are hiding there. Attics, therefore, should be carefully searched.

3. In buildings that have no basements a significant number of people hide in small spaces under the floor. Such spaces must be broken into from the outside or searched by police dogs (a police dog named Asta thus distinguished itself in Pinsk). A hand grenade could also be thrown into the space; any Jews left alive will then immediately crawl out.

4. Because innumerable people hide in camouflaged ditches around the buildings, the ground surrounding the buildings should be probed with sharp instruments.

5.   It is recommended that young Jews be enlisted to point out these hiding places, with the promise that they will be allowed to live if they do.

Captain of the Police Guard
and Commander of the Sauer Company

Executioners

1

Unteroffizier Peter Maiguart was an acrobat in the circus prior to the war. He took part in the march on Paris and then was assigned to garrison duty in Poland. After 22 June 1941 he was on the Eastern Front. His last duty assignment was to serve as commander of the 6th Section of the 1st Company of the 1st Battalion, 536th Regiment, 384th Division.

He relates the following:

"In early August 1941 we came to the city of Gadyach in the Poltavsk district. One day Sergeant Major Chozgrebe lined us up and said: 'The Major is entrusting you with a great responsibility. You have proven yourselves to be good soldiers, and now you must prove yourselves worthy of the trust placed in you.' We set out down the Gadyach-Lokhvitsa highway. Five hundred meters outside of town was a camp for Jews. Opposite the camp, along the right side of the road, a large pit had been prepared; it was about seven meters long and three meters deep. The police began escorting Jews out to the edge of the pit. Under Chozgrebe's command, four other soldiers and I participated in this action. We lined people up facing the pit. Our rifles were pointed at the back of the Jews' heads. Several women were holding children by the hand. We started murdering the children. The business proceeded slowly, since six of us were missing. I had to shoot a young teenage girl, among others. In German she said to me: 'How can you murder people?' I answered: 'Orders.' Then I shot her. Altogether I shot twenty-five people that day, maybe more; I cannot say exactly how many. Others shot more."

2

Lance Corporal Peter Goriza, of the field gendarmes in the 359th Infantry Division, relates the following:

"The first ones we shot were communists and Jews. After December 1941 we started shooting women and children. I took part in the cleansing of Pinsk, Priluk, and Sevsk. Before we shot them, we lined them up facing the pit. The operation was usually carried out early in the morning and did not last more than two or three hours. I personally shot about 150 civilians and 200 prisoners of war. In Pinsk I remember personally shooting 30 people; some of them were Jews; the rest were communists. I considered such shooting to be justified for the security of our army; I have strong nerves."

3

This is a statement by Leopold Bischof, a private in the 1st Company of the 28th Chasseur Regiment, 8th Infantry Division:

"In the autumn of 1941 part of Baranovichi was fenced off with barbed wire, and all the Jews were resettled in a ghetto. In early March 1942 the ghetto was surrounded. Everyone in the buildings there was loaded into trucks and taken to a warehouse for confiscated goods. At the warehouse was a large pit that had been dug for storing ammunition. The Jews were forced to remove their warm clothing; then they were shot."

4

This is from the diary of Otto Werger, Staff Sergeant in the 2nd Battalion of the 3rd Guard Regiment:

"6 September 1941. We arrived in Stary Bykhov. Completely destroyed. Two hundred fifty Jews were shot.

"22 October 1941. A certain Unteroffizier who has just come from Kiev told us that eighty thousand Jews were shot at a pit in Kiev. They say this was done by order of the Führer.

"1 January 1942. A secret order has been issued: to undertake the mass extermination of the Jews in the occupied territories. Four thousand Jews were shot in Smolensk to usher in the New Year."

From the diary of Senior Staff Sergeant Johann Richter, Fourth Battalion, 40th Infantry Division:

"6 July 1941. Matula dug up a body in the Jewish cemetery. Hofsteter wiped off the skull with his fingers. Matula placed it on a stump and crushed it with an axe."

From the Deposition of Captain Salog, Police Regiment Commander

Preparations for shooting the Jewish population were doubtlessly made ahead of time. And, as I discovered later, they consisted of the following:

1. The concentration of the Jewish population.

2. The designation of a Jewish quarter.

3. The compilation of precise lists.

4. The gathering together of the Jews from various population points.

5. The selection of a site to do the shootings.

Six-pointed stars that could be clearly seen had to be painted on the walls of buildings where Jews lived.

The site for the shootings was selected jointly by the chief of the SD (the main executioner), the chief of the gendarmes, and the district commissar. How many days prior to the shootings the site was selected, I cannot say. Judging from the time when the chief of the gendarmes left for Staraya Ushitsa, it must have been three or four days. The SD chief left for Staraya Ushitsa the same day; there they worked out the details with the district commissar.

From personal observations I know that prior to such events the gendarme chief would often spend hours with the district commissar and the chief of the SD; even more often the SD chief would go to see the chief of gendarmes and would have frequent telephone conversations with the district commissar. On such occasions the doors leading from the room where the sergeant majors and I worked to the gendarme chief's main office were carefully closed, and one of the officer workers stood guard. Then the gendarmes warned us that we were not to disturb the chief.

Saturday was always the day selected for the shootings. Why I cannot say. I always got evasive answers to such questions.

I do not know about the first shootings that were carried out in Kamenets-Podolsky in 1941 and in early 1942.

On the word of others I do know the following about one of the larger mass shootings of the Jews:

During the first days of the occupation of the Western Ukraine, Bessarabia, and Northern Bukovna they started transporting Jews to Kamenets-Podolsky. A large group of Jews from Czechoslovakia joined them later and were shot here in Kamenets. The figures on how many were shot vary from eight to ten to twelve thousand. Whether this figure includes the Jews of Kamenets-Podolsky I cannot say.

I personally know of two mass shootings of Jews, citizens of the USSR, that took place in Kamenets-Podolsky in 1942.

In August 1942, while serving a company commander of a gendarme police squad in Kamenets-Podolsky, my subordinates and I participated for the first time in a mass shooting of Jews from the cities of Staraya Ushitsa and Studenitsa. The second time was in Kamenets-Podolsky in September 1942. In November 1942 there was a mass shooting in the vicinity of the Cossack barracks (a training battalion).

Since I was company commander, on the eve of the shooting gendarme chief Lieutenant Reich ordered me through 1st Company commander Krubasik to call out about fifty policemen from my company. At the same time I was ordered to phone the troop commander in Staraya Ushitsa and found out whether he understood the order from the chief of the gendarme post in Staraya Ushitsa about forming a police unit from his troops. The troop commander told me he understood everything and had made the necessary arrangements in cooperation with the chief of the gendarme post, Sergeant Major Kunde of the cavalry, and with the district chief of Staraya Ushitsa.

[He could not tell me what they spoke about over the phone, just as I could not ask him about it. We had both been warned about such things—he by the chief of the gendarme post and I by the gendarme chief.]

When I asked what we would be doing, Krubasik replied: "We shall all know about that tomorrow."

We were ordered to take along ten cartridges for each rifle, plus an extra belt of machine gun cartridges. In addition we took along a sub-machine gun and three automatic weapons. Ten to twelve gendarmes, about fifty policemen from Krubasik's company, and some from my company drove out. Members of the SD and the criminal police went out separately from us.

When we arrived in the village of Grushka, we found that policemen from the Zelenye Kurilovtsy and Privorottya districts were already completely assembled.

Lieutenant Reich and three gendarmes took a car to Staraya Ushitsa; the chief of the SD and four of his men rode in a second car. They ordered the rest of the gendarmes and police to go to bed.

After rising the next morning, we drove out to Staraya Ushitsa in two trucks at dawn. Around one and a half kilometers before reaching Staraya Ushitsa our trucks were stopped and the police were lined up in formation. Here Lieutenant Reich announced our assignment and the purpose of our trip: to gather together all the Jews of Staraya Ushitsa and Studenitsa and escort them to the execution site, which was not far from the main highway.

The SD chief, the gendarme chief, and the district commissar had agreed upon the site for the shooting ahead of time, during one of the trips the SD chief and the gendarme chief had made to Staraya Ushitsa.

All the Jews of Staraya Ushitsa were assembled in the town square, which was cordoned off by gendarmes and policemen. All the men, all the elderly, and all the children, with the exception of nursing infants, were separated from the women in the square. They were ordered to take a seat on the ground and not to talk with one another.

Any attempt to say something was cut short with a shout and a blow from a rifle butt or a club.

The chief of the SD and the chief of gendarmes announced to the Jews that they were going to Kamenets-Podolsky.

[In some instances the women were allowed to take along clothing for themselves and their children, since, when they got the order to immediately assemble in the square, many had left their apartments barefoot and wearing hardly anything.]

In the process of gathering people in the square, many were found hiding in their apartments. People tried to escape by hiding in cellars and attics that they had prepared for such a purpose, having stocked them with food and clothing ahead of time.

Everyone found was beaten with rifle butts and clubs.

[In one instance a Jew caught hiding in an attic was shot and killed on the spot.]

The sick and the elderly who could not walk out into the square were led or carried by their relatives; if there were no relatives, then we ordered other Jews to carry them.

One elderly woman, sixty or seventy years old, came walking out of her room very slowly; she was driven into the street with blows to her back from a rifle butt.

Then shots were fired; screams of despair broke out, and women and children started crying. It was difficult to stop their screaming and crying; clubs and rifle butts had to be used on them.

The chiefs of the SD and the gendarmes gave their orders and drove off in their cars to the execution site. The orders were as follows:

1. To send trucks to Studenitsa in the Staraya Ushitsa region to pick up the Jews living there.

Three or four trucks were sent to Studenitsa with a unit of fifteen to twenty policemen led by a representative of the SD, whose rank and name I do not know; Peucker, the Hauptwachmeister of the gendarmes was also with them. As they finished shooting the Jews of Staraya Ushitsa, they brought in the Jews of Studenitsa; there were eighty-to-a hundred of them. Eight border guards reinforced the convoy guard.

2. To set up a guard for all the apartments vacated by the Jews.

I gave the police troop commander the job of organizing this guard; after taking care of it, he went to the execution site.

3. The district chief was ordered to prepare lunch for the fifty to sixty men in the police and gendarme units. Lunch was to be ready at twelve o'clock.

The convoy columns were set up like this: two gendarmes walked five to ten paces in front of the first row of the column of Jews, with thirty to thirty-five policemen on the sides (three or four paces from the column). The guards in the rear of the column were to prod along the ones who lagged behind. This they accomplished with the help of shouts and blows from rifle butts or clubs, which they remembered to take along with them when they left Staraya Ushitsa. I walked in the rear with a gendarme, a Wachmeister radio operator, and a policeman.

The march through Staraya Ushitsa, from the square to the outskirts, went more or less peacefully, without any incidents. But as soon as the column got outside the city, one could hear the, at first quiet, then increasingly louder weeping of the children; next the women started crying. [It continued almost unceasingly the rest of the way.] Despite all measures taken to restore quiet—kicks, blows from rifle butts, and threats of being shot—the crying and screaming would stop for a moment only to start up again even louder. The women and old people were whispering prayers; others quietly whispered to one another. Some tossed bundles of their belongings to the side of the road, but the police picked them up and threw them into the cart. All along the way we repeated to the Jews several times the lie that they were being taken to Kamenets-Podolsky.

One to one and a half kilometers out of Staraya Ushitsa I saw cars parked along the road. As I later found out, it was the district commissar Reindl and his men. The SD chief and the gendarme chief were talking to them.

Once the column had reached the cars and the gendarme in front had reported to the district commissar, the SD chief pointed in the direction where the column was to move on, that is, toward the pit; the entire column turned in that direction.

At the moment when the column turned toward the pit a general outcry rose up. No shouts or blows from rifle butts, no kicking, could stop those cries. The shrill, penetrating screams of the women mingled with the weeping of the children as they pleaded with their mothers to hold their hands. The screaming would subside and then rise up again even louder. [And so it continued down the path of one to two hundred meters leading to the pit, all the way to the execution site.]

The pit was about twelve by six meters and about one and a half meters deep. One the side facing Kemenets-Podolsky there was an entrance to the pit about two meters wide, with a slope leading down to the bottom. The ones doomed to death passed through this entrance.

At this point, realizing that the promise to be taken to Kemenets-Podolsky was a lie, the Jews started throwing away their cigarette cases, rings, and earrings; they tore up their documents, photographs, letters, papers with notes, and other things.

If a Jew should try to escape, it was not permitted to shoot inside the cordon. The order was to wait until the Jew got outside the cordon, turn to face him, and only then open fire. In order to make it possible to fire from the pit, the two men who were closest to the escapee were to step aside and thus create an opening through which the others could shoot.

A second, inner cordon was set up right next to the Jews, who were thus squeezed as tightly as possible into a single group. The previous arrangement was maintained, with the men standing in front and the women behind. This ring closed tighter at the pit, where the executioner stood with his machine gun.

If one can put it this way, the execution process consisted of the following elements:

As I mentioned above, the mass of people doomed to death stood packed tightly together fifteen to twenty meters from the pit. All of them, including the women and children, were stripped naked and, prodded by blows, were driven into the pit in groups of five.

Along the edge of the pit stood several gendarmes, who in turn used their clubs and rifle butts to move the people down the pit toward the executioner. The executioner's name was Paul; I do not know his last name. After drinking a good deal of liquor, he ordered the victims to lie face down; then he shot them in the back of the head at pointblank range. The next group of five would lie down with their heads on the bodies of their fellow Jews to be murdered in the same manner, receiving "one coffee bean" in the head, as the Germans would say. Above the pit stood a "counter," one of the criminal policemen who would put a small cross (the designated marker) next to each group of five.

The truth must be told that there were frequently instances when, instead of five people, a family of six to eight—despite the orders and despite being beaten half to death—would go into the pit together; then they would be marked off with a cross as if it had been only five.

Not far from the pit gendarme chief Lieutenant Reich, the chief of the SD (whose name I do not know), and Commissar Reindl stood giving various orders. They would egg on their subordinates, sometimes laughing when the blows would hit their mark, as a huge number of blows fell upon the heads and backs of Jews who were already dazed; or else they would stand there stone-faced and silently gaze upon the spectacle of the slaughter. Sometimes they would turn away from the pit and, their hands thrust into their pockets, quietly discuss something. After spending about two hours at the pit, Reindl shook hands with the leaders, saluted all the others, and smiled; then he got into his car and headed for Kamenets-Podolsky.

The shooting went on.

The picture would not be complete if I did not say something about the condition of those who were doomed to death.

After the executioner had fired his first shots, the mass of people fell silent; then, realizing the horror of their situation, their voices rose in such a cry that the heart stopped beating and the blood ran cold.

They shouted threats and curses of retribution. The old ones called out to God and asked Him for revenge.

On the way into the pit and from within the pit itself, under blows from clubs and rifle butts, the men cried out: "Long live the homeland of all peoples: the Soviet Union!"

There were also cries of "Death to the one-eyed wolf Adolf!"

Several old people and several women went insane. These people—their eyes crazed and open wide, paying no attention to the blows—slowly moved forward, their arms at their side. They stumbled, fell, and got up again; then, when they reached the executioner, they came to a halt and froze, saying not a word and making not a move. Only a blow from a machine gun or a kick from an executioner would send such a victim to the bottom of the pit.

The gendarmes violently tore small children away from their mothers and threw them into the pit. One little boy, three or four years old, undressed himself and walked up to the pit. A gendarme grabbed him by the arm and, after signaling the executioner, threw the child into the pit. The executioner fired and hit the child in mid-air. Many women wanted to hide their nakedness and would not take off their slips. Their slips were torn from their bodies, and they were beaten. Several young woman and teenage girls were especially ridiculed. They spit in the faces and eyes of several gendarmes and one of the SD men. The men viciously struck the girls in the face and breasts and kicked them in the genitals with their boots.

Socks and stockings were ripped from the legs of women and children with sticks and rifle butts.

Many women begged for the lives of their children to be spared.

Many ripped their clothing, tore their hair, and bit their arms.

Some men tried to escape. Running in a zigzag pattern and already completely naked, a middle-aged man bolted for some bushes on the northwest side of the execution site. He got seventy to a hundred meters beyond the second cordon, when shots from a rifle and a sub-machine gun killed him.

A second man had taken off his shoes and outer clothing, when he tried to run off in the same direction; but he did not make it past the second cordon and was also murdered.

None of the women tried to escape. As they undressed, the Jews condemned to death tore their fine shoes and clothing to shreds and buried their valuables in the ground. But the experienced SD men kept a sharp lookout for this and stopped the Jews' attempts to destroy their valuables. Valuables recovered from the dirt or from the grass were handed over to a special "collector" from the SD.

Families, relatives, and even acquaintances said farewell to one another, shook hands, and kissed. Sometimes people stood under a rain of blows while embraced in a farewell kiss. There were families that held tightly to one another, their children in their arms, as they went into the pit.

As the shooting was drawing to an end, when the bottom of the pit was full, the executioner stood at the passageway and ordered his victim to run over the bodies; then he shot him. If he missed and the victim was still alive, then shots from rifles and pistols positioned above the pit would finish the him off.

There were times when someone who had been shot was still moving under the bodies of his brothers for ten or fifteen minutes.

Under the direction of the SD men, the policemen began shaking out and examining the shoes and clothing that had belonged to the people who had been shot. They were especially thorough in their examination of the clothing. This was done because they there might be valuables in the pleats of the clothing, in the lining, or in the waistbands of the trousers.

All the valuables were collected into a sack kept by one of the SD men. They filled the sack with cigarette lighters, penknives, leather briefcases, cigarette cases, and wallets.

The items that were new—dresses, handkerchiefs, boots, coats, and even material that had not been sewn—were divided among the men who took part in the execution. Sometimes they tore things from one another, and they had heated arguments.

On that day approximately four hundred citizens of the Soviet Union were shot; among them were men and women of all ages, even children. It took about four hours (from seven or eight in the morning until eleven or twelve).

The second mass shooting of the Jews of Kamenets-Podolsky that I know about and took part in was in November or December 1942; I know about it because my subordinates and I were in the second cordon.

At that time the ghetto, which was in the vicinity of Svyato-Yurskaya and Zelenaya Streets, contained around 4,800 Jews; the overwhelming majority of them were specialists in various professions, including medicine.

I found out about this shooting on the preceding morning from gendarme chief Lieutenant Reich. Going through 1st Police Company commander Wachmeister Krubasik, Reich ordered me to summon members of the staff of the 2nd Police Company, which I commanded, by evening. The procedure for this mass murder was the same as for Staraya Ushitsa; it differed only in a few details, of which I shall speak below.

As soon as the cordon had been set up (within five to ten minutes after Reich's arrival), three trucks full of Jews from the ghetto pulled up. The trucks were covered with tarpaulins; fifty to sixty Jews were unloaded, escorted by gendarmes and SD men. They were sent to the execution site, where they were ordered to undress. The shooting went on until 17:00 or 18:00, or about twelve hours. Groups of forty to sixty Jews were hauled in.

As I later discovered, soldiers from the Kamenets-Podolsky garrison were holding drills throughout the entire city—in parks and squares, in the stadium and the marketplace, and in the villages closest to the execution site. They conducted the drills in small groups around the size of a platoon. At that time the German garrison at Kamenets-Podolsky consisted of two to three thousand young, inexperienced soldiers. They were going through basic training and later left for the front.

The people who dug the pits were taken back to their barracks.

Two executioners from the SD took turns "working" there; when one of them grew tired he would take a break and go climb into a truck, where a snack and some vodka had been prepared for him. Then the other one would take his place. Thus they alternated during the whole time of the shooting. The executioners were not the only ones to fortify themselves with vodka. From time to time the gendarmes or the Gestapo were sent to the trucks, where they would crawl into a cab to eat a sandwich, drink some vodka, and have a smoke. Then they would go back to the execution site.

As I indicated above, there was only one escape attempt. A middle-aged man was shot down after running seventy to a hundred meters beyond the second cordon.

From conversations I had, I found out that on the night before the shooting about five hundred people had escaped from the ghetto.

Apparently the Jews had found out about the shooting on the day before it was to take place. More than two hundred people were also discovered in hiding places in the ghetto. A short while later they too were shot. When and where, I do not know.

I also do not know how many of those who escaped were caught. In 1943 six to eight Jews were brought to the gendarme headquarters. I saw one of them, an agronomist named Hartman. They brought him in the summer of 1943 from the village of Lyantskorun in the Chemerovetsky region, where a local peasant woman has been hiding him in an attic. I do not remember her name. Captain Otto ordered him to be turned over to the SD.

Valuables and other belongings were collected, as before; the valuables went to the SD, while the new things went to the executioners.

This time approximately four thousand citizens of the Soviet Union were annihilated, including the elderly, the sick and the invalids, men and women, professionals, small children, and even infants.

Among the victims of the shooting were twenty to thirty Russians from the prison; I am not sure of the exact number, as I had left town four times. They were loaded into a truck with the Jews and were shot in groups of six to eight people.

Kamenets-Podolsky
25 May 1944

Excerpts from the Diary of Prisoner of War Karl Johannes Drexel, Lance Corporal, [513th Reserve Battalion, Lublin Regiment, GG Division]

1 April 1942. Promoted to Private First Class.

25 September 1942. Assigned to the 2nd Company of the 513th Reserve Battalion in Chelm; housed in a training barracks.

From 15 October to 30 October 1942. On leave.

1 November 1942. The campaign against the Jews. Ten thousand were shot, from the most elderly old man to the smallest infant. They were all thrown into carts and hauled off to mass graves. A cruel sight.

3 November 1942. Jews are being hunted down. Every day three to four thousand Jews are annihilated. They are herded down their last mile in columns. With their eyes full of tears they cross over into the next world. Those who lag behind are killed on the spot. They are gassed and electrocuted. Ninety thousand Russians have perished from typhus and dysentery. They are wrapped in barbed wire and then dragged through the swamps.

6 November 1942. Morning. Three and a half thousand Jews. Grenades are strung together and thrown into their living quarters. Day and night. Five Jews. A heartrending, nerve-wracking experience. A cold night.

8 November 1942. A mother and the child she held in her arms were beaten to death with a rifle butt. They do not enjoy the protection of the law.

12 November 1942. I was in the ghetto and then at the mass graves. The living and the dead are being pillaged. For four days the Jews have been subjected to inhuman treatment. We were given smelling salts. Children and old people, women who had just given birth, were forced to stand on their knees; barely alive, looking like skeletons, they were dragged out and shot at random. People perished in the midst of the cruelest suffering, such as humanity has never known. Homes were ravaged. Bodies lay inside the buildings for six days. Both men and women were forced to undress. It was a sight horrible to behold. [In spite of all this, I managed to sneak into the buildings. I was looking for people to shoot and thus put them of their misery.] Not a single soldier went into this ghetto. The doors and windows creak.

20 November 1942. Forty Jews were dragged out of their hiding places. No girls were found.

4 December 1942. The dead lie all around. Old buildings are being demolished. An epidemic of dysentery and typhus has broken out.

10 December 1942. A partisan took a shot at our company commander.

12 May 1943. We set out to fight the partisans.

4 June 1943. A battle with bandits in Zamoshe. We marched on Whitsuntide.

[12 March 1943. Assigned as a guard in Lublin.

11 December 1943. At the base in Ulanov.

16 January 1944. At the base in Krasnikhin.

From the Deposition of Private First Class Christian Farber

Last year, before I was captured (in November 1942), I was a witness to terrible savagery perpetrated in one of the large villages near Chelm.

A certain SS unit cruelly murdered about three hundred people, including men, women, and children; most of them were Jews. Small groups of men were lined up in front of a pit that they themselves had dug. They were slaughtered with machine guns. Others met the same fate. Terrible moans and cries could be heard, since not all of them had been killed by the machine gun fire. These people who were seriously wounded were buried alive along with the others. Among the SS men, Sergeant Major Josef Schmidt of Freiburg particularly distinguished himself as a murderer. If a man or a woman should try to escape, the SS would chase after them and shoot them down like rabbits. They would grab little children by the legs and crush their heads against a wall.

One young girl was hiding in the hayloft of a barn behind a beam. When the SS found her there, one of them climbed up to the loft while the others formed a circle down below with their bayonets raised. The one in the loft prodded the girl with his bayonet until she had no choice but to jump down. She was literally riddled with bayonets. When I asked the SS man in charge, Lieutenant Karl Dehr (from Ludwigshafen, near Mannheim), why such cruel things were done, he answered: "We threw the Jews out of Germany, and now we must exterminated them from here as well." Toward the end all the livestock were driven out of the village, and every last building was burned to the ground.

[Christian Farber, Private First Class, Shoemaker, 3rd Company,
347th Infantry Regiment (Schwitzingen, near Mannheim)]

An Excerpt from the Protocol of the Cross-Examination of the Prisoner of War Lance Corporal Erich Heubaum,
[1st Company, 173rd Infantry Regiment, 87th Infantry Division]

"I arrived in the city of Lvov in April 1942 and worked there as a driver. My car was in the service of the railroad administration in Lvov.

"In May and June of 1942 all the fascist newspapers in Lvov ran articles calling for the extermination of the city's sixty thousand Jews. By that time ninety thousand Jews had already been hauled off and shot.

"The order to exterminate the rest of the Jews came in June. First part of the city was marked off for a ghetto. It was surrounded by barbed wire, and all the Jews were herded into its borders. Then in a small wood near the railroad station a camp was set up; Jews were taken there in groups of up to a thousand to be shot. At first groups of the condemned were taken from the ghetto to the camp during the day. But since this created a disturbance among the rest of the population and aroused the indignation of some of the soldiers and army officers, they started conducting the shootings at night. Those who could not walk—the sick, the elderly, and the children—were assembled on the railroad platform and shipped off to the camp. Then, at night, they were all shot with machine guns.

"Many of the doomed hid in the ghetto and did not want to leave. At that point the SS surrounded the ghetto and set it on fire. I saw this myself. I saw people running out of burning buildings and jumping out of windows. The SS shot them all with machine guns. The street was covered with dead bodies for three hundred meters. The dead lay piled on top of each other.

"When I saw a young mother jump from the window of a burning building with a baby in her arms and how they started shooting at her, I turned away; it was more than I could take, so I decided to go home...

"For several days afterward the city was filled with the smell of burning bodies.

"I also saw peaceful citizens exterminated with gas. I would drive telephone operators to a small station in Rava-Russkaya, a town located twenty kilometers away. An underground barracks was built in the woods near the train station. I once saw a group of Jews brought in while I was at the station. The train cars were covered; the people were reaching out the windows and begging for water, but they were not allowed to have any. That evening those people were driven into the woods. Strangers in the area who happened to be at the station were forced to stay inside. SD units surrounded the woods.

"There all those people, regardless of age or sex—men, women, old people, and children—were stripped naked and driven into the underground barracks. Three quarters of an hour later the men from the next group were forced to go in and drag out the bodies. Then the next group was driven into the barracks.... Every evening approximately three hundred people were slaughtered in this manner.

"For eight days I witnessed this scene. An SS man named Karl Horst from Saxony told me that these Jews were being gassed. He took part in the operation. Sturmbannführer Herbst of Breslau supervised the executions."

From the Deposition of the Prisoner of War Corporal Heinrich Michael Wenkriech, [54th Field Engineer Battalion, Tank Grenadier SS, Netherland Division, on the Savagery of the German Fascist Invaders in the Ukraine (from 6 December 1941 to 18 March 1942)]

"At that time I was serving with the gendarmes in the Romanian army. We were attached to groups consisting of a company of field police and a unit assigned to maintain order.

"We were assigned to the occupied territory stretching from Rybnitsa on the Dniester to Golta on the Bug. Units already stationed there were about to go on leave, and we were sent to replace them. Under the command of a lieutenant, the troops were quartered in the village of Kruty. The area of troop activity was spread out over several population centers: Semenovka, Moina, Labushna, Kodyma, Frantsyushka, Aleksandrovka, and other cities.

"In all these areas the Jewish people, including women and children, were removed from their residences and placed in barracks without windows or doors. The Jews had all their possessions taken away from them. They were given no food; they went hungry, and many of them starved to death.

"The military authorities ordered the Jews to be moved to another area; they had to go on foot under a heavy guard. It was freezing cold, and all their warm clothing, including their shoes had been taken away from them; most of them were barefoot.

"There were about 350 of them altogether. A Romanian corporal named Gavrila was in command of the convoy. He boasted that he would torture three hundred people to death, and then he would be able to transfer to another position.

"Mothers walked along the road carrying their children in their arms. Whenever they collapsed from exhaustion and could go no further, Gavrila shot them. He did the same to the old and the weak. At night the Jews were locked inside barns. The next morning we generally found thirty to forty of them suffering from frostbite. They were also shot. When the convoy reached Birzuli, it was barely half its original size.

"Since there were many bodies lying in the streets of the village, typhus broke out. We were ordered to bury the bodies rather than leave them in the streets. The Russian population was assembled and ordered to dig pits large enough to hold a hundred people. The Jews who had been shot were dragged into these pits; often some who were still alive were buried with the dead. One of these graves is located along the road from Kruty to Budai. I know of another one near Kodyma...

"On orders from the troop commander, I personally shot a woman fifty to sixty years old. I did not know the reason why.

"As far as I know, in the area where our unit operated not a single Jew survived. Some were shot where they lived, others in the camps."

From the Deposition of Wolfgang Janiko, [1/3ʳᵈ Company, 368ᵗʰ Infantry Regiment, 122ⁿᵈ Infantry Division (a Draftsman from Leipzig), Koburgerstrasse, 91]

I was witness to the execution of Jews when I was stationed at the headquarters of the 281ˢᵗ Guard Division in July 1941 in Resenke (Latvia). There were approximately seven thousand Jews in the city; they were all arrested and systematically "liquidated" (about three hundred per day).

I once witnessed such an execution. And what I saw was horrible. The site where this savagery took place was not far from the city. A large canal, very long and deep, had been dug there. Latvian auxiliary troops under German command ordered thirty to thirty-five of the poor victims to stand along the edge of the canal (they ranged in age from small children to old men and women). The order rang out: "Fire!" And the first victims fell into the canal (shot in the back of the head).

The next group lay the bodies in layers along the bottom of the canal and covered them with lime chloride; then they too were led up to the edge of the canal to be shot. One of our comrades even took a photograph; after the others saw it, however, the troops were forbidden to observe the executions.

The experience had an indescribable effect on us; to this day no other images from the war can erase it. At the time Lieutenant-General Bayer was commander of the division. It must also be noted that all valuables were taken from the victims and confiscated before they were taken from the prison to the execution site. These shootings of the Jews took place in Resenke (now known as Rozitten). I do not know the name of the commandant in charge of the executions.

W. Janiko

Wolfgang Janiko wrote and signed this report in my presence after my conversation with him.

E. S. Fabri, Instructor, Camp 27
Translated by Stern, 14 April 1943

From the Protocol of the Cross-Examination of the Prisoner of War Private First Class Albert Ender, [14ᵗʰ Company of the 195ᵗʰ Assault Regiment, 78ᵗʰ Assault Division]

"I know that the German army perpetrated numerous crimes on Russian soil.

"In the fall of 1941 all the Jews of Kirovograd was ordered to pack a day's worth of provisions and report to the district commissar. Once they had all gathered there, they were taken out to the anti-tank ditches and shot. Among them were Russians as well. It is said that approximately 35,000 people were murdered there. Many were hanged with a sign that read, "Thief." I saw them myself. Sometimes they would hang six, eight, or ten people at the same time; that was very common. All of this was done by the hands of the SS.

"The same scenes were repeated in Dnepropetrovsk.

"In Uman I lived with a Jewish woman. One day the SS arrived at four in the morning; they took her and told me that she was to be liquidated. She never came back.

"When I was in Krasnodon and Tikhoretsk in the summer of 1942 I saw placards announcing that any Jews who did not report to the district commissar would be shot immediately. The civilians sometimes asked us why the Jews were being annihilated. The regular soldiers could reply only by throwing up their arms.

2637"

24 September 1944

Fund No. 1, Case 35, Sheet 4

Protocol of the Interrogation of Wilhelm Sudbrak

1.	Last name, first name:	Wilhelm Sudbrak
2.	Year of birth:	1905
3.	Place of birth:	Aikel, near Wanne-Aikel (Westphalia)
4.	Nationality:	German
5.	Education:	College level
6.	Party affiliation:	None
7.	Assignment:	Soldier of the 15th Company, 195th Assault Regiment, 78th Assault Division
8. Time and place of capture:		Surrendered voluntarily, 24 June 1944, in the Bryukhovtsy region
9. Marital status:		Married

I have been warned about the consequences of giving false testimony and of refusing to testify, according to Statutes 92 and 95 of the Criminal Code of the RSFSR.

(Signature)

Testimony

From the beginning of the German-Soviet war until May 1943 I served in an administration camp for Russian prisoners of war (Stalag) located in the Ukraine. Between one and five thousand prisoners passed through this camp.

At our camp—as at other camps such as the camp at Slavutsky, for example—political workers and Jews were turned over to SS police units. Officially the SS police took commissars and Jews under their protection, but in fact these people were exterminated. All of our people knew about it, even though it was a top secret affair, and no one had the right to divulge the facts concerning the extermination of the prisoners. Sonderführer Fastl, the translator for our camp, was immediately taken away somewhere after he had told me over the telephone about the SS murdering seventeen Jews. The rumor was that he had been arrested.

In the winter of 1941 – 1942 there were twelve to thirteen thousand Russian prisoners of war in the Kovel camp. The prisoners were driven to the camp over several hundred kilometers on foot; they were poorly fed, and they had no sanitation facilities. As a result of all this, many of them died from exhaustion and typhus. At that time the head of the camp was Major Otto. The situation was the same at Vladimi-Volynsky (a camp for officers) and other camps. I learned these facts from my involvement with documents dealing with camp provisions. I do not know of a single instance of anyone being held accountable by Hitler's government for any of the mass murders of prisoners.

In September 1941 as many as eighteen thousand Jews were exterminated in Rovno in a single day.[6] I heard about it from many of our officers.

The same thing was done with the Jews in Kovel in the summer of 1942. Many people also knew about this.

None of these actions was the result of the maliciousness of any individual person or camp administrator. This systematic slaughter of people was supervised by Hitler's government. One fact in particular proves it: when the district commissar in Kovel delayed carrying out an order to exterminate the Jews in 1942, he was called back to Berlin. He was put on trial and, as we were told, was executed.

Fund No. 1, Case 35, Sheet 38

Notes

1. England adopted the Jewish statute in 1275, by which British King Edward I attempted to radically alter the way of life and livelihood for the Jews by severely curtailing their rights. It led to massacres of the Jews and their expulsion from England on 18 July 1290. The statute was not repealed until 1846.
2. On 4 July 1946 forty-two Jews were slaughtered in a pogrom that broke out in the Polish town of Kielce in the wake of a blood libel (the accusation that Jews killed Christian children to use their blood to make matzah). Of the 25,000 Jews who had lived in Kielce before the war, only two hundred returned. Within three months after the pogrom more than 100,000 Jews had fled the Polish territory.
3. Ilya Pavlovich Trainin (1887 – 1949) was an attorney and member of the Academy of sciences of the USSR. During the war he served as director of the Institute of Law of the Academy of Sciences. Gathering many documents on Nazi war crimes, he worked closely with the Jewish Anti-Fascist Committee.
4. This document, as well as other documents from the 3rd Battalion of the 15th Police Regiment, was published in September 1943 under the title "Report of Captain Sauer on the Mass Murder of the Jewish Population of the City of Pinsk" in the collection *The Documents Accuse: A Collection of Documents on the Monstrous Crimes of the German Fascist Invaders of Soviet Territories*, pp. 34-36.
5. Between September and November of 1942 the Third Battalion of the 15th Police Regiment shot 44,837 people, of whom 41,848 were Jews.
6. The Aktion in Rovno took place 6 – 8 November 1941, when 21,000 to 23,000 Jews were slaughtered.